D0230635

# Dubai
## The Complete **Residents'** Guide

www.du.ae

In association with
add life to life

Passionately Publishing...

**EXPLORER**

# Visitor Mobile Line
# Your passport to the UAE

## Buy the du Visitor Mobile Line for only AED 70

- AED 20 recharge card
- UAE visitor guide
- tourist maps
- travel wallet

- 90 day validity with option to renew
- option to migrate to other packages
- more savings with Pay by the Second

Buy yourself a line, or one for your friends and family.
Available at the airport or at any du shop or authorised dealer throughout the UAE.

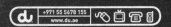
+971 55 5678 155
www.du.ae

UAE
mini maps

UAE
mini guide

du
©

add life to life

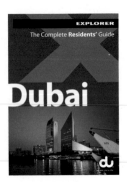

**Dubai Explorer  2008/12th Edition**
First Published 1996
2nd Edition 1997
3rd Edition 1998
4th Edition 2000
5th Edition 2001
6th Edition 2002
7th Edition 2003
8th Edition 2004
9th Edition 2005
10th Edition 2006
11th Edition 2007
**12th Edition 2008   ISBN 10 9948-03-385-X   ISBN 13 978-9948-03-385-1**

**Copyright © Explorer Group Ltd,** 1996, 1997, 1998, 2000, 2001, 2002, 2003, 2004, 2005, 2006, 2007, 2008.
All rights reserved.

Front Cover Photograph – Dubai Creek – Victor Romero

Printed and bound by Emirates Printing Press, Dubai, United Arab Emirates.

**Explorer Publishing & Distribution**
PO Box 34275, Dubai
United Arab Emirates
**Phone**      +971 (0)4 340 8805
**Fax**         +971 (0)4 340 8806
**Email**      info@explorerpublishing.com
**Web**        www.explorerpublishing.com

While every effort and care has been made to ensure the accuracy of the information contained in this publication, the publisher cannot accept responsibility for any errors or omissions it may contain.
No part of this publication may be reproduced, stored in a retrieval system, or transmitted, in any form or by any means, electronic, mechanical, photocopying, recording or otherwise, without the prior permission in writing of the publisher.

# Welcome

Well done you! Mabruk! (it's Arabic). By picking up this glorious book you've taken the first step to making life in Dubai a whole lot easier. Consider Dubai to be like a new gadget. It looks great and it's very exciting, but now and again you can't quite figure out how it works. Well, this is the manual.

The book is divided into six chapters, so whether you're looking for info on visas or volleyball teams, charity shops or chip shops, you'll quickly be able to find the answers.

First up is **General Information**, a sensible starting point for getting your bearings. This chapter gives an overview of the UAE and Dubai in particular, covering the geography, history, environment and culture of the country. There's also stacks of useful numbers, such as embassies, banks and airlines.

Next is the **Residents** chapter, and oh, what a chapter. From the moment you arrive in Dubai to the day you're packing your bags and moving on, Residents will walk with you every step of the way: each bureaucratic battle you face; every bit of red tape you try to cut through, and all the headaches and hurdles you encounter. You'll be given a tour of potential places to live, as well as a wealth of health info and a double session on Dubai's schools. Finally the chapter screeches to a halt with a bus-load of facts on transportation, including how to get your very own motor. Phew.

Now it's time to get out and about with the **Exploring** chapter. Dubai's different neighbourhoods are covered, with parks, beaches, art galleries and museums visited along the way. There's a checklist of absolute must-dos, and we even went out of our way to list some of the best holiday hotspots within easy reach of the UAE.

Sporty (and not so sporty) types will enjoy teaming up with the **Activities** chapter. From the cerebral (such as chess) to the downright exhausting (kitesurfing, anyone?), it's all here. And when you need some hard-earned pampering, the city's finest spas are reviewed for your relaxation.

On to **Shopping**, and our tireless bargain-hounds have trawled the malls and scoured the souks to prove Dubai's reputation as a shopping paradise is richly deserved. Whether it's the debut of Harvey Nics, or a stationers in Satwa with a particularly fine range of new pens, it's all here.

And what to do once the sun goes down? Better turn to the **Going Out** chapter, with reviews of the best restaurants, bars, cafes and clubs. You can search by cuisine, or choose from a selection of venues with a distinctive unique selling point, such as the best cocktails, or an alfresco experience like no other.

If all that advice has left you dizzy, then you'll be relieved to find a whole heap of **Maps** at the back of the book. Featuring both vector maps and satellite imagery, this section covers the city in pinpoint detail. Throughout the book you'll see that companies and locations have a map reference listed – turn to the relevant map and you'll be halfway to reaching your destination.

So there you have it. That covers just about everything. But if you think we've missed something (perhaps your favourite campanology class?) then go to www.explorerpublishing.com, fill in the Reader Response form, and share the knowledge (and love) with your fellow explorers.

Finally, it just remains for us to say a big, fat thanks, because let's face it, without our lovely readers, all our hard work would be in vain.

**The Explorer Team**

# Where are we exploring next?

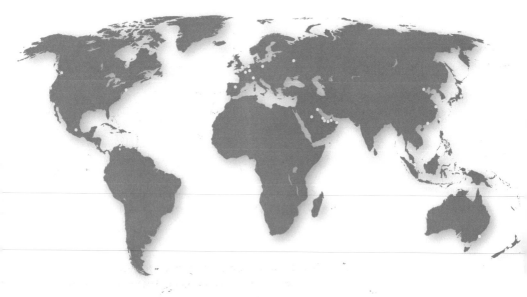

- Abu Dhabi
- Amsterdam
- Bahrain
- Barcelona
- Beijing*
- Berlin*
- Brussels*
- Dubai

- Dublin
- Geneva
- Hong Kong
- Kuala Lumpur*
- Kuwait
- London
- Los Angeles*
- Mexico City*

- Moscow*
- New York
- New Zealand
- Oman
- Paris
- Qatar
- San Francisco*
- Saudi Arabia*

- Shanghai
- Singapore
- Sydney
- Taipei*
- Tokyo*
- Vancouver*

* Available 2008

## Where do you live?
Is your home city missing from our list? If you'd love to see a residents' guide for a location not currently on Explorer's horizon please email editorial@explorerpublishing.com.

## Advertise with Explorer...
If you're interested in advertising with us, please contact sales@explorerpublishing.com.

## Make Explorer your very own...
We offer a number of customization options for bulk sales. For more information and discount rates please contact corporatesales@explorerpublishing.com.

## Contract Publishing
Have an idea for a publication or need to revamp your company's marketing material? Contact designlab@explorerpublishing to see how our expert contract publishing team can help.

# www.explorerpublishing.com

Life can move pretty fast, so to make sure you can stay up to date with all the latest goings on in your city, we've revamped our website to further enhance your time in the city, whether long or short.

## Keep in the know...

Our Complete Residents' Guides and Mini Visitors' series continue to expand, covering destinations from Amsterdam to New Zealand and beyond. Keep up to date with our latest travels and hot tips by signing up to our monthly newsletter, or browse our products section for info on our current and forthcoming titles.

## Make friends and influence people...

...by joining our Communities section. Meet fellow residents in your city, make your own recommendations for your favourite restaurants, bars, childcare agencies or dentists, plus find answers to your questions on daily life from long-term residents.

## Discover new experiences...

Ever thought about living in a different city, or wondered where the locals really go to eat, drink and be merry? Check out our regular features section, or submit your own feature for publication!

## Want to find a badminton club, the number for your bank, or maybe just a restaurant for a hot first date?

Check out city info on various destinations around the world in our residents' section – from finding a pilates class to contact details for international schools in your area, or the best place to buy everything from a spanner set to a Spandau Ballet album, we've got it all covered.

## Let us know what you think!

All our information comes from residents which means you! If we missed out your favourite bar or market stall, or you know of any changes in the law, infrastructure, cost of living or entertainment scene, let us know by using our Feedback form.

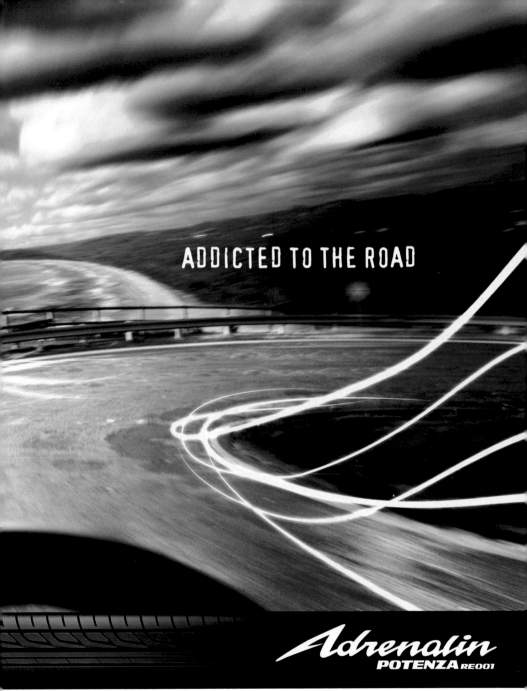

ADDICTED TO THE ROAD

*Adrenalin*
**POTENZA** *RE001*

PASSION
*for EXCELLENCE*

otenza-adrenalin.com
ridgestone-mea.com
lserkal.com

*Nasser Bin Abdullatif Alserkal* Est.

# Heart Care Made in Germany

We pride ourselves in our ability to think, analyze and diagnose. Our complete team has been trained at international institutions. Our experience and commitment is what makes the difference in quality health care.

**Dr. Klaus T. Kallmayer MD, MA**
FACC, FESC, FSCAI

**Dr. Caspar A. Boerner MD**
FESC

**Dr. Helmut W. Lange MD**
FACC, FESC

- **Efficient and hassle-free consultation and test process**
- **Permanent out and in-patient care offered in Dubai**
- **Pediatric cardiology from the age of five upwards**
- **Expertise in difficult and critical conditions**

MOH#1605/2/10/30110/2007

## German Heart Centre
Bremen

**Branch of German Teaching Hospital located at: Dubai Healthcare City**
**Call + 971 - 4 - 362 47 97**

Member of European Society of Cardiology, American College of Cardiology, Society for Coronary Angiography and Interventions, Deutsche Gesellschaft fuer Kardiologie, Society for Cardiac MRI.

# DUBAI
# GREEN COMMUNITY

## SINCE WE WENT TO THE COURTYARD, WE GOT RID OF THAT BIG PIECE OF WHITE FURNITURE IN THE KITCHEN.

Come and relax in the welcoming atmosphere of the Green Community. A variety of dining options to suit all occasions offering you plenty of occasions to share good moments between friends and family and, also, to make new friends! You will enjoy it so much that you might just decide to get rid of your oven as well!

**IT'S THE MARRIOTT WAY.**℠

For restaurant reservations call **04 885 2222** or visit www.marriottdiningatcy.ae

Courtyard by Marriott Dubai
Green Community
Dubai Investment Park, PO Box 63845
Dubai, United Arab Emirates
Fax: +971 4 8852525

# Watch Out...

## Buy 3 Get 1 FREE

Purchase 3 entry tickets and get the 4th FR
Cut out and present this coupon to avail this offer.
*Terms and conditions apply

# Extreme Fun! For Every One!

DREAMLAND
AQUA PARK

Splash, play, laze around,
enjoy good food and do nothing
but have fun at Dreamland Aqua Park.
With 250,000 sq.m of landscaped gardens, over 30
thrilling rides, crazy slides, go-karts, a mini pet land and all yo
favourite restaurants, it's the perfect retreat for the entire family.
Overnight Camping, Tennis Court and WIFI
enabled Zone Now Available

Ras Al Khaimah Highway,
through Emirates Road, Exit 103
Tel: 06 7681888 | www.dreamlanduae.com
Fridays and holidays, strictly for families.

**Jobs Property Cars Nightlife**

Post Your Ads For Free

www.dubaidonkey.com

# Welcome to the desert.

Sun and sand is plentiful in Dubai, but for snow and shopping make a trip to Mall of the Emirates, Dubai's finest shopping resort and the largest mall in the Eastern Hemisphere. With over 450 stores housing the world's leading brands, Ski Dubai - an Alpine themed snow resort, a 14-screen cineplex, a two level family entertainment zone with indoor rollercoasters, and over 75 cafés and restaurants, there are plenty of reasons for you to visit us.

Opening hours: 10am – 10pm (Sun – Wed), 10am – midnight (Thu – Sat)
Carrefour, CineStar and restaurant hours may vary. Please ask for details.
Interchange 4, Sheikh Zayed Road. Tel: 04 409 9000 www.malloftheemirates.com

*Excite*

Kempinski Hotel Mall of the Emirates invites you to discover the world's first and truly complete shopping resort. Situated right next to the hotel, Mall of the Emirates brings you the ultimate in leisure and entertainment with Magic Planet and Ski Dubai, and over 450 international retail brands for an unforgettable shopping adventure, along with 393 luxurious rooms and suites in the hotel. Experience the extraordinary at Kempinski Hotel Mall of the Emirates.

P.O. Box 120679 · Dubai · United Arab Emirates
Tel +971 4 341 0000 · Fax +971 4 341 4500
reservations.malloftheemirates@kempinski.com · www.kempinski-dubai.com

Kempinski Hotel
Mall of the Emirates

DUBAI

*Kempinski*

HOTELIERS SINCE 1897

KEMPINSKI - LEADERS IN LUXURY FOR 110 YEARS

# Have fun out there.

There's fun to be had out there, and Jeep gives you lots of ways to find it. From the open-topp
Wrangler to the spacious powerful Commander, from the sporty luxurious Grand Cherokee, to
trail-blazing Patriot and Cherokee, each Jeep is different but they all drive towards the sa
thing. And when the winds in your hair and the goose-bumps bumping, you'll know you've foun

**trading enterprises**
An Al-Futtaim group company

# CALL TOLL FREE 800-4-I

**m left above:** Commander, Patriot, Wrangler, Grand Cherokee, pass, Cherokee and Wrangler Unlimited.

is a registered trademark of Chrysler LLC.

w.Jeepuae.com | **DUBAI FESTIVAL CITY AND SHEIKH ZAYED ROAD SHOWROOMS OPEN ON FRIDAYS**

# BIGGEST CHOICE OF BOOKS

MAGIC CHOICE OF BOOKS

EXCITING CHOICE OF *BOOKS*

Phenomenal choice of books

UNBEATABLE CHOICE OF BOOKS

 IN FULL COLOUR

SPECIAL CHOICE of books

THRILLING CHOICE OF BOOKS

Encyclopedic choice of Books

BALANCED CHOICE OF BOOKS

FANTASTIC CHOICE of BOOKS

# BORDERS.®

YOUR PLACE FOR KNOWLEDGE AND ENTERTAINMENT

Mall of the Emirates 04 3415758  Deira City Center 04 2957672
Dubai International Finance Center 04 4250371 Muscat City Center 0096895921377

# THE A TO Z OF GOOD HEALTH

- Anaesthesiology
- Antenatal Classes and Breast-feeding Clinics
- Audiology and Speech Therapy
- Cardiology (Interventional & Non-Interventional)
- Cosmetic, Reconstructive and Hand Surgery Dentistry, Periodontics, Orthodontics, Oral Surgery and Dental Implantology
- Dermatology and Laser Skin Surgery
- Dietetics
- Endocrinology and Diabetology
- ENT, Audiology and Speech Therapy
- Gastroenterology
- General and laparoscopic Surgery
- General Practice
- Internal Medicine

- Nephrology
- Neurology
- Neurophysiology
- Neurosurgery
- Nuclear Medicine
- Obstetrics and Gynaecology
- Oncology
- Ophthalmology and Laser Eye Surgery
- Orthopaedics and Physiotherapy
- Paediatrics and neonatology
- Pathology
- Pulmonology
- Radiology and Imaging & Interventional Radiology
- Urology

**AL ZAHRA**
**THE HEALING TOUCH**

Al Zahra Private Hospital, Al Zahra Square, P.O. Box 3499, Sharjah. Tel: 06 5619999. Appointments: 06 5613311. Fax: 06 5616699.
Al Zahra Medical Centre, Sheikh Zayed Road, P.O. Box 23614, Dubai. Tel: 04 3315000. Appointments: 04 3311155. Fax: 04 3314369.
E-mail: alzahra@alzahra.com Website: www.alzahra.com

# become a

virgin important person

V·I·P

Virgin
MEGASTORE

Mall of the Emirates • Deira City Center • Mercato • Burjuman • Abu Dhabi Mall
www.vmeganews.com

**AED 25-30 EACH**

DAN BROWN
DAN BROWN
DAN BROWN
STEPHEN KING
STEPHEN KING    THE GUNSL
STEPHEN KING
STEPHEN KING
ROBIN COOK

Books Plus gives you the incredible chance to own best-selling titles of your favourite authors for as little as Dhs. 25 each. Keep checking out your nearest Books Plus store for the season's best bargains, all round the year. And grab them before the racks get empty!

**5 stores across the UAE**
Lamcy Plaza Tel: 04 3366362, 3349514 ▪ Town Centre, Jumeirah Tel: 04 3442008 ▪ Spinneys Mall, Jumeirah Tel: 04 940278 ▪ Greens Centre Tel: 04 3674388 ▪ Al Reef Mall, Deira Tel: 04 2227547 ▪ Dubai Marina Tel: 04 3606196 ▪ Ibn attuta Mall, China Court Tel: 04 3685375 ▪ Al Jimi Mall, Al Ain Tel: 03 7633503 ▪ Arabian Ranches Tel: 04 3606198 Greens Community Tel: 04 8853250 ▪ Springs Community Center Tel: 04 3605703 ▪ George Mason University Tel: 7 2225526 ▪ Mirdif Tel: 04 2886735 ▪ Dubai Festival City Tel: 04 2325563 ▪ Academic City Tel: 04 4291393

**BOOKSPLUS**
BOOKS ▪ STATIONERY ▪ NOVELTIES
"Reader's No. 1 Choice"

" Today a Reader
Tomorrow a Leader "

## JASHANMAL BOOKSTORES

Abu Dhabi: Abu Dhabi Mall, Level 3, Hamdan Street, Tel: 6443869, Dubai: Mall of the Emirates, Tel: 34067
The Village Mall, Jumeirah, Tel: 3445770, Caribou Coffee, Uptown Mirdiff Tel: 2888376, Dubai Marina Wa
Jashanmal Department Store, Wafi City, Level 2, Tel: 3244800, Sharjah: Sahara Centre, Tel: 5317898,
Bahrain: Seef Mall, West Wing, Tel: 17581632, Al Aali Shopping Complex, Tel: 17582424

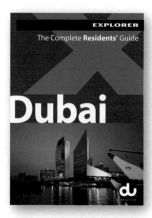

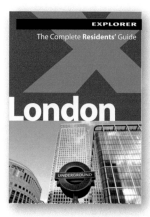

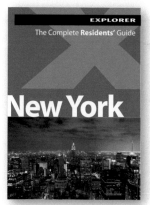

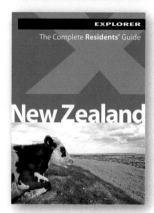

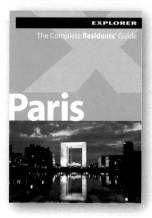

# Tired of writing your insider tips…

## …in a blog that nobody reads?

The Explorer Complete Residents' Guide series is growing rapidly, and we're always looking for literate, resident writers to help pen our new guides. So whether you live in Tuscany or Timbuktu, if writing's your thing, and you know your city inside out, we'd like to talk to you.

Apply online at www.explorerpublishing.com

Abu Dhabi · Amsterdam · Bahrain · Barcelona · Beijing · Berlin · Dubai · Dublin · Geneva
Hong Kong · Kuala Lumpur · Kuwait · London · Los Angeles · New York · New Zealand · Oman
Paris · Qatar · Shanghai · Singapore · Sydney · Tokyo · Vancouver

# EXPLORER

www.explorerpublishing.com

The world's
most respected
news, features,
business and
sports coverage
now here in the
Middle East.

# THE ✦ TIMES  THE SUNDAY TIMES

## PRINTED DAILY IN THE MIDDLE EAST

To subscribe, call 04 3642897
or visit www.thetimesme.com

SAB
media
Local Licensee

# Contents

# Contents

# life... made out of seconds

## Pay by the Second
More calls, more talktime, more control.
National mobile voice calls 0.5 fils per second.
International mobile voice calls are charged by the second as per published tariffs.

 +971 55 5678 155
www.du.ae

add life to life

# General Information

## Geography

The United Arab Emirates (UAE) is situated on the eastern side of the Arabian Peninsula, bordering Saudi Arabia and the Sultanate of Oman, and with coastlines on both the Arabian Gulf and the Gulf of Oman. The country comprises seven emirates – Abu Dhabi, Ajman, Dubai, Fujairah, Ras Al Khaimah, Sharjah and Umm Al Quwain. Abu Dhabi is by far the largest emirate, occupying over 80% of the country. With an area of 3,885 square kilometres, the emirate of Dubai is the second largest.

The coast is littered with coral reefs and more than 200 islands, most of which are uninhabited. The interior of the country is characterised by sabkha (salt flats), stretches of gravel plain, and vast areas of desert. However, to the east rise the Hajar Mountains, ('hajar' is Arabic for rock). Lying close to the Gulf of Oman, they form a backbone through the country, from the Musandam Peninsula in the north, through the eastern UAE and into Oman. The highest point is Jebel Yibir at 1,527 metres. The Rub Al Khali, or Empty Quarter, occupies a large part of the south of the country. Common to the UAE, Saudi Arabia, Oman and Yemen, it's the largest desert in the world, covering an area roughly the same size as France, Belgium and the Netherlands. The Rub Al Khali consists of stark desert, salt flats, occasional oases, and spectacular sand dunes that rise to more than 300 metres. The emirate of Dubai is of course best known for its modern, rapidly expanding city, but visitors will also find a landscape that varies from vast stretches of desert to rugged mountains.

## History

The Arabian (or Persian) Gulf was an important trading post as far back as the Kingdom of Sumer in 3000BC. Sumer, located in the area between the Tigris and Euphrates Rivers in present-day Iraq, is believed to be the birthplace of modern civilisation. This great kingdom had influence, if not control, over trading points throughout the Gulf, and probably further. Deira/Dubai was one of these key positions, a safe haven before entering the narrow Strait of Hormuz and the open sea.

### Development Of Islam

Dubai's early existence is closely linked to the arrival and development of Islam in the greater Middle East region. Islam developed in modern-day Saudi Arabia at the beginning of the seventh century AD with the revelations of the Quran being received by the Prophet Muhammad. Military conquests of the Middle East and North Africa enabled the Arab empire to spread the teachings of Islam from Mecca and Medina to the local Bedouin tribes. Following the Arab Empire came the Turks, the Mongols and the Ottomans, each leaving their mark on local culture and all championing Islam.

---

**Trusty Companion**

A fab companion guide for your time exploring Dubai and the UAE is Explorer's *UAE Road Map.* It's clear, easy to use and gets you from A to B on time.

---

**UAE Fact Box**

**Coordinates:** 24º00' North 54º00' East

**Borders:** 410km with Oman and 457km with Saudi Arabia

**Total land area:** approx. 83,000 sq km

**Total coastline:** 1,318km

**Highest point:** 1,527m

**Total land area:** 3,885 sq km

**Total Dubai coastline:** 60km, but new offshore projects will add over 1,000km

---

**2**

**Sheikh Maktoum bin Rashid Al Maktoum**

*Sheikh Maktoum bin Rashid Al Maktoum was Ruler of Dubai and Vice President and Prime Minister of the UAE from November 1990 until he passed away in January 2006. The eldest son of Sheikh Rashid bin Saeed Al Maktoum, he worked closely with his father during his reign, overseeing the development of modern Dubai. He was known as a philanthropist and was an internationally respected statesman. He is also remembered for his success as a racehorse owner and was a co-founder, along with his two brothers, of the Godolphin stables.*

**Emirs Or Sheikhs?**

*While the term emirate comes from the ruling title of 'emir', the rulers of the UAE are called 'sheikhs.'*

*Dubai Marina from Emirates Hills*

## The Trucial States

After the fall of the Muslim empires, both the British and Portuguese became interested in the area due to its strategic position between India and Europe, and for the opportunity to control the activities of pirates based in the region, earning it the title the 'Pirate Coast'. In 1820 the British defeated the pirates and a general treaty was agreed by the local rulers, denouncing piracy. The following years witnessed a series of maritime truces, with Dubai and the other emirates accepting British protection in 1892. In Europe, the area became known as the Trucial Coast (or Trucial States), a name it retained until the departure of the British in 1971.

## A Growing Trade

In the late 1800s Dubai's ruler, Sheikh Maktoum bin Hasher Al Maktoum, granted tax concessions to foreign traders, encouraging many to switch their base of operations from Iran and Sharjah to Dubai. By 1903, a British shipping line had been persuaded to use Dubai as its main port of call in the area, giving traders direct links with British India and other important trading ports in the region. Dubai's importance as a trading hub was further enhanced by Sheikh Rashid bin Saeed Al Maktoum, father of the current ruler of Dubai, who ordered the creek to be dredged, thus providing access to larger vessels. The city came to specialise in the import and re-export of goods, mainly gold to India, and trade became the foundation of this emirate's wealthy progression.

## Independence

In 1968 Britain announced its withdrawal from the region and oversaw the creation of a single state consisting of Bahrain, Qatar and the Trucial Coast. The ruling sheikhs, particularly of Abu Dhabi and Dubai, realised that by uniting forces they would have a stronger voice in the wider Middle East region. Negotiations collapsed when Bahrain and Qatar chose to become independent states. However, the Trucial Coast remained committed to forming an alliance, and in 1971 the federation of the United Arab Emirates was born.

## Formation Of The United Arab Emirates

The new state comprised the emirates of Dubai, Abu Dhabi, Ajman, Fujairah, Sharjah, Umm Al Quwain and, in 1972, Ras Al Khaimah (each emirate is named after its main town). Under the agreement, the individual emirates each retained a certain degree of autonomy, with Abu Dhabi and Dubai providing the most input into the federation. The leaders of the new federation elected the ruler of Abu Dhabi, His Highness Sheikh Zayed bin Sultan Al Nahyan, to be their president, a position he held until he passed away on 2 November 2004. His eldest son, His Highness Sheikh

**Modern Dubai**

*Trade and commerce are still the cornerstones of Dubai's success, with the traditional manufacturing and distribution industries now joined by financial, media, IT and telecom businesses. With so many world-class hotels and leisure and entertainment options, the city is also becoming an increasingly popular tourist destination, with visitor numbers expected to reach 15 million by the year 2010.*

**Sheikh Zayed bin Sultan Al Nahyan**

*Sheikh Zayed bin Sultan Al Nahyan was not only revered by his peers but also adored by his public. He ruled the UAE for 33 years and in that time oversaw major developments to the nation's economy and pioneered the extension of privileges to expatriates. Sheikh Zayed embraced change without compromising the principles of Arabic heritage and culture. He was a well-respected international figure and passionate about the environment. When he passed away in November 2004, the entire population, from locals to expats of every nationality, mourned.*

Khalifa bin Zayed Al Nahyan, was then elected to take over the presidency. Despite the unification of the seven emirates, boundary disputes have caused a few problems. At the end of Sheikh Zayed's first term as president, in 1976, he threatened to resign if the other rulers didn't settle the demarcation of their borders. The threat proved an effective way of ensuring cooperation, although the degree of independence of the various emirates has never been fully determined.

## The Discovery Of Oil

The formation of the UAE came after the discovery of huge oil reserves in Abu Dhabi in 1958 (Abu Dhabi has an incredible 10% of the world's known oil reserves). This discovery dramatically transformed the emirate. In 1966, Dubai, which was already a relatively wealthy trading centre, also discovered oil.

Dubai's ruler at the time, the late Sheikh Rashid bin Saeed Al Maktoum, ensured that the emirate's oil revenues were used to develop an economic and social infrastructure, which is the basis of today's modern society. His work was continued through the reign of his son, and successor, Sheikh Maktoum bin Rashid Al Maktoum and by the present Ruler, Sheikh Mohammed bin Rashid Al Maktoum.

### Dubai Timeline

| | |
|---|---|
| 1799 | Al Fahedi Fort is built (estimated) |
| 1833 | The Maktoum family settles in Dubai |
| 1835 | Maritime Truce signed between the Trucial States and Britain |
| 1892 | Dubai falls under the protection of Britain |
| 1950s | Oil is discovered in the Trucial States |
| 1963 | Maktoum Bridge is built, becoming the first bridge across the creek |
| 1966 | Commercial quantities of oil discovered off the coast of the UAE. Dubai's first hotel, The Carlton (now The Riviera), is built |
| 1967 | The Shindagha Tunnel is built, providing an alternative to Maktoum Bridge for crossing the creek |
| 1970 | Al Fahedi Fort is converted into Dubai Museum |
| 1971 | Britain withdraws from the Gulf and Dubai becomes independent. The United Arab Emirates is born, with HH Sheikh Zayed bin Sultan Al Nahyan as the leader. The UAE joins the Arab League |
| 1973 | Dubai and the other emirates launch their single currency, the UAE dirham |
| 1981 | The Gulf Cooperation Council is formed, with the UAE as a founding member |
| 1990 | After the death of his father, Sheikh Rashid bin Saeed Al Maktoum, Sheikh Maktoum bin Rashid Al Maktoum becomes the ruler of Dubai |
| 1999 | The doors of the Burj Al Arab, the tallest hotel in the world, open to the public for the first time |
| 2001 | Construction starts on Palm Jumeirah |
| 2004 | Sheikh Zayed bin Sultan Al Nahyan dies and is succeeded as ruler of the UAE by his son, Sheikh Khalifa bin Zayed Al Nahyan |
| 2006 | Sheikh Maktoum bin Rashid Al Maktoum dies and is succeeded as Ruler of Dubai and Prime Minister of the UAE by his brother, Sheikh Mohammed bin Rashid Al Maktoum |
| 2007 | Burj Dubai becomes world's tallest building |

# The most sivilised way to London.

Arrive 30 mins before departure.

Executive terminal in Dubai.

Private terminal in London.

Private security channel.

Flat bed.

Ladies only toilets.

Travel with just 99 other people.

Call 800 044 0224 toll free 24 hours.

fly SILVERJET .com

VERY SIVILISED

## United Arab Emirates Overview

The UAE is considered the second richest Arab country, after Qatar, on a per capita basis. According to World Bank figures for 2006, the UAE's Gross National Income (GNI) per capita was US$23,950. The country has just under 10% of the world's proven oil reserves (most of it within Abu Dhabi emirate) and the fourth largest natural gas reserves. Recent record fuel prices have helped the UAE's GDP grow at over 8% a year. GDP for 2006 was Dhs.599 billion, and the 2007 estimate was Dhs.697 billion. In 2006, Dubai contributed more than 40% of the UAE's non-oil revenue. The UAE's wealth is not solely reliant on oil revenue though, and in 2005 oil accounted for just 35.7% of overall GDP. Trade, manufacturing, tourism and construction are playing an increasingly important part in the national economy. The country's main export partners are Saudi Arabia, Iran, Japan, India, Singapore, South Korea and Oman. The main import partners are Japan, USA, UK, Italy, Germany and South Korea.

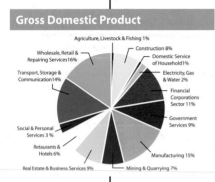

**Gross Domestic Product**

- Agriculture, Livestock & Fishing 1%
- Construction 8%
- Wholesale, Retail & Repairing Services16%
- Domestic Service of Household1%
- Transport, Storage & Communication14%
- Electricity, Gas & Water 2%
- Financial Corporations Sector 11%
- Social & Personal Services 3 %
- Government Services 9%
- Retaurants & Hotels 6%
- Manufacturing 15%
- Real Estate & Business Services 9%
- Mining & Quarrying 7%

## Dubai Overview

Whereas 20 years ago oil revenues accounted for around half of Dubai's GDP, in 2006 the oil sector contributed just 5.5%. It is expected that by 2010 oil will account for less than 1% of total GDP. Dubai's rulers have known for many years that the oil would run out, and so embarked on ambitious projects to diversify the emirate's economy. Today, trade, manufacturing, transport, construction and real estate are the main contributors to Dubai's strong, growing economy. Indeed, the latest figures show that the construction and real estate sectors between them account for almost a quarter of total GDP. In 2006, Dubai's GDP was in excess of Dhs.167 billion, an increase of 19% on the previous year's figure.

One concern with regard to the economy's growth is rising inflation. According to the International Monetary Fund (IMF), inflation in the UAE is estimated at 8%. However, factors such as rising rents – especially in Dubai – mean the cost of living is increasing far more rapidly for residents. In fact, inflation in 2006 at 9.3% was the highest in the last two decades.

### Trade

A long trading tradition, which earned Dubai its reputation as 'the city of merchants' in the Middle East, continues to be an important consideration for foreign companies looking at opportunities in the region today. It is reflected not just in an open and liberal regulatory environment, but also in the local business community's familiarity with international commercial practices and the city's cosmopolitan lifestyle. Strategically located between Europe and the far east, Dubai attracts multinational and private companies wishing to tap the lucrative Middle Eastern, Indian and African markets (which have a combined population of over two billion). Annual domestic imports exceed US$17 billion and Dubai is the gateway to over US$150 billion (annual) in trade.

*Dubai Creek*

### Growth

The pace of economic growth in Dubai over the last 20 years has been incredible – trade alone has grown at

## Quick Facts

- Dubai Shopping Festival attracted 3.5 million visitors in 2006/7.
- Dubai Government aims to attract 15 million visitors a year to Dubai by 2010.
- By 2010, tourism is expected to contribute 20% to the UAE's GDP.
- 28 million passengers passed through Dubai International Airport in 2006. The initial estimate for 2007 was 33 million.
- Dubai International Airport will soon have capacity to handle 70 million passengers a year.
- By 2015, Al Maktoum International Airport will also have the same passenger capacity.
- The Palms, World, and Dubai Waterfront will add more than a thousand kilometres to Dubai's coastline collectively.
- Value of projects and developments planned for next five years is estimated at more than US$30 billion.
- Dubai currently has over 370 hotels and hotel apartments, offering over 26,000 rooms.
- Rumour has it that up to 25% of the world's cranes are currently in Dubai.

more than 9% per annum over the past 10 years. Looking to the future, Dubai stands poised for further growth with the development of many multi-billion dollar coastal extension projects (such as the three Palm Islands projects, The World, and Dubai Waterfront) plus new business and financial ventures. Legislation and government institutions have been designed so that bureaucracy is minimised and there's a positive business environment. Government officials take an active role in promoting investment in Dubai and decisions are taken (and implemented) swiftly. In recent years government departments have also placed increasing importance on improving customer service levels, particularly in the free zones such as Internet City, Media City and Healthcare City, which foster a community environment for specific industries and are very easy to set up and operate in.

However, don't be fooled by the healthy economy into believing that the average expat coming to work in Dubai will automatically be on a huge salary. The wealth isn't spread evenly and except for highly skilled professionals, the salaries for most types of jobs are dropping. This downward trend is attributed in part to the willingness of workers to accept a position at a very low wage. While the UAE GDP per capita income was estimated at approximately Dhs.88,000 in 2006, this figure includes all sections of the community and the average labourer, of which there are many, can expect to earn as little as Dhs.600 (US$165) per month.

## Employment

While the unemployment level of the National population in the UAE is lower than that of many other Arab states, there are still a significant number of local Nationals out of work (over 30,000, according to some estimates). This is partly due to a preference for public sector work and partly because of qualifications, and salary expectations, not matching the skills required in the private sector. However, the government is trying to reverse this scenario and reduce unemployment in the local sector with a 'Nationalisation' or 'Emiratisation' programme (which is common to countries throughout the region). The eventual goal is to rely less on an expat workforce, which will be achieved by improving vocational training and by making it compulsory for certain types of companies, such as banks, to hire a set percentage of Emiratis. In another attempt to attract more Nationals to the private sector, the government has a pension scheme where private companies are required to provide a pension for their National employees. The IMF has also encouraged GCC countries to reduce public sector wage levels to encourage locals into the more competitive private sector. This advice doesn't seem to have been heeded though, as 2005 saw the Dubai government sanction a 25% salary increase for public sector employees, who benefited again in 2007 from a generous settlement.

## Leading Industries

The leading industries in Dubai include trade, manufacturing, transport, construction, real estate, energy, telecommunications, finance and tourism. Other sectors such as publishing, recruitment, advertising and IT, while not as developed in terms of size, are undergoing something of a boom (aided in part by the various free zones).

7

# Tourism Developments

Dubai is well ahead of many other cities in the Middle East in terms of travel and tourism. Its hotels and hotel apartments accommodated 6.44 million guests in 2006, an increase of 5% on the previous year. The mix of visitors at the moment is roughly 40% business traveller and 60% leisure, but the ratio of leisure travellers is set to increase as Dubai strives to reach its target of attracting 15 million visitors a year by 2010.

# Key Dubai Projects

Dubai is certainly the place to be if you're an ambitious architect – the city is home to some of the most exciting building projects, ranging from the practical to the utterly unbelievable. Just a few years ago when the first of the Palm Island projects was announced, it seemed an impossible task (p.16), yet now there are residents living on Palm Jumeirah, and various other projects have since been planned that make the Palm look small by comparison.

**Tourist Hotspot**

The development of high-end tourist amenities and visitor attractions, in conjunction with an aggressive overseas marketing campaign, means that Dubai is swiftly becoming a popular holiday destination. The city is also attracting a lot of business in the MICE (meetings, incentives, conferences and exhibitions) market. The government's plan is to attract 15 million visitors a year by 2010, and 40 million a year by 2015.

---

**Dubailand**
*Emirates Road*

## Al Barari
*www.albarari.com*

Nestling on the edge of Dubailand and bordering a conservation area, Al Barari is a development of 330 luxury villas, a boutique hotel, health resort and commercial space for nature lovers. Around 80% of the development will be left 'unconstructed', with areas of woodland, botanical gardens, themed gardens, lakes and streams.
**Size** 14 million square feet
**Completion** The first villas will be handed over mid 2008

---

**Extending around Jebel Ali and Dubai World Central**

## Arabian Canal
*www.limitless.ae*

A man-made waterway that will run from the new Dubai Waterfront development, past Al Maktoum International Airport, before linking back up with the Arabian Gulf at Dubai Marina. It will be the largest and most complex civil engineering project undertaken in the Middle East, sparking a myriad of new waterside communities.
**Size** 75km long, 150 metres wide
**Completion** End of 2010

---

**Near Dubailand**
*Emirates Road*

## Bawadi
*www.bawadi.ae*

This colossal, Dhs.200 billion development will offer 60,000 hotel rooms in 51 hotels. The plan is to produce the world's longest shopping and hospitality area that will conveniently allow visitors to walk from one end to the other. Asia Asia, the showpiece of Bawadi, is a hotel that will provide 6,500 rooms, a shopping mall and entertainment facilities. It aims to be more environmentally friendly than comparable developments.
**Size** 40 million square feet
**Completion** Unknown

---

**Interchange 1**
*Sheikh Zayed Road*

## Business Bay
*www.businessbay.ae*

Business Bay is based around an extension to the creek that will stretch up to Sheikh Zayed Road at Interchange 2 before continuing to the sea. This self-contained city aims to become the commercial and business capital for the region. Construction has already begun on more than 70 towers; when finished, the development will be home to 220 towers, including the Emirates Park Towers Hotel, set to be the tallest hotel in the UAE.

**Size** 64 million square feet
**Completion** The entire project by 2015

*Dubai Creek* ◀

## Creek Crossings

Dubai's motorists breathed a sigh of relief in 2007, with the opening of the 13 lane Business Bay Bridge and the smaller six lane Floating Bridge, spanning the creek next to Maktoum Bridge. Work is also underway on a much bigger Garhoud Bridge (which will total 13 lanes), and the government has announced two further bridges to ease congestion. Shindagha Bridge will run close to Shindagha Tunnel, while a fifth bridge will connect Deira and Bur Dubai between Shindagha and Maktoum Bridges. The plan is to have 47 lanes crossing the creek by 2008, and a staggering 100 by 2020.

**Completion** The new Garhoud Bridge is expected to open in 2008

*Opposite Festival City* ◀
*Jadaf*

## Culture Village

www.dubai-properties.ae

With architectural emphasis on heritage, Culture Village is set to become a hub for art and culture lovers. The mixed development will feature residential, commercial and retail zones. The commercial district will house academies for art, music, dance and crafts, while the retail district will feature hotels and restaurants, art and craft galleries. There will also be an outdoor amphitheatre and traditional dhow yard.

**Size** 40 million square feet
**Completion** First buildings completed in 2008

*Interchange 1* ◀
*Sheikh Zayed Road*

## Downtown Burj Dubai

www.emaar.com

Burj Dubai, the heart of this vast Emaar development, became the tallest building in the world in July 2007, dominating the landscape in the process. When completed, the tower will house retail outlets, offices, exclusive apartments and eight international chain and boutique hotels. The Downtown development will also be home to Dubai Mall, a lake and park, business and residential complexes.

**Size** The Burj Dubai tower's estimated height is around 800 metres
**Completion** Burj Dubai by 2008, other developments 2008 and 2009

*Between Arabian* ◀
*Ranches and*
*International City*
*Emirates Road*

## Dubailand

www.dubailand.ae

With individual themed 'worlds', this aims to be the biggest tourism, leisure and entertainment attraction on the planet. There will be theme parks, a Sports City, numerous hotels, the largest shopping mall in the world (Mall of Arabia), a snowdome, Formula One World and much, much more. The Bawadi project (p.8) alone will have 51 hotels.

**Size** 278.71 square kilometres/two billion square feet
**Completion** The Autodrome is already open. Phase one, incorporating all the necessary infrastructure and seven other projects is expected from 2008

### Really Tax Free?

Do taxes exist in Dubai? Yes and no. You don't pay income or sales tax, except when you purchase alcohol from a licensed liquor store – when you'll be hit with a steep 30% tax. The main tax that you will come across is the municipality tax of 5% on rent and 10% on food, beverages and rooms in hotels. The rest are hidden taxes in the form of 'fees', such as your car registration renewal and visa/permit fees.

9

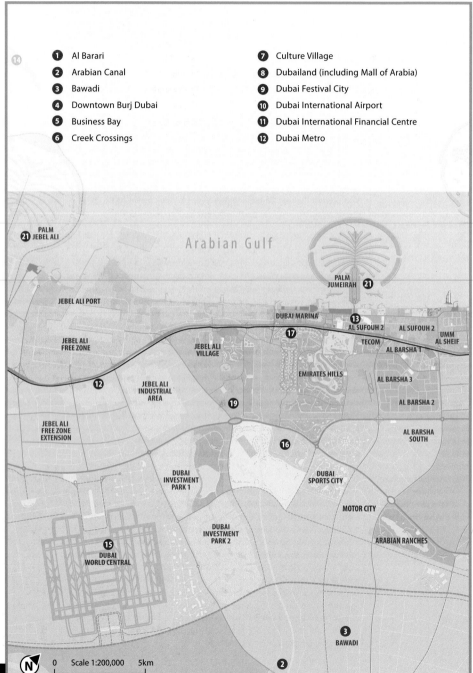

1 Al Barari
2 Arabian Canal
3 Bawadi
4 Downtown Burj Dubai
5 Business Bay
6 Creek Crossings

7 Culture Village
8 Dubailand (including Mall of Arabia)
9 Dubai Festival City
10 Dubai International Airport
11 Dubai International Financial Centre
12 Dubai Metro

Arabian Gulf

21 PALM JEBEL ALI

PALM JUMEIRAH 21

JEBEL ALI PORT

DUBAI MARINA

13

AL SUFOUH 2    AL SUFOUH 2    UMM AL SHEIF

17

TECOM

JEBEL ALI FREE ZONE

AL BARSHA 1

JEBEL ALI VILLAGE

EMIRATES HILLS    AL BARSHA 3

12

JEBEL ALI INDUSTRIAL AREA

AL BARSHA 2

19

JEBEL ALI FREE ZONE EXTENSION

AL BARSHA SOUTH

16

DUBAI INVESTMENT PARK 1

DUBAI SPORTS CITY

MOTOR CITY

DUBAI INVESTMENT PARK 2

ARABIAN RANCHES

15

DUBAI WORLD CENTRAL

3

BAWADI

N    0    Scale 1:200,000    5km

2

© Explorer Group Ltd. 2007

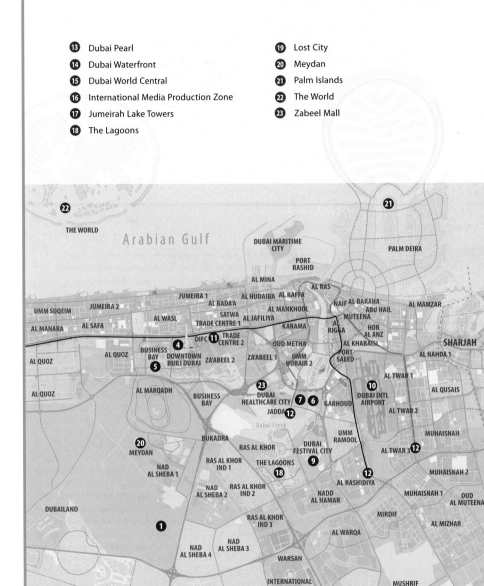

13 Dubai Pearl
14 Dubai Waterfront
15 Dubai World Central
16 International Media Production Zone
17 Jumeirah Lake Towers
18 The Lagoons

19 Lost City
20 Meydan
21 Palm Islands
22 The World
23 Zabeel Mall

22 THE WORLD

Arabian Gulf

21 PALM DEIRA

DUBAI MARITIME CITY

PORT RASHID

AL MINA

AL RAS

JUMEIRA 1
AL HUDAIBA AL RAFFA
NAIF AL BARAHA
AL MAMZAR

UMM SUQEIM
JUMEIRA 2
AL BADA'A
AL MANKHOOL
ABU HAIL
MUTEENA

AL WASL
SATWA AL JAFILIYA
TRADE CENTRE 1
AL RIGGA
HOR AL ANZ

AL MANARA
AL SAFA
DIFC 11 TRADE CENTRE 2
KARAMA
AL KHABAISI
SHARJAH

4
AL QUOZ
AL QUOZ
BUSINESS BAY
DOWNTOWN BURJ DUBAI
ZA'ABEEL 2
ZA'ABEEL 1
OUD METHA
UMM HURAIR 2
PORT SAEED
AL NAHDA 1

5

AL QUOZ
AL MARQADH
BUSINESS BAY
23 DUBAI HEALTHCARE CITY
7 6
GARHOUD
10 DUBAI INTL AIRPORT
AL TWAR 1
AL QUSAIS

12
JADDAF
AL TWAR 2

Dubai Creek
UMM RAMOOL
MUHAISNAH

20 MEYDAN
BUKADRA
RAS AL KHOR
DUBAI FESTIVAL CITY
AL TWAR 3 12

NAD AL SHEBA 1
RAS AL KHOR IND 1
THE LAGOONS
9
12
MUHAISNAH 2

NAD AL SHEBA 2
RAS AL KHOR IND 2
18
AL RASHIDIYA
MUHAISNAH 1
OUD AL MUTEENA

DUBAILAND
NADD AL HAMAR
MIRDIF

1
RAS AL KHOR IND 3
AL WARQA
AL MIZHAR

NAD AL SHEBA 4
NAD AL SHEBA 3
WARSAN

INTERNATIONAL CITY
AL WARQA
MUSHRIF

DUBAI SILICON OASIS
INTERNATIONAL CITY (PHASE 2)
WARSAN
WADI AL AMARDI

8
DUBAILAND
ACADEMIC CITY

© Explorer Group Ltd. 2007

*Beside Dubai Creek* ◀

## Dubai Festival City
*www.dubaifestivalcity.com*

A huge mixed-use development, featuring housing, offices, schools, hotels, retail, entertainment, a marina, and leisure facilities including a golf course and the region's first W Hotel.

**Size** 6.47 square kilometres, spanning 4km of creek frontage

**Completion** Some elements are already finished including the Festival Waterfront Centre (home to hundreds of shops, plus huge IKEA and ACE stores). The entire project will be completed by 2015

*Nxt Terminal 1* ◀
*Garhoud*

## Dubai International Airport
*www.dubaiairport.com*

Construction is already well underway on the new terminal and two new concourses, one exclusively for Emirates airline, plus a huge cargo terminal. Capacity once complete, the airport will be able to handle 70 million passengers a year, up from its present 28 million.

**Completion** Terminal 3 will open in 2008

*Parallel to Sheikh* ◀
*Zayed Road*
*From Emirates Towers to*
*behind the Dusit*

## Dubai International Financial Centre
*www.difc.ae*

DIFC aims to become a regional and global hub for banks, insurance companies and other financial institutions. The site will feature offices, hotels (including a Ritz-Carlton), apartments and restaurants, and is home to the impressive 'Gate' building and the Dubai International Financial Exchange.

**Size** 450,000 square metres

**Completion** The majority by 2008

*Throughout Dubai* ◀

## Dubai Metro
*www.dubaimetro.info*

Underground, overground, this light-rail network will operate driverless trains on four lines, including two linking Al Maktoum International Airport and Dubai International Airport. The network will include trams on Beach Road and Al Sufouh Road. It is estimated that by 2020, the metro will handle 1.85 million passengers a day (see also Metro p.58).

**Size** Total length of 318km by 2020

**Completion** The first trains should be running by September 2009.

*Near the entrance to* ◀
*Palm Jumeirah*
*Al Sufouh*

## Dubai Pearl
*www.dubaipearl.com*

Dubai Pearl will be neatly contained within a circle of land beside Media and Internet Cities, and promises office towers, freehold apartments, hotels, a shopping mall, an art gallery, and the Royal Hall, set to be the largest performing arts venue in the region.

**Size** The diameter of the circle is 500m

**Completion** End of 2008

*Adjoining* ◀
*Palm Jebel Ali*
*Next to Abu Dhabi*
*border*

## Dubai Waterfront
*www.dubaiwaterfront.ae*

Dwarfing all previous developments, Dubai Waterfront will consist of over 250 individual communities. Madinat Al Arab, another new 'downtown', will feature Al Burj – set to be one of the world's tallest buildings. Phase one sold out (to selected developers) within five days, for a cool Dhs.13 billion. The project is being developed by Nakheel, the firm responsible for the three Palms and The World.

**12**

# Economy

InterContinental, Festival City

Sports City, Dubailand

Palm Jumeira

Burj Dubai

Dubailand

**Size** 81 square kilometres, it will add 880km of new coastline
**Completion** First phase by 2010

## Dubai World Central

*Inland from Jebel Ali Port*

www.dubaiworldcentral.ae

Originally called Jebel Ali International Airport City, this will be a self-contained urban centre, based around a new airport with six runways. The first phase includes Dubai Logistics City, a regional hub for air, sea, and road freight. Once complete, DWC will feature commercial and residential areas, a science and technology park and a golf resort. It is expected to handle 120 million passengers a year by 2050.
**Size** DWC will eventually cover around 140 square kilometres
**Completion** The airport is expected to become operational in 2008

## International Media Production Zone

*Btn Autodrome and Green Community*
*Emirates Road*

www.impz.ae

This project is a free zone, not unlike Dubai Media City, but dedicated solely to the media production industry. The first phase will focus on the printing and publishing. Located off the E311 Emirates Road, the development will eventually house hotels, retail outlets, and residential and commercial towers.
**Size** 4 square kilometres of land
**Completion** 2008 onwards

## Jumeirah Lake Towers

*Between Interchanges 5 & 6*
*Sheikh Zayed Road*

www.jumeirahlaketowers.ae

A collection of 87 residential and commercial towers, grouped around a central lake. It is the first mixed-use development to become a free zone and will be a freehold project. The development will also be home to buildings belonging to the Dubai Multi Commodities Centre (www.dmcc.ae).
**Size** 87 towers between 35 and 45 floors high
**Completion** Some towers already finished; others to follow by 2008

## The Lagoons

*Close to Ras Al Khor Wildlife Sanctuary*
*Dubai Creek*

www.lagoons.ae

The lagoons is seven artificial islands under construction on the edge of Dubai Creek. The creek will be extended inland to create a new environmentally friendly development area, providing a range of housing as well as shopping centres, marinas, office space, cultural focal points (including an opera house) and five-star hotels.
**Size** 70 million square feet
**Completion** 2010

## Lost City

*Next to Ibn Battuta Mall*
*Jebel Ali*

www.nakheel.ae

A luxurious residential and commercial site boasting architecture influenced by South America, Persia and Asia. The area will have freshwater streams, cycling paths and an 18 hole golf course designed by Greg Norman.
**Size** 5.6 kilometres
**Completion** tbc

## Meydan

*Near Nad Al Sheba golf course*

www.meydan.ae

This new urban centre will incorporate a racecourse aimed at superseding the existing Nad Al Sheba track. The project aspires to create a 'horseracing city', with a

# monster
## property selection

With over 5,000 properties to choose from and the largest sellers' network in the region including the only certified consultants in the industry - real estate **is towering real high.**

• Residential    • Commercial    • Short-term Rentals    • Property Management

+971 4 344 7714        bhomes.com        betterhomes

business park, residential areas and shopping arcades. Due to become the new home of the Dubai Racing Club, Meydan will be linked to the creek by a canal, and will boast its own marina.

**Size** 15 million square feet

**Completion** 2010

*Off Dubai's coastline*
*Jebel Ali, Jumeirah*
*and Deira*

## Palm Islands

*www.thepalm.ae*

These three palm tree-shaped islands will extend out into the Arabian Gulf and increase Dubai's coastline by hundreds of kilometres. They will feature thousands of villas and apartments, numerous hotels, leisure and entertainment attractions, and retail outlets aplenty.

**Size** Trunk lengths: Jumeirah – 2km, Deira – 12.5km, Jebel Ali – 2.4km

**Completion** The first homes on Palm Jumeirah were released in 2007; land reclamation on Palm Deira is at 20% and will be completed in 2013; Jebel Ali's first properties should be complete by 2013

*3km off Dubai's coast*
*Between Jumeirah and*
*Deira Palm Islands*

## The World

*www.theworld.ae*

These 303 artificial islands in the Arabian Gulf will broadly represent a map of the world. The islands, varying in size, were offered for sale to individual buyers, who could then develop them as they wished. The islands will feature mansions, villas and apartments.

**Size** 9km east to west, 6km north to south

**Completion** Reclamation to be completed by 2008, construction by 2009

*Near Al Wasl Hospital*

## Zabeel Mall

*www.zabeelmall.ae*

Spread over eight storeys, this new mall will feature 280 retail outlets, 30 food and beverage outlets, a children's entertainment centre and an eight-screen cinema. The complex will also include 120 serviced apartments with facilities.

**Size** 400,000 square feet

**Completion** 2009

## International Relations

The UAE remains open in its foreign relations, and is firmly committed to the support of Arab unity. HH Sheikh Khalifa bin Zayed Al Nahyan is very generous with the country's wealth when it comes to helping Arab nations and communities that are in need of aid.

The UAE became a member of the United Nations and the Arab League in 1971. It is a member of the International Monetary Fund (IMF), the Organisation of Petroleum Exporting Countries (Opec), the World Trade Organisation (WTO) and other international and Arab organisations. It is also a member of the Arab Gulf Cooperation Council (AGCC, also known as the GCC), whose other members are Bahrain, Kuwait, Oman, Qatar and Saudi Arabia. Pioneered by the late Sheikh Zayed bin Sultan Al Nahyan, the UAE had a leading role in the formation of the AGCC, in 1981, and the country is the third largest member in terms of geographical size, after Saudi Arabia and Oman. All major embassies and consulates are represented either in Dubai or in Abu Dhabi, or both. The UAE does not officially recognise the state of Israel.

**Thinking of Buying?**

If you're dazzled by the array of dream homes in Dubai and want to get in on the property market, check out the *Dubai Red-Tape Explorer*. This informative guide explains the legal and financial procedures involved with buying property in the emirate.

## Government & Ruling Family

The Supreme Council of Rulers is the highest authority in the UAE, comprising the hereditary rulers of the seven emirates. Since the country is governed by hereditary rule there is little distinction between the royal families and the government. The Supreme Council is responsible for general policy matters involving education, defence, foreign affairs, communications and development, and for ratifying federal laws. The Council meets four times a year and the Abu Dhabi and Dubai rulers have effective power of veto over decisions.

The Supreme Council elects the chief of state (the President) from among its seven members. The current president is the ruler of Abu Dhabi, Sheikh Khalifa bin Zayed Al Nahyan. He took over the post in November 2004 from his late father, Sheikh Zayed bin Sultan Al Nahyan.

The Supreme Council also elects the Vice President of the UAE, currently Sheikh Mohammed bin Rashid Al Maktoum, Ruler of Dubai. The president and Vice President are elected and appointed for five-year terms, although they are often re-elected time after time, as was the case with Sheikh Zayed. The president appoints the prime minister (currently Sheikh Mohammed bin Rashid Al Maktoum) and the deputy prime ministers (currently Sheikh Sultan bin Zayed Al Nahyan and Sheikh Hamdan bin Zayed Al Nahyan). The emirate of Dubai is currently ruled by Sheikh Mohammed bin Rashid Al Maktoum, Vice President and Prime Minister of the UAE (who is considered the driving force behind Dubai's exponential growth) and his brother Sheikh Hamdan bin Rashid Al Maktoum, the UAE Minister of Finance and Industry.

The Federal National Council (FNC) reports to the Supreme Council. It has executive authority to initiate and implement laws and is a consultative assembly of 40 representatives. The Council currently monitors and debates government policy but has no power of veto.

The individual emirates still have a degree of autonomy, and laws that affect everyday life vary between them. For instance, if you buy a car in one emirate and need to register it in a different emirate, you will first have to export and then re-import it. All emirates have a separate police force, with different uniforms and cars.

## Dubai Ruling Family Tree

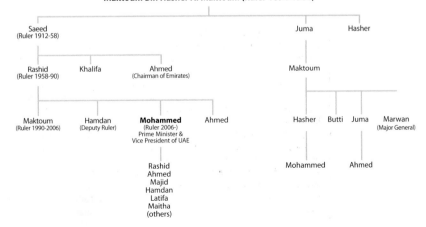

**Maktoum Bin Hasher Al Maktoum (Ruler 1894-1906)**

Saeed (Ruler 1912-58)

Juma    Hasher

Rashid (Ruler 1958-90)    Khalifa    Ahmed (Chairman of Emirates)    Maktoum

Maktoum (Ruler 1990-2006)    Hamdan (Deputy Ruler)    **Mohammed** (Ruler 2006-) Prime Minister & Vice President of UAE    Ahmed    Hasher    Butti    Juma    Marwan (Major General)

Rashid Ahmed Majid Hamdan Latifa Maitha (others)    Mohammed    Ahmed

## Population

All figures below are for National and expat residents.

- According to figures released from the 2005 national census, the population of the UAE stands at 4,104,695. This is a 74.8% increase on the 1995 census figure of 2,411,041.
- The UAE's population is made up of 20.1% Nationals and 79.9% expatriates.
- It is estimated that Dubai's population had risen to 1,422,000 by the end of 2006, compared with 674,101 in 1995 and 276,301 in 1980. This means that 31.8% of the total population of the UAE lives in Dubai.
- By 2017 it is estimated that the population of Dubai will have reached 3 million.
- The annual growth rate for Dubai is approximately 8%, and 7.5% for the UAE.
- In 2006, 292,000 new residents entered Dubai (800 per day).
- 73.4% of Dubai's population is male and 26.6% is female.
- A recent Dubai Municipality statistical survey revealed that the average size of a UAE National household is 7.6 members, while that of an expat is 3.7.
- According to the United Nations Development Program (UNDP), the UAE has the highest life expectancy in the Arab world at 72.2 years for males and 75.6 years for females.

*Source: www.tedad.ae*

### UAE Population Age Breakdown

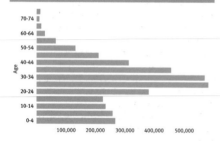

### UAE Population by Emirate

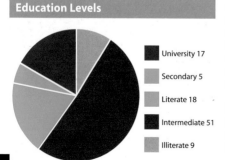

### Education Levels

University 17
Secondary 5
Literate 18
Intermediate 51
Illiterate 9

## National Flag

The UAE flag comprises three equal horizontal bands: green at the top, white in the middle and black at the bottom. A thicker, vertical band of red runs down the hoist side. The colours on the flag are common to many of the Arab nations and they symbolise Arab unity and independence.

In a nation continually striving for world records, it is no surprise that when the 30 year anniversary celebrations were marked on National Day 2001, one of the world's tallest flagpoles was erected in Abu Dhabi and the world's largest UAE flag was raised at Union House in Jumeira, Dubai.

## Local Time

The UAE is four hours ahead of UCT (Universal Coordinated Time – formerly known as GMT). There is no altering of clocks for daylight saving in the summer, so when Europe and North America loses an hour, the time in the UAE stays the same. During this period the time difference is one hour less, so when it is 12:00 in the UAE it is 09:00 in the UK instead of 08:00 during the winter. The table opposite shows time differences between the UAE and various cities around the world (not allowing for any daylight savings in those cities).

## Social & Business Hours

Social hours differ greatly in Dubai, with some people waking up early and working a straight shift (usually from 08:00 to 17:00 or 09:00 to 18:00, with an hour for lunch),

## Time Zones

| | |
|---|---|
| Athens | -2 |
| Auckland | +8 |
| Bangkok | +3 |
| Beijing | +4 |
| Canberra | +6 |
| Colombo | +2 |
| Denver | -11 |
| Doha | -1 |
| Dublin | -4 |
| Hong Kong | +4 |
| Johannesburg | -2 |
| Jordan | -2 |
| Karachi | +1 |
| Kuwait City | -1 |
| Lebanon | -2 |
| London | -4 |
| Los Angeles | -12 |
| Manama | -1 |
| Mexico City/Dallas | -10 |
| Moscow | -1 |
| Mumbai | +1.5 |
| Munich | -3 |
| Muscat | 0 |
| New York | -9 |
| Paris | -3 |
| Perth | +4 |
| Prague | -3 |
| Riyadh | -1 |
| Rome | -3 |
| Singapore | +4 |
| Sydney | +6 |
| Syria | -2 |
| Tokyo | +5 |
| Toronto | -9 |
| Wellington | +8 |

while others work a split shift (working from 09:00 to 13:00, then taking a long lunch break before returning to work from 16:00 to 19:00). Years ago, most of Dubai closed for a long period over lunch, opening again in the late afternoon. Even shops would close their doors at 13:00 and return for evening trading. However, these days the majority of larger shops and shopping centres are open throughout the day and into the evening, generally closing at 22:00. It is only the more traditional, smaller street traders that still close for three or four hours in the afternoon.

Friday is the Islamic holy day and therefore a universal day off for offices and schools. Consumer demand means that the hospitality and retail industries are open seven days a week. In 2006 the five-day working week for government departments and schools was set as Sunday to Thursday, bringing them into line with much of the private sector. There are still private companies which have retained the traditional Saturday to Wednesday working week, while others work five and a half days a week and some operate a six-day week, taking only Friday as a rest day. Government offices are generally open from 07:30 to 14:00, Sunday to Thursday. Private sector office hours vary between split shift days, which are generally 08:00 to 13:00, reopening at either 15:00 or 16:00 and closing at 18:00 or 19:00; or straight shifts, usually 09:00 to 18:00, with an hour for lunch.

Independent shop and souk opening times are usually based on split shift hours, while outlets in the big shopping malls remain open all day. Closing times are usually 22:00 or midnight, while some food shops and petrol stations are open 24 hours a day. On Fridays, many places are open all day, apart from prayer time (11:30 to 13:30), while larger shops in the malls only open in the afternoon from either 12:00 or 14:00.

Embassies and consulates are usually open from 07:30 to 14:30, but they may designate specific times and days for certain tasks (such as passport applications), so it's best to call before you go. Most embassies now take a Friday/Saturday weekend. All will have an emergency number on their answering service, website or on their office doors.

*UAE flag*

### Ramadan Hours

According to labour law, all companies are obliged to shorten the working day by two hours during Ramadan. Even though this is to assist Muslim employees who are fasting, the law makes no distinction in this regard between Muslim and non-Muslim employees. So technically, even expats are entitled to a shorter working day. However, many international companies do not follow this principle, and labour lawyers would advise you not to make a fuss if you are not given a shorter working day. Some lucky expats do get to work shorter hours during Ramadan, and many businesses, schools and shops change their hours slightly.

Dubai's traffic has a totally different pattern during Ramadan: instead of being gridlocked in the mornings and quiet in the afternoons, the mornings are almost jam-free and you'll sail through all the usual trouble spots, while in the afternoons the roads are totally clogged. Night-time activity increases during Ramadan, with many shops staying open later (until midnight or even 01:00) and the city's many shisha cafes and some restaurants staying open until the early hours.

**Lunar Calendar**
*The Hijri calendar is
based on lunar months;
there are 354 or 355
days in the Hijri year,
which is divided into 12
lunar months, and is
thus 11 days shorter
than the Gregorian
year. There are plenty of
websites with
Gregorian/Hijri calendar
conversion tools, so you
can find the equivalent
Hijri date for any
Gregorian date, and
vice versa. Try
www.rabiah.
com/convert.*

# Public Holidays

The Islamic calendar starts from the year 622AD, the year of Prophet Muhammad's migration (Hijra) from Mecca to Al Madinah. Hence the Islamic year is called the Hijri year and dates are followed by AH (AH stands for Anno Hegirae, meaning 'after the year of the Hijra').

As some holidays are based on the sighting of the moon and do not have fixed dates on the Hijri calendar, Islamic holidays are more often than not confirmed less than 24 hours in advance. Most companies send an email employees the day before, notifying them of the confirmed holiday date. Some non-religious holidays are fixed according to the Gregorian calendar. It should be noted that the public sector often gets additional days off for holidays where the private sector may not (for example on National Day the public sector gets two days of official holiday, whereas private sector companies take only one day). This can be a problem for working parents, as schools fall under the public sector and therefore get the extended holidays, so your children will usually have more days off than you do. No problem if you have full-time home help, but if not then you may have to take a day's leave.

| Public Holidays | |
|---|---|
| Eid Al Adha (4) 2007 | Dec 20 Moon |
| New Year's Day (1) | Jan 1 Fixed |
| Islamic New Year's Day (1) 2008 | Jan 10 Moon |
| Prophet Muhammad's Birthday (1) 2008 | Mar 20 Moon |
| Lailat Al Mi'Raj (1) 2008 | Jul 31 Moon |
| Eid Al Fitr (3) 2008 | Oct 2 Moon |
| UAE National Day (2) | Dec 2 Fixed |
| Eid Al Adha (4) 2008 | Dec 9 Moon |

The table above lists the holidays and the number of days they last. This applies mainly to the public sector, so if you work in the private sector you may get fewer days per holiday.

The main Muslim festivals are Eid Al Fitr (the festival of the breaking of the fast, which marks the end of Ramadan) and Eid Al Adha (the festival of the sacrifice, which marks the end of the pilgrimage to Mecca).

Mawlid Al Nabee is the holiday celebrating the Prophet Muhammad's birthday, and Lailat Al Mi'raj celebrates the Prophet's ascension into heaven.

# Photography

While it may lack the picturesque countryside of England or the quaint scenery of Europe, Dubai is still full of fascinating sights that you will want to capture with your camera. Normal tourist photography is acceptable but, like anywhere in the Arab world, it is courteous to ask permission before photographing people, particularly women. In general, photographs of government buildings, military installations, ports and airports should not be taken. See also Camera Equipment in Shopping (p.414).

*Dubai Creek Skyline*

## Climate

Dubai has a subtropical and arid climate. Sunny blue skies and high temperatures can be expected most of the year. Rainfall is infrequent and erratic, usually falling on an average of only 25 days per year, mainly in winter (December to March), but it often seems like less. While the number of days with rain can get as high as 18 per month in extreme cases, the average is five days per month through the winter, and when it does rain, it is not usually for very long or very heavily. However in the Hajar Mountains the amount of rainfall can be much higher, and flash floods in the wadis are not unheard of.

The last few years have not been particularly wet (2005-06 had only 74mm of rain), but compared to the previous few years they were a lot wetter. Between 2000 and 2003 total annual rainfall was as low as 8.8mm, less than 10% of the usual annual total. As it is not seen very often, heavy rainfall can really take its toll on the city within a relatively short period. Not all roads have adequate drainage, and even those that do are not designed for massive downpours and can get blocked by sand, resulting in waterlogging. In addition many of Dubai's drivers are not accustomed to wet conditions, and tend to respond by putting their hazard lights on, meaning you rarely know which direction they are heading.

Temperatures range from a low of around 10°C (50°F) in winter to a high of 48°C (118°F) in summer. The mean daily maximum is 24°C (75°F) in January, rising to 41°C (106°F) in August. Climatic changes have not had a marked effect, but local urbanisation and industrialisation factors, such as the vast increase in the amount of tarmac roads and large buildings since weather records began in the 1960s, have caused a slight increase in temperatures, especially the minimum temperature in winter.

During winter there are occasional sandstorms when the sand is whipped up off the desert. This is not to be confused with a shamal, a north-westerly wind that comes off the Arabian Gulf and can cool temperatures down. Sandstorms cover anything left outside in gardens or on balconies and can even blow inside, so make sure your doors and windows are shut.

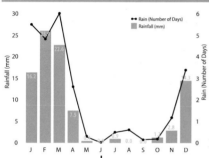

**Temperature & Humidity**

Humidity
Average Max. Temp
Average Min. Temp

**Rainfall**

Rain (Number of Days)
Rainfall (mm)

Surprisingly, mornings can get very foggy and humid especially in spring and autumn, but by mid-morning the sun invariably burns any cloud away. Humidity is usually between 50% and 65%, being slightly lower in the summer than the winter. However, when combined with the high summer temperatures, even 60% humidity can produce extremely uncomfortable conditions. The most pleasant time to visit Dubai is in the cooler winter months, when temperatures are perfect for comfortable days on the beach and long, lingering evenings outside. For up to date weather reports, log on to www.dubaiairport.com/dubaimet, or www.dubaitourism.co.ae.

## Flora & Fauna

As you would expect in a country with such an arid climate, the variety of flora and fauna is not as extensive as in other parts of the world. Still, a variety of plants and animals have managed to adapt to a life of high temperatures and low rainfall. Despite its sandy and rocky nature the UAE is adorned with many parks and green belts, and Dubai is no exception. The municipality has an extensive greening programme in place and areas along the roads are unusually colourful for a desert environment, with grass, palm trees and flowers being constantly maintained by an army of workers and round-the-clock watering. The city also boasts a large number of well-kept parks (see p.268).

### Flora

The region has about 3,500 endemic plants, which is perhaps surprising considering the high salinity of the soil and the harsh environment. The most famous is, of course, the date palm, which is also the most flourishing of the indigenous flora and provides wonderful seas of green, especially in the oases. Heading towards the mountains, flat-topped acacia trees and wild grasses create scenery not unlike that of an African savannah. The deserts are often surprisingly green in places, even during the dry summer months, but it takes an experienced botanist to get the most out of the area.

### Fauna

Indigenous fauna includes the Arabian leopard and the ibex, but sightings of them are extremely rare. Realistically, the only large animals you will see are camels and goats (often roaming dangerously close to roads). Other desert life includes the sand cat, sand fox and desert hare, plus gerbils, hedgehogs, snakes and geckos.

### Birds

Birdlife in the city is a little limited – this isn't a place for hearing a dawn chorus, unless you're extremely lucky. However, recent studies have shown that the number of species of birds is rising each year, due in part to the increasing lushness of the area. This is most apparent in the parks, especially in spring and autumn, as the country lies on the route for birds migrating between central Asia and east Africa. You can also see flamingos at the Khor Dubai Wildlife Sanctuary at the southern end of Dubai Creek.

### Marine Life

Off the coast of the UAE, the seas contain a rich abundance of marine life, including tropical fish, jellyfish, coral, the dugong ('sea cow') and sharks. Eight species of whale and seven species of dolphin have been recorded in UAE waters. Various breeds of turtle are also indigenous to the region. These include the loggerhead, green and hawksbill turtles, all of which are under threat. These are seen by divers off both coasts, and for swimmers or snorkellers, quite commonly just off the east coast at places such as Snoopy Island, and sometimes in Khor Kalba (p.297).

*See Them For Yourself*
*To get close to the flora and fauna of the UAE, you really need to go looking for them in the right places. On close inspection, you'll find that the sand dunes, mountains and wadis are full of hardy creatures that survive despite harsh conditions. Get out of the city and into some natural habitats – and don't forget to take a copy of the **UAE Off-Road Explorer** with you – it's the ultimate guide to the best off-road routes in the region.*

## Environmental Issues

The UAE has an internationally recognised commitment to the environment, which started under the late Sheikh Zayed. He set up the Zayed International Prize for the Environment and was awarded the WWF's (World Wide Fund for Nature) Gold Panda Award in 1997. However, despite this interest and enthusiasm at federal level, the UAE was recently announced as the worst country in the world for environmental impact in the Living Planet Report by the WWF (topping the table with the biggest 'ecological footprint' per person). The average resident of the UAE consumes more than double the amount of energy of citizens in countries such as France and the UK, and more than even America, traditionally the worst ecological offender.

Perhaps as a result of living in a nation inhabited by a vast majority of expatriates, the average UAE resident feels little responsibility towards the country's environment. There is a pressing need for residents to start making a personal contribution to reduce the impact of their prescence. It is being increasingly recognised throughout the world that the time left to be able to make a difference to the future of the planet is decreasing, and it will require everyone to get involved or the earth could well become a very different place for future generations. From turning your air conditioning down a degree or two and switching off electrical appliances when not in use to recycling as much of your waste as possible, there are plenty of things that are easy to do and can make the difference to the UAE's 'footprint'.

### Environmental Issues & Ecosystem

Despite efforts being made, there are some serious environmental issues facing the UAE. The massive scale of development being pursued in Dubai on gigantic projects such as the Palm Islands and Dubai Waterfront is changing the coastline of Dubai and its ecosystem immeasurably, while the desert is being swallowed up by Dubailand and other leisure and residential developments. In 2001, the Dubai government banned any further development along the coast without prior permission, although that seems something of a paradox in light of the projects that have already been granted permission. Conservationists have suggested that the massive construction for projects in the Arabian Gulf will destroy coral reefs and fish stocks, as well as damaging breeding grounds for endangered species such as the hawksbill turtle. In 2007, it was announced by Nakheel that it was becoming difficult to source sand for the land reclamation from inside UAE waters for these projects as so much has already been taken. Changes to the coastal environment have been on such a colossal scale that effects on marine life have been significant. Another result of these developments is the possible downsizing of future projects due to lack of sand.

*Khor Dubai flamingos*

The developers, however, argue that the sites will attract sealife, and point to the recent increase in fish and marine life witnessed around the crescent on the Palm Jumeirah. One strange by-product is that due to this crescent being six kilometres out to sea, certain species of shark that wouldn't normally come so close to the land have been spotted around the beaches. Also, while the UAE desert is not exactly teeming with wildlife, the animals that do survive are being affected by all the development and once gone from the country will be very difficult to reintroduce. While many conservationists slate the rapid expansion of Dubai's infrastructure, the issue remains contentious. Many other countries enjoyed their boom-time in the early part of the last century

23

when environmental issues were not as prominent as they are today, so in some ways it seems unfair that the UAE shouldn't be allowed to develop as other nations have. Then again, the UAE has the advantage of being able to learn from the experience of others, and if there had been more environmental awareness during the industrialisation of leading nations, the world would probably not require such drastic environmental measures. Whatever side you are on, it's safe to say that there are some green issues that could, and should, be given more consideration.

### Picture Perfect

*Images of Dubai* showcases the aesthetic and lush wonders of Dubai in breathtaking images that capture the marvels of the emirate and the diversity of its landscapes.

### Water Usage & Desalination

The lower than average rainfall over the last few years and the increasing demand for water from the UAE's growing population have compounded problems with the decreasing water table, which is at a record low. It was estimated in 2004 that the amount of water taken out of the ground was around 880 million m3 per year, while the amount going back in could be as low as 20 million m3. The water table has decreased by an average of one metre a year for the past 30 years, and if extraction of water from the ground continues at this rate, there is a very real danger of this water drying out completely. As the water table decreases, saltwater moves inland to fill the gap. This contaminates the fresh water stored underground, especially near the coast where the increasing salinity of the ground affects the fertility of the soil, hampering farming. It has even affected places as far inland as the Hajar Mountains, where inland freshwater wells have started to dry up in areas close to Masafi, home of the country's most famous brand of bottled water. One major factor is that the UAE currently has the highest water consumption per capita in the world, using an estimated 133 gallons a day, which is 150% of the amount used by the United States. To provide the ever-growing population of Dubai with water, a complex of desalination plants (the biggest in the world) were recently set up in Jebel Ali to boost production. However, considering the projected growth of Dubai, both businesses and residents need to help reduce the amount of water that is wasted. Charity starts at home, so why not do your bit by saving water wherever you can (for example turn off the tap as you're brushing your teeth) and encourage your company to take similar measures.

### Dolphin Friendly?

One proposed project that has come under widespread criticism is 'Dolphin Bay,' due to open in November 2008 as part of Palm Jumeirah's Atlantis. Animal welfare organisations have been critical of how the star attractions would have to be captured from the wild. They contend that no dolphinarium could ever be big enough to house these magnificent marine creatures, who can swim up to 100km per day in the wild. To find out more about dolphins in captivity, log on to www.wdcs.org.

### Environmental Organisations

Various organisations have been formed to protect the environment, as well as to educate the population on the importance of environmental issues. The Environment Agency Abu Dhabi (www.ead.ae) was established in 1996 to assist the Abu Dhabi government in the conservation and management of the emirate's natural environment, resources, wildlife and biological diversity. This organisation was previously known as the Environmental Research & Wildlife Development Agency (ERWDA) before it was renamed in 2005. Sir Bani Yas Island off Abu Dhabi is home to an internationally acclaimed breeding programme for endangered wildlife. There is also an active branch of the WWF in Dubai (04 353 7761). In addition, The Breeding Centre for Endangered Arabian Wildlife in Sharjah (06 531 1212) has a successful breeding programme for endangered wildlife, particularly the Arabian leopard. See also Environmental Groups (p.338).

# Culture & Lifestyle

**Cross Culture** ◀

The Sheikh Mohammed Centre for Cultural Understanding (04 353 6666) was established to help bridge the gap between cultures and give visitors a clearer appreciation of the Emirati way of life. It organises tours of Jumeira Mosque (p.259) where you can learn about Islam.

## Culture

Dubai's culture is firmly rooted in the Islamic traditions of Arabia. Islam is more than just a religion; it is a way of life that governs even mundane everyday events, from what to wear to what to eat and drink. Therefore, the culture and heritage of the UAE is closely linked to its religion. Unfortunately, Islamic fundamentalism has come to the forefront of the media in recent times and has lead many people around the world to adopt a very extreme, blanket view of the religion. However, in contrast to this image, the UAE is tolerant and welcoming; foreigners are free to practise their own religion, alcohol is served in hotels and the dress code is liberal. Women face little discrimination and, contrary to the policies of Saudi Arabia and Iran, are able to drive and walk around unescorted.

Among the most highly prized virtues are courtesy and hospitality, and visitors are likely to experience the genuine warmth and friendliness of the Emirati people. Luckily, the negative view of Islam that has affected many Muslims living abroad has not had an impact on Dubai, and you will find various nationalities, whether Muslim, Hindu or Christian, working and living side by side without any conflict. To Muslims, like many other religions and cultures, the family unit is very important, and elders are respected for their experience and ability to give advice. Many generations will live together in the same house. Polygamy is practised in the UAE, with Islam allowing a man to have up to four wives at one time, providing he has the financial and physical means to treat each of them equally.

The rapid economic development over the last 30 years has changed life in the Emirates beyond recognition. However, the country's rulers are committed to safeguarding their heritage against any erosion that could be caused by the speed of development and increased access to outside cultures and influence. They are therefore keen to promote cultural and sporting events that are representative of their traditions, such as falconry, camel racing and traditional dhow sailing. Arabic culture in poetry, dancing, songs and traditional art is encouraged, and weddings and celebrations are still colourful occasions of feasting and music.

### Poetry

Poetry is an integral and historically important part of Arabic culture. The ancient form of poetry is called Nabati, and is also known as Bedouin poetry. It is a rich form of literature slightly removed from classical Arabic. HH Sheikh Mohammed bin Rashid Al Maktoum is a renowned poet, and a patron of poetry competitions. The Palm Jebel Ali will feature water-homes constructed on stilts that when viewed from above spell out the following verse written by Sheikh Mohammed: 'Take wisdom from the wise, not everyone who rides a horse is a jockey. It takes a man of vision to write on water, great men rise to great challenges.'

## Language

Other options **Learning Arabic** p.222, **Language Schools** p.354

Arabic is the official language of the UAE, although English, Hindi, Malayalam and Urdu are commonly spoken. Arabic is the official business language, but English is so widely used that you could conduct business here for years without learning a single word of Arabic. Most road signs, shop signs and restaurant menus are in both languages. The further out of town you go, the more you will find just Arabic, both spoken and on street and shop signs.

Arabic isn't the easiest language to pick up, or to pronounce. But if you can throw in a couple of words here and there, you're more likely to receive a warmer welcome or at least a smile – even if your pronunciation is terrible.

See the table on p.26 for a list of useful Arabic phrases.

## Basic Arabic

| General | |
|---|---|
| Yes | na'am |
| No | la |
| Please | min fadlak (m) / min fadliki (f) |
| Thank you | shukran |
| Please (in offering) | tafaddal (m) / tafaddali (f) |
| Praise be to God | al-hamdu l-illah |
| God willing | in shaa'a l-laah |

| Greetings | |
|---|---|
| Greeting | |
| (peace be upon you) | as-salaamu alaykom |
| Greeting (in reply) | wa alaykom is salaam |
| Good morning | sabah il-khayr |
| Good morning (in reply) | sabah in-nuwr |
| Good evening | masa il-khayr |
| Good evening (in reply) | masa in-nuwr |
| Hello | marhaba |
| Hello (in reply) | marhabtayn |
| How are you? | kayf haalak (m) / kayf haalik (f) |
| Fine, thank you | zayn, shukran (m) / zayna, shukran (f) |
| Welcome | ahlan wa sahlan |
| Welcome (in reply) | ahlan fiyk (m) / ahlan fiyki (f) |
| Goodbye | ma is-salaama |

| Introduction | |
|---|---|
| My name is... | ismiy… |
| What is your name? | shuw ismak (m) / shuw ismik (f) |
| Where are you from? | min wayn inta (m) / min wayn inti (f) |
| I am from... | anaa min... |
| America | ameriki |
| Britain | braitani |
| Europe | oropi |
| India | al hindi |

| Questions | |
|---|---|
| How many / much? | kam? |
| Where? | wayn? |
| When? | mataa? |
| Which? | ayy? |
| How? | kayf? |
| What? | shuw? |
| Why? | laysh? |
| Who? | miyn? |
| To/for | ila |
| In/at | fee |
| From | min |
| And | wa |
| Also | kamaan |
| There isn't | maa fee |

| Taxi / Car Related | |
|---|---|
| Is this the road to... | hadaa al tariyq ila... |
| Stop | kuf |
| Right | yamiyn |
| Left | yassar |
| Straight ahead | siydaa |
| North | shamaal |
| South | januwb |
| East | sharq |
| West | garb |
| Turning | mafraq |
| First | awwal |
| Second | thaaniy |
| Road | tariyq |
| Street | shaaria |
| Roundabout | duwwaar |
| Signals | ishaara |
| Close to | qarib min |
| Petrol station | mahattat betrol |
| Sea/beach | il bahar |
| Mountain/s | jabal/jibaal |
| Desert | al sahraa |
| Airport | mataar |
| Hotel | funduq |
| Restaurant | mata'am |
| Slow Down | schway schway |

| Accidents | |
|---|---|
| Police | al shurtaa |
| Permit/licence | rukhsaa |
| Accident | haadith |
| Papers | waraq |
| Insurance | ta'miyn |
| Sorry | aasif (m) / aasifa (f) |

| Numbers | |
|---|---|
| Zero | sifr |
| One | waahad |
| Two | ithnayn |
| Three | thalatha |
| Four | arba'a |
| Five | khamsa |
| Six | sitta |
| Seven | saba'a |
| Eight | thamaanya |
| Nine | tiss'a |
| Ten | ashara |
| Hundred | miya |
| Thousand | alf |

## Religion

Islam is the official religion of the UAE, and is widely practised. The Islamic holy day is Friday. The basis of Islam is the belief that there is only one God and that Prophet Muhammed is his messenger. There are five pillars of the faith which all Muslims must follow: the Profession of Faith, Prayer, Charity, Fasting and Pilgrimage. Every Muslim is expected, at least once in his or her lifetime, to make the pilgrimage (Hajj) to the holy city of Mecca (also spelt Makkah) in Saudi Arabia.

### Places of Worship

| | | |
|---|---|---|
| Arab Evangelical Church of Dubai | 04 884 6630 | Jebel Ali |
| Church of Jesus Christ of Latter-Day Saints | 04 395 3883 | Oud Metha |
| Emirates Baptist Church International | 04 349 1596 | Jumeira |
| Holy Trinity Church (Church of England) | 04 337 0247 | Oud Metha |
| Marthoma Syrian Church of Malabar | 04 884 5233 | Jebel Ali |
| New Frontiers International New Covenant Church | 04 335 1597 | Oud Metha |
| St. Francis of Assisi Roman Catholic Church | 04 884 5104 | Jebel Ali |
| St. Mary's Roman Catholic Church | 04 337 0087 | Oud Metha |
| United Christian Church of Dubai | 04 344 2509 | Al Wasl |
| | 04 884 6623 | Jebel Ali |

Additionally, a Muslim is required to pray (facing Mecca) five times a day. The times vary according to the position of the sun. Most people pray at a mosque, although it's not unusual to see people kneeling by the side of the road if they are not near a place of worship. It is considered impolite to stare at people praying or to walk over prayer mats. The modern-day call to prayer, transmitted through loudspeakers on the minarets of each mosque, ensures that everyone knows it's time to pray. In Dubai, the plan is to build enough mosques so that people don't have to walk more than 500 metres to reach one.

Islam shares a common ancestry with Christianity and many of the prophets before Muhammad can be found in Christian as well as Muslim writings.

Under Islamic Shariah law, Muslim men are allowed to marry non-Muslim women, but a Muslim woman is not allowed to marry a non-Muslim man.

While the predominant religion is Islam, Dubai is tolerant of many other denominations, and the ruling family has, on numerous occasions, donated plots of land for the building of churches. Current churches include the Evangelical Church, Holy Trinity, United Christian Church and St Mary's (Roman Catholic), plus the various churches grouped together in a complex at Jebel Ali. There's also a Hindu temple in Bur Dubai.

### Ramadan

Ramadan is the holy month in which Muslims commemorate the revelation of the Holy Quran (the holy book of Islam). It's a time of fasting and Muslims abstain from all food, drinks, cigarettes and unclean thoughts (or activities) between dawn and dusk. In the evening, the fast is broken with the Iftar feast. Iftar timings are found in all the daily newspapers.

All over the city, festive Ramadan tents are filled to the brim each evening with people of all nationalities and religions enjoying shisha, traditional Arabic mezze and sweets. In addition to the standard favourite shisha cafes and restaurants around town, the five-star hotels erect special Ramadan tents for the month.

The timing of Ramadan is not fixed in terms of the western calendar, but each year it occurs around 11 days earlier than the previous year, with the start date depending on the sighting of the moon (see Public

### Arabic Family Names

*Arabic names have a formal structure that traditionally indicates the person's family and tribe. Names are usually taken from an important person in the Quran or someone from the tribe. This is followed by the word bin (son of) for a boy or bint (daughter of) for a girl, and then the name of the child's father. The last name indicates the person's tribe or family. For prominent families, this has Al, the Arabic word for 'the', immediately before it. For instance, the President of the UAE is His Highness Sheikh Khalifa bin Zayed Al Nahyan. When women get married, they do not change their name.*

### Call to Prayer

There are five calls to prayer throughout the day. They are Fajr at dawn, Juma in the middle of the day, Asr at mid-afternoon, Maghrib at sunset, and Isha at nightfall. The English translation of the call to prayer (Adhan) is something along the lines of 'God is most great, God is most great. There is no God except God, there is no God except God. Mohammed is the messenger of God, Mohammed is the messenger of God. Come to prayer, come to prayer, come to salvation, come to salvation. God is great, God is great. There is none worthy of worship except God.'

27

Holidays on p.20). In 2008, Ramadan is expected to commence on September 1 or thereabouts. Non-Muslims are also required to refrain from eating, drinking or smoking in public places during daylight hours as a sign of respect. Failure to do so could upset people or lead to an official complaint. If a passing policeman spotted you he'd most likely stop to explain what was expected. If you are uncooperative you may end up being taken to the police station.

During Ramadan the sale of alcohol in most outlets is restricted to after dusk, and office hours are cut (always for Muslims, sometimes for non-Muslims), while shops and parks usually open and close later. In addition, no live music or dancing is allowed (so nightclubs

*Deira Souk mannequin*

tend to close for the entire month) and cinemas limit daytime screenings of films. Ramadan ends with a three-day celebration and holiday called Eid Al Fitr, the feast of the breaking of the fast. For Muslims, Eid has similar connotations as Diwali for Hindus and Christmas for Christians.

## National Dress

*Dressing Down*

*Sharjah has a less liberal attitude to dress code and moral behaviour. 'Indecent dress' includes anything that exposes the stomach, back or legs above the knees. Tight-fitting, transparent clothing is also best avoided, as are acts of vulgarity, indecent noises or harassment.*

On the whole, the local population wear their traditional dress in public. For men this is the dishdash(a) or khandura: a white full length shirt dress, which is worn with a white or red checked headdress, known as a gutra. This is secured with a black cord (agal). Sheikhs and important businessmen may also wear a thin black or brown robe (known as a bisht or mishlah), over their dishdasha at important events, which is equivalent to the dinner jacket in western culture.

In public, women wear the black abaya – a long, loose black robe that covers their normal clothes – plus a headscarf called the sheyla. The abaya is often of very sheer, flowing fabric and may be open at the front. Some women also wear a thin black veil hiding their face and/or gloves, and older women sometimes still wear a leather mask, known as a burkha, which covers the nose, brow and cheekbones. Underneath the abaya, women traditionally wear a long tunic over loose, flowing trousers (sirwall), which are often heavily embroidered and fitted at the wrists and ankles. However, these are used more by the older generation and modern women will often wear the latest fashions from international labels under their abayas.

### National Weddings

Weddings in the UAE are very large, serious affairs. Homes are lit from top to bottom with strings of white lights and the festivities last up to two weeks. Men and women celebrate separately, normally in a hotel ballroom or convention centre, depending on the number of guests.

The government-sponsored Marriage Fund, based in Abu Dhabi, assists Nationals with marriage, from counselling and financial assistance (long term loans up to Dhs.70,000 for a UAE National man marrying a UAE National woman) to organising group

**Big Weddings**
*High dowries and extravagant weddings may be a thing of the past, as the government has placed a ceiling of Dhs.50,000 on dowries, and lavish weddings can result in a prison sentence or Dhs.500,000 fine.*

weddings to keep costs down. With so many UAE Nationals studying abroad, and so many expats in Dubai, inter-cultural marriages are increasingly common. The Marriage Fund strongly advises Nationals to marry fellow Nationals (in an effort to preserve the culture and reduce the number of UAE spinsters), although it is easier for a National man to marry a non-National woman than it is for a National woman to marry a non-National man.

## Food & Drink

Other options **Eating Out** p.496

You can eat your way around the world in Dubai – it is home to every cuisine imaginable, from European and American to Indian and Asian. Not only can you feast on exotic cuisines in the city's numerous five-star outlets, you can also find cheaper options at the many street cafes and independent restaurants. You'll also find all the obligatory fast-food outlets such as McDonald's, KFC, Pizza Hut and Burger King here. In terms of food shopping, the mix of nationalities is once again advantageous – supermarkets tend to stock a range of products from around the world to keep their multinational client base happy. Spinneys and Park n Shop stock British and South African products, Safestway stocks more American products, and Choithram has a mix of both. Carrefour and Géant are both huge and stock products from just about everywhere (although not as specialised as the smaller stores). Fruit and vegetables are imported from around the world, and so can be a bit more expensive than buying local produce. There is some local produce available, mainly cucumbers, tomatoes, aubergines, courgettes, green peppers and potatoes, and these items are extremely cheap. For a more colourful food-buying experience, head to the fruit and vegetable market off Emirates Road where you can buy vast quantities of various fruits and vegetables at low prices. The fish market in Deira is also worth a trip – not only will you find a seemingly unlimited range of fresh fish and seafood at low prices, but you can also soak up the authentic atmosphere.

### Arabic Cuisine

On your first trip back to your home country you may find yourself craving the distinctive Arabic cuisine that's so easily available throughout Dubai. Most of the Arabic food available here is based predominantly on Lebanese cuisine. Common dishes are shawarmas (lamb or chicken carved from a spit and served in a pita bread with salad and tahina), falafel (mashed chickpeas and sesame seeds, rolled into balls and deep fried), hummus (a creamy dip made from chickpeas and olive oil), and tabbouleh (finely chopped parsley, mint and crushed wheat). And to round off your meal, you must sample the extensive variety of fresh juices.

### Emirati Cuisine

There are also opportunities to sample the local Emirati food. The legacy of the UAE's trading past means that local cuisine uses a blend of ingredients imported from around Asia and the Middle East. Spices such as cinnamon, saffron and turmeric along with nuts (almonds or pistachios), limes and dried fruit add

**Dates**
As one of the very few crops that thrive naturally across the Middle East, date palms have been cultivated as an invaluable source of nutrition for up to 5,000 years. It's said that in some countries the Bedouin way of life was sustained primarily by dates and camel milk up until as recently as the mid 20th century. Along with their high energy content, dates are also high in fibre, potassium, vitamins, magnesium and iron and contain negligible quantities of fat, cholesterol and salt. Even just five dates per day provide enough nutrition for the recommended daily portions of fruit or vegetables.

interesting flavours to Emirati dishes. Dried limes are a common ingredient in Arabic cuisine, reflecting a Persian influence. They are dried in the sun and are used to flavour dishes, either whole or ground in a spice mill. They impart a distinctively musty, tangy, sour flavour to soups and stews.

### Eating Arabic Style
*Culturally speaking, eating in the Middle East is traditionally a social affair. Whether eating at home with extended families, or out with large groups, the custom is for everybody to share a veritable feast of various dishes, served in communal bowls. Starters are generally enjoyed with flat Arabic bread, and main courses are often eaten with the fingers.*

### Arabic Coffee
*The serving of traditional coffee (kahwa) is an important social ritual in the Middle East. Local coffee is mild with a distinctive taste of cardamom and saffron, and it is served black without sugar. It is served with dates, to sweeten the palate between sips. It is considered polite to drink about three cups of the coffee when offered (it is served in tiny cups, about the size of an egg cup).*

## Pork

Pork is taboo in Islam. Muslims should not eat, prepare or serve pork. In order for a restaurant to serve pork on its menu, it should have a separate fridge, preparation equipment and cooking areas. Supermarkets also require pork to be sold in a separate area; you can buy pork mainly from Spinneys, Park n Shop and Choithram, but you have to find the screened-off pork section first. All meat products for Muslim consumption have to be 'halaal', which refers to the method of slaughter.
As pork is not locally produced you will find that it's more expensive than many other meats.

## Alcohol

Alcohol is only served in licensed outlets associated with hotels (restaurants and bars), plus a few leisure clubs (such as golf clubs and sports clubs) and associations. Restaurants outside of hotels that are not part of a club or association are not permitted to serve alcohol.
Nevertheless, permanent residents who are non-Muslims can obtain alcohol for consumption at home without any difficulty. All they have to do is get a liquor licence (see p.90 for the procedure).

## Shisha

Smoking the traditional shisha (water pipe) is a popular and relaxing pastime enjoyed throughout the Middle East. It is usually savoured in a local cafe while chatting with friends. They are also known as hookah pipes or hubbly bubbly, but the proper name is nargile. Shisha pipes can be smoked with a variety of aromatic flavours, such as strawberry, grape or apple, and the experience is unlike normal cigarette or cigar smoking. The smoke is 'smoothed' by the water, creating a much more soothing effect (although it still causes smoking related health problems).

Smoking shisha is one of those things during your time in Dubai that should be tried at least once, especially during Ramadan, when tents are erected throughout the city and filled with people of all nationalities. You can buy your very own shisha pipe from the Arabian souvenir shops or from Carrefour supermarket, and once you get to grips with putting it all together you can enjoy the unique flavour anytime you want. See also Shisha Cafes (p.572).

*Shisha pipes*

# In Emergency

If you need to see a doctor during your stay in Dubai, there are two options: private or government. If you have medical insurance, check out p.182 in the Residents chapter for an overview of the private hospitals. If you are happy with a government-run hospital, there is either Rashid Hospital (04 337 4000), the main emergency hospital for Dubai, located next to Dubai Creek, or the Iranian Hospital (04 344 0250), a government-affiliated hospital on Al Wasl Road in Satwa. Dial 999 for emergency services if you need an ambulance, or you can make your own way there if you are well enough. Treatment at Rashid Hospital is free for all emergencies, and costs Dhs.100 for a consultation with a doctor. Medicines prescribed can be bought at any chemist. Iranian Hospital charges Dhs.50 for consultations and it usually offers free medicine from the pharmacy in the hospital. In case you need medical help for children, Al Wasl Hospital (04 324 1111) is renowned as one of the best places for paediatric care in the Middle East, government or private, and is located near the Wafi interchange.

| Emergency Services | | |
| --- | --- | --- |
| Al Wasl Hospital | 04 324 1111 | Hospital |
| Ambulance | 998 /999 | Emergency Services |
| American Hospital | 04 336 7777 | Hospital |
| Cedars Jebel Ali International Hospital | 04 881 4000 | Hospital |
| Department for Tourist Security | 800 4438 | Police Services |
| DEWA Emergency | 991 | Emergency Services |
| Dubai Police Emergency | 999 | Emergency Services |
| Dubai Police HQ | 04 229 2222 | Police Services |
| Fire Department | 997 | Emergency Services |
| Iranian Hospital | 04 344 0250 | Hospital |
| Life Pharmacy | 04 344 1122 | 24 hour pharmacy |
| Municipality Emergency Number | 04 223 2323 | Emergency Services |
| Rashid Hospital | 04 337 4000 | Hospital |
| Rashidiya Pharmacy | 04 285 0692 | 24 hour pharmacy |
| Welcare Hospital | 04 282 7788 | Hospital |

# Women

Women should face few, if any, problems while travelling in the UAE. One of the most annoying occurances is the tendency of men in the region to stare unashamedly at women, which can make you feel uncomfortable. Rest assured that in most cases this habit, while infuriating, is borne more out of curiosity rather than sexual deviance, and poses little danger to women. A directive straight from Sheikh Mohammed himself orders men who are caught harassing women to be punished, and 'named and shamed' by having their photos printed in the newspaper.

In contrast with the more radical views of neighbouring Saudi Arabia, the UAE, along with most of the other smaller Gulf states, offers women the same rights as men including travelling alone, driving, owning and renting cars and dressing as they please. However, it is courteous to dress with a little modesty in consideration for local customs. If you venture into the other parts of the country, people in small villages in particular tend to be a lot more conservative.

# Children

Other options **Kids' Clothes** p.436, **Kids' Items** p.436

Dubai is an excellent place for children: safe, with good facilities, and a lot on offer to keep them amused. Hotels and shopping malls are well equipped, offering everything from babysitting services to state-of-the-art amusement centres. Discounted rates for children are common so always ask. The health clubs belonging to hotels often have separate kids' clubs for hotel guests and health club members. Child-friendly restaurants vary between just having a children's menu to offering activities or separate areas for families. Some places tend not to have many high chairs, so it's best to ask when making reservations. To find a restaurant or cafe that is

**31**

## Embassies & Consulates

| | | |
|---|---|---|
| Australian Consulate | 04 508 7100 | 7 C3 |
| Bahrain Embassy | 02 665 7500 | 1 D2 |
| British Embassy | 04 309 4444 | 9 B3 |
| Canadian Consulate | 04 314 5555 | 8 F3 |
| Chinese Consulate | 04 394 4733 | 8 C4 |
| Czech Embassy | 02 678 2800 | 1 D2 |
| Danish Consulate | 04 222 7699 | 9 C4 |
| Egyptian Consulate | 04 397 1122 | 9 A4 |
| French Consulate | 04 332 9040 | 7 F2 |
| German Consulate | 04 397 2333 | 9 A4 |
| Indian Consulate | 04 397 1222 | 9 A4 |
| Iranian Consulate | 04 344 4717 | 7 F1 |
| Irish Embassy (Saudi Arabia) | +966-1488 2300 | na |
| Italian Consulate | 04 331 4167 | 10 A1 |
| Japanese Consulate | 04 331 9191 | 10 A1 |
| Jordanian Consulate | 04 397 0500 | 9 A4 |
| Kuwaiti Consulate | 04 397 8000 | 9 A4 |
| Lebanese Consulate | 04 397 7450 | 7 F1 |
| Malaysian Consulate | 04 335 5528 | 10 D2 |
| Netherlands Consulate | 04 352 8700 | 8 F3 |
| New Zealand Consulate | 04 331 7500 | 7 F2 |
| Norwegian Consulate | 04 353 3833 | 9 A1 |
| Omani Consulate | 04 397 1000 | 9 A4 |
| Pakistani Consulate | 04 397 0412 | 9 A4 |
| Philippine Consulate | 04 266 9643 | 14 C3 |
| Qatar Consulate | 04 398 2888 | 8 C4 |
| Russian Consulate | 04 223 1272 | 9 C4 |
| Saudi Arabian Consulate | 04 397 9777 | 9 A4 |
| South African Consulate | 04 397 5222 | 9 A4 |
| Spanish Embassy | 02 626 9544 | 1 D2 |
| Sri Lankan Consulate | 04 398 6535 | 8 C2 |
| Swedish Embassy | 02 621 0162 | 1 D2 |
| Swiss Consulate | 04 329 0999 | 10 A1 |
| Thai Consulate | 04 349 2863 | 7 C2 |
| US Consulate General | 04 311 6000 | 10 A1 |

recommended for eating out with children, look out for the 'Kid Friendly' icon in reviews in the Going Out section (p.495). One part of Dubai life that is particularly good for families with young children is Friday brunch, with many outlets providing special entertainment for the little ones while mum and dad make repeat trips to the buffet (see Friday Brunch on p.573). The best time of year in Dubai for kids is the winter, as they can enjoy outside activities. One of the best events of the year is the Dubai Shopping Festival (p.68), which takes place in January/February. There is much more on offer than just shopping, with events and attractions organised across town. In summer, when the weather can be uncomfortable, there are still a good number of indoor activities to keep your little ones occupied. The Dubai Summer Surprises (p.70) festival offers all sorts of fun-filled activities for the whole family.

The city is dotted with numerous surprisingly green parks, and its beach parks (p.267) are well equipped with sports and amusement facilities. Water activities, horse riding, sports clubs and other adventure sports are all catered for and there is also a wide variety of amusement centres, water parks and theme parks. See the Directory in the Exploring section (p.274) for more details.

## People With Disabilities

In keeping with its philosophy of being 'The City that Cares', Dubai is starting to consider the needs of disabled visitors more seriously. Dubai International Airport is well equipped for disabled travellers, with automatic doors, large lifts and all counters accessible by wheelchair users, as well as several services such as porters, special transportation and quick check-in to avoid long queues. Dubai Transport has a few specially modified taxis for journeys from the airport and around town. Handicapped parking spaces do exist, but are often taken up by ignorant drivers who don't need the facility.

Most of Dubai's five-star hotels have wheelchair access; for places with specially adapted rooms for the disabled, look out for the icon on the Hotels table (p.44). In general, facilities for disabled guests are limited, particularly at tourist attractions. Wheelchair ramps are often really nothing more than delivery ramps and therefore have steep angles. When asking if a location has wheelchair access, make sure it really does – an escalator is considered 'wheelchair access' to some.

The Dubai Department of Tourism and Commerce Marketing (DTCM) is responsible for improving access for the physically challenged (www.dubaitourism.ae/disabled).

## Dress

No matter how cosmopolitan Dubai becomes, there are still people outside the Middle East of the opinion that it is a conservative city where women have to cover

**Smoke Signals**
*Smoking is now banned
in all government
departments, public
buildings and shopping
malls (with designated
smoking areas remaining
in some places). In
November 2007 all
restaurants and cafes
became smoke-free
environments, though
some may decide to
create non-intrusive areas
for smokers. Many
restaurants and cafes
appeared unprepared for
the ban, and it is unclear
whether it will be strictly
enforced. You will be fined
in Dubai if you are seen
throwing a cigarette butt
onto the street.*

their faces and wear long black robes. Nothing could be further from the truth. Although the UAE is a Muslim country, there is no need for women to cover up. It is another common misconception that local women are poor, downtrodden souls who are forced by their domineering husbands to hide themselves behind shrouds of black and full veils – the truth is that UAE women are well educated, well respected, and increasingly outspoken, and those that wear headscarves or veils do it mostly out of choice and respect for their religion.

There are no real restrictions on dress codes in Dubai (as opposed to in neighbouring emirate Sharjah, where things are more conservative and both men and women should dress appropriately). However, topless sunbathing for women is a definite no-no, and any clothing that reveals the bits only your mother, husband or doctor should see are best left at home. But with the beautiful climate, shorts and T-shirts are acceptable, as are dresses or tops with spaghetti straps. When going to places frequented by Muslims, it is courteous to dress more modestly and during Ramadan, more sensitivity should be shown too. During the cooler months (October to April), it is often necessary to wear a light jacket or cardigan as the temperature drops into the low teens. Everything in the city is air conditioned, and sometimes indoor temperatures can be uncomfortably cold.

**Stare**
As annoying and infuriating as it is to have someone blatantly stare at you, the good news is that these stares are not really sexual in nature – they are more the result of curiosity. The bad news is that there is little you can do to stop this strange little quirk of living in the region. Your best defence is to avoid wearing tight or revealing clothing, particularly in certain areas such as the Gold Souk.

## Crime & Safety
Other options **In Emergency** p.31

While the crime rate in Dubai is very low, a healthy degree of caution should still be exercised. Keep your valuables and travel documents locked in your hotel room or in the hotel safe. When in crowds, be discreet with your money and wallet; don't carry large amounts of cash on you and don't trust strangers. Money and gem-related scams run by con men are on the increase so don't be bullied into anything.

With the multitude of driving styles converging on Dubai's roads, navigating the streets either on foot or in a vehicle can be a challenge. When walking, you need to be really aware of the traffic, as cars tend to do unpredictable things and don't give pedestrians the space or consideration you might be used to. When crossing roads use designated pedestrian crossings wherever possible (jaywalking is actually illegal), and make sure all cars are actually going to stop for you before crossing.

*Burj Al Arab and Madinat Jumeirah*

If you plan on driving yourself, make sure you know the rules of the road, exercise extreme caution as traffic accidents are an all too common occurrence on Dubai's busy roads, always pay much more attention to your mirrors than you would do normally, and know what's happening around you at all times. For what to do in the event of an accident, see In Emergency on p.31. Never drive without the correct documentation and insurance.

## Police

In an effort to better serve Dubai's visitors, the Dubai Police has launched the Department for Tourist Security. It acts as a liaison between you and Dubai Police, although in general police officers are extremely helpful. They are calm and understanding, and speak a multitude of languages. Its website (www.dubaipolice.gov.ae) is easy to navigate, helpful, and has extensive information on policies and procedures. For assistance, call the toll free number (800 4438). In 2007, a new hotline number was launched for people suffering problems on the beach (04 203 6398). These could include sexual harassment or annoyance by quad bikes. For other emergency services call 999 for Police or Ambulance and 997 for Fire.

### Travel Insurance

All visitors to the Emirates should have travel insurance – just in case. Choose a reputable insurer with a plan that suits your needs and the activities you plan to do while in Dubai, especially if they involve extreme sports such as quad biking, diving or skiing. There is every chance that no accidents or illnesses will befall you while you're here, but this is one of those things in life that's better to have and not need, than to need and not have. A good travel insurance policy will not only cover you for illness and injury, but also for loss or damage to your luggage. Just be sure to read the small print – many policies don't cover costs if you injure yourself while under the influence of alcohol or while partaking in extreme sports.

*Money Matters*
*There has been talk of restrictions on the import and export of large amounts of any currency since the events of 11 September 2001. Do your homework before you attempt to carry wads of cash into or out of Dubai. The current limit for undeclared cash that can be brought into the country is Dhs.40,000.*

## Lost & Stolen Property

To avoid a great deal of hassle if your personal documents go missing, make sure you keep one photocopy with friends or family back home and one copy in a secure place, such as a safe. There are a lot of honest people in Dubai who will return found items. If you have no luck, then try the Dubai Police (999) or the Department for Tourist Security (800 4438 – toll free) to report the loss or theft; you'll be advised on a course of action. If you've lost something in a taxi, call the taxi company (p.58). If you lose your passport, your next stop should be your embassy or consulate. See p.32 for a list of all embassies and consulates in Dubai.

## Dubai Tourist Info Abroad

The Dubai Department of Tourism and Commerce Marketing operates 14 offices overseas, which promote Dubai to both travellers and businesses. They participate in travel fairs and exhibitions as well as conducting orientation workshops for travel agents in various countries interested in Dubai (www.dubaitourism.ae).

### Dubai Tourism Offices Overseas

| Australia & NZ | Sydney | +61 2 9956 6620 |
| Far East | Hong Kong | +852 2827 5221 |
| France | Paris | +33 1 4495 8500 |
| Germany | Frankfurt | +49 69 710 0020 |
| India | Mumbai | +91 22 4002 7114 |
| Italy | Milan | +39 02 5740 3036 |
| Japan | Tokyo | +81 3 5367 5450 |
| Russia, CIS & Baltic States | Moscow | +7 495 980 0717 |
| Saudi Arabia | Jeddah | +966 2 652 4283 |
| Scandinavia | Stockholm | +46 8 411 1135 |
| South Africa | Johannesburg | +27 11 785 4600 |
| Switzerland & Austria | Ittigen-Bern | +41 31 924 7599 |
| UK & Ireland | London | +44 20 7839 0580 |
| USA | New York | +1 212 575 2262 |

**With AXA**
**Be Travel Confident**

# Travel Smart Insurance
## Comprehensive protection while you discover the world

Wherever you travel, you can count on AXA to ensure you have the most relaxing trip possible. Travel Smart Insurance is an affordable plan to cover the cost of travel emergencies, from medical to trip cancellation... and much more.

**INSURANCE**

Call 800 4845
www.axa-gulf.com

**Motor - Healthcare - Home - Travel - Yacht - Golf - Relocation**

Be Life Confident

## Places To Stay

In addition to a high number of luxurious five-star hotels, Dubai has plenty of four, three, two and one-star hotels, hotel apartments and youth hostels. A new hotel seems to spring up every few months – 22,000 rooms are planned before the end of 2008 – and local folk have often wondered how all of Dubai's hotels are going to stay in business. But in true 'if you build it, they will come' style, room occupancy rates have soared over the last few years (currently an annual average of 85% – one of the highest in the world), and there are certain times of the year when you can't find a hotel vacancy for love nor money. At the end of 2006, there were more than 31,000 hotel rooms in Dubai, which hosted 6,441,670 guests during 2006.

## Hotels

Other options **Main Hotels** p.38, **Weekend Break Hotels** p.310

Dubai has a vast array of hotels ranging from one of the most superlative and opulent hotels in the world, the Burj Al Arab (p.38), with a published price, or rack rate, in the region of Dhs.11,000 for a night in a standard suite, right down to the cheapest hotels in areas such as Deira costing under Dhs.100 a night. While the hotels at the higher end of the market offer superb surroundings and facilities, those at the cheaper end vary – and you get what you pay for. For people arriving in Dubai on a holiday package, hotels are normally five or four star, but if you are looking for cheaper accommodation at the lower end of the market, make sure you check out the hotel and have a look at one of the rooms before checking in. Remember that, as with anywhere else in the world, you can usually get a discount on the rack rate or published price if you negotiate.

Hotels in Dubai can be split into beach hotels (grouped along the coast to the south of the creek entrance), creek hotels (offering a great central location from which to explore and loads of atmosphere) and city hotels, often used by business travellers or tourists for good value accommodation with access to business districts and shopping areas. Most are located within a 30 minute journey from Dubai International Airport. The larger hotels all offer an airport shuttle service as well as a minibus service to the main tourist spots around the city. A taxi ride from the airport to most hotels will cost between Dhs.40 and Dhs.70. Road transport in Dubai is usually quite fast and the majority of journeys around town will only take 20 to 30 minutes, costing about Dhs.30 to Dhs.40 (for more information, see Taxis on p.58). With so many luxury hotels and resorts in Dubai, there's no reason why you can't combine a stay in a central Dubai hotel with a few nights at a desert resort, such as Bab Al Shams (p.44) or Al Maha Desert Resort & Spa (see p.44).

The Dubai Department of Tourism & Commerce Marketing (DTCM) oversees a hotel classification system that gives an internationally recognised star rating to hotels and hotel apartments so that visitors can judge more easily the standard of accommodation they will receive.

The DTCM also operates an internet reservation system for Dubai's hotels on its website (www.dubaitourism.com). This enables guests to reserve rooms online and allows them to take a virtual tour of the hotel before they book. Alternatively, the DTCM Welcome Bureau at the airport offers instant hotel reservations, often at greatly discounted rates. For food and beverage outlets that can be found in Dubai's hotels, refer to the Index at the back of the book. Just look up the hotel name, and all of its restaurants and bars that are featured in the book will be listed underneath.

For a list of sports and leisure facilities available at a particular hotel, refer to the Club Facilities table (p.386).

**Easy Visa**

*If you are not one of the nationalities listed on p.77, your hotel should be able to arrange a visit visa for you. The visa will be deposited at the airport for collection on arrival. The cost is around Dhs.180 for a regular visa, or Dhs.280 for an urgent visa.*

**DIY Dubai**

*Although a relatively new concept in Dubai, self catering can be more cost effective than hotels, and the accommodation comes equipped with everything from towels to teabags. Check out www.selfcatering dubai.com for online listings of properties.*

# Traditional
# Dinner Cruise
# by the Creek

*al mansour dhow*

The Radisson SAS Hotel, Dubai Deira Creek's legendary Al Mansour Dhow welcomes you aboard to experience an unforgettable dinner cruise featuring a sumptuous buffet with a spread of Arabian cuisine and live performances by our Oud player while you enjoy Dubai Creek's beautiful sights for only Dhs. 175 per person.

\* Boarding daily at 8 pm

Radisson SAS Hotel, Dubai Deira Creek
aniyas Road, P.O. Box 476, Dubai, UAE
or Bookings, please call 04-205 7033
nfocenter.dxbza@radissonsas.com
eiracreek.dubai.radissonsas.com

*Radisson* SAS
HOTEL, DUBAI DEIRA CREEK

## Main Hotels

### Al Bustan Rotana Hotel

*Nr Dubai Intl Airport*
*Garhoud*
*Map 13 E1*

**04 282 0000** | *www.rotana.com*
Located in the centre of Dubai, minutes away from the creek, Dubai International Airport, and Deira City Centre, this hotel provides easy access for tourists and business travellers alike. A member of 'The Leading Hotels of the World', it is renowned locally for having particularly good restaurants including Benihana (Japanese), Blue Elephant (Thai), Come Prima (Italian), and nightclub, Oxygen.

### Burj Al Arab

*Nr Madinat Jumeirah*
*Umm Suqeim*
*Map 6 B1*

**04 301 7777** | *www.burj-al-arab.com*
Architecturally unique, resembling a billowing sail, the world's tallest hotel stands at 321 metres high on its own man-made island, and is dramatic, lavish and exclusive. Guests are looked after by a host of butlers. If you intend to dine at the Burj you will need to make a reservation. Try afternoon tea at Sahn Eddar (Dhs.190) or a drinks package at Sky View Bar (Dhs.200 for two drinks and canapes).

### Crowne Plaza

*Sheikh Zayed Rd*
*Trade Centre 1*
*Map 7 F2*

**04 331 1111** | *www.crowneplaza.com*
The well-established Crowne Plaza is a 560 room hotel with offices and furnished apartments next door in the Commercial Tower. Situated in the Trade Centre area, the complex has its own shopping mall, the Nautilus Health Club, as well as bars, restaurants and cafes including Trader Vic's for great cocktails, Harvester's Pub, Wagamama, the trendy noodle bar chain, and Zinc, a nightclub to queue for.

### Dubai Marine Beach Resort & Spa

*Opp Jumeira Mosque*
*Jumeira*
*Map 7 F1*

**04 346 1111** | *www.dxbmarine.com*
The only beach hotel close to the centre of Dubai, this independent property has 195 villa-style rooms nestled among lush, green landscaped gardens, waterfalls and streams. The grounds offer three swimming pools, a spa, a health club and a small private beach. The restaurants and bars are perennially popular nightspots, especially the Ibiza-esque Sho Cho and beautiful hangout, Boudoir.

### Emirates Towers Hotel

*Shk Zayed Rd*
*Trade Centre 2*
*Map 7 F3*

**04 330 0000** | *www.jumeirah.com*
Recently awarded 'Best Business Hotel in the Middle East', this hotel stands 305 metres high, with 400 rooms on 51 floors, and is the third tallest hotel in the world. Sophisticated and elegant, the hotel tower is twinned with the larger office tower behind it. Between these two, the Boulevard shopping mall provides some top-end retail and an assortment of excellent restaurants, cafes and bars.

**Nr Trade Centre R/A**
*Trade Centre 1*
*Map 8 A4*

## Fairmont Dubai ▶ p.499

*04 332 5555* | *www.fairmont.com*

At night this grand hotel is hard to miss thanks to its glowing pyramids that change colour. The architecture is based on the traditional Arabian windtowers. The interior is even more inspirational, with water features and glass-fronted lifts offering views over the atrium. There's a classy rooftop pool, the excellent Willow Stream Spa and some of the finest restaurants in town including Spectrum on One.

**Nr Garhoud Bridge**
*Umm Hurair*
*Map 13 C1*

## Grand Hyatt Dubai

*04 317 1234* | *www.dubai.grand.hyatt.com*

The Grand Hyatt has 674 spacious and high-tech rooms and an excellent range of facilities within its 37 acres of attractively landscaped grounds. The sheer size is amazing, and from the air the buildings spells out the word 'Dubai' in Arabic. There's a health spa, fitness centre, and many restaurants, cafes, and bars including one of Dubai's more popular nightclubs, The MIX.

**Dubai Marina**
**West Marina Beach**
*Marsa Dubai*
*Map 5 B2*

## Grosvenor House

*04 399 8888* | *www.grosvenorhouse.lemeridien.com*

Grosvenor House has high standards of service and a range of facilities in a 45 storey tower. Taking advantage of its location in Dubai Marina, this hotel attracts people for its lauded flagship restaurant Rhodes Mezzanine and the the trendy Buddha Bar. Facilities are good, especially as guests can also make use of the beach and swimming pools at Le Royal Meridien Beach Resort.

**Dubai Marina**
**West Marina Beach**
*Marsa Dubai*
*Map 5 B1*

## Habtoor Grand Resort & Spa   *3994221*

*04 399 5000* | *www.habtoorhotels.com*

On the site of the former Metropolitan Resort & Beach Club, the Habtoor Grand Resort & Spa offers 442 beautifully furnished, spacious rooms and suites with garden or sea views. Pools, restaurants and bars are set amid the hotel's tropical gardens bordering the Arabian Gulf. Food and beverage options include The 25th, a fine-dining restaurant, and pub The Underground.

**Nr Economic Dept**
*Deira*
*Map 11 C1*

## Hilton Dubai Creek

*04 227 1111* | *www.hilton.com*

With very flash yet understated elegance and high quality service, this ultra-minimalist hotel was designed by Carlos Ott and features interiors of wood, glass and chrome. Centrally located and overlooking the creek with splendid views of the Arabian dhow trading posts, the hotel has two renowned restaurants in Glasshouse and Gordon Ramsay's Verre. Hilton also have a beach resort on Jumeirah Beach in the Dubai Marina area.

*Nr Galleria Mall*
*Deira*
*Map 9 D1*

## Hyatt Regency Hotel

*04 209 1234* | *www.dubai.regency.hyatt.com*

After its refurbishment of a few years back, the Hyatt Regency is looking a lot smarter. Restaurants such as Miyako (Japanese), Focaccia (Mediterranean) and Shahrzad (Persian) are all excellent while Al Dawaar offers Dubai's only revolving restaurant, with views of the creek and coast. All 400 guest rooms and serviced suites have a creek view.

*Dubai Festival City*
*Nr Garhoud Bridge*
*Map 13 D2*

## InterContinental Dubai Festival City

*04 701 1111* | *www.ichotelsgroup.com*

This hotel, opened in November 2007, will have five restaurants and two bars when completed – including the Eclipse Bar, with panoramic views of Dubai, and a restaurant run by Michelin-starred chef Pierre Gagnaire. Offering extensive spa facilities and indoor access to Festival Waterfront Centre, all 498 rooms and suites will have a view of either Dubai Creek or the Festival Marina.

*Jct 9, nr Jebel Ali*
*Shooting Club*
*Jebel Ali*
*Map 2 D4*

## Jebel Ali Golf Resort & Spa

*04 883 6000* | *www.jebelali-international.com*

Just far enough out of Dubai to escape the city's hustle and bustle, this fully equipped resort offers luxurious surroundings and a peaceful atmosphere. Its two properties, Jebel Ali Hotel and The Palm Tree Court & Spa, are set in 128 acres of lush, landscaped gardens, with a private beach, marina, spa, and one of the region's original golf courses. Guests can also enjoy horse riding and watersports.

*Jumeirah Beach Rd*
*Umm Suqeim*
*Map 6 B1*

## Jumeirah Beach Hotel

*04 348 0000* | *www.jumeirah.com*

Along with the Burj Al Arab and the Wild Wadi Water Park, this exclusive hotel is one of Dubai's landmarks. Built in the shape of an ocean wave with a dynamic and colourful interior, the hotel has 618 rooms, all with a sea view. It has some of the classiest joints in town including Uptown for happy hour cocktails and a great view of the Burj, The Apartment for superb French food, and La Veranda for recommended beach-side dining.

*Nxt to Hamarain*
*Shopping Centre*
*Deira*
*Map 11 E1*

## JW Marriott Hotel

*04 262 4444* | *www.marriott-middleeast.com*

This hotel is located in the bustling heart of Deira. A grand staircase, detailed marble floors and natural lighting provided by the Middle East's largest skylight are all impressive, as is the landscaped indoor 'town square'. The Marriott boasts 305 rooms and 39 suites. Favourite eateries include Cucina and The Market Place, while Champions is one of Dubai's best bars for sports fans.

**Mall of the Emirates**
*Barsha*
*Map 6 A3*

## Kempinski Hotel Mall of the Emirates ▶ p.xv

04 409 5199 | www.kempinski-dubai.com

Part of the Middle East's first indoor ski resort, the hotel has 395 deluxe rooms and 15 unique ski chalets overlooking the slopes. There's something for everyone, from a Wellness Spa, infinity pool and ski slope to a fitness centre, tennis court and access to watersports through the sister Kempinski Hotel Ajman. The adjoining Mall of the Emirates has over 400 shops, a 14 screen cinema, a huge entertainment centre for children and a community theatre and arts centre.

**Opp Dubai Airport T1**
*Garhoud*
*Map 13 E1*

## Le Meridien Dubai

04 282 4040 | www.lemeridien-dubai.com

Le Meridien, one of Dubai's first five-star hotels, has an ultra convenient location, just across from the Dubai airport and a stone's throw from the Aviation Club. Its 383 rooms don't have exquisite views, but benefit from luxury standards and service. It is home to a fitness studio, tennis courts, the superb Natural Elements spa, and a popular array of restaurants, including the Meridien Village Terrace.

**Nr Media City**
*Al Sufouh*
*Map 5 C1*

## Le Meridien Mina Seyahi Beach Resort ▶ p.577     399 4141

04 399 3333 | www.lemeridien-minaseyahi.com

This hotel has one of the longest stretches of private beach in Dubai, its own marina and a variety of water activities such as sailing and waterskiing. The 211 rooms come with views of the sea or the landscaped grounds and the clincher for families is the Penguin Club, which entertains kids. There is also the popular Barasti Bar right on the beach and the reliable Italian restaurant, Bussola.

**Nxt Burj Al Arab**
*Umm Suqeim*
*Map 6 A2*

## Madinat Jumeirah

04 366 8888 | www.madinatjumeirah.com

This extravagant resort has two hotels, Al Qasr and Mina A'Salam, with 940 luxurious rooms and suites, and the exclusive Dar Al Masyaf summer houses, all linked by man-made waterways navigated by abras. Nestled between the two hotels is the Souk Madinat, which has over 75 shops within its labyrinth network of passageways. There is also a total of 45 bars, restaurants, cafes and the Trilogy nightclub.

**Opp American Hospital**
*Oud Metha*
*Map 10 D3*

## Mövenpick Hotel Bur Dubai ▶ p.545

04 336 6000 | www.movenpick-hotels.com

Located near Lamcy Plaza and Wafi City, this hotel offers a high standard of service in keeping with the chain's Swiss background. Although you can dine in the impressive lobby, you shouldn't miss the chance to eat at Fakhreldine, one of Dubai's best Lebanese restaurants. And the nightclub downstairs, the well-known Jimmy Dix, is a great place for a laid-back night out.

**41**

*Jumeira Road*
*Al Sufouh*
*Map 5 C1*

## One&Only Royal Mirage ▸ p.526

*04 399 9999* | *www.oneandonlyroyalmirage.com*
Blessed with an intimate atmosphere, this resort is home to three different properties; The Palace, Arabian Court and Residence & Spa. The hotel features unparalleled service and dining, and a luxury spa treatment here is the ultimate indulgence. Try delectable Moroccan cuisine in the opulent Tagine, mingle with the rich and famous at Celebrities, or enjoy late nights at Arabian nightclub Kasbar.

*Downtown Burj Dubai*
*Map 7 D4*

## The Palace – The Old Town ▸ p.494

*04 428 7888* | *www.sofitel.com*
Situated close to Burj Dubai, The Palace hotel is one of the most luxurious additions to the city's hospitality scene. The palatial development boasts 242 deluxe rooms, including 81 suites, and offers traditional Arabic architecture juxtaposed with modern technology. There are three upmarket restaurants, including Asado, an extensive spa, butler service for all rooms and even a lake, not to mention great views of the world's (current) tallest building.

*Dubai Creek Deira*
*Creekside, Deira*
*Map 11 B4*

## Park Hyatt Dubai ▸ p.513

*04 602 1234* | *www.dubai.park.hyatt.com*
The Park Hyatt Dubai enjoys a prime waterfront location next to Dubai Creek Golf & Yacht Club. Mediterranean and Moorish in style with low buildings, natural colours and stylish decor, the hotel is illuminated by candles at night. All 225 rooms have a balcony or terrace with great views. Traiteur and The Thai Kitchen are fine restaurants and the hotel's luxurious spa provides pampering in private rooms.

*Baniyas Rd*
*Nr Dubai Municipality*
*Deira*
*Map 9 B3*

## Radisson SAS Hotel, Deira Creek ▸ p.37

*04 222 7171* | *www.radissonsas.com*
Traffic and parking can be a hindrance, but the popular restaurants, offering seafood, Italian, Japanese and Chinese, make the trip worthwhile. At the Seafood Market you pick your seafood and have it cooked to your preference, while Kubu Bar is the crux of cocktail cool. Located on the creekside in Deira in what was the longstanding and popular InterContinental.

*Wafi City*
*Umm Hurair*
*Map 10 D4*

## Raffles Dubai

*04 324 8888* | *www.raffles.com*
Part of the Wafi City complex, Raffles Dubai opened in October 2007. The hotel when fully completed will feature 248 guest rooms and suites and the RafflesAmrita Spa with a unique Botanical Sky Garden – an oasis of exotic flowers and orchids around a pool. The nine food and beverage outlets will offer a mix of international and far eastern cuisine and afternoon tea will be served in the Raffles Lounge.

## Renaissance Hotel ▶ p.537

*Salahuddin Rd*
*opp Muraqabat*
*Police Station*
*Map 11 E1*

*04 262 5555* | *www.renaissancehotels.com*

Slightly off the beaten track in the nothern side of Deira (Hor Al Anz), this hotel features 244 rooms and 37 suites, as well as 11 meeting rooms. Offering all the plush services you'd expect from a five-star hotel, such as limo service and valet dry cleaning, there are also four restaurants in the building – including the all-inclusive institution that is... Spice Island (p.536).

## The Ritz-Carlton Dubai

*Nxt to Royal Meridien*
*Dubai Marina*
*Map 5 B1*

*04 399 4000* | *www.ritzcarlton.com*

Although the Ritz stands low in comparison to the marina towers behind, it offers stunning Mediterranean architecture. The 138 guest rooms all enjoy a view of the Gulf and their own private balcony or patio. Afternoon tea in the Lobby Lounge is a must; lots of yummy scones and pastries in a posh but comfortable setting. For dining there's Splendido Grill and La Baie – both equally delicious.

## Shangri-La Hotel

*Shk Zayed Rd*
*Trade Centre 1*
*Map 7 E3*

*04 343 8888* | *www.shangri-la.com*

This 43 storey hotel is located on Sheikh Zayed Road, close to all of Dubai's main attractions, with fantastic views of the coast and the city. There are 301 guest rooms and suites, 126 serviced apartments, a health club and spa, two swimming pools and a variety of restaurants and bars including majestic Morrocan Marrakesh and seafood specialist, Amwaj.

## Sheraton Dubai Creek Hotel

*Next to National*
*Bank of Dubai*
*Deira*
*Map 9 B4*

*04 228 1111* | *www.sheraton.com/dubai*

The 255 room Sheraton, like other hotels in this part of town has undergone refurbishments in recent years. Its location on the bank of the creek means that most rooms have beautiful views. Ashiana is renowned as one of the best traditional Indian restaurants in Dubai, Creekside is a favoured Japanese restaurant and Vivaldi shines as a wonderful Italian restaurant with great views.

## Sofitel City Centre Hotel ▶ p.589

*Nr Deira City Centre*
*Al Garhoud*
*Map 11 C3*

*04 294 1222* | *www.deiracitycentre.com*

Adjoining one of the Middle East's largest and busiest shopping centres, Deira City Centre, this hotel is great if you're in town for a shopping spree. Some of the 327 rooms have a good view over the greens of Dubai Creek Golf & Yacht Club and the hotel also features conference facilities, serviced apartments, four restaurants and an English pub, as well as all the outlets in Deira City Centre.

## Resorts

*37km from*
*Arabian Ranches RA*
*Map 1 E2*

### Bab Al Shams Desert Resort & Spa

*04 832 6699* | *www.babalshams.com*

Bab Al Shams, which translates as 'The Gateway to the Sun', is an elegant desert resort in a traditional Arabic fort setting and is home to the region's first authentic open air Arabic desert restaurant, Al Hadheerah. There's a kids' club with camel rides and falcon shows. Health and leisure facilities including the luxurious Satori Spa, an infinity swimming pool and bar with breathtaking views over the dunes.

*Approx 75km from*
*Dubai*
*Dubai – Al Ain Rd*
*Map 1 E2*

### Emirates Al Maha Desert Resort & Spa

*04 832 9900* | *www.al-maha.com*

Set within a 225 sq km conservation reserve, this luxury getaway describes itself as 'The World's first Arabian eco-tourism resort'. Al Maha resembles a typical Bedouin camp, but conditions are anything but basic. Each suite has its own private pool, and guests can enjoy fine dining on their own veranda. Activities include horse riding, camel trekking, falconry and up-close views of rare wildlife.

## Hotels

| Five Star | Beach Access | Phone | Website | Map |
|---|:---:|---|---|---|
| Al Bustan Rotana Hotel | – | 04 282 0000 | www.rotana.com | 13 E1 |
| Al Murooj Rotana Hotel & Suites | – | 04 321 1111 | www.rotana.com | 7 E3 |
| Bab Al Shams Desert Resort & Spa | – | 04 832 6699 | www.babalshams.com | 1 E2 |
| Burj Al Arab | ✓ | 04 301 7777 | www.burj-al-arab.com | 6 B1 |
| Coral Deira | – | 04 224 8587 | www.coral-deira.com | 11 D1 |
| Crowne Plaza | – | 04 331 1111 | www.dubai.crowneplaza.com | 7 F2 |
| Dhow Palace Hotel | – | 04 359 9992 | www.dhowpalacedubai.com | 8 E3 |
| Dubai Marine Beach Resort & Spa | ✓ | 04 346 1111 | www.dxbmarine.com | 7 F1 |
| Dusit Dubai | – | 04 343 3333 | www.dusit.com | 7 E3 |
| Emirates Al Maha Resort & Spa | – | 04 832 9900 | www.al-maha.com | 1 E2 |
| Emirates Towers Hotel | ✓ | 04 330 0000 | www.jumeirah.com | 7 F3 |
| Fairmont Dubai  ▶ p.499 | – | 04 332 5555 | www.fairmont.com | 8 A4 |
| Grand Hyatt Dubai | – | 04 317 1234 | www.dubai.grand.hyatt.com | 13 C1 |
| Grosvenor House | ✓ | 04 399 8888 | www.grosvenorhouse.lemeridien.com | 5 B2 |
| Habtoor Grand Resort & Spa | ✓ | 04 399 5000 | www.habtoorhotels.com | 5 B1 |
| Hilton Dubai Creek | – | 04 227 1111 | www.hilton.com | 11 C1 |
| Hilton Dubai Jumeirah | ✓ | 04 399 1111 | www.hilton.com | 5 A1 |
| Hyatt Regency Hotel | – | 04 209 1234 | www.dubai.regency.hyatt.com | 9 D1 |
| InterContinental Dubai Festival City | – | 04 701 1111 | www.ichotelsgroup.com | 13 D2 |
| Jebel Ali Golf Resort & Spa | ✓ | 04 883 6000 | www.jebelali-international.com | 2 D4 |
| Jumeirah Beach Club Resort & Spa | ✓ | 04 344 5333 | www.jumeirah.com | 7 C1 |
| Jumeirah Beach Hotel, The | ✓ | 04 348 0000 | www.jumeirah.com | 6 B1 |
| JW Marriott Hotel | ✓ | 04 262 4444 | www.marriott-middleeast.com | 11 E1 |
| Kempinski Mall of the Emirates  ▶ p.xv | – | 04 409 5199 | www.kempinski-dubai.com | 6 A3 |
| Le Meridien Dubai | – | 04 282 4040 | www.lemeridien-dubai.com | 13 E1 |
| Le Meridien Mina Seyahi Beach Resort  ▶ p.577 | ✓ | 04 399 3333 | www.lemeridien-minaseyahi.com | 5 C1 |
| Madinat Jumeirah | ✓ | 04 366 8888 | www.jumeirah.com | 6 A2 |
| Metropolitan Palace Hotel | – | 04 227 0000 | www.habtoorhotels.com | 11 C1 |
| Mövenpick Hotel Bur Dubai  ▶ p.545 | – | 04 336 6000 | www.movenpick-hotels.com | 10 D3 |

PERFECT LOCATIONS
COMPLETE COMFORT

## Nuran Serviced Residences, Comfort at your fingertips

From complimentary broadband internet to various amenities and services like home entertainment system, DVD player, washer/dryer, fully equipped kitchen and 5-star housekeeping services, we have left nothing out to ensure your stay is uniquely enjoyable and comfortable.

## www.nuran.com

Tel: 800 NURAN  +9714 4223666 Fax: +9714 4223667
Dubai, UAE.
Email: reservations@nuran.com
GDS code XL

NURAN
SERVICED RESIDENCES

NIGHT & DAY, ALWAYS

SUMMIT
HOTELS & RESORTS

## Hotels

| Five Star | Beach Access | Phone | Website | Map |
|---|---|---|---|---|
| One&Only Royal Mirage ▶ p.526 | ✓ | 04 399 9999 | www.oneandonlyroyalmirage.com | 5 C1 |
| Park Hyatt Dubai ▶ p.513 | – | 04 602 1234 | dubai.park.hyatt.com | 11 B4 |
| Radisson SAS, Dubai Deira Creek ▶ p.37 | – | 04 222 7171 | www.radissonsas.com | 9 B3 |
| Radisson SAS, Dubai Media City ▶ p.529 | – | 04 366 9111 | www.radissonsas.com | 5 C2 |
| Raffles Dubai | – | 04 324 8888 | www.dubai.raffles.com | 10 D4 |
| Renaissance Hotel ▶ p.537 | ✓ | 04 262 5555 | www.renaissancehotels.com | 11 E1 |
| Ritz-Carlton, Dubai | ✓ | 04 399 4000 | www.ritzcarlton.com | 5 B1 |
| Shangri-La Hotel | ✓ | 04 343 8888 | www.shangri-la.com | 7 E3 |
| Sheraton Dubai Creek Hotel & Towers | – | 04 228 1111 | www.sheraton.com/dubai | 9 B4 |
| Sheraton Jumeira Beach Resort & Towers | ✓ | 04 399 5533 | www.starwoodhotels.com | 4 F1 |
| Sofitel City Centre Hotel ▶ p.589 | – | 04 294 1222 | www.deiracitycentre.com | 11 C3 |
| Taj Palace Hotel | – | 04 223 2222 | www.tajpalacedubai.co.ae | 11 C1 |
| The Monarch Dubai | – | 04 501 8888 | www.themonarchdubai.com | 8 A4 |
| The Montgomerie, Dubai | – | 04 390 5600 | www.themontgomerie.com | 5 B3 |
| The Palace – The Old Town ▶ p.494 | – | 04 428 7888 | www.sofitel.com | 7 D4 |

| Four Star | Beach Access | Phone | Website | Map |
|---|---|---|---|---|
| Al Khaleej Palace Hotel | – | 04 223 1000 | www.alkhaleejhotels.com | 9 C4 |
| Arabian Courtyard Hotel | – | 04 351 9111 | www.arabiancourtyard.com | 9 A2 |
| Ascot Hotel | – | 04 352 0900 | www.ascothoteldubai.com | 8 F2 |
| Carlton Tower, The | – | 04 222 7111 | www.carltontower.net | 9 B3 |
| Courtyard by Marriott Green Community ▶ p.xi | – | 04 885 2222 | www.marriott.com | 2 D4 |
| Dubai Grand Hotel | – | 04 263 2555 | www.dubaigrandhotel.ae | 14 C1 |
| Four Points Sheraton | – | 04 397 7444 | www.fourpoints.com | 8 F3 |
| Golden Tulip Al Barsha | – | 04 341 7750 | www.goldentulip.com | 5 F3 |
| Hatta Fort Hotel ▶ p.289 | – | 04 852 3211 | www.jebelali-international.com | 1 F2 |
| Holiday Inn Downtown | – | 04 228 8889 | www.holiday-inn.com/downtowndubai | 11 D1 |
| Ibis World Trade Centre | – | 04 332 4444 | www.accorhotels.com | 7 F3 |
| Jumeira Rotana Hotel | – | 04 345 5888 | www.rotana.com | 8 A2 |
| La Maison d'Hôtes | – | 04 344 1838 | www.lamaisondhotesdubai.com | 7 D1 |
| Lotus Hotel | – | 04 227 8888 | www.lotus-hotel-dubai.com | 9 C4 |
| Marco Polo Hotel | – | 04 272 0000 | www.marcopolohotel.net | 9 E3 |
| Metropolitan Hotel | – | 04 343 0000 | www.habtoorhotels.com | 7 B3 |
| Millennium Airport Hotel | – | 04 282 3464 | www.millenniumhotels.com | 13 E1 |
| Novotel World Trade Centre | – | 04 332 0000 | www.accorhotels.com | 7 F3 |
| Oasis Beach Hotel | ✓ | 04 399 4444 | www.jebelali-international.com | 5 A1 |
| Palm Hotel, The | – | 04 399 2222 | www.thepalmhoteldubai.com | 5 C2 |
| Ramada Hotel | – | 04 351 9999 | www.ramadadubai.com | 8 F3 |
| Regent Palace Hotel | – | 04 396 3888 | www.ramee-group.com | 8 F4 |
| Riviera Hotel | – | 04 222 2131 | www.rivierahotel-dubai.com | 9 B3 |
| Rydges Plaza Hotel | – | 04 398 2222 | www.rydges.com | 8 A3 |
| Towers Rotana Hotel | – | 04 343 8000 | www.rotana.com | 7 E3 |
| Traders Hotel, Deira | - | 04 265 9888 | www.shangri-la.com | 11 E1 |

| Three Star | Beach Access | Phone | Website | Map |
|---|---|---|---|---|
| Admiral Plaza | – | 04 393 5333 | www.admiralplazahotel.com | 8 F2 |
| Ambassador Hotel | – | 04 393 9444 | www.astamb.com | 8 F1 |
| Arabian Park Hotel | – | 04 324 5999 | www.arabianparkhotel.com | 13 B1 |
| Astoria Hotel | – | 04 353 4300 | www.astamb.com | 8 F2 |
| Claridge Hotel | – | 04 271 6666 | na | 9 D3 |
| Comfort Inn | – | 04 222 7393 | www.hotelcomfortinn.com | 9 C4 |
| Imperial Suites Hotel | – | 04 351 5100 | www.imperialsuiteshotel.com | 8 F2 |
| Lords Hotel | – | 04 228 9977 | na | 9 C4 |
| Nihal Hotel | – | 04 295 7666 | www.nihalhoteldubai.com | 9 D3 |
| Princess Hotel | – | 04 263 5500 | www.princesshoteldxb.com | 14 B2 |
| Ramee Guestline Hotel | – | 04 229 9111 | www.ramee-group.com | 11 C1 |

## Hotels

| Two Star | Beach Access | Phone | Website | Map |
|---|---|---|---|---|
| New Peninsula Hotel | – | 04 393 9111 | na | 8 F1 |
| Phoenicia Hotel | – | 04 222 7191 | www.phoeniciahoteldubai.com | 9 C2 |
| President Hotel | – | 04 334 6565 | www.presidentdubai.com | 8 F3 |
| Ramee International Hotel | – | 04 224 0222 | www.ramee-group.com | 9 C2 |
| San Marco | – | 04 272 2333 | www.sanmarcohoteldubai.com | 9 D2 |
| Seashell Inn | – | 04 393 4777 | www.seashellinnhotel.com | 8 E2 |
| Vendome Plaza Hotel | – | 04 222 2333 | www.vendomeplaza.com | 11 C1 |
| **One Star** | | | | |
| Deira Park Hotel | – | 04 223 9922 | www.deiraparkhotel.com | 9 C2 |
| Vasantam Hotel | – | 04 393 8006 | www.vasantabhavan.com | 8 F2 |

## Hotel Apartments

| Deluxe | Phone | Area | Website |
|---|---|---|---|
| Al Bustan Residence | 04 263 0000 | Al Qusais | www.al-bustan.com |
| Al Faris Hotel Apartment 3 | 04 336 6566 | Oud Metha | www.alfarisdubai.com |
| BurJuman Rotana Suites | 04 352 4444 | Bur Dubai | www.rotana.com |
| Capitol Residence Hotel Apartments | 04 393 2000 | Satwa | www.capitol-hotel.com |
| Chelsea Tower Hotel Apartments | 04 343 4347 | Trade Centre 1 | www.chelseatowerdubai.com |
| Coral Boutique Hotel Apartments | 04 340 9040 | Al Barsha | www.coral-boutiquehotel.com |
| Golden Sands X | 04 359 9000 | Karama | www.goldensandsdubai.com |
| Grand Hyatt Hotel Apartments | 04 317 1234 | Umm Hurair | www.dubai.grand.hyatt.com |
| Khalidia Hotel Apartments | 04 228 2280 | Deira | www.khalidiapalacehotel.ae |
| Marriott Executive Apartments | 04 213 1000 | Deira | www.execapartments.com |
| Nuran, Al Majara Serviced Residences ▶ p.45 | 04 422 3666 | Dubai Marina | www.nuran.com |
| Nuran, Al Alka Serviced Residences ▶ p.45 | 04 422 3666 | The Greens | www.nuran.com |
| Rihab Rotana Suites | 04 294 0300 | Garhoud | www.rotana.com |
| Savoy Crest Hotel Apartments | 04 355 4488 | Bur Dubai | www.savoy.ae |
| Sofitel City Centre Residence | 04 294 1333 | Garhoud | www.deiracitycentre.com |
| Wafi Residence | 04 324 7222 | Umm Hurair | www.wafiproperties.com |
| Waterview Executive Apartments | 04 295 0000 | Creekside, Deira | www.waterviewdubai.com |
| **Standard** | | | |
| Al Deyafa Hotel Apartments | 04 228 2555 | Deira | www.aldeyafa.com |
| Al Mas Hotel Apartments | 04 355 7899 | Bur Dubai | www.almashotelapartments.com |
| Atrium Suites | 04 266 8666 | Abu Hail | na |
| Desert Rose Hotel Apartments | 04 352 4848 | Bur Dubai | www.imperialsuiteshotel.com |
| Embassy Suites | 04 269 8070 | Deira | na |
| Golden Sands III | 04 355 5551 | Bur Dubai | www.goldensandsdubai.com |
| Ramee Guest Line Hotel Apartments | 04 355 3344 | Bur Dubai | www.ramee-group.com |
| Tower No. One | 04 343 4666 | Trade Centre 1 | www.numberonetower.com |
| Winchester Hotel Apartments | 04 355 0111 | Bur Dubai | www.winchester.com |

## Hotel Apartments

A cheaper alternative to staying in a hotel is to rent furnished accommodation. This can be done on a daily, weekly, monthly or yearly basis. The longer you rent the better the rate and there is a wide variety, and standard, of options in all areas of the city. One advantage is that the place can feel more like home than a hotel room, particularly on longer stays, so it's especially popular with people on short-term contracts or those first arriving in Dubai. Usually the apartments come fully furnished, including everything from bed linen to cutlery, plus a cleaning service. Additionally, there may be sports facilities, such as a gym and a swimming pool, in the building. For the cheapest, try Al Mas, Desert Rose, Embassy Suites and the Winchester Hotel.

47

## Backpacking

On first inspection Dubai doesn't seem like a backpackers' paradise, due to the luxury hotels and relatively expensive shopping. But many independent travellers have found that Dubai is a good gateway to South East Asia and Australia. There are four youth hostels spread over the Emirates, although many backpackers opt for low-star hotels (which are cheaper in town than they are on the beachfront). With cheap public transport, a myriad of local independent restaurants serving traditional fare for a pittance and so many free sights, Dubai can easily be explored on a budget. For a list of hostels, see right.

## Hostels

The Dubai Youth Hostel, located on Al Nahda Road near Al Mulla Plaza in the north of the city, provides the cheapest accommodation in town. A four-star wing was added to the hostel in 2002, almost tripling the number of rooms. In the old wing, there are 53 beds available for Dhs.60 per night (YHA members) or Dhs.75 (non-members), including breakfast, in one of 20 very clean, two-bed dormitory rooms. Beds in the new wing are Dhs.85 for members and Dhs.100 for non-members, including breakfast. Check-in is always open.

Accommodation is available for men, women and families. Annual membership costs Dhs.100; family membership is Dhs.300 and for groups of more than 25, the yearly charge is Dhs.1,000. Women travelling alone should check availability, since the management reserves the right to refuse bookings from single women when the hostel has a number of men staying. The hostel is well served by a cheap, regular bus service into the centre of Dubai and reasonably priced taxis are plentiful. By car, the hostel is about 15 minutes from Airport Terminal 1. Hostels are also located in some of the other emirates, including two in Sharjah and one in Fujairah.

| Hostels | |
| --- | --- |
| Dubai Youth Hostel | 04 298 8161 |
| Fujairah Youth Hostel | 09 222 2347 |
| Khor Fakkan Youth Hostel | 09 237 0886 |
| Sharjah Youth Hostel | 06 522 5070 |

## Campsites

Other options **Camping** p.326

### Clever Camping

*For the lowdown on camping in the UAE, get your hands on a copy of the UAE Off-Road Explorer. It's the definitive guide to outdoor living, and features recommended camping spots, what to take, and what to do when you get there. It's also packed with informative maps, life-saving tips and inspiring photography.*

There are no official campsites in the UAE, but fortunately there are plenty of places to camp informally. Near Dubai, the desert dunes on the way to Hatta are a good option, as are the mountains a little further on. Jebel Ali beach used to be a popular place, but the construction of Palm Jebel Ali and Dubai Waterfront has now closed access completely. Saih Ash Shaib beach, further down the coast towards Abu Dhabi past Jebel Ali Beach, is now a popular beach camping location. For a fun weekend out of Dubai with all the facilities, Dreamland (p.274) in Umm al Quwain offers camping in provided tents or 'cabana' huts, with access to the pools and all the rides, and food and drink is included in the deal.

UAE mountain campsites

## Getting Around

Other options **Exploring** p.235

Cars are the most popular method of getting around Dubai and the Emirates, either by private vehicle or by taxi. There is a reasonable public bus service, and walking and cycling are possible, but the soaring summer heat and multiple-lane roads put most people off. There are a few motorcyclists on the roads, but most of them are courageous couriers or fearless fast food delivery drivers, as Dubai's aggressive road users make it unsafe for two wheelers. There are no trains and trams yet, but 2009 will see Dubai's first metro running both under and above ground (see Metro on p.58).

The city's road network is excellent, although a little complicated and at certain times of the day packed with traffic jams. The majority of main roads have two or more lanes that are all well signposted, and Dubai is probably the easiest emirate to navigate. Blue or green signs indicate the main areas or locations out of the city and brown signs show heritage sites, places of interest and hospitals. Many streets are rarely referred to by their road names. People often rely on landmarks such as shops, hotels or notable buildings. Often roads are referred to by their nickname, such as Bank Street or Trade Centre Road.

Dubai is a relatively easy city to negotiate. The creek divides Bur Dubai (to the south) and Deira (to the north). The creek currently has five main crossing points: Shindagha Tunnel, Maktoum Bridge, Garhoud Bridge, Business Bay Bridge and the Floating Bridge. The creek can also be crossed by a pedestrian foot tunnel near Shindagha, or by boat (the common water taxis are known locally as abras). Dubai is growing away from the creek though, and in general the new developments have good, modern road networks, often completed before the houses.

To ease the pressure on inner-city roads the E311 Emirates Road was built at a cost of Dhs.150 million. This connects Abu Dhabi directly to Sharjah and the northern Emirates. The E44 Al Khail Road was also built with the hope of further relieving the congestion on Sheikh Zayed Road. There is a ban on all trucks on main routes at busy times of the day. More bypasses, or ring roads, are planned, extending further out into the desert, in an effort to keep traffic away from the city's streets. With new interchanges and the underground track and stations for the metro being constructed, lane closures, contra-flows and hold-ups are an unfortunate reality for many.

### Explorer Online

Now that you own an Explorer book you may want to check out the rest of our product range. From maps and visitor guides to restaurant guides and photography books, Explorer has a collection of carefully crafted products just waiting for you. Check out our website for more. **www.explorer publishing.com**

### Salik

In 2007, the Roads and Transport Authority (RTA) unveiled the Salik road toll system in an effort to cut congestion on Sheikh Zayed Road. The scheme met much resistance when it launched, with many people complaining about this new 'tax', and increased journey times on alternative routes as drivers tried to avoid the tolls. Some drivers have celebrated as their daily commute time has been slashed, while traffic on other roads remains as bad as ever, if not worse. Motorists buy a 'tag' (Dhs.100, including Dhs.50 of credit) from any petrol station, and attach it to their windscreen. There are two toll gates – the Al Barsha gate after Mall of the Emirates and another by Garhoud Bridge. The system automatically deducts Dhs.4 from a user's account each time they pass beneath a gate, up to a daily limit of Dhs.24. An SMS warning will be sent when credit is running low. Accounts can be topped up at petrol stations, and eventually via ATMs, phone and online. Visit www.salik.ae or call 800 72545. Rumours started circulating in late 2007 about a second set of tolls set to be introduced soon, and new signs under wraps have been spotted, so keep your eyes peeled.

**49**

## Air

### New Horizons

*Two more of Europe's major airlines now offer direct flights from Dubai. Low-cost carrier Aer Lingus (www.aerlingus.com) flies three times a week from Dubai to Dublin, and Virgin Atlantic (www.virgin-atlantic.com) offers daily flights from Dubai to London. Both have extensive networks of onward connections.*

Dubai's location at the crossroads of Europe, Asia and Africa makes it an easily accessible city. London is seven hours away, Frankfurt six, Hong Kong eight, India three, and Nairobi four. Most major cities have direct flights to Dubai, many with a choice of operator. There are also direct flights to North America and Australia. Dubai International Airport is a world renowned airport, handling over 28 million passengers in 2006. An ambitious $540 million expansion programme has transformed the already excellent airport into a state-of-the-art facility, ready to meet the needs of passengers for the next 30 years. Work is well underway on an even larger third terminal due to service all Emirates flights. See Key Projects (p.8) for more information.

Currently, more than 110 airlines take advantage of Dubai's open skies policy, operating to and from over 160 destinations. Dubai's award winning airline, Emirates (www.emirates.com), is based here and operates scheduled services to over 90 destinations. The airline's growth is staggering and is synonymous with the development of Dubai itself.

### Dubai World Central

Construction is well underway on Dubai's second airport (Al Maktoum International Airport) and the first phase is expected to open in 2008, although it will cater just for freight. But by 2050 it will have the capacity for 120 million passengers a year. For more information on one of the city's biggest projects, see p.12.

## Airlines

| | | |
|---|---|---|
| Aer Lingus | 04 316 6752 | www.aerlingus.com |
| Air Arabia | 06 508 8888 | www.airarabia.com |
| Air France ▶ p.51 | 02 294 5899 | www.airfrance.co.ae |
| Air India | 04 227 6787 | www.airindia.com |
| Air Mauritius | 04 221 4455 | www.airmauritius.com |
| Air New Zealand | 04 209 5521 | www.airnewzealand.com |
| Air Seychelles | 04 295 1511 | www.airseychelles.com |
| American Airlines | 04 393 3234 | www.aa.com |
| Austrian Airlines | 04 294 1403 | www.aua.com |
| British Airways | 04 307 5777 | www.britishairways.com |
| Cathay Pacific | 04 295 0400 | www.cathaypacific.com |
| CSA Czech Airlines | 04 295 9502 | www.czechairlines.com |
| Egypt Air | 04 228 9444 | www.egyptair.com |
| Emirates | 04 214 4444 | www.emirates.com |
| Etihad Airways | 02 505 8000 | www.etihadairways.com |
| Etihad Holidays | 800 2277 | www.etihadairways.com |
| Delta Airlines | 04 397 7281 | www.delta.com |
| Gulf Air | 04 271 3222 | www.gulfairco.com |
| KLM Royal Dutch Airlines | 04 319 3777 | www.klm.com |
| Kuwait Airways | 04 228 1106 | www.kuwait-airways.com |
| Lufthansa | 04 316 6642 | www.lufthansa.com |
| Malaysia Airlines | 04 397 0250 | www.malaysiaairlines.com |
| Olympic Airlines | 04 222 8689 | www.olympicairlines.com |
| Oman Air | 04 351 8080 | www.oman-air.com |
| Pakistan International Airlines | 04 222 2154 | www.piac.com.pk |
| Qantas | 04 316 6652 | www.qantas.com |
| Qatar Airways | 04 229 2229 | www.qatarairways.com |
| Royal Brunei Airlines | 04 351 9330 | www.bruneiair.com |
| Royal Jet Group | 02 575 7000 | www.royaljetgroup.com |
| Royal Jordanian Airlines | 04 294 4322 | www.rja.com.jo |
| Saudi Arabian Airlines | 04 229 6111 | www.saudiairlines.com |
| Singapore Airlines | 04 223 2300 | www.singaporeair.com |
| South African Airways | 04 397 0766 | www.flysaa.com |
| Swiss | 04 294 5051 | www.swiss.com |
| Thai Airways | 04 268 1702 | www.thaiair.com |
| United Airlines | 04 316 6942 | www.ual.com |
| Virgin Atlantic | 04 406 0600 | www.virgin-atlantic.com |

There are currently two terminals, located on different sides of the airport (a 15 to 30 minute taxi ride, depending on the traffic, and there's also a shuttle bus). Both terminals offer car rental, hotel reservations and bureau de change services. Most of the better-known airlines use Terminal 1, but a selection of over 20 airlines operate from Terminal 2, primarily serving the former Soviet countries. For up-to-date flight information, call 04 216 6666.

Duty Free shops are located in both the arrivals and departures halls, although the arrivals hall outlet is limited. All travellers have the opportunity to enter the Dubai Duty Free raffle to win a luxury car, which can be shipped anywhere in the world (tickets are Dhs.500 each, but only 1,000 tickets are sold).

Launched in November 2003, Etihad Airways, the national airline of the UAE (based in Abu Dhabi), has ambitious growth plans. Within 30 months of start-up it was offering 30 routes; the aim is for 70 routes by 2010. Destinations served include Sydney, Toronto, New York, London, Manchester, Paris and Johannesburg. For more information, visit www.etihadairways.com. Another relative

**AIR FRANCE**

making the sky the best place on earth

- 60 secs: buy your ticket
- 20 secs: choose your seat
- 30 secs: print your boarding card

**Take off quicker with our e-services.**

Seat
8B

AIR FRANCE KLM

Call Air France on 04 602 54 00 (Dubai) or 02 621 58 10 (Abu Dhabi) **www.airfrance.com/ae**

**Airport Bus**
*The RTA, in conjunction with the Dubai Department of Civil Aviation, operates airport buses to and from Dubai International Airport every 30 minutes, 24 hours a day. There are two loop routes: Route 401 services Deira, while Route 402 serves Bur Dubai. The fare is Dhs.3. Call 800 9090 for details, or log on to www.rta.ae.*

newcomer is the budget airline Air Arabia, based in Sharjah (www.airarabia.com). The attractions of this airline are reduced costs and 'ticketless' travel. While neither fly directly to or from Dubai, they do provide an alternative for coming to the UAE and travelling within the region, often at more affordable rates. Abu Dhabi is a 90 minute drive from Dubai, and Sharjah is 45 minutes away.

### Lose The Liquids

The new international regulations on fluids in carry on luggage are enforced at Dubai Airport. All liquids, gels and aerosols must be kept in containers smaller than 100ml. Those containers must then be kept in transparent, re-sealable bags. Any liquids, gels or aerosols not in compliance will be thrown out upon entering the terminal.

## Boat

Opportunities for getting around by boat in the Emirates are limited unless you wish to travel by dhow. Crossing the creek by abra is a common method of transport for many people in Dubai, with the number of passengers in 2006 estimated at nearly 26 million. The RTA (Roads & Transport Authority) recently upgraded the abra stations for boarding and alighting, and also raised the fare from 50 fils (the same price it had been for 20 years) to Dhs.1. Another recent addition to the creek was a fleet of air-conditioned water buses. These operate on four different routes crossing the creek, with fares set at Dhs.4 per trip, and are estimated to carry two million passengers in the first year. A 'tourist' route also exists, with a 45 minute creek tour costing Dhs.25.

Further plans are being looked at to extend the routes to Festival City and into Business Bay, and there has been talk of a coastal service between Dubai and Sharjah, and further off-shore to link all the new island developments. There's also the possibility of seeing solar-powered abras in the future, which will maintain the traditional look without the diesel fumes. Yet a further possibility is the introduction of water taxis that can be booked like a normal cab. There is a cruise ship terminal at Port Rashid, currently the only dedicated complex in the region.

It is possible to travel from Dubai, Sharjah and Ras Al Khaimah to several ports in Iran by boat, including a hydrofoil and traditional dhow option. Prices vary between Dhs.130 and Dhs.250, and the journey time can be up to 12 hours depending on the travel option chosen. For more information, contact the Oasis Freight Agency on 04 352 5000.

*RTA bus*

## Bus

There are currently over 60 bus routes through the main residential and commercial areas of Dubai, with the services available recently being clarified with a colour coding system. While the buses are air-conditioned and modern they do tend to be rather crowded. The Roads & Transport Authority (RTA) is in the process of doubling the number of buses in service (up to a total of 1,200, which will include double deckers and articulated buses), to serve 95% of the city and hopefully increase usage among the city's population from 6% to 30%. It is also introducing air-conditioned bus stops – the first was installed in Jumeira in December 2006. The plan is to build over 800, and the first few hundred shelters should be completed by April 2008. Efforts are also being made to display better timetables and route plans at bus stops and stations to encourage people to use this inexpensive method of transport (www.rta.ae).

# Getting Around

The main bus station is near the Gold Souk in Deira and in Bur Dubai on Al Ghubaiba Road near the Plaza Cinema. Buses run at regular intervals, starting between 05:00 and 06:00 and going until midnight or so. Fares are cheap at between Dhs.1 and Dhs.3 per journey, and are paid to the driver when you board, so try to have the exact change ready. Monthly discount tickets and e-Go cards are also available. Buses also go further afield to Khawaneej, Al Awir, Hatta, and even Oman, for very reasonable prices – a one-way ticket to Hatta, which is 100 kilometres away, is Dhs.7, while Dubai to Muscat takes six hours and costs Dhs.50.

The E1 service links Dubai and Abu Dhabi. From early morning to late at night, buses operate every 40 minutes between Al Ghubaiba and Abu Dhabi Central bus stations, and the two-hour journey costs Dhs.15 each way. There is also a service to and from Al Arouba Rd and Al Wahda in Sharjah to both Bur Dubai and Deira, which runs every 10 minutes.

In addition to taxis, Dubai Transport Corporation also offers a minibus service to other emirates of the UAE. The buses are modern, air conditioned and offer a good value service to Ajman, Umm Al Quwain, Ras Al Khaimah, Fujairah, Al Ain and Abu Dhabi. Unfortunately, at present these services only carry passengers on the outward journeys. Anyone wishing to return to Dubai by public transport must make alternative arrangements. The Road and Transport Authority call centre number is 800 9090. The RTA website (visit www.rta.ae) has very comprehensive route plans, timetables and fares .

### e-Go Card

This electronic smart card helps bus passengers save time and avoids the hassle of small change. Available for Dhs.5, the e-Go card can be topped up with credits (Dhs.20 for the first time and multiples of Dhs.10 thereafter). When placed on the ticket machine in the bus, the ticket amount is automatically deducted, and the balance is adjusted and stored. Alternatively you can buy a monthly pass for Dhs.90 at the bus station that allows unlimited travel for the whole month, but not on all routes.

## Car

Other options **Transportation** p.223

Over the past two decades Dubai has built, and is still building, an impressive network of roads. The Municipality estimates that, in the last 10 years, the number of roads in Dubai has doubled. The roads to all major areas are excellent and an eight lane highway heads south-west from the city to Abu Dhabi, which takes about 90 minutes to reach. Despite this, the sheer volume of traffic has become a definite problem. In 2007, Dubai overtook Cairo as the most congested city in the Middle East, with the average commuter spending one hour and 45 minutes per day in their car. With annual growth of traffic levels at 25% and the number of new vehicles being registered among highest of any city in the world, it doesn't look like it will be getting much easier anytime soon.

Particularly busy spots include roads leading in and out of the city centre, and routes across the creek, due to the fact that the number of crossings are limited and the roads leading to them don't seem to be able to cope with the load. There are currently four bridges and a road tunnel linking the two main districts on either side of the creek, with plans underway to increase the number of crossings. Rush hour on Sheikh Zayed Road and on Maktoum Bridge across the creek is close to total gridlock. Only time will tell whether the increasing number of measures being implemented in Dubai will solve the horrendous traffic jams.

*Traffic Jam Session*
*Avoid a traffic jam by tuning in to any of the following radio channels: Al Arabiya (98.9 FM), Al Khallejiya (100.9 FM), Dubai 92 (92.00 FM), Channel 4 FM (104.8 FM), and Emirates 1 FM (99.3FM, 100.5 FM). Regular updates about the traffic situation on main roads are provided throughout the day, forewarning you if a certain road is blocked so you can take an alternative route.*

**Zero Tolerance**

*Dubai Police exercises a strict zero tolerance policy on drinking and driving. This means that if you have had anything to drink, you are much better off taking a taxi home or getting a lift. If you get into an accident, whether it is your fault or not, and you fail a blood-alcohol test you could find yourself spending a night in a police cell before a trial in Dubai Courts, after which a jail sentence will most likely be applied. In addition, your insurance is automatically void. Police have increased the number of random drink-driving checks. You should also be aware that alcohol may still be in your system from the night before. Think very carefully about driving the morning after a boozy evening.*

## Driving Habits & Regulations

While the infrastructure is superb, the general standard of driving is not. The UAE has one of the world's highest death rates per capita due to traffic accidents. According to Dubai Police, one person is killed in a traffic related accident every 48 hours, and there is one injury every four hours – not the most encouraging of statistics. Drivers often seem completely unaware of other cars on the road and fast, aggressive driving, swerving, pulling out suddenly, lane hopping, tail-gating or drifting happen far too regularly.

One move to help the situation on the roads was a ban placed on using handheld mobile phones while driving. Predictably the sales of hands-free systems rocketed before people went back to their old bad habits.

In Dubai, cars are driven on the right-hand side of the road, and it is mandatory to wear seatbelts in the front seats. Children under 10 years of age are not allowed to sit in the front of a car, although you'll still see people driving with their children on their lap and kids climbing over the seats and on the dashboard. The fine for this is Dhs.100 and four black points.

Details of fines for any traffic violations are found on the Dubai Police website (www.dubaipolice.gov.ae). Speeding fines are Dhs.200 and parking fines start at Dhs.100. You are also issued a certain number of black points against your licence according to the particular violation – get 12 points and you have to reapply for your licence. Most fines are paid when you renew your annual car registration. However, parking tickets appear on your windscreen and you have a week or two to pay; the amount increases if you don't pay within the time allotted on the back of the ticket.

Try to keep a reasonable stopping distance between yourself and the car in front; you also need to be more aware of the other cars on the road and check your mirrors frequently. You may consider yourself the safest of drivers but with so many bad drivers on the road it pays to be extra cautious.

If you wish to report a traffic violation, call the Traffic Police's toll free hotline (800 4353). The Dubai Police website (www.dubaipolice.gov.ae) offers all information relevant to driving, such as traffic violations, road maps and contact numbers. For complete information on highway codes, safety and Dubai's road rules, check out the Safe Driving Handbook available from the Emirates Motor Sports Federation (04 282 7111).

## Speed Limits

Speed limits are usually 60 to 80 kph around town, while on main roads and roads to other emirates they are 100 to 120 kph. The speed limit is clearly indicated on road signs. Both fixed and movable radar traps, and Dubai Traffic Police, are there to catch the unwary violator. In 2005, 754,111 fines were given for speeding – an increase of 36% from 2004. On-the-spot traffic fines for certain offences have been introduced, but in most cases you won't know you've received a fine until you check on the website or renew your vehicle registration.

## Driving Licence

To drive a rental vehicle you must provide either an international driving permit or a temporary Dubai licence, which you can only get if you are from one of the countries listed on the transfer list (see p.88).

If you want to drive a privately owned vehicle, you must first get a temporary Dubai licence. Unless you have a Dubai driving licence, either permanent or temporary, you are not insured to drive a private vehicle. For permanent licences, see Driving Licence in the Residents section (p.88). For more information on licences and the procedures involved, see the *Dubai Red-Tape Explorer*.

## Lane Discipline ◀

*As so many different nationalities converge on Dubai's roads, there are bound to be some major differences in driving styles, and lane discipline is often absent. There is little etiquette for overtaking and cars tend to swerve from the far right to far left lanes in a bid to avoid the slow-paced jalopy trundling along in the middle lane. Aggressive driving is a real problem and you can expect to get incessantly flashed by a speed demon behind you despite there being a truck to your right, leaving you with nowhere to go.*

## Accidents

If you are involved in a traffic accident, however minor, you must remain with your car at the accident scene, report the incident to the Traffic Police and then wait for them to arrive. Unfortunately when you have an accident, you become a star attraction and the passing traffic will slow down to a crawl so that rubberneckers can have a good look at your mishap. Stationary vehicles that block the road after an accident as they wait for the police can cause serious tailbacks. If the accident is minor and no one is injured you should move your vehicle out of traffic while you wait for the police – you may be fined for blocking the road otherwise. When the police arrive you will have to explain how the accident happened. If the vehicles have been moved though, and there is a discrepancy between your version and the other driver's, it could be harder to fight your case.

Stray animals (mostly camels) are something else to avoid on some of the quieter roads in the UAE. If the animal hits your vehicle and causes damage or injury, the animal's owner should pay compensation, but if you are found to have been speeding or driving recklessly, you must compensate the animal's owner, which can be expensive. See Traffic Accidents (p.232).

### Highway To Hell

Despite the relatively diminutive size of the city, the average number of road traffic accidents in Dubai is high at around 125 per month, including 18 fatalities (figures released by Dubai Police). So stay alert. You have to keep your wits about you at all times and try to predict the random manoeuvres of other drivers before they happen.

## Non-Drivers

In addition to dealing with bad drivers, you will find that many pedestrians and cyclists also seem to have a death wish. The few cyclists who do brave the roads will often be cycling towards you on the wrong side of the road, invariably without lights. Pedestrians often step out dangerously close to oncoming traffic and a lack of convenient, safe crossings makes life for those on foot especially difficult. However, the number of pedestrian footbridges and pedestrian-operated traffic lights are gradually increasing.

## Parking

In most areas of Dubai parking is available and people rarely have to walk too far in the heat. Increasing numbers of 'pay and display' parking meters are appearing around the busier parts of the city. The areas are clearly marked and the charge is either Dhs.1 or Dhs.2 for an hour. Try to have loose change with you since there are no automatic change machines available. You can also use prepaid cards that can be bought in post offices and shops; for Dhs.42.50 you get Dhs.50 worth of parking and for Dhs.80 you get parking to the value of Dhs.100. Alternatively, you can buy a card that is displayed on the vehicle's windscreen. Type A parking cards can be used in all parking areas and cost Dhs.700 for three months, Dhs.1,300 for six months and Dhs.2,500 for a year. Type B parking cards restrict you to off-street parking in designated areas and cost Dhs.450 for three months, Dhs.800 for six months and Dhs.1,500 for a year.

Parking meters operate from 08:00 to 13:00 and from 16:00 to 21:00, Saturday to Thursday. The authorities began converting the city's meters to a new hi-tech variety during 2007; in time these will accept payment from mobile phones, allowing you to top up your parking remotely. Failure to buy a ticket is likely to land you with a Dhs.100 fine. If you return to your parked car to find that someone has inconsiderately double-parked behind you, you can call 04 269 4848 and report them.

**55**

**Plastic Isn't Fantastic**
*Customers can't use credit or debit cards to purchase fuel or shop items from Emarat, ENOC or EPPCO station, so make sure you have enough cash.*

## Petrol Stations

Petrol stations in the UAE are numerous and run by Emarat, EPPCO and ENOC (Adnoc in Abu Dhabi). Most offer extra services, such as a car wash or a shop selling all those necessities of life that you forgot to buy at the supermarket. The pump price is controlled by the government, and the majority of visitors find petrol far cheaper than in their home countries – prices in late 2007 were Dhs.6.25 per gallon for Special (95 octane), Dhs.6.75 for Super (98 octane), and Dhs.9.00 for diesel.

### Blood Money

If you are driving and cause someone's death, you may be liable to pay a sum of money, known as 'blood money', to the deceased's family. The limit for this has been set at Dhs.200,000 per victim and your car insurance will cover this cost (hence the higher premiums). However, insurance companies will only pay if they cannot find a way of claiming that the insurance is invalid (if the driver was driving without a licence or under the influence of alcohol). The deceased's family can, however, waive the right to blood money if they feel merciful.

**What's In A name?**
*To make navigation even more difficult, places may not be referred to by their official name. For instance, Al Jumeira Road is often known as Beach Road, and Interchange One, on Sheikh Zayed Road, is invariably called Defence Roundabout. Recently, Sheikh Hamdan bin Rashid Al Maktoum ordered certain streets around Dubai to be given the names of prominent Arab cities, such as Amman Road, Cairo Road and Marrakech Road, to demonstrate the strong ties that exist between the UAE and other Arab nations.*

## Car Hire

All the main car rental companies, plus a few extra, can be found in Dubai. It is best to shop around as the rates vary considerably. The larger, reputable firms generally have more reliable vehicles and a greater capacity to help in an emergency (an important factor when dealing with the aftermath of an accident). Depending on the agent, cars can be hired with or without a driver, and the minimum hire period is usually 24 hours. Prices range from Dhs.80 a day for

### Car Rental Agencies

| | | |
|---|---|---|
| Autolease Rent-a-Car | 04 282 6565 | www.autolease-uae.com |
| Avis | 04 295 7121 | www.avisuae.com |
| Budget Rent-a-Car | 04 295 6667 | www.budget-uae.com |
| Diamond Lease ▶ p.225 | 04 343 4330 | www.diamondlease.com |
| Dubai Exotic Limo | 04 286 8635 | www.dubaiexoticlimo.com |
| EuroStar Rent-a-Car ▶ p.57 | 04 266 1117 | www.eurostarrental.com |
| Hertz | 04 282 4422 | www.hertz-uae.com |
| National Car Rental | 04 283 2020 | www.national-me.com |
| Thrifty Car Rental | 800 4694 | www.thriftyuae.com |
| United Car Rentals | 04 266 6286 | na |

smaller cars to Dhs.1,000 for limousines. Comprehensive insurance is essential; make sure that it includes personal accident coverage, and perhaps Oman cover if you're planning on going exploring.

To rent a car, you are usually required to produce a copy of your passport, a valid international driving licence or a Dubai licence, and two photographs. The rental company may be able to help arrange international or temporary local licences for visitors.

## Cycling

Other options **Cycling** (Activities, p.329)

Cycling can be a very efficient way of commuting as it avoids a great deal of traffic and is a very cheap mode of transport, however for most people in Dubai, the car rules, and bikes are used only by those on lower incomes. A lot of care is needed when cycling in the UAE as some drivers pay little attention to anything else, even other cars, and much less cyclists. Also, in the hotter months, cycling is more arduous and it should be remembered that you won't arrive anywhere fresh after pedalling in temperatures as high as 45°C.

In the quieter areas, many of the roads are wide enough to accommodate cyclists as well as cars, and where there are footpaths, they are often wide and in good

# Show that you've arrived.
# Even before you start your journey.

Let the world gaze at you in respect as you whiz by in a Eurostar car. As one of the leading car rental companies in the UAE, we are equipped to fulfill your every travel need. You have a whole range of quality vehicles to choose from. Showrooms and outlets across Abu Dhabi and Dubai. 24 hour rental desk at Abu Dhabi airport. Most of all, a team of professionals who make it their business to put you in the driver's seat.

**EuroStar®**
RENT-A-CAR
Best Deals on Wheels®
www.eurostarrental.com

Dubai, P.O. Box - 7065, Tel: 04 2661117, Fax: 04 2665561
Sheikh Zayed Road, Tel: 04 3434543, Fax: 04 3434991
Jebel Ali, Tel: 04 8811778, Fax: 04 8811776
Abu Dhabi, P.O. Box - 859
Tel: 02 6455855, Fax: 02 6442140 / 6451414
Abu Dhabi Airport, Tel: 02 5757674, Fax: 02 5757673

condition. Dubai's Roads and Transport Authority (RTA) has decided to try to encourage cycling in the busy districts of Deira and Bur Dubai by adding dedicated lanes and parking areas for cyclists. There is even talk of a network of cycle lanes that would eventually be extended to other parts of the city.

## Metro

**Train Of Thought**
*Plans have been mooted for an 'Emirates Railway', a national rail network, as well as a proposed Arabian rail network for the future, which will connect the UAE to the rest of the GCC and countries to the north. However, both projects are still very much at the feasibility stage, and it remains to be seen when, or if, they will go ahead.*

There are currently no trains in the UAE, but work on the Dubai Metro transit system is already underway. It aims to be the largest driverless metro system in the world, and will be focused on two lines; the Red Line starts at Dubai airport and travels alongside Sheikh Zayed Road to the new developments in the south of the city and Jebel Ali, while the Green Line services the city centre. The Red Line will have 28 stations, including four underground at Bur Juman, Al Rigga, Port Sayed and Union Square, while the Green Line will have 14 throughout Bur Dubai and Deira. Some of the current problems on the roads in the centre of Dubai are due to the construction of the underground stations in these areas. The Red Line is scheduled to open on 9 September 2009 after a three-month trial period, with the Green Line estimated to be completed by March 2010. Purple and Blue lines are also being considered by the Roads and Transport Authority (RTA). It is hoped the Purple Line will provide an express line between Dubai International Airport and Dubai's second airport (Al Maktoum International Airport at Jebel Ali) and the Blue Line will follow Emirates Road. An extension of the Red Line to Abu Dhabi and Sharjah is also being considered. The metro is planned to connect with the increasing amount of other public transport in the city, including buses and abras, and the light rail network on Palm Jumeirah that is already on the way to completion. See Key Projects (p.8) for more information.

## Taxi

**Illegal Pickups**
*There is an illegal taxi system, where unlicensed drivers in unmarked cars tout for passengers at the roadside. These cars are unregulated and are not insured to carry passengers. This practice is not looked upon favourably by Dubai Police and hefty fines are levied on convicted drivers.*

If you don't have a car, taxis are the most common way of getting around. In 2000, the Dubai Transport Corporation decided to take over the entire taxi business in Dubai and private taxis were phased out by the end of the year. There are now seven companies operating more than 6,000 metered taxis with a fixed fare structure. The cars are all beige with different coloured roofs: Dubai Taxis are red, National Taxis are yellow, Cars Taxis are blue, Metro Taxis are brown, Al Arabia are green, City Taxis are white and Hatta Taxis are gold. Not all taxis have been changed so far, so some still sport their old livery, but all have the company logo on the doors and the individual taxi numbers on each car. A fleet of 'ladies taxis' was launched in 2007, with distinctive pink roofs. These cars have female drivers and are meant for female passengers only.

The pickup fare ranges from Dhs.3 to Dhs.7, depending on the time of day and taxi company, and whether you order a taxi by phone, although the starting fare inside the airport area is an extortionate Dhs.25. It is also possible to hire a taxi for 12 or 24 hour periods. Towards the end of 2002, three non-metered taxi companies were once again permitted to work on Dubai's roads. Falling under a franchise of Dubai Transport, non-metered cabs operated by Dubai Taxi, Khaibar Taxi and Palestine Taxi allow customers the option of bargaining the fare down. If you do choose this type of taxi, try to find out what the normal cab fare should be first and agree on the fare before the ride. For the least hassle, you might be better off taking one of the more common metered taxis.

### Taxi Companies

| | |
|---|---|
| Al Marmoom Tourist Taxi | 04 347 6650 |
| Arabia Taxi | 04 285 5566 |
| Cars Taxis | 04 269 3344 |
| Dubai Transport Corporation | 04 208 0808 |
| Emirates Taxi | 04 339 4455 |
| Gulf Radio Taxi | 04 223 6666 |
| Metro Taxi Co. LLC | 04 267 3222 |
| National Taxis | 04 339 0002 |
| Sharjah Delta Taxis | 06 559 8598 |

Taxis can be flagged down by the side of the road or you can make a Dubai Transport taxi booking by calling 04 208 0808. If you make a booking, you will pay a slightly higher starting fare (usually only Dhs.3 more than the standard starting fare). The DTC automated phone system stores your address after the first time you call. Each subsequent time you ring from that number, just listen to the prompts, hit 1, and a cab will be dispatched automatically, (or hit 2, then enter a later time using the phone's keypad). All DTC taxis now have GPS too, so the nearest car can reach you in the shortest time (in theory). Alternatively, if you drop Dhs.1 into one of the 15 electronic booking machines dotted around town, a taxi is immediately sent to the machine's location.

To make life a little more confusing, taxi drivers in Dubai occasionally lack any knowledge of the city and passengers may have to direct them. Start with the area of destination and then choose a major landmark, such as a hotel, roundabout or shopping centre. Then narrow it down as you get closer. If you are going to a new place, try to phone for instructions first. It's also helpful to take the phone number of your destination with you, in case you're going around in circles trying to find it. If your taxi driver is well and truly lost, ask him to radio his control point for instructions.

If your journey could take you through one of the Salik (toll) gates, the taxi driver should give you the option of taking an alternative route. If you choose the Salik route, the Dhs.4 charge will be added to your fare.

There's no minimum distance or fare on a journey, although there have been reports of some taxi drivers asking where you are going before you get into their cab, and refusing to take you if you're only going a short distance. Taxi companies insist that their drivers are obliged to accept any fare, whether it is five kilometres or 50. So either give your destination after you get inside the taxi, or you can make a note of the taxi number and report it.

## Walking

Other options **Hiking** p.349

Cities in the UAE are generally very car oriented and not designed to encourage walking. Additionally, summer temperatures of over 45ºC are not conducive to spending any length of time walking through the city. The winter months, however, make walking a pleasant way to get around and people can be found strolling through the streets, especially in the evenings. Most streets are lined with pavements and there are pedestrian paths either side of the creek, along the seafront in Deira and Jumeira, as well as in the parks throughout the city.

### Warning

If you're new in Dubai, or even if you are taking a taxi to a new place for the first time, it can be a good idea to get an idea of how much the journey should cost before you even get in the cab (not from the driver), and even a rough idea of the route. Occurrences are very rare, but some taxi drivers have taken their fares 'for a ride', so to speak. If you are in any doubt that your driver isn't taking you where he should, either take his number from his ID card or the taxi number and tell him you will be calling the company to complain, or just get out at the earliest opportunity. To make sure you are in the right, it's best to pay him off the amount on the meter, and then take the matter up with the company. The company's contact number will be on the outside of the car.

### Mini Marvels

Explorer *Mini Visitors' Guides* are the perfect holiday companion. They're small enough to fit in your pocket but packed with loads of useful info. With detailed maps, visitors' information, restaurant and bar reviews, the lowdown on shopping and all the sights and sounds of the city, these mini marvels are a holiday must.

59

**Top Tip**
Common payment systems accepted around Dubai are: American Express, Cirrus, Global Access, MasterCard, Plus System and Visa.

## Money

Cash is still the preferred method of payment in the Emirates, although credit and debit cards are now widely accepted. Foreign currencies and travellers' cheques can be exchanged in licensed exchange offices, banks and hotels (as usual, a passport is required for exchanging travellers' cheques). Cheques are a bit more tricky; although strict enforcement of laws regulates the bouncing of cheques, many places still won't accept them.

If you're shopping in the souks and markets in Dubai, or in smaller shops, you're better off paying cash; even if a shop does accept other forms of payment, paying cash will help your bargaining stance.

## Local Currency

The monetary unit is the dirham (Dhs.), which is divided into 100 fils. The currency is also referred to as AED (Arab Emirate dirham). Notes come in denominations of Dhs.5 (brown), Dhs.10 (green), Dhs.20 (light blue), Dhs.50 (purple), Dhs.100 (pink), Dhs.500 (blue) and Dhs.1,000 (browny-purple). The denominations are indicated on the notes in both Arabic and English.

Coins are a bit trickier because the amount is written in Arabic only. Fortunately, there are only three different coin denominations in regular use: the Dhs.1, the 50 fils, and the 25 fils. All are silver in colour. The Dhs.1 coin is nearly 2.5cm in diameter and almost always has a traditional coffee pot imprinted on one side. On the other side, you will be able to read the English words 'United Arab Emirates', but everything else is in Arabic.

The 50 fils coin is seven-sided rather than circular, and usually has a picture of an oil refinery on one side. The 25 fils coin is circular but smaller than the Dhs.1 coin and usually has a picture of a small antelope on one side.

You may come across older versions of the Dhs.1 and 50 fils coins that are still in circulation, and this can be confusing because the old Dhs.1 coin is bigger than the new one, and the old 50 fils coin is the same size as the new Dhs.1 coin. Because 5 fils and 10 fils coins are rarely available, you will often not receive the exact change – sometimes this will work in your favour, sometimes it will work against, but it probably averages out in the end.

To see examples of the UAE's banknotes, visit the website of the Central Bank of the UAE (www.centralbank.ae) and click the 'currency' link on the left.

The dirham has been pegged to the US dollar since 1980, at a mid rate of US$1 to Dhs.3.6725 (see the exchange rates table on p.62). Kuwait deregulated their currency from the dollar in 2007, and the UAE, along with several other Gulf states, looks increasingly likely to consider doing the same. However, for the time being, the UAE Central Bank has stated that it will maintain ties to the dollar, and would only make a move along with other Arab countries. Another issue even more on the cards is a single currency for the GCC, although it looks likely that this will not happen until later than the initial target of 2010.

*Sheikh Zayed Road office towers*

# Current Account? Savings Account? Fixed Term Deposit? Investments? Offshore Banking? NRI Banking?

## We have the answer

Whether you want to grow your savings, conduct routine financial transactions or bank overseas, Barclays has the answer for you.

Call 800 BARCLAYS (800 22725297) or SMS 'ACC' to 4422

**BARCLAYS**

**Banking reinvented**

Terms and Conditions apply.
Barclays Bank PLC is Registered in England: Registered No. 1026167. Registered Office: 1 Churchill Place London England E14 5HP.

## Main Banks

| | | |
|---|---|---|
| ABN AMRO Bank | 04 351 2200 | www.abnamro.ae |
| Abu Dhabi Commercial Bank | 04 295 8888 | www.adcb.com |
| Arab Bank | 04 295 0845 | www.arabbank.com |
| Bank of Sharjah | 04 282 7278 | www.bankofsharjah.com |
| Barclays Bank Plc ▶ p.61 | 04 362 6700 | www.barclays.co.uk |
| BNP Paribas | 04 222 5200 | www.bnpparibas.ae |
| Citibank – Middle East | 04 324 5000 | www.citibank.com/uae |
| Dubai Islamic Bank | 04 295 9999 | www.alislami.ae |
| Emirates Bank International | 04 225 6256 | www.emiratesbank.ae |
| Habib Bank AG Zurich | 04 221 4535 | www.habibbank.com |
| HSBC Bank Middle East ▶ p.109 | 800 4722 | www.uae.hsbc.com |
| Lloyds TSB Bank Plc ▶ p.107 | 04 342 2000 | www.lloydstsb.ae |
| Mashreqbank | 04 217 4800 | www.mashreqbank.com |
| National Bank of Abu Dhabi | 04 267 9993 | www.nbad.com |
| National Bank of Dubai | 04 222 2111 | www.nbd.com |
| RAKBANK | 04 224 8000 | www.rakbank.ae |
| Standard Chartered Bank – Middle East | 04 352 0455 | www.standardchartered.com |
| Union National bank | 800 2600 | www.unb.co.ae |

## Banks

A well-structured and ever-growing network of local and international banks, strictly controlled by the UAE Central Bank, offers a full range of commercial and personal banking services. Transfers can be made without difficulty as there is no exchange control and the dirham is freely convertible. To open a bank account in the UAE (with a few exceptions), you usually have to be a resident. Normal banking hours usually are Saturday to Thursday 08:00 to 13:00 or 14:00 (some banks also keep later hours). For more information on services offered by banks in the UAE, refer to Bank Accounts in the Residents section (p.106).

## ATMs

Most banks operate ATMs (Automatic Teller Machines, also known as cash points or service tills) that accept a wide range of cards. Most ATMs, although linked to a specific bank, are part of a central network so you can use any bank card in them. They usually display a range of symbols indicating which networks they are linked to (Cirrus, Visa Electron, etc). You will probably pay a minimal charge if you use an ATM that does not belong to your bank for cash withdrawals and balance enquiries (usually only a dirham or two). Most shopping centres and large supermarkets have at least one ATM, some petrol stations have one in the forecourt or inside the 24 hour shop, and a few hotels have one in their lobby. For international cards, the exchange rates used in the transaction are normally competitive and the process is faster and much less hassle than traditional travellers' cheques.

## Money Exchanges

Money exchanges can be found all over Dubai, offering good service and reasonable exchange rates, often better than the banks. You'll find at least one in all major

## Exchange Rates

| Foreign Currency (FC) | 1 Unit FC = x Dhs | Dhs.1 = x FC |
|---|---|---|
| Australia | 3.38 | 0.3 |
| Bahrain | 9.74 | 0.1 |
| Bangladesh | 0.05 | 18.7 |
| Canada | 3.83 | 0.26 |
| Cyprus | 9.05 | 0.11 |
| Denmark | 0.7 | 1.41 |
| Euro | 5.28 | 0.18 |
| Hong Kong | 0.47 | 2.11 |
| India | 0.093 | 10.71 |
| Japan | 0.03 | 31.28 |
| Jordan | 5.19 | 0.19 |
| Kuwait | 13.24 | 0.07 |
| Malaysia | 1.09 | 0.91 |
| New Zealand | 2.82 | 0.35 |
| Oman | 9.53 | 0.1 |
| Pakistan | 0.06 | 16.54 |
| Philippines | 0.08 | 11.93 |
| Qatar | 1 | 0.99 |
| Saudi Arabia | 0.98 | 1.01 |
| Singapore | 2.53 | 0.39 |
| South Africa | 0.55 | 1.78 |
| Sri Lanka | 0.03 | 30.3 |
| Sweden | 0.57 | 1.73 |
| Switzerland | 3.14 | 0.31 |
| Thailand | 0.11 | 8.6 |
| UK | 7.58 | 0.13 |
| USA | 3.67 | 0.27 |

# Take the right decision

## Swift Transactions. Global Destinations.

┌─────────────── **Our Service Ranges** ───────────────┐

Demand Draft ✦ Electronic Transfer ✦ Telex Transfer ✦ Travelers Cheques ✦ Foreign Currency Sale and Purchase
Door to Door Delivery ✦ DHL ✦ Cash Against Credit Card ✦ Al Ahli Filahza ✦ Rush Money to Egypt
MoneyGram ✦ Instant Cash ✦ ARY Speed Remit ✦ Travelex Money Transfer ✦ EzRemit

└──────────────────────────────────────────────────────┘

الـفـردان لـلـصـرافة
## AL FARDAN EXCHANGE
*It's about service*

### Call Toll Free: 800 - AFEX (800-2339)

-mail: exchange@alfardangroup.com    www.alfardanexchange.com

shopping malls and in some popular shopping districts (such as Karama or the Gold Souk). Exchange centres are usually open from 08:30 to 13:00, and again from 16:30 to 20:30.

Hotels will usually exchange money and travellers' cheques at the standard (non-competitive) hotel rate. For more details about exchanges, refer to the table below, which lists some of the biggest names in town. Visit their website or call to find out the location of the nearest branch.

### Exchange Centres

| | | |
|---|---|---|
| Al Ansari Exchange | 04 397 7787 | www.alansariuae.com |
| Al Fardan Exchange ▶ p.63 | 04 351 3535 | www.alfardangroup.com |
| Al Ghurair Exchange | 04 222 2955 | www.alghurairexchange.com |
| Al Rostamani International Exchange | 04 332 7444 | na |
| First Gulf Exchange | 04 351 5777 | www.fgb.ae |
| Orient Exchange Company | 04 226 7154 | www.orientxchange.com |
| Wall Street Exchange Centre | 800 4871 | www.wallstreet-corp.com |

## Credit Cards

Most shops, hotels and restaurants accept the major credit cards (American Express, Diners Club, MasterCard and Visa). Smaller retailers are sometimes less likely to accept credit cards and if they do you may have to pay an extra 5% for processing (and it's no use telling them that it's a contravention of the card company rules – you have to take it or leave it). Conversely, if you are paying in cash, you may sometimes be allowed a discount – it's certainly worth enquiring.

The general rule concerning the loss or theft of credit cards is to contact the bank as soon as possible and report the missing card. Once you have reported the loss it is highly unlikely that you will be held liable for any further transactions made on the card. As a consequence of ATM fraud, banks have now set a limit on the amount of cash you can withdraw per day in order to limit the financial damage of stolen credit cards (the amount varies from card to card). In addition to these measures, banks also advise the public on how to prevent credit card crime. A frequent problem is that people do not change their pin when they get the card. This is vital for secrecy, and banks also suggest you change your pin on a regular basis even after the initial necessary change.

**Map Marvel**
The *Abu Dhabi Mini Map* is perfect for storing in your car or briefcase. With a large overview map on one side and two detailed maps on the other, it's an indispensable tool for navigating the emirate. Another bonus is the quick restaurant and shopping guide for those nights where you need nothing more than a perfect meal or some new shoes.

## Tipping

Tipping practises are similar at all hotels, bars and restaurants around Dubai. No matter who you tip or how much, it's all shared with the other staff. It's not usually possible to tip a certain individual you are particularly impressed with, as they won't get it, and they could get into trouble if they keep it for themselves. It is, however, still worth tipping and all tips, even though they are shared, are greatly appreciated. An increasing number of restaurants now also include a service charge on the bill, although it's not clear whether this ever sees the inside of your waiter's pockets. The usual amount to tip is 10% and this covers most services. It is however entirely up to the individual whether to tip and it is not a fixed expectation as you find in other countries. See Going Out for more information (p.495).

For taxi drivers it is regular practice to round up your fare as a tip, but this is not compulsory, so feel free to pay just the fare, especially if he drives like a maniac. For tipping when collecting your valet-parked car at hotels, around Dhs.5 is average. At petrol stations, especially when you get your windows cleaned, it's common practice to give a few dirhams as a tip. To avoid any confusion, wait for them to give you your change, and then hand them back their tip.

**Censorship**
*International
magazines are available
in bookshops and
supermarkets, at greatly
inflated prices. All
international titles are
examined by the censor
and anything offensive
is crossed out with a big
black marker. Even
pictures of mothers
lovingly breastfeeding
their newborns in
Mother & Baby will be
blacked out.*

## Newspapers & Magazines

The UAE has a growing number of daily English language newspapers. Until 2004, there were three main players: *Gulf News*, *Khaleej Times* and *Gulf Today*, all available for Dhs.2 every day, except for Fridays when a glossy magazine is included and the price goes up to Dhs.3. All three titles are of somewhat dubious quality compared with the top newspapers in other countries, with *Gulf News* being better in terms of design, writing and editorial comment. These newspapers are all government mouthpieces to varying degrees, and so you will rarely read anything critical of the UAE

*Sheikh Zayed Road skyline*

government, any member of the royal family or the interests of big business in the region. However, recent years have seen a big shake-up in the industry, starting in 2004 with the launch of *7Days*. Although it started out as a weekly paper, this tabloid-size publication is now distributed free of charge six days a week, and features local and international, business and entertainment news and a sports section. It has pushed some of the boundaries of press freedom in the country, which should benefit the industry in the long run. *Emirates Today* was launched in 2005, claiming to be the first newspaper to truly follow the principles of freedom of the press (principles that are advocated fully by Sheikh Mohammed). It contains some interesting human interest pieces and weekly columns. The glossy magazine inserted into the paper on Fridays, called *etc.*, offers some good reading. In 2007, Al Nisr Group (the publisher of *Gulf News*) launched *Xpress*, a free, weekly tabloid. This new title features a good mix of local news and human interest stories. Arabic language newspapers published in the UAE include *Al Bayan*, *Al Ittihad* and *Al Khaleej*. An international edition of UK broadsheet, *The Times*, is also printed and distributed in Dubai.

The local magazine industry is thriving, with new titles being added seemingly every month. For info on Dubai's social scene and upcoming events, get your hands on *Time Out Dubai* (published weekly), *Connector* or *What's On* (both published monthly). *Aquarius* is a monthly magazine that also lists upcoming events and special offers in Dubai, with a health and beauty theme. *Aquarius* and *Connector* are distributed free of charge to certain outlets (you can usually pick up a copy in schools, doctors' offices and hair and beauty salons) or sold in bookshops and supermarkets if you can't find a free copy.

*VIVA* and *Emirates Woman* are monthly women's magazines with interesting features, beauty news and fashion spreads. These were recently joined by Middle

**Pushing The Limits**
A final word on local magazines in Dubai: don't expect to find anything too similar to *FHM* or *GQ* just yet. Censorship laws are relaxing slowly, but they are still light years away from allowing local magazines with scantily clad women in provocative poses. Local men's mag *FO!* had its licence revoked after just two issues – supposedly for not sticking to its business plan but whispers in the industry claim it had more to do with the pictures that appeared in the second issue, despite a warning following the first.

**65**

East editions of the monthly fashion magazine *Harper's Bazaar* and glossy weekly, *Grazia*. For technology and gadget news, there is also a local edition of *Stuff* magazine. The freehold housing boom is reflected in the number of homeowners' and decor magazines available, including *Inside Out* and *Emirates Home*. *Living in the Gulf* is the Spinneys in-house magazine and is full of family related topics and good recipes; it is available from Spinneys supermarkets for just Dhs.3. Other interesting local magazines include *Emirates Bride*, *Arabian Business* and *Gulf Marketing Review*.

With Dubai being such a sociable place full of so many people just dying to be seen, no discussion of the magazine industry would be complete without making mention of *Ahlan!*, *Society Dubai*, *OK Middle East* and *Hello! Middle East*. These glossy magazines feature syndicated articles on celebrity lifestyles (browse through six-page spreads of so-and-so, star of such-and-such, relaxing in their glamorous home) as well as society pages with photographs of local party-goers out on the town. While the Middle East editions of *OK* and *Hello!* have not quite reached the same status as their UK counterparts, it still might be fun to phone home and tell your mum that you're in this week's edition of *OK*.

### International Press

Foreign newspapers, mostly French, German, British and Asian, are available in supermarkets and bookshops, although they are more expensive than at home (about Dhs.8 to Dhs.12) and slightly out of date. One exception is *The Times*. An international edition of this daily UK title is now available on the morning of publication for Dhs.7. Other titles are available through Todaily (www.todaily.com), which releases international newspapers on the published date. Limited copies are available in Carrefour and Spinneys, but if you log onto its website you can subscribe to more than 200 titles from around the world.

### Books

Other options **Websites** p.67, Books (Shopping, p.414)

As well as this residents' guide, Explorer Publishing also produces the *Dubai Mini Explorer* – a guidebook that is small in size, but packed full of all the information visitors need to know about Dubai. In terms of other tourist publications, publishers such as Time Out, Lonely Planet and Footprint have visitors' guides to Dubai and the United Arab Emirates.

If you want to read more about Dubai, the UAE and the Middle East region in general, there are plenty of books to choose from. Explorer Publishing also publishes the *Abu Dhabi Explorer*, as well as guides to Bahrain, Kuwait, Oman and Qatar. It also produces a range of regional activity guides, such as the *UAE Off-Road Explorer*, *Oman Off-Road Explorer* and the *Oman Trekking Explorer*. The *Dubai Red-Tape Explorer* guides you through the ins and outs of bureaucracy in Dubai and is essential for anybody trying to get settled in the city.

If you are looking for beautiful photographs of the region, have a look at *Images of Dubai and the UAE*, *Images of Abu Dhabi and the UAE*, *Sharjah's Architectural Splendour* and *Dubai: Tomorrow's City Today*. *Dubai Discovered* is a condensed pictorial tour of Dubai, featuring stunning images and published in five languages (English, French, Russian, Japanese and German). For a fascinating historical tour back in time, read *Telling Tales: An Oral History of Dubai*. All these photography books are published by Explorer Publishing and are available in bookshops and supermarkets. For a different perspective, read any of Wilfred Thesiger's books on his experiences in the deserts of the Middle East.

**Cultural Corner**

*Dubai Community Theatre & Arts Centre (DUCTAC), based in Mall of the Emirates, is well worth a visit. Art displays, theatre performances, and all kinds of classes are on offer, ranging from salsa to ballet dancing. (www.ductac.org).*

# Further Reading

## Websites

The table below lists various websites on Dubai and the UAE in general, which should be of interest to residents and visitors.

### Websites

| Dubai Information | |
|---|---|
| www.7days.ae | Local newspaper |
| www.ameinfo.com | Middle East business news |
| www.arabianwildlife.com | The UAE's flora and fauna |
| www.dnrd.gov.ae | Dubai Naturalisation & Residency Department |
| www.dubai.ae | Official Dubai eGovernment portal |
| www.dubaiairport.com/dubaimet | Dubai's current weather and five day forecast |
| www.dubaicityguide.com | Updated daily lists of upcoming and current events |
| www.dubaiclassified.com | Buying, selling, jobs and services |
| www.dubaidonkey.com ▶ p.xiii | Free listings website – jobs, property, cars and more |
| www.dubaikidz.biz | Great site for kids' info |
| www.dubaitourism.ae | Department of Tourism & Commerce Marketing |
| www.dubizzle.com ▶ p.173 | Dubai's largest website for classifieds, properties and jobs |
| www.du-fam.com | A new site and forum especially for families in Dubai |
| www.expatbrats.com | Dubai's online magazine for teens & kids |
| www.expatgossip.com | A lively chatboard with lots of members |
| www.expatwoman.com | General information on living in UAE, woman's perspective |
| www.explorerpublishing.com | Publisher of Residents' Guides |
| www.godubai.com | Covers all the events and news of Dubai |
| www.government.ae | UAE Government 'e-portal' – lots of good info |
| www.gulf-news.com | Local newspaper |
| www.howdoidubai.com | Information on living in Dubai |
| www.khaleejtimes.com | Local newspaper |
| www.roomservice-uae.com | Deliveries from your favourite restaurants |
| www.sheikhmohammed.ae | His Highness Sheikh Mohammed Bin Rashid Al Maktoum |
| www.sheikhzayed.com | A site dedicated to the life of the late UAE President |
| www.souk.ae | The middle east's online market |
| www.souq.com | UAE auction and marketplace |
| www.timeoutdubai.com | Time Out Dubai |
| www.uaeinteract.com | UAE Ministry of Information & Culture |
| www.uaemall.com | Shop online in the UAE |
| www.yellowpages.ae | Yellow pages on the net |
| **Business/Industry** | |
| www.e4me.ae | View and pay phone bills online |
| www.dcci.org | Dubai Chamber of Commerce & Industry |
| www.dewa.gov.ae | Dubai Electricity & Water Authority |
| www.dm.gov.ae | Dubai Municipality |
| www.du.ae ▶ p.171 | Dubai's newest telephone and internet services provider |
| www.dubaiairport.com | Dubai International Airport |
| www.dubaidutyfree.com | Dubai Duty Free |
| www.dubaipolice.gov.ae | Dubai Police Headquarters |
| www.dwtc.com | Dubai World Trade Centre |
| www.dxbtraffic.gov.ae | Dubai Traffic Police – great for viewing traffic fines |
| www.e4me.ae | Veiw and pay phone bills online |
| www.emirates.net.ae | Emirates Internet – Dubai's original internet service provider |
| www.etisalat.ae | Dubai's original telephone service provider |
| **Embassies** | |
| www.dwtc.com/directory/governme.htm | Embassies in Dubai |
| www.embassyworld.com | Search Engine for World's Embassies |

## Annual Events

Throughout the year, Dubai hosts a number of well-established annual events, some of which have been running for years. Whether you're keen to chill out to jazz performances from international artists, show off your prized pooch, or watch the world's best tennis stars, the emirate offers some great experiences. Some of the most popular and regular fixtures on Dubai's social calendar are described below.

*All year round*
*Various Locations*

### Exhibitions
*www.dubaitourism.ae*

With the increasing importance of MICE (meetings, incentives, conferences, exhibitions) tourism to Dubai, there are currently two large state-of-the-art exhibition spaces showcasing a variety of exhibitions each year. These are the Airport Expo (Map 13 F3) and the exhibition halls at the Dubai World Trade Centre (Map 10 A1). For details of exhibitions in Dubai, contact Dubai's Department of Tourism & Commerce Marketing (04 223 0000).

*January*
*Public Holiday*

### Islamic New Year's Day

Islamic New Year's Day marks the start of the Islamic Hijri calendar. It is based on the lunar calendar and should fall on 10 January in 2008.
See also Public Holidays (p.20).

*January*
*Al Ain Airport*

### Al Ain Aerobatic Show
*www.alainaerobaticshow.com*

This five-day annual air show takes places at the Al Ain International Airport and sees participation from flying daredevils from around the world. There is a spectator grandstand for plane enthusiasts and those looking for a fun day out. Both military and civilian planes take part in the aerobatic displays.
There is also a biennial airshow event in Dubai (the next will be November 2009).

*January*
*Dubai International*
*Convention &*
*Exhibition Centre*

### The Wellbeing Show 2008
*www.fairs-exhibs.com*

The bigger, brighter Wellbeing Show is moving from Jumeirah Beach Hotel to Dubai International Convention and Exhibition Centre. With demonstrations, seminars and workshops on looking and feeling good, fitness and health, food and nutrition, and mind, body and soul, this exhibition is a must for anyone looking to turn over a new leaf in the new year.

*January*
*World Trade Centre*

### Dubai Marathon
*www.dubaimarathon.org*

Normally held in January (good for working off that festive tummy), the Dubai Marathon now offers a full marathon as well as a 10km road race and 3km charity run. The event attracts all types of runners, with the emphasis more on fun and participation than competition.

*January to February*
*Various Locations*

### Dubai Shopping Festival
*www.mydsf.com*

A combination of a festival and a shopping extravaganza, Dubai Shopping Festival, or DSF as it is popularly known, is hard to miss as buildings and roads are decorated with coloured lights. There are bargains galore in the participating outlets. Highlights include spectacular fireworks each evening, the international wonders of Global Village and numerous raffles. It's a great (although sometimes rather congested) time to be in the city of Dubai.

## Swim The Burj
**February**
*Burj Al Arab*

www.msf.uae.ae

This event, organised by Medecins San Frontieres, gives you the chance to do a sponsored swim around the spectacular Burj Al Arab hotel. It is 1km in total, great fun and all for a very good cause. There's a serious race for those who are very competitive swimmers, and a fun swim. Lifeguards are on hand and the number of participants is strictly limited. For more details, call 04 345 8177.

## International Property Show
**February**
*Dubai International Convention & Exhibition Centre*

www.internationalpropertyshow.ae

Featuring everything to do with buying international property, this show is particularly popular among expats who are looking to invest overseas. The 2008 exhibition will feature property from the Middle East and around the world.

## Dubai Pet Show
**February**
*Nad Al Sheba*

www.dubaipetshow.com

Held at Nad Al Sheba (usually on a Saturday) and sponsored by Pedigree Chum and Whiskas, the Pet Show is a popular family outing and the only show of its kind in the Middle East. You are guaranteed to see both pedigree and crossbreed dogs of every shape, size and colour imaginable. One of the most popular events is the 'Dog Most Like its Owner' competition – the likenesses are often uncanny. The demonstration by the police dog unit is also fascinating.

## Terry Fox Run
**February**
*Wonderland*

www.dubaiterryfoxrun.com

Last year, thousands of individuals ran, jogged, walked, cycled, wheeled and even rollerbladed their way around an 8.5km course for charity. The proceeds go to cancer research programmes at approved institutions around the world. The 2008 run will be held on 15 February – check the local media for contact details nearer the time.

## Dubai Tennis Open
**February/March**
*Aviation Club*

www.dubaitennischampionships.com

Usually held from the middle of February, the US$1,000,000 Dubai Duty Free Tennis Open is a popular and well-supported event. It is firmly established on the international tennis circuit and offers the chance for fans to see top seeds, both male and female, in an intimate setting. The Williams sisters, Rafael Nadal, Roger Federer and Maria Sharapova have all graced Dubai's courts in past tournaments. Held at the tennis stadium at the Aviation Club, so in between matches you can nip to the Irish Village for a pint.

## Dubai International Jazz Festival
**March**
*Dubai Media City*

www.chilloutproductions.com

If you are looking for a night of chilled moods, then this is the place to be. Established as an annual event over the last few years, this nine-day festival attracts a strong line-up of top artists from all around the world, and grows in popularity each year. It will be held in Dubai Media City and Madinat Jumeirah outdoor amphitheatre, and will feature performances from internationally recognised artists.

## Dubai World Cup
**March**
*Nad Al Sheba*

www.dubaiworldcup.com

The Dubai World Cup is billed as the richest horse race in the world – last year's total prize money was over US$15,000,000. The prize for the Group One Dubai World Cup

**69**

race alone was a staggering US$6,000,000. It is held on a Saturday to ensure maximum media coverage in the west. With a buzzing, vibrant atmosphere, it's a great opportunity to dress up and dig out your favourite hat.

## Great British Day
*March*
*Emirates Golf Club*

www.britbiz-uae.com

With a village fete atmosphere, cream teas and fish and chips, the Great British Day guarantees a good family day out. It is organised by the British Business Group and is usually held on a Friday. Thousands of people of all nationalities attend the event and enjoy competitions, bouncy castles, live music, handicraft stalls and a terrific fireworks display as the grand finale.

## Powerboat Racing
*March*
*DIMC*

www.dimc-uae.com

The UAE is well established on the world championship powerboat racing circuit – in Abu Dhabi with Formula I (Inshore) and in Dubai and Fujairah with Class I (Offshore). These events make a great spectacle, ideal for the armchair sports fan. Events in Dubai are held at the Dubai International Marine Club (DIMC, 04 399 4111).

## Dubai International Boat Show 2008
*March*
*DIMC*

www.boatshowdubai.com

If you love big boats then this is the event for you – even if you don't have the big bucks to afford one. Dubai International Boat Show, the largest marine industry exhibition in the Middle East, is a classic showcase of yachts and boats from both local and international builders, together with the latest innovations in marine equipment and accessories.

## Dubai Masters Football Cup
*April*
*Aviation Club*
*Garhoud*

www.mastersfootballdubai.com

Watch former stars relive their glory days, as ex-Liverpool, Manchester United, Celtic and Rangers players compete for their former clubs in an evening of televised six-a-side matches. Legends such as Ian Rush and Lee Sharpe still have the silky skills that once electrified the crowds at Old Trafford and Anfield. Standard tickets cost Dhs.125.

## Bride Show Dubai
*April*
*World Trade Centre*

www.thebrideshow.com

The Bride Show is the largest bridal exhibition in the region, and brings the whole wedding industry together. Brides can browse through dresses, choose photographers and entertainment, pick their honeymoon destinations and meet wedding organisers. It's a must-do before you say 'I do'.

## Dubai Worldwide Property Show
*May*
*Grand Hyatt*

www.dubaishows.com

This event showcases the latest developments on offer from property developers and real estate agents from around the world.

## Dubai Summer Surprises
*June to August*
*Various Locations*

www.mydsf.com

Dubai Summer Surprises is held to attract visitors during the hot and humid summer months. Aimed at families, it offers fun packed activities, generally held in climate-controlled facilities, such as shopping malls, specially constructed areas and hotels. Events are based on food, heritage, technology, family values and education.

## GITEX

**October**
*Dubai International Convention & Exhibition Centre*

www.gitex.com

One of the largest and most successful international exhibitions for computing, communications systems and applications in the information technology industry, Gitex gets bigger and bigger every year. The five-day exhibition has been running for 25 years and is renowned for its Gitex Computer Shopper where the public can snap up some great deals on technology.

## UAE Desert Challenge

**October & November**
*Jebel Ali Racecourse & Empty Quarter*

www.uaedesertchallenge.com

This is the highest profile motorsport event in the country and is often the culmination of the World Cup in cross country rallying. Following prestigious events, such as the Paris – Dakar race, this event attracts some of the world's top rally drivers and bike riders who compete in the car, truck and moto-cross categories. The race takes place in several stages across the harsh and challenging terrain of the desert, including a spectator event in Dubai. For more details call 04 266 9922.

## Camel Racing

**October to April**
*Nad Al Sheba*

The sight of these ungainly animals is an extraordinary spectacle, especially as racing camels can change hands for as much as Dhs.10 million. This sport suffered a bit of bad press due to the use of child jockeys, but that has all changed with the introduction of robot camel jockeys. Morning races take place throughout the winter at the Nad Al Sheba club and start very early; you need to be there by 07:00 as the races are over by 08:30. Admission is free.

## Dhow Racing

**October to May**
*DIMC*

www.dimc-uae.com

This traditional Arabic sport is great to watch; there is something enigmatic about wooden dhows gliding gracefully over the water, especially when they're racing. The vessels are usually between 40ft and 60ft in length and are either powered by men (up to 100 oarsmen per dhow) or by the wind. Fixed races are held throughout the year as well as on special occasions, such as National Day. Most events are held at Dubai International Marine Club.

## Desert Rallies

**November**
*Various Locations*

www.emsf.ae

The highest profile event is the Desert Challenge (above), which is the climax of the World Cup in Cross Country Rallying. It attracts top rally drivers from all over the world and is usually held in October or November, depending on other events. There are numerous other events throughout the year; contact EMSF (04 282 7111).

## Dubai Rugby Sevens

**December**
*Exiles Rugby Club*

www.dubairugby7s.com

This three-day event is a very popular sporting and spectator fixture. With alcohol on sale at the stadium, the party atmosphere carries on until the small hours. Top international teams compete for the coveted 7s trophy (the Dubai tournament is usually the first leg of the IRB Sevens Tournament), while local teams from all over the Gulf try their luck in the various competitions, including women's rugby. This has become one of the biggest sporting and partying weekends of the year in Dubai and attracts more than 65,000 spectators over three days.

**December**
*Starts at Dubai
Autodrome*

## Fun Drive
www.gulf-news.com

If your idea of fun is venturing through the wilderness of the UAE with 750 other four-wheel drives, then this event is for you. Spread over two days, the Fun Drive is a popular and very sociable, guided off-road trip. Early booking is advised. Contact the *Gulf News* Promotions Department for more information. *Gulf News* also organises a daytrip Fun Drive.

**December**
*Nad Al Sheba*

## Horse Racing
www.dubairacingclub.com

Nad Al Sheba racecourse is one of the world's leading racing facilities and home to the Dubai World Cup race. Racing takes place at night under floodlights, and usually begins at 19:00 (except during Ramadan when it is at 21:00). General admission and parking are free, and the public has access to most areas with a reserved area for badge holders and members. The clubhouse charges day membership on race nights at Dhs.60. Everyone can take part in free competitions to select the winning horses, with the ultimate aim of taking home prizes or cash.

**December**
*Dubai International
Convention &
Exhibition Centre*

## Mother, Baby & Child Show
www.motherbabyandchild.com

Mums and kids will love this show, featuring exhibits by child-friendly companies and lots of entertainment for the little ones. Make sure you pick up a plastic bag at the entrance, because as you walk round you get given loads of samples and giveaways.

**December**
*Sharjah Expo Centre*

## Sharjah World Book Fair
www.swbf.gov.ae

This annual event, one of the oldest and largest book fairs in the Arab World, takes place at the Sharjah Expo Centre and boasts participation from 35 countries. Thousands of titles in Arabic, English and many other languages are displayed by private book publishers, governments and universities.

**December**
*Madinat Jumeirah*

## Dubai International Film Festival
www.diff.ae

Having debuted in December 2004, this has become a hotly anticipated annual event and marks a great achievement for the film industry in Dubai. Last year it was hosted at Madinat Jumeirah and attracted some well-known industry players such as Morgan Freeman, Orlando Bloom and Sarah Michelle Gellar. The festival brings together a collection of international films, including those from the Arab world.

Rallying in the desert

Supercar on display

# Great things can come in small packages…

Perfectly proportioned to fit in your pocket, these marvellous mini guidebooks make sure you don't just get the holiday you paid for, but rather the one that you dreamed of.

**Explorer Mini Visitors' Guides**
Maximising your holiday, minimising your hand luggage

Abu Dhabi • Amsterdam • Bahrain • Barcelona • Beijing • Berlin • Dubai • Dublin • Geneva •

**EXPLORER**

# Visitor Mobile Line
# Your passport to the UAE

Buy the du Visitor Mobile Line
for only AED 70

- AED 20 recharge card
- UAE visitor guide
- tourist maps
- travel wallet
- 90 day validity with option to renew
- option to migrate to other packages
- more savings with Pay by the Second

Buy yourself a line, or one for your friends and family.
Available at the airport or at any du shop or authorised
dealer throughout the UAE.

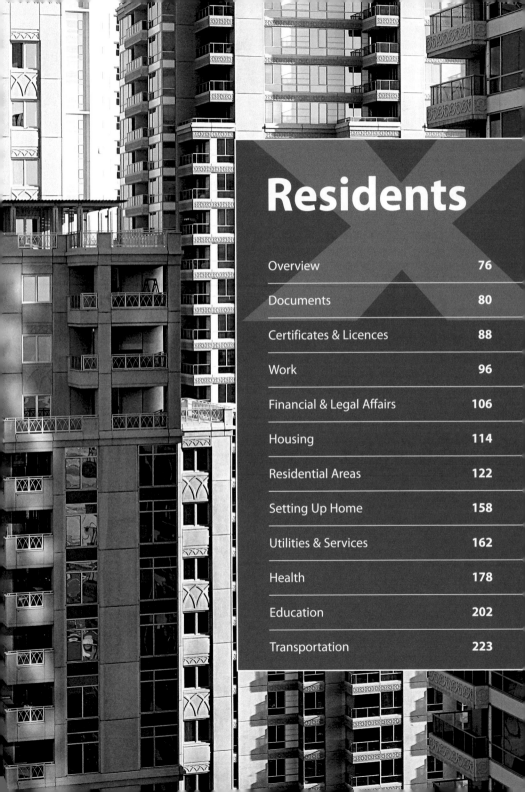

# Residents

# Residents

**Drinking in DXB**
While drinking alcohol is forbidden for Muslims, it is served in the many bars, clubs and restaurants throughout Dubai. However, you won't find a booze aisle in your local supermarket, although some people have made the mistake of stocking up on 0% alcohol beers that line the shelves. Two companies operate liquor stores, but you'll need a licence to buy alcohol (see p.408).

## Overview

Dubai is without a doubt a destination of the 21st century. Read any article about the fastest growing city in the region and it's almost guaranteed you'll see the words 'ambitious', 'record-breaking' and 'staggering'. This meteoric growth has not gone unnoticed, and each year thousands of expats arrive to claim a slice of the action. Dubai certainly has a lot to offer, and this book aims to provide you with all the information needed to make the most of your new life here and minimise the bureaucracy.

The Residents chapter takes you through every imaginable aspect of living here – whether you are reading this as you sit in the comfort of your home country, contemplating a sojourn abroad, are fresh off the plane with your whole life in a suitcase, have called Dubai home for months or even years, or are about to say your bittersweet farewells.

One thing you do need to remember is that procedures and laws change regularly, often in quite major ways. Changes are generally announced in the newspapers and can be implemented overnight – so be prepared for the unexpected.

## Considering The United Arab Emirates

Living in Dubai has much to offer. The sun shines almost every day, the shopping and leisure facilities are impressive, and the salaries are taxfree. Of course, there are hassles and annoyances, but for many these are outweighed by the positives.

**Combat Culture Shock**
It will definitely reduce culture shock if you know as much about Dubai as possible before arriving. This book, of course, is one of the most comprehensive sources of information, but you may also find the websites listed on p.67 of some interest.

But, with Dubai's dizzying growth and rising popularity, the expat experience has changed in recent years. Whereas once it was easy for expats to get work, more competition means employers can be pickier. And with candidates arriving from all over the world, salaries are dropping. But opportunities remain, particularly in engineering and construction.

The cost of living is on the up too, with rents seeing significant increases. To make it worthwhile you may need to hold out for a good expat package with housing, schooling, and medical expenses included. These generous packages are not as common as they were. Before jumping on the first plane, test the job market by sending some emails to potential employers and monitoring the overseas appointments pages and recruitment websites (p.102).

You also need to consider how you're going to enter the country and stay here. To remain in Dubai on a permanent basis you need a residency permit (often called a visa), and to get this you need a 'sponsor'. For employed people, their company will be their sponsor. These employees should then be able to sponsor members of their family (subject to certain conditions, see p.84). If you don't have work lined up, you may be able to enter on a visit visa (see p.80), but this is for a limited period only.

**And in 80th place...**
In a report by Mercer Human Resource Consulting in 2007, Dubai ranked number 80 in a list of the world's most liveable cities – up five places from 2006. The survey was based on a number of quality of life factors including security, infrastructure, and the availability of goods and services. The world's most liveable city was Zurich, followed by Geneva and Vancouver.

## Before You Arrive

If you're coming to Dubai to work, or even just to look for work, you should have any qualification certificates and important documents (such as your marriage certificate, and kids' birth certificates) attested in your home country. This can be quite a lengthy process, and involves solicitors and the UAE foreign embassy.

Property owners may consider selling up before the move, but don't be hasty. It may be wise to test the water and give yourself a year before you commit long-term – although many people have come for a year or two and are still in the country five years later. If you do own property in your home country you could consider letting for the first year, until you've settled in. You also need to get your financial affairs in order, such as telling banks and building societies, and the tax office. Speak to your pension company too – moving abroad could have implications on your contributions (see

Financial & Legal Affairs, p.106). If you've got kids you should start researching schools as soon as possible. New schools are opening all the time to keep up with Dubai's growing population, but places are not guaranteed, so get your name down in plenty of time (see Education, p.202). Finding a place to live is one of the most important tasks in moving to a new country so if possible you should take your time and explore all the different residential areas Dubai has to offer (see p.124). A good idea is to arrange temporary accommodation, maybe in a furnished apartment (see p.117), while you look for your perfect home. If you have been employed from your home country some companies will pay for this initial accommodation. When you do move it's likely you'll want to bring more than just a suitcase with you, so speak to shipping and/or relocation companies, and book well in advance (for more information, see p.160). If you're coming to look for employment, do your homework before you arrive. Contact recruitment agencies and sign up with online job sites as far in advance as possible. There may also be agencies in your home country that specialise in overseas recruitment. The Work section (p.96) should give you some handy information.

*Visa on Arrival*
*Citizens of the following countries receive an automatic visa on arrival: Andorra, Australia, Austria, Belgium, Brunei, Canada, Cyprus, Denmark, Finland, France, Germany, Greece, HongKong, Iceland, Ireland, Italy, Japan, Liechtenstein, Luxembourg, Malasyia, Malta, Monaco, Netherlands, New Zealand, Norway, Portugal, San Marino, Singapore, South Korea, Spain, Sweden, Switzerland, United Kingdom, United States of America and Vatican City*

## When You Arrive

The list of things you'll have to deal with in the first few weeks can be a little daunting, and you may well be in for a lot of form filling, queuing, and coming and going. Try not to let it spoil things though, because you'll hopefully soon be a fully fledged resident enjoying your new life, and all that boring bureaucracy will be a distant memory. Some of the key issues you should be covering are listed below.

• Residency/visas – if you're on an employment or residency visa, you'll apply for a health card, take the medical test, and get your residency permit (see p.83). If you're on a visit visa, either sort out your sponsorship (by a company or family member) or be prepared to make 'visa runs' (p.82). It is expected that from late 2007 a UAE ID card will be introduced for all residents, which will combine your labour, health and e-gate cards in one (p.82).
• Furnish your new home and get connected – for advice on furnishings and how to get the water, electricity, phone and TV connected, see p.169 and p.170
• Buy a car – for advice on what's available, how to go about it, and the registration process, see Vehicles, p.230
• Licences – get your driving licence, and get a liquor licence if you want to buy alcohol. See licences on p.88 and p.90.
• Register with your embassy – it's always worthwhile letting your embassy know you're living here. See the table on p.32
• Get acquainted – to help you settle in and find like-minded individuals, consider joining a social group.

## Essential Documents

For many procedures you'll have to produce your 'essential documents.' At the very least these are:
• Original passport
• Passport photocopies (including photo page and visa page if appropriate)
• Passport photographs

Depending on the procedure, you may also have to show a copy of your labour contract, a salary certificate, a tenancy contract, and a no objection certificate (NOC) from your company or sponsor. It's also a good idea to make copies of all your original documents and store them in a safe place.

You're going to need a lot of photographs over the coming months, as just about everything you do requires a copy of your passport and a photograph – whether you're applying for a health card, getting a phone connection or joining your local

77

gym. To save time and money, when you have your photos done ask for the original negative or a CD. Duplicate photos can then be made easily. There are hundreds of photo shops all over Dubai that offer this service, and you'll pay around Dhs.20 for a dozen pictures.

Often when renting a house or opening a bank account you may have to produce a salary certificate from your employer to confirm that you are employed and earn the minimum salary requirement. You may have also be asked for an NOC (no objection certificate) from your employer when renting a property, buying a car, opening a bank account or applying for your driving licence although it is not always a requirement. Either way, any paperwork provided by your employer should be on a company letterhead, signed and stamped with the company stamp to make it undeniably 'official'.

## When You Leave

Rather than just jetting off, there are certain things that have to be wound up before you leave, such as:

- Electricity and Water – give DEWA at least two days' notice before you leave the property. They'll take a final reading and return your security deposit (p.117).
- Landlord – make sure the place is spick and span, otherwise you may lose some of your deposit. The landlord may also require a clearance certificate from DEWA to prove you've paid all the bills.
- Sell your car – not always a straightforward job, and the second-hand garages can smell a departing expat a mile off so be prepared for lots of ridiculously low offers. For a list of used car dealers, see p.227.
- Shipping – just as when you arrived, the more notice you can give the removal/relocation company the better. For a list of companies, see p.160.
- Sell your home contents – sometimes easier (and cheaper) than shipping them half way across the world. The beauty of Dubai is that it is still a transient city, so there are often leavers looking to sell and newcomers looking to buy. You can put a notice on supermarket noticeboards or even have your own garage sale.

Red tape, unfamiliar bureaucracy and living out of a suitcase can make expat life a little stressful at the start, but year-round sunshine, golden sandy beaches, modern facilities, first-class shopping and some of the region's best restaurants and bars can make it all worthwhile.

*The Gardens*

We know what turns you on

...dmit it, you'd love to get your hands on an Audi, Porsche or
...lkswagen. Well, you'll find them all at Al Nabooda Automobiles LLC.
...o drop in, and get turned on.

AL NABOODA LLC
AUTOMOBILES

DRIVEN BY
PROFESSIONALISM

...Box 10773, Dubai, UAE. **Corporate Office/ Volkswagen Showroom:** Tel: 04-3386999 Fax: 04-3388890, **Audi Showroom:** Tel: 04-3475111 Fax: 04-3473443,
**Porsche Showroom:** Tel: 04-3213911 Fax: 04-3211554, **Sharjah:** Tel: 06-5422241 Fax: 06-5422243, **Fujairah:** Tel: 09-2221066 Fax: 09-2224692.

# Entry Visa

**Visitors** ◀

*If you live in Dubai and friends or family want to visit you, but they don't qualify for an automatic visit visa on arrival (see p.77), there are various options. If they are staying in a hotel, most hotels offer a visa service. If they are flying with Emirates, the airline can arrange a 60 day visit visa (for an extra fee). Or you can arrange a visa for them – you'll need their passport copy, your own passport with your residency permit, your employment contract showing your salary or a salary certificate for free zone workers, and sometimes your tenancy contract (not always required). Minimum salary requirements apply: A total salary of Dhs.4,000 plus housing allows you to sponsor your parents, Dhs.5,000 plus housing and your siblings can come too, and Dhs.8,000 means you can arrange visas for friends. Apply at the Immigration Department. Once the visa is approved, fax a copy to your visitors and deposit the original at the airport.*

Visa requirements for entering Dubai vary greatly between different nationalities, and regulations should always be checked before travelling since details can change with little or no warning. GCC nationals (Bahrain, Kuwait, Qatar, Oman and Saudi Arabia) do not need a visa to enter Dubai. Citizens from many other countries (including the UK, USA, Australia, Canada and many EU countries) get an automatic visa upon arrival at the airport (see the full list of 35 countries on p.77). The entry visa is valid for 60 days, although you can renew for a further 30 days (see Visa Renewal, p.80).

Holders of British overseas passports issued in Hong Kong or China are also entitled to a visa on arrival at Dubai International Airport.

Expats with residency in other GCC countries, who do not belong to one of the 35 visa on arrival nationalities but who do meet certain criteria (professions such as managers, doctors and engineers), can get a non-renewable 30 day visa on arrival – check with your airline before flying.

People of certain nationalities who are visiting the Sultanate of Oman may also enter Dubai on a free-of-charge entry permit. The same criteria and facilities apply to Dubai visitors entering Oman (although if you have Dubai residency you will pay a small charge). Citizens of eastern European countries, countries that belonged to the former Soviet Union, China and South Africa can get a 30 day, non-renewable tourist visa sponsored by a local entity, such as a hotel or tour operator, before entry into the UAE. The fee is Dhs.100 for the visa and an additional Dhs.20 for delivery.

Other visitors can apply for an entry service permit (exclusive of arrival/departure days), valid for use within 14 days of the date of issue and non-renewable. Once this visa expires the visitor must remain out of the country for 30 days before re-entering on a new visit visa. The application fee for this visa is Dhs.120, plus an additional Dhs.20 delivery charge.

For those travelling onwards to a destination other than that of the original departure, a special transit visa (up to 96 hours) may be obtained free of charge through certain airlines operating in the UAE.

A multiple-entry visa is available to visitors who have a relationship with a local business, meaning they have to visit that business regularly. It is valid for visits of a maximum of 30 days each time, for two years from date of issue. It costs Dhs.1,000 and should be applied for after entering the UAE on a visit visa. A fee of Dhs.200 per visit applies to the multiple entry visa. For an additional Dhs.150, a multiple entry visa holder is eligible for the e-Gate service (see p.82). Companies may levy a maximum of Dhs.50 extra in processing charges for arranging visas. The DNATA (Dubai National Airline Travel Agency) visa delivery service costs an extra Dhs.20.

## Visa Renewals

Visit visas valid for renewal may be extended for a further 30 days at the Department of Immigration and Naturalisation (04 398 1010), Karama, near the Dubai World Trade Centre Roundabout. The fee is Dhs.500. At the end of this period, you must either leave the country and arrange for a new visit visa from overseas or, for certain nationalities, leave and re-enter the country on a 'visa run' (see p.82).

While the current rules generally grant a 60 day visa free of charge to the 35 nationalities listed on p.77, discrepancies do sometimes occur, and there have been suggestions that the UAE Naturalisation and Residency Department plans to tighten the visit visa rules. Proposals include charging a fee, and limiting some nationalities to a non-renewable 30 day visit visa. A further proposal is the introduction of a 'ban' after the expiry of all visit visas. This would force the visitor to leave the UAE and remain out of the country for a period of one month or more before re-entering on a new visa. But, Dubai wants to attract many millions of tourists over the coming years, so logically the

# They Mean the World to You

We understand the importance of making your relocation experience as smooth as possible. After all, we're not just relocating your possessions, we are helping to relocate the most precious things in your life. Crown Relocations is a leading provider of domestic and international moving and settling-in services with over 100 locations in more than 45 countries.

*Well Connected. Worldwide.*™

**Dubai**
Tel: (971) 4 289 5152
Fax: (971)4 289 6263
Email: dubai@crownrelo.com

**Abu Dhabi**
Tel: (971)2 674 5155
Fax: (971)2 674 2293
Email: abudhabi@crownrelo.com

**Bahrain**
Tel: (973)17 227 598
Fax: (973)17 224 803
Email: bahrain@crownrelo.com

**Egypt**
Tel: (202) 580 6628
Fax: (202) 580 6601
Email: cairo@crownrelo.com

**Kuwait**
Tel: (965) 299 7850
Fax: (965) 299 7800
Email: kuwait@crownrelo.com

**Qatar**
Tel: (974) 462 1115/1170/1439
Fax: (974) 462 1119
Email: doha@crownrelo.com

**Turkey**
Tel: (90) 212 347 4410
Fax: (90) 212 347 4413
Email: istanbul@crownrelo.com

*Please Visit* **www.crownrelo.com**
*for details.*

**CROWN**
R E L O C A T I O N S

procedures should be simplified. Rules and regulations do have a habit of changing without notice so you are best advised to check with the UAE consulate or embassy in your home country, or at least ask the airport official stamping your passport how long you're allowed to stay.

**Fully Fledged Resident**
*After entering Dubai on an employment or residency visa, you have 60 days to complete all of the procedures involved in becoming a resident (although it's unlikely to take anywhere near that long). If you need to leave the country again before the process is completed, you should be able to do so as long as you have the entry visa that was stamped in your passport when you first entered. It's probably best though if you avoid booking any holidays in those first few weeks.*

## Visa Run

The 'visa run' basically involves exiting and re-entering the country to gain an exit stamp and new entry stamp in your passport. You can simply fly to a neighbouring country and back into Dubai. Driving over the border into Oman is another alternative as you can get your passport stamped at the border near Hatta, but both of these options are only possible for those on the list of 35 countries (see p.77). If you do drive to the Hatta border, you must also make sure that your car insurance covers Oman – take your insurance documents to prove it, otherwise you'll get stung for some temporary cover. Visa run flights are usually to Doha, Manama or Muscat and you return an hour or so later, usually on the same plane. Passengers remain in transit in the airport and hence do not need a visa for the country they fly to. There are several flights daily and the cost is about Dhs.400 for a return ticket, depending on the season. Flights are offered by Emirates (04 214 4444), Gulf Air (04 271 3222), Qatar Airways (04 229 2229) and Air Arabia flying from Sharjah (06 558 0000). If you do fly from Sharjah to Oman you will be charged Dhs.60 for your visa, whereas visitors from Dubai get their visa for free.

## UAE-Gate

The UAE-Gate service allows UAE and GCC nationals, as well as people with a valid residence permit to pass through both the departures and arrivals halls of Dubai International Airport without a passport. Swipe your smart card through an electronic gate and through you go, saving a great deal of time otherwise spent in long queues. Applications for a card are processed within minutes at Dubai International Airport, in the DNATA buildings (one on Sheikh Zayed Road and one in Deira near Deira City Centre), or the DNRD office on Trade Centre Road. You'll need your passport, containing the valid residence permit and you will be fingerprinted and photographed. The UAE-Gate card costs Dhs.200 and is valid for two years. Payment can be made by cash or credit card. For further information, contact 04 316 6966.

**The Health Card**
*The health card entitles you to subsidised health care at government-run hospitals and clinics. The health card must be renewed each year, but you only need to take a new medical test when your visa is up for renewal.*

# Health Card

Once you have the correct visa (either an employment visa or a work visa), the next step to becoming a fully fledged resident is to apply for a health card and take the medical test. If you entered Dubai on a visit visa, you must transfer your visa either by exiting and re-entering, or paying Dhs.500 to the Immigration Department for 'visa amendment.' It may seem to be the wrong way round, but you actually get your health card before taking the medical test (although you can now do both on the same day). If you're in employment your company PRO should take care of most of the paperwork, and will certainly be able to get the health card for you as well as advise you where to go (and sometimes accompany you) for the medical test. Some employers provide additional private medical insurance and, as in many countries, this is regarded as preferable to state care.

To apply for a health card yourself, pick up an application form at any public hospital, (see p.180) such as the Iranian, Al Baraha (commonly known as Kuwaiti Hospital), Maktoum or Rashid Hospital, or the Ministry of Health. It makes sense to go to Rashid Hospital though, as that is where you will have to submit everything, unless you're on a free zone permit (see p.83) in which case you may be directed to another hospital. Take the application form (typed in Arabic) to the health card section at Rashid Hospital, along with your passport and passport copies, a copy of your visa (employment or residency), and two passport photos. The fee is Dhs.310, plus a typing fee of around Dhs.20, and in return you'll get a health card and a blank form for the medical test.

**Improved Service** ◀

*The Department of Health & Medical Services are attempting to improve their procedures by embracing the internet. Results of medical tests can be retrieved online and health cards can be renewed using the Express HC service. You will need to register on www.dohms.gov.ae to use this service. However, it can be somewhat temperamental and you may find yourself doing it the old fashioned way anyway, but it is still worth a couple of clicks*

## Medical Test

Check with your employer which hospital to go to, or ask at Rashid Hospital when applying for your health card. The two most common options are Maktoum Hospital and Al Baraha (Kuwaiti) Hospital, which despite their ramshackle appearances are relatively well run. You will need your health card, a copy of the receipt for the Dhs.310 paid at Rashid Hospital, the test form filled out in Arabic (there are typing offices around Dubai who'll do this for Dhs.20 or so), and two passport photos. The test fee is Dhs.210. Submit all the forms, take a ticket and wait your turn. If you're lucky you'll only have a short wait, but if it's busy you may be there for many hours – the best time is usually first thing in the morning, and midweek is quieter. Blood will be taken (nurses use this to test for HIV and Hepatitis). If your test is positive you will be called back for another test – if this test confirms that you are HIV positive or have Hepatitis, you will be detained and deported to your home country. Getting called back for a second test does not automatically mean that you have something to worry about. Often samples are mixed in batches and one test will be run per batch, and if any blood within that specific batch is diseased everyone within that group will need to be tested again. If you are at all nervous about undergoing the test then it may be a good idea to go to your local doctor and get tested before you leave your home country.

After your blood test you might have to have a chest X-ray to test for tuberculosis. There are changing rooms, although if these are full you might have to change in the corridor. Ladies are given a gown, but if you go in a T-shirt, you don't have to wear the gown and can just remove your bra instead. After the tests are finished, collect a receipt – this will tell you when to return to collect your results (usually three or four days later).

**Make Sure Your** ◀
**PRO is a pro**

*In Dubai a PRO is your company's 'man who can' – he liaises with various government departments and carries out those tiresome admin procedures. The PRO knows the system inside out, and will take care of all visa, residency, health card, and labour card applications. He might even help you get your driving licence. There is a move towards allowing only UAE Nationals to work as PROs in the future; bad news for the thousands of non-Nationals already employed in this field.*

## Residence Visa

Once you have your health card and the results of your medical test, you can go to the Immigration Department to process your residency. While you will often hear this referred to as your visa it is actually your residency permit – the visa is what allows you to enter the country in the first place.

There are two types of residence permit, one for when you are sponsored for employment, and the other for residence only (for example when you are sponsored by a family member who is already sponsored by an employer). The new property-owner visa falls into the latter category, with the developer acting as your sponsor for as long as you own the property. This will only be available to property owners with no other sponsorship options. If you are working in Dubai and buy a property, you will remain on your employment residency. The property-owner visa has no employment rights. Once a resident, if you leave the UAE it can only be for a period of less than six months at any one time, otherwise your residency will lapse. This is particularly relevant to women going back home to give birth, or children studying abroad. If the residency is cancelled, the original sponsor can visit the Immigration Department and pay Dhs.100 for a 'Temporary Entry Permit' which will waive the cancellation and allow the person to re-enter Dubai. You'll need their passport copy, and will have to fax them a copy of the permit before they fly back.

## Sponsorship by Employer

Your company PRO should handle all the paperwork, meaning you probably won't have to visit the Immigration Department yourself. He'll take your passport, employment visa (with entry stamp), medical test results, attested education certificates, copies of your

**83**

company's establishment immigration card and trade licence, and three passport photos. For a fee of Dhs.300 (plus typing fees) the Immigration Department will process everything and affix and stamp the residency permit in the passport. This may take up to 10 days, during which time you'll be without your passport, but for an extra Dhs.100 they can do it on the same day. Your company is obliged to pay these fees for you. When arranging your residency, the company will apply directly for your labour card (see p.85). The Ministry of Labour website (www.mol.gov.ae) has a facility for companies to process applications and transactions online.

To be accepted by the authorities here, your education certificates must be verified by a solicitor or public notary in your home country and then by your foreign office to verify the solicitor as bona fide. It's a good idea to have this done before you come to Dubai, but Empost does offer a verification service at a cost of Dhs.500 per degree. The minimum turnaround time you can expect for this service is two weeks.

**Older Children** ◄

*For parents sponsoring children, difficulties arise when sons (not daughters) turn 18. Unless they are enrolled in full-time education in the UAE they must transfer their visa to an employer, or the parents can pay a Dhs.5,000 security deposit (one-off payment) and apply for an annual visa. Daughters can stay on their father's sponsorship until they get married.*

## Family Sponsorship

If you are sponsored and resident in Dubai you should be able to sponsor your family members, allowing them to stay in the country as long as you are here. It's unlikely that your company will assist you with this, and the process is quite tedious. To sponsor your wife or children you will need a minimum monthly salary of Dhs.3,500 plus accommodation, or a minimum all-inclusive salary of Dhs.4,000. Only what is printed on your labour contract will be accepted as proof of your earnings, so make sure you're happy with this before starting the job.

To apply for residency visas for your family, you'll need to take your passport, a passport copy of the family member(s), and your labour contract to the Family Entry Permit counter at the Immigration Department. After submitting all the documents, as return after a couple of days to collect the visa. Send a copy by fax to the family member, then deposit the original at the visa counter in Arrivals at the airport. When they arrive they swap their copy for the original. Once in Dubai on the correct entry visa, your family member must now apply for a health card and take the medical test to continue the process.

With the medical test out of the way, you then return to the Immigration Department with all the essential documents as before, plus the medical test result and the attested birth certificate (if sponsoring a child) or attested marriage certificate (if sponsoring your spouse). For Dhs.300 (plus typing) the application will be processed and around five days later the passport – with the residency permit attached – will be ready for collection (for an additional Dhs.100, you can ask for the process to be completed on the same day).

If the family member is already here in Dubai on a visit visa you can still apply for the residency entry visa as above. Once it is processed, the family member either exits the country and re-enters with the correct visa, or you can pay Dhs.500 to have the visa swapped over.

If you are resident under family sponsorship and then get a job, you won't need to change onto your employer's sponsorship, but your new company will need to apply for a labour card on your behalf – see Labour Card (p.85)

It may be possible for a woman to sponsor her husband and children, for instance if she is employed in a certain profession (such as a doctor or teacher) and earning a high wage, but it is important to check this in advance before accepting any job offer.

In most cases the husband/father will be the 'head of the family' and therefore the sponsor. There are similar constraints when a resident wishes to sponsor his or her parents. A special committee meets to review each case individually – usually to consider the age of parents to be sponsored and their health requirements. In the case of a woman sponsoring her husband or a resident sponsoring their parents, even when a visa is granted it is only valid for one year and is reviewed for renewal on an annual basis.

**Maids & Dependants** ◀
*If you are processing a
health card for a maid,
driver or cook, you will
need to pay an
additional fee,
(Dhs.60–100), to have
him or her vaccinated
against hepatitis. There
will also be a small
typing fee (see Domestic
Help, p.162). Only
children over the age of
18 need to take the
medical test; for under
18s you simply apply for
the health card, and can
then proceed directly
with the next stage of
the residency process*

*Dubai Media City*

## Sponsoring A Maid

To sponsor a maid you must have a salary above Dhs.6,000 per month, and be able to provide the maid with housing and the usual benefits including an airfare home at least every two years. The process is very similar to sponsoring a family member (see above), the main differences being the additional costs involved – you have to pay a 'maid tax' of around Dhs.5,000 per year.

## Sole Custody/Single Parents

If you have sole custody of your child and wish to sponsor him or her, in addition to the documents listed above you may also need a letter from the other parent stating the child's name, passport number and nationality, and that they have no objection to the child living with you in the UAE. The letter must be endorsed by the legal authority that issued the sole custody, and attested. If you have no way of contacting the other parent (or if they are deceased), then the attested divorce/sole custody paperwork (or death certificate) should suffice.

# Labour Card

To work in the UAE you are legally required to have a valid labour card. The labour card can only be applied for once you have residency, but for employees on company sponsorship the process starts way before that. Before you are even granted an employment visa to enter the country, your company will have to get approval from the Ministry of Labour. You then enter on an employment visa, get a health card, take the medical test, and get the residency stamp in your passport. The company PRO then takes all of the relevant paperwork to the Ministry of Labour where the actual labour card will be issued (even though it has 'work permit' printed on the back). The card features your photo and details of your employer. You're supposed to carry the card with you at all times but it is highly unlikely that you will ever be asked to produce it. The process can also be quite slow, and it's possible you may not receive your card for a few weeks, or even months, after starting work. The labour card costs Dhs.1,000 (paid by your company) and is usually valid for three years. It must be renewed within 60 days after expiry. Failure to do so will result in a fine (which your company will be liable for) of Dhs.5,000 for each year the card has expired.

If your employer is arranging your residency you will need to sign your labour contract before the labour card is issued. This contract is printed in both Arabic and English. It's not necessarily your agreed 'contract' as such – most employees will sign a more comprehensive contract. Unless you read Arabic it may be advisable to have a translation made of your details, since the Arabic is the official version in any dispute. However, if there is any discrepancy, the judge would want to know why your company got the details wrong in the first place. (see Employment Contracts, p.104).

*Working On Family Sponsorship*

If you are on a family residency and then decide to work for your employer, not your visa sponsor, will need to apply for a labour card. You'll need to give your employer the usual documents including a letter of no objection (NOC) from your sponsor (usually your husband or father), your passport with residency stamp, attested certificates (if appropriate), passport photos, and usually a photocopy of your sponsor's passport. The Labour Card will cost your employer Dhs.1,000, and must be renewed annually.

*Holiday Jobs*

Expat students who wish to work in Dubai during the summer holidays should apply to the Department of Naturalisation & Residency for a permit allowing them to work legally. Location: Ministry of Labour, near Galadari roundabout, (04 269 1666).

## Free Zones

Employees of companies in free zones have different sponsorship options depending on the free zone. For example, in Jebel Ali you can either be sponsored by an individual company or by the free zone authority itself. Whether the Jebel Ali Free Zone, Dubai Internet City, Media City, Knowledge Village, Healthcare City or the Dubai Airport Free Zone, the respective authority will process your residency visa/permit directly through the Immigration Department, without having to get employment approval from the Ministry of Labour. This speeds up the process significantly, and residency permits can sometimes be granted in a matter of hours. Once Immigration has stamped your residence permit in your passport, the free zone will issue your labour card – this also acts as your security pass for entry to the free zone. A big advantage of working in a free zone is the lack of red tape encountered if you move jobs to another free zone company. This is because the free zone is actually your sponsor, so when you switch jobs to another employer you won't be switching sponsors. A free zone residency permit is valid for three years, and the labour card either one or three years, depending on the free zone. Designed to encourage investment from overseas, free zones allow 100% foreign ownership and offer exemption from taxes and customs duties. An added attraction is relative lack of red tape. For more information on setting up a business in a free zone, refer to the Business chapter of the *Dubai Red-Tape Explorer*.

## ID Card

The Emirates Identity Authority (EIDA) have been given the responsibility of initiating a UAE ID card system in which all residents, nationals or not, must be in the possession of one. The process is ongoing with new centres opening up to deal with the extra administration. This will undoubtedly become seen as a national responsibility as it aims to secure personal identities and cut down on things such as fraud. This will eventually replace other cards, such as your health card and labour cards, but you will still have to aply for them until the identity card is firmly introduced. So far the UAE has won the Information Security Award for the ID card programme which is known officially as the Population Registry and Identity Card Programme (PRIDC). The finalised fee structure for the ID card is Dhs.100 for nationals, which will be valid for five years. Expat rates are linked to the length of their visas, a resident with a one year visa will also pay Dhs.100, one year or more is Dhs.200 and three years Dhs.300. For more information on location of offices and the latest ID card news releases, visit www.emiratesid.ae.

**Picture Perfect**

They say a picture can speak a thousand words so if you're can't sum up the sights and sounds of a city in a sentence then grab a copy of one Explorer's stunning *Photography Books*. Showcasing a unique view of the city, make sure the next time you go on holiday you take home more than just your memories.

# Never taking a chance with your customer's sentiments

OUR INTERNATIONAL NETWORK NOT AFFILIATED TO FIDI: QATAR • KUWAIT • DELHI • MUMBAI • CHENNAI • BANGALORE • KOLKATTA • HYDERABAD • PUNE

At Interem, we are absolutely committed to giving your customers the highest quality of service at all times. We take extra care and walk that extra mile to ensure an absolutely hassle-free experience for both you and your customers.

Our state-of-the-art relocation procedures, precise planning and co-ordination, and the resources of a global network, enables us to handle everything from packing, documentation, customs formalities and finally unpacking and setting up your customer's new home.

Move with us and you'll never take a chance with your customer's sentiments.

306, Office Court, Oud Metha Road, P.O. Box 50965, Dubai, UAE, Tel: +9714 8070581/584 / 8815154, Fax: +9714 8070580
E-mail: albert@freightsystems.com   Website: www.freightsystems.com

International Credentials:

INTERNATIONAL PACKAGING SERVICES • COMPREHENSIVE RELOCATION SERVICES • SHORT & LONG TERM STORAGE FACILITIES

# Driving Licence

Other options **Transportation** p.223

Other options **Transportation** p.223

**Traffic Police Offices**
• Traffic Police HQ: near
Galadari Roundabout,
Dubai-Sharjah Road
(04 269 2222)
• Bur Dubai Police
Station: Sheikh Zayed
Road, Junction 4
(04 398 1111)

Until you get full residency you can drive a hire car, provided you have a valid international licence (this only applies to those countries on the transfer list below) – a driving licence from your country of origin is not acceptable. In order to drive a private vehicle, you must obtain either a temporary or permanent Dubai driving licence, and as soon as your residence visa comes through you will need to switch to a Dubai licence.

## Temporary Licence

You cannot drive a privately registered vehicle on an international or foreign driving licence, as the vehicle is only insured for drivers holding a UAE driving licence. However, you can get a temporary UAE licence, even if you are not a resident here, which allows you to drive a privately owned car. Visitors to Dubai, or those who are waiting for their residency permit to be processed, can apply for a six-month temporary licence. If you belong to one of the nationalities listed below, the procedure is fairly straightforward. At the Traffic Police office visit the typing office to have the application form filled out in Arabic. Then go to the counter with your passport (original and copy), your visa (visit, employment or residency), your foreign licence (original and copy) and two passport photos. You should also take an eye test certificate, although this isn't always needed. The cost of the licence is Dhs.110. You'll have your picture taken and the licence should be ready a few minutes later. For UK licence holders you need to take the card and the paper counterpart. It has been known for officials to ask for your license to be authenticated by your consulate. In this case, oblige and visit your consulate – otaining a letter of approval should not take long at all.

## Permanent Licence

Once you have your residence permit you must apply for a permanent (10 year) Dubai licence. Nationals of the countries listed in the margin can automatically transfer their driving licence, as long as the original is valid. Take your existing foreign licence, your passport (with residency stamp), an eye test certificate (or have an eye test done on the premises), and the Dhs.110 fee to the licensing office of the Traffic Police. Again, have the typing office fill out the application in Arabic (for a small fee), and take everything to the counter. Depending on how busy it is, you may have quite a wait before being seen by an officer, although women will probably find the que in the ladies section shorter. Your photo will be taken and you'll get your licence there and then.

## Driving Test

If your nationality is not on the automatic transfer list you will need to sit a UAE driving test to be eligible to drive in Dubai, regardless of whether you hold a valid driving licence from your home country or not.

Much of the driving test process has been handed over to five authorised driving institutes, so you can apply for a learner's permit at the driving school directly, instead of going to the Traffic Police. You can even begin the process at the post office, who have teamed up with Emirates Driving Institute to offer prepaid packages.

Some driving institutions insist that you pay for a set of prebooked lessons. In some cases, the package extends to 52 lessons and can cost up to Dhs.3,000. The lessons must be taken on consecutive days and usually last 30 to 45 minutes. Other companies offer lessons on an hourly basis, as and when you like, for around Dhs.35 per hour. Women are required to take lessons with a female instructor, at a cost of Dhs.65 per hour. If a woman wants to take lessons with a male instructor she must have NOCs from her husband/sponsor and the Traffic Police.

**Automatic Licence Transfer**
Australia, Austria, Bahrain, Belgium, Canada, Cyprus, Czech Republic, Denmark, Finland, France, Germany, Greece*, Iceland, Ireland, Italy, Japan*, Korea*, Kuwait, Netherlands, New Zealand, Norway, Oman, Poland, Portugal, Qatar, Saudi Arabia, Singapore, Slovakia, South Africa, Spain, Sweden, Switzerland, Turkey, United Kingdom, United States.
*Citizens of these countries require a letter of approval from their consulates.

ART
FASHION
FOOD
ENTERTAINMENT
LIFESTYLE

# FROM FINE ART
# TO THE ART OF FOOD

Appreciate the work of local artists in a 14th century souk and
the finest cuisines from around the world, all in one place.

WWW.WAFI.COM

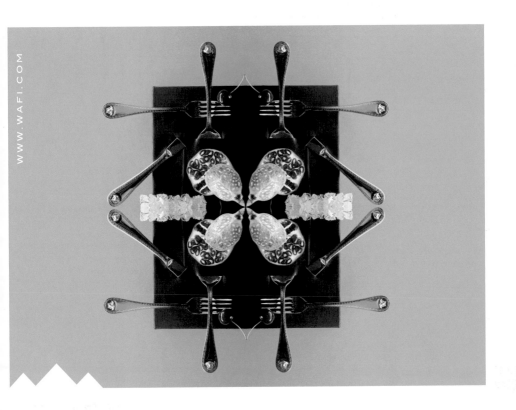

**Eye Tests**

*To get your eyes tested, visit one of the many opticians around Dubai and tell them you need an eye test certificate for the driving licence. Many have signs in the window indicating that they do eye tests for driving licences. It costs around Dhs.25 and you'll need to take along two passport photos.*

You will take three different tests on different dates. One is a Highway Code test, another includes parking and manoeuvres, and the third is a road test. Before you are issued with your permanent driving licence you will have to attend two compulsory hour-long road safety lectures, the cost of which is incorporated into the price of your lessons. For detailed, step-by-step information on licence procedures, refer to the *Dubai Red-Tape Explorer.*

Always carry your Dubai driving licence when driving. If you fail to produce it during a police spot check you will be fined. You should also ensure you have the car's registration card in the car. Licences can be renewed at the Traffic Police as well as other sites around Dubai including Al Safa Union Co-Op (04 394 5007), Al Tawar Union Co-Op (04 263 4857) and Jumeirah Plaza (04 342 0737).

### Motorcycle Licence

The rules for riding a motorbike in Dubai are similar to those for driving a car – if you have a transferable licence from your home country you can get either a six-month temporary licence or a 10 year permanent one (see the list of nationalities listed on p.88).

### Off-Road Licence

Drivers working for tour companies who go off-roading in the desert must pass a desert driving course. For the time being, ordinary drivers who like to go off road don't need to take the test, although they can go on desert driving courses offered by most of the driving schools. Likewise, there are no licence requirements for riding a motorbike off road.

| Driving Schools | |
|---|---|
| Al Ahli Motor Driving School | 04 272 2595 |
| Al Ain Driving Institute | 04 331 1667 |
| Al Amal Driving School | 04 226 3058 |
| Belhasa Driving School | 04 881 7171 |
| Dubai Driving School | 04 271 7654 |
| Emirates Driving Institute | 04 263 1100 |
| Galadari Motor Driving Centre | 04 267 6166 |

## Liquor Licence

Other options **Alcohol** p.408

Dubai probably has the most liberal attitude towards alcohol of all the emirates. You won't be able to buy alcohol at the supermarkets for home consumption, but you can apply for a liquor licence to buy it from licensed shops. In public, only hotels are licensed to serve alcoholic drinks in their bars and restaurants, as are some private clubs and associations. Independent restaurants generally do not have a liquor licence. You don't need a liquor licence to drink at a hotel or a club, but you will require valid ID to prove you are 21 or older.

To get a liquor licence you must be a non-Muslim and a resident of Dubai. The first thing you need to do is pick up an application form from the two licensed liquor store chains in Dubai, A&E and MMI. Complete the form (include your spouse's details, photograph and signature if you would like them to be able to use the licence too) and have it signed and stamped by your employer. Return to the outlet with the following documents: passport copy, residence permit copy, labour contract copy (the Ministry of Labour one, in Arabic and English), tenancy contract copy (or a letter from your employer if you're in company accommodation), one passport photo and the fee of Dhs.150. (When you first submit your form make sure you tear off the strip at the bottom; when you go to collect your licence hand the slip back.)

The liquor store will process your application through the Dubai Police on your behalf. The licence allows you to spend a limited amount on alcohol per month. The amount is based on your monthly salary, and is at the discretion of the police. The process takes around 10 days, and the outlet will contact you when the licence is ready. The card has

# THINKING OF A FEW COLD ONES TONIGHT?

Did you know that as a resident of Dubai you need a licence to have a drink at home? Fortunately it's now easier than ever to get one. That's because we do all of the processing for you, no queues, no hassle. Simply obtain a form from any MMI shop or for more information please call 04 343 3687.

*bringing more to life*

• SHEIKH ZAYED ROAD • DUBAI SILICON OASIS • AL WASL • TRADE CENTRE RD • IBN BATTUTA MALL • DEIRA • BUR DUBAI • GREEN COMMUNITY • KARAMA • MALL OF THE EMIRATES

a chip that records each transaction, so you can't spend over your limit. Limits are usually generous, and you should be able to buy enough booze on your limit to last you for at least a month. However, if you are planning a big party, it's a good idea to stockpile supplies for a few months.

Buying alcohol from liquor shops can be expensive, as you have to pay an additional tax of 30% on top of the listed price. The range, however, is excellent. For a list of branches of MMI and A&E liquor stores, see p.90 in the Shopping section.

It is possible to buy alcohol without a licence in some of the neighbouring emirates, such as from Ajman's 'Hole in the Wall' near the Ajman Kempinski, the Barracuda Resort in Umm Al Quwain (next to the Dreamland Aqua Park), and Centaurus in Ras Al Khaimah (see p.408 in Shopping). However, it is illegal to transport alcohol around the emirates without a liquor licence. This law is enforced particularly strictly in Sharjah and while there are no regular roadblocks, if you're unfortunate enough to get stopped for anything, you may have all your alcohol confiscated. Drinking on the beach and in public parks is not tolerated, whether you have a licence or not. While there may be cheaper alternatives, it is still worth having a liquor licence so you can nip out for supplies when you run dry, and so that you can drink at home without any worries.

*New Babies* ◀ | # Birth Certificate & Registration
:--|:--

*Babies born abroad to expatriate mums with UAE residency are required to have a residence visa or a visit visa before entering the UAE. The application should be filed by the father or family provider, along with the essential documents, a salary certificate and a copy of the birth certificate*

Every expat child born in the UAE should be registered with their parents' embassy (if the parents are from different countries you can choose which one to register your child with). You need to get a passport for your baby and apply for its residency permit within 120 days. If you don't get the residency within that time, you will have to pay a fine of Dhs.25 for every day that you go over the limit.

The hospital that delivers the baby will prepare an official 'notification of birth' certificate (this will be in Arabic) upon receipt of hospital records, photocopies of both parents' passports and marriage certificate, and a fee of Dhs.50. To get the birth certificate, take the birth notification to the Birth Certificate Office at Al Baraha Hospital.

## Adoption

While you can't adopt a UAE National baby, many couples in Dubai adopt children from Africa, Asia and Far Eastern countries. Adoption regulations vary according to which country the child comes from, but once you clear the requirements of that country, and formalise the adoption process, you will have no problems bringing your new child into the UAE on your sponsorship. Check with your embassy about the procedure for applying for citizenship of your home country for your new child. If you are considering adopting a child, a good starting point is to contact the Adoption Support Group (04 360 8113).

# Marriage Certificate & Registration

## Getting Married In Dubai

A few years ago organising a wedding in Dubai may have been a bit of a challenge, but thanks to the trusty rules of supply and demand, weddings are becoming big business. Everything your heart desires for a dream wedding is here, and in comparison to the big bucks weddings in other countries, things here are little more affordable – relatively. For more information on wedding dresses and accessories, as well as cakes and invitation cards, see p.449 in the Shopping section.

While many hotels offer wedding packages, they mainly extend to the reception – The Royal Mirage (04 399 3999) and the Ritz-Carlton (04 399 4000) are the hot favourites, although the high-rise construction sites right next door could take a bit of the shine off your dream day. The Radisson SAS Creek also offers a tailored wedding service (04

**Living in Sin**
*Under UAE law an
unmarried couple may
not live together.
However, it is a fact that
many, many unmarried
couples do live together
in Dubai without
getting into trouble.
Dubai is a liberal place,
and the authorities
seem to accept that this
law is widely flouted. It
would also be virtually
impossible to enforce
this rule on the millions
of tourists that descend
on Dubai each year
from all around the
world. No hotel will
question whether a
couple checking in are
married or not. The only
foreseeable problem
could be if you got into
trouble with the police
over another matter,
and they decided to
punish you for this too,
but you'd have to be
quite unlucky.*

A wedding planner could be your fairy godmother (especially when your family support network is miles away). Sarah Feyling is an expert wedding planner based in Dubai who will help you every step of the way – from the paperwork to the seating plan (www.theweddingplanner.ae).

*Dubai Courts*

Upscale & Posh offers a tailored service for flowers and wedding reception decorations (www.upscaleandposh.com).

Brides needn't worry about missing out on the princess treatment. Most spas offer tailor-made services for brides.

When it comes to hair and makeup there are a number of excellent salons dotted around Dubai, as well as a number of independent specialists. Maria Dowling (04 345 4225) is an excellent bridal hair stylist who will come to your house or hotel to do your hair on the day of the wedding. Wenda Oosterbroek (050 343 8161) is a CIBTAC qualified makeup artist with experience in bridal makeup. She offers trial makeup sessions where she works with the bride to find the perfect look, and on the big day she will do the bridal makeup at your home or hotel.

THE One (for a list of branches see p.573) offers wedding gift registries. To set up the list you go around the store with a member of staff and select the items that you want (you can also add gift vouchers to the list).

### The Paperwork

Before going ahead with a wedding you should consult your embassy or consulate for advice, especially regarding the legality of the marriage back home. In nearly all cases a marriage that is legally performed in Dubai will be recognised elsewhere in the world, but it's always best to check. In addition, you may need to inform your embassy of your intention to marry. The British Embassy in Dubai, for example, will display a 'notice of marriage' in the embassy waiting room for 21 days prior to the marriage (along the same lines as 'the banns' being published in a parish newsletter for three successive Sundays). Afterwards, providing no one has objected, they will issue a 'certificate of no impediment' that may be required by the church carrying out your ceremony.

**Wedding
Photographers**
*Robeya Polley (050
494 4297), Simon
Charlton (050 518
4241), Sue Johnston
(050 564 5519) & Tom
Percy (050 654 0063)
are the snappers to
call to capture that
special day.*

Muslims: A Muslim marrying another Muslim can apply at the marriage section of the Dubai Courts, next to Maktoum Bridge. You will need two male witnesses and the bride should ensure that either her father or brother attends as a witness. You will require your passports with copies, proof that the groom is Muslim and Dhs.50. You can marry there and then. A Muslim man can marry a non-Muslim woman, but a non-Muslim man cannot marry at the court. The situation is more complicated for a Muslim woman wishing to marry a non-Muslim man and this may only be possible if the man first converts to Islam. Call the Dubai Courts (04 334 7777) or the Dubai Court Marriage Section (04 303 0406) for more information.

Christians, Catholics and Anglicans: Christians can either have a formal church ceremony with a congregation, or a small ceremony that must take place in a church, followed by a blessing at a different location, such as a hotel.

Your church may require that you have someone witness you signing a 'legal eligibility for marriage' document (a legal paper signed under oath) at your embassy or consulate. You may also need to attend at least three sessions of premarital counselling.

At the official church ceremony you will need two witnesses to sign the marriage register and the church will then issue a marriage certificate. You will need to get the certificate translated into Arabic by a court-approved legal translator. Take this, and the original, along with your essential documents to the Notary Public Office at the Dubai Courts. They will certify the documents for a fee of about Dhs.80. Next you will need to go to the Ministry of Justice (near CompuMe and Chili's in Garhoud) to authenticate the signature and the Notary Public seal. Just when you think it's all over you still have to go to The Ministry of Foreign Affairs (behind the distinctive Etisalat building in Deira) to authenticate the seal of the Ministry of Justice. Now you just need to pop back to your embassy for final legal verification.

*Shotgun Weddings*
*It is illegal to have a baby out of wedlock in the UAE. If you are unmarried and fall pregnant, you have two choices: march down the aisle asap or leave Dubai. You'll be asked for your marriage certificate when you give birth (and even earlier if you are having your prenatal checks at a government hospital). If there is a significant discrepancy in the dates, you will probably face many questions and a lot more paperwork*

Catholics must also undertake a marriage encounter course, which usually takes place at the busy St Mary's Church in Oud Metha (04 337 0087) on a Friday. At the end of the course you are presented with a certificate. You should then arrange with the priest to undertake a pre-nuptial ceremony (which will require your birth certificate, baptism certificate, passport and passport copies, an NOC from your parish priest in your home country and a donation, and the filling out of another form). If you are a non-Catholic marrying a Catholic you will need an NOC from your embassy/consulate stating that you are legally free to marry. A declaration of your intent to marry is posted on the public noticeboard at the church for three weeks, after which time, if there are no objections, you can set a date for the ceremony. The cost of the service will be Dhs.50. Anglicans should make an appointment to see the chaplain at Holy Trinity Church (04 337 0247). You will need to fill out forms confirming that you are legally free to marry and take your essential documents along (p.77). If you have previously been married you will need to produce either your divorce certificate or the death certificate of your previous partner. Fees differ depending on your nationality and circumstances but are around Dhs.1,000 for the ceremony and an additional Dhs.1,000 if you wish to hold the ceremony outside the church. You'll pay Dhs.50 for any additional copies of the marriage certificate that you want. If you're not overly concerned about sticking to a particular doctrine, but want a church wedding, the Anglican ceremony is simpler to arrange and less time consuming than its Catholic equivalent.

These marriages are recognised by the Government of the UAE but must be formalised. To make your marriage 'official', get an Arabic translation of the marriage certificate and take it to the Dubai Court. Filippino citizens are required to contact their embassy in Abu Dhabi before the Dubai Court will authenticate their marriage certificate. Hindus can be married through the Hindu Temple and the Indian Embassy (04 397 1222). The formalities take a minimum of 45 days.

## Death Certificate & Registration

### In The Event Of A Death

In the unhappy event of a death of a friend or relative, the first thing to do is to notify the police by dialling 999. The police will fill out a report and the body will be taken to hospital where a doctor will determine the cause of death. The authorities will need to see the deceased's passport and visa details. On receipt of the doctor's report, the hospital will issue a death certificate declaration for a fee of Dhs.50. Take the declaration and original passport to the police who will issue a letter addressed to Al Baraha (Kuwaiti) Hospital. This letter, plus death declaration, original passport and copies should be taken to Al Baraha Hospital, Department of Preventative Medicine, where an actual death certificate will be issued. If you are sending the deceased home you should also request a death certificate in English (an additional Dhs.100) or appropriate language – check this with your embassy. Take the certificate to the Ministry of Health and then to the Ministry of Foreign Affairs to be registered officially.

### Registering A Death

As well as notifying the police, you should contact the relevant embassy or consulate as soon as possible (see p.32 for a list of embassies). The embassy will be able to provide practical help, support, and advice on local procedures and any repatriation if required. The embassy can also assist with registration of the death in the deceased's country of origin, and can also issue its own death certificates. Although it is not always obligatory to register the death with the embassy, for probate purposes a death certificate from the home country, or a consular report of death, may be mandatory. The embassy will need to see the original passport and the local death certificate and the embassy certificate could cost up to Dhs.700. The deceased's visa must also be cancelled by the Immigration Department. To do this take the local death certificate, original cancelled passport and embassy-issued death certificate.

### Investigation & Autopsy

Dubai Police will investigate in the case of an accidental or suspicious death, and it's likely that an autopsy will be performed at a government hospital. If you're unhappy with the outcome of an investigation you could hire a private investigator, but this is a bit of a grey area so seek advice from your embassy or consulate.

### Returning The Deceased To Their Country Of Origin

You will need to book a flight through DNATA (04 211 1111), get police clearance from airport security to ship the body out of the country, and an NOC from the embassy. The body needs to be embalmed and you must get a letter to this effect from the police. Embalming can be arranged through Al Maktoum Hospital for Dhs.1,000, which includes the embalming certificate. The body must be identified before and after embalming, after which it should be transferred to Cargo Village for shipping and this will cost Dhs.100. Cargo fees will range from Dhs.1,000 to Dhs.10,000 and a coffin costs about Dhs.750. The following documents should accompany the deceased: local death certificate, translation of the death certificate, embalming certificate, NOC from the police, embassy/consulate death certificate and NOC, and cancelled passport.

**Local Burial**
A local burial can be arranged at the Muslim or Christian cemeteries in Dubai. The cost of a burial is Dhs.1,100 for an adult and Dhs.350 for a child. You will need to get a coffin made, as well as transport to the burial site. Cremation is also possible, but only in the Hindu manner and with the prior permission of the next of kin and the CID. For more information refer to the **Dubai Red-Tape Explorer**.

*Hospital, Healthcare City*

# Working In Dubai

Expat workers come to Dubai for a number of reasons: to advance their career, for a higher standard of living, to take advantage of new career opportunities or most commonly for the lifestyle and the experience of living and working in a new culture. Whatever the reason, there are various advantages of working here.

While the biggest bonus of working in Dubai may seem to be tax-free salaries, the benefits of not paying tax has been somewhat outweighed for some nationalities by the increasing weakness of the dirham (it remains pegged to the US dollar) against other currencies, especially the UK pound and the euro. This has resulted in salary packages being less lucrative than they were four or five years ago which, coupled with the constantly increasing rents, means disposable income isn't as impressive as it once was. However, there are other distinct benefits and these are what make people stay.

**Jobs Online** ◀

*As well as the usual recruitment websites, two other sites worth checking out for jobs online or before you arrive in Dubai are the listings section of locally based www.dubaidonkey.com or the local version of the global recruitment site www.bayt.com*

## The New Dubai

The boom that Dubai is undergoing, even in just the last few years, means that the job market is constantly changing. At the very senior end of the scale there remain some idyllic opportunities and huge packages that attract the big players, and these are predominantly in the construction, aviation and finance industries.

However, for positions lower than senior management, the image of cushy expat life in the Gulf is changing, with much more competition in all areas of the market and an increasing number of people looking for work in Dubai. Not so long ago foreign expats could walk in to jobs that they could only dream of back home, but these days the market is much more competitive. All-inclusive packages with accommodation and education allowances are also not as common, although basic benefits still apply (such as annual flights home and 30 calendar days leave).

Work-wise, there are still a lot of great job prospects in Dubai and in many respects it is a land of opportunities for skilled professionals. It is also easier to change industries, as skill sets are less 'pigeon-holed' than in other countries.

Jobs in certain industries (such as construction and real estate) are likely to be much more available in the UAE due to the continued efforts to establish Dubai as a tourist and business centre.

## Working On A Visa

One of the main differences about working in Dubai as opposed to your country of origin is that you need to be sponsored by an employer, which often leaves some people feeling tied or uncomfortably obligated to their employer. If you leave the company your current visa will be cancelled and you will have to go through the hassle of getting a new residency permit (for you and your family, if they are on your sponsorship).

## Setting Up Business In Dubai

As well as the opportunities within companies, there are many people who start their own business here. With an economy that can best be described as 'exploding' rather than just 'growing', there are plenty of opportunities for small businesses in Dubai. Unless you are setting up your business in one of Dubai's free zones, you will need a local partner (although a new draft law that changes this is expected to be approved shortly) and the bureaucracy will no doubt frustrate you at times. But if you have the necessary drive and ambition, Dubai is a great platform for starting up your own business.

In addition to the various government departments specifically responsible for providing commercial assistance to enterprises in Dubai, there are various business

# We've seen a lot of changes since 1979. (Thankfully!)

*Technology, interior design, style*; many things about the office environment have changed since 1979.

One thing that hasn't changed is the commitment and excellent service that has kept BAC at the forefront of the UAE's recruitment industry for nearly 30 years.

We were the first recruitment consultancy in the world to obtain ISO 9001 quality certification, and have successfully placed over 20,000 candidates. We work closely with the best employers and recruit across all major sectors. Whether you're new to Dubai, or are looking for your next career move, please visit our website or forward your CV to **recruit@bacme.ae**

Your Search Partner | **ISO9001:2000 Certified**

**EXECUTIVE RECRUITMENT**

Tel: +971 4 3375747   Fax: +971 4 3376467   Email: recruit@bacme.ae

www.bac.ae

groups that help facilitate investments and provide opportunities for networking with others in the community. Some business groups and councils provide information on trade with their respective countries, as well as on business opportunities both in Dubai and internationally. Most also arrange social and networking events on a regular basis.

Before you set up, contact the Dubai Chamber of Commerce (04 228 0000) and the Dubai Economic Department (04 222 9922). Both can offer excellent advice. Embassies or consulates can also be a good business resource and may be able to offer contact lists for the UAE and the country of representation. For information and details, refer to the *Dubai Red-Tape Explorer,* the *Dubai Commercial Directory*, or the *Hawk Business Pages*.

**Read Between The Lines**

*If a job ad says 'UK/US candidate preferred', that usually means they are looking for a white, western-employee. Similarly, 'ability to speak Arabic an advantage' actually means 'Arabs only'.*

## Networking

With Dubai still being a relatively small city, made up of communities that are smaller still, networking is critical, even across industries. Everyone seems to know everyone and getting in with the corporate 'in-crowd' definitely has its plus points. Business acumen here can, at times, be more important than specific industry knowledge so it pays to attend business events and trade shows. Make friends in government departments and this will often land you in the front line of opportunities. Likewise, bad news is rarely made public here, so staying in tune with the grapevine can help prevent wrong decisions.

## Business Culture & Etiquette

Despite its status as a cosmopolitan, modern metropolis, Dubai is still an Arab city in a Muslim country. Even if your counterpart in another company is an expatriate, the head decision maker may be a UAE National who could quite possibly take a different approach to business matters. Your best bet when you're just starting out in Dubai's

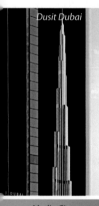

Dusit Dubai

Sheikh Zayed Road Towers

Media City

business circles is to observe closely, have lots of patience and make a concerted effort to understand the culture and respect the customs.

Tea and coffee are a very important part of local custom and it may be considered rude to refuse this offer of hospitality during a meeting. Tilting the small Arabic coffee cup back and forth several times with your fingers will signal that you do not want another refill. Don't be too taken aback if you find time-keeping flexible and if people walk in during your meeting for a chat.

Although proper dress is important for all business dealings, the local climate has dictated that a shirt and tie (for men) is sufficient for all but the most important of business encounters; women usually choose a suit or a skirt and blouse and nothing too revealing.

**Escape Red Tape!**
You know the drill: join the queue, get the form, get it typed, join the queue again, wait for ages, get told you're at the wrong counter, join the queue again, wait for ages, get told you have the wrong documents, start again tomorrow! Get this handy guide to all things bureaucratic and cut corners, jump queues and get things done. Easy peasy.

## Working Hours

Hours differ dramatically between companies, with start and finish times varying. Straight shifts vary from 07:30 to 14:00 for government organisations to the common 09:00 to 18:00 for private companies. Most retail outlets tend to be open from 10:00 to 22:00 but often operate shifts. Teachers start early at around 07:30 and classes finish at 14:00, although like in any job, paperwork can add to the day's work. Although less common nowadays, some offices and shops operate split shifts, which allow for a longer break in the afternoon (hours are usually 08:00 to 13:00 and 16:00 to 19:00). The maximum number of hours permitted per week according to UAE Labour Law is 48, although some industries, such as hospitality and retail, have longer stipulated hours. Annual holiday allowance starts at one calendar month per year, or 22 working days. Some employees, especially those in management, have more than this and long service usually adds to holiday allowance. Friday is the Islamic holy day and therefore a universal day off for offices and schools. Consumer demand means that the hospitality and retail industries are open seven days a week. As for the second weekend day, in 2006 the five-day working week for government

| Business Councils & Groups | |
|---|---|
| American Business Council | www.abcdubai.com |
| Australian Business in the Gulf (ABIG) | www.abiguae.com |
| British Business Group | www.britbiz.uae.com |
| Canadian Business Council | www.cbc-dubai.com |
| Danish Business Council | www.danishbusinessdubai.com |
| French Business Council | www.fbcdubai.com |
| German Business Council | www.gbcdubai.com |
| Iranian Business Council | www.ibcuae.org |
| Lebanese Consulate | www.leconse.com |
| South African Business Council | www.sabco-uae.org |
| Swedish Business Council | www.swedchamb.com |
| Swiss Business Council | www.swissbcuae.com |

departments and schools was set as Sunday to Thursday, bringing them into line with much of the private sector. There are still private companies which have retained the traditional Saturday to Wednesday working week, while others work five and a half days a week and some operate a six-day week, taking only Friday as a rest day.

Public holidays (see p.20) are set by the government, while the timing of religious holidays depends on the sighting of the moon. The labour law states that all employees (even non-Muslims) are entitled to a shorter working day during Ramadan, although labour lawyers would advise you not to insist on this right if you are non-Muslim or not fasting.

## Finding Work

Dubai's current boom means that many industries are opening up and expanding, often quite rapidly, and therefore recruitment is a priority.

The good news for job hunters is that new opportunities are constantly emerging, and if you are prepared to be flexible you may find yourself in your dream job.

People are often seconded to Dubai by companies based in their home country or are recruited from their country of origin, but there are increasing numbers of people who arrive here with their partners or spouses and then begin to look for work. There's also a fair share of career hopefuls who start looking for work opportunities after visiting Dubai on holiday or to stay with friends and family here.

**Know Your Rights**
You might be able to get a copy of the UAE Labour Law from your employer, or you can order it through the Ministry of Labour & Social Affairs (04 269 1666). However, with constant amendments to the law, it is usually best to seek legal advice. The UAE Labour Guide, published in 2002 by the Ministry, outlines rights of workers.

### Finding Work Before You Come

While it is often easier to find a job once you are here, it's worth looking from your home country before you leave. There are a number of companies that recruit abroad, and you may even find Dubai jobs advertised in the media.

If you are lucky enough to find a job this way it's likely that the company will pay for your flight to Dubai, provide help with relocation costs, and start the paperwork involved in becoming a resident.

Alternatively, have a good search on the internet; there are plenty of job sites with Dubai listings. Local paper, *Gulf News,* has an excellent appointments section and has just started publishing online, so try www.khaleejtimes.com, as well as www.jobsindubai.com, www.uaestaffing.com, www.gulfjobsites.com and www.bayt.com. Browse vacancies listed on websites of recruitment firms such as Charterhouse and IQ Selection (p.102).

If you know the industry that you want to work in, it is worth investigating Dubai companies within that sector and contacting them with your CV. Word of mouth is a particularly useful tool here.

**Before You Make a Move**
If you have an NOC from your previous employer, and the Ministry of Labour approves the move, your visa transfer should be hassle-free. But this is one area where laws change frequently so it's best to check with the Labour Department or a lawyer first.

### Finding Work While You're Here

It is undoubtedly easier to look for a job once you are here. Your first step should be to get your hands on the *Gulf News* appointments supplement, published on Sundays, Tuesdays and Thursdays, or the *Khaleej Times* Appointments on Sundays, Mondays and Wednesdays. It is also a good idea to register with a recruitment agency (p.102) and to contact companies directly and start networking.

Thanks to Dubai's relatively small size the more people you meet the more likely you are to bump into someone who just happens to work somewhere that has a vacant position that you might be able to fill. Many large Dubai-based companies have vacancy listings on their websites, so if you have a company in mind, see if they have anything available.

*Etisalat Building*

### Recruitment Agencies

There are numerous recruitment agencies in Dubai. To register, check with the agency to find out if they take walk-ins, although most only accept CVs via email and will then contact you for an interview. Invariably when you go for the agency interview you will also have to fill out an agency form summarising your CV and will need a few passport photos. The agency takes its fee from the registered company once the position has been filled. It is illegal for a recruitment company to levy fees on candidates for this service, although some might try this.

Isn't it time that you looked for a more rewarding career?

Sales & Marketing • Advertising, Media & PR • FMCG • Banking & Finance
Human Resources • Emiratisation • Executive Secretarial
IT & Telecommunications • Construction & Engineering • Oil & Gas

At iQ selection we are passionate
about selecting the right job for you.
**www.iQselection.com**
Tel: + 971 4 329 7770

iQ selection

Should you be suitable for a job the agency will mediate between you and the employer and arrange all interviews. However, don't rely too heavily on the agency finding a job for you. More often than not, agencies depend on candidates spotting a vacancy that they have advertised in the paper. There is no reason why you can't sign up with more than one agency – just don't be surprised when they both try to put you forward for the same job. In this case it is at your discretion which agency you want to represent you. Below is a list of recruitment agencies based in the UAE. Some of these agencies specialise in certain industries so do your research and register accordingly.

## Recruitment Agencies

| | | |
|---|---|---|
| BAC Middle East ▶ p.97 | 04 337 5747 | www.bacme.com |
| Bayt | 04 391 1900 | www.bayt.com |
| Charterhouse ▶ p.103 | 04 332 5116 | www.charterhouse.ae |
| Clarendon Parker | 04 391 0460 | www.clarendonparker.com |
| Grafton Recruitment | 04 367 1939 | www.grafton-group.com |
| IQ Selection ▶ p.101 | 04 329 7770 | www.iqselection.com |
| Job Scan | 04 355 9113 | www.jobscan.ae |
| Job Track | 04 397 7751 | www.jobtrackme.com |
| Kershaw Leonard | 04 343 4606 | www.kershawleonard.net |
| Search | 04 268 6100 | www.searchinternational.net |
| SOS Agency | 04 396 5600 | www.sos.co.ae |
| Talent Management Consultancy | 04 335 0999 | www.talentdubai.com |

## Voluntary & Charity Work

There are a number of opportunities to do voluntary or charity work in Dubai and the organisations listed below are always looking for committed volunteers. If it's environmental voluntary work you're after, the Emirates Environmental Group (www.eeg-uae.org) organises regular campaigns.

### Volunteer Organisations

Feline Friends is a non-profit organisation that helps cats in the UAE. Volunteers rescue and re-home stray cats and kittens, promote the control of street cats by sterilisation and provide care and relief to sick and injured cats and kittens. Volunteers are needed for rescues and also for fostering cats until homes can be found for them. Call 050 451 0058 or visit www.felinefriendsuae.com.

K9 Friends helps care for and re-home unwanted dogs from all over the UAE. It is run by a dedicated group of volunteers. Running costs are met entirely through donations from the public, as well as corporate sponsors. If you are interested in volunteering, contact them in Dubai on 04 347 4611 or visit their site at www.k9friends.com.

Médecins Sans Frontières (MSF) is an international, independent, non-profit emergency medical relief organisation that relies on volunteers to provide aid in any way they can. If you would like to become involved locally with their fund-raising or awareness campaigns, call them on 04 345 8177 or visit www.msfuae.ae

Foresight is an organisation formed to raise funds for research and to improve the lives of visually impaired people in the UAE and throughout the world. Contact 04 391 1443 or the website (www.foresightrp.com) for more info.

Riding for the Disabled was set up to provide physical and mental stimulation through gentle horse riding for children with special needs. They are always on the lookout for reliable, committed volunteers to lead the horses and assist the riders. For more information visit www.rdad.ae.

All As One is a non-profit organisation, staffed by volunteers, whose primary concern is to care for the abandoned, disabled, abused and destitute children of Sierra Leone in

**Need Some Direction?**

The *Explorer Mini Maps* pack a whole city into your pocket and once unfolded are excellent navigational tools for exploring. Not only are they handy in size, with detailed information on the sights and sounds of the city, but also their fabulously affordable price mean they won't make a dent in your holiday fund. Wherever your travels take you, from the Middle East to Europe and beyond, grab a mini map and you'll never have to ask for directions.

# know the right move

Charterhouse's progressive and structured approach to Executive Search and Selection has positioned us as the leading recruiter in the Middle East. Our focus and expertise continues to raise recruitment standards in a challenging and rapidly developing market looking to attract new talent and skill sets.

Our contingent and search recruitment models cater for diversity of functional coverage whilst allowing our reach and expertise to deliver at all levels across middle and senior management positions.

## CHARTERHOUSE
PARTNERSHIP

MIDDLE EAST · AUSTRALIA · EUROPE · ASIA

**Your partner in recruitment**

Charterhouse Partnership Dubai     Charterhouse Partnership Abu Dhabi
T: +9714 332 5116                              T: +9712 414 6635

For more details log onto www.charterhouseme.ae

the All As One Children's Centre. It depends on donations, child sponsorship, and fundraising events to fund operating costs. For more, visit www.allasone.org.

## Employment Contracts

Accepting an expat posting can have its pitfalls, so before you sign your contract pay special attention to things such as probation periods, accommodation, annual leave, travel entitlements, medical and dental cover, notice periods, and repatriation entitlements. There is often confusion over the offer letter and the contract – an offer letter should give details of the terms of the job you are being offered, such as salary, leave, hours and other benefits – if you accept the terms of this offer, it becomes a legally binding contract. You may be asked to sign an additional Ministry of Labour contract that accompanies your residency application, but the initial offer letter is, in effect, your contract.

The UAE labour law allows for an end-of-service gratuity payment for employees. The rules are a bit convoluted, but basically, an employee on a fixed-term contract, who has completed one or more years of continuous service, will be entitled to 21 days' pay for each of the first five years of service, and 30 days' pay for each additional year. If the employee is on an 'unlimited duration' (open-ended) contract and terminates it of his own accord, he will get a third of the gratuity for a service period of between one and three years, two thirds for three to five years, and the full amount if service exceeds five years. Leaving before the end of your fixed-term contract or getting fired could result in you losing your gratuity. Gratuity payments are worked out according to your basic salary, which is why employers will often split your salary into various categories (basic, housing, transport and utilities). You will still get the same cash salary at the end of every month, but because your basic salary is much lower than your total salary, your gratuity payment is lower.

It is common for companies to have three or six-month probation periods written into employment contracts. Some companies may delay the residency process illegally until the probation period is up, which can make settling in difficult – no residency means you can't sponsor family members, buy a car or get a bank loan. You may also not be eligible for sick leave or annual leave during your probation period. All of these matters should be discussed with your future employer before signing your contract.

*Emirates Towers*

## Labour Law

The Labour Law outlines everything related to employee entitlements, employment contracts and disciplinary rules. The law tends to favour employers, but it also clearly outlines employee rights.

Labour unions and strikes are illegal, although there have been some protests by labourers in the past. Rather than being punished, the labourers achieved some results. The employers concerned were forced to pay wages immediately or remedy living conditions, and a hotline was set up for other unpaid workers to report their employers. Also, an amended federal labour law looks likely to allow the formation of labour unions (trade unions have long existed in some other Gulf countries). If you find yourself in the situation where you have not been paid, you can file a case with the UAE Labour Department who will take the necessary action.

You could also get a lawyer to deal with the claim on your behalf (see p.113 for a list of law firms). Although lawyers are expensive in Dubai, the employer will have to bear the cost if the case is settled in your favour.

*Maternity Leave*

Maternity leave for public sector staff has been cut, from three months to two. Government workers can now claim up to 60 days off, fully paid. Previously, new mums were entitled to 30 days paid, 30 days on half pay, and 30 days unpaid. Private sector workers can claim up to 45 days on full pay, once they've completed one year of continuous service (it's Article 30 of the UAE Labour Law, if your boss needs reminding). This can only be used directly before and after the birth. Those who have been with their employer for less than a year can claim 45 days on half pay. Proud Papas in the public sector now get three days off.

## Changing Jobs

Until recently, anyone leaving a job and cancelling their visa faced the possibility of being 'banned' for six months. Fortunately the banning rules have been relaxed, so as long as you remain on good terms with your employer, and he gives you permission to leave your job (in the form of a no objection certificate or NOC), you should be able to switch to a new job.

However there are catches: if you have a PhD or masters degree you can change jobs as many times as you like, but you are limited to two moves if you have a bachelor's degree and only one move if you have no tertiary qualifications. And you still need that crucial agreement from your previous sponsor – the all-important NOC.

To change sponsors, pick up the relevant forms from the Ministry of Labour and get them typed in Arabic. Get the forms signed and stamped by both your previous and new employers, and submit them along with the trade licence and establishment card of your new company. Everything goes to the Immigration Department who will amend your visa. In most cases your new employer will take care of this procedure for you.

There are some exceptions where you can transfer your sponsorship without the approval of your current sponsor, such as death of your sponsor, change of company ownership or company closure. Regulations differ in the free zones, as you are technically sponsored by the free zone authority (FZA) rather than the company. Therefore if you move to another company within the free zone, there is no need to transfer your visa.

*Capital Gains Tax* ◀

*Even though you are no longer resident in your home country, you may still be liable for capital gains. UK citizens may find the HM Revenue and Customs site helpful – www.hmrc.gov.uk*

## Company Closure

Employees who face the unlucky situation of company bankruptcy or company closure are entitled under UAE Labour law to receive their gratuity payments and holiday pay, but you will need to speak to the labour department for the proper process as it is rather complex. An employee of a firm that has been closed is allowed to transfer sponsorship to a new employer if they are able to find a new job, but if not their visa will be cancelled and they will have to leave the country. To transfer the visa they'll need an attested certificate of closure, issued by the court and submitted to the Ministry of Labour & Social Affairs (04 269 1666). Consult the appropriate government offices to get your paperwork right, or consider investing in the services of a lawyer that specialises in labour issues (see p.113 for a list of lawyers).

*Banks by the creek*

## Bank Accounts

Dubai is full of reputable banks that offer current, deposit and savings accounts as well as credit cards and loans. Most of them also offer the convenience of online banking, so you can check balances, transfer money, and pay bills with just a few clicks of the mouse. There are plenty of ATMs (cashpoints) around Dubai and most cards are compatible with the central bank network (some also offer global access links). You may pay a small fee for using another bank's ATM but it should never be more than a few dirhams. To open an account in most Dubai banks, you need a residence visa or to have your residency application underway. The bank employee dealing with your application will require your original passport, copies of your passport (personal details and visa) and an NOC from your sponsor. Some banks set a minimum account limit – this can be around Dhs.2,000 for a deposit account and as much as Dhs.10,000 for a current account. This means that at some point in each month your account balance must be above the minimum limit. Although credit cards are widely available, Dubai banks don't provide an overdraft facility. If you don't have a residence visa, meBANK (an offshoot of Emirates Bank) will open an account for you and provide an ATM card, but not a chequebook. meBANK also allows you to apply online for an account (www.me.ae).

A number of laws passed recently aim to combat money laundering. The UAE Central Bank monitors all incoming and outgoing transfers, and banks and currency exchanges are required to report transfers over a certain limit. Additionally, if you need to send more than Dhs.2,000 by international transfer you may have to show a valid passport.

## Banking Comparison Table

| Name | Phone | Web | Online Banking | Tele-Banking |
|------|-------|-----|----------------|--------------|
| ABN AMRO Bank | 04 351 2200 | www.abnamro.ae | ✓ | ✓ |
| Abu Dhabi Commercial Bank | 04 800 2030 | www.adcb.com | ✓ | ✓ |
| Arab Bank | 04 295 0845 | www.arabbank.com | ✓ | ✓ |
| Bank of Sharjah | 04 282 7278 | www.bankofsharjah.com | na | na |
| Barclays Bank Plc ▶ p.61 | 04 362 6700 | www.barclays.co.uk/dubai | ✓ | ✓ |
| BNP Paribas | 04 222 5200 | www.bnpparibas.ae | ✓ | ✓ |
| Citibank – Middle East | 04 324 5000 | www.citibank.com/uae | ✓ | ✓ |
| Dubai Islamic Bank | 04 295 9999 | www.alislami.ae | ✓ | ✓ |
| Emirates Bank International | 04 225 6256 | www.emiratesbank.ae | ✓ | ✓ |
| HSBC Bank Middle East ▶ p.109 | 04 800 4722 | www.uae.hsbc.com | ✓ | ✓ |
| Lloyds TSB Bank Plc ▶ p.107 | 04 342 2000 | www.lloydstsb.ae | ✓ | ✓ |
| Mashreqbank | 04 217 4800 | www.mashreqbank.com | ✓ | ✓ |
| meBANK | 04 316 0316 | www.me.com | ✓ | ✓ |
| Middle East Bank | 04 316 0316 | www.emiratesislamicbank.ae | ✓ | ✓ |
| National Bank of Abu Dhabi | 04 267 9993 | www.nbad.com | ✓ | ✓ |
| National Bank of Dubai | 04 222 2111 | www.nbd.com | ✓ | ✓ |
| Standard Chartered Bank – Middle East | 04 352 0455 | www.standardchartered.com | ✓ | ✓ |
| Union National bank | 04 800 2600 | www.unb.co.ae | ✓ | ✓ |

Lloyds TSB | for the journey...

Personal, Business & Corporate Banking

# The best of British on your doorstep...

Wherever you are in life, we can help you get to where you want to be. Whether that means setting up a new home or growing your business, Lloyds TSB has a full range of services to meet all of your Personal, Business and Corporate Banking needs.

Get in touch
## +971 4 342 2000

Visit
## www.lloydstsb.ae

Or call into any of our locations

Lloyds TSB Bank plc has a license issued by the UAE Central Bank to carry on banking business in the United Arab Emirates. Lloyds TSB Bank plc, (Registered in England & Wales). Registered Number 2065, 25 Gresham Street, London EC2V 7HN. Lloyds TSB Bank plc is authorised and regulated by the Financial Services Authority for investments in the UK. Rules and regulations made under the Financial Services and Markets Act 2000 for the protection of investors, including the Financial Services Compensation Scheme, do not apply to the investment business of companies within the Lloyds TSB Group carried out from offices outside the United Kingdom. Lloyds TSB Bank plc is a wholly-owned subsidiary of Lloyds TSB Group plc whose office is Henry Duncan House, 120 George Street, Edinburgh EH2 4LH.

All applications for finance are subject to status.                                                                LTS-2576D

## Cost of Living

| | |
|---|---|
| Apples (per kg) | Dhs.6 |
| Bananas (per kg) | Dhs.3 |
| Barber haircut (male) | Dhs.25 |
| Bottle of house wine (restaurant) | Dhs.150 |
| Bottle of wine (off-licence) | Dhs.40 |
| Burger (takeaway) | Dhs.12 |
| Bus (10km journey) | Dhs.2 |
| Can of dogfood | Dhs.4 |
| Can of soft drink | Dhs.1 |
| Cappuccino | Dhs.12 |
| Car rental (per day) | Dhs.100 |
| Carrots (per kg) | Dhs.4 |
| CD Album | Dhs.60 |
| Chocolate bar | Dhs.2 |
| Cigarettes (pack of 20) | Dhs.7 |
| Cinema ticket | Dhs.30 |
| Cleaner (per hour) | Dhs.25 |
| Digital photo printing (4x6) | Dhs.1 |
| Dozen eggs | Dhs.7 |
| Fresh beef (per kg) | Dhs.20-25 |
| Fresh chicken (per kg) | Dhs.15 |
| Fresh fish (per kg) | Dhs.15-20 |
| Golf (18 holes) | Dhs.450 |
| House wine (glass) | Dhs.25-40 |
| Large takeaway pizza | Dhs.40 |
| Loaf of bread | Dhs.4 |
| Local postage stamp | Dhs.1 |
| Milk (1 litre) | Dhs.5 |
| Mobile to mobile call (local, per minute) | 30 fils |
| New release DVD | Dhs.85 |
| Newspaper (international) | Dhs.15 |
| Newspaper (local) | Dhs.2 |
| Orange juice (1 litre) | Dhs.4 |
| Pack of 24 asprin/paracetamol tablets | Dhs.7 |
| Petrol (gallon) | Dhs.6.25 |
| Pint of beer | Dhs.20 |
| Postcard | Dhs.3 |
| Potatoes (per kg) | Dhs.3.50 |
| Rice (1 kg) | Dhs.7 |
| Salon haircut (female) | Dhs.90 |
| Salon haircut (male) | Dhs.70 |
| Shawarma | Dhs.3 |
| Six-pack of beer (off-licence) | Dhs.25 |
| Strawberries (per punnet) | Dhs.6 (seasonal) |
| Sugar (2 kg) | Dhs.5 |
| Taxi (10km journey) | Dhs.20 |
| Text message (local) | 18 fils |
| Tube of toothpaste | Dhs.4 |
| Water 1.5 litres (restaurant) | Dhs.10 |
| Water 1.5 litres (supermarket) | Dhs.1.50 |

## Financial Planning

Many expats are attracted to Dubai for the tax-free salary and the opportunity to put a little something away for the future. When choosing a financial planner in Dubai there are some key points to bear in mind: most importantly you should ensure that they are licensed by the Central Bank of the UAE, so that you have some recourse in the event of a dispute. You should also consider the company's international presence – if you leave Dubai you still want to be able to reach the company and enjoy the same access to advice and information, and your investments. Finally it may be better to use an independent company or advisor who is not tied to a specific bank or savings company, and therefore will objectively offer you the full range of savings products on the market.

Before leaving your home country you should contact the tax authorities to ensure that you are complying with the financial laws there. Most countries will consider you not liable for income tax once you prove you're a UAE resident (a contract of employment is normally a good starting point). However, you may still have to fulfil certain criteria, so do some research before you come (if you are already here, check with your embassy). You may be liable for tax on any income you receive from back home (for example if you are renting out your property).

### Pensions

If you have a pension scheme in your home country, it may not be worth continuing your contributions once you come to Dubai, but rather to set up a tax-free, offshore savings plan. It is always advisable to speak to your financial adviser about such matters before you make any big move.

## Offshore Accounts

While offshore banking used to be associated with the very wealthy or the highly shady, most expats now take advantage of tax efficient plans.

An offshore account works in much the same way as a conventional account, but it can be adjusted specifically for you. Money can be moved where it will produce the best rewards, and cash accessed whenever and wherever you need it, in your desired currency. Offshore accounts allow for management through the internet, and over the phone, in a range of currencies (most commonly in US dollars, euros or pounds sterling). If you are travelling outside the UAE, try to make sure that your account comes with 24 hour banking, internationally recognised debit cards, and the ability to write cheques in your preferred currency. To open an account, there is usually a minimum balance of around $10,000. Do

**Winner**

Best Offshore Bank Group

**Wherever you are on your expat journey, HSBC Bank International is with you every step of the way.**

At HSBC Bank International, we understand that as an expat, it is sometimes difficult to manage your finances both at home and while you are here in the Middle East.

As one of the HSBC Group's specialist providers of offshore banking services, our team at our representative office on Jumeriah Beach Road is exclusively available to help you make the most of your money through our HSBC Premier service.

Call +971 4 407 9789

Email dubai.repoffice@hsbc.com

Click www.offshore.hsbc.com

**HSBC**

The world's local bank

Issued by HSBC Bank International – Dubai Representative Office. HSBC Bank International Limited is regulated by the Jersey Financial Services Commission to carry on deposit-taking business under the Banking Business (Jersey) Law 1991 and regulated for General Insurance Mediation, Collective Investment Schemes & Investment Business. Communications may be monitored and/or recorded for security/ service improvement purposes. ©HSBC Bank International Limited. 2007. All Rights Reserved.        MC7165BYDUBSP

**Financial Advisors**

| | | |
|---|---|---|
| deVere Partners (PIC) | 04 343 3878 | www.pic-uae.com |
| Investment Consultants | 04 312 4334 | www.prosperity-uae.com |
| Mondial (Dubai) L.L.C. – | | |
| Financial Partners International | 04 331 0524 | www.mondialdubai.com |
| Prosperity Offshore Investment Consultants | 04 312 4334 | www.prosperity-uae.com |

some thorough research before opening an account, and check the potential tax implications in your home country. It is important to seek independent financial advice, and not just the opinion of the bank offering you an acount. Lloyds TSB (www.lloydstsb.ae) and HSBC (www.hsbc.ae) both offer good offshore services, but will of course, only advise on their own products. To open your account, you may have to produce certain reports or documents from your chosen country. However, for those willing to do the research and undertake the admin, offshore banking can prove to be a lucrative investment.

## Taxation

The UAE levies no personal income taxes or withholding taxes, but the IMF is helping the UAE to plan the introduction of VAT, probably by 2010. This would no doubt be unpopular, and could hamper attempts to attract foreign investment, but the IMF is advising Middle Eastern governments to introduce tax reforms in order to diversify their resources.

The only noticeable taxes you pay as an expat are a 5% municipality tax on rental accommodation and a 30% tax on alcohol bought at Dubai liquor stores. The municipality tax is included in your DEWA bill, and if you don't pay your utilities will be cut off. This has resulted in some complaints – tax is meant to cover refuse collection, street lighting and community road networks, but people renting freehold properties also pay maintenance to cover these things so it's understandable why some people have objections. There is also a 10% municipality tax and a 10% service charge in hotel food and beverage outlets, but you'll find that these are usually incorporated into the displayed price.

## Legal Issues

The country's constitution permits each emirate to have its own legislative body and judicial authority. Dubai has thus retained its own judicial system, including appellate courts (courts of appeal), which are not part of the UAE federal system. There are three primary sources of UAE law, namely federal laws and decrees (applicable in all emirates), local laws (laws and regulations enacted by the individual emirates), and Shariah (Islamic law). Generally, when a court is determining a commercial issue, it gives initial consideration to any applicable federal and/or local laws. If such federal and local laws do not address the issue, Shariah may be applied. Moreover, Shariah generally applies to family law matters, particularly when involving Muslims.

### Divorce

Statistics show that the UAE has one of the highest divorce rates in the Arab world. To counter this, bodies such as the State Marriage Fund have launched schemes offering education and counselling services to National couples. Expats can get divorced in Dubai, and in some cases the procedure can be relatively straightforward. However, expat couples wishing to divorce may also be governed by the laws of their home country (if the couple has mixed nationalities the home country of the husband applies), so it is advisable to seek legal advice. A husband who sponsors his wife has the right to have her residence visa cancelled in the event of divorce.

### Mini Marvels

Explorer *Mini Visitors' Guides* are the perfect holiday companion. They are small enough to fit in your pocket but beautiful enough to inspire you to explore. With area information, detailed maps, visitors' information, restaurant and bar reviews, the lowdown on shopping and all the sights and sounds of the city these mini marvels are simply a holiday must.

### Speedy Seperation

*Under Shariah law a Muslim man can divorce his wife without cause by stating 'I divorce you' three times over the course of three months. Classical Shariah states that a woman can divorce a man under very limited conditions, including if he is insane, suffers from leprosy, or is infertile at the time of marriage.*

# HADEF AL DHAHIRI & ASSOCIATES
## LEGAL CONSULTANTS AND ADVOCATES

## REGIONAL EXPERTISE

## INTERNATIONAL STANDARDS

Hadef Al Dhahiri & Associates provides comprehensive legal service to the UAE business community. Our 70 lawyers, based in Abu Dhabi and Dubai, qualified in primary western and middle eastern jurisdictions. We represent leading international and regional clients in the following practice areas:

Banking & Finance
Commercial
Corporate
Dispute Resolution
Employment
Engineering & Construction
Insurance & International Trade
Intellectual Property
Maritime & Transportation
Mergers & Acquisitions
Private Equity
Projects & Energy
Real Estate
Regulatory
Technology & Media

### www.hadalaw.com

**Dubai:** Level 5, Building 3, Burj Dubai Square, Tel: +971 4 429 2999

**Abu Dhabi:** 12th Floor, Blue Tower, Tel: +971 2 627 6622

*Getting A Will*

Having a valid will in place is one of those essential things that everybody should do. It is especially important to seek legal advice when drawing up your will if you become a property owner in Dubai. This is one area where the law is rather complicated – under Shariah law, the basic rules as to who inherits property after someone's death differ to 'western' rules. For example, in the event of your death it may be the case that your sons (or brother, if you don't have any sons) are first in line for inheritance and your wife could end up with nothing. Therefore it is better to make sure that you have a clear last will and testament in place. A Dubai-based lawyer will be able to assist you with a locally viable will. See the table opposite for a list of law firms.

*Adoption*

Although adoption is not recognised in the Muslim community, many expats based in the UAE have found it relatively straightforward to adopt children from Asia and the Far East. Once you successfully meet all the requirements in your adopted child's home country, you should have little trouble bringing your child back to the UAE and applying for a residence visa. Check the regulations involved in securing your citizenship for your child; your embassy will be able to help. Contact the Adoption Support Group (04 349 3970) for more information.

*Tips for Women*

The following general tips are useful for women in Dubai:
• Stick to the dress code; tight, revealing clothing equals unwanted attention.
• Be careful when out alone at night, especially after a few drinks.
• Never get into an unmetered taxi; and always take down the taxi number.
• As long as you exercise due care and attention Dubai is a safe place for women.

# Crime

Dubai is known for having a low crime rate – in fact for many expats it is still the number one benefit of living here. It would be naive to think that there was no crime, as there are cases of theft, rape and even murder, but these occur on such a small scale that they rarely affect the quality of life of the average expat.

The most common reason for expats getting on the wrong side of the law is driving under the influence of alcohol. In the UAE there is a zero-tolerance policy – forget blood alcohol ratios or 'one safe pint'. If even a sip of alcohol has passed your lips, you are not allowed to drive. While there are few spot checks, if you have even a minor accident, and even if you were not at fault, you might be breathalysed and the consequences can be serious. Even driving the morning after a heavy night is risky, since you will still have alcohol in your system. You will be arrested, and the usual penalty is minimum thirty days in prison. You should bear in mind too that your insurance company could refuse to pay the claim if you were in an accident, even if you were not to blame. It's just not worth the risk – cabs are cheap and there are plenty of them.

Taking illegal narcotics is an absolute no-no – even the smallest amounts of marijuana or hashish could earn you a prison sentence of four years or more. This will almost certainly be followed by deportation. If you are found guilty of dealing or smuggling, you could be looking at a life sentence, or even the death penalty (although this is uncommon). Even some medications that are legal in your home country, such as codeine and temazepam, may be banned here – check before you come, and if you are in any doubt, try and find an alternative or at least have a copy of the prescription and a letter from your doctor. You can see a list of approved drugs on the Ministry of Health website (www.moh.gov.ae) although it is not known how frequently this list is updated or how reliable it is.

Harming others, whether physically or verbally, will get you into trouble – at the very least a heavy fine, but if the other person was injured a jail term may be in order. If the victim chooses to drop the charges then you will be released. If you are detained for being drunk and disorderly you may spend a night in the cells, but if you are abusive you could be looking at a fine or longer sentence.

**Neighbourhood Watch**
*In their efforts to maintain and promote a safe community the Dubai Police launched Al Ameen, a confidential toll free telephone service where you can report anything suspicious. For example if you have seen someone hanging around your property or loitering at cashpoints you can pass the information on anonymously by calling 800 4888 or emailing alameen@eim.ae.*

## Traffic Accidents & Violations

If you are involved in a traffic accident in which someone is seriously injured or killed, it's possible that you'll be detained until the circumstances are ascertained. If you are found to have been at fault (and especially if under the influence of alcohol) you're likely to spend time in prison.

If you are held responsible for someone's death you'll remain in prison until the blood money has been paid to the victim's family, or until the family grants you a pardon. Make sure your insurance covers you for blood money, but be aware that insurance companies will do all they can to get out of paying it.

## Arrest

If you are arrested you will be taken to a police station and questioned. If it's decided that you must go to court the case will go to the public prosecutor who will set a date for a hearing. For a minor offence you may get bail, and the police will keep your passport and often the passport of another male resident who is willing to vouch for you. Police stations have holding cells, so if you don't get bail you'll be held until the hearing. All court proceedings are conducted in Arabic, so you should secure the services of a translator. If sentenced you'll go straight from court to jail.

Upon being arrested you are advised to contact your embassy or consulate. They can liaise with family, advise on local legal procedures and provide a list of lawyers, but they will not pay your legal fees. The consulate will try to ensure that you are not denied your basic human rights, but they cannot act as lawyers, investigators, secure bail, or get you released.

**Other Common Crimes**
*The following acts are definite law breakers, and although many of them are often overlooked, they are still against the law:*
• *Buying alcohol without a liquor licence*
• *Bouncing cheques*
• *Eating, smoking or drinking in public during daylight hours in Ramadan (including non-Muslims)*
• *Living together if not married*
• *Kissing in public or lewd behaviour*
• *Homosexual behaviour*
• *Distributing religious material (non-Muslim)*

## Doing Time

Most prisoners will find themselves in the new Central Jail near Al Awir, which was moved from its old location in Al Wasl in 2006. Short-term or temporary male prisoners may be held in an 'Out Jail', while long-term prisoners are likely to go to the main Central Jail.

Conditions inside the old jail were described as basic but bearable, but the new complex has much improved conditions, with the reported overcrowding in the old jail a thing of the past.

Inmates are given three meals a day, and there's a small snack shop with limited opening hours. Prisoners are allowed occasional access to payphones, so if you are visiting an inmate a few phone cards will be appreciated.

Prisoners are generally allowed visits once a week. Thursdays are reserved for visits to Arab detainees, and Fridays are for other nationalities. Men and women are not allowed to visit together – men can visit from 10:00 to 11:00 and women from 16:00 to 17:00. If you are a woman you may not be allowed to visit a man who is of no family relation to you. Times are subject to change so it's best to check by calling the Department of Punitive Establishments (04 344 0351). In late 2007 there was a clampdown on drinking and driving with whispers of increased jail sentences, so always remember the law is zero tolerance.

| Law Firms | | |
|---|---|---|
| Afridi & Angell | 04 330 3900 | www.afridi-angell.com |
| Al Sharif Advocates & Legal Consultants | 04 262 8222 | www.dubailaw.com |
| Al Tamimi Advocates & Legal Consultants | 04 295 3366 | www.tamimi.com |
| Hadef Al Dhahiri & Associates ▶ p.111 | 04 429 2999 | www.hadalaw.com |
| Musthafa & Almana Associates | 04 312 4051 | www.musthafa-almanalawyers.com |
| Trench & Associates | 04 355 3146 | www.trenchlaw.com |

**113**

# Housing

The first decision you need to make in terms of housing in Dubai is whether you want to buy or rent. It is only since 2002 that expats have been able to own property in Dubai, and apartments and villas are being snapped up as quickly as they come on the market. The second decision is whether you would prefer to live in a villa or an apartment, and the third is what area you would like to live in. This chapter gives a detailed description of all the residential areas in Dubai, as well as the ins and outs of the processes involved in buying and renting.

## Renting In Dubai

Despite expats now being able to buy property in Dubai the property market is still in its infancy and many choose to continue renting. New residents arriving in Dubai to start a new job may be given accommodation (or a monetary allowance) as part of their package. Your allowance may not always be high enough to rent a place in the area you want, so many expats choose to top up the amount out of their own pockets. If your contract provides specific accommodation but you would prefer the cash equivalent, it is worth asking as most employers are willing to be flexible.

Rents have risen steadily over the past few years , with 2005 seeing some severe increases – up to 40% in some cases. A decree was passed by Sheikh Mohammed in late 2006 limiting rental increases to 7% per year for existing tenants, but this means some landlords have hiked rents for new tenants as there is no limit on what they can charge.

Reports in summer 2007 suggested that the government will introduce fixed three to five-year tenancies in a bid to keep costs down, but there would be no enforcement. Like any major city Dubai has an enormous range of accommodation options, and many residential areas each with its own pros and cons (see p.117 for details). Prices quoted are intended to illustrate going rates, but bear in mind that negotiation is part and parcel of the deal and that there are still finds to be had, particularly if you talk to colleagues and friends. Another reason for chatting to other expats is to find out what makes some areas more popular than others. Speaking to your colleagues about commuting times to work is also a good idea before you decide on an area.

**Renting Smart** — Always check the paperwork: to avoid disputes with your landlord, the Rent Committee advises that both parties produce a written agreement. This contract reduces the risk of either party falling out on the rental terms discussed. Remember to get a copy of the estate agent's identification card and make sure you save copies of all receipts, contracts and other documents.

**Pay Out or Get Out** — Rent increases are a hot topic. While the Rent Committee aims to help, landlords still hold a great deal of power. Keep all documentation and offers in writing to continue paying the rent at an acceptable rate and know that you cannot be evicted without a court order.

| Real Estate Agents | | |
|---|---|---|
| Al Futtaim Real Estate | 04 211 9111 | www.al-futtaim.com |
| Alpha Properties | 04 228 8588 | www.alphaproperties.com |
| Arabian Homes | 04 295 3838 | www.arabianhomes.org |
| Arenco Group | 04 355 5552 | www.arencore.com |
| Asteco Property Management | 04 403 7777 | www.astecoproperty.com |
| Better Homes ▶ p.15 | 04 344 7714 | www.bhomes.com |
| Cluttons LLC | 04 334 8585 | www.cluttons.com |
| Damac Properties | 800 326 22 | www.damacproperties.com |
| Dubai Government Real Estate | 04 398 6666 | www.realestate-dubai.gov.ae |
| Dubai Luxury Homes | 04 303 9300 | www.dubailuxuryhomes.com |
| Dubai Property Group | 04 262 9888 | www.dubaipropertygroup.com |
| House Hunters Real Estate Brokers | 04 340 1940 | www.househuntersdubai.com |
| Landmark Properties | 04 331 6161 | www.landmark-dubai.com |
| Oryx Real Estate | 04 351 5770 | www.oryxrealestate.com |
| Property Shop, The | 04 345 5711 | www.propertyshopdubai.com |
| Rocky Real Estate | 04 353 2000 | www.rocki.com |
| Sherwoods | 04 343 8002 | www.sherwoodsproperty.com |
| The Specialists ▶ p.115 | 04 331 2662 | www.dubaiuae.com |
| Union Properties | 04 885 1555 | www.up.ae |
| Vakson Real Estate | 04 349 5111 | www.vakson.com |

# your shortcut to better living...

Finding that perfect property can be a difficult experience. Whether you are looking to lease or to buy, the Real Estate Specialists can give you advice in your search for the ideal property, be it your future home or a financial investment. Our team is committed to finding the right property for you.

- Real Estate
  Sales, Leasing, Management & Investment

- Relocation
  Settling in, Orientation & Cultural training

- Interior Decoration
  Curtains, Soft Furnishings & Upholstery

- Maintenance
  A/C, Plumbing, Electrical, Painter & Handyman

## the specialists
complete real estate solutions
property · relocation · furnishings · maintenance

**T +971 4 331 2662** P. O. Box 44644 Dubai U.A.E.
www.thespecialistsdubai.com

Finding A Home

*There are a number of ways to find suitable accommodation, the most obvious of which is via a real estate agent (see p.114). But this isn't the only, or necessarily the best, option. If you have the time it is worth checking classified ads. An an even better bet is to drive around a few areas and look out for 'To Let' signs displayed on vacant villas; these will display the phone number of either the landlord or the letting agent. Often this extra effort when looking for a home can result in a 'real find' and many proud barbecues to come.*

# The Lease

Your lease is an important document and in addition to the financial terms will state what you are liable for in terms of maintenance as well as what your landlord's responsibilities are. Therefore it is important that you read the contract and discuss any points of contention before you sign on the dotted line. The following points are often open to negotiation:

## Housing Abbreviations

| | |
|---|---|
| BR | Bedroom |
| C.A/C | Central air conditioning (usually included in the rent) |
| D/S | Double storey villa |
| Ensuite | Bedroom has private bathroom |
| Ext S/Q | Servant quarters located outside the villa |
| Fully fitted | Includes appliances (oven,refrigerator, washing machine) |
| Hall flat | Apartment has an entrance hall (ie,entrance doesn't open directly onto living room) |
| L/D | Living/dining room area |
| Pvt garden | Private garden |
| S/Q | Servant quarters |
| S/S | Single storey villa |
| Shared pool | Pool is shared with other villas in compound |
| W.A/C | Window air conditioning (often indicates an older building) |
| W/robes | Built in wardrobes (closets) |

- Tenants usually pay rent via a number of post-dated cheques – typically two or three. If you can afford to pay the whole year up front, use it as a bargaining tool to reduce the annual rent.
- Try to negotiate a fixed rate for two, three, or more years – that way you won't get any nasty shocks with rent increases after your first year.
- Make sure you agree who is responsible for maintenance. Some rents might be fully inclusive of all maintenance and repairs, while you could negotiate a much cheaper rent (particularly on older properties) if you agree to carry out any maintenance work.
- While not common, some landlords will include utility expenses in the rent.
- Security deposit amounts vary, but are usually around Dhs.3,000 to Dhs.5,000 (although some landlords will ask for up to Dhs.20,000).
- The landlord must give written notice of any rent increase at least one month in advance. If your landlord does try to increase the rent unfairly then there are government channels to dispute rent matters (see below).

Rent Committee

*Dubai Municipality Building, Deira 04 206 3917.*

## Rent Disputes

In late 2006 Sheikh Mohammed capped rent increases for the year at 7% for existing tenants. At the time of going to print the rent cap for 2007 had yet to be announced. There have been reported cases where landlords refused to renew leases because they were 'renovating' or needed the place for their 'brother'. Although there is a Rent Committee, many people have simply put up with the increase, fearing that they would incur costs in arguing it, and could lose anyway. However, the Rent Committee has ruled in favour of the tenants in many instances and you should know that you cannot be thrown out of your home without a court order, even if your lease is up (provided, of course, that you are still paying rent at the rate agreed in your tenancy contract). In the case of a rent dispute, you can approach the Rent Committee who will arbitrate between you and your landlord. You can lodge your complaint in the Dubai Municipality building in Deira, opposite the Sheraton hotel (opening hours are 09:00 to 14:30, Sunday to Thursday) or call 04 206 3917 for more information. Take your passport copy, the tenancy contract, and any correspondence. Any non-Arabic paperwork will have to be translated. The official will fill in the form outlining your complaint, and you'll then have to pay a hefty fee – around 4% of the existing annual rent, plus an extra Dhs.100. Both parties will be instructed to attend on a given date. If you're lucky the landlord may well back down at this stage.

There have been mixed reports about the Rent Committee; some have reported success and others failure. But on the whole the outcome is often in the tenants favour.

# Main Accommodation Options

## Apartment/Villa Sharing

For those on a budget the solution may be to share an apartment or villa. Obviously the rent will be lower, and it may be the only affordable method of living in a plush five-bedroom villa (until you get that pay rise). The down side is the lack of privacy, and not having somewhere to call your own. You may also have to deal with the hassle of finding new housemates if someone moves out (and covering their share of the rent in the meantime). If you're looking to share, the noticeboards at supermarkets in the area or property classifieds in the local press are a good place to start. But, landlords and the municipality are beginning to clamp down on these shared homes. Some tenants in areas such as Al Barsha and Jumeirah, which are allotted as family accommodation spots, have been forced out by their landlords. In the most extreme cases, power and water have been disconnected to get them out. The Rent Committee will be little help where such homes are mixed, because strictly speaking, unmarried and unrelated men and women are not allowed to live together.

*Renter's Nightmare*

*Most leases are fixed for one year. Leave before the year is up, and you will probably have to pay a penalty or lose the months you've already paid for as the year's rent is usually paid upfront. (Some landlords allow you to pay in two or three instalments with post-dated cheques). If you really want to get out of your lease you may be able to sub-let the place to new tenants, although this can only be done with your landlord's consent.*

## Standard Apartment

Dubai apartments come in various sizes from studio to four bedroom, with widely varying rents to match. Newer apartments usually have central air conditioning (C A/C) and older ones have the noisier window air conditioners, where the unit is built into the wall. C A/C is usually more expensive, although in some apartment buildings your air-conditioning costs are built into the rent.

Top of the range apartments often come semi-furnished (with a cooker, fridge and washing machine), and have 24 hour security, satellite TV, covered parking, private gym and swimming pool. In some cases there are additional facilities on site, such as a restaurant, shop and laundry.

One downside is that you're at the mercy of your neighbours to some extent, especially those upstairs (a disadvantage of marble/ceramic floors is that every scraped chair and stiletto heel is amplified through your ceiling). Depending on the area, parking may be a problem too – check to see if you get a space.

## Villa

Most people's dream of expat life is to have a beautiful villa where you can spend lazy days by the pool and balmy evenings around the barbie. This lifestyle doesn't come cheap, and smart villas are snapped up pretty quickly. The good news is that if you look hard enough and use the grapevine, you might find the perfect villa that won't break the budget. Depending on the area, size and age of the villa it may be cheaper than some apartments, even if air-conditioning costs will be higher.

Villas differ greatly in quality and facilities. Independent ones often have bigger gardens, while compound villas are usually newer and often have shared facilities like a pool (and even a gym).

## Hotel Apartment

A hotel apartment is expensive, but ideal if you need temporary, furnished accommodation. There's a large concentration in Bur Dubai, but one or two are cropping up out of town. They can be rented on a daily, weekly, monthly or yearly basis. Water and electricity are also included in the rent (see p.117).

# Other Rental Costs

Extra costs to be considered when renting a home are:
• Water and electricity deposit (Dhs.2,000 for villas, Dhs.1,000 for apartments) paid

**On The Move**
*If you're moving within Dubai, you can use a moving company or hire a few guys with their own truck from downtown Bur Dubai. The latter is a cheaper option but requires constant supervision to ensure damage is kept to a minimum. Agree a price upfront to avoid a dispute later – work on around Dhs.50-70 per hour including two men.*

directly to Dubai Electricity & Water Authority (DEWA) and fully refundable on cancellation of the lease.

- Real estate commission – around 5% of annual rent (one-off payment).
- Maintenance charge – varies, but could be around 5% of annual rent (may be included in the rent).
- Municipality tax – 5% of annual rent.
- Fully refundable security deposit – Dhs.1,500-Dhs.5,000.

If you're renting a villa don't forget that you may have to maintain a garden and pay for extra water. It's worth asking the landlord or the previous tenants what the average DEWA bills are for a particular property. With your landlord's permission you could have a borehole installed to save money on water bills. To have a well dug and a pump fitted, expect to pay around Dhs.3,000.

Often the more popular accommodation has waiting lists that are years long. To secure an immediate tenancy many people offer the landlord 'key money': a down payment of several thousand dirhams to secure the accommodation (in other words, jump the queue).

## Purchasing A Home

In 2002 the rules surrounding property purchase were opened up allowing foreign nationals to purchase freehold property in Dubai, but only in certain developments. As a result a property boom ensued, with villas selling out within minutes, even though construction hadn't even started. It's safe to say that a majority of properties have been bought by investors looking to make a bob or two in resale or renting, although plenty of residents have bought their dream homes in Arabian Ranches and Emirates Hills. Although prices have shot up, what you get for your money is still pretty good compared with some other cities around the world. One thing buyers have been frustrated by is the constant delays.

There is also some ambiguity around the term 'freehold' – at the time of writing the property developer remains the legal owner of the property and the law does not clearly confirm a foreigner's right to legally own the freehold title to a Dubai property, although an amendment law has been drafted (see Real Estate Law, p.120). As with buying any property, legal assistance is recommended and many legal firms in Dubai now have departments that deal specifically in real estate law.

**Property-Owner Visa**
*The registered owner of the property will be entitled to a residency permit which will be valid for as long as he/she owns the property, but it must be renewed every three years. The property developer will handle the process, but you will have to pay the fees and costs vary (expect to pay around Dhs.5,000 for three years). The visa holder will then be able to sponsor immediate family (spouse and children), subject to the usual immigration rules and laws (p.84). The permit is only for residency and has no employment benefits.*

### Escrow Accounts

Trust accounts became mandatory in late 2007 for new, off-plan properties. Projects started after August 2007 cannot accept payment directly from buyers. Instead, buyers will pay into trust (or escrow) accounts, monitored by the Land Department, with money only released when building commitments are met. The move is designed to stop developers from disappearing with investors' money, and assure buyers that their 20m pool won't end up a 5m pond.

### The Process

Once you find your dream home it is worth seeking legal advice to help you in the purchase process. As a start, you have to be at least 21 years old to purchase property in Dubai.

For new, off-plan developments, it's worth speaking directly to developers and visiting their presentation centres and show homes. You may have to register in order to be eligible for new launches and often this is done at the sales centre where you give basic details and a copy of your passport. On the day of the launch you need to take your passport and copies and complete the contracts. You also have to pay a deposit or down payment at this stage, which is usually 10% of the purchase price, but may be up

## Main Developers

| | | |
|---|---|---|
| Abyaar Real Estate ▶ p.IFC | 04 343 7727 | ww.abyaar.com |
| ARY | 04 226 3535 | www.arymarinaview.com |
| B&M FZ CO | 04 299 6968 | www.larivieratower.com |
| Continental Properties | 04 222 5586 | www.continentalrs.com |
| Damac Properties Co. LLC | 04 332 2005 | www.damacproperties.com |
| Dubai Properties | 04 390 0094 | www.dubai-properties.ae |
| Emaar Properties PJSC ▶ p.129 | 04 367 3333 | www.emaar.com |
| Fortune Group | 04 331 6789 | www.fortunetower.com |
| Nakheel Properties | 04 390 3333 | www.nakheel.ae |
| Saba Real Estate | 04 330 0086 | www.saba-re.com |
| Trident International Holdings | 04 883 0555 | www.tihglobal.com |

to 25%. Often, only a cheque is accepted. Further payments are then scheduled depending on the timescale of the development, normally around 15% every six months until completion. For those buying off-plan, a new law has been introduced to protect their investments. Payments will now be made into escrow accounts that are managed by banks instead of directly to the property developer. Funds will only then be released when construction has reached a satisfactory level. If you're buying as an investment, check if there are any limitations on reselling. Joint ownership is possible, but only with next of kin (mother, father, husband, wife, son, daughter) and both parties must be present to complete the formalities. It's important that you do your homework before you begin the purchasing process as not all mortgage lenders will give finance on all developments.

**Getting Out Early ◀**

*When arranging your home finance, check whether there are penalties for early redemption of the mortgage – they could be up to 2% of the mortgage value. Life insurance isn't always mandatory, but some banks insist you take out one of their policies which may involve a medical at their chosen Dubai clinic which can be inconvenient if you're arranging the mortgage from overseas.*

## Mortgages

Soon after the government announced the granting of freehold status of residential property to expats, mortgage plans were introduced for those wishing to purchase. The maximum mortgage granted is Dhs.5 million and financing companies offer up to 90% of the purchase price or valuation to UAE Nationals, up to 80% to GCC and foreign national residents, and a ceiling of around 60% for non-residents. Mortgages must be paid back in monthly instalments within a maximum of 25 years (though 15 year mortgages are more popular), and rates are comparable to international norms, although the rate is often a little higher for non-residents. The mortgage amount depends on the chosen mortgage plan and is limited to an amount no greater than 60 times the monthly household income (husband and wife's combined). Currently not all banks offer mortgages and some of those that do only do so for specific developments. Tamweel now offers 'pre-approved home finance', meaning you can get the go ahead for a mortgage before you actually choose a property, which speeds up the process (as well as gives you peace of mind during your home hunting), and gives people applying for those new releases that are often snapped up very quickly a distinct upper hand.

## Mortgage Providers

| | | |
|---|---|---|
| Abu Dhabi Commercial Bank | 02 696 2222 | www.adcb.com |
| Amlak Finance | 04 800 4337 | www.amlakfinance.com |
| Barclays Bank ▶ p.61 | 04 362 6888 | www.barclays.com |
| Dubai Bank | 04 332 8989 | www.dubaibank.ae |
| Dubai Islamic Bank | 04 295 9999 | www.alislami.ae |
| Emirates Bank International | 04 225 6256 | www.emiratesbank.ae |
| HSBC Bank Middle East ▶ p.109 | 04 800 4722 | www.uae.hsbc.com |
| Lloyds TSB Bank Plc ▶ p.107 | 04 342 2000 | www.lloydstsb.ae |
| Mashreqbank | 04 217 4800 | www.mashreqbank.com |
| National Bank of Dubai | 04 222 2111 | www.nbd.com |
| RAKBANK | 04 224 8000 | www.rakbank.ae |
| Tamweel | 04 295 2259 | www.tamweel.ae |

## Other Purchasing Costs

Most property owners will pay a maintenance charge to cover the upkeep of the building, gardens and any shared facilities. In some developments, this charge is fixed, but other developers charge between Dhs.6 and Dhs.15 per square foot per year. In a big villa, this could add up to quite a substantial amount. Another consideration is the

**119**

transfer fee. If you're buying on the secondary market, the developer will require a percentage of the sale price. This is usually around 2% but can be as high as 7%. The buyer is responsible for this fee, but it may be possible to negotiate with the seller to share the cost. The buyer and seller will also owe a fee to the real estate agent (if one was used), and this is likely to be around 1% of the selling price. You will also pay lawyer's fees, if you have opted to use a lawyer.

## Moving Tips

* Get more than one quote - companies will often match lower quotes to get the job.

* Make sure that all items are covered by insurance and get item specific insurance for your valuables.

* Make sure that you have a copy of the inventory and that each item in each box is listed.

* While you may not want to tell the packers how to do their jobs, it's much easier to insist on items being repacked if you're not happy than having to claim for them.

* It may sound odd but take photos of the process as it goes along, then if you do have to make a claim there'll be photographic evidence.

* Any customs restricted goods (DVDs, videos or books) should be carried with you, it's much easier to open a suitcase in an air-conditioned airport than empty a box outside in the sun.

## Real Estate Law

A law was passed in March 2006 allowing non-GCC expats the right to buy 99 year leasehold and freehold property in designated areas. This means that expatriates can now register title deeds with the Dubai Land Registry. So, you get the land, as well as the building on it.

But, laws are constantly changing, and it's important that you get advice from a law firm specialising in real estate before you sign on the dotted line. Sale and purchase contracts should be reviewed thoroughly by your lawyer. Hadef Al Dhahiri & Associates (www.hadalaw.com) and Trench & Associates (www.trenchlaw.com) have dedicated real estate departments.

The term 'freehold' doesn't mean the same as in most other countries. For example, there may be restrictions on selling the property or making any structural changes to it. In some areas, you may not even be able to paint the outer walls.

Most developments levy annual service charges, and significant transfer fees when selling the property. Problems may also arise in the event of the owner's death, since under Shariah law (which UAE courts will apply, particularly in family law matters) it may not necessarily be transferred to the spouse. Your lawyer may be able to establish an offshore company which may avoid application of Shariah law.

Be aware that the market here is underdeveloped, so risks are potentially higher. But, if you have plans to stay in Dubai long-term, and can afford the down payment, buying can be a much better option than renting. Just don't forget to factor in maintenance, finance fees and other transfer costs. The best advice when purchasing in Dubai is to get a good lawyer.

*Deira apartments*

Moving back to
Boston with husband,
daughter, three dogs
and two containers
of treasured
possessions.
When?
Tomorrow.

Simplify your life

Relocating can be a trying experience with so much to plan, organize and accomplish. There is also less time to spend on things that really matter like friendships or special places you've enjoyed. This is why Writer Relocations provides unparalleled move support so that you can continue to enjoy life right until the time you leave.

Writer Relocations
P.O. Box 34892
Dubai, UAE
Phone: 04 340 8814  Fax: 04 340 8815
writerdubai@writercorporation.com
www.writercorporation.com

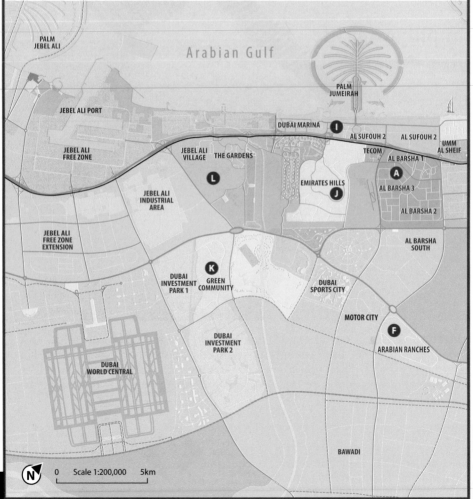

© Explorer Group Ltd. 2007

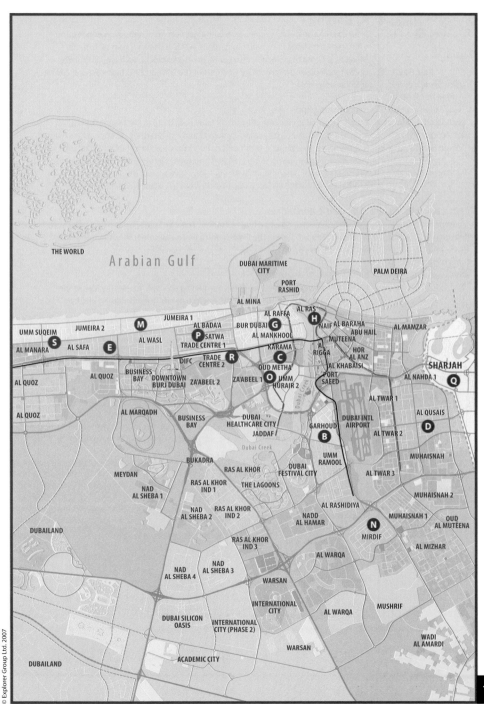

THE WORLD

Arabian Gulf

DUBAI MARITIME CITY

PALM DEIRA

PORT RASHID

AL MINA

JUMEIRA 1

AL RAFFA

AL RAS

UMM SUQEIM

JUMEIRA 2

**M**

AL BADA'A

BUR DUBAI

**G**

**H**

NAIF AL BARAHA

ABU HAIL

AL MAMZAR

**S**

**P** SATWA

AL MANKHOOL

MUTEENA

AL MANARA

AL SAFA

AL WASL

TRADE CENTRE 1

KARAMA

AL RIGGA

HOR AL ANZ

**E**

DIFC

TRADE CENTRE 2

**R**

**C**

AL KHABAISI

SHARJAH

AL QUOZ

BUSINESS BAY

DOWNTOWN BURJ DUBAI

ZA'ABEEL 2

OUD METHA

**O** UMM

PORT SAEED

AL NAHDA 1

**Q**

AL QUOZ

AL QUOZ

ZA'ABEEL 1

HURAIR 2

AL TWAR 1

AL MARQADH

BUSINESS BAY

DUBAI HEALTHCARE CITY

GARHOUD

**B**

DUBAI INTL AIRPORT

AL QUSAIS

**D**

JADDAF

AL TWAR 2

BUKADRA

Dubai Creek

UMM RAMOOL

AL TWAR 3

MUHAISNAH

MEYDAN

RAS AL KHOR

DUBAI FESTIVAL CITY

MUHAISNAH 2

NAD AL SHEBA 1

RAS AL KHOR IND 1

THE LAGOONS

AL RASHIDIYA

MUHAISNAH 1

OUD AL MUTEENA

NAD AL SHEBA 2

RAS AL KHOR IND 2

NADD AL HAMAR

**N**

DUBAILAND

MIRDIF

AL MIZHAR

RAS AL KHOR IND 3

AL WARQA

NAD AL SHEBA 4

NAD AL SHEBA 3

WARSAN

MUSHRIF

INTERNATIONAL CITY

AL WARQA

DUBAI SILICON OASIS

INTERNATIONAL CITY (PHASE 2)

WARSAN

WADI AL AMARDI

ACADEMIC CITY

DUBAILAND

© Explorer Group Ltd. 2007

*Map p.5*
*Area* **A** *p.122*

# Al Barsha

Al Barsha has two distinct zones, each with their own accommodation options. The main area offers large villas with big gardens, while Al Barsha 1, near Mall of the Emirates, is home to a growing number of apartment blocks. Both are particularly handy for Media and Internet City workers but the E44 and E311 highways make most of Dubai accessible.

**Best Points**
*Villas are larger and often much better value than in other areas on this side of town. Access to Sheikh Zayed Road is easy, and Mall of the Emirates is nearby.*

## Accommodation

Accommodation is mainly in the form of fairly new, three to five bedroom villas. Around 75% of the houses are locally owned and inhabited, the neighbours are quiet and the villa area is popular with families. Prices for villas start at Dhs.120,000 for a three bedroom and go up to Dhs.180,000. You could pay up to Dhs.350,000 for a four-bedroomed place. Apartments Al Barsha 1 start from around Dhs.80,000 for a one bedroom and Dhs.100,000 for a two bedroom but get snapped up quickly.

**Worst Points**
*Some parts of the area are a bit isolated and lacking in convenient shopping and leisure facilities.*

## Shopping & Amenities

Mall of the Emirates houses a huge Carrefour. There's a Lulu's Hypermarket nearby, and an Organic Foods & Cafe in the Greens. You'll find a few 'corner shops' in the area and two petrol stations.

## Entertainment & Leisure

Apart from numerous cafes, two foodcourts and a ski slope, the nearby Mall of the Emirates also houses the Kempinski Hotel which has its own restaurants and bars. The Marina and Madinat Jumeirah are only a short drive away.

## Healthcare

The only private clinic in the area is the Medical Specialist Centre in the new Khoury Building near Sheikh Zayed Road (340 9495). The nearest government clinic is in Umm Suqeim, and the nearest emergency hospital is Rashid Hospital (see p.182).

## Education

There are a few schools in Al Barsha, including Dubai American Academy and Al Mawakeb. Many other schools can be found in nearby areas, such as Wellington International School off Sheikh Zayed Road, JESS in Arabian Ranches and Dubai College in Al Sufouh.

*Al Barsha Villa*

**Travelling Times**
*Airport – 40 mins*
*Media City – 10 mins*
*Trade Centre – 20 mins*

## Traffic & Parking

Traffic isn't bad although Interchange 5 and the traffic lights near the Greens are hotspots. Sheikh Zayed Road is affected by slow traffic during rush hour. It's easy to get onto the E44 or E311. Parking is easy; finding a taxi less so.

## Safety & Annoyances

In general, Al Barsha is safe. Street lighting is almost non-existent, however. Massive power lines run through the the the area, which might put people some people off.

*Map p.13*
*Area* **B** *p.123*

# Garhoud

With its central location, range of villas and suburban feel, it's no surprise that Garhoud is such a popular residential area. It's handy for both central Dubai and downtown Deira, although this does mean that traffic can be a problem at peak times. Finding available accommodation isn't always easy, and there's not much in the way of new construction. Being only two minutes away from the airport means it's popular with airline staff and frequent travellers, but also that there is a chance of aircraft noise depending on the wind direction. Rents are slightly lower than some other central areas but they have began to creep up like everywhere else.

**Best Points**
*It is conveniently situated just 10 minutes from the Trade Centre, close to Deira, the airport and Sharjah. It is also home to some excellent entertainment options, including the Irish Village, Century Village and Aviation Club.*

**Worst Points**
*Traffic congestion in the area is very bad at peak times. The area's proximity to the airport means noise and fumes can be a problem.*

*Al Bustan Rotana Hotel*

## Accommodation

The area on top of the hill has nice, older villas, usually with well-established gardens and plenty of character. They are also relatively cheap considering the central location. The price for a three bedroom ranges anywhere between Dhs.150,000 and Dhs.250,000, and will depend on the age of the villa. The biggest problem is finding somewhere vacant. Away from the airport, lower down the hill, there are some newer villas, predominantly in compounds, that are similar in standard and price to villas in other areas of Dubai. The usual size is four bedroom, which goes for an average of Dhs.220,000. The whole area is home to a mix of nationalities with airline staff monopolising the accommodation. There are apartments in the Al Garhoud Complex by the Casablanca Road next to the Al Bustan Rotana Hotel. The average price is currently Dhs.95,000+ for a two-bedroom apartment. Across the road from this complex, near the Irish Village and tennis stadium, there are some apartments but they are used for Emirates staff accommodation.

## Shopping & Amenities

The small shopping street in Garhoud has two good supermarkets as well as a laundry, a pharmacy, photo shop, and an ATM. There are also several small restaurants that offer takeaway and delivery. Less than a 10 minute drive away is Deira City Centre (p.454) which offers everything from washing machines to wellington boots. Along Casablanca Road there are several car cleaners, tyre shops and petrol stations, while the area near Welcare Hospital has a massage centre, beauty salons and hairdressers.

## Entertainment & Leisure

Kids will love the park in Garhoud; it has a skate ramp, a sandy football pitch and some good playground equipment. For indoor activities, Magic Planet in Deira City Centre is a large amusement centre, with an 11 screen cinema.

In terms of eating out, Garhoud residents are spoilt for choice – there are many excellent restaurants and bars in the Al Bustan Rotana, the Le Meridien Dubai, the

**125**

Millenium Airport Hotel, Century Village and the Irish Village. It's one of the few residential areas where you can actually walk to the pub.

### Healthcare
Although there are no government clinics in the area, there are good private facilities such as Welcare Hospital, and two of the main government hospitals, Al Wasl and Rashid, are only a short distance away across the creek. See p.180.

### Education
Several schools are located along the road on the southern edge of Garhoud including Deira International School, American School of Dubai and Cambridge International School. Many other schools are accessible, in areas like Umm Hurair, Al Twar, and Festival City. Yellow Brick Road Nursery and Montessori Nursery are in the neighbourhood. For more information on education see p.202.

**Travelling Times**
Airport – 2 mins
Trade Centre – 10 mins
Media City – 30 mins

### Traffic & Parking
Apart from the horrors of Garhoud Bridge, traffic area the general area is bearable and there are usually no problems around the residential roads. Parking is easy and it is a safe area for kids and pedestrians. Taxis are easy to find, and the fare to the Trade Centre is about Dhs.20.

### Safety & Annoyances
On the whole Garhoud is a great area, very peaceful and suburban, with wide roads, plenty of quiet streets and grassy areas suitable for children to play in or for people to walk, cycle or jog along. Crime is low, and the only main annoyances are the congestion of the Garhoud Bridge and the occasional noisy aircraft overhead.

*Roadside Garhoud*

Map p.10
Area **C** p.123

# Karama

Near the heart of downtown Dubai lies Karama, its convenient location means it is a thriving commercial area with plenty of amenities. The price you pay is a lack of peace and quiet and lots of traffic. There are many low-cost restaurants, supermarkets, shops and the Karama Market (p.445), which sells a wide range of goods. Reasonable rents make Karama a good choice for Dubai residents on a budget.

**Best Points**

*Right in the centre of Dubai, Karama is a convenient place to live with masses of shops and restaurants on your doorstep. The rest of Bur Dubai and Deira is only a short, inexpensive taxi ride away.*

## Accommodation

Most accommodation is in low-rise blocks with apartments ranging from studios to three bedrooms. Prices can be as low as Dhs.30,000 for a one bedroom in the older buildings. The most desirable buildings are along Zabeel Road or in the area along Trade Centre Road, opposite Spinneys. You can get two and three-bedroom apartments for around Dhs.75,000 and Dhs.120,000 respectively, but in a new building with facilities you could pay up to Dhs.90,000 and Dhs.135,000. Availability tends to be in the newer buildings – the older, cheaper apartments are snapped up through word of mouth.

**Worst Points**

*Parking is limited, even for residents, and traffic in the evenings gets pretty congested, especially around Karama Market.*

## Shopping & Amenities

Everything is on your doorstep here. On Trade Centre Road there is a Spinneys and a Union Co-Op. There are plenty of small grocery shops, a fish market and of course the well known Karama Market. The recently expanded BurJuman Mall provides good shopping, while cheap-and-cheerful Avenue (p.473) and Sana (p.475) are nearby. There are also beauty salons, barbershops, laundries, video rental shops and independent fitness clubs. The area is near the central post office as well as several banks and ATMs.

## Entertainment & Leisure

There is not much in the way of greenery, but there are several small public areas between buildings and next to the main shopping area. Zabeel Park (p.271) is close and can be accessed via a footbridge. Karama has an incredible, diverse selection of restaurants to suit all budgets. Eating out, takeaways and home deliveries from the Arabic, Indian, Filippino, Sri Lankan and Pakistani restaurants around Karama Market and along Trade Centre Road are popular. For bars, Karama houses one of Dubai's perennial guilty pleasures – the Rock Bottom Café (p.584) – while the Trade Centre area with its cafes, restaurants (many licensed), bars and nightclubs is only a five-minute cab ride away.

## Healthcare

Karama is convenient for many reasonably priced medical centres, doctors and dentists and is also just a few minutes away from Rashid Hospital for emergencies. For more information on healthcare facilities see (p.178).

## Education

Although there are no popular schools or nurseries in the area, there are plenty of options close by and reaching them should be relatively easy.

**Travelling Times**

*Airport – 15 mins
Trade Centre – 5 mins
Media City – 25 mins*

## Traffic & Parking

Traffic is a nightmare at peak times. Parking is limited and driving around in heavy traffic looking for a spot is frustrating. It's best to walk, and it's very easy to get round Karama on foot. Keep your wits about you though on the busy roads and remember it is not a very child-friendly area in terms of traffic.

## Safety & Annoyances

Karama is busier than many other residential areas and there is significant traffic noise. Roads are packed and trying to get in or out of the area during busy times is a hassle.

127

Map p.14
Area **D** p.123

# Al Qusais (incl. Al Twar & Al Nahda)

Al Qusais accommodation

Al Qusais is situated on the edge of Dubai. The area's biggest selling point is the lower rents. It's very close to the border with Sharjah so if you're commuting in and out of Dubai be prepared for a lot of traffic. The main street has developed considerably and is now home to several supermarkets and small shopping centres as well as an increasing number of flashy government buildings.

**Best Points**

Cheap accommodation compared with other parts of Dubai, easy parking with plenty of free spaces and limited traffic problems.

**Worst Points**

The traffic heading to Dubai can reach gridlock at peak times on the Dubai to Sharjah Road, and other roads such as Emirates Road (E311) can also get pretty congested.

## Accommodation

Accommodation is mainly apartment blocks around Al Nahda Road. These range from studios to four-bedroom places in new buildings with similar facilities to new buildings in Karama or Oud Metha. It is still possible to get a one bedroom for about Dhs.50,000, but more common is a three bedroom at upwards of Dhs.100,000. There are few villas in this area available for rent.

## Shopping & Amenities

There are several larger supermarkets and hypermarkets including Lulu's Hypermarket, Union Co-Op and Emirates Cooperative Society, as well as plenty of smaller supermarkets for convenience items. The Al Bustan Centre is home to a selection of shops. There is also a number of ATMs and lots of pharmacies.

## Entertainment & Leisure

The Qusais nightlife isn't going to set your social calendar on fire, and most people head for nearby Deira for a good night out. Fantasy Kingdom in the Al Bustan Centre is a large amusement centre, and with plenty of open sandy areas and parks, this is a good area for kids. For eating out, there is a good choice of cheap restaurants serving Arabic, Indian and Pakistani food, as well as fast-food outlets such as Pizza Hut and Hardees.

## Healthcare

There are several private clinics in Qusais as well as the Zulekha Hospital (04 267 8666).

## Education

There are a number of schools under construction in the area that should attract students from other areas.

**Travelling Times**

Airport – 10-15 mins
Media City – 40 mins
Trade Centre – 20 mins

## Traffic & Parking

The roads are good and most have footpaths. Traffic is not a problem and neither is parking in Qusais, although getting in and out of the area can be challenging at busy times. During rush hour it can get crazy on Sharjah-Dubai routes.

## Safety & Annoyances

This is a pretty safe area, the only annoyance being some noise from aircraft and the problems with the traffic at rush hour.

# ONE GLOBAL DESTINATION
# DOWNTOWN BURJ DUBAI

Welcome to the most prestigious square kilometre on the planet.
A place where architectural wonders and highbrow homes rub shoulders with leisured elegance and simple joie de vivre.

- A development spanning 45 million sq. m.
- 30,000 ultra luxurious homes to choose from
- First Armani Hotel along with other world-class hotels
- Breathtaking landscaped gardens
- **Burj Dubai**: The world's tallest tower
- **Burj Dubai Lake and Park**: Soothing waters and beautiful stretches of green
- **The Old Town Island**: An exclusive refuge with Arabesque homes, quaint markets, courtyards and charming alleyways
- **The Dubai Mall**: One of the largest malls in the world including a dazzling aquarium, fashion show arena, gold souk, and an ice rink
- **Burj Dubai Boulevard**: The shimmering thread that holds the whole of Downtown Burj Dubai together with endless shopping and entertainment

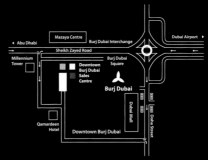

For more information please visit the Downtown Burj Dubai Sales Centre
or call 800-EMAAR (+971 4 366 1688)

www.downtownliving.ae

DOWNTOWN BURJ DUBAI

EMAAR

*Map p.7*
*Area* **E** *p.123*

# Al Safa & Al Wasl

These residential areas are separated from the beachside districts of Jumeira and Umm Suqeim by Al Wasl Road, with everything between Safa Park and Satwa officially known as Al Wasl, while Al Safa 1 & 2 lie between Safa Park at the north and Al Manara Street, which comes off Interchange 3. Housing is mainly large villas at high prices. Facilities are very good, and while you will usually need a car even to go to the local shops, just about everything you need is only a few minutes away.

**Best Points**
*This is a quiet area (especially around the roads off or behind Al Wasl) and close to many areas of the city including Bur Dubai, Dubai Marina, Jumeira and the beach. There are all kinds of shops, amenities and facilities close at hand.*

## Accommodation

Safa consists mostly of villas, usually three bedroomed, but bigger villas are available. Styles range from independent villas to villas in small, older compounds with unique character and established greenery. There are also some attractive new compounds (although there are a few that are a bit prison-like in their austerity). At the top end there are the massive local family homes. You do find some old bungalows, but these are predominantly occupied by local families. Safa 1 and 2 are where most rental villas are found. Prices for both areas start from around Dhs.160,000 and go up, up and up.

**Worst Points**
*The lack of small 'corner shops' that can be reached on foot, and (depending on the location of your house) most journeys need to be done by car.*

## Shopping & Amenities

Most houses are only a few minutes drive from one or more of the large supermarkets or shopping centres, with the Safa area having Union Co-Op and Choithram supermarkets opposite Safa Park, the Spinneys Centre along Al Wasl Road towards Umm Suqeim and the Park n Shop centre half way between the two on Al Wasl Road. All three centres have smaller auxiliary shops in or around them with a variety of facilities including video rental, cafes, restaurants, takeaways, bookshops, ATMs, chemists, liquor shops, hair and beauty salons and florists.

In the centre of Al Wasl, just beside Sheikh Zayed Road, there is the Mazaya Centre, with a Spinneys supermarket, a branch of Gulf Greetings as well as Homes R Us and Pier Import for home goods. Almost next door is the large Safestway supermarket. Beach Road in Jumeira is also just a few minutes away with shopping opportunities such as Palm Strip, Town Centre and Mercato. There is also a 24 hour pharmacy on Al Wasl Road, ATMs all over the place, banks in Jumeira, several veterinary clinics, a public library near Safa Park and a post office.

## Entertainment & Leisure

The huge, verdant spread of Safa Park is a popular attraction (see p.270). A second smaller park, Al Safa 2 Park, is located on Street 8A near Umm Suqeim School for Girls in Safa 2, and is open for ladies and children only through the week and families only at the weekend. There are plenty of cafes in or around the supermarkets and shopping centres, and numerous popular takeaways and small restaurants around Park n Shop and in the Safa area.

## Healthcare

Both Al Wasl Road and the nearby Jumeira Road have lots of medical centres, doctors and dentists, but these are mostly all private. There is one government clinic on Al Attar Road (Al Safa Clinic), and the excellent value Iranian Hospital is just down Al Wasl Road towards Satwa. For a list of hospitals see p.180.

## Education

Safa 1 has several schools including Jumeirah English Speaking School, The English College, Emirates English Speaking School, Jumeirah College and Jumeirah Primary School as well as nurseries including The Palm Nursery and Kangaroo Kids. The proximity to Sheikh Zayed Road makes Wellington International School a popular choice, and the highway means access to other schools is easy too. For a list of schools see p.202.

For a list of schools see p.202.

**Travelling Times**
Media City – 20 mins
Trade Centre – 10 mins
Airport – 20 mins

## Traffic & Parking

This is usually an easy area to move around in and get in and out of, although Al Wasl Road can get congested between Safa and Satwa at peak hours. Most villas have ample parking and there's usually plenty of room at the supermarkets. Walking is not a common way of getting around, but there are plenty of quiet streets for a stroll or walking the dog. And the open areas add a bit of space and provide places for kids to play. There are usually plenty of taxis swarming around Al Wasl Road but if you live in one of the back streets you will most likely have to give clear directions on how to get to your home.

## Safety & Annoyances

This is a safe area, although there have been reported cases of petty theft. Keep doors and windows secure to deter opportunists.

Semi-detached housing in Al Wasl

Area **F** p.122

# Arabian Ranches

One of Emaar's many residential developments, Arabian Ranches is located away from the centre of town, off the Emirates road near Dubai Autodrome. This is an all-villa project set among lush greenery, lakes and the Arabian Ranches Golf Course, with a range of luxury facilities that all add up to some pretty fine living. Although it is a bit out of town it is still just a 15 minute drive from shopping and dining options.

## Accommodation

Arabian Ranches is made up of villas of various sizes from two bedrooms to four bedrooms, for which you won't get much change from Dhs.270,000. Most of the villas were bought by people who now live in them, rather than rent them out. Telephone, internet and TV services are provided by du.

## Shopping

The Village Community Centre is conveniently located on the estate, housing Le Marche supermarket, a chemist, bookshop, petshop, laundry, bank, ATM, a liquor store, a DVD rental machine and several cafes, restaurants and fast-food outlets, most of which do home delivery.

## Entertainment & Leisure

Around the estate are several pools, basketball hoops, tennis courts, BBQ pits and grassy areas. The shopping centre has a good range of cafes and restaurants, many of which offer takeaway and home delivery. There is also The Arabian Ranches Golf Course, an 18 hole golf course with a pro shop, a clubhouse and the Ranches Restaurant and Bar, offering views out over the golf course from their terrace. The Autodrome and Dubai Polo and Equestrian Club are close by and offer fun on four wheels, or four legs.

## Healthcare

There are no local healthcare facilities and the nearest medical centres are in Umm Suqeim (government) or Al Barsha (private), while the nearest hospitals are probably in the Oud Metha/Umm Hurair area of Bur Dubai.

## Education

Apart from the branch of Jumeirah English Speaking School (JESS) next to the shopping centre, there is no other choice in the Ranches at present. Otherwise, it isn't too far to Al Barsha and Emirates Hills.

## Traffic & Parking

Your main access road is the Emirates Road (E311), which can be a bit hair-raising and congested at times. Traffic builds up as you enter or leave the Ranches.

## Safety & Annoyances

Security is good, with guards and barriers at the entrance to each estate, though residents may get tired of being stopped every day.

**Best Points**
This is one of the most popular areas for buyers and it isn't difficult to see why. It feels like a community, enclosed, safe, neighbourly with all the everyday facilities that you might need.

**Worst Points**
It is still a bit of a construction site, with some roads not completed and trucks clogging up the roads.

**Travelling Times**
Airport – 25 mins
Media City – 25mins
Trade Centre – 20 mins

*Villas at Arabian Ranches*

*Map p.8*
*Area* **G** *p.123*

# Bur Dubai & Al Mankhool

Bur Dubai is a bit of a concrete jungle with mid-size apartment blocks and virtually no green spaces, but many of the apartments have excellent facilities and spacious interiors. Bur Dubai is also popular because of its convenient central location. One of the most popular areas is Al Mankhool (also known as Golden Sands), but there are also some nice apartment blocks in the Al Hamriya area (across Bank Street from the BurJuman Mall). Nearer the creek and further west towards the sea, the buildings are generally a lot older with fewer facilities and limited parking, although those with balconies facing in the right direction do have beautiful views of the creek.

### Best Points

*Good access to central Dubai and everything you need within easy reach and the rare pleasure of being able to walk around – be it to the bank, shopping centre, restaurant or bar.*

### Worst Points

*Not a particularly attractive area, with few open spaces. Also has a lack of community feel due to the fact that nearly all the buildings are blocks of flats with no shops or services in inner Mankhool. All amenities are mainly located on the roads surrounding this block, Bank Street and Trade Centre Road. On occasion it can be an unpleasant place for women to walk at night due to sleazy guys cruising the area on the prowl for certain illicit nocturnal encounters.*

## Accommodation

The area is dominated by apartments in a mix of new and old medium-rise buildings from studios to large flats with several bedrooms. Some of the larger apartments are used as company flats. Rents in the newer buildings have risen to nearly the same as in other areas of Dubai, but the older the accommodation the cheaper it gets. A two-bedroom apartment in a new building could set you back around Dhs.100,000 but for that you should expect excellent facilities. A one-bedroom apartment in an older building starts at Dhs.55,000 while a two bedroom will be around Dhs.70,000, depending on the age of the building and range of facilities offered.

## Shopping & Amenities

There are two large Spinneys supermarkets in the area, as well as a Union Co-Op on Trade Centre Road, a Choithram on Mankhool Road and a huge Carrefour in Al Shindagha near the mouth of the creek. On and around Bank Street (Khalid Bin Al Waleed Road), there are a number of banks and ATMs, some smaller food stores, clothing shops, cafes, independent restaurants and sports stores. The BurJuman Centre (p.452) provides a huge range of shops and both Al Ain Plaza and Al Khaleej Centre on Mankhool Road are well known for computers and electronic goods. The souk area of Bur Dubai will stimulate the senses with its bright lights, noise, and hustle and bustle, or head to Karama for its market shops full of bargain designer copies and Arabian souvenirs.

## Entertainment & Leisure

You're so centrally located in Bur Dubai that you are just a short cab ride away from some of Dubai's best nightlife areas. There are also some good outlets right on your doorstep: The Arabian Courtyard Hotel on Al Fahedi Street and the Ascot Hotel on Bank Street both have various outlets, with Waxy O'Conners (in the Ascot) worth a special mention for one of Dubai's liveliest Thursday nights and biggest (and cheapest) Friday brunches. There is also the Regent Palace Hotel on the Karama side of Trade Centre Road, where the Rock Bottom Café is always good for a night out and a great venue for live music. There are also many small independent eateries on Bank Street and further into Bur Dubai.

## Healthcare

Both in Bur Dubai and in neighbouring Karama you can find a number of small medical centres. Rashid Hospital (government) is just a stone's throw away in Umm Hurair. Some popular private medical centres are just a few minutes away, including American Hospital and those in the newly opened, expansive Healthcare City (see p.178).

**133**

### Education

There are no schools in the area itself, but the central location means that there is plenty of choice nearby (see p.204).

(see p.204)

**Travelling Times**
Airport – 15 mins
Media City – 25 mins
Trade Centre – 5-10 mins

### Traffic & Parking

Bur Dubai has seen an increase in traffic and it's getting a lot more difficult to find parking, especially in the Mankhool area and the shopping areas in the heart of old Bur Dubai. Getting around the residential areas away from the main roads is not too bad during the day, but it gets congested at rush hours. The main roads get clogged up especially at traffic lights, but you'll soon find yourself little shortcuts which save loads of time. For pedestrians, it is generally a relatively safe area to get around as long as you stick to the pedestrian crossings at the traffic lights.

### Safety & Annoyances

Women may feel uneasy walking the streets, especially in the evening when there seem to be quite a few people just loitering around. There are very few cases of anything sinister going on, and so there is not really anything to fear, but just as in any city in the world, it pays to keep your wits about you.

Traditional windtowers

Bur Dubai bustling streets

Map p.9
Area **H** p.123

# Deira

Deira is not a hugely popular residential area for expats in higher income brackets, probably because of the horrendous traffic and general congestion. The heart of Deira is built up with a mix of old apartment blocks and hardly any open spaces or public greenery, while nearer the creek there are lots of new buildings offering modern upmarket apartments, many with spectacular views across the creek. Rents are relatively low in some of the more built up areas, while the creekside dwellings cost big bucks. One of the great things about Deira is the fact there are so many things to explore on your doorstep, such as the dhow wharfage and the atmospheric souks.

**Best Points**
*It is a good area for shopping and amenities, and the rents are generally cheaper than just over the creek in Bur Dubai.*

**Worst Points**
*The traffic is probably worse here than anywhere else in Dubai and with the southern end of Dubai attracting more and more residents, Deira is seen by some as being 'on the wrong side of the track'.*

## Accommodation

Although Deira does have some areas with villas (Abu Hail, Al Wuheida), they are almost exclusively inhabited by locals, with the areas closer to the creek full of apartments where most expats in the area congregate. In the heart of Deira, you'll pay around Dhs.45,000 for a studio apartment and Dhs.75,000 for two bedrooms, but these often are in older buildings and are not what you might call salubrious. The creekside area just north of Maktoum bridge offers a great standard of accommodation and is used by professional expats of all nationalities. There are many executive apartments with great views over the creek, impressive landscaping and good facilities – but prices here tend to be high, with a standard two-bedroom costing around Dhs.95,000 and a one-bedroom, furnished, serviced apartment costing upwards of Dhs.18,000 per month.

### Deira is Not Dead
This is the oldest and one of the most atmospheric parts of town. Many might have forgotten its charms as Dubai expands, but it's a great place to explore along the bustling corniche, through the souks, in heritage sites and the restaurants and bars of the modern creek-side hotels.

## Shopping & Amenities

Deira has lots to offer with popular malls like Al Ghurair City (p.466), Reef Mall (p.470) and Deira City Centre (p.454) being the most popular. All have good supermarkets (Spinneys, Al Maya and Carrefour respectively) as well as many other shops. Being an older area of town, there are also plenty of smaller groceries, pharmacies, dry-cleaners and laundry services on most of the streets. Deira's main post office is close to Al Ghurair Centre and there are many banks on Al Maktoum Road.

## Entertainment & Leisure

Within a small area, there's a good choice of hotels, including the InterContinental, Hilton and Sheraton Creek, the JW Marriott, Renaissance, Traders and Metropolitan Palace, all of which offer a great choice of dining outlets, bars and nightclubs. The traffic later in the evening will usually ease off, allowing you to get out and about a bit more easily.

For cheap eats, Al Rigga Street has a great range of independent restaurants along with some fast food places, and the Al Ghurair Centre has some particularly nice cafes on the terrace. Traffic and parking in this area can get a bit crazy at night on weekends. There are some pleasant walking areas by the creek and along the corniche towards Mamzar Park, which is gigantic and great for weekends, especially with the beach chalets available for daily rental.

**135**

*Healthcare*
Local healthcare is provided by Dubai Hospital near the corniche, while Dubai's foremost emergency hospital, Rashid Hospital, is just across Maktoum bridge in Umm Hurair. There is also the choice of many small private medical clinics, although the larger private hospitals tend to be located on the Bur Dubai side of the creek (see p.182).

*Education*
There are not many recognised expat schools in Deira – the area tends to attract more singletons looking for a city dwelling than people with kids looking for a family home.

**Travelling Times**
*Airport – 10 mins*
*Media City – 40 mins*
*Trade Centre – 20 mins*

*Traffic & Parking*
Dreadful. Congestion and bottlenecks over the bridge can double or triple your journey time. Even getting from A to B within Deira itself can be a challenge – if you are just going down the road it may easier to walk. Taxis are popular, especially since parking is difficult.

*Safety & Annoyances*
The main annoyance for people living in Deira is the traffic problems. Apart from that, it is a relatively safe place to live. Single women may find it is not quite as pleasant as other areas in Dubai, mainly due to unwanted attention from men seeking the company of a 'lady'.

*Creekside Dubai*

**Map p.5**

**Area ❶ p.122**

# Dubai Marina & Al Sufouh

Dubai Marina introduces modern luxury living to the area while Al Sufouh has a little more history. This entire area is undergoing dramatic changes, not least the building of the Palm Jumeirah out into the Gulf. The Marina's official name is Marsa Dubai (Marsa is Arabic for port or harbour) but you'll hardly hear anyone call it that.

**Best Points**

*One of the most desirable areas in Dubai at the moment, especially for its proximity to entertainment and leisure facilities. In Al Sufouh you can find palatial villas (with a price tag to match). This area is the perfect location for Media and Internet City and Knowledge Village.*

## Accommodation

In the Marina it's almost all apartments, with just a few townhouses. A two-bedroom apartment in Jumeirah Beach Residence will set you back more than a million dirhams to buy, while renting a similar property in the Marina towers costs around Dhs.160,000. Dubai Marina was the first freehold development in the UAE, and many people bought places purely for investment. In the many towers that make up the Jumeirah Beach Residence there are still some apartments available for purchase directly from developers, and many are also available on the secondary market.

Al Sufouh, on the other hand, is all villas. Some are new, some are old, but most are expensive. For a decent four-bedroom villa you won't get much change from Dhs.210,000.

**Worst Points**

*Rents and purchase costs are high and the massive development going on both in the Marina and around the entrance to the Palm means lots of noise and disruption. Traffic is building in the area and will increase once everyone has moved into the Palm and Jumeirah Beach Residence.*

## Shopping & Amenities

On Marina Walk, alongside all the restaurants, there's a Spinneys supermarket, a pharmacy, a bookshop, a classy florist, and a liquor store, plus a number of ATMs. In the cooler months, Friday is Marina Market day, with stallholders selling arts and handicrafts.

Ibn Battuta, Madinat Jumeirah, and Mall of the Emirates are just a few kilometres away. There's only a bit of free beach left along this stretch, by the hotels at the Marina, but this too will become part of the Jumeirah Beach Residence beach club (although public access may still be possible). However, the free beaches in Umm Suqeim and Jumeira are not too far. There's not much greenery to speak of in this area – the nearest park is near the beach in Umm Suqeim.

## Entertainment & Leisure

Plenty of options: the older hotels on the coast (including the Ritz Carlton and the Hilton Jumeirah), as well as the soon-to-be-extended Grosvenor House, all have some excellent restaurants and bars. Marina Walk has a number of decent-enough spots including Chandelier (p.507) and Johnny Rockets (p.502). The Marina also has a health spa above the parade of shops in Marina Walk. Most hotels have beach clubs and leisure facilities, although it's not cheap to become a member, and many have waiting lists. There are many bars and restaurants at the Madinat, and the Hard Rock Café is next to Media City. Entertainment and leisure options will multiply with the opening of the Palm. The Emirates Golf Club is just over the road.

## Healthcare

The nearest government clinic is Umm Suqeim, and the nearest government hospital is Rashid. The Neuro Spinal hospital opposite Jumeira Beach Park has round-the-clock A&E, and their own ambulance. In the other direction, the Cedars Hospital at Jebel Ali also offers 24 hour emergency care. For more information on hospitals, see p.180.

## Education

There is Dubai College in Al Sufouh, as well as the American University of Dubai and the many educational establishments within Knowledge Village. There's also the

Wellington International School and the International School of Choueifat in Al Sufouh. See p.216.

**Travelling Times**
Airport – 40 mins
Media City – 10 mins
Trade Centre – 20 mins

## Traffic & Parking

Getting in and out of the area has been greatly improved by the opening of a new interchange near Media City. The morning and evening traffic coming from Internet City, Media City and Knowledge Village can get busy in certain hotspots. Parking depends on whether you have access to your building's car park, although there's an underground car park by Marina Walk.

In Al Sufouh you should have plenty of room to park outside your villa.

## Safety & Annoyances

Security is good, with many apartment blocks having 24 hour security and underground parking. The biggest annoyance is the ongoing construction in the Marina, and the roads around Jumeirah Beach Residence, which can cause traffic delays and extra noise at night.

*Sunset over the Marina's construction*

*Sky high Marina views*

Map p.5
Area **J** p.122

# Emirates Hills

Part of the burgeoning 'new Dubai', Emirates Hills is a desirable address with a range of villa-style houses in The Springs, The Lakes and The Meadows and apartments in The Greens. Tree-lined streets and pathways, attractively landscaped lakes, gardens and pool/recreation areas make it perfect for those who want to escape the chaos of city life and enjoy the peace and quiet of this surburb-style area (although there is the inevitable construction noise). Convenient for those working in Media and Internet Cities and Jebel Ali Free Zone, it is also popular for those working in the centre of Dubai, as the morning and evening commute only takes 20-30 minutes against the flow of traffic.

**Best Points**

*You can buy or rent here and the whole area is nicely landscaped, attractive, safe, and has that 'out of town' feel.*

## Accommodation

The Greens, on the edge of Emirates Hills, offers a range of one to four bedroom apartments, which are well appointed but a bit small for the money. A one bedroom rents for around Dhs.90,000 and a three bedroom for around Dhs.160,000. Generally the style and quality of all houses in Emirates Hills is good, although they all look the same. Mid-range villas with two bedrooms rent from about Dhs.115,000 or sell at around Dhs.1.7 million. Even with the lack of individuality, for most people the advantage of being able to buy here and the community feel beats more spacious options available elsewhere. Telephone, internet and TV services are provided by du (see p.170).

**Worst Points**

*Insects. The lush landscaping has provided the perfect habitat for a thriving insect population including mosquitos and spiders, even some dangerous species, so care is needed. Also you can get slow moving traffic in and out of Emirates Hills during rush hour. The junction between Barsha and The Greens is a bottleneck, but has been eased since the opening of the new interchange at the Marina.*

## Shopping & Amenities

The Greens has a range of shops, including Choithram and Organic Foods & Café. Within Emirates Hills you'll find three centres, each anchored by a supermarket. There's Choithram at the Springs end, a large Spinneys at Spinneys Town Centre in the middle and a Spinneys Market in Meadows. Each centre has a Hayya! gym, a beauty salon, a pharmacy and ATMs. Between them all, you should find everything you need, from laundry services to fast food and fine dining or coffee shops to video rentals. Town Centre boasts stores such as Beyond the Beach, Mothercare, Pets Delight and Tavola. Other nearby supermarkets include Spinneys (Dubai Marina), Géant (Ibn Battuta) and Carrefour (Mall of the Emirates).

## Entertainment & Leisure

Each estate within Emirates Hills has a recreation area and swimming pool, offering pleasant places to relax and for kids to play. Dubai's two latest and greatest shopping malls are both about 10 minutes away and between them have a huge range of shops, cafes, restaurants and foodcourts, as well as leisure facilities such as Ski Dubai in Mall of the Emirates and the 21 screen cinema (including Dubai's first IMAX screen) at Ibn Battuta Mall. For eating out, there's the licensed Academy Restaurant and Bar at Montgomerie Golf Club, plus all the options at The Greens, Emaar Business Park and Dubai Marina.

## Healthcare

There are currently no medical facilities in the vicinity – although there is a new private medical centre in Al Barsha, or the government clinic in Jebel Ali. Otherwise it's a bit of a drive to get to the main government and private facilities (see p.180).

## Education

There are lots of new schools springing up, although demand is high and it can be tough to get in anywhere. Waiting lists for a place in the most sought-after schools and nurseries are long, and it is best to sign up well in advance. Schools already open include Emirates School, Dubai British School, Regent School and Dubai International Academy, while the Kids' Oasis in Emirates Hills is the only pre-school in the immediate area. For more information on schools see p.202.

**Travelling Times**
*Airport – 35 mins*
*Media City – 10-20 mins*
*Trade Centre – 25 mins*
*(depending on area)*

## Traffic & Parking

Within the area the traffic is fine, although speed bumps slow things down. Getting in and out through the new Interchange on Sheikh Zayed Road can be a problem at rush hour. This is not helped by the fact that the work on the metro system will not be completed until late 2008. The traffic lights where Sheikh Zayed Road meets the 'back road' past The Greens is a nightmare during peak hours. An alternative route onto the Al Khail Road (E44) can be a lot quicker. The main road through Emirates Hills has landscaped, shaded pavements which makes the area great for pedestrians and children.

## Safety & Annoyances

There really are few annoyances – apart from the traffic. In addition the area is well guarded by security and is pleasant to stroll around.

The Springs

The Greens

*Townhouses*

Area **K** *p.122*

# Green Community

The Green Community lives up to its name. An oasis of green in the desert, this new development is especially good for families, and homes are hard to come by. Built by Union Properties, the apartments and houses are sold on a 90 year leasehold (see www.up.ae for details). It's a bit out in the sticks (or sand), but it's the perfect choice for people working in the Jebel Ali Free Zone.

**Best Points**
*The sprawling greenery and splendid peace and quiet.*

**Worst Points**
*The distance is the real downer, especially as it makes travelling times and taxi fares a little on the high side.*

## Accommodation
There is a wide variety including villas, townhouses, and apartments. The original Green Community was so well received that developer Union Properties built a new phase – Green Community West. For a four-bedroom villa you can expect to pay around Dhs.240,000 in rent.

## Shopping & Amenities
The Market is the Green Community's new shopping centre (p.470). As well as a jewellers, clothes shops, and home furnishing outlets, there's a pharmacy, a florist, a dry cleaners, a card shop, a book shop, an optician, and a branch of Ace. It is also home to a Choithram supermarket, and Ibn Battuta mall is not too far away.

## Entertainment & Leisure
The Courtyard by Marriott and the neighbouring Market are the focal points for dining out, with a number of coffee shops, good restaurants and places for a quick bite with licensed outlets in the hotel. There's top-class golf courses nearby at Emirates Hills, Jebel Ali and Arabian Ranches.

## Healthcare
The Green Community Medical Centre (04 885 3225) upstairs in The Market is a private clinic with full-time doctors, plus visiting specialists. The nearest government-run clinic is at Jebel Ali. For emergencies the Cedars Hospital within the Jebel Ali Free Zone is nearest – they have their own ambulance too. For government A&E care it's quite a trip to Rashid Hospital.

## Education
New primary school The Children's Garden (349 8806) offers a bilingual curriculum in English/German or English/French. There are various primary & secondary schools nearby in Emirates Hills and Jebel Ali.

**Travelling Times**
*Airport – 40 mins*
*Media City – 20 mins*
*Trade Centre – 30 mins*

## Traffic & Parking
Traffic within the Community itself is not a problem. Parking is adequate. The biggest headache is that there's only one main road, the E311 Emirates Road, linking the Green Community to Jebel Ali and the rest of Dubai. This road is often clogged with trucks that come to a standstill in the nearside lane. It will cost around Dhs.65 for a taxi to Trade Centre and up to Dhs.100 to the airport.

## Safety & Annoyances
The Green Community is a great place for families, as the gated complex is very safe. Just don't let little ones wander into the water.

**141**

Map p.4
Area ⓛ p.122

# Jebel Ali & The Gardens

There was a time when the Jebel Ali area was not really considered a part of Dubai, but a 'satellite' town that grew up around the port. Today though, with the centre of Dubai moving ever further south-west, it's closer to the action. A great location for people working in the Jebel Ali Free Zone and Media and Internet Cities, it's also well connected to the major road networks.

**Best Points**

The area remains relatively peaceful and as yet has not become overly crowded. It is close to Media and Internet Cities and Jebel Ali Free Zone.

**Worst Points**

You will feel a little bit far out of town here, although there are many entertainment and leisure options nearby in the developing areas in and around the Marina.

## Accommodation

In Jebel Ali village it's a mixture of old single-storey villas and newer villas in compounds. The Gardens is a complex of very affordable one, two and three-bedroom apartments.

Jebel Ali village rents were traditionally pretty cheap given its out-of-town location, but have gone up in recent years. If you can find one of the older villas you might be lucky enough to get it for around Dhs.100,000, but a smart four-bedroom pad in one of the complexes will cost upwards of Dhs.130,000.

The Gardens is the exception to the Dubai rental rule – from day one the rents were set by the developer Nakheel, and they were low. The best bit is they haven't gone up a great deal since. So for a two-bedroom apartment you'll pay around Dhs.50,000 plus a Dhs.4,000 annual air-conditioning fee. The bad news? Nakheel closed the waiting list once it reached 3,000, and they are extremely hard to find.

## Shopping & Amenities

Ibn Battuta shopping mall is right on the doorstep. The range of shops is massive, and includes a big Géant hypermarket and a multiplex cinema featuring an Imax screen. In Jebel Ali, the little shopping centre near the Al Montazah Complex has an Abela supermarket, a dry cleaners, hair salons and an internet cafe. As you enter Jebel Ali, there's a Choithram supermarket and a pharmacy. Jebel Ali Village has a lovely green park, complete with a pond and ducks. In The Gardens there are also lots of green spaces, with cricket pitches and badminton courts, while the Jebel Ali Village Riding Centre offers horse riding for all ages.

## Entertainment & Leisure

For dining and leisure options there are the cinema, foodcourt and some decent restaurants in the Ibn Battuta Mall (although restaurants are not licensed). Jebel Ali Club is licensed though, and is a popular spot for local residents. It has a bar and restaurant with outdoor terrace, plus leisure facilities including a pool, gym, and squash and tennis courts. The Jebel Ali Hotel and Spa is also nearby, and so is the shooting club (p.180).

## Healthcare

The Jebel Ali Clinic is the local government health clinic. There's the private Al Montazah Medical Clinic near the shops, and a branch of Al Rafa Poly Clinic (04 882 4470) in building 27 in the Gardens. Jebel Ali Hospital (884 5666), near the shops, has an emergency department and can dispatch their own ambulance. Cedars-Jebel Ali International Hospital in JAFZ also has A&E and an ambulance, but as these are private you'll have to pay for treatment in both cases. The nearest government A&E is Rashid Hospital. For more information on hospitals see p.218.

## Education

There are several schools in the area, such as Jebel Ali Primary, Winchester School and Delhi Private School (in the Gardens). See p.204 for more information.

**Travelling Times**
Airport – 40 mins
Media City – 15 mins
Trade Centre – 30 mins

## Traffic & Parking

Not a huge problem with traffic or parking – in both areas it can get busy around rush hours, and traffic will build up when you're leaving the Gardens and Jebel Ali village, but for commuters working in Dubai you'll be against the flow of busy traffic so shouldn't hit too many delays. Media and Internet City workers will face problems while work goes on at the interchanges for the Palm Jumeirah. You can expect to pay around Dhs.60 for a taxi to Trade Centre and Dhs.80 to the airport.

## Safety & Annoyances

Jebel Ali village and the complexes are especially good for families, as there's not much through-traffic. The Gardens is also a safe area, with plenty of security guards doing the rounds. These same security personnel could in fact prove to be the most annoying aspect of living in The Gardens – because the apartments are so sought-after, tenants may be tempted to sub-let when they leave. This is very much against the rules, and to discourage it the security guards are always on the lookout for signs of people moving in or moving out. If you're caught carrying a washing machine out to your car, you'd better have a good excuse.

*The Gardens*

Map p.7
Area **M** p.123

# Jumeira

The actual area of Jumeira occupies a prime nine-kilometre strip of coastline stretching south-west from the port area, but the name has been hijacked to such an extent that new residential and commercial developments bearing the Jumeira tag are cropping up for miles around. Even the Palm Jumeirah doesn't connect with Jumeira, but actually extends from the area of Al Sufouh. (Admittedly though, this whole stretch of beach is known as Jumeira Beach). Jumeira itself is characterised by quiet streets lined with sophisticated villas, golden beaches (some free, some paid-for), and good access to lots of shopping.

**Best Points**

*This is location, location, location – it's close to the beach, close to the shops, close to Dubai and close to many a resident's heart.*

## Accommodation

The ultimate location for that dream villa in the sun, Jumeira property attracts some of the highest rents in the city. There's a mixture of huge 'palaces', independent villas, and villas in compounds with shared facilities. It's all low-rise, and hardly an apartment in sight. For a three-bedroom, stand-alone villa you can expect to pay anywhere in the region of Dhs.200,000 to Dhs.250,000 depending on the age and specific location. You can however get the odd villa in an older compound for around Dhs.150,000.

**Worst Points**

*In keeping with the rest of Dubai, traffic can be heavy at certain times of day, but it's bearable. The only other downside to living in this desirable area is the sky-high rents you have to pay for the privilege.*

## Shopping & Amenities

There are shopping centres all along Beach Road, the biggest of which is the popular Mercato with well-known brands and a Spinneys supermarket. There's also a big Union Co-Op and a Choithram opposite Safa Park, and the Spinneys Centre just the other side of Al Wasl Road. There's another Choithram supermarket on Beach Road as well as the large Spinneys near the mosque end. Just a few kilometres along the coast you've got Madinat Jumeirah, and it's not that far to the Mall of the Emirates. You'll find lots of laundries, dry cleaners and tailors dotted along Beach Road, as well as a high concentration of art galleries and boutiques. You've got Empost on Al Wasl Road for postal services, a few petrol stations, and plenty of banks and ATMs.

**Jumeira or Jumeirah?**

*Jumeira or Jumeirah? According to the 'official' spelling used by Dubai Municipality, it's Jumeira, so that's what we use when referring to this area. However, many hotels, parks, clubs, schools, and residential developments have added an 'h' to the end, so don't be surprised if you see the two different spellings side by side throughout the book.*

## Entertainment & Leisure

There are plenty of independent restaurants and cafes, especially in the shopping centres along Beach Road. The Lime Tree Cafe is fabulous, although it can get a bit too busy on weekends and during lunchtimes. Not far up Beach Road is the Jumeirah Beach Hotel, the Burj Al Arab, and Madinat Jumeirah with a host of glittering gourmet delights and beautiful bars.

There are many beaches, although the public ones are crowded on weekends. The Jumeirah Beach Park charges Dhs.5 entry, but it is worth it for the lack of crowds and the additional facilities. Safa Park is nearby, and is undoubtedly one of the most picturesque parks in Dubai. Mercato Mall has an 11 screen cinema.

## Healthcare

Al Safa Clinic (04 394 3468) opposite Safa Park (next to the library) is the nearest government health clinic. Emirates Hospital, opposite Jumeirah Beach Park, has a 24 hour walk-in clinic to deal with common ailments, but they do not accept emergency cases. The Neuro Spinal Hospital in the same building does have a 24 hour emergency department though. Jumeira is known for being home to countless beauty salons and private medical facilities, including dentists, physiotherapists and cosmetic surgery centres. For more information on hospitals, see p.182.

## Education

There are numerous nurseries in Jumeira, and Jumeirah Primary School, Jumeirah College and Jumeirah English Speaking School are all in the neighbourhood. Easy access to road networks means even outlying schools are fairly easy to reach. For more details of these schools, see p.213.

**Travelling Times**
Airport – 20 mins
Media City – 20 mins
Trade Centre – 10 mins

### Traffic & Parking

Although it's been widened in recent times, Jumeira Road (more commonly known as Beach Road) gets very busy at rush hour, with traffic leaving Internet and Media Cities often bringing things to a crawl in the evenings. Mercato's popularity often leads to jams along that stretch too, especially on a Friday evening.

Getting from one side of Beach Road onto the other can be tricky for both pedestrians and drivers. Speed bumps and cameras along the length of the road do have the desired effect of slowing most of the traffic down. Streetside parking if you're located behind Beach Road shouldn't be a problem, but if your villa is near Mercato you may find people parking across your drive at busy times.

### Safety & Annoyances

Small pockets of construction are noisy. In general roads and pavements are very good, and mostly well-lit, but the fast traffic, even in the suburbs, means you probably wouldn't want your kids playing out in the street.

Housing on Beach Road

Development on Jumeira Beach

*Map p.15*
*Area* **N** *p.123*

# Mirdif & Rashidiya

For many years Mirdif was one of Dubai's best-kept secrets – a quiet neighbourhood, nice villas, low rents, and not as far out of town as it may appear. Alas, the secret is out; new residential and retail developments are cropping up, and rents are on the rise. Rashidiya is another of Dubai's older areas, with street after street of traditional single-storey villas. Al Warqa is sparsely populated but growing, and International City is home to some of Dubai's most affordable freehold properties.

**Best Points**

*The rents are certainly lower here than in many other areas of Dubai, and both Mirdif and Rashidiya still have that local, neighbourhood surburb feel. Unfortunately though rapid growth means that many of the open desert areas that surround this residential hotspot have been taken over by property development.*

## Accommodation

In Mirdif it's a mix of independent villas and small compounds, with the odd large compound community. The new, and rather large, Uptown Mirdiff development offers apartments on a 99 year leasehold basis as well as townhouses for sale and rent. If you can find one, a decent three-bedroom villa should cost around Dhs.120,000 to Dhs.160,000 a year and, depending on whether it's a stand-alone or in a compound, may have a little garden or shared pool.

Al Warqa has an ever-increasing number of independent villas, but still lots of 'desert' in between. Rashidiya has an older feel, with smaller single-storey villas, some of which have then been divided into rooms to provide low-cost staff accommodation. A three bedroom villa will go for between Dhs.120,000 and Dhs.140,000, while a four bedroomed place will probably cost around Dhs.150,000.

International City is a new residential development behind the Dragon Mart on the Dubai–Hatta Road (E44). Each of its areas reflects the architectural style of a different country or region (hence the name), and when finished in 2008 the development will be home to 60,000 residents. Cheaper than many other properties for sale in Dubai, a one-bedroom apartment in International City will sell for around Dhs.500,000.

**Worst Points**

*Watch the skies – parts of Mirdif are right under the flight path to the airport, great for plane-spotters, not so great for everyone else, so choose that villa carefully.*

## Shopping & Amenities

Mirdif has several little clusters of shops, selling the basics, as well as the impressive Uptown Mirdif. For your weekly shop there's also a Spinneys and WestZone supermarket. Rashidiya has the Bin Sougat Mall (p.466), with a small Spinneys supermarket, a pharmacy, an excellent stationery shop, and perfume, clothes and cosmetics stores. The main post office serving the area is in Rashidiya. In Al Warqa there's a big 'Mars' supermarket, with an internet cafe behind it. Deira City Centre is just 10 minutes away and Festival City sports an IKEA, HyperPanda, and numerous fashion stores and boutiques in its waterfront malls.

Next to the big mosque on Mirdif's Street 15 there's a DVD rental shop and a place for internet access at Dhs.7 per hour. Rashidiya Library has a small selection of English language books, and you can also surf the web for Dhs.3 per hour. The Elyazia beauty salon in Mirdif offers pedicures and manicures, hair styling, waxing and more.

Uptown Mirdiff is the area's big draw. Its pleasant piazza-style courtyards are home to numerous stores including Mothercare, Early Learning Centre, Accessorize, Adidas, Beyond the Beach and Pumpkin Patch. There's also a pet shop, a Starbucks, a huge foodcourt, and several restaurants including the excellent Gourmet Burger Kitchen.

## Entertainment & Leisure

Mirdif has its share of good independent restaurants such as Oregano (Italian) and Open House (Indian). Your takeaway options range from Mexican, Chinese, pizza and Indian to a traditional chippy. Uptown has a huge foodcourt that's sure to undo all your hard work at the local Fitness First.

Mushrif Park is so big that you actually drive around it rather than walk, and it features a train, swimming pools and tennis courts. Rashidiya has a quiet park with lots of greenery and swings and slides, but it's ladies and children only except Fridays and holidays. lots of trees and paths and a playground.

## Healthcare
Rashidiya Clinic is the government health facility serving the area. The nearest government hospital is Rashid, with 24 hour emergency services. The private Welcare Hospital is nearer, also with round-the-clock A&E.

## Education
There is a choice of nurseries in Mirdif including Small Steps, Super Kids and Emirates British Nursery. Uptown Primary is recommended. Other new schools include the Sharjah American International School in Al Warqa, Royal Dubai School in Muhaisnah, and the American Academy for Girls in Mizhar.

**Travelling Times**
*Airport – 5 mins*
*Media City – 30 mins*
*Trade Centre – 20 mins*

## Traffic & Parking
Within Mirdif, Rashidiya and Al Warqa the traffic is minimal, although the main road through Mirdif is often used as a shortcut for Emirates Road traffic heading to Sharjah. There's no problem with parking as most villas have plenty of room out front or on the driveway (if it hasn't been dug up for roadworks). It's not easy to flag down a taxi in these areas so you will need to call for one (04 208 0808).

## Safety & Annoyances
Generally safe, but some people drive too fast around the neighbourhood streets. Burglaries do occur, mainly opportunist, so don't leave windows or patio doors open. Emirates Road gets clogged, and of course the airport is fairly close so aircraft noise can be a nuisance.

*Uptown Mirdif*

147

*Map p.10*
*Area* ◉ *p.123*

# Oud Metha & Umm Hurair

Oud Metha has the advantage of being centrally located, within easy reach of the highways, plenty of shops and restaurants within walking distance or just minutes by car, as well as Lamcy Plaza and the Wafi City complex of shops and restaurants. Accommodation is mainly in nice four-storey apartment blocks, and not as densely packed in as in other 'inner-city' areas. There is a fair amount of construction going on but at present apartments are not easy to find.

**Best Points**
*Convenient central location with easy access.*

## Accommodation

It is all apartments in this part of town and they are usually in four-storey buildings. Sizes range from studio to three-bedroom although the most common are one and two. Annual rents range from Dhs.75,000 (if you're really lucky) to Dhs.90,000 (if you're in the new buildings) for a one bedroom, Dhs.90,000 to Dhs.120,000 for a two bedroom and around Dhs.130,000 for a three bedroom, obviously with facilities increasing and improving in the higher priced buildings. It can be quite a challenge to get into one of the cheaper buildings, with vacancies filled as soon as they have gone on the market.

**Worst Points**
*Small-scale construction affects some residences with noise and blocking roads, but lack of accommodation is probably the biggest problem.*

## Shopping & Amenities

This small area is packed with all you'll need, including a large Lals supermarket inside Lamcy Plaza on the top floor, and plenty of good medium-sized supermarkets, convenient smaller groceries, pharmacies and a Spinneys Market in the area. There are also plenty of dry cleaners and laundries scattered through the area as well as some good video rental stores and a post office counter in Lamcy Plaza. ATMs for many banks can be found in Lamcy Plaza and Wafi City along with branches for a couple of banks in the area including National Bank of Dubai near Movenpick Hotel. Several of Dubai's churches can also be found in the area.

## Entertainment & Leisure

The area around Lamcy Plaza has some great independent restaurants, such as Lemongrass and Lan Kwai Fong, and there are licensed restaurants in Movenpick, Grand Hyatt and the Wafi complex. These were joined in late 2007 by Dubai's latest luxury hotel, Raffles. Cheaper options include the foodcourt in Lamcy with some branches of local chains and the big fast food names, and there are numerous local shawarma joints around Oud Metha. For bars and nightclubs there is the low key, fun-packed Jimmy Dix in the Movenpick, and The Mix at the Grand Hyatt, one of Dubai's superclubs.

For relaxation there are numerous health spas, Moroccan baths, hairdressers and beauty salons located in this area are as well as several social clubs. For the more energetic there are plenty of places offering sports and activities including Al Nasr Leisureland (home to a bowling alley), the health clubs at Movenpick, Grand Hyatt and Wafi, many small gyms dotted around, and billiard halls.

There is a small park on Umm Hurair Road close to Dubai TV, while Creekside Park and Zabeel Park are both just five minutes away. In addition, there are amusement centres at Al Nasr Leisureland, Lamcy Plaza and Wafi City, Children's City at Creekside Park and the 12 screen Grand Cineplex cinema next to the Grand Hyatt. Streetside shisha cafes are popular with residents and also draw plenty of people to the area.

## Healthcare

Dubai's two main government hospitals, Rashid and Al Wasl, are both nearby, but there are also several popular private medical centres such as American Hospital, the

Canadian Specialist Medical Centre and the newly opened Health Care City, home to many medical facilities (see p.178).

### Education

The main street between Oud Metha and Umm Hurair is home to some of Dubai's largest schools such as the Indian High School and Dubai English Speaking School, a popular school for western children living all over Dubai. For more information on schools, see p.212.

**Travelling Times**
Airport – 10 mins
Media City – 20 mins
Trade Centre – 5-10 mins

### Traffic & Parking

While traffic tends to be a bit of a headache in most central areas there is the benefit of various alternative access routes. The only regular places to watch out for slow traffic are by Lamcy Plaza and through the main roundabout in Umm Hurair coming from the Wafi interchange. The area has some good free parking, in shopping centre carparks, on side roads, and on empty patches of sandy ground. The municipality carpark close to Lamcy is now metered.

In rush hour Sheikh Zayed Road suffers the usual problems towards Garhoud Bridge and Sharjah and towards Media City, but Maktoum Bridge can be a viable alternative to Garhoud at certain times of the day.

### Safety & Annoyances

Sometimes at weekends there can be some noise from cars driving around at night, but a good police presence is addressing the problem.

Oud Metha apartments

Map p.7
Area **P** p.123

# Satwa

A mixture of accommodation and a great central location makes Satwa (and the adjoining neighbourhoods of Al Bada'a, Hudheiba & Al Jafilya) a popular choice. For that idyllic peaceful villa you'll probably need to head further along the coast to Jumeira, Al Wasl and Umm Suqeim, but for singles or couples, Satwa's lively bustle can be rather endearing, and its main street, Diyafah is a blissful pedestrian paradise compared with the rest of Dubai.

**Best Points** ◀
*The good central location, lots of facilities and amenities within walking distance, and many more places just a short drive away.*

**Worst Points** ◀
*The traffic on Diyafah Street (both vehicular and pedestrian).*

## Accommodation

There is a selection of apartment blocks on Diyafah Street and Al Hudeiba Street (Plant Street), all of which are no higher than seven or eight storeys. In addition there's a number of low-rent rooms above shops around the one-way system. Surprisingly you'll also find a fair few villas too, some old, traditional and run down, others more modern and expensive. For a two-bedroom apartment on Diyafah Street you can expect to pay around Dhs.85,000. Prices for smart villas, however, are not much cheaper than Jumeira – starting at roughly Dhs.180,000 for a three bedroom.

## Shopping & Amenities

There are plenty of shops and supermarkets on Diyafah Street, while the nearest 'big' supermarkets include Spinneys on Beach Road and Safestway on Sheikh Zayed Road. Dune Centre on Diyafah Street has a few shops (including a place to hire formal evening wear should you ever need it), a DVD rental shop and an internet cafe. The new Al Ghazal Shopping Complex has more than 70 outlets offering fashion and homewares, plus a nail bar, pharmacy and health clinic.

The one-way system is one of the best areas in Dubai for cut-price textiles and tailors. The multitude of tailors located here are great for upholstery and cushions too. You just take along your measurements and they'll run you up some snazzy 'majlis' style cushions. For the handyman, DIY gear and tools abound and Satwa is one of the best places for car spares such as batteries, and small repairs – pull into the small car park next to the mosque construction site and you'll have half a dozen guys on the bonnet offering to fix your car. Just be prepared to haggle.

'Plant Street' (real name Al Hudeiba Street) has a number of shops that sell plants (surprisingly) as well as pots and other such garden equipment as well as a range of picture framing and soft funishing shops

## Entertainment & Leisure

Rydges Plaza on Diyafah Street has some popular casual favourites, including Aussie Legends, Billy Blues, Cactus Cantina and Il Rustico. The Jumeira Rotana has the ever-popular Boston Bar where ladies' nights certainly draw in the crowds, while the nearby Capitol Hotel is home to Henry J. Beans.

Diyafah Street has some great independent restaurants too, including Al Mallah and Sidra for yummy shawarmas, falafel and juice. There's a few Indian and Chinese places, plus KFC, Pizza Hut and Burger King. Also virtually in any direction there is a whole range of enticing hotspots, be it in Jumeira, Bur Dubai or on Sheikh Zayed Road.

## Healthcare

The Iranian Hospital on Al Wasl Road is very close and has an excellent A&E department plus a walk-in GP service with free medication. Also the Rashid government hospital isn't too far. The Neuro Spinal Hospital on Beach Road has a 24 hour A&E and its own ambulance while the Belhoul Hospital on Diyafah Street specialises in surgery. The new Al Bada'a Clinic (government) is behind Chelsea Tower. There are also a number of pharmacies on the main roads. For more information on hospitals see p.180..

### Education

While there aren't any popular expat schools within Satwa there are a number in Jumeira and Al Wasl, as well as various nurseries, which are easily accessible. See 204

**Travelling Times**
Airport – 15 mins
Media City – 20 mins
Trade Centre – 5 mins

### Traffic & Parking

Diyafah Street gets pretty busy, especially in evening rush hour, and on a Friday night when drivers and pedestrians seem to spend hours cruising up and down. The one-way system is constantly busy too, with too much lane swapping and reversing out into oncoming traffic. Diyafah Street and the one-way system have metered parking, but spaces can be hard to come by. However there are a few sandy areas outside buildings where you can park.

### Safety & Annoyances

Around some of the older areas there may be one or two undesirables, and occasional break-ins have been reported in older villas. You may get annoyed by the traffic on the main roads and by the sheer volume of cars and people around the one-way system. If you like neon lights and hustle and bustle though, this could be right up your alley.

Satwa shopping

Satwa at night

## Sharjah

*Map p.12*
*Area* ⓠ *p.123*

Dubai's neighbouring emirate is an attractive location for many mainly due to the significantly lower rents, which can be up to half what you'd pay in Dubai. As you'd expect in any city, there's a wide range of accommodation options, from small apartments to big villas.

**Best Points**

*The low rents are a real draw for people looking for budget accommodation. The city also has a fairly quiet, community feel.*

### Accommodation

Downtown it's all high-rise apartment blocks. Some have been around a few years and so facilities will be a little basic. Newer blocks command higher rents. As you venture out of town there's some big independent villas, and smaller, older villas too.
For a one-bedroom apartment in town you could pay as little as Dhs.40,000, while a three-bedroom villa can be found for Dhs.100,000.

**Worst Points**

*At rush hour the E11 linking Sharjah and Dubai becomes the world's longest car park. Journey times of two hours are not uncommon. Sharjah is the only 'dry' emirate, so there's no bars or licensed restaurants, and the city is certainly not as liberal as Dubai, so you should behave and dress accordingly.*

### Shopping & Amenities

Dubai may be famous for its shopping, and Sharjah isn't bad either. Sharjah City Centre, Sharjah Mega Mall, and the Sahara Centre all feature a host of international brands and stores (such as M&S and Debenhams), and there are plenty of smaller shopping centres catering to all tastes and budgets. For a slightly more traditional shopping experience, the big Central Souk (aka Blue Souk) has rows of jewellery shops and stores selling Arabian knick-knacks and pretty much anything you could imagine. The Souk Al Arsah in the Heritage Area is another traditional Arabian market (although it now has a roof and doors and is pleasantly air-conditioned). Sharjah also has fruit, vegetable and fish markets in Al Jubail beside the water, with many stalls offering a variety of fresh produce.
For your everyday shopping needs, there's a big Carrefour hypermarket in the City Centre mall and a Spinneys in the Sahara Centre. You'll also find no end of small grocery stores dotted around the residential areas, as well as dry cleaners and laundries.

### Entertainment & Leisure

Sharjah does have a reputation for being a bit quiet, and many expats head for Dubai at night. That said, Sharjah does have its share of dining and leisure options, with a number of good independent restaurants. You'll also find branches of well-known chains and fast-food restaurants, and the shopping malls all have foodcourts.

*Sharjah at dusk*

A particularly popular option for expats in Sharjah is the Sharjah Wanderers Sports Club. They have a host of sporting and leisure facilities (including two grass pitches), and, perhaps most importantly, licensedbars and restaurants, (yes, lisenced, selling alcohol, in Sharjah.) The club is only accessible to members, and guests of members. For more info visit www.sharjahwanderers.com.

Cinemas in Sharjah include the Star Cineplex at City Centre and Century Cinema at the Sahara Centre. For spending time outdoors, Sharjah has some big green parks, attractive corniches, and good beaches, and the Qanat Al Qasba is a lovely spot for a leisurely stroll. The Heritage and Arts areas are certainly worth a visit, with plenty of art galleries and museums showing how life used to be.

## Healthcare

Sharjah has a number of government health clinics for subsidised medical care, plus private clinics and hospitals. The two government hospitals with emergency facilities are the Qassimi (06 538 6444) and Kuwaiti hospitals (06 524 2111), while Al Zahra, Zulekha (06 565 8866), and the Central Private (06 563 9900) are the main private hospitals with 24hr emergency care.

## Education

Sharjah English School is a primary school for English-speaking children (06 552 2779), and Wesgreen International School (06 537 4401) teaches the curriculum of England and Wales from kindergarten through to secondary. The Sharjah American International School (06 538 0000) teaches the American curriculum. The Lycée Georges Pompidou de Sharjah (06 552 3430) is a French school for children from 3 to 18 years old, and the German School Sharjah (06 567 6014) offers the German curriculum to the same age group.

Sharjah University City is home to a number of higher education institutions including the American University of Sharjah (06 515 5555). For more information, see p.202.

**Travelling Times**
Airport – 15 mins
Media City – 45 mins
Trade Centre – 25 mins
(on a clear run!)

## Traffic & Parking

Thousands of people make the journey between Sharjah and Dubai every day, and the roads simply can't handle the volume of traffic. The notorious E11 Al Ittihad Road links central Sharjah and central Dubai, crossing Dubai Creek over Garhoud Bridge, and for most of the morning it's nose to tail leaving Sharjah and the same in the other direction once evening arrives. The E311 Emirates Road is one alternative, but it's a long way round, and it too becomes very busy at rush hour. Traffic within Sharjah itself suffers as a result, with delays at the big interchanges.

Finding your way around is a challenge, and whoever's in charge of the signposts in Sharjah clearly has a sense of humour.

Parking downtown can be tricky, as there's not really enough to go round. Much of the roadside parking is metered too, and as the parking bays are 'end on', you really have to look out for people reversing out into the oncoming traffic. The local taxis are not always as clean or modern as those in Dubai, but they are significantly cheaper and fairly easy to flag down in the built-up residential areas. The main companies are Delta Taxi (06 559 8598) and Emirates Taxi (06 539 6666). One problem you may well encounter is that your driver has been in Sharjah for less time than you have, and therefore will have no idea where he's going.

## Safety & Annoyances

Crime is not common. Downtown is a bit of a concrete jungle so not ideal for families, but out of town is quieter. Sharjah is catching up with the construction boom, so you may experience noise and disruption.

**153**

Map p.7
Area ®️ p.123

# Trade Centre

The strip between Trade Centre Roundabout and Interchange One is home to some of Dubai's biggest, brightest and boldest towers, both residential and commercial, plus some of the most impressive hotels in town. Being so close to all the action it's a popular area, and rents are high as a result. This part of Sheikh Zayed Road has often been compared to Hong Kong because of its architecturally splendid skyscrapers.

**Best Points**
The proximity to so many entertainment venues is a definite plus point as is the easy access to all of Dubai. There is even the possibility of a sea view if you're high enough and facing the right direction.

## Accommodation

It's pretty much all apartments in a mix of styles and luxury levels, but all are on the expensive side. Most should have some sort of leisure facilities in the building. Rents can be Dhs.90,000 for a one bedroom and Dhs.170,000 for a three bedroom.

## Shopping & Amenities

While there are no huge malls as such in the immediate vicinity (the nearest are probably Deira City Centre or Mercato on Jumeira Road) there are two decent shopping centres: the Crowne Plaza 'Holiday Centre', with a few clothes shops, an optician, pharmacy, and a fairly big Choithram supermarket; and the Boulevard at Emirates Towers, with a selection of designer clothes outlets, jewellery and perfume shops. There's also an optician, a nail bar, a men's spa and a cigar shop.

**Worst Points**
There is always traffic and lots of hustle and bustle, so it's not really a place to retreat.

Otherwise there are plenty of smaller shops catering to all your everyday needs. Many of the towers have grocery or convenience stores on the ground floor, and there are supermarkets such as Lifco for weekly shops. Spinneys on Trade Centre Road or in Mazaya Centre and Safestway supermarket (which stocks US brands) aren't a million miles away. There's an MMI liquor store behind Pizza Hut and plenty of banks and ATMs including NBD on both sides, HSBC, Mashreqbank and a Thomas Cook money exchange. There's a machine to pay police fines in the Boulevard at Emirates Towers. The hotels have spas, gyms and leisure facilities (although they don't come cheap), and many residential and office towers will have some sort of fitness facilities.

**Defence Roundabout**
You'll often hear Sheikh Zayed Road's Interchange One referred to as Defence Roundabout, as the army HQ was previously situated nearby. A planned overhaul of this busy junction includes bridges, flyovers, and a new name – Burj Dubai Interchange – although the old Defence title will no doubt live on for many years.

The nearest post office is on Al Wasl Road, but Mail Box in the lobby of Al Durrah Tower offers a range of postal services and PO boxes, and you can rent a PO box at the Emarat garage on Al Safa Street. The new Satwa Park has sports facilities and a bit of greenery and Safa Park isn't too far away.

For car care, just down Al Safa Street there's a Grand Lube for all your automotive lubrication needs, plus repairs, tyres, and a car wash. Emarat, right next door, also has a car wash (reputedly the best in Dubai) and offers oil changes.

## Entertainment & Leisure

With a high concentration of hotels and independent restaurants, the options are almost endless. Dining wise, at one end of the scale (and the street) you've got the five-star finery of the Fairmont while at the other you'll find a little taste of England in the shape of 'The Chippy.'

Some of Dubai's favourite bars, restaurants and clubs are along this strip, including Spectrum on One in the Fairmont, Teatro and Long's Bar in the Towers Rotana and Trader Vic's and Zinc in the Crowne Plaza. The Loft, run by the same people who run Lotus One, is a nightclub next to Fibber McGee's.

Arabica and Zyara are good cafes for local food and shisha and Saj Express is good for cheap Arabic food. French Connection has good food, tea, coffee and bakery products, plus free wireless web access if you're eating there. Shakespeare & Co is a favourite thanks to its unique bohemian decor and interesting outside space. There are also bowling lanes and a pool hall just by Interchange 1 on the Satwa side.

### Healthcare

Al Zahra Medical Centre in Al Safa Tower has a number of departments including family medicine and dentistry. The nearest emergency care is either Rashid or Iranian hospital or the private Neuro Spinal Hospital. The new Al Bada'a Clinic (government) is behind Chelsea Tower. The Doha Pharmacy near 21st Century Tower is open 24 hours and there are quite a few other pharmacies dotted around. For information on hospitals, see p.182.

### Education

There are no international schools in the area, but several schools and nurseries can be found nearby in Satwa and Jumeira. For more information on schools see p.202.

**Travelling Times**
*Airport – 10 mins*
*Media City – 20 mins*

### Traffic & Parking

Parking is not bad if you have a card to access your building's car park, otherwise it's either find a sandy spot between the towers (these are disappearing as more buildings go up) or pay for metered parking on the street. Traffic is a problem in this area, as the E11 Sheikh Zayed Road is a main thoroughfare linking Sharjah and 'old' Dubai with Jebel Ali, and Media and Internet Cities. During rush hour the traffic is crawling, towards Jebel Ali in the morning, and towards Sharjah in the evening. The two interchanges (Trade Centre Roundabout and Defence Roundabout) are busy too, especially the latter which is being upgraded. If you're on one side of Sheikh Zayed Road, it could take about 20 minutes to drive to the building directly opposite. Traffic is even worse if there's a major event or exhibition (such as Gitex) going on at the Trade Centre.

### Safety & Annoyances

There are pavements but watch out for speeding drivers on the service roads. The only way to cross Sheikh Zayed Road on foot is via the bridge linking the Trade Centre with the Fairmont, or the pedestrian underpass further down near the Crowne Plaza. Living here can be a bit noisy if you're on one of the lower floors facing the road. Trucks are not allowed on Sheikh Zayed Road so there's no thundering lorries at all hours.

Sheikh Zayed Road

155

*Map p.6*

# Umm Suqeim

*Area* **S** *p.123*

This is a desirable area mainly because it is close to the beach and all the amenities you could wish for, while still remaining relatively peaceful. Plus it is slightly cheaper than neighbouring Jumeira (only just). There are no high-rises either (not counting the Burj Al Arab hotel) and Umm Suqeim is within easy reach of the major road networks, and midway between the old centre of Dubai in Deira and the new Dubai emerging further along the coast towards the marina. This is an ever popular choice for expats with kids but the rents are on the steep side.

**Best Points**

*Easy access to the beach, shopping, entertainment facilities and plenty of nice big villas – perfect for families.*

## Accommodation

Villas, villas, villas. Ranging from traditional, old single-storey dwellings and smart multi-bedroom villas to palatial mansions. If you're extremely lucky you may hear about an old (perhaps run-down) villa going for Dhs.120,000, but for this price you can expect to have to pay for any maintenance and repairs. In fact, you hear stories of people spending a fair amount to make their cheap villa more liveable, only for the owner to then up the rent once they see how nice it is. For a detached four or five-bedroom villa, you'll be paying at least Dhs.250,000.

**Worst Points**

*The rents are high and the traffic on Beach Road can be bad at rush hour, but apart from that there is little else to criticise about the area.*

## Shopping & Amenities

The modern but traditional Souk Madinat Jumeirah is on the Umm Suqeim-Al Sufouh border and makes for a nice shopping trip. There's a well-stocked Choithram supermarket (04 348 1864) on Al Wasl Road, with a dry cleaners, a good little florist, and a shop that sells CDS, DVDs, and videos. You can also rent videos from here (but not DVDs). Outside there's an HSBC ATM, and Al Faisal Pharmacy (04 348 5102) next door, open 07:30–24:00 seven days.

Showcase Antiques (348 8797) opposite the Dubai Municipality building on Jumeira Road (known as Beach Road) has a big selection of furniture, decorative items, old doors and chests, and ancient weapons. Kids' clothes shop Stitches (04 348 6110) on Beach Road does school uniforms and there are various grocery stores, pharmacies, laundries, tailor's shops and Mercato Mall (p.462).

Spinneys Centre is also nearby (p.472), and the enormous Mall of the Emirates (p.460) is just across Interchange 4 on Sheikh Zayed Road.

There are long stretches of golden sandy beach open to the public – the section immediately north of the Jumeirah Beach Hotel is the nicest, and busiest as a result. There are new lifeguard centres being constructed at intervals along the beach. Walking and jogging around the residential areas is popular as they are pretty quiet, but the best place has to be the beach. There are also occasional areas of sand and scrub for dog walking, and one or two have goal posts for a kick-around. Umm Suqeim Park on the seafront is a pleasant oasis of green with a kids' playground, picnic areas, benches, a cafe, and toilets. Saturday to Wednesday it's open between 08:00 and 23:00, but only to ladies and children. On Thursday, Friday and holidays it is open 08:00 to 23:30 for families only (no men on their own).

Umm Suqeim Library is primarily an IT centre with plenty of smart new PCs with internet access costing Dhs.3 per hour. You can also study for the International Computer Driving Licence (ICDL) here.

## Entertainment & Leisure

With the Burj Al Arab, Jumeirah Beach Hotel, and Madinat Jumeirah all on the doorstep, the entertainment and dining options are plentiful. At the opposite end of the spectrum, but no less enjoyable, there are places such as the Buqtair 'restaurant', a Portakabin opposite the fishing harbour in Umm Suqeim 1. The guys here do a mean fish curry made with the morning's catch. The Chalet Restaurant on Beach Road is great

**156**

for traditional Arabic food and juices. The nearest cinema is at Mercato, and the Wild Wadi water park is next to the Jumeirah Beach Hotel.

### Healthcare

The nearest hospital with a 24 hour emergency room is the private Neuro Spinal Hospital opposite Jumeirah Beach Park in Jumeira 2. For general medical care there is The Umm Suqeim Clinic (government) as well as many specialists and dentists along Beach Road including Advanced Chiropractic & Massage Clinic (04 348 8262) and the Euro American – Cosmetic Surgery and Telesurge Center (04 348 5575). For more information on hospitals, see p.182.

### Education

The biggest secondary school is Emirates International School, but there are lots of other schools in nearby Jumeira. There are plenty of nurseries including Emirates British Nursery, Alphabet Street Nursery, British Curriculum Children's Nursery and Le Petit Poucet (a French nursery, 04 348 4451). For more information on schools, see p.202.

**Travelling Times**
*Airport – 25 mins*
*Media City – 5 mins*
*Trade Centre – 15 mins*

### Traffic & Parking

During rush hour and the school-run, Beach Road up to Media City is pretty busy, as is Al Wasl Road, but it does flow. Parking is fine off the main roads, but tricky now on Beach Road after it was widened by one lane each way.

### Safety & Annoyances

Umm Suqeim is generally pretty safe and secure, and a great area for families, but there are the occasional instances of petty burglary so keep doors locked. Beach Road can be noisy and busy.

*Umm Suqeim housing*

*Burj Al Arab*

### Start Afresh

*Prices for furniture and appliances in Dubai are pretty reasonable so it may make sense to furnish your new home with new items (see Home Furnishings, p.432). There's also a good second-hand market thanks to the transient nature of expat life in Dubai (see Second Hand Items, p.444). When, and if, the time comes when you want to return home, you'll most certainly be shipping a packed container.*

# Moving Services

When hiring from abroad, Dubai employers sometimes offer help (such as a shipping allowance or furniture allowance) but the city is also well served by relocation specialists. If you're planning to arrive with more than a suitcase, you'll need to send your belongings by air or by sea. Air freight is faster but more expensive. Sea freight takes longer but it's cheaper, and containers can hold a huge amount.

Some well known removal firms are in Dubai, and if you use a reputable company you'll probably have fewer worries about breakages and loss. Everything you ship will need to be checked by customs and you must be present to collect your goods – air freight at Cargo Village in Garhoud and sea freight at Jebel Ali Port. Be sure to have your own copy of the inventory so that you know exactly what is in each box. And be patient.

The process for sea freight is a little longer but some agencies will do the customs clearing for you, and arrange delivery to your home. In the hot summer months, you'll be glad of the reduced hassle.

Once your freight is ready for collection (you'll get a call or letter), go to the agent's office and pay the administration and handling charges. Keep these documents. The Bill of Lading number must be marked on all paperwork and entered into the customs computer system.

Then, go to Dubai Customs House, on Al Mina Road. The staff are helpful and the procedure is fairly straightforward, so ignore the touts outside. When the papers have been stamped and the Port Clearance received (there are fees at each stage) head down to Jebel Ali port. If you need a truck to transport the boxes, there's an area at the sea end of Kuwait Street or in Al Quoz where you can hire one. Jebel Ali is huge, so make sure you have the phone number of the warehouse and good directions; a day pass will be issued at the gate. At the warehouse, if the consignment has been stamped 'need to be inspected', load up and take it to the police inspection area by the main gate; it's up to the officer whether they'll need to be x-rayed or not. If there's any doubt about whether any of your DVDs, videos and books comply with UAE censorship laws, they'll be taken to the Department of Information and viewed. If they're passed you'll be

## Removal Companies

| | | |
|---|---|---|
| Ahmed Saleh Packing | 04 285 4000 | www.albannagroup.com |
| Allied Pickfords ▶ p.159 | 04 408 9555 | www.alliedpickfords.com |
| Blue Line | 06 562 5111 | na |
| Crown Relocations ▶ p.81 | 04 289 5152 | www.crownrelo.com |
| DASA International Movers | 04 334 4545 | www.dasadxb.com |
| Gulf Agency Company (GAC) ▶ p.161 | 04 881 8090 | www.gulfagencycompany.com |
| Interem (Freight Systems Co. Ltd) | 04 807 0583 | www.freightsystems.com |
| ISS Worldwide Movers | 04 303 8645 | www.iss-shipping.com |
| Movers Packaging | 04 267 0699 | na |
| Southeast Cargo Packagers | 04 359 9885 | www.secpacme.com |
| Writer Relocations ▶ p.121 | 04 340 8814 | www.writercorporation.com |

## Smooth Moves

* Get more than one quote - some companies will match lower quotes to get the job.
* Make sure that all items are covered by insurance.
* Make sure that you have a copy of the inventory and that each item is listed.
* Don't be shy about requesting packers to repack items if you are not satisfied.
* Take photos of the packing process, to use for evidence if you need to make a claim.
* Carry customs restricted goods (DVDs, videos or books) with you: it's easier to open a suitcase in an air-conditioned airport than empty a box outside in the sun.

# moving?

## relax.
### we carry
### the
# load. SM

### Door to door moving with Allied Pickfords

Allied Pickfords is one of the largest and most respected providers of moving services in the world, handling over 50,000 international moves every year.

We believe that nothing reduces stress more than trust, and each year thousands of families trust Allied Pickfords to move them. With over 800 offices in more than 40 countries, we're the specialists in international moving and have the ability to relocate you anywhere anytime. Move with Allied to Allied worldwide.

## Call us now on +971 4 408 9555
## www.alliedpickfords-uae.ae
## general@alliedpickfords.ae

Your Chance to Earn Airmiles for using Allied Pickfords

**ALLIED PICKFORDS**®
*The Careful Movers*™

notified when they are ready for collection, otherwise, they'll be destroyed. The release papers will be issued at the office where the inspection stamp was issued. If you need storage in Dubai call Sentinel Storage in Al Quoz on 04 340 6962.

## Relocation Companies

| | | |
|---|---|---|
| Allied Pickfords ▶ p.159 | 04 408 9555 | www.alliedpickfords.com |
| Crown Relocations ▶ p.81 | 04 289 5152 | www.crownrelo.com |
| Dailys Relocation | 04 343 7428 | www.dailys.ae |
| Enigma Relocation | 04 394 6710 | www.enigmadubai.com |
| Global Relocations | 04 352 3300 | www.globalrelocations.com |
| In Touch Relocations | 04 321 5701 | www.intouchdubai.com |
| Interem (Freight Systems Co. Ltd) | 04 807 0583 | www.freightsystems.com |
| SIRVA-Middle East | 04 338 3600 | www.sirva.com |
| Southeast Cargo Packagers | 04 359 9885 | www.secpacme.com |
| The Specialists ▶ p.115 | 04 332 4111 | www.dubaiuae.com |
| Writer Relocations ▶ p.121 | 04 340 8814 | www.writercorporation.com |

## Furnishing Accommodation

Other options **Second-Hand Items** p.444, **Home Furnishings & Accessories** p.432

**Create A Dream Home**
*New city, new house, new start – an interior designer can make your new abode look just like the one you've always pictured it in your mind. See p.432.*

Whether you're renting or you've bought somewhere, you'll need some furniture. Most properties, including rentals, are unfurnished, and don't even have basic white goods such as a cooker or fridge. Not all villas have fitted cupboards and wardrobes. Dubai is home to many furniture shops, ranging from Swedish simplicity at IKEA to rich Indian teak at Marina Gulf Trading. Alternatively, head to one of the carpentry workshops on Naif Road or in Satwa. For more information on where to buy beautiful furniture, see p.432.

### Second-Hand Furniture

The population of Dubai is still fairly transitory, and with so many arrivals and departures, there's a constant stream of second-hand items out there. There are a number of small shops, mainly in Karama, Naif and Satwa that sell second-hand furniture, but you might find even better bargains from scouring the supermarket noticeboards or online classifieds. Try www.dubizzle.com, www.expatwoman.com or www.websouq.com – people list their items for sale on these sites and it is quite surprising what you can pick up. Alternatively, keep your eyes peeled for signs advertising garage sales in your neighbourhood.

## Household Insurance

Crime and natural disasters are not a big concern for Dubai's residents, but insuring your household goods against theft or damage is still wise. See the table below for a list of reputable insurance companies. To create a policy, the insurance provider will need your home address, a list of household items and valuation, and invoices for anything worth more than Dhs.2,500. Cover usually includes theft, fire and storm damage. You can also insure personal items outside the home. Costs vary, but as a guideline you can expect to pay around Dhs.1,500 per 1.2sqm for building insurance, Dhs.250 for up to Dhs.60,000 worth of home contents and Dhs.850 for up to Dhs. 60,000 worth of personal possessions.

## Household Insurance

| | | |
|---|---|---|
| AXA Insurance ▶ p.229 | 800 4845 | www.axa-gulf.com |
| Greenshields Insurance ▶ p.181, 231 | 04 397 4464 | www.greenshield.co.ae |
| Millennium Insurance | 04 335 6552 | www.milleniuminsurancegroup.com |
| National General Insurance (Healthnet) | 02 667 8783 | www.ngi.ae |
| Oman Insurance | 04 262 4000 | www.tameen.ae |
| Royal & Sun Alliance Insurance | 04 334 4474 | www.royalsunalliance.com |

# GAC Dubai International Moving
## Quality, Reliability, Flexibility

Relocation in itself is a challenge. And we believe that you already have enough to do without worrying about your forthcoming move. That's why when it comes to moving your home or office, GAC treats each item with care and every move with pride.

With more than 30 years of experience in moving household goods in and out of the Middle East, GAC provides comprehensive, high quality door-to-door services for any relocation need. Moves are professionally planned, starting with a free initial survey and recommendations on the most efficient shipment mode. All necessary services, including professional export packing, custom built crating, forwarding and secure storage facilities, are also provided.

 **www.gacworld.com**

**Gulf Agency Company (Dubai) L.L.C**   P O Box 17401, Jebel Ali, Dubai, United Arab Emirates
Tel: + 971 4 881 8090   Fax: + 971 4 805 9342   Email: gacremov@emirates.net.ae

## Laundry Services

There are no self-service laundrettes, but laundries are everywhere. As well as dry cleaning and laundry, they all offer an ironing service. If you have specific instructions, make sure these are noted when you drop off your laundry – creases in trousers are standard, so if you don't want them pressed into your jeans, speak up. Compensation policies for lost or damaged items vary, but losses are rare, even in the places that look most disorganised. Large chains normally have a free pick-up and delivery service. The average laundry costs are reasonable. Expect to pay Dhs.8 for a shirt, Dhs.25 for a suit and Dhs.35 for a quilt.

| Laundry Services | | |
| --- | --- | --- |
| Black & White | Oud Metha | 04 337 5111 |
| Butler's | Al Garhoud | 04 282 0712 |
| | Emirates Hills | 04 366 3359 |
| | Jebel Ali Village | 04 884 6312 |
| | Trade Centre 1 | 04 332 8900 |
| | Umm Suqeim | 04 348 3186 |
| Champion Cleaners | Abu Hail | 04 265 4981 |
| | Al Garhoud | 04 282 8297 |
| | Al Rashidiya | 04 285 2822 |
| | Downtown Bur Dubai | 04 224 6403 |
| | Emirates Hills | 04 368 4890 |
| | Jebel Ali | 04 368 5564 |
| | Jumeira | 04 394 0986 |
| The Cleaners | Deira | 04 295 8367 |
| | Downtown Bur Dubai | 04 355 9958 |
| | Jumeira | 04 394 3058 |
| Dubai Laundry | Al Karama | 04 336 4158 |
| | Jumeira | 04 349 3510 |
| Snow White Laundry | Al Rashidiya | 04 289 4993 |
| | Al Satwa | 04 342 0626 |
| White Way | Mirdif | 04 272 4165 |

## Carpet Cleaners

Wall-to-wall carpets are rare in this part of the world, but many homes do sport loose rugs and carpets. When they're looking a bit grubby, the following companies can pay you a visit, give you a quote, and take the carpets away to be cleaned, returning them a couple of days later.

| Carpet Cleaners | | |
| --- | --- | --- |
| Modern Cleaning Methods | Al Rashidiya | 04 285 1668 |
| Royal Carpet Cleaning & Painting | Downtown Bur Dubai | 04 393 5038 |
| Spotless | Trade Centre 1 | 04 331 8827 |

## Domestic Help

Other options **Entry Visa** p.80

Domestic help is readily available in Dubai, whether full or part-time, and there are a number of options available, depending on your needs. Legally, a housemaid may only be employed by the individual who sponsors her, but in practice many maids take on cleaning or babysitting for other families; if you are caught you face a hefty fine but the law seems rarely to be enforced. If you are looking for someone part time, but want to stay within the law, see below for a list of domestic help agencies.

## Domestic Help Agencies

When your busy lifestyle leaves no time for those tiresome household chores, help is just a phone call away. Many companies in Dubai provide cleaners and maids on an hourly basis, and for around Dhs.20 to Dhs.30 per hour they'll take care of all your sweeping, mopping, dusting, washing, and ironing. Most companies stipulate a minimum number of

| Domestic Help Agencies | |
| --- | --- |
| Dialamaid | 04 398 0850 |
| Home Comfort Services | 04 272 2135 |
| Home Help | 04 355 5100 |
| Molly Maid | 04 398 8877 |
| Ready Maids | 04 339 5722 |
| Sky Maid Services | 04 332 4600 |

hours, usually two or three per visit. For an apartment, three hours a week should be enough, while bigger villas may need four or five hours worth of cleaning each week. If you're considering sponsoring your own maid full-time, see p.85.

# thirsty?

| Babysitting & Childcare | |
| --- | --- |
| Home Help | 04 355 5100 |
| Ready Maids | 04 339 5722 |
| Sky Maid Services | 04 332 4600 |

# Babysitting & Childcare

Childcare is the dilemma that faces all working parents. Options here are fairly limited, and there is no network of childminders. You could hire a full or part-time maid, if you can find someone who you are comfortable leaving the children with. Or another parent may be willing to take care of your child for a fee (while there are mums who do this in Dubai they don't advertise their services, so word-of-mouth is the way to go). The information board on www.expatwoman.com is a good place to start. Domestic help agencies also offer babysitting services. Ask around your neighbourhood to see if there is a maid who is available for evening babysitting, or try the nurseries – classroom assistants are often looking for extra work.

## Domestic Services

Having maintenance work done is often just a matter of a phone call to the landlord. Otherwise, plumbers, handymen and electricians are easy to find. Smaller, local firms often advertise by slapping stickers on your gate or door. Burooj 2000 operates across

| Domestic Services | | |
| --- | --- | --- |
| Al Salam Sanitary & Electrical | Al Qusais | 04 261 5977 |
| Berkeley | Various Locations | 04 339 3111 |
| Brightest Trading | Al Satwa | 04 331 0822 |
| Burooj 2000 | Mirdif | 04 288 7665 |
| Hassan Foulad Plumbing Works | Al Rashidiya | 04 285 9187 |
| Hitches & Glitches | Various Locations | 800 426 34 |
| Howdra | Various Locations | 04 285 4308 |
| Island King | Al Karama | 04 334 6555 |
| Speedy Home Repairs | Various locations | 050 298 8340 |
| Those Pool Guys | Al Quoz | 04 339 0418 |
| Treisha | Al Quoz | 04 347 6730 |

Dubai and does plumbing, painting and air-conditioner servicing. Howdra is also city wide and offers maid and ironing services along with heavier work. Hitches & Glitches operates in the Meadows, Springs and Emirates Hills areas and can provide 24 hour general maintenance on an annual contract. For garden maintenance, try a service company like Berkeley, which will maintain your garden for a monthly fee. Alternatively independent gardeners may knock on your door, and they usually charge around Dhs.250 per month, to water and tidy your garden every day. If you have a swimming pool, for around Dhs.300-500 per month you can get twice weekly visits to clean the pool and balance the chemicals. Try Those Pool Guys or Island King.

## Pets

*Pet Crimes*

*While rare, there have been reports of dogs being stolen, either to be sold to unscrupulous pet shops, or for dog fighting. Ensure your garden is secure and don't let your dog roam around on the street.*

The attitude towards pets in Dubai is mixed so it's sensible to keep your pet under control. Pets are prohibited from parks and beaches, so there aren't many places where you can walk your dog, other than the streets in your area. While uncommon, there are a number incidents of animal abuse, which can be reported to the Municipality (04 289 1114). Dubai has several pet shops and they vary enormously in quality. Smaller outlets are usually not for the faint-hearted.

### Cats & Dogs

Dubai has a significant problem with strays. Feline Friends (050 451 0058) and K9 Friends (04 347 4611) are hard-working animal charities that take in as many as they can, and they are always on the lookout for help (see p.167).

You should inoculate your pet annually against rabies, and register it with the municipality (04 289 1114), which will provide plastic neck tags. If the municipality picks up an animal without a tag, it is treated as a stray. You can have your pet microchipped, but with no national register the plastic tag is your best bet. The municipality's clampdown on strays has been successful and the UAE is now considered to be free from rabies (so pets can travel to the UK under the 'Pet Passport' scheme and are subject to a reduced quarantine in Australia and New Zealand).

# Dubai Kennels & Cattery

# Just come 'n meet us
## (owners welcome too.)

Global Relocations & Transit Care
Boarding & Daycare
Collection & Delivery
dogs, cats, birds, rabbits . . .
and other creatures, too . . . since 1983

04 285 1646 • info@dkc.ae • www.dkc.ae

DKC is a member of AATA, IPATA and ABKA

**Sleek Salukis**

*The saluki is the breed most commonly associated with the region; they are used in traditional forms of hunting. The Arabian Saluki Center (www.arabian saluki.ae) can provide information of all aspects of the care of these animals. Many 'desert dogs' descend from the Saluki. If you'd like to adopt your own desert dog, contact K9 Friends (www.k9friends.com).*

Most areas have street cats, which tend to be harmless and keep a lid on rodent problems. The municipality is currently working on trapping the cats and sterilising them before re-releasing them – it's the first authority in the region to do so. Feline Friends is active in trapping and sterilising street cats, and should be contacted if your area is overrun. Sterilised street cats usually have part of their ear removed to distinguish them from unsterilised cats.

Whether you live in a villa or an apartment you should check with your landlord what the pet policy is before you move in. When walking your dog, keep it on a short leash, as many workers and children are frightened of them.

## Birds & Fish

Birds are popular and are sold in all the pet shops. A wide variety of species is available, from budgies to macaws. For those interested in keeping fish, the pet shops of Dubai have a huge selection, and all the equipment you will need.

## Pet Shops

The standard of pet shops in Dubai ranges from the passable to the awful. Pet lovers are better off avoiding the smaller ones, predominantly in Satwa, as they tend to pay little regard to the health or welfare of the animals. There are laws governing pet shops but the maximum penalty for those contravening them is the closure of the shop for a day – hardly a deterrent. It's illegal for puppies to be offered for sale before they are 16 weeks old but in many cases the papers have been altered and the animal is younger; the origin of the animals is also altered and many come from Eastern European 'puppy farms' where conditions are inhumane. A much better option is to get your pet from K9 Friends or Feline Friends instead. All their animals have been sterilised and inoculated.

### Veterinary Clinics

| | | |
|---|---|---|
| Al Barsha Veterinary Clinic | Al Barsha | 04 340 8601 |
| Al Safa Veterinary Clinic | Umm Suqeim | 04 348 3799 |
| Al Zubair Animal Care | Sharjah | 06 743 5988 |
| Animal Care Centre Sharjah | Sharjah | 06 543 6280 |
| Deira Veterinary Clinic | Deira | 04 258 1881 |
| Energetic Panacea | Jumeira | 04 344 7812 |
| European Veterinary Center | Trade Centre 2 | 04 343 9591 |
| Jumeirah Veterinary Clinic | Jumeira | 04 394 2276 |
| Modern Veterinary Clinic | Umm Suqeim | 04 395 3131 |
| Veterinary Hospital | Jumeira | 04 344 2498 |

**Pet Watch**

*PetWatch Dubai is an online community for promoting responsible pet ownership in the UAE. Run by volunteers and designed to ease the burden on K9 Friends and Feline Friends, they can help answer your questions, connect you with others and also act as a reference point for contacts and advice. For more information or to join the pet network, check out their website: www.petwatchweb.com*

## Vets & Kennels

Standards of care at Dubai's veterinary clinics are reasonably high. Prices do not vary dramatically, but the Deira Veterinary Clinic and Al Barsha Veterinary Clinic are a little cheaper than the rest. Dubai Municipality has a veterinary services department, which treats and vaccinates animals and issues identity tags. It is located next to Mushrif Park. Kennels are generally of a good standard, although spaces are limited during peak times (summer and Christmas). An alternative is to use an at-home pet-sitting service – someone will come into your house at least once a day to feed and exercise your pet for a reasonable fee (for a bit extra they might even water your plants).

## Bringing Your Pet To Dubai

Imported dogs and cats must be older than 120 days – this ensures that they are old enough to have had rabies vaccinations. Pets flying into Dubai must travel as cargo – animals are no longer permitted to travel as excess baggage.

**Feline Friends (050 451 0058) and K9 Friends (04 347 4611)**

Feline Friends is a non-profit organisation, aiming to improve the lives of cats by rescuing and rehoming stray cats and kittens. It has a 24 hour telephone answering service as well as a comprehensive website, www.felinefriendsuae.com. K9 Friends helps to rehome stray and injured dogs, many of which are abandoned family pets looking for a second chance. See www.k9friends.com for more information.

# K9 FRIENDS

Associated member of

K9 Friends is a voluntary organisation that rescues and rehomes stray and abandoned dogs here in the UAE. Our finances are solely dependent on fund raising and donations kindly given by the general public.

**If you can:-**
* Give a dog a home
* Foster a dog until a permanent home can be found for it.
* Help with fund raising and marketing or organising events.
* Give some of your time to help with our rescue dogs.
* Sponsor a kennel or a dog on an annual basis to help pay expenses.

Please give us a call on **04 347 4611** email us at **k9@emirates.net.ae** **www.K9friends.com**

**Your help would be greatly appreciated**

Proud Supporters of K9 Friends

## Pets Boarding/Sitting

| | | |
|---|---|---|
| Al Zubair Animal Care | 06 743 5988 | Boarding |
| Creature Comforts | 050 695 9480 | Petsitting |
| The Doghouse, | 04 347 1807 | Boarding |
| Dubai Kennels & Cattery (DKC) ▶ p.165 | 04 285 1646 | Boarding |
| Pet Partner | 050 774 2239 | Petsitting |
| Petland Resort | 04 347 5022 | Boarding |
| Pets At Home | 04 331 2186 | Petsitting |

Dubai Kennels & Cattery (04 285 1646), The Doghouse (04 347 1807) and Katie O' Sullivan (050 477 8759) are pet relocation specialists that can help.

Otherwise, you need an import permit from the Ministry of Environment and Water, Vet Quarantine Section (04 222 8161). They will need to see the owner's passport and residence visa (or employment offer letter), the pet's vaccination certificate (showing rabies vaccination) and a government-issued health certificate. You also need proof that the animal has been microchipped. After receiving the import permit, you can book the flight. You must also present a certificate of good health to authorities on arrival. Animals will be taken to the Cargo Village for collection.

### Taking Your Pet Home

The process can be quite lengthy, taking a minimum of seven months for the UK. All countries require a health certificate – this is issued by the Ministry of Environment and Water, Vet Section and should be taken to the government vet at Cargo Village not more than seven days before departure. For this you will need the animal's vaccination card showing a valid rabies inoculation (some countries require additional vaccinations or blood tests).

## Pets Grooming/Training

| | | |
|---|---|---|
| Al Safa Veterinary Clinic | 04 348 3799 | na |
| Creature Comforts | 050 695 9480 | Grooming |
| Doghouse, The | 04 347 1807 | Grooming |
| Duncan Robertson | 04 348 3799 | Training |
| Gail Gordon | 04 349 9879 | Grooming |
| Paws Canine Training Centre | 050 784 5350 | Training |
| Petland Resort | 04 347 5022 | Grooming |
| Shampooch Mobile Pet Grooming | 04 344 9868 | Grooming |

These must have been done not less than 30 days before departure and no later than the expiry date set out by the manufacturer.

You will also need an airline-approved travel box (available through Dubai Kennels & Cattery and The Doghouse). Most airlines allow animals to travel either as accompanied baggage or cargo, but check with the airline beforehand.

*Canine friends*

# Electricity & Water

**Apartments Are Cool...**
You can expect a higher
A/C bill in a villa – not
only is it probably bigger
than your average
apartment, but many
apartment buildings
include air-conditioning
costs in the rent.

Dubai Electricity and Water Authority (DEWA) is the sole provider of water, electricity and sewerage. When you sign up for connection to your new home you will need to pay a deposit (Dhs.2,000 for a villa and Dhs.1,000 for an apartment), which is fully refundable when you leave the property. DEWA charges a standard rate per unit, currently 20 fils per unit for electricity, 3 fils per unit for water and 0.5 fils per unit for sewerage. Your DEWA bill also includes the municipality housing tax, which is 5% of the rental value of the property and covers refuse collection and utilities maintenance. Your DEWA bill will fluctuate depending on the time of year – the need for round the clock air conditioning in summer equals a high bill. If you have a garden to water it will probably need doing twice a day in summer. It might be possible to have a borehole installed in your garden, meaning you have access to free groundwater. Installation will set you back around Dhs.1,000. Once it's done you should notice a marked decrease in your DEWA bill, although there is a chance of the borehole becoming brackish after a few years.

## Electricity
The electricity supply in Dubai is 220/240 volts and 50 cycles and the socket type is the same as the three-pin British system. Many appliances are sold with two pin plugs which can either be changed or used with an adaptor which are widely available and can be bought for a couple of dirhams from Carrefour.

### Water

**Hot Water**
The water in your cold
taps can get so hot in
summer that you can
turn off your water
heaters. You know
winter's coming when
you have to turn the
water heater on again.

Tap water is desalinated sea water and is perfectly safe to drink although most people choose mineral water, mainly because it tastes better. Bottled water is cheaper than in your home country, especially the locally produced brands.

| Water Suppliers | |
|---|---|
| Al Madina Drinking Water Supply | 04 267 0710 |
| Al Rawi Pure Drinking Water | 04 347 7112 |
| Culligan International | 800 4945 |
| Desert Springs | 800 6650 |
| Falcon Spring Drinking Water | 04 396 6072 |
| Nestle Pure Water | 800 4404 |
| Oasis Drinking Water | 884 5656 |

Bottled water, both local and imported, is served in hotels and restaurants. Most people end up buying a water cooler or pump and getting the five-gallon bottles of purified water to drink at home. You usually pay a Dhs.30 deposit for each bottle, and around Dhs.7 for a refill.

# Gas

There are still no gas mains in Dubai, even though gas is the most popular method for cooking. Individual gas canisters need to be purchased and attached to the cookers. There are a number of gas suppliers. They can also connect up the supply, but let them know so that they can bring the pipes and regulators needed. Gas bottles come in three sizes: most houses use the medium size, the small are better in apartments and the large are really only for industrial use – they are enormous. The canisters initially cost around Dhs.300 and refills are usually Dhs.60 (keep your receipt so that you can get your deposit back). There is usually a gas van around your area at all times so chances are that if you run out of gas in the middle of cooking your chips, one call to your local gas man and he can be with you in less than 20 minutes.

| Gas Suppliers | |
|---|---|
| Honest Hands Gas | 04 285 6586 |
| Lahej Gas Distribution LLC | 04 337 6686 |
| New City Gas Distributors | 04 351 8282 |
| Oasis Gas Suppliers | 04 396 1812 |
| Salam Gas | 04 344 8823 |
| Union Gas Company | 04 266 1479 |

**169**

## Sewerage

Much of Dubai now has mains sewers but there are areas where houses are still serviced by septic tanks. These are regularly emptied by municipality contractors, but should you have a problem, contact your landlord or local municipality office. All sewage has to be treated, hence the charges on the DEWA bill even for houses not on the main sewer network.

## Rubbish Disposal and Recycling

Dubai's per capita domestic waste rate is extremely high, with some estimates saying that each household generates over 1,000kg of rubbish per year. Fortunately, rubbish disposal is efficient, with municipality trucks driving around each area and emptying skips daily. Just empty your household bins into the skips (there is usually one on every street). If you don't have a skip on your street, contact the municipality on 04 206 4234 to request one. Recycling efforts are poor but slowly improving. There are over 40 recycling points where you can dump your glass bottles, aluminium cans and paper. Most of these are in schools and shopping centres (such as at Spinneys in Emirates Hills), but there's also one in Deira (in the carpark near Samsung) and one at Knowledge Village. Emaar also offers residents in their developments an excellent recycling collection service called Earth Watch (050 347 4576, earthwatch@emaar.ae).

## Telephone

*Don't Forget The Prefix*
*You have to dial the 050 for Etisalat mobile numbers even if you're dialling from one yourself. That's because mobile numbers from du begin with 055. Prefixes are as follows: 04 – Dubai, 02 – Abu Dhabi, 03 – Al Ain, 06 – Sharjah, 050 – Etisalat mobile, 055 – du mobile*

Telecoms in the UAE witnessed competition for the first time, with the entry of second operator, du. du launched mobile services in Feb 2007, followed by Call Select, which allows users to save on calls made from existing Etisalat landlines. Emaar properties currently have their internet, telephone and TV needs met by du (who replaced Dubai Internet City Telecom, the previous provider of these services). Mobile phone users can now choose between du and Etisalat, who both offer monthly or pay-as-you-go packages. Plans are in the pipeline for broadband and pay TV services. To get info on all the procedures related to phones and the internet, refer to the *Dubai Red-Tape Explorer*.

### Landline Phones

du launched a landline service in which you can tailor the features to suit your own personal needs. du aims to create a personal flexibility for customers and although the service is still expanding these initiatives are proving popular. Customers have the choice of 10 existing landline features and once subscribed you are free to cancel you subscription to these whenever you like. Some of the options include three-way call conferencing, incoming call barring and caller ID. Check the du website at

### Area Codes & Useful Numbers

| Area or Description | Code or Number |
|---|---|
| Abu Dhabi | 02 |
| Ajman | 06 |
| Al Ain | 03 |
| Directory Enquiries (du) | 199 |
| Directory Enquiries (Etisalat) | 181 |
| du Contact Centre (from du phones) ▶ p.171 | 155 |
| du Contact Centre (other phones) ▶ p.171 | 04 369 9988 |
| Dubai | 04 |
| Etisalat Contact Centre | 101 |
| Etisalat Information | 144 |
| Fault Reports (Etisalat) | 171 |
| Fujairah | 09 |
| Hatta | 04 |
| Jebel Ali | 04 |
| Mobile Telephones (du) | 055 |
| Mobile Telephones (Etisalat) | 050 |
| Operator | 100 |
| Ras al Khaimah | 07 |
| Sharjah | 06 |
| Speaking Clock | 140 |
| UAE Country Code | 971 |
| Umm Al Quwain | 06 |

# add life to business

with our dedicated business telecommunications division

At du, we know that being a CEO and a great daddy are both full time jobs. That's why we've introduced du business – a telecommunications division dedicated to providing your company tailor-made solutions that take care of the business side of your life.

Dedicated account managers | Fair and transparent billing | Business help desk | Tailored business solutions

### Cheap Calls Not Allowed

*Sites like Skype.com that allow you to make cheap international calls via the internet have been blocked by the TRA (the local telecoms regulator). This has provoked anger, since the proxy is only supposed to block sites that offend the religious, political, moral or cultural values of the UAE, rather than ones that hurt the operators' profits. UK supermarket Tesco has an internet phone service that has so far evaded censure. Go to www.tesco.com/internetphone for more.*

### Personal Delivery

*For a fee, you can have post collected from your PO box and delivered (in a sealed satchel) to your home or office. There is also a collection service that includes the price of stamps. See www.emiratespost.com.*

www.du.ae for regular special offers and updates on packages and promotions. To install a landline with Etisalat you must apply directly with a completed application form, a copy of your passport and residence visa, a no objection letter from your sponsor, and Dhs.245 (inclusive of first quarterly rental). Taking the number of the landline closest to your house can help pinpoint your location. Telephone calls between landlines in Dubai are free, but there is a nominal charge for calls to Jebel Ali. Depending on the time of day, calls to elsewhere in the UAE cost between Dhs.0.12 and Dhs.0.24 per minute; calls to mobiles cost between Dhs.0.18 and Dhs.0.24. Off-peak timings are 14:00 to 16:00 and 19:00 to 07:00, Saturday to Wednesday; and all weekend from 14:00 on Thursday to 07:00 on Saturday. Off-peak rates are applicable all day on public holidays. Off-peak timings for mobile calls are 14:00 to 16:00 and midnight to 07:00 every day. The tariffs for international calls vary from country to country but there is some variation in peak timings, depending on country.

| Telecomms Companies | | | |
| --- | --- | --- | --- |
| du ▶ p.74 | 04 369 9988 | www.du.ae | |
| Etisalat | 101 | www.etisalat.ae | |

## Emaar & Nakheel

du provides services to many Emaar and Nakheel properties, both business and residential (eg Dubai Marina, Arabian Ranches, Emirates Hills, the Greens/Springs/Lakes, and Jumeirah Islands). Currently, villas and apartments are equipped with multiple sockets for telephone, internet and TV signals. To apply, you will need a copy of your passport and tenancy agreement. The fees include a one-off installation charge (Dhs.200) plus line rental of around Dhs.15 per month. Call charges are comparable with Etisalat's. In addition, internet packages are available from 64 kbps to up to 2mbps. As it's not a dial-up connection you don't need a modem – instead you need an Ethernet (network) card – this is built into most computers. And because it's not dial-up, the connection is always on. The du internet service doesn't fall under the Etisalat proxy, so you may have access to some banned sites, but this is constantly under review. The du offices can be contacted on 04 390 5555. Keep an eye on www.du.ae for updates on all new services and information.

# Internet

Other options **Websites** p.67, **Internet Cafes** p.572

If you live in an Emaar property, your internet is currently provided by du (www.du.ae). It offers a range of 'always on' internet packages to its Emaar residents, ranging from 64kbps (Dhs.75 per month) to 2mbps (Dhs.349 per month). There is a Dhs.200 installation fee. It is expected that internet services from du will be offered to other areas shortly – check www.du.ae for details. Emirates Internet & Media (www.eim.ae, 800 6100), a subsidiary of Etisalat, is the other provider in Dubai. The internet is accessible from any standard Etisalat phone line using a 56k modem. You can also get an ISDN line (128 kbps) or an ASDL line (256-512 kbps). To get connected you will need a landline, a copy of your passport and residence visa, and a completed application. The initial charge is Dhs.100 for dialup, Dhs.200 for ISDN (plus Dhs.415 for modem) and Dhs.200 for ADSL (plus Dhs.275 for modem). Rental charges are typically Dhs.20 per month, plus an hourly rate (Dhs.1.80 peak, Dhs.1 off-peak). For more information, see the *Dubai Red-Tape Explorer*.

## Dial & Surf

This facility allows you to surf without subscribing to the Etisalat internet service. All that's needed is a computer with a modem and a regular phone (or ISDN) line – no account number or password is required. In theory, you then simply dial 500 5555 to gain access. However, in practice it may not be quite so straightforward, since there are

# dubizzle.com
## Buy Sell Find Anything

(you need me)

100's of fresh properties, classifieds, and jobs listed every day.
If you're not on **dubizzle.com**, you're the only one.

different set-ups depending on your software. If you have difficulties, contact the helpdesk (800 5244). The charge of 12 fils per minute is made for the connection and billed to the telephone line from which the call is made.

## Bill Payment

Bills are mailed monthly and are itemised. du bills can be paid at the sales office in Media City, at one of the drop boxes dotted around Emaar developments, or via bank transfer or credit card. The bill can be checked online (www.telecom.dic.ae). You have 30 days from the date of the invoice to settle the bill. Etisalat bills can be paid online (www.e4me.ae for phone bills, www.eim.ae for internet bills), by phone banking, at Etisalat offices or at one of the payment machines in most shopping centres. You have 10 days to settle your landline bill, and 45 days to settle your mobile bill.

### Bill Enquiry Service

It is possible to get the current amount due on your Etisalat phone bill - just dial 142 from the phone in question and you will be given the balance.

**Sending Gifts Home** ◄ ## Post & Courier Services

*If you would rather not chance the post, Gift Express provides a selection of gifts that can be sent to most countries. (www.giftexpress.ae)*

There is currently no postal delivery service to home addresses, although there are plans for Dubai's streets to be named so a home delivery system can be introduced. For the time being, everyone has their mail delivered to a PO box. Mail is first delivered to the Central Post Office and then distributed to clusters of PO boxes in various areas. To get your own, fill in the application form and pay the annual fee (Dhs.150); you will be given a set of keys (Dhs.10 per key) to access your own box. Many people have mail delivered to their company's PO box.

Empost will send you notification by email when you receive registered mail or parcels in your PO box. For an extra Dhs.9 you can have the item delivered to your door. However, you might have to pay customs charges on international packages. Letters and packages do occasionally go missing and, if the item has not been registered, there's little that you can do apart from wait – some turn up months after they are expected. Empost offers a courier service for both local and international deliveries. Delivery times are guaranteed and packages can be tracked. Registered mail is a relatively inexpensive alternative, and can also be tracked via the reference number.

## Radio

The UAE has a number of commercial radio stations broadcasting in a range of languages, including Arabic, English, French, Hindi, Malayalam and Urdu. Daily schedules can be found in the local newspapers.

There are four English language music stations, all operating 24 hours a day. Dubai 92 (92.0FM), Channel 4 (104.8 FM) and Emirates Radio 1 (99.3FM & 100.5FM) all play a mixture of old and new popular music, and have regular news broadcasts. If you're more into ELO than Eminem, you might prefer Emirates Radio 2 (90.5FM & 98.5FM), which plays adult contemporary music mixed with news and talk shows.

Most shows are locally produced but there are some syndicated shows (Dubai 92 airs a number of dance music programmes at the weekend, featuring international DJs such as Roger Sanchez, Judge Jules, Carl Cox and Pete Tong).

Dubai Eye (103.8FM) is Dubai's first major talk radio station, with a good mix of news, talk, and sport. There are some interesting shows with topics relevant to residents of Dubai. QBS Dubai (97.5FM & 102.6FM) focuses on radio plays and jazz music.

Umm Al Quwain's Hum FM (106.2FM) broadcasts mainly in Hindi with a bit of English, and if you want to hear Arabic music, tune in to 93.9FM. You can also listen to the BBC World Service in English between 09:00 and 18:00 on 87.9FM.

# CROSS
# BORDERS
# WITHOUT
# BARRIERS.

**Whether you're connecting with family and friends or sending goods for business, you'll find all the help you need to cross borders without barriers at any of our UAE offices.**

**Toll free 800 DHL**

**Missed the Start?** ◄
*It's so annoying when
you turn on the TV only
to find that the movie
you've been dying to
see for ages started
half an hour ago. The
'Super Movies' channel
shows recent films that
start one hour later on
'Super Movies + 1'.*

# Television

The local television channels in Dubai generally leave a little to be desired. There have however been developments and the revamped One TV (formerly Ch 33) now shows a respectable line up of British and American programmes. The MBC channels also have a good selection. You can catch some classic films from the '80s and '90s on MBC2, various children's programmes such as the Tweenies, Bob the Builder, Barney and Tom and Jerry on MBC3, and comedies, dramas, news and chat shows (such as Oprah, Charmed, Frasier, Friends, Dead Zone, CBS News and 60 Minutes) on MBC4.

Most Dubai residents subscribe to one of the satellite networks (see below). Look out for Entertainment Plus, a supplement published on Wednesday inside Gulf News. It provides a comprehensive listing of what's on for the next week. You'll also find TV listings in Time Out, Ahlan! and 7Days.

## Satellite TV & Radio

Do your homework before you choose a satellite provider – your choice will depend on what kind of TV you just can't live without. For example, Sky News is only available on Orbit and FirstNet, while MTV and VH1 are only available on Showtime. Popular British soaps Eastenders and Coronation Street are both available, but only on Orbit and Showtime respectively. FirstNet was always the choice for Premiership football fans, but Showtime bought the rights for the start of the 2007/08 season. It's possible to flick between every Premiership match as Showtime spreads coverage on Saturdays and weekday nights across its channels. Pictures and commentary are taken from English channels. FirstNet is good for reality show addicts (catch up with current episodes of American Idol, The Bachelor, For Love or Money and The Apprentice on the Star World channel). Showtime seems to be in the lead for popular American sitcoms, with the recent addition of Desperate Housewives and Lost to their schedules, but Brits might choose Orbit for BBC Prime and shows such as The Weakest Link, Strictly Come Dancing and Changing Rooms (it's also great for the kiddies' shows on CeeBeebies). Showtime is renowned for getting the best films sooner, although other providers also provide a variety of movie channels.

One new entrant in 2007 was City 7. It is the first UAE based, English language channel, and offers a mix of locally produced news and lifestyle shows and imported dramas and comedies. The news programmes feel a little like provincial news in the UK or US, and still tend to show an excessive reverence to the movements of UAE's rulers, but do have a local flavour that is unavailable elsewhere in English. It is available (normally for free) from all of the above satellite providers.

### Satellite Radio

Depending on your satellite provider, you may get some radio stations through your decoder. Various channels are available, including Virgin Radio from the UK and the BBC World Service. You can also get access to a variety of music channels – from country to pop. You get 10 Music Choice channels on Showtime, and 20 on Orbit. For more information on Dubai's local radio stations, see p.174.

| Satellite & Cable Providers | | |
| --- | --- | --- |
| Arabtec SIS | 04 286 8002 | www.sisuae.com |
| Bond Communications | 04 343 4499 | www.bondcommunications.com |
| Emirates Cable TV & Multimedia E-Vision | 800 5500 | www.emiratescatv.co.ae |
| Eurostar Group | 04 808 7777 | www.adduniverse.com |
| FirstNet | 03 766 1144 | www.adduniverse.com |
| Orbit | 04 405 9999 | www.orbit.net |
| Showtime | 04 367 7000 | www.showtimearabia.com |

*Traditional Arabian design*

# General Medical Care

The general standard of healthcare in the UAE is high, both in the public and private sectors. As in most countries, private healthcare is seen as preferable (English speaking, shorter waiting times and more comfortable inpatient facilities) and is likely to be mandatory under new UAE laws. So even though residents qualify for subsidised state care, you might want to consider health insurance. Emergency treatment in government hospitals is free, regardless of nationality or whether you have a health card. When you get your health card (see p.82) it will list a clinic or hospital to which you are assigned, although you're not obliged to use this one.

## Emergency Services

Rashid Hospital is the main hospital for medical emergencies and has a well-equipped accident and emergency (A&E) department. Dubai Hospital also has an emergency section. Al Wasl Hospital offers emergency services to women and children under the age of 12, and is especially recommended for maternity and paediatric emergencies, although they do not deal with trauma cases. The Iranian Hospital has a busy A&E. While finding a place to get emergency treatment is easy, getting there is more problematic as Dubai's paramedic services are under-developed, to say the least. Ambulance response times are variable but can be up to 30 minutes (compared with around four minutes in a large UK city like Birmingham).

## Government Healthcare

In Dubai, the Department of Health and Medical Services (www.dohms.gov.ae) runs the following hospitals: Dubai, Rashid, Al Baraha (aka Kuwaiti), Maktoum and Al Wasl. Dubai Hospital is renowned as one of the best medical centres in the Middle East, while Al Wasl is a specialised maternity and paediatric hospital. DOHMS also operates a number of outpatient clinics. The Iranian Hospital, while not funded by the UAE government, also provides subsidised healthcare.

## Private Healthcare

Dubai's various private hospitals and clinics have high standards. American Hospital (p.184), Welcare Hospital (p.186), and Al Zahra Private Hospital (p.184) are popular. But be aware, that if you don't have the money, the Hippocratic oath can go out of the window. Your best bet is to make sure that you have health insurance, but at the same time not all companies cover treatment in all of Dubai's private hospitals so always check with your insurance company before receiving treatment.

## Health Insurance

Following Abu Dhabi's ruling that all employers must provide health insurance for full-time employees and their dependents, it is expected that Dubai will follow suit. The new law is apparently being discussed but is not expected to be implemented until 2008 at the earliest. Your employer may already provide health insurance in addition to the healthcare available to those with a government health card. Levels of cover

**Sidebar:**

**Prevention Is Better Than Cure**
Well Woman and Well Man clinics are available at a number of clinics and hospitals including the Welcare and American Hospitals. In addition to Well Man and Well Woman services, Al Zahra Private Medical Centre also offers Well Child assessments.

**Screening Programmes**
Many hospitals and clinics in Dubai, including the American and Welcare Hospitals, have breast screening programmes and clinics where women can learn the proper method for self-examination. You could also learn how while enjoying a spot of pampering, with the therapists at Sensasia Spa (p.396) being trained to instruct women in self-screening.

**Healthcare City**
This new development is home to some of the world's most renowned health facilities, and will serve as a hub for treatment, prevention, education and research. See www.dhcc.ae.

### Health Insurance Companies

| | | |
|---|---|---|
| Alico Middle East | 06 556 2566 | www.alico.com |
| Alliance Insurance | 04 605 1111 | www.alliance-uae.com |
| Allianz Worldwide | 04 332 9929 | www.allianz.com |
| AXA Insurance ▶ p.229 | 800 4845 | www.axa-gulf.com |
| Greenshield Insurance ▶ p.181, 231 | 04 397 4464 | www.greenshield.co.ae |
| Lifecare International (BUPA) ▶ p.179 | 04 331 8688 | www.bupa.com |
| Mednet | 800 4882 | www.mednet-uae.com |
| National General Insurance | 04 222 2772 | www.ngi.ae |
| Nextcare | 04 286 9311 | www.nextcare.co.ae |

BUPA
international
Scheme Adviser UAE

LIFECARE
INTERNATIONAL

the  world  health  service

# Whether you're
## at **home** or **living**
## or **working abroad**...

. . you'll want to be sure that you and your
family are securely covered for medical treatment.

Wherever you are, you need to be confident
that you can get instant access to quality
health cover if you fall ill or become injured.

BUPA International is part of the global
BUPA network which looks after the health
of nearly 8 million members worldwide

- Nearly 35 years' experience
- 24 hour multi-lingual helpline open
  365 days a year
- Dedicated website for members
- 5,500 participating hospitals
  and clinics worldwide
- Cover throughout the world
- Direct settlement

LIFECARE INTERNATIONAL INSURANCE BROKERS
BUPA INTERNATIONAL SCHEME ADVISOR, U.A.E.
Tel: 04-3318688  Fax: 04-3318001  E-mail: info@lifecareinternational.com
P.O. Box: 71208, Dubai, U.A.E.

***Free Breast Tests***
*All women in Dubai, be they nationals, expats or visitors, have access to free breast cancer screening. Call 02 621 5525 for more information and to arrange a screening.*

vary depending on the policy – check what you're entitled to. Dental care and screening tests (such as for breast cancer) aren't usually provided as standard, and you may need to have been on the policy for a year before you can receive maternity cover.

## Pharmacies

Most pharmacies are open from around 09:00 to 22:00, Saturday to Thursday (although some close for lunch between 13:00 and 16:00). Most are also open on Fridays, from 16:00 to 22:00. There is a rota system for pharmacies to stay open 24 hours, so there is always at least one pharmacy in every emirate open round the clock. Call 04 223 2323 to find out which pharmacy is open, consult the daily papers, or check on the Dubai Police website (www.dubaipolice.gov.ae).

# Main Government Hospitals

Government healthcare in the UAE is of a high standard and all expats qualify for subsidised care as long as they have a government health card. Refer to p.82 for more information on applying for your health card. The following major government hospitals offer a high level of treatment.

*Nr Naif Road*
*Al Baraha*
*Deira*
*Map 9 F2*

## Al Baraha Hospital
*04 271 0000*
Commonly referred to as the Kuwaiti Hospital, this large government hospital is situated on the Deira side of the Shindagha Tunnel, on the right-hand side. You're not likely to use this hospital for treatment, but you might need to come here for your blood test when processing your residency (Maktoum and Al Bahara Hospitals are the most common 'blood test' hospitals), or for a birth certificate.

*Nr Fish Roundabout*
*Deira*
*Map 9 D3*

## Al Maktoum Hospital
*04 222 1211 | www.dohms.gov.ae*
Opened in 1949, this was the first modern healthcare facility in the region. The place is showing its age, but the facilities are adequate. Today however, the only reason you're likely to visit Maktoum Hospital is to go for the health test for your medical card (there's no emergency or surgical departments). You'll first have a blood sample taken, and then walk to another building to have the chest x-ray. Maktoum Hospital also has a department that carries out embalming. For more information on the medical test, see p.83.

*Oud Metha Rd*
*Bur Dubai*
*Map 10 D4*

## Al Wasl Hospital
*04 324 1111 | www.dohms.gov.ae*
Al Wasl specialises in obstetrics, gynaecology, paediatrics and paediatric surgery. The hospital has an emergency department that provides 24 hour care, seven days a week to women and children up to the age of 12 years. This includes medical, surgical and non-trauma cases, it also includes women with serious problems relating to pregnancy and gynaecology. There is a walk-in clinic for emergencies, but trauma and orthopaedic cases cannot be treated here. You'll be charged Dhs.100 for a non-emergency case if you hold a valid heath card; if you don't hold a valid heath card you will be charged Dhs.200 to see a doctor. For expat residents admitted in an emergency without a valid heath card the charge is Dhs.100 a day as well as your medication bill on top. A deposit of Dhs.500 must be paid for the first five days if the patient came

| Government Health Centres & Clinics | | |
|---|---|---|
| Al Safa Clinic | Al Safa | 04 394 3468 |
| Jebel Ali Clinic | Jebel Ali | 04 884 6489 |
| Jumeirah Health Centre | Jumeira | 04 342 1005 |
| Rashidiya Clinic | Al Rashidiya | 04 285 7353 |
| Umm Suqeim Clinic | Umm Suqeim | 04 394 4461 |

Reviving house plants from the brink of death

Warm clothes coming out of the tumble dryer

ooking up in the sky and finding stuff - planes, birds, funny shaped
ouds, grand pianos about to fall on my head

Finding glitter on me from an unknown source

e in awhile, life throws each of us a curve ball. And while there's no way of protecting ourselves from the unforeseen,
an plan ahead. With medical coverage options including local & international plans, inpatient & outpatient care,
·gency evacuation/repatriation and optional dental & maternity benefits, your insurance can cover you when and
·r which circumstances you desire. Greenshield Insurance removes the financial burden, so you can focus on life.
a free consultation, call Michelle on 04.397.4464 or email michelle@greenshiled.co.ae

GREENSHIELD
I N S U R A N C E

• **Medical** • **Education** •**Travel**• **Motor**• **Savings** • **Property and Fire** • **Bankers Blanket Bond**• **Product Liability**

through the A&E but was not diagnosed as an emergency case. A deposit of Dhs.1,500 is required upon admission if you want a private room plus a Dhs.300 per day charge. If you don't have a valid heath card, non-emergency operations can cost anywhere from Dhs.2,000 to Dhs.6,000 based on the type of operation you require. Al Wasl is a popular choice for expat couples who are having a baby in Dubai and don't have medical insurance to cover the pre-natal care and delivery charges in a private hospital.

**Nr Baraha Hospital** ◀
*Al Baraha*
*Map 9 F3*

## Dubai Hospital
*04 271 4444* | *www.dohms.gov.ae*

Dubai Hospital has a number of outpatient clinics including gynaecology, orthopaedics, dermatology, paediatrics, ophthalmology, ENT (ear, nose and throat) and general medicine. They also undertake general surgery and cardiac surgery as well as dentistry. The A&E department will take patients whether you're a critical emergency or not. The charges for treatment are Dhs.100 to see a doctor if you have a valid heath card, Dhs.200 to see a doctor if you don't have a valid health card and an additional charge of Dhs.300 per day for private rooms. Only emergency cases without a health card are exempt from charges. Other in-patients without a health card who were diagnosed as non-emergency upon admission will be charged Dhs.100 a day.

**Al Wasl Rd** ◀
*Jumeira*
*Map 7 F1*

## Iranian Hospital
*04 344 0250* | *www.irhosp.ae*

If you haven't already seen the mosaic-fronted Iranian Hospital then you may want to take a look - even if not from a medical point of view. The building itself – at the Satwa end of Al Wasl Road – is an impressive sight. The hospital is in fact affiliated to the Red Crescent Society of Iran and therefore isn't strictly a UAE government hospital. It offers its own health card and the fees are very reasonable. If you have this, there's a Dhs.40 charge to be seen by a doctor as an outpatient and a Dhs.50 charge if you don't have the health card. In addition, some of the medicines which they prescribe are free. On the downside the hospital is rather busy.

**Nr British Council** ◀
*Downtown Bur Dubai*
*Map 10 F2*

## Rashid Hospital
*04 337 4000* | *www.dohms.gov.ae*

Rashid Hospital is the main government hospital for accident and emergency, trauma and intensive care patients and paramedic services in Dubai. They have inpatient and outpatient care for elective and emergency surgery and cover virtually all surgical treatments. The hospital provides diagnostic facilities including laboratory testing (haematology, biochemistry, bacteriology and serology), radiology testing (mammography, CT and MRI scan as well as a nuclear medicine unit) plus a well-equipped physiotherapy and social affairs unit.

**Health At Home** ◀
*New healthcare service Health Call (04 363 5343) will send a doctor to your home 24 hours a day should you need a consultation from a team of North American and European certified doctors. For more information check out www.health-call.com.*

## Main Private Hospitals

In addition to the government-funded hospitals, Dubai has a growing number of private hospitals offering world-class medical care. Almost every conceivable treatment and procedure is available, to treat all conditions. Many private hospitals have 24 hour emergency departments too, and may even have their own ambulances.

| Dermatologists | |
|---|---|
| Al Karama Star Medical Centre | 04 335 5105 |
| Al Moosa Medical Centre | 04 345 2999 |
| Al Noor Poly Clinic | 04 223 3324 |
| Al Rustom's Skin & Laser Clinic | 04 349 8800 |
| Al Zahra Private Medical Centre ▶ p.xix | 04 331 5000 |
| Atlas Star Medical Centre | 04 359 6662 |
| Belhoul European Hospital | 04 345 4000 |
| Belhoul Speciality Hospital | 04 273 3333 |
| Derma Health Int'l Medical Centre | 04 224 3786 |
| Dr Mahaveer Mehta Skin Medical | 04 221 9300 |
| Dr Mohamed Al Zubaidy Clinic | 04 227 7533 |
| Dr Simin Medical Clinic | 04 344 4117 |
| Jumeira Prime Medical Centre | 04 349 4545 |
| Medica | 04 282 8338 |

Ministry of Health Ads Approval #2327/2/12/30/12/2007

# Dubai Cosmetic Surgery
complete make-over experts

**COSMETIC LASER CLINIC**

Laser Hair Removal
Tattoo Removal
Laser Veins Removal
Photo Rejuvenation
Birth Marks Removal
Freckles & Age Spot
Melasma & Rosacea

**COSMETIC SURGERY CLINIC**

Facial Enhancement
Body Contouring
Breast Cosmetic Surgery
Botox & Fillers
Hair Transplant
Rhinoplasty
LPG (Cellulite Treatment)

**COSMETIC DENTISTRY CLINIC**

Complete Smile Makeover
Teeth Whitening (Brite Smile)
Porcelain Veneers
Teeth contouring & reshaping
Tooth Colored Restoration
Dental Implants
Crown & Bridge Procedure

NEW CLINIC

**SKIN CARE CLINIC**

Microdermabrasion
Chemical & Herbal Peels
Facials
Pigmentation
Dark Circles Around The Eyes
Rejuvenation Treatment
Anti-Aging Treatment

*Live Beautifully...*

Dubai Cosmetic Surgery, Al Wasl Rd., (Al Manara, Umm Suqeim area) **Dubai**, United Arab Emirates, **Tel. +971 4 348 5575,** Fax. +971 4 348 6292
**UAQ, Tel. +971 6 766 5536,** Email: info@dubaicosmeticsurgery.com visit us at www.dubaicosmeticsurgery.com for more information

In addition to the government-funded hospitals, Dubai has a growing number of private hospitals offering world-class medical care. Almost every conceivable treatment and procedure is available, to treat all conditions. Many private hospitals have 24 hour emergency departments too, and may even have their own ambulance. One other number worth noting is Health Call (see Private Clinics table below). The firm can send round a European or North American certified GP for house calls at short notice.

*Al Zahra Sq*
*Sharjah*
*Map 2 F2*

## Al Zahra Hospital ▶ p.xix

*06 561 9999* | www.alzahra.com

Al Zahra Hospital in Sharjah operates a 24 hour GP clinic and emergency unit, with consultants on call around the clock. There is also Al Zahra Private Medical Centre situated in Al Safa Tower on Sheikh Zayed Road (Trade Centre 1) in Dubai. This offers outpatient services covering a range of medical and surgical disciplines including cardiology, dentistry, dermatology, ENT, family/general practice, gastroenterology, general and laparoscopic surgery, internal medicine, neurology, obstetrics & gynaecology, ophthalmology, orthopaedics, paediatrics and physiotherapy. They also offer various health packages and check-ups including Well Woman, Well Man, and Well Child assessments, cardiac fitness assessments, and maternity packages.

### Diagnostics

| | | |
|---|---|---|
| Al Shifa Al Khaleeji Medical Center | Deira | 04 294 0789 |
| Al Zahra Private Medical Centre ▶ p.xix | Trade Centre 1 | 04 331 5000 |
| Allied Diagnostic Centre | Al Satwa | 04 332 8111 |
| American Hospital | Oud Metha | 04 336 7777 |
| Apollo Medical Diagnostic Centre | Deira | 04 227 0001 |
| Dr Leila Soudah Clinic | Jumeira | 04 395 5591 |
| German Heart Center ▶ p.x | Umm Hurair | 04 362 4797 |
| Gulf Plastic Surgery Hospital | Deira | 04 269 9717 |
| Medic Polyclinic | Downtown Bur Dubai | 04 355 4111 |
| Medical Imaging Department | Downtown Bur Dubai | 04 309 6642 |
| Welcare Hospital | Al Garhoud | 04 282 7788 |

*Oud Metha Rd*
*Opp Movenpick Hotel*
*Oud Metha*
*Map 10 E3*

## American Hospital

*04 336 7777* | www.ahdubai.com

The American Hospital has excellent facilities for both in and outpatients. It has top-of-the-range diagnostic equipment and the doctors and nurses are from all corners of the world. The hospital has an A&E, operating rooms, intensive care and a neonatal intensive care. It offers maternity packages for prenatal care and delivery in the labour ward which is equipped with private rooms. In addition to gynaecology and obstetrics, the hospital's outpatient clinics include paediatrics, family medicine, internal medicine, cardiology, ophthalmology and an excellent neurology clinic. There is also a wide range of elective and emergency surgery available including reconstructive surgery, urology, orthopaedics, and microsurgery.

### Private Health Centres & Clinics

| Name | Address | Area | Phone |
|---|---|---|---|
| Al Borj Medical Centre | Mazaya Centre | Al Quoz | 04 321 2220 |
| Al Zahra Private Medical Centre ▶ p.xix | Shk Zayed Rd | Trade Centre 1 | 04 331 5000 |
| Allied Diagnostic Centre | Al Diyafa St. Satna R/A | Al Satwa | 04 332 8111 |
| Belhoul European Hospital | Dhiyafa Street | Al Satwa | 04 345 4000 |
| Dr Akel's General Medical Clinic | Magrudy Shopping Mall | Jumeira | 04 349 4880 |
| Dubai London Clinic | Al Wasl Rd | Jumeira | 04 344 6663 |
| Dubai Medical Village | Jumeirah Rd | Jumeira | 04 395 6200 |
| Dubai Physiotherapy Clinic ▶ p.197 | Al Wasl Rd | Jumeira | 04 349 6333 |
| German Heart Center ▶ p. x | Dubai Health Care City | Umm Hurair | 04 362 4797 |
| Health Call ▶ p.185 | Dubai Healthcare City | Oud Metha | 04 363 5343 |
| Health Care Medical Centre | Markaz Al Jumeira | Jumeira | 04 344 5550 |
| Jebel Ali International Hospital | Dugas Rd | Jebel Ali | 04 881 4000 |
| Manchester Clinic | Jumeira Beach Rd | Jumeira | 04 344 0300 |
| New Medical Centre | Salah Dean St | Deira | 04 268 3131 |
| Prime Medical Center | Salahuddin Rd | Deira | 04 349 4545 |

# Health Call
### your health, your call

# Specialized in house calls 24/7

## We are a team of North American and European board certified doctors providing comprehensive primary healthcare

### House Calls

- Our doctors come fully equipped to your home, office or business at your convenience to examine and treat you and also to provide you with basic medication during the visit.

- Languages spoken by doctors include English, French, Dutch, German and Arabic

Located at Dubai Healthcare City

### Services offered at the clinic:

- Family Medicine
- General physical check-up
- Well Woman check-up
- Sports Medicine

- Well child check-up
- Executive check-up
- Insurance check-up
- Vaccinations

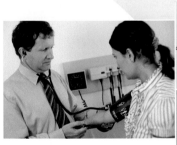

24/7

# Call us 24/7 on 04 363 5343

info@health-call.com

Dubai Healthcare City, Ibn Sina Building, Block B, 5th floor, Clinic 502, P.O. Box 505032, Dubai, U.A.E.

MOH:2212/2/12/31/12/07

## Belhoul Speciality Hospital

*Al Khaleej Rd*
*Deira*
*Map 9 D2*

**04 273 3333** | *www.belhoulspeciality.com*

The Belhoul Speciality Hospital has a new nephrology department offering four state-of-the-art dialysis machines for kidney disorders. The latest diagnostic equipment is also on offer such as MRI, CT scan, digital radiography, cathlab and gamma camera. Other specialities include ophthalmology, interventional cardiology and cardiac surgery, general and laparoscopic surgeries, dental work, gynaecology and obstetrics, and paediatrics. The hospital has an emergency room and its own ambulance.

## Cedars Jebel Ali International Hospital

*Off Int 6*
*Sheikh Zayed Rd*
*Map 3 F2*

**04 881 4000** | *www.cedars-jaih.com*

Cedars Jebel Ali International Hospital is situated near to the Jebel Ali Free Zone. Services include a 24 hour emergency clinic and dedicated ambulance, family medicine, pediatrics, gynecology, dentistry, day surgeries, cardiology, dermatology, and a 24 hour pharmacy. To call their ambulance telephone 881 4000 or 881 8816.

## Emirates Hospital

*Jumeirah Beach Rd*
*Jumeirah*
*Map 7 B1*

**04 344 6678** | *www.emirateshospital.ae*

Mainly deals with in-patient care and specialises in acute disorders. They do not deal with all patients in need of treatment and consultation on chronic illnesses such as cancer or diseases of the brain, nor do they admit trauma patients or have a maternity unit. The care that they do administer includes plastic surgery, gastric banding, gastric balloon, cardiology, osteoporosis pain management, pediatrics, diabetes. They also operate a 24 hour walk-in clinic. It is possible to book an appointment online.

## Neuro Spinal Hospital

*Jumeirah Beach Rd*
*Jumeira*
*Map 7 B1*

**04 342 0000** | *www.nshdubai.com*

The Neuro Spinal Hospital has an emergency room that is open around the clcok. It is prepared for all spinal, neurosurgical and neurological emergencies. There are also two other emergency rooms for general examination and minor injuries. The Neuro Spinal Hospital has a stroke centre for treatment of acute cerebro-vascular accidents. They also have their own ambulance which can be dispatched by calling 04 315 7777.

## Welcare Hospital

*Nr Aviation Club*
*Al Garhoud*
*Map 11 C4*

**04 282 7788** | *www.welcarehospital.com*

The Welcare hospital offers in and outpatient care in a modern and asthetically pleasing atmosphere. They cover a wide range of surgical and medical services including cardiac surgery, dermatology, ENT, general and prosthetic dentistry, general surgery, neurology, obstetrics, gynecology, pediatrics & neonatology, physio, plastic & cosmetic surgery and urology. Special services include a contact lens clinic, diabetic clinic, holiday dialysis, home call consultations (specialist and GP), laser treatment (eyes), MRI/LT scan and maternity packages as well as Well-Man and Well-Woman packages. Their prenatal and delivery care is considered to be one of the best in Dubai. Welcare do postnatal packages for you and your baby which is a nice way to meet other new mums.

## Zulekha Hospital

*Nr Dubai Women's*
*College*
*Al Qusais*
*Map 14-D1*

**04 267 8866** | *www.zulekhahospitals.com*

This hospital and diagnostic centre has both out-patient and in-patient facilities, including a 24 hour emergency department and a fully equipped intensive care unit. Other speciality departments include general surgery, orthopaedics, internal medicine, obstetrics & gynaecology, paediatrics, dermatology, cardiology, and neurology.

# Dr. Michael's Dental Clinic

## Dazzling **Dentistry**

Jumeirah Clinic :

Dr. Christina Formenius, DDS (Sweden)
Dr. Gabriel Harutunian, DDS, Implant Specialist (USA)
Dr. David Carrington, BChD, MSc, FDS, MOrthRCS,
Orthodontics - Braces (UK)
Dr. Alexander Tosev, DDS (Sweden)
Dr. Louis Paul Querel, DMD (Canada)
Dr. Seema Shah, BDS, MFDS RCS, Pediatric (UK)
Dr. Gun Ingrid Norell, DDS (Sweden)
Felicia Bjurfjall, Dental Hygienist (Sweden)
Noel Matney, RDH Dental Hygienist (Canada)

Umm Suqeim Branch :

Dr. Michael Formenius, DDS (Sweden)
Dr. Robert Barksenius, DDS (Sweden)
Dr. Mette Dyhr Rothmann, DDS (Denmark)
Dr. Sadegh  Mirzadeh, DDS (Sweden)
Dr. Eva Ingegerd Gorton, DDS (Sweden)
Dr. Farshid Sadeghi, Endodontist (Holland)
Beverley Watson, Dental Hygienist (UK)

Dr. Michael's is now in
Umm Suqeim and Jumeirah

Jumeirah Clinic : Al Wasl Road , Tel :(+9714) 3 49 59 00 , reception1@drmichaels.com
Umm Suqeim Branch : Al Wasl Road , Tel :(+9714) 3 94 94 33 , reception2@drmichaels.com

# Maternity

Other options **Maternity Items** p.438

**Skin Sense**

*The strong sun in Dubai means you should be especially wary of any new moles or irregular marks that appear on your skin, or if existing moles change or grow in size. Welcare Hospital runs a skin cancer awareness clinic staffed by fully-trained dermatologists, and the Belhoul Speciality Hospital also has dedicated dermatology experts. A number of clinics also specialise in looking after your skin, including Derma Health International (04 224 3786) and Mahaveer Mehta Medical Centre (04 221 9300).*

Every expatriate child born in the UAE must be registered at the Ministry of Health within two weeks and hold a residence visa within four months of birth, otherwise you may not be able to take the child out of the country. See Birth Certificates & Registration (p.92) for more details about the process.

There are various considerations when deciding where to give birth. If you have your heart set on a water or home birth you may want to consider going home, since these options aren't available in the UAE. If you decide that you would rather have the baby in your home country, keep in mind that airlines do have restrictions on taking heavily pregnant passengers, so check when their cut-off date is. However, if you do decide to have your baby here you will find the level of care is excellent. The *Dubai Red Tape Explorer* lists the procedures you'll need to follow as well as the costs you can expect. The Al Wasl Hospital may lack some of the private hospital frills but it has an excellent reputation for maternity care and paediatrics. Before you decide on a government hospital check their policy regarding husbands and family members in the labour ward. Certain hospitals may not allow your husband to be with you in the labour ward (although he can be present at delivery and often, if you are persuasive and there are no local ladies admitted, they will allow you access). All government hospitals now charge expatriates for maternity services and delivery, and costs vary depending on the package you choose. Private hospitals will be more expensive, although if you shop around you may be surprised to find that in some cases the difference between government and private is not as great as you might think. No matter which you choose, if you have medical insurance check that it covers maternity costs – some have a limitation clause (you need to have been with the insurer for at least 12 months before conception) and some may not cover any costs at all. Private hospitals offer maternity packages that include prenatal care, delivery and postnatal care for you and the baby. But remember that the price you are quoted by the hospital is for the basic, 'best-case-scenario' delivery, and if you have additional requirements, such as an epidural (when the anaesthetist must be present) or an assisted delivery (when the paediatrician must be present), you will be charged extra. If you give birth by caesarean section, the cost is usually significantly higher and the hospital stay is longer (five days, compared to two days for standard delivery).

Maternity leave in the UAE is short compared to some other countries. Although a new mother is entitled to 45 days leave on full pay (whether this is calendar days or working days depends on your employer), a lot of employers here are not that flexible about giving further leave, even on an unpaid basis, so it's worth discussing this with your employer as early as possible. New dads are not entitled to any paternity leave (unlike the UK where you get two weeks), so will have to take annual leave if they want to help with the sleepless nights and nappy changing.

**Working Mums**

*Mums that have been in a private sector job for more than one year can claim up to 45 days maternity leave on full pay. This can only be used directly before and after the birth. See Labour Law, p.104, for more.*

## Maternity Hospitals & Clinics

| | | |
|---|---|---|
| Al Wasl Hospital | 04 324 1111 | Government |
| Al Zahra Private Medical Centre ▶ p.xix | 04 331 5000 | Private |
| American Hospital | 04 336 7777 | Private |
| Belhoul European Hospital | 04 345 4000 | Private |
| Dr Akel's General Medical Clinic | 04 349 4880 | Private |
| Dr Fakih Gynaecology & Obstetrics Center | 04 349 2100 | Private |
| Dr Leila Soudah Clinic | 04 395 5591 | Private |
| Dubai Hospital | 04 271 4444 | Government |
| Dubai London Clinic | 04 344 6663 | Private |
| General Medical Centre | 04 349 5959 | Private |
| Medlink Clinic | 04 344 7711 | Private |
| Royal Medical Centre | 04 345 6780 | Private |
| Welcare Hospital | 04 282 7788 | Private |

# Cut through Dubai's bureaucracy...buy the book

A comprehensive instruction manual
to setting up home, finding a job, getting
married, having a baby, starting a business...
in other words getting a life.

**Dubai Red-Tape**
A complete step-by-step handbook

Abu Dhabi • Amsterdam • Bahrain • Barcelona • Beijing • Berlin • Dubai • Dublin • Geneva
Hong Kong • Kuala Lumpur • Kuwait • London • Los Angeles • New York • New Zealand • Oman
Paris • Qatar • Shanghai • Singapore • Sydney • Tokyo • Vancouver

**EXPLORER**

www.explorerpublishing.com

## Gynaecology & Obstetrics

| | |
|---|---|
| Al Aliaa Poly Clinics | 04 349 3600 |
| Al Diyafa Modern Medical Centre | 04 345 4945 |
| Al Wasl Hospital | 04 324 1111 |
| Al Zahra Private Medical Centre ▶ p.xix | 04 331 5000 |
| American Hospital | 04 336 7777 |
| Belhoul European Hospital | 04 345 4000 |
| Dr Akel's General Medical Clinic | 04 349 4880 |
| Dr Fakih Gynaecology & Obstetrics Center | 04 349 2100 |
| Dr Leila Soudah Clinic | 04 395 5591 |
| Dr Taher H Khalil Clinic | 04 268 7655 |
| Dubai Gynaecology & Fertility Centre | 04 334 4300 |
| Dubai London Clinic | 04 344 6663 |
| General Medical Centre | 04 349 5959 |
| Jumeira Prime Medical Center | 04 349 4545 |
| Jumeirah Family Clinic, The | 04 344 8844 |
| Manchester Clinic | 04 344 0300 |
| Medlink Clinic | 04 344 7711 |
| Royal Medical Centre | 04 345 6780 |
| Welcare Hospital | 04 282 7788 |

Having a baby in Dubai as opposed to returning to your home country for the birth has its advantages. The level of care in both the private and government hospitals is of a very high standard, both for prenatal, delivery and postnatal care. In addition if you stay in the country then you have the benefit of developing a relationship with your obstetrician during your prenatal care which will make the delivery all the more comfortable when the time comes (midwives, although they take an active role, are not qualified in Dubai to deliver babies and your obstetrician must deliver the baby). In addition, if you do decide to have your baby in Dubai you benefit from not being separated from your husband. Without paternity leave it's unlikely that you husband will be able to accompany you back home and stay until you and baby are ready to board a plane. Also there is no guarantee that you'll deliver on your due date so it makes the trip very hard to plan. Plus, if you have to have an emergency caesarean this could make the recovery period a lot longer and therefore delay your return to Dubai.

Whatever you decide to do there are numerous mother and baby groups in Dubai that will help you to settle into your new role as a mother (see p.361).

## Paediatrics

Most public and private hospitals and medical centres have full time paediatricians on staff, with a growing number having devoted paediatric departments. The American Hospital and Welcare Hospital (both private) have teams of specialist paediatric doctors, while Al Wasl Hospital (government) has dedicated paediatric surgeons and neurodevelopment therapists that care for children with special needs and learning difficulties. The Dubai Community Health Centre (04 395 3939) also provides professional services such as speech therapy and social skills training for children with special needs.

### Paediatrics

| | |
|---|---|
| Dr Abed Aydin | 04 336 7777 |
| Dr Anil Gupta | 04 336 7777 |
| Dr Badi Alatasi | 04 282 7788 |
| Dr Carole Chidiac | 04 349 5020 |
| Dr Ejaz Wasseem | 04 344 7711 |
| German Heart Center ▶ p.x | 04 362 4797 |
| Health Call ▶ p.185 | 04 363 5343 |
| Dr Keith Nichol | 04 394 1000 |
| Dr Marie-France Petermans | 04 362 4711 |
| Dr Michael Loubser | 04 349 5959 |

## Dentists & Orthodontists

Dentistry in Dubai is, like most other medical services, of a high standard and various practitioners offer dental surgery, cosmetic cleaning and check-ups. Prices match the level of service, which is always high, and standard health insurance packages generally don't cover dentistry, unless it's an emergency treatment brought about by an accident. You may be able to pay an additional premium to cover dentistry, but the insurer may first want proof that you've had regular, six-monthly check-ups for the previous two or three years.

If you have a health card you're entitled to dentistry by your assigned hospital, and if they don't have a dental section, they'll refer you to another public hospital that does, such as Rashid Hospital. You will be charged Dhs.100 for the visit, as well as for any other services that are performed, such as cleaning and filling. Service is generally professional and good, but the rates may not be any lower than at a private dental clinic.

*Do You Like My smile ?*

# Talass

مركز طَلَس لتقويم وطب الأسنان
**ORTHODONTIC & DENTAL CENTER**

# Trust The Experts...

* Airflow Cleaning * Tooth Whitening * Cosmetic Fillings * Ceramic Veneers
* Crown & Bridge Work * Invisible Braces * Dental Implants * Maxillo-Facial Surgery
* Cosmetic Facial Surgery * T M Joint Treatment * Root Canal Treatment * Family & Children Dentistry

Jumeira Beach Road - Dubai U.A.E.
Sat - Wed : 10AM - 2AM & 3PM - 8PM
Tel : 04 - 349 2220

**www.talass.com**

MOH – 1916/2/11/30/11/07

For a standard filling you could be looking at paying anywhere between Dhs.50 and Dhs.1,000. If it is root canal treatment that you need, expect to part with anything from Dhs.600 to Dhs.3,000. A number of practices, including Talass Orthodontic & Dental Center and the American Dental Clinic, specialise in cosmetic dentistry using crowns, veneers and teeth whitening to give you a smile to be proud of. Dr Michaels Dental Clinic has a range of international doctors based in both its Jumeirah and Umm Suqeim branches so that you'll always feel completely comfortable with the doctor who treats you.

| Dentists & Orthodontists | | |
|---|---|---|
| Al Zahra Private Medical Centre ▶ p.xix | | 04 331 5000 |
| American Dental Clinic | | 04 344 0668 |
| British Dental Clinic | | 04 342 1318 |
| British Medical Consulting Centre | | 04 344 2633 |
| Charly PolyClinic | | 04 337 9191 |
| Clinic for Orthodontics & Aesthetic Dentistry | | 04 330 0220 |
| Dr Michaels Dental Clinic ▶ p.187 | | 04 349 5900 |
| Drs Nicolas & Asp Clinic ▶ p193 | | 04 394 7777 |
| Dubai London Clinic | | 04 344 6663 |
| Emirates Hospital | | 04 349 6666 |
| General Medical Centre | | 04 349 5959 |
| Health Care Medical Clinic | | 04 344 5550 |
| Jumeira Beach Dental Clinic | | 04 349 9433 |
| Modern Dental Clinic | | 04 228 2784 |
| Swedish Dental Clinic | | 04 223 1297 |
| Talass Orthodontic & Dental Center ▶ p.190 | | 04 349 2220 |
| The Dental SPA Family & Cosmetic Dentistry | | 04 395 2005 |

| Cosmetic Treatment & Surgery | |
|---|---|
| Al Rustom's Skin & Laser Clinic | 04 349 8800 |
| American Hospital | 04 336 7777 |
| Belhoul European Hospital | 04 345 4000 |
| British Medical Consulting Centre | 04 344 2633 |
| Cosmesurge | 04 344 5915 |
| Dubai Cosmetic Surgery ▶ p.183 | 04 348 5575 |
| Dubai Medical Village | 04 395 6200 |
| Emirates Hospital | 04 344 6678 |
| Euro Gulf Medical Center | 04 331 3544 |
| Gulf American Clinic | 04 344 2050 |
| Gulf Plastic Surgery Hospital | 04 269 9717 |
| Manchester Clinic | 04 344 0300 |
| Welcare Hospital | 04 282 7788 |

## Cosmetic Treatment & Surgery

Dubai is becoming known as a destination for cosmetic surgery thanks to the heightened awareness of image through an influx of people, the rapid growth of the media and all those with expendable money. The city now boasts a growing number of clinics that specialise in reducing, reshaping, removing and enlarging various parts of your anatomy. The private hospitals also offer cosmetic services including aesthetic and reconstructive surgery. Many of the independent clinics are located in Jumeira, especially along the Beach Road. One of these is Dubai Medical Village (04 395 6200) whose dedicated team of surgeons offer a range of surgical procedures, eye care, and laser treatment including hair removal. If you want a bit of sprucing and don't fancy slicing, a lot of the cosmetic clinics will do botox and other non-surgical treatments.

*Healthcare City*

**"CARING IS OUR CONCERN"**

دكـتــورنـيـقــولا وآ ســب

# DRS. NICOLAS & ASP

## SPECIALISED DENTAL CARE FOR ALL THE FAMILY

**GENERAL DENTISTRY**
DR E NICOLAS, USA
DR SVEN ASP, SWEDEN
DR JOAN ASP, SWEDEN
DR TOMAS VON POST, SWEDEN
DR CLAS OSKARSSON, SWEDEN
DR CHRIS JOHANSSON, SWEDEN
DR E. IZABELA, POLAND
DR KARIM FEKIH, FRANCE
DR DIANE FARHANG, FRANCE
DR HELEN KHATIB, UK
DR RUBY GHAFFARI, USA
DR CATARINA FAERBOM, SWEDEN
DR NASTARAN KARAMI, GERMANY
DR FARMAN POUR, SWEDEN

**ORTHODONTICS (BRACES)**
DR ROLF LINDMAN, SWEDEN
DR BRITTANY NICOL, AUSTRALIA
DR TANJA NAKOVICS, GERMANY
DR AHMAD ISMAIL, FRANCE

**ORTHODONTICS & CLEFT LIP & PALATE**
DR SALAM AL-KHAYYAT, TURKEY

**SURGERY & IMPLANTS**
DR DAVID ROZE, FRANCE

**ENDODONTICS**
DR DIANE FARHANG, FRANCE
DR DAVID ROZE, FRANCE

**PROSTHODONTICS (CROWN & BRIDGE)**
DR MATTHIEU GABRIELE, FRANCE

**PAEDIATRIC DENTISTRY**
DR AGNES ROZE FRANCE

**DENTAL HYGIENE**
KATE PASZKOWSKA, POLAND
AHLEH MAHTABPOUR, IRAN

**ORAL MAXILLOFACIAL SURGERY & IMPLANTS**
DR DIRK NOLTE, GERMANY
DR THOMAS TKOTZ, GERMANY

MOH: 2286/2/12/30/1/08

**JUMEIRAH DENTAL : 04 394 7777**

**24/7 Emergency Hotlines**
Dental: 050 551 7177 • Medical: 050 640 7695

**GREEN COMMUNITY**
**DENTAL + MEDICAL**
04 885 4440

**MARINA WALK**
**DENTAL + MEDICAL**
04 360 9977

**MIRDIF**
**DENTAL**
04 288 4411

**DHCC**
**DENTAL**
04 362 4788

enquiries@nicolasandasp.com

## Opticians & Ophthalmologists

| Opticians & Ophthalmologists | |
|---|---|
| Al Zahra Private Medical Centre ▶ p.xix | 04 331 5000 |
| American Hospital | 04 336 7777 |
| Atlanta Vision Clinic | 04 348 6233 |
| Barakat Optical | 04 329 1913 |
| Gulf Eye Centre | 04 329 1977 |
| Moorfields Eye Hospital ▶ p.195 | 04 429 7888 |
| Welcare Hospital | 04 282 7788 |

## Opticians & Ophthalmologists

You're never far from an optician in Dubai, with most of the malls having at least one outlet. The bigger branches such as Al Jaber Optical in Deira City Centre (04 295 4400) and Yateem in the BurJuman Centre also carry out the eye test required for a driving licence (see Driving Licence, p.88). Most opticians stock a good range of contact lenses and the necessary solutions. Barakat Optical on Sheikh Zayed Road will even deliver disposable lenses. For a list of opticians see Eyewear (p.425).
For eye problems requiring specialist treatment many hospitals and clinics offer consultations and are able to carry out appropriate treatment, especially Moorfields Eye Hospital (04 429 7888), the American Hospital Dubai (04 336 7777) and the Welcare Hospital (04 282 7788) which all have well-equipped ophthalmology departments. A number of clinics and medical centres offer laser eye surgery, such as Moorfield Eye Hospital, Al Zahra Private Medical Centre, the Gulf Eye Centre and the Atlanta Vision Clinic.

## Alternative Therapies

There is a well-balanced choice of spiritual and holistic therapies available in Dubai. The Dubai Herbal & Treatment Centre (04 335 1200) offers a full range of Chinese, Indian and Arabic herbal medicines. The facility, which is unique in the GCC region, currently caters to outpatients only, but there are plans to expand the facility to offer inpatient services. Natural medicine can be very specialised, so when consulting with someone make sure that you ask questions and explain your needs and expectations to ensure practitioners can help with your situation. Prices vary but are generally comparable to western medicine, and most insurance companies will not cover the costs. As always, word of mouth is the best way of establishing who might offer the most appropriate treatment (posting a query on www.expatwoman.com could turn up some recommendations).
There is also a range of clinics providing 'well-being' services, such as U Concept (04 344 9060) in the Village Mall, Jumeira. U Concept offers a 'unique lifestyle service', combining personal training, nutritional advice, and a range of treatments. You can agree on a 12 week programme to help you achieve your personal health and fitness goals and cope with stress. It even has the option of having freshly prepared healthy food delivered to your home.
The UAE Ministry of Health grants licences to and administrates qualified practitioners of alternative medicine through its dedicated department for Traditional, Complementary and Alternative Medicine.
On the following pages are some of the services offered, and the main practitioners in Dubai.

### Quitting Is For Winners

Although it sometimes seems impossible to escape the smoke in Dubai, there are groups and organisations that exist solely to help people kick their addiction to nicotine. The Ministry of Health has a number of Quit Smoking clinics as do some of the private hospitals such as Emirates Hospital. There are also organisations such as I Quit Smoking (IQS), which can be reached on 800 3100, that help smokers by giving them a programme to follow and support.

### Acupressure/Acupuncture

Acupressure involves the systematic placement of pressure with fingertips on established meridian points on the body. This therapy can be used to relieve pain, soothe the nerves and

| Acupressure/Acupuncture | |
|---|---|
| Cedars Jebel Ali International Hospital | 04 881 4000 |
| Dubai Herbal & Treatment Centre | 04 335 1200 |
| Dubai Physiotherapy Clinic ▶ p.197 | 04 349 6333 |
| Gulf American Clinic | 04 349 8556 |
| House of Chi & House of Healing | 04 397 4446 |
| King China Acupuncture Center | 04 398 5548 |

stimulate the body, as determined necessary by the therapist. Acupuncture is an ancient Chinese technique that uses needles to access the body's meridian points. The technique is surprisingly painless and is quickly becoming an alternative or complement to western medicine as it aids ailments such as asthma, rheumatism and other serious diseases.

www.moorfields.ae

Long recognised as a global centre of visionary excellence,
Moorfields Eye Hospital is now open in Dubai.

For over 200 years patients from all over the world have travelled great
distances to London to benefit from Moorfields Eye Hospital's unrivalled
reputation for ground-breaking research and treatments which have
revolutionised eye health.

Now world-class help is closer at hand. If you have a sight-related problem
or are seeking LASIK or cosmetic surgery around the eyes, please contact us
today to arrange a consultation with a highly qualified ophthalmologist at
our brand new, state-of-the-art hospital in Dubai Healthcare City.

**Call 04 429 7888 or visit www.moorfields.ae today for more information.**

Moorfields
Eye Hospital Dubai

LASIK │ CATARACT │ COSMETIC │ RETINA │ CORNEA │ GLAUCOMA          2206/2/12/30/12/2008

## Aromatherapy

| | |
|---|---|
| Cleopatra's Spa | 04 324 7700 |
| Essensuals Aromatherapy Centre | 04 344 8776 |
| Haven, The | 04 345 6770 |
| Marie France Beauty Salon | 04 344 8739 |
| Six Senses Spa | 04 366 6818 |

*Aromatherapy*

Essential oils derived from plants and flowers can be used in many ways to add balance to your health. Specialists use oils when delivering massages as well as a number of other methods to address your needs. While no certification is required to practise aromatherapy, it's a healthy decision to make sure your practitioner has studied plants and can make the best choices for you. For cosmetic and relaxing purposes alone, aromatherapy facials or massagse are recommended, which many spas and salons offer. While these are intended to be for pleasure rather than health related, they can work wonders on your soul!

## Healing Meditation

| | |
|---|---|
| Art of Living | 04 344 9660 |
| Dubai Community Health Centre | 04 395 3939 |
| GMCKS Pranic Energy Healing Centre | 04 336 0885 |
| SSY (Siddha Samadhi Yoga) | 04 344 6618 |

*Healing Meditation*

Meditation can offer inner peace as well as a disease-free mind and body. With various breathing techniques, movements and mantras, group and individual meditation sessions can be a powerful tool in healing and stress relief. Growing numbers of Dubai's residents are trying meditation as a means to unwind.

## Homeopathy

| | |
|---|---|
| Holistic Healing Medical Centre | 04 348 7172 |
| Jumeirah Prime Medical Center | 04 349 4545 |
| Medlink Clinic | 04 344 7711 |
| Rays Medical Centre | 04 397 3665 |

*Homeopathy*

Homeopathy strengthens the body's defence system. Natural ingredients are used to address physical and emotional problems. The discipline extracts elements from traditional medicines of various origins but was recently organised into a healthcare system in Europe. Practitioners undergo disciplined training and some are also western medical doctors.

*Reflexology & Massage Therapy*
Other options **Massage** p.398

Reflexology is a detailed scientific system, with Asian origins, that outlines points in the hands and feet that impact other parts and systems of the body. In addition to stress reduction and improved health, the pressure applied to these points directly addresses issues in those specific corresponding parts of the body. While many spas and salons offer massage and reflexology, the listed centres have a more focused approach to the holistic healing

## Reflexology & Massage Therapy

| | |
|---|---|
| Bliss Relaxology | 04 286 9444 |
| Cleopatra's Spa | 04 324 7700 |
| Dubai Herbal & Treatment Centre | 04 335 1200 |
| Dubai Physiotherapy Clinic ▶ p.197 | 04 349 6333 |
| Essensuals Aromatherapy Centre | 04 344 8776 |
| Feet First | 04 349 4334 |
| Haven, The | 04 345 6770 |
| Healing Zone, The | 04 394 0604 |
| Herbalpan Ayurvedic Centre | 04 321 2553 |
| House of Chi & House of Healing | 04 397 4446 |
| Marie France Beauty Salon | 04 344 8739 |
| Thai Relaxation Therapy Centre | 04 321 2345 |
| Welcare Hospital | 04 282 7788 |

qualities of reflexology and massage. For a listing of spas that offer massage for relaxation and beauty, see p.390.

*Rehabilitation & Physiotherapy*

Many Dubai residents lead an active lifestyle, working hard and then playing hard. But accidents and injuries do happen, so whether you got roughed up playing rugby, pulled something in the gym or simply tripped over the cat you'll be pleased to hear

# Dubai Physiotherapy & Family Medicine Clinic

- Family Medicine

- Physiotherapy

- Osteopathy

- Acupuncture

- Nutrition

- Therapeutic Massage

**Dubai Physiotherapy & Family Medicine Clinic**

Al Wasl Road, Jumeirah (opposite Belhasa Driving School & Jumeirah Post Office)
PO Box 74638, Dubai, UAE
**Tel: 04 349 6333  Fax: 04 344 8617**
E-mail: dxbphys@emirates.net.ae

Open from 8 am to 7 pm, Sunday to Thursday
8 am to 5 pm, Saturday

| Rehabilitation & Physiotherapy | |
| --- | --- |
| Al Zahra Private Medical Centre ▶ p.xix | 04 331 5000 |
| American Hospital | 04 336 7777 |
| Dubai Physiotherapy Clinic ▶ p.197 | 04 349 6333 |
| General Medical Centre | 04 349 5959 |
| Gulf American Clinic | 04 344 2050 |
| Health Care Medical Centre | 04 344 5550 |
| OrthoSports Medical Center ▶ p.199 | 04 345 0601 |

that the city has some excellent facilities to help you on the road to recovery. The OrthoSports Medical Center (04 345 0601) in Jumeira specialises in orthopaedic and sports medicine, offering physiotherapy, hydrotherapy and orthopaedic surgery to international standards.

## Back Treatment

Back problems plague many people, whether they are young and fit sports fanatics or sedentary people in their later life. Luckily, treatment is widely available in Dubai with excellent specialists from all around the world practising here.

Chiropractic and osteopathy treatments concentrate on manipulating the skeleton in a non-intrusive manner to improve the functioning of the nervous system or blood supply to the body. Chiropractic is based on the manipulative treatment of misalignments in the joints, especially those of the spinal column, while osteopathy involves the manipulation and massage of the skeleton and musculature. Craniosacral therapy aims to relieve pain and tension by gentle manipulations of the skull to balance the craniosacral rhythm. Pilates is said to be the safest form of neuromuscular reconditioning and back strengthening available. It is also a form of exercise that's gaining popularity. Check with your gym to see if they offer any classes.

| Back Treatment | |
| --- | --- |
| Advanced Chiropractic Health Center | 04 348 8262 |
| Al Zahra Private Medical Centre ▶ p.xix | 04 331 5000 |
| Canadian Chiropractic & Natural Health Centre | 04 342 0900 |
| Clark Chiropractic Clinic | 04 344 4316 |
| Dr Akel's General Medical Clinic | 04 349 4880 |
| Gulf American Clinic | 04 349 8556 |
| House of Chi & House of Healing | 04 397 4446 |
| Neuro Spinal Hospital | 04 342 0000 |
| OrthoSports Medical Center ▶ p.199 | 04 345 0601 |
| Osteopathic Health Centre | 04 344 9792 |
| Pilates Studio, The | 04 343 8252 |
| Specialist Orthopaedic Surgery Centre | 04 349 5528 |

## Nutritionists & Slimming

With such a variety of dining options in Dubai, and with the emphasis very much on lounging and relaxing, it's easy to let your diet suffer and pile on the pounds. Thankfully, a number of slimming clubs and nutritionists are on hand to help:

- 8 Weeks to a New You is for people wanting to lose weight and improve their general health and wellbeing, and the programme offers regular exercise sessions and individual nutrition consultation. Courses are held at the Fairmont Hotel.
- Shapes at Knowledge Village describes itself as the biggest weight and inch-loss facility in the UAE. Nutritionists and dieticians will devise a personal diet and exercise plan, and the club offers more than 100 fitness classes a week to choose from.
- Hypoxi All Body Solutions is the only outfit in Dubai offering the revolutionary HypoxiTherapy, a fast acting way to lose cellulite and fat from your stomach, waist, hips, thighs and buttocks, by exercise combined with vacuum suction. Loved by celebrities, this method is immediate and painless. They have a number of machines around Dubai including the Aviation Club (04 282 4122) and Le Meridien (04 702 2466).
- Right Bite offers a tailor-made healthy eating service. Low calorie, low fat and low cholesterol meals, devised by their own dieticians, are freshly prepared and delivered to your door.
- Good Habits helps people lose weight through healthy eating. Meetings are held every week at various locations all over Dubai, and often include food tasting and cookery demos. Exercise classes are also organised.

...be fit

MOH:1240/2/9/30/9/2007

**orthopedic surgery** ● **sports medicine** ● **osteopathy** ● **physiotherapy** ● **hydrotherapy**

www.orthosp.com

# ORTHOSPORTS

## MEDICAL CENTER
THE SPORTS MEDICINE SPECIALISTS

BEACH ROAD JUMEIRA    TEL: 04-345 0601  FAX: 04-345 0028

## Nutritionists & Slimming

| | |
|---|---|
| 8 Weeks to a New You | 04 849 0198 |
| American Hospital | 04 336 7777 |
| Dubai London Clinic | 04 344 6663 |
| Emirates Hospital | 04 344 6678 |
| Good Habits | 04 344 9692 |
| Hypoxi All Body Solutions | 04 204 5032 |
| Manchester Clinic | 04 344 0300 |
| Right Bite | 04 351 4453 |
| Shapes Weight-Loss Club & Health Spa | 04 367 2137 |
| Welcare Hospital | 04 282 7788 |

- The Welcare Hospital provides a dietary counselling service, where a team of dieticians and nutritionists will educate and evaluate the patient's eating habits, and then point them in the right direction with a unique diet plan.
- The American Hospital offers a food and nutrition service managed and provided by ADNH Compass. The Hospital also runs a Diabetic Centre of Excellence.
- Emirates Hospital has a weight reduction programme that uses liquid supplements and a very low calorie diet. The Hospital has dietician and nutrition experts who specialise in medically supervised weight reduction programmes, obesity in children, obesity in diabetic patients and patients with high blood pressure or cholesterol.

## Counsellors & Psychologists

| | |
|---|---|
| Belhoul European Hospital | 04 345 4000 |
| Comprehensive Medical Centre | 04 331 4777 |
| Dr Roughy McCarthy Psychology Clinic | 04 394 6122 |
| Dr Suzie Hachez | 050 624 9050 |
| Dubai Community Health Centre | 04 395 3939 |
| Health Call ▶ p.185 | 04 363 5343 |

# Counselling & Therapy

Even the most resilient of personalities can be affected by expat culture shock or homesickness. Whatever the origin of the stress, a new environment takes some getting used to, and can be demanding on your nerves. The good news is there are a number of support groups (p.200) where problems can be shared (and halved) and much needed ears bent. If your troubles run deeper, then you may benefit from some therapy and there are a number of counsellors and psychologists in Dubai that will help you deal with emotional problems. Many doctors will also treat cases of child psychology or children with behavioural issues such as ADHD. The Dubai Community Health Centre (395 3939) is a non-profit organisation that offers workshops and other psychiatric services at competitive rates. The Centre is the GCC region's first dedicated mental health centre, and also specialises in educational psychology for children and adults, marriage and family counselling, as well as yoga and reiki programmes. In addition there are a number of psychiatrists in Dubai who deal with the diagnosis and treatment of more chronic mental illnesses.

## Psychiatrists

| | |
|---|---|
| Belhoul European Hospital | 04 345 4000 |
| Belhoul Speciality Hospital | 04 273 3333 |
| British Medical Consulting Centre | 04 344 2633 |
| Dr Adnand Clinic | 04 398 9740 |
| Dr Akel's General Medical Clinic | 04 349 4880 |
| Dr EJ Voerman | 04 394 6122 |
| Dubai Community Health Centre | 04 395 3939 |
| Health Call ▶ p.185 | 04 363 5343 |
| Jumeirah Prime Medical Center | 04 349 4545 |
| Welcare Hospital | 04 282 7788 |

*Table4six ◀*

*To help you meet new people, Table4six (www.table4six.net) will reserve a table at a Dubai restaurant and then invite six of its members to dinner. Upon joining you can specify your preferences, including how often you want to be invited.*

# Support Groups

Living away from your family can be challenging, however, there are support groups offering a hand through the difficult patches. There is also the Dubai Community Health Centre (04 395 3939) which provides space for support group meetings.

- ADHD (Attention Deficit Hyperactive Disorder). Meetings every second Sunday (04 335 5578).
- Adoption Support Group (04 360 8113). Meetings held once a month. Call Carol for further info.
- Alcoholics Anonymous (AA) (04 344 1542 - 24 hour hotline). Information on weekly meetings can be found on www.aainarabia.com
- All 4 Down's Syndrome (050 880 9228 - 24 hour hotline). Providing support to families whose lives have, in some way, been affected by Down's Syndrome. The group holds social mornings every Sun morning between 10:00 and 12:00 at Favourite Things, Palm Strip Jumeirah.
- UAE Down's Association (050 748 0633) run by Mrs Iman.

## Support Groups

| | |
|---|---|
| Adoption Support Group | 04 394 6643 |
| Alcoholics Anonymous | 04 344 1542 |
| All 4 Down's syndrome | 050 880 9228 |
| Breastfeeding Telephone Support Group | 050 453 4670 |
| City of Hope | cityofhope18@gmail.com |
| Diabetic Support Group | 04 309 6876 |
| Fertility Support Group | 050 632 4365 |
| Mother to Mother | 050 452 7674 |
| Overcomers Outreach | 04 342 1302 |
| Pastoral Counselling | 050 422 0251 |
| SANDS Support Group | 04 348 2801 |
| Special Families Support | 04 393 1985 |
| Still Birth & Neo Natal Death Society | 04 884 6309 |
| Twins, Triplets or More! | www.twinsormore.20m.com |

***Single Dubai Female***
*The Bridget Jones Club Dubai is a social group of more than 400 single women that get together for various events and activities. They welcome members of all ages and nationalities and are always looking for suggestions on new activities. Visit http://thebridgets.com.*

- Bullied kids and their parents can learn how to deal with bullying as a family. Call Salomi on 050 657 0866.
- City of Hope (04 394 2650 or 050 651 6511). Not a support 'group' as such, but a project providing shelter for women and children of all nationalities who have been the victim of abuse. They are in the process of applying for a licence, but as yet remain 'unofficial'. The shelter is staffed entirely by volunteers, and the project is reliant on donations and support. Contact on above number Sat to Wed 08:15 to15:30, or by emailing cityofhope18@gmail.com.
- Diabetic Support Group (04 309 6954). Meets every three months on a Wednesday evening at 17:30. Based at the American Hospital Dubai. Contact Caroline.
- Mother 2 Mother (04 348 3754 or 050 452 7674). Support, friendship, fun and advice for all mothers, from those who are expecting to those who have already delivered.
- Overcomers Outreach (04 342 1302). A group for those affected directly or indirectly by the abuse of any mood altering chemical, or obsessive/compulsive behaviour.
- Pastoral Counselling (050 422 0251 or 04 297 3221). A support service available whatever the problem, with the aim of restoring the joy and significance of living.
- SANDS Support Group. A UK-based charity for those families experiencing pregnancy loss either through still birth, neonatal death or late miscarriage. Contact Angela 04 348 2801, Anita 04 394 0384, or June 04 884 6309. SANDS also offer hospital and home visits.
- Special Families Support (04 393 1985 or 050 726369) has monthly meetings for the families of special needs children. Contact Ayesha Saeed on the above numbers or contact Guelsen (050 454 1940).

*American Hospital*

The Complete **Residents'** Guide

## Knowledge Village

Knowledge Village (www.kv.ae) is a key part of Dubai's commitment to improving educational services and attracting more international students to the country as well as providing opportunities for local students to study here rather than abroad (see p.218).

# Education

The education system is varied, with many international schools to choose from, and more opening every year. But, as there is no government-funded education for expat children, all these schools charge fees.

Other parents are always a good source of advice, as are company HR departments. Also, consider posting a query on one of the expat websites (see p.67) – just bear in mind that advice won't necessarily be objective. It's also a good idea to visit a few schools before you make your decision. Most of the top schools operate waiting lists and you may not be able to get your child into your first choice. You may also have to pay a fee to be registered on the waiting list, which is non-refundable.

After-school activities are common and include things such as gymnastics, swimming, ballet, Arabic classes, horse-riding, rugby, golf, football and tennis. Most are free. The school terms are similar to education systems in the UK and USA, with autumn (mid September – mid December), spring (early January - early April) and summer (mid April – early July) terms.

In most cases you will need the following documents in order to enrol your child:
• Application form
• Copies of student and parents' passports – both information page and residence visa stamp
• Passport photographs (usually eight)
• Copies of student's birth certificate
• School records for the past two years
• Current immunisation records and medical history
• Official transfer certificate from the student's previous school detailing his/her education. Original transfer certificates must contain the following details:
• Date of enrolment
• Year of placement
• Date the child left the school
• School stamp
• Official signature

The Ministry of Education also requires the following documents for any student enrolling in any school in Dubai:
• Original transfer certificate (to be completed by the current school)
• Most recently issued original report card

If the student was attending a school anywhere other than the UAE, Australia, Canada, Europe or USA, the transfer certificate and the most recently issued original report card must be attested by the Ministry of Education, Ministry of Foreign Affairs and the UAE embassy in that country.

## Personal Tutoring

Power Tutoring support school-age students by providing specialised private tutoring after school hours. They offer a variety of subjects and cirricula, have focused exam and revision timetables and offer small group sessions or one-on-one study. Located in Knowledge Village, they can be contacted on 04 364 3080. Or visit them at www.powertutoring.com.

# Nurseries & Pre-Schools

Some nurseries accept babies from as young as three months, although most prefer to accept children who are at walking age (around 12 months). Fees vary dramatically and so do timings so it's best to call around and visit a few nurseries to get an idea of what's available. As a general rule of thumb, most nurseries are open for four or five hours in the morning and charge anything from Dhs.3,000 to Dhs.12,000 per year. The more popular nurseries have long waiting lists so you should enrol your child before it's even born! Some of the bigger primary schools also have nursery sections - if you've got a primary school in mind for your child, it's worth checking to see if they have a nursery, as this may help you secure a place a few years down the line. There are a number of factors to consider when you are looking for a nursery and it is always a good idea to take your time to visit a number of schools. Try and drop in during the day so that you can have a look at the facilities while there are children in school.

*Homework time*

Many of the nurseries in Dubai operate morning hours which may rule them out if you are working. However many also run late classes for an extra fee. Also a number of them have early bird drop-offs and have term break classes and summer school. Another factor worth thinking about is whether the school provides meals or not, having to make a packed lunch every morning when you're trying to get ready for work may not be for you!

Some nurseries accept babies from as young as three months, although most prefer to accept children who are at walking age (around 12 months). Fees vary dramatically and so do timings, so it's best to call around and visit a few nurseries to get an idea of what's available. In general, nurseries are open for four or five hours but some offer early starts and late sessions. The more popular nurseries have long waiting lists. Some of the bigger primary schools also have kindergartens. There are a number of factors to consider when you are looking for a nursery and it's always a good idea to visit a number of schools before deciding. Try and drop in during the day so that you can have a look at the facilities while there are children in school. Many of the nurseries in Dubai operate morning hours which may rule them out if you are working, but many also run late classes for an extra fee. Some nurseries have early bird drop-offs and summer school classes during the holidays. Some provide cooked lunch (and breakfast, in some cases).

**Nr Post Office**
*Jumeira*
*Map 7 D3* 🔟

## Al Safa Nurseries
**04 344 3878** | www.safanurseries.com
This nursery follows the Montessori teaching method. Activities include educational play, singing, playhouse activities and water play. The choice of Arabic or French as a second language is introduced to children above the age of 3. Field trips are arranged throughout the year, and there are annual event days. Late classes run until 14:00.
Age range: 12 months – 4 years
Other branches: Safa II (04 344 3878)

**Al Manara St**
*Rd 8*
*Umm Suqeim*
*Map 6 D2* 🔟

## Alphabet Street Nursery
**04 348 5991**
Alphabet Street employs a mix of the Montessori teaching method and the Early Years & Foundation Stage Programme (UK), to develop each child's communication, control, and coordination. They offer flexible early morning drop off, with the possibility of a 07:30 start, and also provide holiday care during the holidays. Late class available until 17:30.
Age range: 14 months – 5 years

**Nr Choithram**
*Al Wasl Rd*
*Umm Suqeim*
*Map 6 C2* 🔟

## Baby Land Montessori
**04 348 6874** | www.babylandnursery.com
Baby Land uses Montessori methods to encourage learning through play and exploration. Children participate in a series of practical activities especially designed to improve independence, concentration, hand/eye coordination, fine motor skills, patience and judgement. Baby Land offers late classes until 16:00 and a summer school.
Age range: 12 months – 4 1/2 years

**Barclays Personal Loans**

# All banks have charges
# But we don't hide ours

We understand that when it comes to your money, cute surprises aren't so cute. At Barclays, we make sure everything is loud and clear. No hidden charges and no extra payments.

**To apply for a loan call 800 BARCLAYS (800 22725297) or SMS 'LOAN' to 4422**

Subject to approval. Terms and Conditions apply.
Barclays Bank PLC is Registered in England: Registered No. 1026167. Registered Office: 1 Churchill Place London England E145HP.

**BARCLAYS**
**Banking reinvented**

## British Orchard Nursery

*Villa 20a*
*Street No. 33*
*Al Mankool*
*Bur Dubai*
*Map 8 D3* **18**

04 398 3536 | *www.britishorchardnursery.com*
This nursery follows the British national curriculum, and the guidelines of OFSTED, the schools regulator in the UK. Timings are from 08:00 to 12:30 and there are two out of school day care clubs, Little Apples and Breakfast Club, which run from 07:30 to 17:00. Parents can also log on to a secure website and see what their children are up to through the in class CCTV.

## Emirates British Nursery

*Umm Suqeim*
*Map 6 B2* **37**

04 348 9996 | *www.ebninfo.ae*
Emirates British Nursery regards playtime as an important factor in a child's early development. Both (the other is in Mirdif) locations are spacious and well planned, with multilingual staff and an in-house nurse. A summer school (a lifesaver for working mums!) is available during July and August. Late class available until 15:00.
Age range: 11 months – 4 years

## Jumeirah Infants Nursery School

*Nr Jumeira Post office*
*Jumeira*
*Map 7 D2* **57**

04 349 9065 | *www.jinschools.com*
One of the oldest nurseries in Dubai, Jumeirah Infants Nursery follows the standards set by UK OFSTED (Office for Standards in Education) and individual care and attention is given in a safe and balanced environment. Late class available until 16:00.
Age range: 8 months – 4 years

## Kids' Island Nursery

*Off Beach Rd*
*Umm Suqeim*
*Map 6 F1* **56**

04 394 2578 | *www.kidsislandnursery.com*
Kids' Island aims to create a relaxed and caring atmosphere, in which children follow the British curriculum. The nursery is open all year round, thanks to their summer school. They have large, outdoor shaded play areas, an activity room and playroom. Late class available until 13:30.
Age range: 12 months – 4 years

## Kids Cottage Nursery School ▶ p.207

*Off Beach Rd*
*Umm Suqeim*
*Map 6 F2* **44**

04 394 2145 | *www.kids-cottage.com*
This cheerful nursery with good facilities offers an activities based curriculum for children over the age of 12 months. Parents can check up on their kids via a webcam (access is password protected). Late class available until 13:30.
Age range: 12 months – 4 years

## Ladybird Nursery

*Nr Post Office*
*Al Wasl*
*Map 7 C2* **58**

04 344 1011
Ladybird strikes an interesting balance between a traditional nursery and a Montessori school, by providing the usual bright and cheerful environment, toys, dressing up clothes and soft play. Late class available until 13:30.
Age range: 18 months – 4 years

## Little Land Montessori

*Beach Rd*
*Umm Suqeim*
*Map 6 D1* **42**

04 394 4471 | *www.littleland-montessori.com*
Jointly owned by a neonatal specialist and a qualified Montessori teacher, this professional team has created a relaxing environment for little ones. The six classes are split according to age. A late class is available until 14:00.
Age range: 15 months – 4 years

KIDS COTTAGE NURSERY

DUBAI

# Where
# "Good Beginnings Never End."

* Warm, caring & friendly environment

* Experienced, qualified & dedicated teachers

* British Foundation Curriculum

* Spacious play areas & bike path

* Bright & well equipped classrooms

## Kids Cottage Nursery
## 04-3942145
www.kids-cottage.com

*Nr Safa Park*
*Al Safa*
*Map 7 B2* 55

## Palms Nursery School

*04 344 7017* | *www.palmsnursery.com*
This nursery has seven classrooms and play areas plus a soft play classroom. The curriculum is intended to help children acquire the skills and values that enable them to develop socially, physically and emotionally. Late class available until 13:30.
Age range: 22 months – 4 years

*Nr Mall of the Emirates*
*Al Barsha*
*Map 6 A4* 54

## Seashells Nursery

*04 341 3404* | *www.seashellsnursery.com*
Seashells follows the British Curriculum, has two indoor playrooms, an indoor gym, a project room for cooking and fun experiments and outdoor shaded play areas. The children can join in library, show and tell and recycling activities and field trips.
Age range: 18 months – 4 years

*Nr Al Wasl Rd*
*Jumeira*
*Map 7 F1* 61

## Small World Nursery

*04 345 7774* | *www.smallworldnurserydubai.com*
Small World offers a balanced educational structure, combining academic learning with physical education. The well equipped facilities include a library, sandy play area, a role playing room and outside play areas. There is a late class until 13:30.
Age range: 18 months – 4 years
Other branches: Small World II, also in Jumeira (04 349 0770)

*Off Street 15*
*Mirdif*
*Map 2 F2* 71

## Superkids Nursery

*04 288 1949* | *www.superkids-nursery.com*
Super Kids is a small but popular nursery that serves the growing Mirdif community. The focus is on providing a warm, cosy 'home away from home' environment. Facilities include a large, shaded outside play area, an activity gym and a music room. Hot lunch and transport are optional extras. Early bird class from 07:30 and late class available until 17:00
Age range: 11 months – 5 years

*Dubai Media City*
*Al Sufouh*
*Map 5 C2* 28

## Tender Love and Care

*04 367 1636* | *www.tenderloveandcare.com*
A popular option for people working in Internet and Media cities, this nursery has weekly activity plans and parents are notified of the monthly theme. Facilities include a gymnasium and garden. The nursery has a daily 'drop in' service, and a late class until 18:00.
Age range: 11 months – 4 years

*Nr Irish Village*
*Al Garhoud*
*Map 13 E1* 68

## Yellow Brick Road Nursery

*04 282 8290* | *www.yellowbrickroad.ws*
This huge and very popular nursery (with a long waiting list) accommodates 180 children in nine classes and a dedicated baby room. Children are taught the British nursery curriculum as well as enjoying outdoor play and swimming in the paddling pool. A cooked breakfast and lunch is provided. Late class available until 19:00.
Age range: 4 months – 5 years

## **Primary & Secondary Schools**

Primary school ages are from 4 1/2 years to 11 years, and secondary is from 11 years to 18 years. In addition to the documents listed on p.202, your child may also be required to take a short entrance exam and there may even be a physical examination and a family interview. Translated school certificates must have the student's name spelled exactly as it is found on the student's school record and passport. Most national curriculum syllabuses can be found in Dubai schools, covering GCSEs, A levels, French and International Baccalaureate and CNEC as well as the American and Indian equivalent. Standards of teaching are usually high and schools have excellent facilities with extracurricular activities offered. The international schools will often employ teachers who have been trained in, and have teaching experience from, the country relevant to the curriculum being offered. You should think carefully about what curriculum you want your kids to study. If you're coming from the UK it makes sense to go for a school teaching the British curriculum as the transition should be seamless. Likewise if and when you return home (or move to another country) you want your child to be able to slot right back into the schooling system. The Ministry of Education regularly inspects schools to ensure rules and regulations are being upheld, and most schools insist on a school uniform.

Hours: Most schools are open from 08:00 to 13:00 or 15:00, from Saturday to Wednesday. Ramadan hours are shorter - usually starting an hour or so later and finishing an hour earlier.

Fees: Primary school fees can range from Dhs.10,000 to Dhs.30,000 per year, while secondary school fees can range from Dhs.15,000 to Dhs.55,000 per year. Other costs may include a deposit or registration, medical fees, excursion fees and arts/activity fees.

## Al-Mizhar American Academy for Girls

*11A St*
*Mizhar 1*
*Mirdif*
*Map 15 D2* **73**

**04 288 7250** | *www.aag.ae*

American curriculum for girls from Kindergarden to Year 12. Based in Mizhar (near Mirdif), the school is equipped with a range of facilities including swimming, basketball, football, volleyball, drama and the band. A swimming pool, gymnasium, well-resourced library, computer labs, interactive whiteboards, art studios, music studios, science labs, and a mini auditorium are all present. The girls-only policy is intended to encourage potential and avoid gender stereotypes found in co-ed schools.
Age range: primary & secondary
Curriculum: American

## American School of Dubai

*Street 53B*
*Building 30*
*Al Wasl*
*Map 7 E2* **59**

**04 344 0824** | *www.asdubai.org*

The American School of Dubai is an independent, non-profit school offering top-quality education according to the American curriculum. The huge campus includes around 70 classrooms as well as two separate buildings for kindergartens. Other facilities include a media centre, swimming pool, computer labs, art rooms and two gymnasiums. Students partake in a range of sports including tennis, basketball, football, as well as other activities such as drama, sailing, scouts, dance and music.
Age range: primary & secondary
Curriculum: American

## Australian International School

*Opp Shj Univeristy*
*Malihard Rd*
*Dubai-Sharjah border*
*Sharjah*
*Map 2 F2*

**06 558 9967** | *www.ais.ae*

This school is run in partnership with the State of Queensland. Facilities have been customised to complement the Australian curriculum, and include large activity rooms, teaching areas for art and music, computer labs, a comprehensive library, conference rooms, a swimming pool and a multi-purpose hall and gym area. School clubs are encouraged in activities such as reading, chess, drama, music, arts and sports.
Age Range: primary
Curriculum: Australian

**209**

**Opp mosque**
5th Rd
Al Garhoud

## Cambridge International School

*04 282 4646* | www.gemscis-garhoud.com

With an attractive campus set in the popular suburb of Garhoud, Cambridge is equipped with excellent recreational facilities including a kindergarten playground, a swimming pool, tennis and volleyball courts, science and computer labs, music and art studios, a library and a canteen. The school currently has around 700 pupils, and a diverse range of professional staff. It follows the National Curriculum of England meticulously and to an extremely high standard, providing its students with an education that is recognised around the world.
Age range: primary & secondary with foundation year
Curriculum: British

**Dubai Festival City**
Al Rashidiya
**Map 5 C4** **31**

## Deira International School

*04 368 4111* | www.diadubai.com

DIS is one of the newer schools in Dubai, and one of two situated within the Dubai Festival City complex. It offers GCSE/IGCSE, A Levels and the British Baccalaureate programme and has the capacity for around 600 students. Facilities within the school include a gymnasium, a full-size track and football field, music rooms, computer and science labs, libraries, a large auditorium and a swimming pool. Although English is the language of instruction the school also offers strong Arabic and Islamic study programmes.
Age range: primary with foundation year
Curriculum: British

**Int 4**
Sheikh Zayed Rd
Al Barsha
**Map 6 A4** **38**

## Dubai American Academy

*04 347 9222* | www.gemsaa-dubai.com

Dubai American Academy provides high quality education to students from more than 60 countries. The school offers the International Baccalaureate Diploma and an enriched American curriculum. In terms of facilities, there is a cafeteria, computer and science labs, a gymnasium, library, swimming pool, athletics track and an auditorium. There's also an after-school programme from 14:45 to 15:45.
Age range: primary & secondary school
Curriculum: American

**Emirates Hills**
**Map 5 A4** **27**

## Dubai British School

*04 3619 361* | www.dubaibritishschool.ae

Dubai British School is situated in several acres of land in the grounds of Emirates Hills. The curriculum is based on the British National Curriculum. The school strongly encourages pupils to participate in the many extra-curricular activities. Facilities at the school include a swimming pool, gymnasium and library.
Age range: primary & secondary with foundation year
Curriculum: British

**Nr Internet City**
Al Sufouh
**Map 5 E2**

## Dubai College

*04 399 9111* | www.dubaicollege.org

Students at Dubai College are encouraged to develop their intellectual, physical, creative and social skills, and therefore the school boasts a diverse range of facilities. Sporting activities include athletics, rugby, football (soccer), netball, tennis and swimming; and non-sporting activities such as music, public speaking and drama are also available. There are currently just over 700 pupils at the school.
Age range: secondary
Curriculum: British

# Orbit
## leading the way

| | |
|---|---|
| **4** | TVMAX Channels |
| **6** | Western Movie Channels |
| **2** | Arabic Movie Channels |
| **8** | Western Entertainment Channels |
| **5** | Arabic Entertainment Channels |
| **5** | News Channels |
| **5** | Sports Channels |
| **7** | Kids Channels |
| **4** | Factual Channels |
| **3** | TV Music Channels |
| **20** | Radio Channels |

super **MEGA** TOTAL ENTERTAINMENT

## AED 189
Monthly

**FREE!**
Decoder & installation
TERMS AND CONDITIONS APPLY
**to subscribe**
call 04 405 9999
or visit our website at www.orbit.net

KUWAIT: 802 999
SAUDI ARABIA: 9 2000 4444
OMAN: 2448 1427
QATAR: 447 7177

## IT'S A **STAR-STUDDED** LINE-UP IN **RAMADAN**

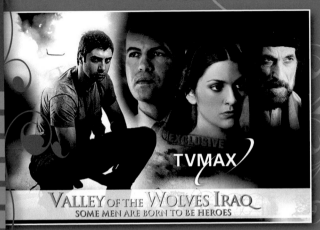

**TVMAX**

VALLEY OF THE WOLVES IRAQ
SOME MEN ARE BORN TO BE HEROES

**59TH PRIMETIME EMMY® AWARDS LIVE ONLY ON ORBIT!**

**007 BOND EXTRAVAGANZA**
ORBIT HAS THE LICENCE TO THRILL
WITH AN EXCLUSIVE PREMIERE LINE-UP OF
**20** BOND MOVIES ON CINEMA CITY
ALSO DON'T MISS CASINO ROYALE IN OCTOBER ON TVMAX

*Nr St Mary's School*
*Oud Metha*
*Map 10 F2*

## Dubai English Speaking School

*04 337 1457* | *www.dessdxb.com*

DESS first opened in a single room of a villa in 1963, and has since grown into a highly respected school with top-class facilities and around 700 pupils. The curriculum is based on the British National Curriculum and prepares students for secondary education either here or in the UK. Facilities and activities include computers, music, swimming, dance, a library and various sports.
Age range: primary
Curriculum: British

*Emirates Hills*
*Map 5 C4*

## Dubai International Academy

*04 232 5552* | *www.disdubai.ae*

Dubai International Academy follows an international curriculum taught in English. The International Baccalaureate programme consists of the primary years programme (PYP), middle years programme (MYP) and the diploma program (DP). The school has over 80 classrooms, as well as music, art, dance and drama rooms, science and computer labs, libraries, swimming pools, playing fields, basketball and tennis courts, and a cafeteria.
Age range: primary
Curriculum: British (International Baccalaureate)

*Meadows Drive*
*Emirates Hills*
*Map 6 C3*

## Emirates International School

*04 362 9009* | *www.eischool.com*

EIS aims to foster independent thinking with a balanced approach to education and an international curriculum. Facilities include fully equipped classrooms, computer and science labs, a library, a theatre and a canteen. Extra curricular activities include drama, music, swimming and basketball.
Age range: primary & secondary
Curriculum: International

*Off Shk Zayed Rd*
*Al Safa*
*Map 7 A3*

## The English College

*04 394 3465* | *www.englishcollege.ac.ae*

English College has a long tradition of academic and sporting excellence. A varied extra-curricular programme offers activities such as chess, rugby, tennis, trampolining, and even rock climbing. Students are encouraged to explore their unique talents. The multicultural environment at the school promotes tolerance and understanding.
Age range: primary & secondary
Curriculum: British

*Nr Park N Shop*
*Al Safa*
*Map 7 C2* 51

## Horizon English School

*04 342 2891* | *www.horizonschooldubai.com*

Horizon opened in 1992 with just 15 pupils, and today it has expanded to a large complex complete with top-class facilities and over 300 children. Students are educated according to the British curriculum, and can choose from afternoon activities such as football, netball, rounders, karate, swimming, dancing, cooking and drama.
Age range: primary
Curriculum: British
Other branches: Safa Horizon School (394 7879)

*Btn Jct no 4 & 5*
*Umm Suqeim*
*Map 6 F2*

## International School of Choueifat

*04 399 9444* | *www.sabis.net*

The school system here is a unique method of education that allows students to learn more in a shorter time and with less effort. New students take placement tests to check

whether they have attained certain standards in English and mathematics.
Age group: primary & secondary with foundation year
Curriculum: British & American

## Jebel Ali Primary School

*Jebel Ali*
*Map 4 C3*

**04 884 6485** | www.jebelalischool.com
This friendly primary school first opened its doors in 1977 and today it educates close to 500 pupils in 22 classes. It occupies two sites, one for infants and one for juniors. Both have access to swimming pools and grassed areas. After-school activities include football, netball, golf, gymnastics, squash, drama, cooking, music and computers.
Age range: primary
Curriculum: British

## Jumeirah College

*Nr Park n Shop*
*Al Safa*
*Map 7 A2*

**04 395 5524** | www.gemsjc.com
Jumeirah College is registered with the DFES, Department for Education and Skills in London. The school offers all the regular sporting and cultural extra curricular activities, as well as some more unconventional pursuits such as trampolining, ballet, waterskiing, horse riding, rock climbing, and karate. There are facilities for tennis, netball, swimming and there is a small, grassed playing field. The campus also has studios for art and ceramics, music rooms and drama facilities.
Age range: secondary
Curriculum: British

## Jumeirah English Speaking School

*Nr Shk Zayed Rd*
*Al Safa*
*Map 7 A2*

**04 394 5515** | www.jessdubai.org
There are four classes in each year group from Foundation I to Year 6. The campus is well equipped, with a gymnasium, music rooms, two playing areas, a football pitch and a swimming pool. Preference will be given to British passport holders, those holding debentures, and those with siblings higher up the school.
Other branch: Arabian Ranches (04 394 5515)
Age range: primary with foundation
Curriculum: British

## Jumeirah Primary School

*Nr Park n Shop*
*Jumeirah Rd*
*Al Safa*
*Map 7 A2*

**04 394 3500** | www.jumeirahprimaryschool.com
This friendly primary school first opened its doors in 1977 and today it educates close to 500 pupils in 22 classes. It occupies two sites, one for infants and one for juniors. Both have access to swimming pools and grassed areas. After-school activities include football, netball, golf, gymnastics, squash, drama, cooking, music and computers.
Age range: primary
Curriculum: British

## Kings' Dubai

*Off Al Wasl Rd (St 17)*
*Umm Suqeim*
*Map 6 B2*

**04 348 3939** | www.kingsdubai.com
Kings' Dubai opened in 2004 and has around 300 pupils. The facilities including a purpose-built auditorium, gymnasium, swimming pool, games court and sports field. The school teaches the British National Curriculum, through an innovative and creative approach with specialist teachers of ICT, PE, music, French and Arabic.
Age range: primary school with foundation
Curriculum: British

## Raffles International School ▶ p.215

▶ p.215

*Next to Spinney's*
*Meadows Drive*
*Map 6 B2* 20

04 427 1200 | www.rafflesis.com

Owned by the real estate giant Emaar, it offers a choice between British A Levels and the American High School Diploma in years 11 and 12, after students complete their IGCSEs (International General Certificate in Secondary Education). There is also the option of taking Raffles own accounting, marketing, or business administration diploma, which is recognised by some universities in the UK, US and Australia. Age range: primary and secondary. Curriculum: British.

## Regent International School

*The Greens Community*
*Emirates Hills*
*Map 5 D3*

04 360 8830 | www.risdubai.com

The school's new complex at The Greens includes state-of-the-art technology, multimedia zones, as well as library, computer, science and language labs. The sporting facilities range from a football pitch, playing fields and gymnasium to a swimming pool. The school also has an auditorium for the performing arts.
Age range: primary & secondary with foundation year
Curriculum: British

## Royal Dubai School

*Off Airport Rd*
*Mirdif*
*Map 15 D2*

04 288 6499 | www.royaldubaischool.com

Royal Dubai School is a brand new school situated on six acres of land in Mirdif. It follows the British curriculum with an internationally recruited teaching team. School facilities are wide ranging and include music and drama studios, art and science rooms, ICT suites and a library. A large, multi-purpose sports hall has been built along with a sports field, a 25m swimming pool and covered play areas.
Age range: primary with foundation year
Curriculum: British

## The Sheffield Private School

*Al Qusais*
*Map 14 D1* 66

04 267 8444 | www.sheffieldprivateschool.com

This is a GEMS managed school that follows the British curriculum. The school prides itself on a happy and supportive environment, especially among the youngest children, who have a separate play area up to the end of the second year. Facilities include music and art studios, an ICT lab, covered play areas, a swimming and a wading pool. The school offers a wide variety of extra-curricular activities and school trips.
Age range: primary with foundation year (eventually up to year 13)
Curriculum: British

## Star International School

*Nr New Airport Terml*
*Al Twar*
*Map 12 B2* 65

04 263 8999 | www.sistwar.com

Located near the new airport terminal building, Star International School follows the British curriculum, supplemented by the international primary curriculum. Day boarding is offered, so you can leave your child at the school under full supervision until 16:30.
Age range: primary & secondary
Curriculum: British

## St. Mary's Catholic High School

*Opp Iranian Club*
*Oud Metha*
*Map 10 F2* 64

04 337 0252 | www.stmarysdubai.com

Founded in 1968, St. Mary's retains the discipline of convent education but welcomes the diversity of all religions at the school. In addition to various sports activities, other activities include drama, music, debating, cookery and chess. Age range: primary & secondary. Curriculum: British.

Licensed by
حكومة دبي
Government of Dubai
هيئة المعرفة والتنمية البشرية
Knowledge and Human Development Authority

EMAAR
EDUCATION

RAFFLES
INTERNATIONAL
SCHOOL

# *Education has a new address.*

Raffles International School in Umm Suquiem has a high academic standard, a well-rounded approach to theoretic and practical learning and extra curricular activities.

We aim to prepare our students for the I.B., A-level, and US High school academic systems. 270 students from over 40 countries are tutored by experienced educators of over 20 nationalities in Arabic and English whilst French and Mandarin are also language options. Other subjects include: I.T. studies, Mathematics, Science, Music, Life skills, Art, Social studies and P.E.

To stimulate our students who range from KG to Grade 12 a number of after-school activities such as photography classes, German language, soccer, basketball, choir, crafts, chess, netball, environment club, tennis and computer club, along with extra mathematics have been created.

All of which makes our school the perfect place to address the educational needs of your child.

### St Andrews International School ▶ p.217

*Villa 19*
*Street 43A, Al Safa 1*
*nr Al Wasl Spinney''s*
*Map 6 F3* **19**

**04 394 5907** | www.sta-college.com

St Andrews follows the International Primary Curriculum and a neuro-developmental programme, based on the belief that children learn better when they have personal coaching to help develop the main senses. Its staff includes occupational, play, speech and educational therapists as well as teachers.
Age range: primary.
Curriculum: international.

### Universal American School Dubai

*Dubai Festival City*
*Deira*
*Map 13 D3*

**04 232 5222** | www.uasdubaiae.com

UASD follows a full American curriculum culminating with the American high school diploma. Arabic language classes are also included. The campus has a gymnasium, Olympic size track and football field, music rooms, art rooms, computer and science labs, libraries, a large auditorium and a swimming pool.
Age range: primary & secondary
Curriculum: American

### Uptown Primary School

*Str 15*
*Uptown Mirdiff*
*Mirdif*
*Map 15 B3*

**04 288 6270** | www.uptownprimary.ae

Uptown primary is a new school in Mirdif. The school offers the International Baccalaureate Primary Years Program (PYP) and Middle Year Programme (MYP). The main language of instruction is English. The school also houses an early learning centre developed specially for the under sixes. Facilities include a swimming pool, gymnasium, library, computer labs, art studies, music rooms, safe play areas and science labs. Uptown Primary also caters for students with special needs, and is staffed by qualified specialists.
Age range: primary and middle years.
Curriculum: British

### Wellington International School

*Opp Mall of the*
*Emirates*
*Al Sufouh*
*Map 5 F3*

**04 348 4999** | www.wellingtoninternationalschool.com

Wellington International School is a brand new GEMS-managed school with HRH Prince Michael of Kent as its patron. Unique features in the school include an observatory, TV station, creative garden and ICT, art and music suites. Other facilities include a large sports hall, gymnasium, health and fitness studio, 25m indoor swimming pool, 300m running track, basketball and tennis courts and two climbing walls. Dance and drama are encouraged through a performing arts programme.
Age range: primary & secondary
Curriculum: British

### The Westminster School

*Al Qusais*
*Map 14 C1*

**04 298 8333** | www.gemsws-ghusais.com

The Westminster school is another GEMS managed school that takes children from key stage 1 (3 years) up to year 12 (16 years). The school has 120 classrooms and a multi-purpose auditorium. Laboratories for biology, chemistry and physics are provided for the more senior pupils along with three computer labs and three libraries. The school offers athletics, basketball, football, hockey, volleyball, gymnastics and table tennis. Children are educated to the highest standards, following the British curriculum.
Age range: primary & secondary with foundation year
Curriculum: British

# St Andrews International School

*in association with the*

## British Institute for Learning Development

## The Creative Approach to Schooling

The St. Andrews International School is a registered International School with FES – the management company for the Royal Dutch Shell Schools – and uses the IPC – UK curriculum.

The IPC allows us to motivate children toward achieving academic skills and their personal goals. It also allows us to develop their 'talents' so the children can increase their ability for intellectual reasoning.

Like the British Curriculum and the International Baccalaureate, it sets 'milestones' – skill achievment levels, for the children to reach through the education journey.

Villa 19, 43a Street, Jumeirah 3
Dubai, PO Box 65725
Tel. 04 394 5907
Email: reception@british-ild.com

## website: www.sta-college.com

*The Gardens*
*Jebel Ali*
*Map 4 D3*

# The Winchester School

**04 882 0444** | *www.thewinchesterschool.com*

The Winchester School started in 2003 and has students from many different countries. Facilities include a multi-purpose auditorium, a sports field, music, art and craft rooms, science and computer labs, a library and audiovisual rooms. For the younger children there's an air-conditioned play area and covered outside area. There are numerous extra-curricular activities including music, dance, drama, outdoor sports and indoor games.
Age range: primary with foundation year
Curriculum: British

## University & Higher Education

Upon leaving school, children of expat families have traditionally returned to their home country to continue with higher education, but Dubai does have a growing number of internationally recognised universities and colleges offering degree and diploma courses in the arts, sciences, business and management, and engineering and technology. There are also a number of opportunities for post-graduate courses. Many institutions are based at Knowledge Village near Media and Internet Cities – for more info visit www.kv.ae. Dubai Academic City, on the outskirts of Dubai, will house a number of tertiary institutions and is due for completion by 2012.

### Professional Training

A number of business schools have also opened recently, offering MBAs and other professional qualification for those looking to advance their careers. A number of UK institutions have shown enthusiasm in tapping in to this potentially lucrative market. The London Business School (www.london.edu/dubai-london) is based in DIFC, as is Cass (www.cass.city.ac.uk/mba/dubai, this used to be known as City University Business School). The latter specialises in energy and Islamic finance. Warwick Business School (www.wbs.ac.uk) has been offering MBAs in Dubai since 2003.

| Universities | | |
|---|---|---|
| American College of Dubai, The | na | 04 282 9992 |
| American University in Dubai | Umm Suqeim | 04 399 9000 |
| American University of Sharjah | Sharjah | 06 515 5555 |
| British University | Al Sufouh | 04 391 3626 |
| Esmod French Fashion University ▶ p.219 | Academic City | 04 429 1228 |
| Manipal Academy of Higher Education | Al Sufouh | 04 391 1988 |
| University of Wollongong | Al Sufouh | 04 367 2400 |

*Opp Dubai Festl City*
*Garhoud*
*Map 13 D1*

## American College of Dubai

**04 282 9992** | *www.centamed.com*

The American College of Dubai offers courses that will provide students with university-level credits allowing them to transfer to institutions in the US, UK, UAE, Canada, Europe, India, or elsewhere around the world. Additionally, Associate Degrees in the Liberal Arts, Business, and Information Technology are also available.

*Shk Zayed Rd – Int 5*
*Umm Suqeim*
*Map 5 C2*

## American University in Dubai

**04 399 9000** | *www.aud.edu*

With its impressive main building that is something of a landmark along Sheikh Zayed Road, the American University Dubai is a well-established university with over 2,000 students of various nationalities. Courses offered include Business, Engineering, Information Technology, Visual Communication, Interior Design and the Liberal Arts.

# FRENCH

# FASHION

# UNIVERSITY

# ESMOD

# DUBAI

+971 (0) 4 429 12 28

WWW.FRENCH-FASHION-UNIVERSITY.COM

*Sharjah Intl Airport St*
*Sharjah*
*Map 2 F2*

## American University of Sharjah
**06 515 5555** | *www.aus.edu*
The American University of Sharjah offers a wide range of undergraduate programmes in areas such as Language, Literature, Communications, Business, Finance, and various engineering degrees. Postgraduate courses are also offered from the schools of Arts and Sciences, Architecture and Design, Business and Management, and Engineering.

*Knowledge*
*Village*
*Al Sufouh*
*Map 5 D2* 74

## British University in Dubai
**04 391 3626** | *www.buid.ac.ae*
The British University In Dubai, established in 2004, is the region's first postgraduate research based university. BUID offers postgraduate degrees including MSC Environmental Design of Buildings, MSC Information Technology and PHD programmes.

*Academic City*
*Map 2 F3*

## Esmond French Fashion University ▶ p.219
**04 429 12 28** | *www.french-fashion-university.com*
The French Fashion University is the only University in the Middle-East fully dedicated to fashion. Accredited by the French Ministry of Education they carry three year BA courses, Fashion Workshops of three and six months, trend forecasting masterclasses, merchandising training sessions for retailers & individuals, and MBA in Fashion Management

*Academic City*
*Map 2 F3*

## Heriot-Watt University Dubai
**04 361 6999** | *www.hw.ac.uk./dubai*
One of the UK's oldest universities, Heriot-Watt has now opened a campus at Academic City in Dubai (with an office at Knowledge Village). The university offers undergraduate and postgraduate courses in business, management, finance, accounting, and IT.

*Knowledge Village*
*Al Sufouh*
*Map 5 D2* 34

## Manipal Academy of Higher Education
**04 391 1988** | *www.mahedubai.com*
Manipal Academy of Higher Education offers certificate programmes, bachelors and masters degree programmes in a range of subjects including information systems, media and communications, and fashion and interior design.

*Knowledge*
*Village*
*Al Sufouh*
*Map 5 D2* 17

## Middlesex University
**04 367 8100** | *www.mdx.ac*
The UK's Middlesex University recently opened a campus at Knowledge Village. Students have the option of studying for single or joint honours degrees, in subjects including accountancy, business studies, tourism, human resource management, marketing and computing science.

*Knowledge Village*
*Al Sufouh*
*Map 5 D2* 33

## SAE Institute
**04 361 6173** | *www.sae-dubai.com*
This respected Australian film, which has branches throughout the world, has an impressive multimedia training institute. SAE offers courses specialising in audio engineering, digital animation and filmmaking.

*Knowledge Village*
*Al Sufouh*
*Map 5 D2* 32

## University of Wollongong ▶ p.221
**04 367 2400** | *www.uowdubai.ac.ae*
The University of Wollongong offers a number of undergraduate and postgraduate programmes in business and IT, in addition to certificates and awards in accounting, banking and management. The university used to be situated along Beach Road, but moved to Knowledge Village in 2005.

# UOWD

## University of Wollongong in Dubai

# 5 Reasons to Choose University of Wollongong in Dubai

1. **UOWD is oldest and most prestigious private university in the UAE, with a proud Australian heritage.**
Established in 1993 by the University of Wollongong Australia, UOWD represented a very early Australian initiative in the UAE. The University of Wollongong was established in Wollongong (80kms south of Sydney) in 1951. Today, it is Australia's leading university with over 22,000 students enrolled in 10 faculties which include a Graduate Medical School. UOW is one of only two universities in Australia to achieve top-tier rankings in every discipline category of the Australian Government's 2008 Learning and Teaching Performance Fund§.

2. **UOWD degrees are accredited in the UAE, GCC and Australia.**
UOWD degree programs are accredited by the UAE Ministry of Higher Education and Scientific Research and are also reviewed by the Australian Universities Quality Agency. Their nationally and internationally recognised qualifications enable UOWD graduates to pursue further education and employment in the private and public sectors around the world.

§ Department of Education, Science and Training's 2008 Learning and Teaching Performance Fund.

3. **UOWD teachers are world-class.**
Our teachers are locally and internationally recruited academics who have extensive experience in the class room as well as in business and industry. They bring years of knowledge in their respective fields as well as the latest developments from their research, into the class room providing students with a stimulating academic environment.

4. **UOWD degrees focus on putting knowledge to work in the real-world.**
Our programs are delivered in a way that seeks to bridge the gap between theoretical models and business realities. Students are given projects based on current issues in the real world and students have the opportunity to attend seminars co-hosted with industry partners.

5. **At UOWD you will belong to an international community.**
UOWD attracts students not just from the UAE and Australia but from all over the world. Approximately 2,500 students comprising more than 80 nationalities are currently enrolled at UOWD and enjoy a quality academic experience and the benefits of a truly international student body.

Block 15, Dubai Knowledge Village
P.O. Box 20183, Dubai, United Arab Emirates
Telephone: + 971 4 367 2400, Fax: + 971 4 367 8047
Email: admissions@uowdubai.ac.ae, Website: www.uowdubai.ac.ae

A Partner Of

DUBAI
KNOWLEDGE
VILLAGE

## Your Australian University in the Emirates

*A Whole Lot Of*
*Knowledge*
*Knowledge Village prides itself on creating an environment conducive to education, the business of education and networking. The operating rules and regulations are relatively straightforward and they simplify the application process for a one-year student's resident visa, too. Some of the tertiary institutions to be found here (in addition to those mentioned above) are: European University College Brussels, Institute of Management Technology, Islamic Azad University, Mahatma Ghandi University, UAE University, Royal College of Surgeons and the University of New Brunswick in Dubai. Find out more on www.kv.ae.*

## Special Needs Education

If your child has physical or learning difficulties, there are several organisations that can help. Some mainstream schools will try to accommodate children suffering from dyslexia, ADHD and other more manageable challenges but are rarely geared up to take students with other needs. Special needs schools operate without government assistance, and therefore rely on donations, sponsorship, grants and help from volunteer workers. All charge tuition fees.

• The Al Noor Centre for Children with Special Needs (04 394 6088, www.alnooruae.org) provides therapeutic support and comprehensive training to special needs children of all ages. The centre also equips its 220 students with work related skills.
• The Dubai Centre for Special Needs (04 344 0966) currently has 130 students, all of which have an individual programme, including physiotherapy, speech therapy and occupational therapy. A pre-vocational programme is offered for older students, which includes arranging work placements. www.dcsneeds.ae
• Rashid Paediatric Therapy Centre (04 340 0005,www.rashidc.ae) includes physical, occupational and speech therapy. In the afternoons, therapists see children on an outpatient basis, also working on early intervention and assisting school children with motor, learning, speech and communication difficulties.
• There is a therapeutic horse riding programme for children with special needs – Riding for the Disabled (www.rdad.ae). The team offers lessons to children from the various special needs schools around Dubai, providing much-needed physical and mental stimulation. Lessons take place at the Desert Palms Polo Club, and include a variety of gentle exercises and short outrides.
• Dubai Autism Centre provides a support network for parents and teacher training for teaching autistic children (04 398 6862, www.dubaiautismcenter.ae).
• The Dyslexia Support Group is run by volunteer mums, and offers advice and support to families. Call 04 344 6657 or 04 344 0738 for more information.
• Senses is a Dubai-based residential and daycare centre for people with special needs, speak to Kerry on 04 394 8765 for more details.

## Learning Arabic

Other options **Language Schools** p.354

English is so widely used in Dubai that you can get by without having to learn a single word of Arabic. However, some say that to enrich the cultural experience of your time in this part of the world, knowing some basic Arabic is helpful. Many expat children have Arabic lessons at school, so it can be useful to know a bit yourself. The language schools listed in the table all offer classes in Arabic, and most teach beginner, intermediate and advanced classes. Arabic classes are available both during the day and in the evenings, so you should be able to find one at a convenient time.

| Learning Arabic | | |
| --- | --- | --- |
| Arabic Language Centre | 04 308 6036 | alc@dwtc.com |
| Berlitz | 04 344 0034 | www.berlitz.com |
| Dar El Ilm School of Languages | 04 331 0221 | darelilm@emirates.net.ae |
| El Ewla Language Academy | 04 391 1640 | www.elewla.com |
| Polyglot Language Institute | 04 222 3429 | www.polyglot.ae |
| Sheikh Mohd Centre for Cultural Understanding | 04 353 6666 | www.cultures.ae |
| University of Wollongong | 04 367 2400 | www.uowdubai.ac.ae |

## Transportation

Other options **Car** p.53, **Getting Around** p.49

Options for public transport are somewhat limited, and so most Dubai expats find that owning a car is essential. There's a comprehensive bus network operated by Dubai Municipality, but it gets busy and more often then not, you'll find yourself having to wait a while for a bus to come along that isn't too overloaded with people for you to get on board. The Municipality is moving fast towards a better public transportation system with metro plans still movng forward and more buses on the roads to take care of the issue of overcrowding, as well as air-conditioned bus shelters, which apparently feature high on the agenda. For information on Dubai's bus services, see p.52 or call 800 9090. Construction work on the Dubai Metro has begun. This is a light rail network that should hopefully ease traffic congestion when it is finished (estimated completion date is 2009). For more information on the Metro project, see p.58.

### Taxi

Dubai has a taxi fleet of around 5,000 licensed taxis, so it's pretty easy to flag one down. You can also order one from Dubai Transport (www.dubaitransport.gov.ae) to come and pick you up where you are. They have a satellite tracking system installed in all their cabs and an automated phone system – to order a taxi call 04 208 0808 and follow the instructions. The first time you call you'll be put through to an operator who will take down the directions to your house; your details are then stored on their database so the next time you call from your home number, simply press '1' on your phone and the taxi will be dispatched straight away. It's also possible to request a bigger taxi for trips to the airport when you might have lots of luggage, although you should book one of these in advance. The Toyota Camry is the standard car model used for taxis.

If needed, you can hire a Dubai Transport cab for longer periods. This costs about Dhs.500 for 12 hours (within Dubai). For more information on taxis, see p.58.

### Driving

Petrol has recently gone up several times, but in comparison with other countries it's still pretty cheap. This means that many people drive gas-guzzlers. Car prices are generally lower than in other countries, so you may have the opportunity to drive in style. Car pooling has not really taken off.

On the roads that connect Sharjah to Dubai the sheer volume of traffic results in gridlock nearly every morning and evening.

Most street parking in Dubai is now governed by parking meters. You pay Dhs.1 or Dhs.2 for one hour, depending on how busy the area is. After feeding your coins into the machine, you get a printed ticket that you must display on your dashboard. The price increases dramatically the longer you park in a spot, so you'll pay Dhs.5 for two hours, Dhs.8 for three hours, and Dhs.11 for four hours (the maximum). Parking is free from 13:00 to 16:00 and 21:00 to 08:00 daily and on Fridays and public holidays.

Dubai drivers are notoriously bad. You can expect lots of overtaking on the inside, dramatic lane-switching manoeuvres, sudden stops, and quite surprising levels of aggression. Your first few weeks of driving will be an ordeal, but you will quickly learn to drive defensively. The important thing is not to let the bad driving keep you from getting out and about – the sooner you get behind the wheel, the sooner you'll get used to it. For more information about driving and driving licences, see p.88.

### Start Your Engines!

If the constant grind of gridlock is making you hate getting behind the wheel then maybe it's time you took to the desert. The Gulf is home to some of the most breathtaking scenery in the Middle East and there is no better way to experience it than bashing dunes and driving through wadis. Grab a copy of the *Off-Road Explorer Guides* (available for Oman and the UAE) and plan your trip today.

*Dubai roads*

**Cash Only**
*In 2007, petrol stations suddenly adopted a 'cash only' policy whereas before you could pay for your petrol by debit and credit card. So make sure you have cash to hand before you fill up, and don't rely on there being an ATM at all petrol stations.*

## Parking Cards

There are several different ways of purchasing pre-paid parking cards for use in parking meters, which save you money and the hassle of always needing the right change at the many paid parking areas in Dubai. The first way is through the post office where you can get pay-as-you-go cards you display in the car – for Dhs.42.50 you get Dhs.50 worth of parking and for Dhs.80 you get parking to the value of Dhs.100. Alternatively, you can buy a card from Dubai Municipality that can be used for an unlimited amount. Type A parking cards can be used in all parking areas – they cost Dhs.700 for three months, Dhs.1,300 for six months and Dhs.2,500 for a year. Type B parking cards restrict you to off-street parking in designated areas – they cost Dhs.450 for three months, Dhs.800 for six months and Dhs.1,500 for a year.

## Salik

In 2007, the Salik road toll system came into effect. It has two gates, one at the Bur Dubai entrance to Garhoud Bridge, another on the Sheikh Zayed Road after Mall of the Emirates for those heading in the direction of Jebel Ali. There are no booths, and no need to stop as you drive through. Instead, drivers stick a tag to their windscreen, which is read by radio frequency as they pass through. It costs Dhs.4 each time. Those that don't have a card will be fined Dhs.50. The kit can be bought from Emarat, EPPCO, ENOC, and ADNOC petrol stations, Dubai Islamic Bank and Emirates Bank.

# Vehicle Leasing

Many people find that they have no other option (due to visa requirements) than to lease a vehicle, and while it may be easier in terms of repairs, re-registration and servicing, long term leasing can be expensive. Most leasing companies include the following in their rates: registration, maintenance, replacement, 24 hour assistance and insurance. Find out which car hire agent your company uses, as you might qualify for a corporate rate.

Leasing is generally weekly, monthly or yearly. Monthly lease prices range from Dhs.1,500 for a small vehicle such as a Toyota Echo, Dhs.1,900 for larger cars like a Honda Accord, and Dhs.3,500 for a 4WD. As the lease period increases, the price decreases, so if you're considering keeping the car for a long period, it may not work out that much more expensive than buying.

| Vehicle Leasing Agents | | |
|---|---|---|
| Auto Assist | 04 391 1933 | na |
| Autolease Rent-a-Car | 04 282 6565 | www.autolease-uae.com |
| Avis | 04 295 7121 | www.avisuae.com |
| Budget | 04 295 6667 | www.budget-uae.com |
| Diamond Lease ▶ p.225 | 04 343 4330 | www.diamondlease.com |
| EuroStar Rent-a-Car ▶ p.57 | 04 266 1117 | www.eurostarrental.com |
| FAST Rent A Car | 04 332 8988 | www.fastuae.com |
| Hertz | 04 282 4422 | www.hertz-uae.com |
| Highway Rent A Car LLC | 04 347 4773 | na |
| National Car Rental | 04 335 5447 | www.national-me.com |
| Thrifty Car Rental | 04 800 4694 | www.thriftyuae.com |
| United Car Rentals | 04 266 6286 | na |

Before you take possession of your leased car, check for any dents or bumps. While many companies will deliver the car to you, you might still have to visit the office to sort out all the paperwork. To hire any vehicle you will need to provide a passport copy, credit card and a valid driving licence (either your Dubai licence, your licence from your home country, or a valid international licence). If you are just visiting Dubai (and have no Dubai driving licence), you might find that a valid international licence is more readily accepted than the licence from your home-country. Many companies offer daily rentals – refer to the table above for the most reputable agents.

## Company Cars

Some people will be given a company car as part of their package, which will no doubt have been bought or leased by the company and therefore will be returned if you leave. Some people are given a lease car by their employer when they first arrive (until

# Experience
# the heights of excellence.

Backed by high quality and professional services, Diamondlease has the latest range of vehicles. Check out the fleet which is complete with the finest marques from across the globe and from a diverse cross section of vehicles in the market - starting from everyday cars to prestigious high-end marques, from four wheel drives to family movers, from coaches to pick-ups. That's why we say with Diamondlease, the choice is unlimited!

## DIAMONDLEASE
### CAR RENTAL

Box 32689, Dubai, U.A.E., E-mail: carlease@emirates.net.ae, Website: www.diamondlease.com

| | | | | |
|---|---|---|---|---|
| Office: | Dubai Airport (24 hrs): | Sheikh Zayed Road (Al Quoz): | Dubai Investment Park: | Knowledge Village: |
| 4 3434330 | Tel: 04 2200325 | Tel: 04 3394500 | Sales Dept.: Tel: 04 8852677 | Tel: 04 3903794 |
| or Grand: | Metropolitan Hotel: | Jebel Ali: | Service Dept.: Tel: 04 8852211 | |
| 4 3995049 | Tel: 04 3434022 | Tel: 04 8814645 | Dhow Palace Hotel: | |
| | | | Tel: 04 3599992 (Ext: 8443) | |
| DHABI | Abu Dhabi Airport: | Mussafah: | | Our Associate |
| a Street Branch: | Tel: 02 5758117 | Tel: 02 5530012 | FUJAIRAH: | in Romania |
| 2 6222028 | | | Tel: 09 2232774 | |

**24 Hours Emergency Service: 04 8852211**

ELITE

ISO 9001: 2000

DUBAI SERVICE EXCELLENCE SCHEME

برنامج دبي للخدمة المميزة

they get their residency formalities sorted out and can buy a car), and others receive a transportation allowance as part of their salary package.

**Second Opinion**

*When buying a used car it's well worth having it checked over by a garage or mechanic. Eppco/ Tasjeel, AAA and Max Garage offer a checking service. Alternatively, speak to the service department at the dealership where the car was originally bought. A thorough inspection will cost about Dhs.250.*

# Buying a Vehicle

You must have a residence visa in order to own a car. Most insurance policies cover multiple drivers (as long as they have a valid UAE driving licence, either temporary or permanent), but check the small print before you let your spouse behind the wheel (see Certificates & Licences, p.88).

## New Car Dealers

Most of the major car makes are available through franchised dealerships in Dubai, with big Japanese and American brands particularly well represented. Expat buyers may be pleasantly surprised by the low cost of new cars – for example, a Jeep Wrangler would cost around $24,000 (approx Dhs.88,150) in the US, over £16,000 (approx Dhs.110,500) in the UK, but as little as Dhs.74,000 here in Dubai. Similarly, the ubiquitous Toyota Land Cruiser would set you back roughly $56,000 (approx Dhs.205,680) in the US and a massive £45,000 (approx Dhs.311,300) in the UK, but Dubai prices start at around Dhs.110,000. For many, this lower initial cost, coupled with cheaper fuel and maintenance, means they can afford something a little more extravagant than they might drive at home.

## New Car Dealers

| | | | |
|---|---|---|---|
| Alpha Romeo, Saab | Gargash Motors | 04 266 4669 | www.gargashme.com |
| Aston Martin, Bentley, Mitsubishi | Al Habtoor Motors | 04 269 1110 | www.habtoormotors.com |
| Audi | Al Naboodah Automobiles (Audi showroom) ▶ p.79 | 04 347 5111 | www.nabooda-auto.com |
| BMW, Rolls Royce, Mini | AGMC | 04 339 1555 | www.bmw-dubai.com |
| Cadillac, Opel, Hummer | Liberty Automobiles Co. | 04 282 4440 | www.liberty.ae |
| Chevrolet, Daihatsu | Al Yousuf Motors | 04 339 5555 | www.aym.ae |
| Chrysler, Dodge, Honda, Jeep, Volvo | Trading Enterprises HQ ▶ p.xvi, xvii | 04 204 7160 | www.alfuttaim.ae |
| Ferrari, Maserati, Jaguar | Al Tayer Motors | 04 266 6489 | www.altayer.com |
| Fiat, Lancia, Ssangyong | Al Ghandi Automotive | 04 266 6511 | www.alghandi.com |
| Ford, Landrover, Mercury, Lincoln | Al Tayer Motors | 04 201 1001 | www.altayer.com |
| Hyundai | Juma Al Majid Est | 04 269 0893 | www.hyundai-motor.com |
| Kia, Renault | Al Majed Motors | 04 269 5600 | www.kia-hypen.com |
| Lexus, Toyota | Al Futtaim Motors | 04 228 2261 | www.toyotauae.com |
| Mazda | Galadari Automobiles | 04 299 4848 | www.mazdauae.com |
| Mercedes | Gargash Enterprises LLC– Mercedes Benz | 04 269 9777 | www.gargash.mercedes-benz.com |
| Nissan, Infinity | Arabian Automobiles- Nissan | 04 295 1234 | www.arabianautomobiles.com |
| Peugeot | Swaidan Trading Co. Peugeot | 04 266 7111 | www.swaidanpeugeot.com |
| Skoda | Autostar Trading | 04 269 7100 | na |
| Suzuki | Al Rostamani Trading (Suzuki) | 04 347 0008 | www.alrostamani.com |
| Volkswagen, Porsche | Al Naboodah Automobiles ▶ p.79 | 04 338 6999 | www.nabooda-auto.com |

## Used Car Dealers

Due to the relatively low price of cars and the turnover of expats in the emirates, there is a thriving second-hand market. Dealers are scattered around town but good areas to start are Sheikh Zayed Road and Garhoud. Expect to pay a premium of between Dhs.5,000 and Dhs.10,000 for buying through a dealer (as opposed to buying from a private seller), since they also offer a limited warranty, insurance, finance and registration.

**Tinted Windows**
*Currently, the government allows you to avoid the sun somewhat by tinting your vehicle's windows up to 30%. Some areas have facilities where you can get your car windows tinted but don't get carried away - remember to stick to the limit. Random checks take place and fines are handed out to those caught in the dark! Tinting in Sharjah is allowed for a fee of Dhs.100 and Ajman residents may tint for Dhs.200 per annum, but only if they are women.*

**Dodgy Drives**
*Finding a taxi in congested areas can be difficult, and in their frustration, many people are using illegal cabs. Be warned though that unlicensed taxis haven't had to meet the safety standards for their cars that legal cabs do. As these cabs are difficult to trace, there have also been cases where drivers have either been the victim of crimes or have perpetrated them.*

One of the biggest used-car dealers in Dubai is 4x4 Motors (www.4x4motors.com), with a large showroom near the airport. Despite the name, they sell saloon cars as well as 4WDs, and offer finance on all purchases. They have been well-established in Dubai for many years and are often the port-of-call for new residents looking to upgrade their vehicle of choice from what they used to drive in their home country. They often have 'nearly new' vehicles that are a year or less old and therefore cheaper than buying from a new car dealer.

Al Futtaim Automall (www.automalluae.com) has three sites in Dubai, and each car comes with a 12 month warranty and a 30 day exchange policy.

Off Road Motors (04 338 4866) on Sheikh Zayed Road also has a good selection of used cars (again, with saloons as well as 4WDs) as do Jumeirah Motors (next to the Mazaya Centre on Sheikh Zayed Road), Western Auto (branches at Al Awir and Deira), Target Auto (near Mazaya Centre), House of Cars (Sheikh Zayed Road), and Sun City Motors (branches near the airport, Al Awir, and Sheikh Zay2466).

The Al Awir complex has a website (www.usedcars.ae) with links to many of the dealers and the ability to search for cars by make, model or year. Al Awir is also home to Golden Bell Auctions (www.goldenbellauctions.com), with sales held each Wednesday evening. All cars up for auction have to undergo a test at the nearby Eppco/Tasjeel garage, and all outstanding fines will have been cleared. The cars are put up for sale by banks and finance companies, showrooms, rental companies, taxi firms and individuals. There's a Traffic Department office on the site so buyers can register their new vehicles on the spot. You have to pay a refundable deposit that allows you to bid, and there are some real bargains to be had. However, you should never forget the handy Latin phrase *caveat emptor* – let the buyer beware. Take along someone who knows their cars, and give any vehicle a thorough going over before you get bidding.

The *Gulf News* and *Khaleej Times* classifieds sections are a good starting place for second-hand cars. There are lots of ads placed by showrooms, but plenty of private ads too. Supermarket noticeboards are another good option. Alongside the adverts for cheap furniture and lost cats, you may just find a bargain motor being sold by an expat leaving town at the end of the week. Most Choithram supermarkets have noticeboards, and the ones at Spinneys are usually pretty big, as is the one at Park n Shop in Al Safa.

## Used Car Dealers

| | | | |
|---|---|---|---|
| 4x4 Motors | Al Garhoud | 04 282 3050 | www.4x4motors.com |
| Al Futtaim Automall | Al Quoz | 04 347 2212 | www.al-futtaim.com |
| Auto Plus | Al Quoz | 04 339 5400 | www.autoplusdubai.com |
| Boston Cars | Al Awir | 04 333 1010 | na |
| Dynatrade | Al Awir | 04 320 1558 | www.dynatrade-uae.com/povd |
| Exotic Cars | Al Quoz | 04 338 4339 | na |
| House of Cars | Al Wasl | 04 343 5060 | www.houseofcarsgroup.com |
| Jumeirah Motors | Al Wasl | 04 343 4449 | na |
| Motor World | Al Awir | 04 333 2206 | na |
| Off Road Motors | Al Quoz | 04 338 4866 | www.offroad-motors.com |
| Quartermile | Al Awir | 04 333 5663 | www.quartermile.net |
| Reem Automobile | Al Wasl | 04 343 6333 | www.reemauto.com |
| Sun City Motors | Al Barsha | 04 340 3050 | www.suncitymotors.com |
| Target Auto | Al Wasl | 04 343 3911 | www.target-auto.com |
| Tony Edwards Motors | Al Quoz | 04 80 0836 | www.temllc.com |
| Western Auto | Deira | 04 297 3737 | www.westernauto.ae |

## Ownership Transfer

To register a second-hand car in your name you must transfer vehicle ownership. You will need to submit an application form, the valid registration card, the insurance certificate, the original licence plates and Dhs.20 to the Traffic Police, plus an NOC from the finance company, if applicable. The seller must also be present with their passport and residence permit (and copies) to sign the form.

| Vehicle Finance | | |
|---|---|---|
| Emirates Bank | 04 316 0316 | www.emiratesislamicbank.ae |
| HSBC ▶ p.109 | 04 228 8999 | www.hsbc.ae |
| Lloyds TSB Bank Plc ▶ p.107 | 04 342 2000 | www.lloydstsb.ae |
| Mashreqbank | 04 217 4800 | www.mashreqbank.com |
| National Bank of Dubai – Abu Dhabi | 02 639 4555 | www.nbd.com |
| RAK Bank | 04 213 0000 | www.rakbank.ae |

## Vehicle Finance

Many new and second-hand car dealers will be able to arrange finance for you, often through a deal with their preferred banking partner. Be aware that this may involve writing out years and years worth of post-dated cheques – make sure they never bounce, or you'll be in trouble with the police. Always ask about the rates and terms, and then consider going directly to one of the banks to see if they can offer you a better deal.

## Vehicle Import

A requirement for cars imported by individuals or private car showrooms that were manufactured after 1997/98, is an NOC from the official agent in the UAE or from the Ministry of Finance and Industry (if no official agent exists). This is to ensure that the car complies with GCC specifications. Additionally, if you are buying a vehicle from another emirate you have to export and import it into Dubai first. This means lots of paperwork, and you'll need your essential documents, the sale agreement, current registration and Dhs.60. You will be issued with a set of temporary licence (export) plates, which are valid for three days – enough time to submit a new registration application in Dubai. Note that export plates are not available for motorbikes.

**To Oman & Back**

*It is wise to check whether your insurance covers you for the Sultanate of Oman as, within the Emirates, you may find yourself driving through small Oman enclaves (especially if you are off-road, near Hatta, through Wadi Bih and on the East Coast in Dibba – see Exploring, p.295). Insurance for a visit to Oman can be arranged on a short term basis, usually for no extra cost.*

## Vehicle Insurance

Before you can register your car you must have adequate insurance, and there are many insurance companies to choose from in Dubai. The insurers will need to know the usual details such as year of manufacture, and value, as well as the chassis number. If you got a real bargain of a car and feel it's worth much more than you paid, make sure you instruct the insurance company to cover it at the market value. However, if the value is higher than they would normally estimate, they may ask to inspect the vehicle. Take copies of your UAE driving licence, passport and the existing vehicle registration card.

Annual insurance policies are for a 13 month period (this is to cover the one-month grace period that you are allowed when your registration expires). Rates depend on the age and model of your car and your previous insurance history, although if you're new in Dubai and insuring a car for the first time, very few companies will recognise any no-claims bonuses you have accrued in your home country. The rates are generally 4 to 7% of the vehicle value, or a flat 5% for cars over five years old. Fully comprehensive cover with personal accident insurance is highly advisable, and you are strongly advised to make

| Vehicle Insurance | |
|---|---|
| Al Khazna Insurance Company | 04 294 4088 |
| Arab Orient Insurance Company | 04 295 3425 |
| AXA Insurance ▶ p.229 | 04 800 4845 |
| Emirates Insurance | 04 299 0655 |
| Greenshield Insurance ▶ p.181, 231 | 04 397 4464 |
| Nasco Karaoglan | 04 352 3133 |
| National General Insurance (Healthnet) | 02 667 8783 |
| Oman Insurance | 04 800 4746 |

# With AXA
# Be Driving Confident

## Motor Perfect Insurance
Comprehensive protection at the best value

Get on the road with AXA's unique comprehensive motor packages. Motor Perfect Insurance gives you extra services and benefits like a no claim bonus, roadside assistance, off-road cover for 4x4 vehicles and much more.

**INSURANCE**

Call **800 4845**
www.axa-gulf.com

**Motor - Healthcare - Home - Travel - Yacht - Golf - Relocation**

Be Life Confident

sure the policy covers you for 'blood money' (see p.56 for more details). For more adventurous 4WD drivers, insurance for off-roading accidents is also recommended

see p.56 for more details

## Registering a Vehicle

All cars must be registered annually with the Traffic Police. There is a one-month grace period after your registration has expired in which to have your car re-registered (hence the 13 month insurance period), but after that you'll face a Dhs.110 fine for each month the registration has expired. Please beware that some second-hand dealers may sell you a car that under normal circumstances would not pass the annual vehicle testing. However, with 'friends' at the test centre, they are able to get the car passed, leaving you stuck when you come to do it yourself the following year.

### The Process

In order to get licence plates for the vehicle, the car must first be tested, then registered with the Dubai Traffic Police. If you have purchased a new vehicle from a dealer, the dealer will register the car for you. You do not need to test a new vehicle for the first two years, although you must re-register it after one year. There are several ways to test your car. Ras Al Khor boasts a five-lane testing centre (Al Ghandi Shamel) that is run in conjunction with the Traffic Police. The centre is paperless and this saves you time in necessary procedures. EPPCO and Emarat offer a full registration service. For an additional fee they will collect your car, test and register it, and deliver it back to you in the same day. Alternatively, an express service, where you bring the car in and enjoy your complimentary drink in the air-conditioned waiting room while they do the process for you, is available. Emarat (04 343 4444) also has five full registration and vehicle testing service centres (called Shamil), where they will test and register your car with the police. You can also pay any traffic fines here.

Remember to take all your essential documents, insurance valid for 13 months, registration card, proof of purchase agreement and vehicle transfer or customs certificate (if applicable) and cash. Before the registration procedure can be completed, all traffic offences and fines against your car registration number must be settled. Try to check your fines before you get your car tested (you can do so on www.dubaipolice.gov.ae), as some of the larger fines cannot be paid at the test centre.

| Registration Service | |
|---|---|
| AAA | 04 266 9989 |
| Echo | 04 396 9929 |
| EPPCO Tasjeel | 800 4258 |
| Midland Cars | 04 396 7521 |
| Shamil | 800 4559 |

**Registration Costs**

Registration with long number plates, Dhs.70. Registration with short number plates, Dhs.50. Registration through a finance company may cost a little more for the convenience. Registration Service Companies: AAA (04 266 9989) Dhs.150. Al Ghandi Shamel (04 333 1204) Dhs.200. Echo Car Registration Service (04 396 9929) Dhs.125. Emarat Shamil (800 4559) Dhs.200. EPPCO Tasjeel (800 4258/04 347 9662) Dhs.200. Midland Cars (04396 7521/2) Dhs.200

## Traffic Fines & Offences

If you are caught driving or parking illegally you will be fined unless the offence is more serious, in which case you may be brought before the courts. You can also be fined Dhs.50 on the spot for being caught driving without your licence, so always keep it with you, along with your vehicle's registration card.

Fines for speeding start at Dhs.200. Running a red light will land you with a Dhs.500 fine and your vehicle will be confiscated for a week if it's your first offence. If you do so again, your car will be confiscated for a longer period of time. You also face being taken to court and losing your licence. Dangerous driving attracts the same penalty. Parking tickets are Dhs.150 if issued

## Breakdowns

In the event of a breakdown, you will usually find that passing police cars will stop to help, or at least to check your documents. It's important that you keep water in your car at all times – the last thing you want is to be stuck in the middle of summer with no air conditioning while you wait for assistance. Dubai Traffic officers recommend, if

*tor Insurance from Greenshield*

# A traffic accident takes place every 3 minutes in Dubai. Make sure you drive in intervals of 2 minutes and 45 seconds.

e in awhile, life throws each of us a curve ball. And while there's no way of protecting ourselves from the reseen, we can plan ahead. With all levels of motor coverage including agency/non-agency repair, third-party lity, personal accident cover (driver & passenger) and specific territory coverage, your insurance can be omised for your individual needs. Greenshield Insurance covers you for the unexpected, so you can focus on ying life. For a free consultation, call Michelle on 04.397.4464 or email michelle@greenshiled.co.ae

GREENSHIELD
INSURANCE

• **Medical** • **Education** • **Travel** • **Motor** • **Savings** • **Property and Fire** • **Bankers Blanket Bond** • **Product Liability**

| Recovery Services/Towing (24 hour) | |
| --- | --- |
| AAA | 04 2669 989 |
| AKT Recovery Service | 04 263 6217 |
| Dubai Auto Towing Services | 04 359 4424 |
| IATC Recovery | 04 800 5200 |

possible, that you pull your car over to a safe spot. If you are on the hard shoulder of a highway you should pull your car as far away from the yellow line as possible and step away from the road until help arrives.

The Arabian Automobile Association (AAA) (04 266 9989 or 800 4900, www.aaa-uae.com) offers a 24 hour roadside breakdown service for an annual charge. This includes help in minor mechanical repairs, battery boosting, or help if you run out of petrol, have a flat tyre or lock yourself out. Mashreq Bank Visa card holders receive free AAA membership. The more advanced service includes off-road recovery, vehicle registration and a rent a car service. It's a similar concept to the RAC or AA in Britain, or AAA in the States. Other breakdown services who'll be able to help you out without membership include IATC (it also offers annual membership), Dubai Auto Towing Services and AKT Recovery.

### Black Points

In addition to a system of fines for certain offences, a black points penalty system operates. If you have a permanent licence and receive 12 black points in one year, your licence is taken away and your car impounded. Driving in a reckless manner or racing will earn you 6 points, as will parking in a handicapped zone or in front of a fire hydrant. Other major offences include overtaking where prohibited, jumping a red light and entering a road dangerously. If you do something particularly dangerous your licence can be taken away immediately. However, the rules are somewhat ambiguous, and erratically applied.

**Blood Money** ◀

As the law currently stands, the family of a pedestrian killed in a road accident is entitled to Dhs.200,000 diya (blood) money. The money is usually paid by the insurance company unless there's any whiff of the driver having been under the influence of alcohol. However an amendment to the law is being considered to put a stop to the terrible trend among desperate lower-income workers of killing themselves to provide for their family. This will mean blood money is not automatically due if the victim was walking across a road not intended for use by pedestrians, such as Sheikh Zayed Road.

## Traffic Accidents

Other options **Car** p.53

Many people who arrive in Dubai and become familiar with the roads by taking a taxi around the city often think they will never be able to drive here. This hesitation is understandable; firstly the road systems seems somewhat complicated when you first arrive and secondly you witness an inordinate amount of accidents – ranging from numerous fender benders to many serious collisions. However, most people do eventually get behind the wheel and invariably find that within a few months they've adopted a very defensive method of driving. It's vital not to become complacent about driving in Dubai, no matter how long you have been doing it. You should always exercise extra care and attention when on the roads as there are more than a few maniacs driving machines that simply have too much horsepower for them. Be vigilant and remember to use your mirrors (and indicators) at all times.

A total of 157 people were killed on Dubai's roads in the first 6 months of 2006, (with Emirates Road considered by police to be the most dangerous highway in the emirate). That's an average of 26 deaths per month. The number of accidents rockets during the holy month of Ramadan, as many drivers are tired, hungry and irritable, and in an even bigger hurry than usual to reach their destination, especially in the late afternoon and evening.

If you are involved in an accident call 999. If the accident is minor and no one has been hurt you need to agree with the other driver where the blame lies and move your cars to the side of the road to avoid obstructing the flow of traffic. You can be fined Dhs.100 for failing to do, so even if the accident wasn't your fault.

The Dubai Police Information Line (800 7777, Arabic & English) gives the numbers of police stations around the emirate. The police will assess the accident and once they have apportioned blame they will give you a copy of the accident report, if it is green then the other party is at fault but if it is pink then you are to blame for the accident.

You will need to submit this form to the insurance company in order to process the claim, or to the garage for repairs. Garages are coming under increasing pressure not to accept any vehicle for repair without a police report of the accident. Police recently announced they will also fine rubberneckers Dhs.100 if caught driving slowly to gawp at accidents. For more details on traffic accidents and procedures see Accidents in General Information, p.55.

## Vehicle Repairs

By law, no vehicle can be accepted for major 'collision' repairs without an accident report from the Traffic Police, although very minor dents can be repaired without a report. Basically, if it looks like you hit another vehicle and you don't have an accident report, the garage could get into trouble if they repair your car.

| Vehicle Repairs | | |
| --- | --- | --- |
| 4x4 Motors | Al Quoz | 04 339 2020 |
| AAA | Al Quoz | 04 347 0400 |
| Central Motors | Abu Dhabi | 02 554 6262 |
| House Of Cars | Al Quoz | 04 339 3466 |
| Icon Auto | Al Quoz | 04 338 2744 |
| Max Garage | Al Quoz | 04 340 8200 |
| X Centre | Al Quoz | 04 339 5033 |

Your insurance company will usually have an agreement with a particular garage to which they will refer you. The garage will carry out the repair work and the insurance company will settle the claim. Generally, there is Dhs.500 deductible for all claims, but check with your insurance company for details of your policy.

If you purchase a new vehicle your insurance should cover you for 'agency repairs,' that is, repairs at the workshop of the dealer selling the car, although this is not a guarantee and you may have to pay a premium. It's worth it though as your car's warranty (two to three years) may become invalid if you have non-agency repairs done on it. Besides accidents and bumps, you may also have to deal with the usual running repairs associated with any car. Common problems in this part of the world can include the air-conditioning malfunctioning, batteries suddenly giving up and tires blowing out. With the air-con it may just be a case of having the system topped up, which is a fairly straightforward procedure. Car batteries don't tend to last too long in the hot conditions, and you may not get much warning, one day your car just won't start, so it's always handy to keep a set of jump leads in the boot. If you do manage to get your car started then take a trip to Satwa, before you know it, your car will be surrounded by guys offering to fix anything and everything. Haggle hard and you can get a bargain for simple repairs and spares – including that new battery.

*Agency Repairs*

*If you purchase a new vehicle your insurance should cover you for 'agency repairs,' that is, repairs at the workshop of the dealer selling the car, although this is not a guarantee and you may have to pay a premium. It's worth it though as your car's warranty (two to three years) may become invalid if you have non-agency repairs. Even if you buy a fairly new second-hand car (less than three years old) it may be an idea to opt for agency repairs, especially if the service history has only agency repairs, in order to protect the value of the car.*

*Business Bay Bridge*

# DUELER
## H/P SPORT

# CHOSEN FOR THE BEST
## For Premium SUVs

**DUELER**
**H/P SPORT**

**BRIDGESTONE**

**Nasser Bin Abdullatif Alserkal Est.**

www.alserkal.com

# Exploring

## Exploring

Known as the City of Gold or the City of Lights, Dubai is a world class metropolis where east meets west, and old meets new. In this chapter, each of its main geographical areas is described in detail, including landmarks, attractions and shopping opportunities. Dubai has many reasons to be proud: it is jam-packed with luxurious five-star hotels, it boasts some of the most innovative and biggest shopping malls, it is one of the region's most happening nightspots, and has a growing collection of heritage sites, museums and places of interest. There are also numerous photographic opportunities: mosques, palaces, dhows, camel and horse racing, sunsets, architecture and windtowers, to name just a few. Just remember to ask permission before taking photos of people, especially local women. Dubai is a cosmopolitan city with something for everyone, and just when you think you've seen it all, a new major project is announced, whether it's the world's tallest building, the largest shopping mall, or a ski slope in the desert.

The Dubai Checklist (p.237) highlights some of the best sites to explore, but you will find many other amazing places on your travels that are not listed here.

Dubai Creek is still considered to be the lifeline of the city – this is where it all started, when early settlers built their mud huts along the gleaming stretch of water that splits the city in two: Deira to the north and Bur Dubai to the south. Today, it is lined with skyscrapers and is a popular destination for visitors and residents – many of whom still commute across the creek on traditional wooden 'abras' (water taxis). The creek is 15km long, about 500m wide, and has three main crossing points: Al Shindagha Tunnel, Maktoum Bridge, and Garhoud Bridge. More bridges are under construction, to help ease traffic congestion across the creek.

On the Bur Dubai side you'll find Oud Metha and Umm Hurair (residential, recreational and commercial areas), Satwa and Karama (both original suburbs of old Dubai), and Jumeira and Umm Suqeim (both originally fishing settlements) along the coast. Further past Umm Suqeim on the way to Abu Dhabi is Jebel Ali, the southern-most point of the city, and famous for its port and free zone. The main road connecting Dubai and Abu Dhabi is Sheikh Zayed Road, a multi-lane highway lined with some impressive skyscrapers in the area now known as Trade Centre.

On the Deira side of the creek, you'll find Garhoud (near the airport), Rashidiya (an older residential and industrial area) and Mirdif. The maps at the back of this book will help you find your bearings wherever you decide to venture.

For more information on what's on offer in Dubai, visit the offical website for Dubai tourism, DTCM at www.dubaitourism.ae. This chapter also covers areas outside of the city, for a list of useful titles in the *Explorer* series, see www.explorerpublishing.com.

**GCC easy as ABC**
*While Dubai and its surrounding emirates have many landscapes and horizons to discover, the other GCC countries are worth visiting while you live in the region. Whether you want to get sporty in Qatar, check out the colourful heritage of Kuwait, find tranquility in the wilderness of Oman or join in the excitement of the grand prix in Bahrain there is a whole host of exploring to be done just a very short haul away. Pick up a copy of the respective Explorer guide and make the most of your trip or trips.*

*Dubai Marina*

## Madinat Jumeirah  p.41

Inspired by traditional Arabian architecture, this stunning resort is a must for shopping, sightseeing and a night out. Lose yourself exploring the maze of alleyways of the traditionally styled, air-conditioned souk, leading to intimate open-fronted boutiques, classy cafes, and charming waterfront bars and restaurants.

## Bastakiya  p.258

Stroll through historical streets for a glimpse of Dubai's past with traditional windtowers, courtyard houses, museums and galleries that characterise this heritage-rich part of the city. Learn ancient facts at the Dubai Museum, stop for a coffee at the Basta Art Cafe or a meal in one of the area's great Arabic restaurants.

## Jumeira Mosque  p.259

Learn more about local culture, Islam and what goes on inside a mosque through organised tours held here four days a week (10:00 sharp). You don't need to book, but it would be wise to call beforehand to confirm. You should also adhere to the conservative dress code.

## Bus Tours  p.279

Think you've seen it all? Think again. View Dubai from the upper floor of a double-decker bus, learning some fascinating facts about the city in the process. The Big Bus allows you to hop on and hop off at various attractions and traditional points of interest. Or try the amphibious Wonder Bus, which sails along the creek and then drives around some of Dubai's land-based attractions.

## Souks  p.483

Still an essential part of life for many people, Dubai's souks should be visited at least once. Check out the Spice Souk for the aromas, the colourful textile souk in Bur Dubai, the Fish Market in Deira or Karama and the Gold Souk to discover why Dubai is called the City of Gold.

## Burj Al Arab  p.28

Venture into the glamour and a cocktail at the Burj and indulge yourself with either Afternoon Tea at Sahn Eddar or Sky View, or a meal at the top class seafood restaurant Al Mahara (complete with simulated submarine ride). Or make use of their special weekend packages during the summer and stay the night in one of the amazing rooms.

## Shop Till You Drop  p.450

Beat the heat, splash some cash and cut a dash in one of Dubai's many shopping malls. No matter where you're from, chances are that Dubai does shopping bigger, better and cheaper. Skim through the Shopping section (p.450) for detailed descriptions of each mall.

## Creekside p.248

Don't miss a walk around the heart of Dubai's trading heritage, exploring the atmospheric area around Dubai Creek. Stroll down the open corniche and past the cruise vessels towards the creekside souk on the Bur Dubai side, or head over to Deira to see dhows being loaded and unloaded on the wharf – the way boxes of assorted goods are left trustingly on the pavement is quite something.

## Abra Ride (Water Taxi) p.52

Take in the panoramic views along both sides of Dubai Creek on a ride from Bur Dubai to Deira by traditional abra. As well as being a great tourist attraction, these functional, traditional vessels are still used as everyday transport for people getting from one side of Dubai to the other.

## Sporting Events p.69

Dubai is becoming a popular destination for some of the world's sporting competitions, with parallel social events of note. The Dubai World Cup offers high-class horseracing, hobnobbing and hats, the Dubai Tennis Championships always attracts some top tennis legends, and the Rugby Sevens has fast and furious action on the field and one of the best social nights off it.

## Cable Car p.266

The next best thing to a scenic flight over the city, the 45 minute ride by cable car travels the full length of Creekside Park suspended 30 feet in the air, and offers great views over the creek to the striking Deira skyline. Definitely one for the cooler months as the cars can get quite hot inside and there's no windows. Not advisable for those suffering from acrophobia.

## Desert Safari p.277

While in Dubai, a trip to the desert is an absolute must. Surfing over the dunes in a car at impossible angles is great fun and part of the essential desert experience, along with a camel ride, climbing a sand dune, sand skiing, star gazing, eating your fill at the BBQ and learning how to belly dance. Plenty of tour operators offer various excursions at competitive prices, so be sure to shop around.

## Global Village p.68

Increasing every year in size and duration, Global Village now has its own site just out of town on Emirates Road, and remains open for nearly five months of the year. Stands and stalls representing countries from around the world offer culture, shows, attractions, and traditional items and food for sale. There is enough to keep kids and adults entertained on multiple visits.

## Dinner Cruises p.510

Experience a truly memorable evening on Dubai Creek, taking in the atmosphere and the views of both the Bur Dubai and Deira sides of the creek from the best vantage point. Dining options vary from lunch, sunset and dinner cruises, and on board entertainment is often included (don't forget your camera).

### Dhow Building p.245

For a glimpse of craftsmen still practising their ancient skills, visit the dhow building yard in Al Jadaf, just to the east of the Garhoud Bridge on the south side of the creek. Watch the mesmerising procedures of dhows being constructed without the aid of drawings or modern equipment, and best of all no nails!

### Shisha p.572

Join in the Arabic social tradition of hanging out at a shisha cafe. A widely favoured pastime with the locals (both men and women in places popular with the younger crowd), shisha consists of tobacco mixed with molasses and a variety of fruity flavourings, which is then smoked from a water pipe.

### Dubai Museum p.264

This is a fantastic and enjoyable museum offering an enlightening stroll through Dubai's past. With displays depicting everything from the fascinating history of the emirate and how traditional life used to be before the discovery of oil just over half a century ago, to views of the wildlife and natural environment of the UAE.

### Heritage and Diving Village p.262

The former fishing village of Shindagha is now home to an increasing number of restored buildings, including the museums in Sheikh Saeed Al Maktoum's House and the Heritage and Diving Village, where you can also see traditional crafts, tribal dances and ceremonies. On the creek side, several local restaurants provide great surroundings for sampling typical Emirati and Arabic fare.

### Camping p.326

One of the best ways to see the natural beauty of the countryside of the UAE, camping gets you away from it all and closer to nature. In the tranquility of the mountains or desert, you can camp almost anywhere you please, and a night under the clear star-studded Arabian skies is an unforgettable experience.

### Ski Dubai p.372

In the city whose imagination knows no bounds, it should come as no surprise to find an enormous ski slope towering above a shopping mall. There are a number of runs, all with real snow, and lessons are available for non-skiers and boarders. Alternatively, you could just go to the Snow Park for a spot of tobogganing and a snowball fight.

### DSF p.68

Dubai Shopping Festival sees Dubai come alive with the ringing of a million cash registers, as shoppers flock to the city for great bargains. It is about much more than shopping though, with attractions, events and special entertainment in malls creating a buzz throughout the city.

**239**

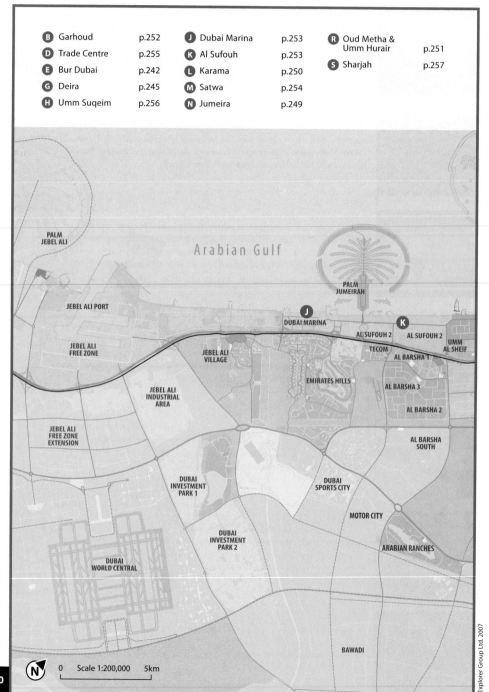

PALM
JEBEL ALI

Arabian Gulf

PALM
JUMEIRAH

JEBEL ALI PORT

**J** DUBAI MARINA

**K**

AL SUFOUH 2    AL SUFOUH 2    UMM
AL SHEIF

JEBEL ALI
FREE ZONE

JEBEL ALI
VILLAGE

TECOM

AL BARSHA 1

EMIRATES HILLS

AL BARSHA 3

JEBEL ALI
INDUSTRIAL
AREA

AL BARSHA 2

JEBEL ALI
FREE ZONE
EXTENSION

AL BARSHA
SOUTH

DUBAI
INVESTMENT
PARK 1

DUBAI
SPORTS CITY

MOTOR CITY

DUBAI
INVESTMENT
PARK 2

ARABIAN RANCHES

DUBAI
WORLD CENTRAL

**N** 0    Scale 1:200,000    5km

BAWADI

© Explorer Group Ltd. 2007

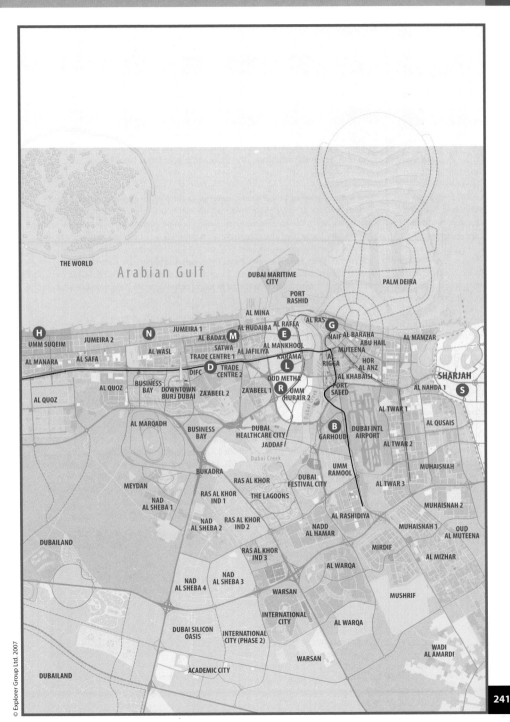

© Explorer Group Ltd. 2007

# Bur Dubai

Area **E**
Map p.240-241

**The Lowdown**
*The centre of Dubai's history and now the centre of its heritage – a great place to explore, especially on foot.*

**The Good**
*The fabulous Bastakiya area, the illuminating Dubai Museum, the atmospheric souks and a ride on an abra over the creek to Deira.*

**The Bad**
*Traffic in rush hour can be slow in downtown Bur Dubai, especially with all the traffic lights, and you're more likely to strike gold in some areas than find a parking space at particular times of the day.*

**The Must Dos**
*A walking tour of the entire area, especially Bastakiya by day and the corniche at night.*

What was once just a flat, sandy area with a sprinkling of palm trees and barasti (palm) houses, is now the bustling heart of the city. Up until only a few years ago, Bur Dubai, and Deira across the creek, were the business districts of the city, but the development of office towers along the prestigious Sheikh Zayed Road, as well as future plans for Burj Dubai and Business Bay, are shifting the business focus to other areas. Bur Dubai is still a residential hotspot, with a multitude of nationalities living in various multi-storey apartment blocks. It also offers great shopping and entertainment options. For exploring, this is one of the best areas in Dubai with both Bastakiya and Shindagha offering atmospheric, historical sites that are great to stroll around, as well as Dubai Museum, the souks and the Bur Dubai Corniche.

*Residential*

Despite the area being a bit of a concrete jungle, it remains very popular with expats of all nationalities. Mostly modern mid-rise buildings house various sizes and styles of apartments, which due to ever-rising rents are becoming increasingly populated by professionals. The quality of accommodation is generally excellent. Residents are well served by a comprehensive selection of shopping malls, supermarkets, smaller shops and other services, as well as restaurants, cafes, bars and nightclubs. There are no green or public spaces and the roads can get blocked with traffic at rush hour, but for its convenient central location, it is hard to beat. For more details, refer to Residential Areas (p.124).

*Retail*

Modern malls, such as BurJuman Centre and the smaller malls on Bank Street and Mankhool Road, contrast with the oldest souks in Bur Dubai near the creek to provide a complete range of shopping choices. Whether you like to buy designer labels, or have your own clothes made up from Indian silk, it's all available here. Likewise, food shopping ranges from bulk-buy bargains in discount stores in the souk, right up to gourmet dates from Bateel in BurJuman.

*Places of Interest*

The area near the mouth of the creek, known as Shindagha, is a good starting point to explore Bur Dubai. Here you can visit Sheikh Saeed Al Maktoum's House (see p.263) and the Heritage & Diving Village (p.262), a two-minute walk from each other, before following the creek inland to Dubai Museum and finishing in the Bastakiya area. On your way through Bur Dubai, you will pass the busy Al Fahedi Street (p.478) near the Astoria Hotel, a great place to shop for electrical goods. Nearby, underneath wooden shaded walkways, is the Textile Souk (p.485) with every type of fabric imaginable.

Facing Dubai Museum (see p.264) is the 'Diwan', the Ruler's office and the highest administrative body of the Dubai government. Built in 1990, the low white building is surrounded by black railings and combines modern materials with a traditional design, including examples of traditional windtowers. Located near the Diwan is the Grand Mosque, which can accommodate 1,200 worshippers and has 54 domes and a 70 metre minaret – presently the tallest in the city. It is possible to walk inland along the edge of the creek, past the Diwan to the Bastakiya district,

**Photo Op**
To the south-west of Bur Dubai is Port Rashid, where you'll find the Dubai Ports Authority building. A large glass and chrome construction imaginatively designed like a paddle steamer, all the paraphernalia of a port can be glimpsed over the surrounding fence.

# Take her away for the weekend...
## before she packs your bags

Covering the UAE and Oman, this luxury guide
to the best weekend breaks is a must-own for
all residents. And with promotional offers
to boot weekend breaks won't break the bank.

**Weekend Breaks in the UAE and Oman**
Now you won't waste another weekend

Abu Dhabi · Amsterdam · Bahrain · Barcelona · Beijing · Berlin · Dubai · Dublin · Geneva
Hong Kong · Kuala Lumpur · Kuwait · London · Los Angeles · New York · New Zealand · Oman
Paris · Qatar · Shanghai · Singapore · Sydney · Tokyo · Vancouver

**EXPLORER**
www.explorerpublishing.com

which is one of the oldest heritage sites in the city (see p.262). Originally known as Bastakiya Chok (square), this area is gradually being reconstructed by Dubai Municipality to pay homage to the traditional Arabian way of life and provide a great little area for tourists to explore the maze of small winding alleys.

From Bastakiya it is possible to follow the corniche up along the creekside where a number of luxury cruise boats moor (you can board one of these for a dinner cruise, see p.510 for more info). The relaxed atmosphere of this area, with its grassy parks often full of people (especially families and children), makes it a great place to view the flashy buildings on the Deira side of the creek and watch the water traffic. For more information on Dubai Creek, refer also to p.248.

Nearby, Bait Al Wakeel was built in 1934 as Dubai's first office building. It currently houses the fishing museum. Numerous embassies are located in this area, while further inland from the creek is the popular BurJuman Shopping Centre (p.452). Located on the busy crossroads of Khalid bin Waleed Road (or Bank Street, as it is popularly known), this already huge mall has recently been extended to triple its original size.

*Take Your Time*
*While in the area, linger for a while and absorb the unique sights, sounds and smells of Bur Dubai over a meal at Kan Zaman (p.507).*

The many sides to Bur Dubai

*Area* **G**
*Map p.240-241*

# Deira

Although Deira has fallen out of favour as a residential area for many expats in recent years, with the creek now seeming to be a barrier as to how far people will move or even travel in search of entertainment, it is still an incredibly atmospheric area with plenty to explore. Narrow convoluted streets bustle with activity while gold, spices, perfumes and general goods are touted in numerous souks. The streets are full of people, especially in the evenings. As the oldest part of the city, there is plenty of heritage around, and while it can be a crazy place to navigate by car, you can avoid the frustrations of the snarled-up traffic if you visit at quieter times of the day. Alternatively, beat the block (and the nightmare of the Maktoum Bridge traffic) and arrive by abra.

*The Lowdown*
*Deira is not dead! This is the oldest and one of the most atmospheric parts of tow. There's plenty to explore along the corniche, through the souks and in the heritage sites, and there are loads of restaurants and bars in the modern creekside hotels.*

## Residential

Perhaps because of the traffic, the rapid southward expansion of Dubai and the opportunity to own property in the Emirates Hills areas, Deira is not as popular a residential area as it once was. Most accommodation is in apartments, with few villas to be found. It is mainly chosen by people seeking more reasonable rents. For more details, refer to Deira under Residential Areas (p.135).

*The Good*
*The ambience of the souks and the corniche with the traditional trade from the dhows still plays a major role in this part of the city.*

## Retail

Still a big draw for shopping locations, both modern and historical, Deira has one of Dubai's largest and most popular malls, in the shape of Deira City Centre (p.452). Shopping in the souks such as the Gold Souk (p.484) and the Spice Souk (p.485) is an essential part of any tourist's stay in Dubai, as well as being an integral part of life for many residents.

*The Bad*
*Worst traffic in Dubai, especially in rush hour and when trying to get over the Maktoum Bridge.*

## Places of Interest

Inland, near the eastern end of the creek, is Deira City Centre. Not only is it a gigantic shopping mall, but it also houses many restaurants and cafes and an 11-screen cinema. It's recent expansion has created 20 more outlets and despite the opening of two other massive malls in the south of the city (Ibn Battuta and Mall of the Emirates), City Centre shows no signs of slowing down (p.452).

*The Must Dos*
*Gold Souk, Spice Souk, Dhow Wharfage, Al Ahmadiya School & Heritage House, Deira Fish Market and the Dubai Creek Golf & Yacht Club.*

Opposite City Centre and bordering the creek for about 1.5 km is an enticing stretch of carefully manicured greenery, home to the Dubai Creek Golf & Yacht Club (p.346), which re-opened in 2005 after extensive landscaping and refurbishment. The impressive golf clubhouse is based on the shape of dhow sails (the image of this famous building is found on the Dhs.20 note), while the yacht club is aptly in the shape of a yacht. This is also the site of one of the city's newest five-star hotels, the Park Hyatt Dubai, which features Mediterranean-style low buildings offering creek views and some great restaurants.

Bordering the creek are some awe-inspiring buildings that seemed years ahead of their time when they were built. The large golf ball that sits atop the Etisalat telecommunications building is testimony to the unique imagination of Dubai's modern architecture. The sparkling glass building housing the National Bank of Dubai (known fondly as the 'pregnant lady') is a sculptural vision, standing tall like a magnificent convex mirror and reflecting the bustling activity of the creek.

It is also in this area that you can find three of Dubai's finest five-star hotels: Hilton Dubai Creek, Sheraton Dubai Creek, and the SAS Radisson Dubai Creek (formerly Hotel Intercontinental Dubai), which recently celebrated its 30th anniversary. Between them, they offer many fantastic dining and nightlife opportunities.

Take a stroll along the dhow wharfage where local traders unload wooden dhows lazily docked by the water's edge, tightly packed with everything from fruit and vegetables to televisions and maybe even a car or two. Often you will find a stack of electrical goods trustingly left on the wharfage – a sight rarely seen elsewhere in the world. This slice of local merchant life is a reminder of Dubai's trading history and a photo opportunity not to be missed.

Take the pedestrian underpass to the left of the abra station on the Deira side to enter the oldest market in Dubai, now mainly selling household items. Nearby is the Spice Souk, where the aroma of saffron and cumin fill the air. You'll find every spice under the sun as well as loose frankincense and other perfumed oils and dried herbs sold for medicinal purposes. The souk spreads over a large area between Al Nasr Square and the Gold Souk where street after street is paved with gold shops whose windows are laden with yellow and white gold and platinum. If it's rugs you want then Deira Tower on Al Nasr Square is worth a visit. About 40 shops offer a colourful profusion of carpets from Iran, Pakistan, Turkey and Afghanistan to suit everyone's taste and pocket. For further information on carpets and gold, refer to the Shopping section (p.420).

> ### Hotel Corniche
> One of Dubai's first hotels, the Hyatt Regency stands in a commanding position on Deira's corniche with great views over the mouth of the creek and out to sea, especially in Al Dawaar, Dubai's only revolving restaurant. The hotel's recent refurbishment has breathed new life into its many outstanding restaurants.

> ### Gold Linger
> The Gold Souk is an Aladdin's Cave of gold shopping. Bargaining is expected, and discounts depend on the season and the international gold rate. Dubai Shopping Festival and Dubai Summer Surprises are the main periods for low prices when huge discounts attract gold lovers from around the world. Individual pieces can be made, or copies done to your own specifications, within a few days. Even if you aren't buying, an evening stroll through the Gold Souk, when it's glistening, is worth the experience.

Closer still towards the sea, set back a little from the main roads by the creek, is a small area being renovated and developed into a tourist area by the Dubai Municipality. It contains the earliest school in the city, Al Ahmadiya School (now the Museum of Education), and the Heritage House next door (see p.260), an excellent example of an Emirati family home. These have been joined by a traditionally styled hotel with a small restaurant, an old-style mosque and a building housing several shops, all located around a small central courtyard renovated in the last few years. In the nearby lanes there are other buildings with preservation orders, awaiting reconstruction to add to the 'Al Souk Al Khabeer' area.

Dubai Municipality has also reconstructed Murabba'at Umm Rayool (the name comes from the Arabic word for 'leg', as the building stands on seven pillars, or legs). This was originally used as a weaponry store and was located on Baniyas Street, but the new building is on Union Square near the Deira taxi stand. This building style dates from 1894.

Another cultural attraction is Dubai's largest and busiest fish market (near the Hyatt Regency Hotel), where you can stock up on the freshest seafood in town at bargain prices. You can pay a 'wheelbarrow man' to follow you and carry your shopping, and someone else to gut your fish. Once you get used to the smell it's a lot of fun. A fish museum has recently been created at Deira Fish Market to give shoppers and tourists more information about the 350 species in the Arabian Gulf, the history of the fishing trade in the UAE, and the types of fishing boats and equipment used by fishermen.

Along the seafront from the Hyatt Regency, you will pass Al Hamriya Port as you continue on Al Khaleej Road, which has plenty of car parking and a spectacular corniche looking straight out over the ocean (the uninterrupted views will soon be obliterated by construction on the Palm Deira, so make the most of them now). Further still is Al Mamzar Beach Park (p.267). The road also follows past the park inland along the lagoon, with a path on the corniche, public beaches and a slipway to launch jet skis and speedboats into the water.

In true Dubai style, development plans are now underway off the coast to reclaim land for the Palm Deira, the third and biggest of Nakheel's Palm Island project. It is set to cover over 80 square kilometres, making it almost as large as Greater London and bigger than Paris or Manhattan. In addition, the 'Abu Hail Development Project' will transform the corniche area by replacing older buildings with smart new residential and commercial units, public utilities and tourist attractions.

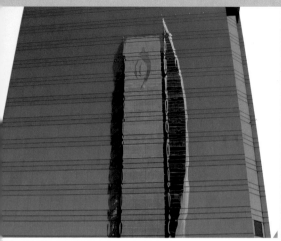

*Lively Deira*

*Creek Tours* ◀

*A cruise on Dubai Creek is a wonderful way to enjoy views of new and old parts of the city side by side. Many of the tours are in traditional wooden dhows, but even these often have air conditioning inside to avoid the summer heat and humidity. In the cooler months, the top deck is the place to be. Prices per adult range from about Dhs.35 for a daytime trip or Dhs.90 for a bargain dinner cruise and up to Dhs.260 for a top-class evening cruise with fine food. For more information see Boat & Yacht Charters p.277 and Dinner Cruises p.510.*

## Dubai Creek

The creek has played a pivotal role in the development of Dubai. The earliest Dubai settlement was near the mouth of the creek, but when it was dredged to create a larger anchorage and to encourage trade, the growing town gradually crept further inland. At present, Dubai Creek has three main crossing points – nearest to the sea is the Shindagha Tunnel, then Maktoum Bridge and furthest inland is Garhoud Bridge. Both bridges can be raised to allow boats through (thereby diverting traffic), but this usually only happens late at night. There is also a pedestrian foot tunnel near Shindagha. There are some parts of creekside Bur Dubai and Deira that are worth exploring on foot. On both sides, there are souks and corniches, and you can cross from one side to the other in a traditional water taxi ('abra'). This short boat ride makes a refreshing change from crossing the creek via one of the often-congested bridges, and it only costs Dhs.1 (the price was recently doubled from an even cheaper 50 fils). It is estimated that around 15,000 people make the crossing every day. For visitors, an abra ride gives a unique perspective of the gleaming, mirrored buildings along the creek, which stand in contrast to the traditional domes and windtowers of 'old Dubai' on the Bur Dubai side. Official one-hour RTA tours of the creek cost Dhs.100 per abra, and are available from the stations, although you may get a slightly cheaper fare if you are prepared to haggle with boat drivers further up the creek - be sure to agree on the price in advance.

For details of areas to explore along the corniches, see p.242 (for the Bur Dubai side) and p.245 (for the Deira side).

### Creek Tours

| Bateaux Dubai ▶ p.511 | 04 399 4994 |
| Danat Dubai Cruises | 04 351 1117 |
| Tour Dubai ▶ p.539 | 04 336 8409 |

*Views across the Creek*

*Loading dhows*

*Traditional abras*

Area **N**
Map p.240-241

**The Lowdown**
*Shops, sandy beaches, sunshine, socialising – Jumeira has it all, which is why it is the original expat area, and home to the infamous, coiffeured 'Jumeira Janes'.*

**The Good**
*Picking from the many malls and shopping centres in Jumeira is tough, but for a shopaholic it's a dream come true. Plus you're just a stone's throw away from the beach and several excellent entertainment options.*

**The Bad**
*The widening of the Beach Road means you can no longer pull over and park outside some of the shops and cafes – robbing the area of some of its character. Even with the extra lane, this road can get very busy, especially at rush hour.*

**The Must Dos**
*The Jumeira Mosque tour for an enlightening glimpse into the culture and religion of the country, a delicious, leisurely breakfast at the Lime Tree Café (see p.570), and a stroll round the piazza-like Mercato mall.*

# Jumeira

Jumeira is a highly desirable residential area, with good access to the beach and plenty of shopping. It's also something of a medical district, with loads of private clinics and surgeries offering everything from sports physiotherapy to tummy tucks. Jumeira Road (aka the Beach Road) runs the whole length of Jumeira (around 9km), and it's here that you'll find most of the shopping centres.

## Residential

The address of choice for Dubai's movers and shakers, Jumeira has some beautiful big villas with rents to match. There's nothing much higher than two storeys (apart from the shopping malls) and very few apartments. Villas are sometimes in compounds with a shared pool, but there are also many independent and semi-detached villas. Occasionally you will find an old villa with slightly more reasonable rent, but these are often snapped up quickly, and often before they even come onto the market (through word of mouth).

## Retail

So many shops, so little time. Drive along the Beach Road and you'll pass plenty. While Mercato Mall is impressive with its renaissance theme, well-known brands, multi-screen cinema and many dining options, the real clincher for Jumeira is the fact that you could almost be shopping on a high street thanks to the side-by-side mini malls. Start at the Jumeirah Plaza and head towards Jumeira Mosque, (a five minute walk if it wasn't for all the retail opportunities that will hypnotise you). There are a number of boutiques and independent shops in the area that you won't find in other malls in Dubai, such as ladies fashion favourite Eve Michelle (04 342 9574), excellent school supplies shop White Star Trading (04 342 2179) and the only stand-alone THE One in Dubai (p.571).

## Places of interest

Jumeira should have something to keep everyone busy. The beautiful Jumeira Mosque (p.259) is certainly worth a visit, and the Majlis Ghorfat Umm Al Sheif makes an interesting diversion. For art lovers there are a couple of galleries (see p.258), and if it's beach you want there's plenty of it. The popular Jumeira Open Beach (by Dubai Marine Beach Resort & Spa) has showers and lifeguards, but unfortunately attracts a few voyeurs so you may prefer to try the more-private Jumeira Beach Park (p.268). Jumeira is one of the few areas of Dubai that makes for a pleasant stroll and whether you walk along the beach or down the shop-laden Beach Road, the excellent Lime Tree Cafe is a good pitstop (p.570). Although there aren't really any major hotels in the area – the Burj Al Arab and Jumeirah Beach Hotel (which are actually in Umm Suqeim) are visible in the distance - Dubai Marine Beach Resort & Spa is the only beach hotel close to the centre of Dubai and is home to some of the city's most stylish venues such as Sho Cho (p.585) and Boudoir (p.578).

*Jumeira Mosque*

249

**Area ❶**

Map p.240-241

# Karama

Karama is well known for having something for everyone. It is primarily a residential area, consisting of relatively low-cost flats in low-rise apartment blocks, but has a great shopping area, the Karama Shopping Complex, very popular with residents and especially visitors to Dubai. It also has a particularly good range of inexpensive restaurants serving tasty cuisine from Arabic and Indian to Sri Lankan and Singaporean.

**The Lowdown**

*A lively area with a community feel, great shopping, and scores of superb low-priced dining options – a must for any visitor to Dubai.*

### Residential

Karama is a good choice for people seeking reasonable rents and a central location. All sizes of apartments (from studio to three bedrooms) are available in the area's many low-rise buildings. It is one of the few places where you can feasibly get around on foot, as you will have all kinds of shops and services right on your doorstep. Access to most of central Dubai is quick and easy. The noise and traffic may put some people off, but in terms of price and convenience it has many fans. For more details, refer to Residential Areas (p.127).

**The Good**

*The shopping! There's plenty of great buys in Karama Shopping Area and the surrounding streets, where bargain prices can be lowered further depending on your haggling skills.*

### Retail

The heart of Karama is an open-air shopping area consisting of two central streets lined with lots of small shops, all with their goods spilling out onto the pavements. This is a great area for buying anything from clothes or suitcases to kitsch fluffy camels or silver jewellery from Oman. The incessant approach from vendors offering 'copy watches, copy handbags, copy DVDs' can be annoying, especially if you are not interested in any of these items. The renovated fish and vegetable markets are also worth a visit for the atmosphere and some reasonably priced, fresh produce, or for cheap or second-hand furniture on the streets nearby. For more details, also refer to Karama Shopping Area (p.480).

**The Bad**

*Traffic and parking can get a bit crazy at night.*

### Places of Interest

The Karama Shopping Area is the main draw for most people. Combine a trip around the market with a cheap meal in one of the many roadside restaurants scattered around. Particularly good examples include Pakistani food at Karachi Darbar (p.552), Sri Lankan food at Chef Lanka (p.558), or Filipino food at Tagpuan (p.516). There are also numerous cheap Indian restaurants serving amazing value 'thali' set meals (for well under Dhs.10) and lots of small Arabic restaurants for shawarma, falafel and fresh fruit juices. The area alongside Trade Centre Road, offers a slightly higher standard, at very reasonable prices. The nearby Zabeel Park opened just across Al Qataiyat Road in late 2005, and is linked by a footbridge from Karama to the area near Trade Centre Roundabout. This park is full of open green spaces in perfect contrast to Karama, as well as recreational areas for kids, a jogging track, a cricket pitch, a boating lake with lakeside restaurants and cafes and other facilities for adults.

**The Must Dos**

*Eat in one of the cheap local restaurants for as little as Dhs.5 per person for a delicious meal, then go shopping for delightful kitsch like a mosque alarm clock, a shisha pipe or a wooden camel.*

Bargain shopping

Area ⓡ
Map p.240-241

**The Lowdown**
*It may be small, but this area has a surprisingly good choice of leisure and recreation for kids and adults, great shopping and numerous options for eating out.*

**The Good**
*Exclusive brand names at Wafi Mall, cheaper shopping in Lamcy, numerous leisure opportunities and some of Dubai's best restaurants – including many independent restaurants where a delicious, authentic meal will cost well under Dhs.100 for two.*

**The Bad**
*Slightly hard to navigate because of all the cloverleaf junctions and hidden slip roads, but you'll get used to it.*

**The Must Dos**
*The Pyramids Complex at Wafi City has a great health club as well as some of Dubai's best restaurants and bars, while Jimmy Dix (p.591) is a firm big night out favourite. Creekside Park is an explosion of greenery and houses numerous leisure activities in a beautiful setting overlooking Dubai Creek.*

# Oud Metha & Umm Hurair

Oud Metha and Umm Hurair are located in the centre of Dubai next to Karama, bordered by the creek to the north, Umm Hurair Road to the west and the E11 (Dubai-Sharjah Road) to the south and east. Within this area, popular for its good quality residential buildings, you'll find a great deal of top-quality shopping, entertainment, recreational, social and educational facilities. Some of Dubai's most popular shopping is found in Wafi City in Umm Hurair and Lamcy Plaza in Oud Metha, with both also offering some great eating out options. You'll also find some of the city's best leisure options with Creekside Park, Al Nasr Leisureland, WonderLand Theme & Water Park and Wafi City.

## Residential

A great central location with easy access to the highways. Accommodation is located mostly in Oud Metha where there are lots of new, low-rise apartment blocks and all the facilities you'll need within easy reach. For more details, refer to Oud Metha & Umm Hurair under Residential Areas (p.148).

## Retail

Oud Metha has the lively Lamcy Plaza, which offers great shopping in a variety of stores throughout its five floors, and is home to Loulou Al Dugong's, a fabulous play area for young children. In Umm Hurair, Wafi Mall is packed with some of Dubai's most exclusive names which pull in the punters, although it always manages to appear quiet and serene in contrast to the frenzy of other malls.

## Places of Interest

Just off Oud Metha Road are a string of social clubs from various countries and two of Dubai's churches. Nearby you'll find Rashid Hospital (the government emergency hospital), the private American Hospital and Al Nasr Leisureland. This complex offers a variety of facilities, including an amusement park (p.273), Fruit & Garden Luna Park (p.270), bowling and an indoor ice rink. As well as The Lodge nightclub, there are also some licensed restaurants just outside the park (try Khazana and Chinese Treasure). The area around Lamcy Plaza has some great independent restaurants, including Lemongrass, Lan Kwai Fong and Russian Home Restaurant. Two great hotels, the Movenpick and the Grand Hyatt, are nearby, as is the mighty shopping, leisure and entertainment complex, Wafi City.

Near Maktoum Bridge and the Dubai Courts you'll find Creekside Park (see p.268). There is another, smaller park in Oud Metha, on Umm Hurair Road near Maktoum Bridge, with children's activities, volleyball and basketball facilities, a jogging track and a small lake. WonderLand Theme & Water Park is a popular amusement park offering various rides and incorporating the SplashLand Water Park (see also p.274).

The Al Boom Tourist Village near Garhoud Bridge is a popular wedding venue for local couples. Visitors can sample local cuisine in Al Dahleez or take a dinner cruise on one of the beautifully illuminated dhows.

Further inland along the creek, just across the road from Al Boom Tourist Village, is a patch of land where you may get to see a traditional wooden dhow being built. Mainly used for trade, these distinctive high bowed vessels take months to construct, but their lifespan can be over a century.

Near Wafi City is the Grand Cineplex, an 11-screen cinema, and the impressive Grand Hyatt Hotel with its opulent lobby resembling a beautiful, lush tropical garden. Also in this area is Dubai Healthcare City, phase one of which is now open. It is a state-of-the-art medical facility being developed in conjunction with top international medical organisations, and will be completed by 2010.

**251**

## Garhoud

**Area B**
**Map p.240-241**

**The Lowdown**
*A small area with currently just a few attractions but worth checking out for all its restaurants, pubs and bars. Dubai Festival City will add masses of options as it gradually expands over the next few years.*

**The Good**
*A great place for eating out and entertainment – especially alfresco – including Century Village, Irish Village, Meridien Village and many others.*

**The Bad**
*Can be tough getting in and out of the area due to the traffic on Garhoud Bridge and on the Dubai-Sharjah Road at certain times of the day.*

**The Must Dos**
*Irish Village is a great place to chill out with a pint outside on the fantastic terrace, while 'next door' Century Village offers some great restaurants, all with alfresco dining.*

The area of Garhoud (aka Al Garhoud) lies to the north of Garhoud Bridge, between the creek and Deira, and is bordered by the airport. The centre has a small, but pleasant and sought-after, residential neighbourhood, while surrounding this is the commercial area to the west bordered by Garhoud Road. The area has some well-known hotels, a few shops, Dubai Tennis Stadium, Century Village, the Irish Village, the Aviation Club, and several large schools to the east.

### Residential

Offering accommodation in a variety of villas, Garhoud is centrally located with good facilities and has a really nice atmosphere. Despite being only a few minutes from the airport, it is a quiet place to live and a great location from which to access most of central Dubai. Rents are reasonable for villas compared to Jumeira and Umm Suqeim, but are on the rise. For more details, refer to Garhoud under Residential Areas (p.125).

### Retail

Not currently one of Dubai's foremost shopping areas (although it is not far from Deira City Centre), Garhoud adds convenience for residents but doesn't offer much to attract shoppers from elsewhere. However, this is set to change with the opening of Dubai Festival City, one of the city's latest shopping and entertainment mega-projects. The first phase opened in late 2005 with a new, bigger IKEA and a Toyota showroom. These were joined in 2006 by the largest ACE outside North America (complete with garden centre), a flagship Plug-Ins, and the enormous HyperPanda supermarket. In 2007, the much-awaited Festival City Mall brought in multiple shops and new brand names.

### Places of Interest

Under Garhoud bridge and alongside the creek is a popular spot for fishing, although the water may not be the cleanest. Also alongside the creek, the massive Dubai Festival City is gradually coming to life, and will continue to open in stages over the next few years. It will eventually include a marina and a 3.2km waterfront promenade, which will be home to 40 water-view restaurants, hotels, family entertainment venues, a 'global village', residential and office space, plus lots more indoor and outdoor shopping.

In the middle of Garhoud is Dubai Tennis Stadium, home to the star-studded annual Dubai Tennis Championships and also doubling as a concert venue on occasion. It also has some very popular venues for eating out and socialising, with the licensed bars and restaurants all having alfresco dining in the pleasant landscaped courtyards and gardens of Century Village and the Irish Village, and at The Cellar just across the lake in the Aviation Club. There are also three hotels in Garhoud with popular outlets including Le Meridien Dubai, Al Bustan Rotana Hotel and Millennium Airport Hotel.

One landmark in Garhoud that will definitely catch your eye is a building shaped like the front half of an aeroplane, which rather appropriately is the training centre for Emirates. Located to the north-east, Dubai International Airport is currently undergoing a massive $4.1 billion expansion.

Garhoud has its very own park that is a haven of peace in a quiet part of the suburb. Entrance to the park is free, and this is one of the few free parks that allows men to enter during the week. It is quite small, and grassy areas are limited, but the children's play areas are huge and packed with the latest and greatest playground equipment.

**Mini Magic**
While *Dubai Explorer* is the ultimate resource for residents, we admit it is a little cumbersome for your guests to take on their sightseeing tours. No fear – give your guests a copy of *Dubai Mini Explorer*, which neatly fits in a back or top pocket, and you won't see them for days – yippee!

Area **J** & **K**

Map p.240-241

**The Lowdown**

*A mainly residential area, with a good selection of eating and drinking options at the many hotels. Also good for those that like messing about on, or in, the water.*

**The Good**

*You're never far from the sound of lapping waves.*

**The Bad**

*The building sites around the marina have more cranes, more dust, and more sun-blocking high-rise towers than anywhere else in Dubai.*

**The Must Dos**

*The bars and restaurants with a view of the Gulf. Lots to recommend, including the Rooftop Lounge at The One&Only Royal Mirage, and the top deck of Bussola at Le Meridien Mina Seyahi for pizza and cocktails.*

## Dubai Marina & Al Sufouh

Previously home to just a handful of waterfront hotels, the Marina (or Marsa Dubai to use its proper title) has seen some of the most intensive of all Dubai's construction in recent years. Apartment buildings are popping up along every inch of the man-made marina, while Jumeirah Beach Residence has squeezed 36 towers into the last stretch of beach available to developers. The coast is home to a number of stunning five-star hotels, such as The Ritz-Carlton and One&Only Royal Mirage. The Hilton Dubai Jumeirah, Sheraton Jumeirah, and Le Meridien Mina Seyahi can also be found here along this strip, as well as Grosvenor House, home to the hip Buddha Bar. Al Sufouh is home to Media City, Internet City and Knowledge Village (which are expanding all the time), but also has isolated clusters of villas and a peaceful air. Before too long though there will be a few new neighbours moving in, as soon the famous Palm Jumeirah opens fully to residents.

### Residential

Apart from a few townhouses and villas, the Marina is all apartments. Depending on the floor number and side of the building, some have great sea views, and are luxuriously finished. In Al Sufouh there are a few compounds of older villas (although these are very pricey) and new ones, too. The Palm (which joins Al Sufouh's coastline) will feature almost every type of accommodation going, although the frond-end signature villas are most desirable.

### Retail

Not a great deal for shoppers in all honesty – Marina Walk has a book shop and a supermarket, but the emphasis seems to be on living, eating and drinking.

### Places of Interest

Marina Walk is worth a stroll, especially at night when diners sit out in front of the many restaurants, and you can gaze out over the gleaming yachts and glittering towers. On Friday and Saturday afternoons from October to April, Marina Walk hosts the Marina Market, with stalls selling clothing, jewellery, gifts and handicrafts.

For beach lovers there is still a stretch of the sandy stuff in front of the existing hotels (although the JBR development will claim a slice for its beach club) and watersports fans are catered for, with Dubai International Marine Club (DIMC) being a prime location for sailing and boating in Dubai. DIMC also hosts legs of the Off-shore Powerboat Racing series, in which Dubai's own Victory Team are world-class contenders. On race days you can take a picnic down to the adjacent beach and watch the high-octane action – it's quite a spectacle. Check the racing calendar at www.dimc-uae.com.

Thrill-seekers may also want to consider parasailing – the Sheraton Hotel has a boat, and the ride will give you an unforgettable bird's eye view of the Marina and Palm Jumeirah.

*Dubai Marina*

**253**

*Area* **N**
*Map p.240-241*

**The Lowdown**
*A central location,
with its fair share of
good-value eateries
and interesting
shopping – just what
you need if you've
overdone the malls.*

**The Good**
*The 'challenge' of
bargain hunting in the
little shops along
Satwa Road and down
Plant Street (or Al
Hudaiba Street).*

**The Bad**
*Not necessarily the
place to come if you're
looking for some peace
and quiet.*

**The Must Dos**
*Dine alfresco at one of
the Arabic cafes for
delicious shawarmas,
falafel and fresh fruit
cocktails while you
watch the world go by.
Al Mallah (p.503)
is particularly
recommended.*

# Satwa

Satwa is an area of contrasts. At one end, quiet suburban streets house smart villas, while just a 15 minute walk away you'll reach Al Diyafah Street and Satwa Road, bustling thoroughfares lined with shops and plenty of inexpensive restaurants and cafes. When the weather is cool enough, it's a great area to wander around – the evenings get particularly busy, and Diyafah Street is the place for people with expensive, customised cars to show off their dubious driving skills.

## Residential

There is quite a mixture of housing options, from a room above a shop to a big, independent villa. Somewhere in the middle there are some decent apartments in low-rise blocks, but the central location means rents are not really on the low side.

## Retail

Satwa is home to textiles and tailors. For a fraction of what you'd pay in a proper shop, you can choose your material and then let one of these guys knock up a made-to-measure masterpiece. There are also plenty of fascinating knick-knack shops selling mostly cheap tat, but a browse is always good for a laugh and there are some genuine bargains to be found. Plant Street is famous for pots and plants (hence the name), dodgy pet shops, and furniture upholstery shops and hardware stores. For grocery shopping, there are small 'corner shops', Lal's supermarket (Plant Street), a tiny branch of Union Co-op (just off Satwa Roundabout) and West Zone supermarket. For anything lacking in these, there's a Spinneys on Beach Road just a few minutes' drive away.

## Places of Interest

At the end of Al Diyafah Street nearest the sea is the Dar Al Ittehad (Union House), where the treaty to create the United Arab Emirates was signed on 2 December 1971. It is also the site of the UAE's largest flag (40m x 20m) on top of a 120m reinforced column – quite unmissable, especially at night.

At the other end of Al Diyafah Street (near the Rydges Plaza Hotel) is the permanently busy Satwa Road. Along here are numerous small shops selling mainly textiles, inexpensive clothes and general household items. You will also find a small area full of car repair shops. If you need a tyre change, new battery, or some minor repairs, this place is worth a visit – they can fix just about anything and everything, and bargaining on price is expected.

Plant Street is between Satwa Road and Al Wasl Road, and is very interesting to explore. This is the place to come at Christmas time, as they stock fir trees.

On Al Wasl Road is the beautiful and intricate Iranian Mosque, with its distinctive blue tiles, arches and pillars mirroring the similarly patterned Iranian Hospital across the road.

If it's greenery you're after, the brand new Satwa Park has been built in the shadow of the skyscrapers on Sheikh Zayed Road, and the smaller Al Khazan and Al Wasl Parks are also oases of greenery with shade and benches. Sporty types can also try a spot of five-a-side football or basketball on the courts along Al Diyafah Street.

*Iranian Mosque*

Etisalat Building

**Area** Ⓓ
**Map p.240-241**

**The Lowdown**
*Dubai's 'strip', where people work hard and then play hard.*

**The Must Dos**
*Vu's bar on the 51st floor of the Emirates Towers Hotel is the ultimate location for a sundowner cocktail and a bird's eye view of the city.*

**The Good**
*So much to do, and all on your doorstep. From this central location you are close to everything, from beaches and malls to nightlife and leisure activities.*

**The Bad**
*With traffic and a lack of pedestrian subways or overpasses, it could take you half an hour to reach a building on the other side of the road.*

## Trade Centre

This lively location is known for the striking architecture of its high-rise residential buildings, office towers, and top-class hotels. From the Trade Centre to Interchange One (known as Defence Roundabout) the Hong Kong-style stretch of Sheikh Zayed Road – all 3.5km of it – is the subject of many a photo, as well as many after-hours tete-a-tetes in the various happening hotspots. With so many residents, tourists, and business people around, this area really buzzes at night, as the crowds flit from restaurants to bars to clubs. During the day there's shopping to be done, with the main draw being Boulevard at Emirates Towers.

### Residential

Tall apartment blocks offer a variety of units and great views, but they don't come cheap. If you're high enough and facing in the right direction, you can see right over the top of Satwa and Jumeira to the sparkling ocean beyond. There are a number of executive apartments that include a housekeeping service. As time goes by, more and more apartment buildings are muscling into this short strip making the parking situation even more dire, but unfortunately not halting the skyscraping rents. For more information on living in the area see p.154.

### Retail

Almost every building has at least a shop or a small selection of them on its ground floor, but many feature mini-shopping centres. The shopping destination of choice for many of Dubai's well-to-do is Boulevard at Emirates Towers. With designer names and designer prices, you can always make do with a bit of window shopping. The Crowne Plaza is also home to The Holiday Centre which has a good (and much cheaper) selection of shops from bookstores to boutiques. Whether you go north or south on Sheikh Zayed Road there are additional shopping opportunities - Wafi City, BurJuman and Deira City Centre are one way and Ibn Battuta and Mall of the Emirates are the other - and either way it shouldn't take you more than 20 minutes. In terms of distance, however, going a few kilometres can take more than a few minutes, thanks to the heavy traffic.

### Places of Interest

At the start of the Sheikh Zayed Road 'business district' is the landmark Dubai World Trade Centre and exhibition halls (illustrated on the Dhs.100 banknote). When it was completed in the 70s the 39 storey tower was by far the tallest building in Dubai. Although it has been surpassed in terms of size and grandeur by a multitude of statuesque skyscrapers, it remains a prominent landmark on this ever-expanding skyline. For a great view, especially in winter when it is less hazy, try the guided tour to the observation deck.

Nearby the Emirates Towers are an impressive address for international business and pleasure in Dubai. At 355 metres, the Office Tower was once the tallest building in the Middle East and Europe. The smaller tower, at 305 metres, houses the Emirates Towers five-star hotel. The views from the 51st floor cocktail bar are spectacular, and the adrenaline-pumping lift ride is not to be missed. Behind the towers is the site of the Dubai International Finance Centre (DIFC), with the distinctive 'Gate' building. DIFC is home to Dubai's very own financial exchange.

Just beyond the first interchange, work is well under way on Burj Dubai, which, at upwards of 700 metres, already claims to be the world's tallest building, even before it's finished. It is due to be completed in 2008.

**255**

*Area* **H**
*Map p.240-241*

# Umm Suqeim

Umm Suqeim is a pleasant family neighbourhood with a good stretch of beach and some top-class leisure and entertainment facilities. It is also home to Dubai's iconic landmark, the Burj Al Arab (currently the tallest hotel in the world), which sits 280m off the coast on its own island. Although not nearly as tall, the area's other luxury hotels are no less impressive, with fine-dining restaurants and some real star bars. Souk Madinat Jumeirah should be on every visitor's itinerary, and Wild Wadi Water Park is a great place to cool down on a hot day.

**The Lowdown**
*Golden beaches, smart villas, posh hotels, a shopping 'souk' and a popular water park.*

**The Good**
*The iconic Burj Al Arab in the background.*

**The Bad**
*Sky-high rents means that living in a villa with a view of the Burj Al Arab is reserved for a few fortunates only.*

**The Must Dos**
*Pick a great bar in Al Qasr, Mina A'Salam or the Jumeirah Beach Hotel, then sit and sip a cocktail and watch the sunset.*

## Residential

Umm Suqeim is a great location for families, thanks to its low-rise villas, many with gardens and courtyards. Some villas are actually so big and fancy they could be described as palaces. Being so close to Internet and Media Cities means the area is popular with high-flyers, and the rents are sky-high too.

## Retail

Until fairly recently there was no real shopping to be had in Umm Suqeim, but that changed with the opening of Souk Madinat Jumeirah. Built to resemble a traditional Arabian market, the souk is a maze of alleyways featuring 75 open-fronted shops and boutiques. For weary shoppers there's endless coffee shops, restaurants and bars.

## Places of Interest

The ultimate place of interest has to be the Burj Al Arab hotel (p.28). If your budget allows, you shouldn't miss the chance to sample its bars and restaurants, or even the health spa. If you prefer your leisure to be free-of-charge, there's plenty of public beach to enjoy – just turn up, pop your towel down and relax. However, if the beach is a little sedate and you fancy some aquatic fun for the whole family, it has to be Wild Wadi (p.274).

*Madinat Jumeirah wind towers*

*Wild Wadi & Burj Al Arab*

## Sharjah

Area **5**
Map p.240-241

**The Lowdown**
Quieter than Dubai, but
still plenty to see and do,
especially for arts and
culture lovers.

**The Good**
Sharjah is a city of
culture, heritage and the
arts, and also boasts an
attractive corniche and
lush green parks.

**The Bad**
Traffic! A 10 kilometre
journey can take well
over an hour, which may
put you off visiting in
the evenings.

**The Must Dos**
Wander around the
Heritage Area and
imagine that you've
stepped back in time. Hats
off to the local
government for restoring
and preserving this
fascinating slice of history.

**Tone it Down**
Sharjah is more
conservative than Dubai,
both in terms of dress
code and behaviour.
Wearing revealing
clothing or kissing and
canoodling might earn
you some disapproving
stares, if not a stern
talking to from the police.
Bear this in mind when
exploring the area.

Before Dubai's rise to prominence as a trading and
tourism hotspot, its neighbour, Sharjah, was one of the
wealthiest towns in the region, with settlers earning their
livelihood from fishing, pearling and trade. The city grew
inland from the original creekside town, but the creek
remains a prominent landmark today. Sharjah is worth a
visit for its various museums and great shopping. In 1998,
UNESCO named Sharjah the cultural capital of the Arab
world due to its commitment to art, culture and
preserving its traditional heritage.

### Residential
Downtown is mainly apartment blocks, while further
inland and along the coast you'll find a mixture of villas
old and new. Rents in Sharjah are generally much
cheaper than those in Dubai, meaning many Dubai
workers live in Sharjah and make the short trip in each day. Short, that is, in terms of
distance (less than 10km 'creek-to-creek'), but because so many thousands hit the road
at the same time, journey times can be infuriatingly long.

### Retail
Big shopping centres and malls are well represented in Sharjah, with the biggest
being Sharjah City Centre, Mega Mall, and the Sahara Centre. All your favourite shops
and brands are here, and you may be pleasantly surprised to find far fewer shoppers
than in Dubai's malls. Sharjah also has numerous good souks, with the Central Souk
(aka Blue Souk) and Souk Al Arsah particularly worth a mention. Beside the creek the
fruit and vegetable markets provide some real atmosphere and colour.

### Places of Interest
Sharjah is built around Khalid Lagoon, (popularly known as the creek), and the
surrounding Buheirah Corniche surrounding is a popular spot for a stroll in the
evening. From various points on the lagoon, small dhows can be hired to see the
lights of the city from the water. One place you shouldn't miss is the Heritage Area, the
fascinating old walled city that is home to numerous museums and the traditional
Souk Al Arsah. The nearby Arts Area is a treat for art lovers with galleries and more
museums. Another must is Qanat Al Qasba, Sharjah's latest attraction with a canal,
performance spaces and waterside restaurants. Another worthy weekend stop-off is
the Sharjah Natural History Museum, see p.266 for more.

### Close Neighbour
Sharjah is of course a
separate city, and emirate,
but it is within easy reach
(traffic depending) of Dubai,
it does have its fair share of
things to see and do, and it is
home to many people who
work in Dubai. Therefore, it
appears here as an extended
'main area' of Dubai, with its
good points and bad points
listed, and details some of the
sights and attractions to
tempt you over the border.

*Sharjah*

# Art Galleries

Other options **Art & Craft Supplies** p.410, **Art** p.408

While there's nothing like the Tate Gallery or the Louvre in Dubai, there are a number of galleries that have interesting exhibitions of art and traditional Arabic artefacts. Most operate as a shop and a gallery, but some also provide studios for artists and are involved in the promotion of art within the emirates. The Majlis Gallery, The Courtyard and the XVA Gallery are all worth visiting for their traditional and unusual architecture alone. They provide striking locations in which you can enjoy a wide range of art, both local and international. Take a look at the Time Out Dubai magazine for details of weekly exhibitions and events.

**Nr Choithram**
*Jumeira*
*Map 7 B1* **9**

## Creative Art Centre

*04 344 4394* | *www.arabian-arts.com*

A large gallery and shop with eight showrooms set in two villas, the Creative Art Centre has a wide range of original art, framed maps, and Arabian antiques and gifts. The selection of antiques includes Omani chests and old doors, much of it 'rescued' in Oman by the gallery owners and then restored in-house. There's also a good selection of old weapons and silver. Lynda Shephard, the managing partner, is a well known artist in both Oman and Dubai and some of her works can be purchased here. The gallery offers a picture-framing service, and they specialise in the restoration of antiques and furniture. The centre can be found set back from Beach Road (take the turning inland between Choithram supermarket and Town Centre shopping mall).

**Al Zomorrodah Bld**
*Al Karama*
*Map 10 E1* **111**

## Four Seasons Ramesh Gallery

*04 334 9090* | *www.fourseasonsgallery.com*

Originally opened in 1970, this company has one of the largest selections of art and photography in Dubai. Located in Block A of the Al Zomorrodah Building on Zabeel Road in Karama, just along from the main post office, the gallery is in one end of the store, which is now largely devoted to selling contemporary furniture. There is a large selection of different types of art exhibited, and for sale, with a mixture from both local and international artists, as well as some interesting photos of Dubai's history.

**Villa 23, St 51,**
**Beh Dubai Zoo**
*Jumeira*
*Map 7 E1* **11**

## Green Art Gallery

*04 344 9888* | *www.gagallery.com*

Housed in an attractive single-storey villa just a stone's throw from the Beach Road, the Green Art Gallery features original art, limited edition prints and hand-crafted work by artists from all over the world. In particular, the gallery draws on those influenced and inspired by the heritage, culture and environment of the Arab world and its people. The managing partners also encourage local artists of all nationalities by guiding them through the process of exhibiting and promoting their work. This is a 'proper' art gallery, with large white minimalist walls and lots of floor space, and makes a great stop-off if you fancy some peace and quiet and a little culture. Seasonal exhibitions are held from October to May.

**Villa 6, Street 49a**
*Al Rashidiya*
*Map 2 C3*

## Hunar Art Gallery

*04 286 2224* | *hunarart@eim.ae*

This gallery exhibits international fine art. Beautifully decorated Japanese tiles, Belgian pewter and glass pieces fill the spaces between ever-changing, contemporary local and world art. Some artists (usually either local artists or those particularly popular at the gallery) receive more regular showings, but typically there is a diverse array of

artists shown. Exhibitions last for around a month, and each one displays either a theme, an artist or a group. The gallery will also, on occasion, display the works of talented local scholars. Many of the pieces in the gallery can be purchased and taken home (but if the piece you buy is part of an exhibition, you can only take it home after the event).

*XVA Gallery*

**Al Faheidi Street**
*Downtown Bur Dubai*
*Map 9 A2* **1**

## The Majlis Gallery
*04 353 6233 | www.majlisgallery.com*
Set in traditional surroundings in the old Bastakiya area of the city, (located on Al Fahedi Street close to Al Fahedi Roundabout), the Majlis Gallery is a converted Arabic house, complete with windtowers and courtyard. Small whitewashed rooms lead off the central garden area and host a variety of exhibitions by contemporary artists. In addition to the fine art collection, there's an extensive range of handmade glass, pottery, fabrics, frames, unusual pieces of furniture and other bits and bobs. The gallery hosts exhibitions throughout the year, but is worth visiting at any time. Open Saturday to Thursday.

**Courtyard, The**
*Al Quoz*
*Map 6 D3*

## Total Arts
*04 228 2888 | www.courtyard-uae.com*
Dubai's biggest gallery occupies two floors of The Courtyard in Al Quoz. It usually exhibits works of art from a variety of cultures and continents, although there is a leaning towards regional talent (particularly Iranian). There are over 300 paintings on permanent display, and regular shows of traditional handicrafts and antique furniture. One of the main attractions here is the beautiful cobbled courtyard itself, surrounded by different facades combining a variety of building styles from around the world.

**Bastakiya**
*Downtown Bur Dubai*
*Map 9 A2* **3**

## XVA Gallery ▶ p.307
*04 353 5383 | www.xvagallery.com*
Located in the centre of the maze-like alleyways of Bastakiya , this is one of Dubai's most interesting art galleries. Originally a windtower house, it is now fully restored and worth a visit for its architecture and displays of local and international art or for a snack in the tranquil shaded courtyard. The gallery focuses mainly on paintings and hosts many different exhibitions throughout the year. From September to June, the gallery hosts free film screenings on Wednesday evenings. XVA can also lay claim to the title of Dubai's hippest hotel – there are eight guest rooms located on the upper floors, where you can chill out in rooftop rocking chairs and gaze over the minarets to the lights of Bur Dubai and beyond.

# Religious Sites

**Jumeira Beach Rd**
*Jumeira*
*Map 7 F1*

## Jumeira Mosque
*04 353 6666 | smccu@eim.ae*
Jumeira Mosque, located at the beginning of the Beach Road, is easily the most beautiful in the city and perhaps the best known. Its image features on the UAE's Dhs.500 banknote. The mosque is especially breathtaking at night when lit. Non-Muslims are not usually permitted entry to a mosque, but the Sheikh Mohammed

**259**

### Ramadan Timings

During Ramadan, timings for many companies in Dubai change significantly. For museums and heritage sites, they usually open slightly later in the morning than usual, and close earlier in the afternoon. Check with the company before you go.

Centre for Cultural Understanding, through its 'Open Doors, Open Minds' programme, organises tours on (Saturday, Sunday, Tuesday and Thursday mornings at 10:00 sharp). Visitors are guided around the mosque and told all about the building, and then the hosts give a talk on Islam and explain the prayer rituals that all Muslims undertake. At the end of the hour-long tour there's a question-and-answer session with the guides. For both visitors and residents this tour provides a fascinating insight into the culture and beliefs of the local population, and is thoroughly recommended during your time in Dubai. Men and women are required to dress conservatively – that means no shorts and no sleeveless tops. Women must also cover their hair with a head scarf or shawl, and all visitors will be asked to remove their shoes before entering. Cameras are allowed, and in fact picture-taking is encouraged. There is a registration fee of Dhs.10 per person, and large groups are able to book their own private tour.

## Heritage Sites

Old Dubai features many fascinating places to visit, all of which offer glimpses into the past when the city was nothing more than a small fishing and trading port. Many of the pre-oil heritage sites have been carefully restored, paying close attention to traditional design and using original building materials. Take an ambient stroll through the Bastakiya area, characterised by the many distinctive windtowers, and marvel at how anyone could have survived in Dubai before air-conditioning. Aside from Dubai, many other areas also offer history fans opportunities to learn more about the region's fascinating past

*Al Khor St, Al Ras*
*Deira*
*Map 9 A1* **4**

### Al Ahmadiya School & Heritage House

*04 226 0286 | www.dubaitourism.ae*

Al Ahmadiya School was the earliest regular school in the city and a visit here is an excellent opportunity to see the history of education in Dubai. Established in 1912 by Mr Ahmadiya for Dubai's elite, this building was closed in 1963 when the school relocated to larger premises. Situated in what is becoming a small centre for heritage in Deira (Al Souk Al Khabeer), it is just behind the Heritage House, an interesting example of a traditional Emirati family house and the former home of Mr Ahmadiya, which dates back to 1890. Both buildings were renovated and converted into museums with the same excellent care and attention as Dubai's other heritage sites. They opened in March 2000, and are now great places for a peek into how life used to be in Dubai's past. Admission to both is free.

*Nr Al Hisn Fort,*
*Kalba – East Coast*
*Kalba*
*Map 1 F2*

### Al Hisn Kalba

*09 277 4442 | www.sharjah-welcome.com*

As you drive along the coast road in Kalba town, you come to the restored house of Sheikh Sayed Al Qassimi, which overlooks the sea. The house is located at the end of a large grassy expanse with swings and small rides for children. On the opposite side of the road is Kalba's Al Hisn Fort, which houses the town's museum and contains a limited display of weapons. Entrance fee: Dhs.2 for individuals; Dhs.4 for families.

*Btn Diwan R/A &*
*Al Faheidi R/A*
*Downtown Bur Dubai*
*Map 9 A2* **3**

### Bastakiya

The Bastakiya area is one of the oldest heritage sites in Dubai and certainly one of the most atmospheric. The neighbourhood dates back to the early 1900s when traders from the Bastak area of southern Iran were encouraged to settle there by tax concessions granted by Sheikh Maktoum bin Hashar, the ruler of Dubai at the turn of the century. The area is characterised by traditional windtower houses, built around courtyards and clustered together around a winding maze of alleyways. The distinctive four-sided windtowers ('barjeel' in Arabic), that can be seen on top of the traditional flat-roofed buildings, are one of the earliest forms of air conditioning.

The whole area is a great place to explore for a few hours, strolling around the peaceful and shaded narrow lanes really takes you away from the bustle of Bur Dubai just streets away. Many buildings have been restored and converted into art galleries, shops, cafes, including Dubai's smallest and most unique guesthouse, a traditionally styled Arabic restaurant, Calligraphy House, Philately House and offices for several non-governmental organisations such as the Sheikh Mohammed Centre for Cultural Understanding, the Journalists' Association and the World Wildlife Fund. To cater to the growing number of tourists visiting this area, a new tourism office was opened in 2006.

An ongoing reconstruction project is gradually turning Bastakiya into a pedestrian conservation area with more and more buildings being restored. Maps of the area (in English and Arabic) are situated opposite Al Musalla Post Office on Al Fahedi Street and also near Al Diwan Roundabout.

**Nr Fujairah Fort**
*Fujairah*
*Map 1 F2*

## Fujairah Heritage Village

This 6,000 square metre heritage village depicts life in the UAE as it was before oil was discovered, with displays of fishing boats, simple dhows, clay, stone and bronze implements and pots, and hunting and agricultural tools. The heritage village is close to Ain Al Madhab Gardens, which are situated in the foothills of the Hajar Mountains just outside Fujairah City. The gardens are fed by mineral springs and this warm sulphur laden water is used in two swimming pools (separate for men and women). Private chalets can be hired on a daily basis. The entrance fee is Dhs.5.

**Hatta town**
*Hatta*
*Map 1 F2*

## Hatta Heritage Village

*04 852 1374 | www.dubaitourism.ae*

Opened to the public in early 2001, Hatta Heritage Village is located an hour's drive south east of Dubai city and a few kilometres from Hatta Fort Hotel. It is constructed around an old settlement and was restored in the style of a traditional mountain village. Explore the tranquil oasis, the narrow alleyways and discover traditional life in the mud and barasti houses. Hatta's history goes back over 3,000 years and the area includes a 200 year-old mosque and the fortress built by Sheikh Maktoum bin Hasher Al Maktoum in 1896, which is now used as a weaponry museum. Entry is free.

*Bastakiya*

| | |
|---|---|
| *Nr Al Shindagha* | **Heritage & Diving Village** |
| ***Tunnel*** | **04 393 7151** \| *www.dubaitourism.ae* |
| *Al Shindagha* | |
| *Map 9 A1* | |

Located near the mouth of Dubai Creek, the Heritage & Diving Village focuses on Dubai's maritime past, pearl diving traditions and architecture. The museum is staffed by real potters and weavers who display their craft the way it has been practised for centuries. There are also a number of shops clustered in one corner selling the usual range of souvenirs. As you wander through, local Arabic women serve up traditionally cooked bread and fried 'doughnuts' – one of the rare opportunities you'll have to sample genuine Emirati cuisine. Camel rides are available most afternoons and evenings. The village is very close to Sheikh Saeed Al Maktoum's House, and is part of the area of Shindagha currently being developed into a cultural centre. Buildings in the area are being renovated and reconstructed to recreate the traditional and simple life in Dubai as it was before modernity took hold. It's particularly lively here during the Dubai Shopping Festival and Eid celebrations, with performances such as traditional sword dancing.

| | |
|---|---|
| *Jumeira Beach Rd* | **Majlis Ghorfat Um Al Sheef** |
| *Jumeira* | **04 394 6343** \| *www.dubaitourism.co.ae* |
| *Map 7 B1* **14** | |

Constructed in 1955 from coral stone and gypsum, this simple building was used by the late Sheikh Rashid bin Saeed Al Maktoum as a summer residence. The ground floor is an open veranda ('leewan' or 'rewaaq'), while upstairs the 'majlis' (Arabic for 'meeting place') is decorated with carpets, cushions, lanterns and rifles. The roof terrace was used for drying dates and even sleeping and it originally offered an uninterrupted view of the sea, although all you can see now is villa rooftops. The site has a garden with a pond and traditional falaj irrigation system, using stone and gypsum channels to direct water from a well. In another corner there's a barasti shelter constructed entirely from palm branches and leaves. The structure has a windtower, designed to channel any available wind down into the building, the Middle East's early and efficient attempt at air conditioning. The Majlis is located just inland from Beach Road on Street 17, beside HSBC bank and Jumbo Electronics – look for the brown Municipality signs. Entry is Dhs.1 for adults and free for children under 6 years. It's closed on Friday mornings.

| | |
|---|---|
| *Nr Arts Area* | **Sharjah Heritage Area** |
| *Sharjah* | **06 569 3999** \| *www.sharjahtourism.ae* |
| *Map 2 C2* | |

The beautifully restored heritage area in Sharjah is a great place for people with an interest in Sharjah's local history. The area includes a number of old buildings: Al Hisn Fort (Sharjah Fort); Sharjah Islamic Museum; Sharjah Heritage Museum (Bait Al Naboodah); the Maritime Museum; the Majlis of Ibrahim Mohammed Al Midfa and the Old Souk (Souk Al Arsah). Here you will see traditional local architecture and life described, depicted and displayed as it was over 150 years ago and up to more recent times. The Majlis of Ibrahim Mohammed Al Midfa, situated between the souk and the waterfront, is a peaceful majlis famous for its round windtower, the only one of its kind in the UAE. Toilets can be found at each venue and there's an Arabic coffee shop in the shady courtyard of Souk Al Arsah. Closed on Mondays.

| | |
|---|---|
| *Bastakiya* | **Sheikh Mohammed Centre for Cultural Understanding** |
| *Downtown Bur Dubai* | **04 353 6666** \| *www.cultures.ae* |
| *Map 9 A2* **3** | |

Located in the Bastakiya area, the cultural centre of Dubai, SMCCU was established to help visitors and residents understand the customs and traditions of the UAE through various activities. These include tours in Jumeira Mosque, (see p.259), a walking tour of the Bastakiya area, Arabic courses, Cultural Awareness programmes and weekly coffee mornings where it is possible to meet UAE Nationals to learn about all aspects of Emirati life. The centre itself is also worth a look for the majlis-style rooms around the courtyard and great views through the palm trees and windtowers.

*Nxt to Heritage* **&** *Diving Village*
*Al Shindagha*
*Map 9 A1* **5**

## Sheikh Saeed Al Maktoum's House

*04 393 7139 | www.dubaitourism.ae*

The modest home of Dubai's much-loved former ruler was once strategically located at the mouth of Dubai's creek but now lies close to the Bur Dubai entrance to Al Shindagha Tunnel. Dating from 1896, this carefully restored house-turned-museum is built in the traditional manner of the Gulf coast, using coral covered in lime and sand-coloured plaster. The interesting displays in many rooms show rare and wonderful photographs of all aspects of life in Dubai pre-oil. There is also an old currency and stamp collection and great views over the creek from the upper floor. Entry is Dhs.2 for adults, Dhs.1 for children and free for under 6 years free.

## Museums

For residents and visitors alike, a visit to one of the museums or heritage sites in the UAE is a great opportunity to discover the culture and history of the country, as well as to catch a glimpse of a fast disappearing way of life. Dubai Municipality plays an active role in preserving Dubai's past and is currently overseeing a huge renovation project which includes 230 of Dubai's old buildings; completion is expected in 2009. Dubai Museum is a gem, while neighbouring Sharjah offers a multiple cultural attractions.

*Opp Etisalat*
*Ajman*
*Map 2 C1*

## Ajman Museum

*06 742 3824 | ajmuseum@eim.ae*

Ajman Museum is interesting and well arranged, with displays described in both English and Arabic. The museum has a variety of exhibits, including a collection of passports (Ajman used to issue its own) and depictions of ancient life, but it's the building itself that will most impress visitors. Housed in a fortress dating back to around 1775, and a former residence of the ruler of Ajman, the museum is a fascinating example of traditional architecture, with imposing watchtowers and traditional windtowers. The fortress served as a police station before becoming the museum in the early 1980s. Closed on Saturdays. Entry is Dhs.4 for adults; Dhs.2 for children under 6 years; Dhs.1 for students. Evening hours are from 17:00 - 20:00 in summer and from 16:00 - 19:00 in winter.

*Al Hisn Ave, Bank St*
*Sharjah*
*Map 2 C2*

## Al Hisn Fort/Heritage Museum

*06 568 5500 | www.sharjah-welcome.com*

It is hard to imagine but this was once an isolated building on the edge of the creek (it was built in 1820). Now this magnificent fort is enclosed by modern high-rise buildings in Sharjah's Corniche, showcasing Sharjah's love of its traditional and distinguished past. The building was originally home to Sharjah's ruling Al Qassimi family, before it was opened by the sheikh to the general public. It was renovated and partially rebuilt after some of it was removed, due to structural changes in the city, in 1969. The fort played an important role in many aspects of life and this can be seen in the rooms throughout the fort, which display social, commercial, military and political developments in Sharjah. Possibly the most fascinating thing about the museum is the incredible photographic history of the Emirate's rulers and people in general – some of the images look as though they could have been taken yesterday and yet the date below reveals them be from as far back as early last century. Built in the traditional courtyard style with three towers on the surrounding walls, the fort links Sharjah's main heritage and arts areas. The museum is closed on Mondays.

**263**

*Nr Bastakiya*
*Downtown Bur Dubai*
*Map 9 A2*

# Dubai Museum
*04 353 1862 | www.dubaitourism.ae*

Located in Al Fahedi Fort, one of Dubai's oldest buildings, which dates back to 1787, Dubai Museum is a highly creative, appealing and well thought-out museum – it is well worth a visit for residents and visitors, to get an overview of Dubai and its history. The fort was originally built as the residence of the ruler of Dubai and for sea defence, then renovated in 1970 to house the museum. The site has also been expanded to include a large area under the courtyard of the old fort. All parts of life from Dubai's past are represented in an attractive and interesting way: walk through a souk from the 1950s, stroll through an oasis complete with falaj, see the way of life in a traditional Emirati house, get up close to the wildlife of the UAE, learn about the archaeological finds from the area or go 'underwater' to discover the part the sea has played in Dubai's growth with its pearl diving and fishing industries. Even if museums aren't your thing, you will find it interesting and informative. It's highly recommended for the whole family. Entry costs Dhs.3 for adults and Dhs.1 for children under 6 years.

*Opp Ruler's Palace*
*Fujairah*
*Map 1 F2*

# Fujairah Museum
*09 222 9085 | www.gia.gov.ae*

This interesting museum offers an insight into Fujairah's history and heritage, which despite being less colourful than its neighbouring emirates is interesting nonetheless. You can see permanent exhibitions on traditional ways of life including the not-so-distant Bedouin culture. There are also artefacts which were found during archaeological excavations throughout the emirate. Some of the items uncovered by local and foreign archaeologists include weapons from the bronze and iron ages, finely painted pottery, carved soapstone vessels and silver coins. The museum is closed on Saturdays. Entry fee is Dhs.3 for adults and Dhs.1 for children.

*Nad Al Sheba*
*Racecourse*
*Al Marqadh*
*Map 16 C3*

# Godolphin Gallery
*04 336 3031 | www.godolphin.com*

The Godolphin Gallery celebrates the Maktoum family's private racing stable, and houses the world's finest collection of racing trophies. The gallery is refurbished every year and incorporates interactive touch-screen consoles, photographs, video presentations and memorabilia from over 10 years of the Godolphin racing stable.

Dubai Museum

Adjacent to Nad Al Sheba Club, the gallery is open throughout the racing season from its start in November until the end of April.

## National Museum of Ras Al Khaimah

*Old town – beh Police HQ*
*Ras Al Khaimah*
*Map 1 E1*

**07 233 3411** | www.rakmuseum.gov.ae

Housed in an impressive fort, the former home of the present ruler of Ras Al Khaimah, this museum has mainly local natural history and archaeological displays, plus a variety of paraphernalia from pre-oil life. Upstairs you can see an account of the British naval expedition against Ras Al Khaimah in 1809, a model of a 'baggala' (a typical craft used in the early 1800s), and excellent examples of silver Bedouin jewellery. Look out for fossils set in the rock strata of the walls of the fort – these date back 190 million years. The building has battlements, a working windtower, and ornate, carved wooden doors. Entrance fees: Adults Dhs.2; children Dhs.1. If you wish to use your camera you need a photo permit costing an extra Dhs.5. The museum is located behind the Police Headquarters in the old town close to the bridge. From Dubai, turn left at the second roundabout after the Clock Roundabout once in RAK and the museum is 100 metres on your right. Open September to May from 10:00 - 17:00, and from June to August from 08:00 – 12:00 and 16:00 – 19:00. The museum is closed on Tuesdays.

## Sharjah Archaeological Museum

*Nr Cultural R/A*
*Sharjah*
*Map 2 C2*

**06 566 5466** | www.archaeology.gov.ae

This hi-tech museum offers an interesting display of antiquities from the region. Linked to a conference centre and used as an educational venue for local schoolchildren, the museum has installed computers in each hall to provide in-depth information on the exhibits. Using well-designed displays and documentary film, the museum traces man's first steps and progress across the Arabian Peninsula through the ages. One area features the latest discoveries from excavation sites in the UAE. Worth a visit for archaeology and history lovers. Admission is free. The museum is closed on Sundays.

## Sharjah Art Museum

*Sharjah Arts Area*
*Sharjah*
*Map 2 C2*

**06 568 8222** | www.sharjahtourism.ae

Opened in April 1997, Sharjah Art Museum dominates the arts plaza area. It was purpose built in a traditional style, chiefly to house the personal collection of over 300 paintings and maps of the ruler, HH Dr Sheikh Sultan bin Mohammed Al Qassimi. Permanent displays include the work of 18th century artists, with oil paintings and watercolours depicting life from all over the Arab world, while other exhibits in the 72 small galleries change frequently. There's also an art reference library, bookshop and coffee shop, and the museum hosts various cultural activities. The museum is closed on Mondays and Friday mornings; Wednesday afternoons are for ladies only. There is no entry fee.

## Sharjah Heritage Museum

*Sharjah Heritage Area*
*Sharjah*
*Map 2 C2*

**06 568 5500** | www.sharjahtourism.ae

Also known as 'Bait Al Naboodah', this two-storey building was once owned by the late Obaid bin Eesa Al Shamsi (nicknamed Al Naboodah), and is a reconstruction of a family home (bait) as it would have been around 150 years ago. Three generations of the Al Naboodah family lived here until 1972. The home is built around a large courtyard, as were many traditional Arabic houses at the time. Each room shows various items such as clothing, weapons, cooking pots and goatskin water bags. You can get a good background knowledge of the house and its history by watching the short documentary film when you first arrive. There is no entry fee. The museum is closed on Mondays.

*Sharjah*
*Heritage Area*
*Sharjah*
*Map 2 C2*

## Sharjah Islamic Museum

*06 568 3334 | www.sharjahtourism.ae*

Sharjah Islamic Museum is home to an unrivalled collection of Islamic masterpieces and manuscripts, representing the cultural history of Muslims over 1,400 years. Housed in a 200 year-old building, the displays are from HH Dr Sheikh Sultan bin Mohammed Al Qassimi's private collection, and include examples of Islamic crafts such as ceramics, manuscripts, jewellery and textiles. In the Honoured Ka'aba Hall there is an impressive collection of gold-plated Qurans and a replica of the curtain that covers the Ka'aba Stone at Mecca. There is also a Science Hall particularly fascinating for its map of the globe, the first of its kind by Al Shareef Al Idrisi (born 1099AD), which appears upside down compared to modern maps. The museum is open during holy days and public holidays. Wednesday afternoons are for ladies and children under 12 only. Closed on Mondays and Friday mornings. There is no entry fee.

*Sharjah*
*Heritage Area*
*Sharjah*
*Map 2 C2*

## Sharjah Maritime Museum

*06 569 3999 | www.sharjahtourism.ae*

This museum is a must for anyone with an interest in nautical history and the development of seafaring in the Middle East, with displays featuring fishing, trading, pearl diving and the construction of the many types of boats native to the UAE. Each room in the museum informs visitors about a different aspect of marine industry. One room contains scale models of the larger ships while in the open courtyard, at the centre of the museum, and also just outside the entrance, there are full-size boats with names and descriptions.

*Jct 8, Sharjah –*
*East Coast Rd*
*Sharjah*
*Map 2 C2*

## Sharjah Natural History Museum

*06 531 1411 | www.sharjahtourism.ae*

This fascinating museum, which combines learning with entertainment, unfolds through five exhibition halls to expose you to the earth's secrets. Exhibits include a 35-metre diorama of the UAE's natural habitat and wildlife; a stunning geological UV light display; a hall showing the interaction between man and his environment, including the museum's best known exhibit: a mechanical camel; plus a botanical hall, and the marine hall. The site also incorporates the Arabian Wildlife Centre (06 531 1999), where you have the chance to see indigenous and endangered species; most famously, the Arabian leopard (photography is forbidden). There is a breeding centre at the same location but in order to allow the animals maximum privacy this is not open to the public. There is also a Children's Farm (06 531 1127) where animals, such as donkeys, camels and goats, can be fed and petted. The facilities are excellent and offer an enjoyable, interactive and educational day out. Picnic areas are available, plus cafes and shops. Great fun for all ages, and a place that you will want to visit again and again. Closed on Mondays. Entry costs Dhs.15 per person, Dhs.30 for families, and includes access to everything.

*Nr TV station*
*Sharjah*
*Map 2 C2*

## Sharjah Science Museum

*06 566 8777 | www.sharjahtourism.ae*

Opened in 1996, this museum is the only interactive science museum in the UAE and offers visitors exhibits and demonstrations, covering subjects such as aerodynamics, cryogenics, electricity, colour and a guided tour of the universe in the Planetarium. There's also a children's area where the under fives and their parents can learn together. Those who are inspired to learn more can visit the Learning Centre, which offers more in-depth programmes on many of the subjects covered in the museum. There is also a cafe and gift shop. School groups are more than welcome. Entry costs Dhs.2 for children aged 2 to 12 years; and Dhs.3-5 for over 12's. Family entry (two adults and four kids) costs between Dhs.8-15. Groups of 20 or more receive a 20% discount.

**Warning!**

*Although the waters off the coast of Dubai generally look calm and unchallenging, very strong rip tides can carry the most confident swimmer away from the shore very quickly and drownings have occurred in the past. Take extra care when swimming off the public beaches where there are no lifeguards.*

# Beaches

Other options **Swimming** p.378, **Parks** p.268, **Parasailing** p.365, **Beach Clubs** p.384

If you love sea breeze in your hair and sand between your toes, you'll be happy to know that there are many beautiful beaches in Dubai. You have a choice between public beaches (limited facilities but no entry fee), beach parks (good facilities and a nominal entrance fee), and (normally part of a hotel or resort – see p.267).

Options for public beaches include Al Mamzar Beach Park (Map 12-D1), which has a cordoned-off swimming area, chalets, jet skis for hire and free beaches along the lagoon to the south. Travelling south past the creek, you'll come to Jumeira Open Beach (Map 7-F1), which is great for soaking up the sun, swimming and people watching. Moving further south brings you to the small beaches between the Dubai Offshore Sailing Club (Map 6-F1), and Jumeirah Beach Hotel (Map 6-B1), previously the place for kite surfers and paramotors. Those looking for more natural beaches used to be able to pay a visit to the expanse of beach past the Jebel Ali Golf Resort & Spa (Map 3-A1), but this previously quiet area is now also being developed. The construction of the trunk of Palm Jebel Ali and the Dubai Waterfront project mean most of these beaches have subsequently been closed to the public.

Regulations for the public beaches seem to be getting more strict. Dogs are banned from the beaches, and so is driving. Officially, other banned beach activities include barbecues, camping without a permit and holding large parties. Contact the Public Parks and Recreation Section (04 336 7633) for clarification.

# Beach Parks

Other options **Parks** p.268

A visit to one of Dubai's beach parks is a perfect way to spend the day – the warm waters, white sandy beaches and stretches of lush greenery will transport you a hundred miles from the stresses of city life.

Both of the beach parks are busy at weekends, especially during winter, although Al Mamzar Park rarely feels crowded because it is so huge. Both parks have a ladies' day when men are not allowed (ladies may enter with their young sons, however). Remember where you are and dress appropriately – swimming costumes and bikinis are totally acceptable, as long as you wear both the top and bottom halves.

Timings often change during Ramadan, when parks usually open and close later in the day. Both parks have lifeguards on duty – when they raise the red flag, it is unsafe to swim and you should take the opportunity to work on your tan instead.

## Al Mamzar Beach Park

**04 296 6201** | www.dm.gov.ae

**Nr Hamriya Port**
*Al Hamriya*
*Map 12 D1*

With its four clean beaches, open grassy spaces and plenty of greenery, Al Mamzar Beach Park is a popular spot and well worth a visit, even for people who don't live in Deira. A large amphitheatre is located near the entrance and paths wind through picnic areas and children's playgrounds. The well-maintained beaches have sheltered areas for swimming and changing rooms

### Kids' Play Areas

When high temperatures drive you indoors, it's good to know that most malls have an indoor play area that should keep kids busy for ages. Most have various facilities and activities to suit a spectrum of ages. Some recommended venues are: Fun Corner - Bin Sougat Mall (04 286 2848), Umm Suqeim (04 394 0315), Reef Mall (04 227 6620); LouLou Al Dugong's - Lamcy Plaza (04 335 2700); Magic Planet - Mall of the Emirates (04 341 4000), Deira City Centre (04 295 4333); Peakaboo - Village Mall (04 344 7122), Mall of the Emirates (04 347 0622).

**267**

with showers. Kiosks near each beach sell food and other small necessities you may have left at home, while near the entrance is a restaurant and a coffee shop. Air-conditioned chalets, complete with a barbecue area, can be rented on a daily basis for Dhs.150-200. There are also two swimming pools and lifeguard patrols. To get around the park you can hire bicycles or take a train tour. During the Dubai Shopping Festival there are activities organised here as well as shows for kids in the amphitheatre. Sadly, the previously clear views out to sea are now somewhat obstructed by the offshore construction on the Palm Deira. Entrance fees are Dhs.5 per person or Dhs.30 per car (including all occupants). Pool fees are Dhs.10 per adult, Dhs.5 per child. Wednesday is family day, which means no single males are allowed.

## Jumeira Beach Park

**Nr Jumeirah Beach Club**
*Jumeira*
*Map 7 B1*

**04 349 2555** | www.dm.gov.ae

With azure seas, a one-kilometre stretch of golden sand and palm trees for shade, Jumeira Beach Park is a popular destination. You can hire a sunbed and parasol for Dhs.20, but they do sometimes run out so get there early or take your own. At either end of the beach there's a cafe selling snacks and drinks, as well as another drinks shop and an icecream parlour. There are showers along the beach and toilets too. Lifeguards are on duty from 08:00 to sunset, after which swimming is not permitted. Away from the beach there are plenty of grassy areas and landscaped gardens, a children's play area, and barbecue pits available for public use. Cycling is not allowed (except for small children) and neither is rollerblading. The park can get really busy at weekends and in the evenings too, especially on public holidays when there's a good atmosphere with friends and families getting together for a barbie. Entry is Dhs.5 per person and Dhs.20 per car. Mondays are for women and children only.  It's open daily from 07:00, closing at 22:30 Sunday to Wednesday, and at 23:00 Thursday to Saturday and on holidays.

## Parks

Other options **Beaches** p.267

Dubai has a number of excellent parks, and visitors will be pleasantly surprised by the many lush green lawns and the variety of trees and shrubs which make the perfect escape from the concrete jungle of the city. In winter months, the more popular green parks can be very busy at weekends. Most have a kiosk or cafe selling snacks and drinks. Alternatively take a picnic or use the barbecue pits provided (remember to take your own wood or charcoal, and food). Creekside Park has an amphitheatre and often holds concerts during public holidays or special occasions, including events during the Dubai Shopping Festival (details are announced in local newspapers two or three days before). Regulations among the parks vary, with some banning bikes and rollerblades, or limiting ball games to specific areas. Pets are not permitted and you should not take plant cuttings. Certain parks have a ladies' day when entry is restricted to women, girls and young boys (check the individual entries) and some of the smaller ones actually ban anyone other than ladies through the week, and allow families only at the weekends. As with the beach parks, opening hours change during Ramadan. Entrance to the smaller parks is generally free, while the larger ones charge up to Dhs.5 per person. Contact the Dubai Municipality by email at publicparks@dm.gov.ae or by telephone on 050 858 9887 for more info.

## Creekside Park

**Nr Wonderland**
*Umm Hurair*
*Map 11 A3*

**04 336 7633** | www.dm.gov.ae

Situated in the heart of the city but blessed with acres of gardens, fishing piers, jogging tracks, BBQ sites, children's play areas, restaurants and kiosks, this is the ultimate in park

*A breath of fresh air*

life. There's also a mini falaj and a large amphitheatre. Running along the park's 2.5km stretch of creek frontage is a cable car system which allows allowing visitors an unrestricted view from 30m in the air. From Gate Two, four-wheel cycles can be hired for Dhs.20 per hour (you can't use your own bike in the park). Rollerblading is allowed, and there are no ladies-only days. Entrance fee: Dhs.5. Cable car: adults Dhs.25; children Dhs.15. Children's City: adults Dhs.15; children Dhs.10.

## Fruit & Garden Luna Park

*Al Nasr Leisureland*
*Oud Metha*
*Map 10 E2* **18**

04 337 1234 | www.alnasrleisureland.ae

This fruity little park offers many attractions that are suitable for everyone, and is an ideal venue for a birthday party. Activities include rides, go-karts, bumper cars and a rollercoaster, and you can combine a visit here with use of the other facilities of Al Nasr Leisureland. Entrance fees are set at Dhs.10 for adults and Dhs.5 for children under the age of 5 years.

## Mushrif Park

*Al Khawaneej Rd,*
*9 km past Dubai*
*Airport*
*Map 15 C4*

04 288 3624 | www.dm.gov.ae

Situated just past Mirdif along the Airport Road, Mushrif Park is a huge desert park full of activities and facilities. The grounds are extensive, and although it is a 'desert park' there are many large stretches of beautiful green lawn. The park has three pools in total: two large pools (one for men, one for women, with no mixing allowed), and a smaller pool for young children that is situated next to the ladies' pool. There are numerous playgrounds dotted around the park, featuring slides, swings, roundabouts and climbing frames, and a central plaza complete with fairground rides and trampolines. There is also an animal enclosure where you can get up close and personal with horses, camels, goats and even a turkey – pony and camel rides are available, starting from Dhs.5 for a short ride. An interesting feature of the park is a mini-town, where you can wander around miniature houses. There is also a train that tours the park in the afternoons (Dhs.2 per ride). No bikes or rollerblades are allowed inside the park, but you can drive aaround it. Entry costs Dhs.3 per person or Dhs.10 per car. Swimming pool entrance is Dhs.10 per adult and Dhs.5 per child. A membership scheme is available.

## Rashidiya Park

*Nr Bin Sougat Ctr,*
*Off Airport Rd*
*Al Rashidiya*
*Map 13 F4*

www.dm.gov.ae

This pretty and peaceful park is where you'll find plenty of expat mums from Mirdif, Rashidiya and the surrounding areas. It has several large grassy areas, divided by paved walkways. There are also two comprehensive play areas for children, featuring a good mix of climbing frames, miniature playhouses, slides, swings and see-saws. Although the play areas are not very shady, there are plenty of other shaded areas in the park where you can go to escape the sun for a while. There is a little shop next to the entrance, selling drinks, snacks and a range of cheap plastic toys that go down well with children. Entrance is free. Saturday to Wednesday is reserved for women and children only – the park gets much busier on weekends when families are allowed.

## Safa Park

*Nr Union Co-op &*
*Choithrams*
*Al Wasl*
*Map 7 B2*

04 349 2111 | www.dm.gov.ae

Spot the giant Ferris wheel opposite Jumeira Library and you've found Safa Park. This beautiful, artistically divided and huge park offers electronic games for teenagers in its large Pavillion, plus (at weekends) bumper cars, a big wheel, a Mini-Train ride, 'Traffic Garden' (buggies and a course), a big trampoline cage and a merry-go-round. It also has volleyball, basketball and football pitches, tennis courts, an obstacle course, barbecue sites, expanses of grassy areas and several play areas with swings. In the centre of the park is an Arabic

Garden and a Lake Promenade with waterfall feature, where rowing-boats can be hired. The lake is home to a bevy of friendly ducks who love being fed, so remember to take along all your old bits of stale bread. You are not allowed to take your own bicycle into the park, but you can hire one inside (Dhs.100 deposit and Dhs.30 for one hour). Rollerblading is allowed. A popular feature of the park is the running track around its perimeter – you don't have to pay to use this and in the early evenings it is very busy with runners and walkers. The track is specially sprung to help you avoid high-impact sports injuries; as you step onto it you'll be able to feel the slightly spongier texture. Tuesday is ladies' day, but there is also a permanent ladies' garden within the park where men are not allowed. The park also houses a Birds' Promenade and a Plant Nursery, and at certain times of year exhibitions are held. During these exhibitions, the entrance fee may rise to Dhs.10, but normally entry costs just Dhs.3, with children under 3 years going in for free.

## Satwa Park

*Beh Al Moosa Towers*
*Trade Centre 1*
*Map 7 E2*

www.dm.gov.ae

This new community park opened its gates in 2006, and while certainly not on the scale of Safa or Zabeel Parks, it does offer some welcome relief and relaxation in the shadows of the SZR skyscrapers. The park has tennis and basketball courts, a grass football pitch, and a running track around its perimeter. There's plenty of shade, seating, and grassy areas, and the kids' play area has the usual array of colourful slides and climbing frames.

## Umm Suqeim Park

*Nr Jumeirah*
*Beach Hotel*
*Umm Suqeim*
*Map 6 C1*

**04 348 4554** | *parks@dm.gov.ae*

This ladies' park is closed to men except for weekends. It is fairly large and has three big playgrounds with some great equipment that kids will love. There are also plenty of shady, grassy areas so that mums can sit and rest while the kids let off steam. In the middle of the park there is a popular coffee shop. Entrance is free.

## Zabeel Park

*Nr Trade Centre R/A*
*Al Kifaf*
*Map 10 C1*

Providing an oasis of greenery in the heart of downtown Dubai, Zabeel Park serves the communities of Karama, Bur Dubai, Satwa and the Trade Centre area. It is also the first park in the Middle East with a 'technology theme', and features three zones: alternative energy, communications and technology. Covering 51 hectares, the huge green area is taken up by recreational areas, a jogging track, a mini cricket pitch, a football field, boating lake, and an amphitheatre. There are a number of restaurants and cafes within the park for some refreshment and a bite to eat. The newest attraction is Stargate – built to resemble a spaceship that has crash-landed. It promises to become a family 'edutainment' centre, with spaces for learning, shopping, dining and exercising. Open from 08:00 weekly, closing at 23:00 Sunday to Wednesday, and at 23:30 Thursday to Saturday. On public holidays the park stays open until midnight. Mondays are reserved for ladies only. Entry costs Dhs.5 (it's free for children up to 2 years). People with disabilities can gain free access.

*Zabeel Park*

## Other Attractions

*Btn Al Khan &*
*Khalid Lagoons*
*Sharjah*
*Map 12 F3*

### Qanat Al Qasba

*06 556 0777 | www.qaq.ae*

The beautiful Qanat Al Qasba is a kilometre-long canal linking Al Khan Lagoon and Khalid Lagoon, with lots of attractions and eateries along its banks. The emphasis is on culture, with an ever-changing calendar including Arabian poetry and film (with English subtitles), art exhibitions and classes, musical events and theatrical performances, either in the dedicated venues or outdoors on the walkways beside the canal. The Tent of Wonders is a permanent 'big top' featuring shows by performers from around the world. There are shops and stalls selling Arabian treasures and souvenirs including woodwork, metalwork and pottery, embroidery, sculpture, and Islamic calligraphy and engraving. When you get hungry, restaurants and cafes with outdoor terraces serve Arabic, Asian and Mediterranean cuisine. Motorised abras provide boat tours up and down the canal, but perhaps the biggest draw, and certainly the most visible, is the Eye of the Emirates – a 60-metre high observation wheel with air-conditioned pods offering amazing views over Sharjah and across to Dubai and beyond. See the website for details of events.

## Amusement Centres

Other options **Amusement Parks** p.273

*Creekside Park*
*Umm Hurair*
*Map 11 A3*

### Children's City

*04 334 0808 | www.childrencity.ae*

Children's City is an educational project that offers kids their own learning zone and amusement facilities, by providing hands-on experiences relating to theory they have been taught at school. There's a Planetarium focusing on the solar system and space exploration, a Nature Centre for information on land and sea environments, and the Discovery Space, which reveals the miracles and mysteries of the human body. Children's City focuses on 5 to 12 year olds, although items of interest are included for toddlers and teenagers.

*Opp Sharjah Airport,*
*Al Dhaid Rd*
*Sharjah*
*Map 2 C2*

### Discovery Centre

*06 558 6577 | www.sharjah-welcome.com*

This colourful centre features a wide range of activities suitable for toddlers and children up to the age of 13, including a soft-play area for the very tiny tots. Children can explore the themed areas and experiment and interact with the exhibits. The underlying aim is to teach youngsters about the biological, physical and technological worlds in a practical way. There is good pushchair access, an in-house cafe and ample parking. Children under 2 years get in for free. Kids under 12 pay Dhs.4 in the mornings and Dhs.7 in the evenings, while over 13s pay Dhs.5 in the mornings and Dhs.10 in the evenings. Family tickets are available (two adults, three children) for Dhs.15 in the mornings and Dhs.30 in the evenings. Open from 09:00 - 14:00 Saturday to Tuesday, and 15:30 - 20:30 Wednesday to Friday. Hours are subject to change, so it's advisable to call ahead to check opening times.

*Children's City*

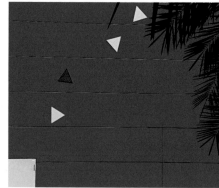

## Encounter Zone

*Wafi Mall*
*Umm Hurair*
*Map 10 D4*

*04 324 7747 | ezone@eim.ae*

With a range of activities for all ages, Encounter Zone is a great stop-off if you want to reward your kids for being good while you have shopped up a storm in Wafi's many boutiques. Galactica is for teenagers and adults and features an inline skating and skateboarding park. Lunarland is for kids aged 1 to 8, and is packed with activities designed especially for younger children, including a small soft-play area for very tiny tots. Prices range from Dhs.5 to Dhs.25, or you can buy a day-pass for Dhs.45. Open from 10:00 to 22:00 Saturday to Tuesday, from 10:00 to 23:00 Wednesday and Thusday, and from 13:00 to 22:00 on Fridays.

## Extreme Fun

*Hamarain Centre*
*Deira*
*Map 11 E1*

*04 262 1110 | www.dubaishoppingmalls.com*

Previously known as City 2000, this is a small centre with lots of video games and a few rides. Entrance is free and all machines are operated by Dhs.1 tokens. Most take two tokens, except for adult simulator games that take three. If all that fun leaves you famished, head to the foodcourt.

## Fantasy Kingdom

*Al Bustan Centre*
*Al Qusais*
*Map 14 B1*

*04 263 2774 | www.al-bustan.com*

Themed as a medieval castle, Fantasy Kingdom offers adventure and excitement for the little ones. The centre has a 24,000 square foot indoor play area, which is divided into sections for different age groups. Younger children can enjoy the merry-go-round, cars to ride and the soft-play area, while older kids can play interactive games, video games, bumper cars, pool and air hockey. There is also a childrens' cafeteria.

## Magic Planet

*Deira City Centre*
*Deira*
*Map 11 C3*

*04 295 4333 | www.deiracitycentre.com*

This blaring, boisterous play area is located to the side of the foodcourt, and is a hugely popular destination for kids accompanying their mums and dads on long shopping trips. There are various rides, including a large merry-go-round and a train, as well as bumper cars and the latest video games. For tinier tots there is a large activity play gym and a small soft-play area. Entrance to Magic Planet is free, and you use the facilities on a 'pay as you play' basis (by loading cash onto a plastic card). For unlimited fun and entertainment, you can buy a Dhs.50 special pass. And if hunger pangs start interfering with playtime, there are over a dozen outlets in the foodcourt where you can refuel.

## Amusement Parks

Other options **Amusement Centres** p.272, **Water Parks** p.274

## Adventureland

*Sahara Centre*
*Sharjah*
*Map 2 C2*

*06 531 6363 | www.adventureland-sharjah.com*

Located on the first floor of the Sahara Centre, you may think this is just another 'amusement corner' to keep the kids happy while you recover from a hard day's shopping, but you'd be wrong. Adventureland is a fully fledged indoor funfair, with an impressive variety of rides and attractions to keep all ages happy. The Quantum Leap ride shouldn't be missed – it's fast and thrilling and not for the faint-hearted, but there's also plenty of sedate rides for the little ones. The centre also features 100 video games and simulators, an internet cafe, a climbing wall, billiards, bowling and a sports cafe. They also have a party room, and offer a number of packages catering to children's parties.

**273**

## Water Parks
Other options **Amusement Parks** p.273

*North of UAQ,*
*on RAK Rd*
*Umm Al Quwain*
*Map 1 E1*

### Dreamland Aqua Park ▶ p.xii
*06 768 1888* | *www.dreamlanduae.com*
With over 25 water rides spread across 250,000 square metres of green, landscaped grounds, Dreamland Aqua Park is one of the largest water parks in the world. Adrenaline junkies will not be disappointed with rides such as the Black Hole, the Kamikaze, and the four 'Twisting Dragons'. For a more leisurely experience there's the lazy river, a wave pool, and a high-salinity pool for floating about. The Aqua Play area has 19 games and attractions for the whole family, and if you prefer not to get wet you can burn rubber on the 400 metre go-kart track. There's a variety of cafes and restaurants, including Saj Zaman, a Lebanese cafe, as well as a licensed pool bar and shisha majlis. Overnight accomodation is aso available, either in a tent (provided for you) or a 'cabana' hut. Admission costs Dhs.80 for adults and Dhs.50 for children under 12, while children under 4 go free. The park is open from 10:00 to 18:00 in winter and from 10:00 to 21:00 in summer (June to September). Fridays and holidays are reserved for families only.

*WonderLand*
*Umm Hurair*
*Map 13 C1* **20**

### Splashland
*04 324 1222* | *www.wonderlanduae.com*
The waterpark within Wonderland in Umm Hurair offers fun for kids or adults with nine rides including slides and twisters, a lazy river, an adults' pool and a children's activity pool with slides, bridges and water cannons. Alternatively, you can just relax by the pool and sunbathe. Lockers and changing rooms are available. Refer to WonderLand Theme & Water Park below for more details of what is available.

*Nr Jumeirah*
*Beach Hotel*
*Umm Suqeim*
*Map 6 B1*

### Wild Wadi Water Park ▶ p.275
*04 348 4444* | *www.wildwadi.com*
Don't miss this world-class water park themed around the adventures of Juha, the mythical friend of Sinbad. Spread over 12 acres beside Jumeirah Beach Hotel, and with the Burj Al Arab towering nearby, the park has 23 aquatic rides and attractions to suit all ages and bravery levels. One of the first you'll encounter is the Wipeout, a permanently rolling wave giving you the chance to show off your body-boarding skills. Less taxing and altogether more relaxing is Juha's Journey, where you just sit back (in either single or double rubber rings) and float through a changing landscape. For thrill-seekers there's the Jumeirah Sceirah – the tallest and fastest freefall water slide outside North America. Depending on how busy it is you may have to queue for some of the rides, but the wait is always worth it. There are two cafes serving drinks and snacks, and once you've paid the entrance fee there is no limit to the number of times you can ride. The park opens at 11:00. The closing time depends on the time of year – 18:00 from November to February, 19:00 from March to May and September to October, and 21:00 from June to August. Admission is Dhs.150 for adults and Dhs.125 for children. There is also a 'sundowner' rate (for the last three hours of opening), when adults pay Dhs.120 and children pay Dhs.95.

*Nr Creekside Park*
*Umm Hurair*
*Map 13 C1*

### WonderLand Theme & Water Park
*04 324 1222* | *www.wonderlanduae.com*
With both an amusement theme park and the Splashland Water Park (see above), Wonderland will keep the most demanding of youngsters happy. The theme park offers indoor and outdoor rides and slides for people of all ages, including The Space Shot, Freefall and Action Arm as well as play areas, trampolines, video and arcade games. Parties and events can be catered for and paintball and go-karting are also available. See also Paintballing (p.365).

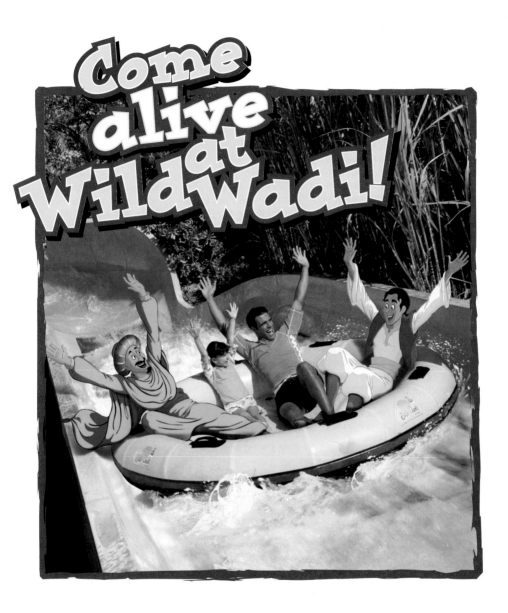

Introducing Summit Surge and Rushdown Ravine, our Family
Master Blaster – an unforgettable up and down journey in a ring
that's made for four. It's just one of the attractions that make
Wild Wadi the most splashtacular day out in Dubai. So come on
down and come alive!

**Tel: 04 348 4444 • www.wildwadi.com**

Wild Wadi is located between Burj Al Arab and Jumeirah Beach Hotel.

## Zoos & Wildlife Parks

**Sharjah Natural History Museum**
*Sharjah*
*Map 2 C2*

### Arabian Wildlife Centre

*06 531 1411 | www.sharjah-welcome.com*

This centre is home to lots of exciting animals and endangered species, such as the Arabian leopard. See the entry on p.266 for The Sharjah Natural History Museum.

**Jumeira Beach Rd**
*Jumeira*
*Map 7 E1*

### Dubai Zoo

*04 349 6444 | www.dubaitourism.ae*

Originally a small private collection of animals, Dubai Zoo was taken over by the Municipality in 1971 and underwent expansion and refurbishment in the mid 1980s. This is an old-fashioned zoo, with lions, tigers, giraffes, monkeys, deer, snakes, bears, flamingos, giant tortoises and other animals housed behind bars in small cages. The curator and his staff do their best with the woefully inadequate space and resources, and look after the animals. Attempts are occasionally made to offload animals by handing them over to other zoos, but despite this numbers are actually increasing as the zoo takes in dangerous and exotic creatures seized at Dubai's ports. The zoo has around 1,200 animals, and space is so tight that cages have even been extended vertically. Visitor numbers are increasing too, with over 400,000 a year on average, and you may find some visitors' treatment of the animals as troubling as the conditions. An early attempt at barrier-free cages was abandoned after people attempted to feed the animals, and threw their rubbish into the enclosures. It could be said that the bars are there now to protect the animals from the public as much as the other way round.

For many years there has been talk of relocating the zoo to much bigger premises – first near Mushrif Park, and more recently to a site within Dubailand – but up to now the plans have never materialised. It can only be hoped that the authorities make good on their promises and build a new zoo with sufficient space and facilities. Until then, those with a more modern attitude to animal welfare are advised to steer clear. Entry costs Dhs.2 per person, while under 2's go free. The zoo is closed on Tuesdays.

Oryx

## Tours & Sightseeing

**Tour-Tastic**
*If you are booking a tour for your family or friends then make sure you ring around to get the best price. Dubai is dedicated to discounts and if you have the right connections, or pretend you do, you can often get a better rate as a resident. Just remember it is all about putting on the charm – not being a cheeky customer.*

As you might expect from a city that is staking its future on the tourism industry, Dubai has numerous tour operators offering an exciting range of city, desert and mountain trips. The following information covers the most popular tours given by the main operators. If there is something specific you have in mind, many operators can tailor a tour to your needs.

When booking your tour, it is useful to book three or four days in advance. Some operators will request a 50% deposit, while others are happy for you to pay the driver the full amount when he picks you up. You can usually expect to pay about Dhs.110 for a half-day city tour, and around Dhs.250 for a desert safari, but prices do vary between operators. Tours usually depart from set pick-up points, such as major hotels, although some operators will actually pick you up from your house. Wear cool, comfortable clothing, and take a hat and sunglasses. Desert or mountain tours require strong, flat-soled shoes, and if you're going into the desert in the cooler months, take a jacket as the temperature can drop considerably after sunset. One last word on desert or mountain tours: these trips often involve some pretty extreme driving over sand dunes or through wadis. If you are pregnant, elderly, sick, are travelling with young children or suffer from motion sickness, inform the tour company so that they can arrange a more gentle route for you.

## Boat & Yacht Charters

Other options **Speedboating** p.377, **Dinner Cruises** p.510, **Dhow Charters** p.333, **Creek Tours** p.248

### Bateaux Dubai ▶ p.511
*Nr British Embassy*
*Downtown Bur Dubai*
*Map 9 B3* 34

*04 399 4994* | *www.bateauxdubai.com*
Bateaux Dubai provides parties of up to 300 people with unobstructed sightseeing from all seats, and offers charters for corporate events and private parties. The vessel can be chartered daily with advance bookings, including weekends and holidays.

### Bluesail Dubai
*Nr British Embassy*
*Downtown Bur Dubai*
*Map 9 B3* 35

*04 397 9730* | *www.bluesailyachts.com*
Bluesail have two 42ft sailing yachts available for private charter and corporate development events including professionally facilitated team building and 'Match Race' incentive days. Bluesail also offer private motor-boat charters on their new 21ft/200hp and 34ft/450hp speed boats, taking in the creek and Dubai's coastline - see Speedboating (p. 377). All vessels are fully insured and equipped with the required safety equipment.

### Bristol Middle East Yacht Solution
*Marina Walk*
*Dubai Marina*
*Map 5 B2 112*

*04 366 3538* | *www.bristol-holding.com*
This Marina-based company offers charters and packages on boats of all kind, from luxury yachts to its old wooden dhow, Captain Jack. Its boats can be hired for any event, including romantic outings for two, right through to weddings and birthaday parties. Fishing trips and watersports can be organised too, and Bristol also puts together land and air tours.

### Cavendish White
*Wafi Residence,*
*Suite G09*
*Umm Hurair*
*Map 10 E4*

*050 624 0684* | *www.cavendishwhite.com*
Cavendish White provide luxury yacht charter, including anything from short blasts to exclusive overnight stays and even holidays on the water. They also own the biggest yacht in Dubai – a whopping 122 feet long beauty, so definitely one to impress business partners or friends. Many cruising options are available (including charter all

over the world), and they provide full catering services. Corporate enquiries are also welcome. The company has a large selection of craft for sale too.

## Charlotte Anne Charters

*Fujairah*
*International Marine*
*Club*
*Fujairah*

*09 222 9007 | www.charlotteannecharters.com*
The Charlotte Anne was built in Denmark in 1949 and has been chartering in Arabian waters for more than a decade. Built entirely of oak, the ship operates exclusive, live-aboard charters to the Musandam region of northern Oman, with particular emphasis on scuba diving at some of the finest, and as yet untouched, dive sites in the region.

## Danat Dubai Cruises

*Nr British Embassy*
*Downtown Bur Dubai*
*Map 9 B3* **37**

*04 351 1117 | www.danatdubaicruises.com*
Boasting a top speed of 18 knots, this 34 metre catamaran is available for group charters, product launches and wedding receptions, and has a capacity of 300 passengers (170 for sit-down functions). Onboard facilities include a dance floor, music system, video monitors, sun deck and two enclosed air-conditioned decks.

## Dusail

*DIMC*
*Al Sufouh*
*Map 5 B1*

*04 396 2353 | www.dusail.com*
Dusail Yacht Charter provides coastline tours aboard their 50ft flagship luxury yacht, Andorra, as well as deep sea, reef or fly fishing packages, and rentals of motor and rigid inflatable boats. Morning cruises depart from Dubai International Marine Club at 10:30, returning at 12:30, while the sunset cruises set sail at 15:30. Light snacks and soft drinks are offered onboard while guests relax and enjoy uninterrupted views of Dubai's coastline.

## El Mundo

*Le Meridien Mina*
*Seyahi, Al Sufouh Rd*
*Al Sufouh*
*Map 5 C1* **21**

*050 452 3202 | www.elmundodubai.com*
El Mundo is a 60 foot catamaran that can be chartered for all manner of occasions, including romantic cruises, corporate events, lunch/dinner cruises around the Palm Jumeirah and 'Fun In The Sun.' Longer charters for snorkelling, dolphin watching or trips to Musandam are also available.

## ENJOY Yachting

*Various locations*

*04 311 6568 | www.uaeyachting.com*
ENJOY Yachting offers a variety of scheduled and bespoke trips allowing visitors and residents to sample the beautiful waters of the Gulf. Embarking from a number of locations throughout Dubai, a private boat charter makes a great romantic trip for two, or could be just the place for a business meeting or presentation with a difference. A sunset trip is also a popular choice. Additionally, perhaps the coolest way to beat Dubai's traffic jams is to ring for your very own powerboat taxi service, with various pick-up and drop-off points between the creek and Dubai Marina. These fast (50kmph) powerboats can be hired from as little as Dhs.500 per hour, inclusive of a skipper (English, German and Arabic speaking) and soft drinks. Alternative contact number: 050 465 0425.

## Jebel Ali Golf Resort & Spa

*Jct 9, nr Jebel*
*Ali Shooting Club*
*Jebel Ali*
*Map 3 A1*

*04 883 6000 | www.jebelali-international.com*
Club Joumana, at the Jebel Ali Golf Resort and Spa, can arrange one or two-hour boat trips for up to seven people on their 36ft fishing boat. Departure is from the private marina at the resort in the morning or afternoon, with prices and timings available on request.

*Al Sufouh Rd*
*Al Sufouh*
*Map 5 C1*

## Le Meridien Mina Seyahi ▶ p.577

**04 399 3333** | *www.lemeridien-minaseyahi.com*

Le Meridien Mina Seyahi operates a variety of charter cruises from their marina. A number of boats are available for trips of different lengths and activities include deep-sea fishing, trawling and sightseeing. Prices are available upon request and all rates include a skipper and equipment.

## Boat Tours

*Various locations*

## Tour Dubai ▶ p.539

**04 336 8409** | *www.tour-dubai.com*

Tour Dubai offers a one-hour creek tour aboard a traditional dhow, including pre-recorded commentary of the area and country's history and places of interest. Commentary is available in English. There are four departures a day, 11:30, 13:30, 15:30 and 17:30, and the price of around Dhs.70 includes transfers to and from your apartment. The company offers a variety of other tours, including private dhow charters (see p.333).

## Bus Tours

*Wafi City*
*Umm Hurair*
*Map 10 D4*

## The Big Bus Company

**04 324 4187** | *www.bigbus.co.uk*

It's not a mirage, there really are eight open air London double-decker buses roaming the streets of Dubai. There's live commentary in English, which includes little known facts such as in 1968 there were only 13 cars in Dubai. It's wise to break the tour at their recommended stops and then hop on the following bus once you've finished exploring. Prices: adults Dhs.150; children Dhs.100 (ages 5 to 15 years); free for children under 5 years; families Dhs.400 (two adults and two children). Tours depart daily with departures every hour from 09:00 to 17:00.

*BurJuman Centre*
*Downtown Bur Dubai*
*Map 8 F4*

## Wonder Bus Tours

**04 359 5656** | *www.wonderbusdubai.com*

The Wonder Bus is an amphibious bus that is capable of doing 120 kph on the road and seven knots on water (life jackets are supplied, if you're nervous). The trips are two-hour mini tours of Dubai, concentrating on the creek, and covering Creekside Park and Dubai Creek Golf Club, under Maktoum Bridge towards Garhoud Bridge, then up the boat ramp and back to BurJuman. The bus is air conditioned and can take 44 passengers. Prices: adults Dhs.115; children Dhs.75 (ages 3 - 12). There are three departures daily: 11:30, 14:30, 17:00 (but this is subject to change depending on the tide).

*Activity Tours*
*If you're an adrenaline junkie, get in touch with Desert Rangers, East Adventure Tours, Mountain High, Off-Road Adventures or Voyagers Xtreme – all of these tour operators offer a great range of activity tours.*

## Desert & Mountain Safaris

Desert safaris are easily the most popular tour available, perhaps because a good safari offers many activities in one day. Starting with an exciting ride up and down some of the desert's biggest dunes, you can try sand skiing before watching the sun set over the desert. After driving a short distance further to a permanent Bedouin-style camp, you are treated to a sumptuous barbecue, followed by shisha, belly dancing, camel rides and henna painting. You can vary the length of your safari, choosing to stay overnight if desired. However, a safari to the mountains is highly recommendable, if only to see how the landscape changes from orange sand dunes to craggy mountains within the space of a few kilometres. The approximate cost for a desert safari is Dhs.150-300 (overnight up to Dhs.500). Many companies offer these types of tour; below is a selection of typical itineraries you can choose from.

**279**

### Dune Dinners

Enjoy some thrilling off-road desert driving before settling down to watch the sun set behind the dunes. Starting around 16:00, the tour passes camel farms and fascinating scenery, that provide great photo opportunities. At an Arabian campsite, enjoy a delicious dinner and the calm of a starlit desert night, returning around 22:00.

### Full-Day Safari

This day-long tour usually passes traditional Bedouin villages and camel farms in the desert, with a drive through sand dunes of varying colours and heights.

*Hiking in the Hajar Mountains*

Most tours also visit Fossil Rock and the mesmerising Hajar Mountains, the highest in the UAE. A cold buffet lunch may be provided in the mountains before the drive home.

### Hatta Pools Safari

Hatta is a quiet, old-fashioned town nestled in the foothills of the Hajar Mountains, famed for its fresh water rock pools that you can swim in. The full-day trip usually includes a stop at the Hatta Fort Hotel, where you can enjoy the pool, landscaped gardens, archery, clay pigeon shooting and nine-hole golf course. Lunch is served either in the hotel, or in the mountains. The trip costs between Dhs.260-345.

### Mountain Safari

This full-day tour takes you north along the coast, heading inland at Ras Al Khaimah and entering the spectacular Hajar Mountains at Wadi Bih. You will travel through rugged canyons onto steep winding tracks, past terraced mountainsides and old stone houses. It leads to Dibba where a highway quickly returns you to Dubai, stopping at Masafi Market on the way. Some tours operate in reverse, starting from Dibba.

### Overnight Safari

This 24-hour tour starts at about 15:00 with a drive through the dunes to a Bedouin-style campsite. Dine under the stars, sleep in the fresh air and wake to the smell of freshly brewed coffee, before heading for the mountains. The drive takes you through spectacular rugged scenery, past dunes, along wadis (dry riverbeds), before stopping for a buffet lunch and returning to Dubai.

## Farm & Stable Tours

Other options **Horse Riding** p.350, **Polo** p.366

**Sharjah Natural History Museum**
*Sharjah*
*Map 2 C2* 76

### Children's Farm

06 531 1127 | www.sharjah-welcome.com
See entry under 'Sharjah Natural History Museum' (p.266). Closed on Mondays.

**Nad Al Sheba**
*Al Marqadh*
*Map 16 A2*

### Nad Al Sheba Club

04 336 3666 | www.nadalshebaclub.com
An early morning visit to the world's top racehorse training facilities at Nad Al Sheba is inclusive of a cooked breakfast, a behind-the-scenes glimpse of the jockeys' facilities

# Experience Wonderful Arabia

* Off-Road Round Trips
* Safari Excursions
* Hatta Mountain Tour
* Musandam Adventure
* Liwa Expedition
* Quad Bike Tours
* Sand Boarding

* Camping
* Dune Drive
* VIP Functions
* Hiking
* 4WD Training
* Camel Riding
* Desert Parties & Team Building

**OFF-ROAD ADVENTURES**

**Off-Road Adventures L.L.C**
*Please visit our website for online reservations or call:*
**website:** www.arabiantours.com, **Hotline:** 04-32 11 377 (24/7)

and a view over the racecourse from the Millennium Grandstand, you'll also get a chance to see horses training. The tour ends with a visit to Godolphin Gallery where the Dubai World Cup is on display. Prices: adults Dhs.170; children Dhs.80 (ages 4-12).

## Helicopter/Plane Charters

Other options **Plane Tours** p.286, **Flying** p.341

*Dubai Intl Airport*
*Map 11 F4*

## Aerogulf Services Company

*04 220 0331* | www.aerogulfservices.com

Viewing Dubai from the air is an exhilarating experience and an ideal way to get a unique perspective of the city. Helicopter tours will show you dhows, parks, the creek, palaces and beaches. The tours operate during daylight hours. Basic rates are Dhs.2,925 for a half hour tour (basic) and Dhs.3,600 for a 'VIP Class' half hour tour. Each helicopter is limited to four passengers.

## Heritage Tours

To find out what life was like in Dubai before the discovery of oil and the frenetic pace of development, try a heritage tour. You will walk through narrow alleyways in old areas, where houses were built close together to maximise shade, and see how, in the days before air conditioning, buildings included windtowers to catch the slightest breeze. Many old buildings have been restored and converted into art galleries and museums, which further illuminate the fascinating and not-too-distant past of the region.

## Hot Air Ballooning

Other options **Plane Tours** p.286, **Flying** p.341

*Nr Claridge Hotel*
*Deira*
*Map 9 D3* **46**

## Balloon Adventures Dubai

*04 273 8585* | www.ballooning.ae

Operating two of the most advanced and largest hot air balloons in the world, with a capacity of up to 40 people, Balloon Adventures offer tours for individuals and groups. Flights begin first thing in the morning between October and May in order to catch the sunrise, and afterwards you can go off-road driving over the dunes with their experienced drivers as part of the trip.

*Dubai Garden Centre*
*Al Quoz*
*Map 6 B3*

## Desert Rangers ▶ p.287

*04 340 2408* | www.desertrangers.com

Desert Rangers operates balloon trips that enable you to sample the absolute stillness and silence as you float over the desert. With flights available at dawn or dusk, you can watch the ever-changing colours of the sand dunes below as they react to the first or last flickers of sunlight. You'll finish this memorable experience with refreshments on landing. It's advisable to book early as these are popular tours. You should also note that flights are subject to weather conditions on the day. From October to May (please enquire about September flights), pick-up time for the morning balloon safari is 04:30. The cost is Dhs.750 per person.

*Dune Centre*
*Al Satwa*
*Map 8 A2*

## Voyagers Xtreme

*04 345 4504* | www.turnertraveldubai.com

This is a great way to celebrate birthdays, anniversaries or product launches. Daily flights for up to 12 people operate every morning over the city, mountains or desert, taking off from Dubai Internet City or Fossil Rock with a fully certified pilot. Trips are weather permitting.

## Main Tour Operators

### Absolute Adventure

*Nr Golden Tulip Hotel*
*Dibba*
*Map 1 F1*

*04 345 9900* | *www.adventure.ae*
For a revitalising weekend doing something different, Absolute Adventure offer dormitory-style camping (food and washing facilities are included), in a traditional stone bungalow just off Dibba beach in Omani territory (no visa required though). Choose from a range of adrenalin pumped activities in unspoilt surrounds such as treks exploring ancient ruins and secret caves, sea kayaking, snorkeling, mountain biking and motor hang gliding. Activity prices start at Dhs.200. Overnight camping costs from Dhs.1,950 for up to 14 people and Dhs150 per extra guest – you can even rent out the whole house!). Dinner costs Dhs.50 per person. See the website for more details or contact Paul on 050 625 9165.

### Arabian Adventures

*Emirates Holiday*
*Bld, Shk Zayed Rd, Jct 2*
*Downtown Bur Dubai*
*Map 7 B3* **49**

*04 303 4888* | *www.arabian-adventures.com*
Offering a remarkably comprehensive range of tours and activities for business or pleasure, Arabian Adventures is a one-stop operator for all your touring needs. It organises itineraries for complete trips and can provide specific services. The tours available include sand skiing, moonlight dhow cruises, city tours, desert safaris, camel riding, wadi and dune bashing among others.

### Desert Rangers ▶ p.287

*Dubai Garden Centre*
*Al Quoz*
*Map 6 B3*

*04 340 2408* | *www.desertrangers.com*
In addition to the standard range of desert and mountain safaris, Desert Rangers offers many more exciting activities and tours. The scope of their activities is huge and covers camel trekking by day or night, sand boarding, canoeing, raft building, deep sea fishing, dhow cruises, camping, hiking, rock climbing, Hatta Pool safari, desert driving courses, dune buggying and helicopter tours of Dubai. It also specialises in initiative tests, team building and multi-activity trips for children, especially schools and youth groups.

### Dubai Tourist & Travel Services

*Al Abbar Bld*
*Downtown Bur Dubai*
*Map 14 B1* **50**

*04 336 7727* | *www.dubai-travel.ae*
An international company founded in 1976, DTTS offer Dubai, Abu Dhabi and Al Ain city and shopping tours, Creek dinner cruises, Sharjah-Ajman cultural tours, East Coast tours, desert and mountain tours to Hatta, Sand skiing and camel riding tours, desert safaris and overnight safaris. Phew!

### East Adventure Tours

*Zomorrodah Bld*
*Al Karama*
*Map 10 E1* **51**

*04 335 0950* | *www.holidayindubai.com*
East Adventure offers city discovery tours with a personal guide/driver as an escort. It's ideal if you are new to Dubai and don't know your way around, as the chauffeur service is available 24 hours a day. They also arrange various trips that showcase the best of the UAE and Oman – choose from a Bedouin desert safari, a dhow dinner cruise, a camel safari or many other activities. For further information, visit the website or contact Mr Ali (050 644 8820).

### Gulf Ventures

*Nr Gold Souq*
*Deira*
*Map 9 B1* **52**

*04 209 5568* | *www.gulfventures.org*
With an impressive 120 years' experience, Gulf Ventures is well established and very knowledgeable about culture, history and the lay of the land. It offers a great variety of exciting and informative tours over a wide area of the UAE and Oman, including Bedouin camps, creek cruises, tours around the east coast, plus activities such as fishing, polo and ballooning, as well as a wide range of city tours.

**283**

## Mountain High

**Al Bakhit Centre**
*Deira*
*Map 11 D2*

*04 266 8661* | *www.mountainhighme.com*

Founded by Dubai resident, Julie Amer, Mountain High organises an exhilarating range of adventure challenges such as worldwide mountain treks, cycling holidays, walking, and Himalayan expeditions to Nepal, Tibet and India. You can also opt for something calmer with their range of holistic and well-being treatments. For more info, call 050 659 5536 or log on to their website.

## Net Tours

**Le Meridien Mina**
*Al Sufouh*
*Map 5 C1* **21**

*050 659 5536* | *www.nettoursdubai.com*

Net Tours offers all Dubai can bestow in terms of adventure; from Mountain tours to theme parks, dhow cruises to safaris. Delve into Dubai's history or trek through the Ras Al Khaimah Mountains or even try sand skiing. in a range of tours. Five desert campsites just 45 minutes from Dubai, allow you to explore the dunes and return to your Bedouin haven in an 'authentic' Arabian adventure that comes complete with air-conditioning, separate restrooms for men and women, internet, satellite connection and even a VIP lounge.

## Oasis Palm Tourism ▶ p.289

**Al Rigga Road,**
**opp. ADCB**
*Deira*
*Map 9 B4* **53**

*04 262 8889* | *www.optdubai.com*

Oasis Palm's desert safari's, dhow dinner cruises and wadi trips come with the typical guarantee of the desired Arabian adventure, alongside the promise of great service and a memorable experience. Their East Coast Tours will take you through the Hajjar Mountains and the strawberry garden in Al Dhaid to one of the oldest mosques in the UAE. They also offer diving trips to the beautiful Khor Fakkan the 'Creek of two jaws' and four hour deep sea fishing trips.

## Off-Road Adventures

**Shangri-La Hotel**
*Trade Centre 1*
*Map 7 E3*

*04 405 2917* | *www.arabiantours.com*

As its name suggests the company offers a wide range of off-road excursions, including desert trips (with dinner at an Arabian camp), wadi and mountain drives, overnight camping, and expeditions to Liwa and the empty quarter. In addition to off-road tours it also arranges watersports and airborne activities, and can offer tailor-made packages for groups.

## Orient Tours ▶ p.285

**Various locations**

*04 282 8238* | *www.orienttours.ae*

Orient Tours offers tours to all major cities in the UAE, including trips to the horse and camel races, desert safaris, sea safaris around Musandam, off-road trips to Hatta and day tours of the majestic dunes of the Empty Quarter in Liwa. They specialise in corporate and educational events and also offer flexible packages catering to individual needs. Established in 1982, Orient Tours has branch offices in Dubai, Sharjah, Abu Dhabi, Muscat & Salalah.

## Planet Travel Tours & Safaris

**Airport Rd**
*Al Garhoud*
*Map 11 D3*

*04 282 2199* | *planet@eim.ae*

Planet Travel Tours and Safaris offer various tours in and around Dubai, as well as along the east coast and other major cities of the UAE. Within Dubai itself they offers coach tours, heritage tours and shopping tours, and outside of the cities it offers safaris and desert tours.

## Sunflower Tours

**Za'abeel Rd**
*Al Karama*
*Map 10 E1* **51**

*04 334 5554* | *www.sunflowerdubai.com*

Sunflower Tours offers the usual desert and city tours, but it also runs camel safaris, fishing trips and helicopter tours. For something really different, book a crab hunting trip with them, or a diving trip to explore the splendour of Musandam and Khasab.

# Golden Memories with a Silver Lining...

## And 25 Years of Excellence.

Established in 1982, Orient Tours celebrates a quarter of a century at the helm of the inbound tourism sector in the United Arab Emirates and the Sultanate of Oman.

With innovation and creativity, Orient Tours has perfected the mystery of how to make you feel different and special in reliving the authentic Arabian experience.

Let Arabia come alive, let Orient Tours show you the secrets of the shifting sands and the wonders of a rich culture.

Golden memories that will capture your imagination for a lifetime.

**ORIENT TOURS LLC**
P O Box 61790, Dubai, United Arab Emirates
Tel: +971 4 2828238, Fax: +971 4 2828154
E-mail: otdxb@emirates.net.ae
**www.orienttours.ae**

*Celebrating the Sands of Time*

*Dune Centre*
*Al Satwa*
*Map 8 A2*

## Voyagers Xtreme

*04 345 4504* | www.turnertraveldubai.com

Voyagers Xtreme provides a range of adventurous activities over land, air and sea. For a trip to remember, try its 'One Wild Week in the Emirates' tour. You will visit places such as the Empty Quarter, Al Ain, the Hajar Mountains, Fossil Rock, the east coast, Dibba, Musandam and Wadi Bih, and enjoy activities as diverse as mountain biking, trekking, desert driving, hot air ballooning, snorkelling and sky diving.

### Other Tour Operators

| | | |
|---|---|---|
| Arabianlink Tours | 06 572 6666 | www.arabianlinktours.com |
| Khasab Travel & Tours | 04 266 9950 | www.khasabtours.com |
| Lama Desert Tours | 04 334 4330 | www.lamadubai.ae |
| Leisure Time | 04 332 7226 | na |
| Oasis Palm Tourism ▶ p.289 | 04 262 8889 | www.optdubai.com |
| Quality Tours | 04 297 4000 | www.quality-tour.com |
| SNTTA Travel & Tours | 04 282 9000 | www.sntta.com |

## Plane Tours

Other options **Hot Air Ballooning** p.282, **Flying** p.341

*Fujairah*
*International Airport*
*Fujairah*
*Map 1 F2*

## Fujairah Aviation Centre

*09 222 4747* | www.fujairahaviation.ae

A bird's-eye view of the coastline, rugged mountains, villages and date plantations is available from the Fujairah Aviation Centre. Flights can accommodate one to three people, and last from 30 minutes to four hours depending on what you want to see. The cost is Dhs.600 per hour.

*Jebel Ali Htl*
*Jebel Ali*
*Map 2 A4*

## Seawings

*04 883 2999* | www.seawings.ae

Get a different perspective of Dubai from an eight-seater Cessna 208 Caravan seaplane. This unique flying experience begins at the Jebel Ali Golf Resort & Spa, and gives you a breathtaking seagull's-eye view of the city's attractions, soaring past and over Dubai Marina, the Jumeira and Jebel Ali Palms, the World and downtown Dubai, before touching down smoothly again on the water at Jebel Ali. Prices start at Dhs.795 for a seat on the half-hour flight, or you can opt for an upgrade with the extended, more luxurious Gold tour. The plane can also be chartered, and the fleet is set to expand with a second aircraft.

*Shopping Tour*
*Dubai has a well-deserved reputation as the shopping capital of the Middle East. From designer clothes, shoes and jewellery in the malls, to electronics, spices and textiles in the souks, everything is available. This half-day tour takes you round some of the hottest shopping spots in Dubai. Whether or not you walk away with some bargains depends on your haggling skills, so start practising!*

## Sightseeing Tours

### Dubai by Night

Enjoy the early evening lights with a tour of the city's palaces, mosques and souks. See the multitude of shoppers of all nationalities, and streets alive with traditional charm, before enjoying dinner at one of Dubai's many excellent restaurants.

### Dubai City Tour

This is a half-day overview of old and new Dubai. Usual sights include souks, the fish market, mosques, abras, Bastakiya windtower houses and thriving commercial areas with striking modern buildings.

### Mosque Tours

For an insight into Islam and a closer look at the amazing architecture of a mosque, you can book a mosque tour through a number of tour operators or directly through the Sheikh Mohammed Centre for Cultural Understanding (see p.262). You will visit the impressive mosque in Jumeira, with tours starting at 10:00, four days a week.

# DESERT RANGERS

## ...and now for something completely different

Desert Rangers is an exciting and innovative company that offers a variety of outward-bound activities and adventure safaris, providing exclusive opportunities for you to try something totally different.

### We can also offer...

- Overnight safaris
- Dune Dinner safaris
- Mountain safaris
- Trekking
- Helicopter safaris
- Deep sea fishing
- Dhow cruising
- Rock climbing

- Dune Buggy safaris
- Sand boarding
- Canoe expeditions
- Hatta pool safari
- Hot air ballooning
- Desert driving courses
- Tailor-made packages
- Team building exercises

and many more...

DESERT RANGERS

DUBAI'S LEADING ADVENTURE SPORTS
AND ACTIVITIES OPERATOR

For more information please give us a call...
PO Box 37579, Dubai, UAE - Tel (+971 4) 3402408 - Fax (+971 4) 3402407
rangers@emirates.net.ae  www.desertrangers.com

## Aerial Tours

What better way to view the sights of Dubai or the desert than from the air? Aerial tours are an expensive but truly memorable way to experience unobstructed views and take some awe-inspiring aerial photos of the many fantastic dunes, buildings and landmarks that make Dubai famous. For further information contact either Desert Rangers (340 2408), Lama Desert Tours (334 4330), Gulf Ventures (209 5568), Aerogulf Services Company (220 0331), Heli Dubai (224 4033), Seawings (see p.286) or Voyagers Extreme (345 4504). A helicopter tour requires a minimum of four people, and costs around Dhs.1,000 per person for a 30-minute tour. A hot air balloon tour costs around Dhs.800 per person. Cessna tours require at least three people, at a cost of Dhs.200 per person, and a tour in a private jet will set you back around Dhs.1,400.

**Tour Operators**
*Almost all tour operators offer the usual tours: city tours, desert safaris and mountain safaris. Some, however, offer more unique activities, such as fishing or diving trips, trips to see the Empty Quarter up in Liwa, helicopter tours and desert driving courses. The main tour operators and those that offer something a little bit different are listed on p.283.*

# Tours Outside Dubai

## Abu Dhabi Tour

The route from Dubai passes Jebel Ali Port, the world's largest man-made seaport, on the way to Abu Dhabi, capital of the United Arab Emirates. Founded in 1761, the city is built on an island. Visit the Women's Handicraft Centre, Heritage Village, Petroleum Exhibition and Abu Dhabi's famous landmark – the corniche. (Full day).

## Liwa Tour

The Oasis of Liwa, a couple of hours from Abu Dhabi, offers an opportunity to experience the desert at its most barren. Liwa borders one of the biggest sand deserts in the world – the Rub Al Khali or 'Empty Quarter'. It is worth seeing for the awesome, landscape and the strange tranquility of such an unspoiled area. This tour is only offered by a few operators (Off-Road Adventures and Voyagers Xtreme, while Orient Tours offers it as part of a package tour).

## Ajman & Sharjah Tour

Ajman is the place to go to see traditional wooden dhows being built. Take in the museum before driving to the neighbouring emirate of Sharjah, where you can shop to your heart's content at the souks. Finish with a wander around the restored Bait Al Naboodah house to see how people lived before the discovery of oil. (Half day).

## Al Ain Tour

Known as the 'Garden City', there are many historical attractions here, from one of the first forts to be built by the Al Nahyan family over 175 years ago, to prehistoric tombs at Hili, said to be over 5,000 years old. Other attractions include Al Ain Museum, the camel market, the falaj irrigation system, which is still in use, and the souk. (Full day).

## Ras Al Khaimah Tour

Drive up country along the so-called Pirate Coast through Ajman and Umm Al Quwain. Explore ancient sites and discover the old town of Ras Al Khaimah and its museum. The return journey passes natural hot springs and date groves at Khatt, via the striking Hajar Mountains. (Full day).

## East Coast

Journey east to Al Dhaid, a small oasis town known for its fruit and vegetable plantations. Catch glimpses of dramatic mountain gorges before arriving at Dibba and Khor Fakkan on the east coast. Enjoy a refreshing swim, then visit the oldest mosque in the UAE. This tour usually visits the friday market for a browse through cheap carpets, clay pots and fresh local produce. (Full day).

Enjoy the thrill and fun of

# Desert Safari

BBQ Dinner-Veg/Non Veg | Arabic Tea/Coffee | Unlimited Soft Drinks | Dune Bashing | Sand Boarding | Camel Riding | Photograph in Local Dresses | Enchanting Belly Dancing Show | Sheesha (Hubbly-Bubbly) | Henna Painting & Lot More...

*Everyday*

## Dhs. 180/- US $ 50/- Per Person

Timings: Pickup: 3:00 PM        Drop Off: 9:00 to 9:30 PM

*Promise of Excellence*

## Dhow Cruise Dinner    Dhs. 140/-

A Dhow Cruise Dinner is truly a romantic person's dream come true. Feast on a selectable choice of aunthetic Arabic and International Buffet Dinner and other entertainment throughout.

### OTHER EXCURSIONS

Dubai City Tour | Hatta Mountain Safari | Abudhabi & Alain City Tour | East Coast Tour | Deep Sea Fishing |

| Burj Al Arab Tour - Dinner - Lunch - Breakfast & Hi Tea |

24 Hrs. Reservation  : Tel: 04-2620644, Mob : 050 - 2531138
E-mail : optdubai@emirates.net.ae, Website : www.opdubai.com

## Oasis Palm
TOURISM L.L.C.

## Out of Dubai
Other options **Weekend Break** p.298

Dubai may have everything from ski slopes and souks to boutiques and beaches but there are a number of interesting and varied areas outside the city that deserve a place in your weekend plans. There are six other emirates in the UAE, all of which warrant exploration. Also within the Dubai enclave, the small town of Hatta is worthy of at least a day trip. While Dubai may be home to skyscrapers and sophisticated living, the landscapes you can discover beyond this modern metropolis are of the more rugged variety. Monstrous mountain ranges, gigantic sand dunes and sprawling wadis are all waiting to be discovered – all you need is a copy of the fantastic UAE Off-Road Explorer, which details a number of awe-inspiring routes across the UAE and beyond.

## Hatta
Other options **Weekend Break** p.298

Perhaps most famous as a destination during a visa run to Oman, Hatta is a small town nestled at the foot of the Hajar Mountains, about 100km from Dubai city and 10km from the Dubai-Oman border. Hatta is still within Dubai though, and is home to the oldest fort in the emirate which was built in 1790. You'll also see several watchtowers on the surrounding hills. On the drive there you'll pass row after row of carpet shops which are great for practising your bargaining skills and for picking up a new rug for the villa. The town of Hatta has a sleepy, relaxed feel, and apart from the ruins and the Heritage Village, there is little to see or do. However, beyond the village and into the mountains are the Hatta Pools where you can see deep, strangely shaped canyons that have been carved out by rushing floodwater.

The Hatta Fort Hotel is an ideal weekend destination. Spacious bungalow-style luxury rooms sit in tranquil gardens with a mountainous backdrop making it the perfect antidote to Dubai's city living. A good range of sports and leisure facilities will leave you refreshed and relaxed. See p.302 for more details on the hotel.

Just off the main road (E44) on the way to Hatta is the famous 'Big Red' sand dune. Estimated to be over 100m high, it's a popular spot for practising dune driving in 4WDs or quad bikes, as well as attempting sand skiing (although the number of Landcruisers and Patrols hitting the hill on a Friday may make you think twice about the skiing). Alternatively, take a walk (if you have the energy) to the top for a great view. For further information on the area around Hatta, refer to UAE Off-Road Explorer from Explorer Publishing. See also: Dune Buggies, p.338; Sand Boarding/Skiing, p.369; and Tour Operators, p.283.

Hatta

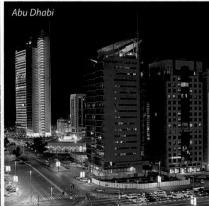
Abu Dhabi

**HATTA FORT HOTEL**
*Your Exclusive Mountain Retreat*

A MEMBER OF

JEBEL ALI INTERNATIONAL
HOTELS

## Picturesque Perfection

Stay in a deluxe chalet-style room overlooking stunning mountain scenery, choose from a range of leisure activities spanning archery to mini-golf and clay shooting to trekking, or indulge your appetite for international cuisine with our fine dining options. Whether you come on holiday or for business, there's so much to delight in at the Hatta Fort Hotel.

For reservations and more information please contact:
Tel: +971 4 852 3211 ✆ Fax: +971 4 852 3561
E-mail: hfh@jaihotels.com
Website: www.jebelali-international.com

**Big Sister** ◀

Just an hour or so away (depending of course where you start from) Abu Dhabi is the perfect weekend getaway for Dubai residents who fancy a change of pace. While the pace may be a bit slower, the shopping and social scene is forever burgeoning. For more information on what the capital emirate has to offer pick up a copy of Abu Dhabi Explorer.

## Abu Dhabi Emirate

Other options **Weekend Break** p.298

Dubai is often mistaken as the capital of the UAE thanks to the 'Sydney Syndrome' (Sydney may be the capital city of Australia in popularity terms, however the capital is Canberra). In actual fact further south is where you'll find the true king of the desert, Abu Dhabi. Oil was discovered in Abu Dhabi before Dubai (1958 compared to 1966) and today accounts for 10% of the world's known crude oil reserves. No surprise then that Abu Dhabi is the richest emirate in the UAE and its main city has the skyline to prove it. In recent years there has been a greater commitment to tourism with a number of developments attracting a greater number of tourists. While there isn't much you can get in Abu Dhabi that you can't get in Dubai, it still has a slightly slower pace that makes a refreshing change from its frenetic neighbour. The city itself lies on an island shaped liked a scorpion and is connected to the mainland by causeways. It is home to numerous internationally renowned hotels, a selection of shiny shopping malls and a sprinkling of culture in the form of heritage sites and souks. Shoppers may be pleasantly surprised to find the malls much less busy than in Dubai, goods and services are often a little cheaper too. For example, a taxi ride from one side of town to the other will set you back around Dhs.5. There are often good deals to be had on hotel breaks too, and quite a few restaurants offer 'all you can eat and drink' deals for much less than you pay in Dubai.

In the cooler months, the newly renovated and extended corniche is a lovely spot for a stroll, and on weekend evenings the area comes alive with families meeting up to enjoy a barbecue and shisha.

### Liwa Oasis

A couple of hours south of Abu Dhabi by car lies the Liwa Oasis, which is situated on the edge of the infamous Rub Al Khali desert (also known as the Empty Quarter). Covering parts of Oman, Yemen, a good chunk of Abu Dhabi emirate and most of southern Saudi Arabia, the Rub Al Khali is actually the largest sand desert in the world. If you appreciate spectacular scenery and enjoy a spot of camping, a trip into the dunes here is possibly one of the most rewarding experiences in the country. The scale is hard to describe, but imagine standing at the top of a 300 metre-high dune (if you can reach the top) and looking out over a 'sea' of sand that stretches to the horizon in every direction. It's desolate and remote, but quite breathtaking and thoroughly recommended. The driving is hard and should only be attempted by experienced off-roaders, in groups, with all the necessary equipment. If you're not up to the challenge yourself, many of the tour companies listed on p.283 organise trips.

### Al Ain

Al Ain is Abu Dhabi emirate's second city. It lies on the border with Oman, with whom it shares the Buraimi Oasis. The shady oasis is a pleasant stretch of greenery among the harsh surroundings, and the palm plantations have plenty of examples of the ancient 'falaj' irrigation system. Al Ain has a variety of sights and attractions to interest visitors. Hili Archaeological Garden is the source of many ancient finds, most of which are now displayed in Al Ain Museum. The museum is worth a visit, with displays of traditional Bedouin life and photographs showing how much the area has changed. The camel market is also a must. Again, arrive early to see the traders haggling over these grunting ships of the desert. Jebel Hafeet, around 15km to the south of Al Ain, is a rather dramatic mountain that rises abruptly from the surrounding flat terrain. A silky smooth road allows you to reach the very top and survey Al Ain and the desert beyond. At the base of the jebel is the surprising sight of Green Mubazzarah, a

# Small but indispensable…

Perfectly proportioned to fit in your pocket, this marvellous mini guidebook makes sure you don't just get the holiday you paid for but rather the one that you dreamed of.

**Abu Dhabi Mini Visitors' Guide**
Maximising your holiday, minimising your hand luggage

Abu Dhabi · Amsterdam · Bahrain · Barcelona · Beijing · Berlin · Dubai · Dublin · Geneva
Hong Kong · Kuala Lumpur · Kuwait · London · Los Angeles · New York · New Zealand · Oman
Paris · Qatar · Shanghai · Singapore · Sydney · Tokyo · Vancouver

# EXPLORER

www.explorerpublishing.com

landscaped park of rolling grassy hills, trees, hot springs, and waterfalls. Accommodation is also available in chalets, either within the park, or around a man-made lake where you can even rent pedalos. Reservations can be made by calling 03 783 8310, and prices range from Dhs.300 a night for a one bedroom chalet during the week, to Dhs.650 for a two bedroom at the weekend.

## Ajman
Other options **Weekend Break** p.298

Ajman is the smallest of the seven emirates, its centre being about 10km from Sharjah, although the two towns merge along the beachfront. Ajman also has two inland enclaves, one at Masfut on the edge of the Hajar Mountains and one at Manama between Sharjah and Fujairah. Ajman is known for having one of the largest dhow building centres in the region. The centre offers a great chance to see these massive wooden boats being built with rudimentary tools, using skills passed down through the generations. The old souk too, is another traditional reminder of a slower pace of life. This quiet emirate has some great beaches and a pleasant corniche, and an increasing number of facilities to tempt the visitor, including the Ajman Kempinski Hotel & Resort, and the Ajman City Centre mall offering a good selection of retail outlets and a cinema. The developers are making their way up the coast too, with Al Ameera Village – a project featuring heritage-styled residential buildings, a mall, and a hotel along Emirates Road.

## Ras Al Khaimah
Other options **Weekend Break** p.298

Ras Al Khaimah (RAK) is the most northerly of the seven emirates, but thanks to the new Emirates Road extension you can make the trip from Dubai in less than an hour. With the majestic Hajar Mountains rising just behind the city, and the Arabian Gulf stretching out from the shore, RAK has possibly the best scenery of any city in the UAE. A creek divides the city into the old town (Ras Al Khaimah proper) and the newer Al Nakheel district.

If you're visiting for the day you should make time to visit the souk in the old town and the National Museum of Ras Al Khaimah, which is housed in an old fort. Manar Mall is a large shopping and leisure complex, housing a cinema complex, family entertainment centre and watersports area. The town is quiet and relaxing, and is a good starting point for exploring the surrounding countryside and visiting the ancient sites of Ghalilah and Shimal. Also worth quick stops are the hot springs at Khatt and the camel racetrack at Digdagga. The town of Masafi, inland towards the east coast, is the source of the bottled water of the same name.

Although relatively unknown and undiscovered (in comparison to Dubai), RAK is in the process of reinventing and rebranding itself with the aim of becoming a popular tourism destination in the coming years. Projects such as Al Hamra Village, Mina Al Arab, Al Marjan Island, Port Arabia (aka Khor Qurm), and the Jebel Jais Mountain Resort will add five-star hotels, sports and leisure facilities (including an outdoor ski slope) and a host of dining and entertainment options (including a branch of the licensed aalcohol , in addition to freehold housing available for purchase by foreigners. The emirate is also to have its own airline. See www.raktourism.com for details.

RAK is the starting or finishing point for a spectacular trip through the mountains via Wadi Bih to Dibba on the East Coast and is also the entry point to the Musandam Peninsula in Oman. Refer to the UAE Off-Road Explorer for further information on exploring these areas. See also: Wadi & Dune Bashing on p.379.

### Big Car? Big Book
If you're sick of being stuck in gridlock traffic in a hatchback then it's high time you got yourself a four wheel drive and headed out to the desert, wadis and mountains of the UAE outback. Pick up a copy of the **UAE Off Road Explorer** and you can find yourself in the wilderness without getting lost!

## Umm Al Quwain
Other options **Weekend Break** p.298

Umm Al Quwain is the second smallest of the Emirates, and has the smallest population. Nestled on the coast between Ajman and Ras Al Khaimah, it's a quiet place where not much has changed over the years. The main industries are still fishing and date cultivation. The emirate has six forts and a few old watchtowers around the town, and a lagoon, with mangroves and birdlife, is a popular weekend spot for boat trips, windsurfing and other watersports. Umm Al Quwain has not escaped the attention of the developers though, and a project currently underway will see over 9,000 homes and a marina emerge on the shore of the Khor Al Beidah wildlife area. What impact this will have on the delicate ecosystem and abundant plant and animal life remains to be seen. Another project under development is the massive Al Salam City on the Emirates Road. When completed it will feature residential districts, towers, commercial units and a shopping mall, and will be home to over half a million residents.

The area north of the lagoon is known for being the 'activity centre' of the region, with a variety of distractions to suit all tastes. Umm Al Quwain Aeroclub offers flying, skydiving, paramotoring and microlighting, and can also arrange 10 minute air tours, either in a Cessna or a microlight, at very reasonable prices. The Emirates Car and Motorcycle Racing Club hosts all types of motorsport events, including the Emirates Motocross Championship that takes place here on a specially built track. The Umm Al Quwain Shooting Club has a firing range, and a 100-square metre outdoor paintballing area with obstacles to dodge around and hide behind (note that reservations should be made at least two days in advance). One of the most popular attractions here is Dreamland Aqua Park – see details below. Another favourite destination for Dubai residents is the adjacent Barracuda Beach Resort, which is particularly popular thanks to its well-stocked duty-free liquor store.

*Fujairah Fort*

*Part of the east coast's rich heritage, Fujairah Fort has undergone a major renovation programme, which was due for completion in 2007. Once complete, it is expected that the fort and buildings nearby will be a museum for the public. Carbon dating estimates the main part of the fort to be over 500 years old, with other sections being built about 150 years later.*

## East Coast
Other options **Weekend Break** p.298

Even of you're only in the UAE for a short time, a trip to the east coast is worth the effort. You can get there in under two hours, and the drive takes you through the interesting scenery of the rugged Hajar Mountains. The east coast and the desert and mountains inland provide plenty of opportunities for sampling the great outdoors, from camping and off-road driving to snorkelling and scuba diving. The diving off the east coast is considered better than that off Dubai, mainly because of increased visibility. Snoopy Island is a favourite spot for snorkelling, where you're guaranteed to see a host of exotic fish species, and perhaps turtles and small sharks if you're lucky. The scuba diving is good too, and many diving schools operating out of Dubai often head east with their students.

### East Coast Made Easy
To reach the UAE's east coast from Dubai takes about an hour and a half by road. The most popular route is to pick up the E88 that runs from Sharjah to Masafi, and then turn left to Dibba or right to Fujairah. A recently opened alternative though is the S116 that heads south-east out of Sharjah, past Fossil Rock and through the Hajar Mountains, hitting the coast at Kalba. It's faster than the E88, it's smooth, it's got tunnels, great scenery, and is so quiet you'll wonder whether it's actually open yet.

### Badiyah
The site of the oldest mosque in the UAE, Badiyah is located roughly half way down the east coast, north of Khor Fakkan. The mosque is made from gypsum, stone and mud bricks finished off with

white washed plaster and its design of four domes, supported by a central pillar, is considered unique. The building is believed to date back to the middle of the 15th century. Officially called Al Masjid Al Othmani, it was restored in 2003, but it must be said that the restoration was more of a renovation, and this ancient mosque now looks quite smart and new. The mosque is still used for prayer, so non-Muslim visitors have to satisfy themselves with a photo from the outside. Built into a low hillside with several recently restored watchtowers on the hills behind, the area is now lit up at night with lovely sodium coloured light. Unless you're an ardent ancient mosque enthusiast, it's probably not worth a special trip from Dubai, but if you're passing it's worth a quick stop and a photo. The village of Badiyah is one of the oldest settlements on the east coast and is believed to have been inhabited since 3000BC.

### Bithna

Set in the mountains about 12 km from Fujairah, the village of Bithna is notable mainly for its fort and archaeological site. The fort once controlled the main pass through the mountains from east to west and is still impressive. The village can be reached from the Fujairah-Sharjah road, and the fort through the village and wadi. The archaeological site is known as the Long Chambered Tomb or the T-Shaped Tomb, and was probably once a communal burial site. It was excavated in 1988 and its main period of use is thought to date from between 1350 and 300BC, although the tomb itself is older. Fujairah Museum has a detailed display of the tomb that is worth seeing, since the site itself is fenced off and covered against the elements. The tomb can be found by taking a right, then a left hand turn before the village, near the radio tower.

**The Dibba Dead**

*A vast cemetery on the outskirts of town is said to be the last resting place of over 10,000 rebels who died in a great battle fought in 633AD, when the Muslim armies of Caliph Abu Baker were sent to suppress a local rebellion and to reconquer the Arabian Peninsula for Islam.*

### Dibba

Located at the northern-most point of the east coast, on the border with Musandam (part of Oman), Dibba is made up of three fishing villages. Unusually, each part comes under a different jurisdiction: Dibba al Hisn is part of Sharjah, Dibba Muhallab is Fujairah and Dibba Bayah is Oman. The three Dibbas share an attractive bay, fishing communities, and excellent diving locations – from here you can arrange dhow trips to take you to unspoilt dive locations in the Musandam (see also Dhow Charters, p.333). The Hajar Mountains provide a wonderful backdrop, rising in places to over 1,800 metres. There are some good public beaches too, where your only company will be the crabs and seagulls, and where seashell collectors may find a few treasures. Dibba is the starting or finishing point for the stunning drive to the west coast through the mountains via Wadi Bih.

### Fujairah

Fujairah was actually part of Sharjah until 1952, making it the youngest of the seven emirates. Its independence makes it the only emirate located entirely on the east coast, and with its golden beaches bordered by the Gulf of Oman on one side and the Hajar Mountains on the other, it's definitely worth a visit. The town is a mix of old and new. Overlooking the atmospheric old town is a fort, which is reportedly about 300 years old, and which will eventually house the artefacts currently on display in the Fujairah Museum once its restoration is complete. The surrounding hillsides are dotted with ancient forts and watchtowers, which add an air of mystery and charm. Most of these also appear to be undergoing restoration work, too. Fujairah is also a busy trading centre, with its modern container port and a thriving free zone attracting major companies from around the world.

Off the coast, the seas and coral reefs make a great spot for fishing, diving and watersports. It is also a good place for birdwatching during the spring and autumn migrations since it is on the route from Africa to Central Asia. The emirate has started to encourage more tourism by opening new hotels and providing more recreational facilities. Since Fujairah is close to the mountains and many areas of natural beauty, it makes an excellent base to explore the countryside and discover wadis, forts, waterfalls and even natural hot springs. An excellent tourist map has been produced by the Fujairah Tourism Bureau (09 223 1554). To get a copy of this map, visit the Tourism Bureau at Fujairah Trade Centre, 9th Floor, Office No. 901, on Sheikh Hamad Bin Abdullah Rd (call ahead for opening times, as these are subject to change). On Friday afternoons during winter, crowds gather between the Hilton Hotel and the Khor Kalba area to watch 'bull butting'. This ancient Portuguese sport consists of two huge bulls going head to head for several rounds, until after a few nudges and a bit of hoof bashing, a winner is determined. It's not as cruel or barbaric as other forms of bullfighting, but animal lovers may still want to avoid it. A new wire fence protects spectators from any angry runaways.

## Thank Crunchie!

When Thursday evening finally rolls around, take inspiration (and discount vouchers!) from *Weekend Breaks* and head off to recharge your batteries. Choose from the hottest selection of hotels, spas and resorts in the UAE and Oman. Bliss.

### Kalba

Just to the south of Fujairah you'll find Kalba, which is part of the emirate of Sharjah and renowned for its mangrove forest and golden beaches. It's a pretty fishing village that still manages to retain much of its historical charm. A road through the mountains linking Kalba to Hatta has recently been completed, creating an interesting alternative to returning to Dubai on the Al Dhaid-Sharjah road.

### Khor Kalba

South of the village of Kalba is Khor Kalba, set in a beautiful tidal estuary (khor is the Arabic word for creek). This is the most northerly mangrove forest in the world, the oldest in Arabia and home to a variety of plant, marine and birdlife not found anywhere else in the UAE. The mangroves flourish in this area thanks to a mix of saltwater from the sea and freshwater from the mountains, but worryingly they are receding due to the excessive use of water from inland wells. For birdwatchers, the area is especially good during the spring and autumn migrations when special species of bird include the reef heron and the booted warbler. It is also home to the rare white collared kingfisher, which breeds here and nowhere else in the world. There are believed to be only 55 pairs of these birds still in existence. A canoe tour by Desert Rangers is an ideal opportunity to reach the heart of the reserve and you can regularly see over a dozen kingfishers on a trip. There is also the possibility of seeing one of the region's endangered turtles. The reserve is a unique area so please treat it with respect. See also: Desert Rangers – Canoeing, p.327; Birdwatching, p.322.

### Khor Fakkan

Khor Fakkan lies at the foot of the Hajar Mountains halfway down the east coast between Dibba and Fujairah. It is a popular and charming town, set in a bay and flanked on either side by two headlands, hence its alternative name 'Creek of the Two Jaws'. It is a favourite place for weekend breaks and day trips and has an attractive waterfront and beach. The iconic 70s-style Oceanic Hotel is a popular choice, and there are plenty of good fishing and diving sites nearby. Khor Fakkan is part of the emirate of Sharjah, and above the Oceanic Hotel the Ruler of Sharjah's Palace is visible high up on the hilltop. The town has a modern port, and its position on the Gulf of Oman means visiting ships don't have to undergo a further 48-hour journey through the Strait of Hormuz to the west coast. The nearby old harbour is an interesting contrast to the modern port. There are some great dive sites just a few minutes from Khor Fakkan, including Shark Island, Martini Island, and the Car Cemetery. See the UAE Underwater Explorer for more details. Set inland in the mountains is the Rifaisa Dam which was built to contain flood water and feed the towns below. Local legend has it that when the water is clear, a lost village can be seen at the bottom of the dam.

## Weekend Breaks

There are plenty of nice spots to escape to just outside of Dubai and many are quite different. With adventure excursions, desert safaris, mountain trekking and posh hotels that are willing to cater for every need you can put up your feet and relax or take the time to explore in your spare time. The UAE can offer myriad trips to keep you occupied.

*Emirates Palace*

## Abu Dhabi

*Al Raha Corniche, Nr Intl' Airport*
*Abu Dhabi*
*Map 1 D2*

### Al Raha Beach Hotel
*02 508 0555* | www.ncth.com
This elegant boutique hotel offers excellent service and unsurpassed comfort in an idyllic beach setting. Choose from one of the 110 luxury rooms or one of 24 beautiful villas (two, three or four bedrooms) for a really relaxing break. The hotel boasts uninterrupted sea views, a private health club with swimming pool, sauna and steam room, and a state-of-the-art spa. Book yourself into one of the magnificent Royal Suites for the ultimate in luxury and a taste of the high life.

*250 km west of Abu Dhabi*
*Jebel Dhanna*
*Map 1 D2*

### Danat Resort Jebel Dhanna
*02 801 2222* | www.ntch.com
Located 250km west of the city of Abu Dhabi, this five-star beach resort is a world away from the hustle and bustle of city life. Apart from beautifully furnished deluxe guest rooms and private waterfront villas, Jebel Dhanna offers a huge range of leisure activities including tennis, squash, golf (on a nine-hole sand course), a temperature-controlled swimming pool and a beautiful stretch of beach where you can enjoy several exciting watersports. It's a good base from which to visit the pristine Sir Bani Yas Island, a natural wildlife reserve just off the coast of Abu Dhabi.

*Corniche Rd*
*Abu Dhabi*
*Map 1 D2*

### Emirates Palace
*02 690 9000* | www.emiratespalace.com
Abu Dhabi's answer to the Burj Al Arab is the ultimate in luxury, perhaps even more ostentatious than its more famous rival. With 12 restaurants, 390 rooms and suites, and an amazing collection of pools and a private beach, all set in 200 acres of lush gardens, it is an incredible place to visit if you want to treat yourself to a weekend of pure indulgence. If you're feeling flash you can book yourself into one of the opulent palace suites, and arrange a limousine service to take you to and from the hotel.

*Corniche Rd*
*Abu Dhabi*
*Map 1 D2*

### Hilton International Abu Dhabi
*02 681 1900* | www.hilton.com
This 10 storey luxury hotel located on Abu Dhabi's Corniche Road is near the financial and business district and several modern shopping malls. Choose from king, queen or twin-bed rooms, all of which have views of either the sea, the landscaped gardens or the city. All rooms have mini bars, hairdryers, air conditioning and satellite TV. There are

three swimming pools and a private beach, as well as a wide range of watersports. Enjoy fine dining at The Pearl, Mediterranean at La Terrazza, good vibes and casual food at Hemingways (which incorporates the Tequilana Discotheque), sophisticated nights and live music at The Jazz Bar, alfresco eating at Coconut Bay or Vasco's, authentic Japanese and Lebanese at Kei and Mawal respectively, and delectable Italian food at world-renowned restaurant chain, BiCE.

*Al Bateen St,*
*Beh Hilton Abu Dhabi*
*Abu Dhabi*
*Map 1 D2*

## Hotel InterContinental

***02 666 6888*** | *www.intercontinental.com*

Adjacent to the marina, this hotel is surrounded by lush parks and gardens. With five restaurants, four bars and 330 deluxe rooms offering views of the city and the Arabian Gulf, the hotel draws many conference and business visitors. Some of the outlets here are definitely worth the trek, and the pool, health club and spa are excellent. At the time of going to press, the hotel was nearing the end of an extensive renovation.

*Al Meena*
*Abu Dhabi*
*Map 1 D2*

## Le Meridien Abu Dhabi

***02 644 6666*** | *www.lemeridienabudhabi.ae*

Renovated in 1998, this hotel has a vast choice of accommodation, from the standard five-star rooms to studios, residence, diplomatic and deluxe suites, and even a presidential suite. The hotel is famous for its modern health club and spa, private beach, and Culinary Village with 15 excellent food and beverage outlets. There is a children's swimming pool, and numerous activities, including tennis, squash and volleyball, just in case you're the active type.

# Ajman

*Along theCorniche*
*Ajman*
*Map 1 E1*

## Ajman Kempinski

***06 745 1555*** | *www.ajman.kempinski.com*

Just a short drive out of frenetic Dubai is the tranquility and calm of Ajman and its renowned leisure resort, the Ajman Kempinski. Relax on half a kilometre of private beach or around the superb pool complete with adjoining children's pool. The hotel has 185 seaview rooms and a diverse range of international restaurants, cafes and bars, plus an art gallery and grand ballroom. The Laguna Club is a comprehensive health and fitness club offering a gym and a range of sports activities, and there is also a spa offering massages and beauty treatments.

# Al Ain

*Al Sarooj District,*
*Hilton St*
*Al Ain*
*Map 1 E3*

## Hilton Al Ain

***03 768 6666*** | *www.hilton.com*

Located near the heart of Al Ain, this ageing hotel, built in 1971, is a good base from which to explore the zoo, museum, Jebel Hafeet and the Hili Tombs. The 202 guestrooms, suites and villas overlook landscaped gardens, while its five bars and restaurants, floodlit tennis/squash courts, a health club and a nine-hole golf course offer plenty to do. Dining options offer you choices from around the world, including Persian, Italian and Tex-Mex.

### Saudi Arabia

The Kingdom of Saudi Arabia has some incredible scenery, fascinating heritage and archaeological sites, and diving locations that are among the best in the world. Sadly, due to the difficulty in obtaining visas and the present security concerns, most western expats are unlikely to ever experience this diverse and intriguing country. Recent press reports suggest that the Kingdom will issue more tourist visas in order to boost tourism industry, and as part of its preparation to join the WTO. Until then, take a look at www.sauditourism.gov.sa and www.saudinf.com to see what you're missing.

**299**

**Al Nyadat Rd**
*Al Ain*
*Map 1 E3*

## Hotel InterContinental Al Ain

*03 768 6686* | *www.interconti.com*

A recent multi-million dollar refurbishment has transformed this hotel into one of the most impressive inland resorts in the UAE. Landscaped gardens, swimming pools, guestrooms, deluxe villas and a Royal Villa with a private jacuzzi, along with many restaurants and bars make this a great leisure retreat. It is especially good for families, as apart from the training pool and family pool, there is also a shaded babies' pool, a large children's playground and a soft-play area.

**Jebel Hafeet**
*Al Ain*
*Map 1 E3*

## Mercure Grand Jebel Hafeet

*03 783 8888* | *www.mercure.com*

Situated near the top of the imposing Jebel Hafeet, this hotel offers the best views of Al Ain from all of its simply decorated rooms. As you sample great Mediterranean food in La Belvedere, you can enjoy amazing views of the city by night. The hotel also has some superb sports and leisure facilities, including an excellent swimming pool.

# Dubai

**Dubai – Al Ain Rd**
*Map 1 E2*

## Al Maha Desert Resort

*04 832 9900* | *www.al-maha.com*

Set within a 225-square-kilometre conservation reserve, this luxury getaway describes itself as 'the world's first Arabian eco-tourism resort' and provides breathtaking views across picturesque dunes. Al Maha is designed to resemble a typical Bedouin camp, but conditions are anything but basic. Each suite is beautifully crafted and has its own private pool. Guests are welcome to dine on their own veranda, with impeccable yet discreet butler service, or in the elegant restaurant. Activities include horse riding, camel trekking and falconry. The resort also has a superb spa.

**Nr Endurance Village**
*Map 2 B4*

## Bab Al Shams

*04 832 6699* | *www.babalshams.com*

Bab Al Shams ('The Gateway to the Sun'), is a beautiful desert resort built in the style of a traditional Arabic Fort. Each of its 115 rooms is decorated with subtle yet stunning Arabian touches, and pristine desert dunes form the backdrop. Al Hadheerah, an authentic, open-air, Arabic desert restaurant, is highly recommended. There is a kids' club, a large swimming pool (complete with swim-up bar), and the luxurious Satori Spa.

# East Coast

**Nr Dibba**
*Al Aqqa*
*Map 1 F1*

## Fujairah Rotana Resort & Spa ▶ p.301

*09 244 9888* | *www.rotana.com*

Located between the Hajar Mountains and the Indian Ocean, the Fujairah Rotana Resort & Spa opened in 2007. It has 250 guest rooms and suites each with its own balcony and view over the sea, and spread around a pool and gardens. The hotel also offers a variety of dining options (from Mediterranean to Middle Eastern), spas, a kid's pool and kid's club, and even meeting facilities.

**Al Ghourfa Rd,**
**North end of the**
**Corniche**
*Fujairah*
*Map 1 F2*

## Hilton Fujairah Resort

*09 222 2411* | *www.hilton.com*

Fujairah lies on the east coast of the UAE and enjoys slightly more moderate weather conditions than Dubai. The Hilton Fujairah, set amid the grand Hajar Mountains, is a relaxing resort with all the facilities needed for a wonderful weekend away. Once you get tired of lounging by the temperature-controlled swimming pool, or activities such

the
EAT HOTELS
THE WORLD

*Wish you were here.*

elcome to the pearl of the Indian Ocean, the Fujairah Rotana
sort & Spa. Our resort provides the ultimate serene setting.
henever the mood strikes, you can relax in the finest rooms, enjoy
astounding array of recreational facilities, including unlimited
ter sports & desert tours or choose from the amazing dining
periences to indulge in delectable cuisine from around the world.
r business, discover a new dimension to your next event. From
sting small meetings, to orchestrating group seminars, we pride
rselves on developing unique experiences. The Fujairah Rotana
sort & Spa will be without a shadow of a doubt a truly relaxing
d inspirational experience.

FUJAIRAH ROTANA
RESORT & SPA
AL AQAH BEACH

THERE'S ONE FOR YOU
P.O.Box 1856, Fujairah, U.A.E., Tel: (971) 9 2449888,
Fax: (971) 9 2449800, Email: fujairah.resort@rotana.com

rotana.com

as tennis, snooker, basketball or the watersports offered on the private beach, you could always explore the rugged splendour of the surrounding mountains. The hotel is great for families, and there is a safe play area for children.

**Nr Dibba**
*Al Aqah*
*Map 1 F1*

## Le Meridien Al Aqah Beach Resort ▶ p.303

**09 244 9000** | www.lemeridien-alaqah.com

About 15km from Dibba, the award-winning Le Meridien Al Aqah Beach Resort is a very popular weekend retreat for Dubai residents, and is just a two-hour drive away. All the rooms have views over the Indian Ocean, and the grounds are characterised by lush foliage and a mountain backdrop. It is particularly geared up for families, with the Penguin Club, kids' pool, and outdoor and indoor play areas. There's an extensive spa at Le Mirage Health Club and entertainment options include a cinema, restaurants and bars, which serve a range of Thai, Indian and European cuisine.

**Al Aqqa, Btn Dibba**
**& Khorfakkan**
*Fujairah*
*Map 1 F1*

## Sandy Beach Hotel & Resort

**09 244 5555** | www.sandybm.com

The appealing Sandy Beach Hotel and Resort is positioned on an idyllic bay amid a stretch of golden sand running along the Indian Ocean. About 30 minutes from Fujairah and an hour and a half from Dubai it is ideally situated for a short break. The ocean and beach are clean and beautiful and there is a 5-Star Padi Dive Centre within the hotel. This is an ideal spot from which to explore Snoopy Island. Choose from a one or two-bedroom chalet, or a luxurious double room.

# Hatta

**Hatta**
*Hatta*
*Map 1 F2*

## Hatta Fort Hotel ▶ p.291

**04 852 3211** | www.jebelali-international.com

The tranquil, extensive grounds at Hatta Fort Hotel cover 80 acres of land with a beautiful oasis of greenery. Hatta Fort is a perfectly isolated mountain retreat that is fully equipped with numerous facilities and activities. There are 50 individual chalet-style rooms and suites, all with patios overlooking the impressive Hajar Mountains. Facilities are wide ranging and include a bar, conference facilities, gift shop, Senses Beauty Salon, a driving range and chipping green, floodlit tennis courts, archery and clay pigeon shooting, a restaurant, and a coffee shop in an open-air gazebo.

# Jazira

**Btn Abu Dhabi**
**& Dubai**
*Abu Dhabi*
*Map 1 E3*

## Golden Tulip Al Jazira Hotel & Resort

**02 562 9100** | www.goldentulipaljazira.com

The Golden Tulip has original architecture and a 7km man-made channel connecting the main hotel to the beach resort, where you can stay in luxury bungalows. The hotel is fully equipped with everything needed for a relaxing retreat. Each room has a large terrace overlooking the swimming pool or the impressive sea channel. There is a special pool for children and a private beach with various watersports. Guests have a number of dining options, from light snacks to a la carte menus.

# Jebel Ali

**Jct 9, nr Jebel**
**Ali Shooting Club**
*Jebel Ali*
*Map 2 A4*

## Jebel Ali Golf Resort & Spa

**04 883 6000** | www.jebelali-international.com

Just far enough out of Dubai to escape the city's hustle and bustle, this fully equipped resort offers 392 luxurious rooms, resplendent surroundings and a peaceful

The sunny side of life.

ABU DHABI • AL KHOBAR • AMMAN • BANGALORE • BEIRUT • CHENNAI
DAMASCUS • DUBAI • JEDDAH • KUWAIT • LATTAKIA • MUMBAI • NEW DELHI

## Sea, sand, fun and sun

Do more, see more, enjoy much more at Le Méridien Al Aqah Beach Resort. Whether you choose to relax on our idyllic beach, cool off in our spectacular swimming pool, go diving, fishing or on safari, or just pamper yourself in our unique spa, everything your heart desires is here. Our spacious rooms all offer breathtaking sea views while our restaurants have something for every taste and mood. For meetings, incentives or corporate events, our superb facilities and wonderful setting simply can't be matched.

- Largest swimming pool in the UAE
- Wide unspoilt beach
- Professional dive centre (with easy access to the best East Coast dive sites)
- Watersports Centre (windsurfing, sailing, water-skiing)
- 218 ocean view rooms
- Rooms starting from 48 sq metres
- Choice of 8 restaurants & bars
- Three floodlit tennis courts
- Penguin Village – children's recreational area with pool
- Gymnasium
- Squash court
- Sauna and steam room
- Jacuzzi
- Wellness centre
- Safaris & mountain excursions
- Boat & dhow trips to Musandam
- Chartered fishing trips
- Mountain, coastal and heritage discovery tours
- Business, meeting & conference facilities.

**All just 90 minutes from Dubai**

Ask about our special offers on Superior Rooms, Royal Club, Conference Packages and Weekends.

Le MERIDIEN
AL AQAH BEACH RESORT
FUJAIRAH

www.lemeridien.com
www.alaqah.lemeridien.com
Tel: +971 (9) 244 9000
e-mail: reservations@lemeridien-alaqah.com
In Partnership with Nikko Hotels International

atmosphere – the perfect place for a weekend break (or longer). The two distinct properties, the Jebel Ali Hotel and The Palm Tree Court & Spa, are set in 128 acres of lush, landscaped gardens, with an 800-metre private beach, a marina, and one of the region's original golf courses. Guests can also enjoy horse riding, shooting and a variety of watersports. There is also a fine range of restaurants, bars and cafes within the grounds and of Dubai itself is close enough to be easily accessible for whatever else you may require from your stay.

## Liwa

**Rub Al Khali Desert** ◄
*Liwa*
*Map 1 C4*

### Liwa Hotel

**02 882 2000** | www.ncth.com

The Liwa Hotel overlooks the Rub Al Khali desert (also known as the Empty Quarter), one of the most stunning panoramas in the world. In contrast to the miles and miles of dunes, the hotel is a luxurious retreat set among lush, landscaped gardens. Facilities include a beautiful pool (a modern oasis in the desert), a sauna, jacuzzi and steam room, as well as tennis and volleyball courts. Kids will love the playground and children's pool. There are several food and beverage options, from an Arabic meal at Al Misyal to a traditional shisha pipe on the Nakheel Terrace.

## Ras Al Khaimah

**Nxt Etisalat, Bin** ◄
**Dahir Rd**
*Ras Al Khaimah*
*Map 1 E1*

### Hilton Ras Al Khaimah

**07 228 8888** | www.hilton.com

The biggest draw of this city hotel is the Hilton Ras Al Khaimah Beach Club, which is just down the road from the four-star hotel and has some attractive leisure facilities. With three pools and a pool bar, there is also a beach with plenty of watersports on offer. For a weekend spent relaxing by the mountains in a quiet part of the UAE, this is well worth a trip. The luxury Hilton Ras Al Khaimah Resort & Spa has just opened next to the beach club, offering a more pampered stay, and the MMI alcohol shop is right nearby too so you can stock up before heading back home.

**Off Road E11** ◄
*Ras Al Khaimah*
*Map 1 E1*

### Al Hamra Fort Hotel & Beach Resort

**07 244 6666** | www.alhamrafort.com

With traditional arabic architecture, and set amongst acres of lush gardens along a strip of sandy beach, this hotel offers a peaceful get-away, just an hour's drive from Dubai. Offering a range of watersports and activities, including 2 floodlit golf courses and an onsite dive centre, there is plenty to keep you entertained, and the 6 main restaurants offer a wide variety of cuisine and atmosphere. There is also a kid's club and babysitting service, making it ideal for families too.

## Umm Al Quwain

**Nr Dreamland** ◄
**Aqua Park**
*Umm Al Quwain*
*Map 1 E1*

### Barracuda Beach Resort

**06 768 1555** | www.barracuda.ae

Many Dubai residents are familiar with the Barracuda Beach Resort, as it is the location of one of the most popular 'hole in the walls' – a place where you can buy tax-free booze. But it is also a pleasant beach resort that is ideal for a quick getaway, particularly if you want to combine it with a booze run. The facilities are built for relaxation; the pool, jacuzzi and children's pool are all situated next to the tranquil lagoon. If you want more activity, the Dreamland Aqua Park (the largest water park in the UAE) is right next door.

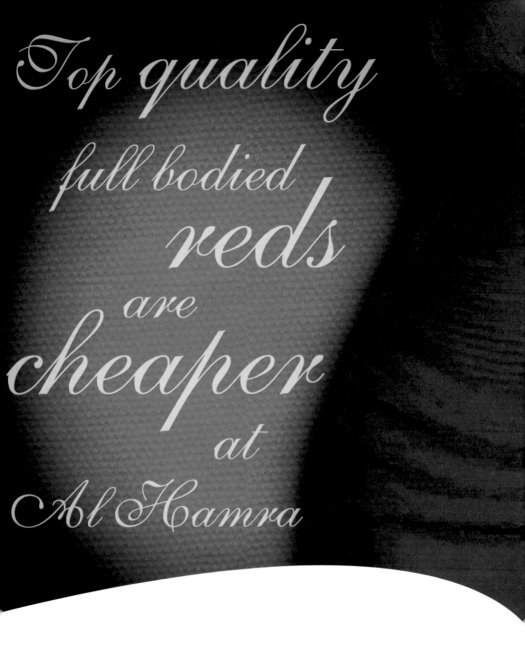

*Top quality full bodied reds are cheaper at Al Hamra*

For the largest selection of professionally stored, tax free wines and other leading brands in the region visit Al Hamra Cellar in Ras Al Khamiah. Located close to the Al Hamra Fort Hotel and Al Hamra Golf Club (junction 119 of the Emirates Road), open 7 days a week.

We advise that you have a current liquor licence to take advantage of the extensive choice, low prices and exciting offers that always greet you at Al Hamra Cellar.'

**For more information call 07 244 7403.**

Al Hamra
CELLAR

*After UAQ*
*Hospital R/A*
Umm Al Quwain
*Map 1 E1*

## Flamingo Beach Resort

*06 765 1185 | www.flamingoresort.ae*

Situated within the popular Umm Al Quwain Tourist Club, Flamingo Beach Resort has a selection of decent quality rooms overlooking the pool and terrace. The pool area includes a jacuzzi and a children's pool. The resort is surrounded by an unpolluted, shallow lagoon interspersed with many green islands that attract a variety of birdlife, including migrating flamingos. You can try a number of watersports activities including paragliding, fishing and cruising the coral reefs in a glass-bottomed boat.

*Follow signs to*
*fish/fruit &*
*vegetable market*
Umm Al Quwain
*Map 1 E1*

## Imar Spa

*06 766 4440 | www.imarspa.com*

The perfect girly weekend getaway, this ladies-only spa haven is in the heart of Umm Al Quwain, in a tranquil, seaside setting. The hotel has a small private beach and terrace for sun lounging and a fabulous temperature-controlled pool and saltwater aqua therapy pool. The hotel offers limited but pleasant accommodation (with only five rooms – two twin rooms and three singles) so booking in advance is advised. Facilities include a gym and workout space, hammam, funky hair salon and an immaculate spa. Treatments on offer include everything from botox to chocolate facials.

## Weekend Breaks – Other Hotels

| Location | Name | Telephone | Email |
|---|---|---|---|
| Abu Dhabi | Beach Rotana Hotel & Towers | 02 644 3000 | www.rotana.com |
| | Hilton International Abu Dhabi | 02 681 1900 | www.hilton.com |
| | Mafraq Hotel | 02 582 2666 | www.ncth.com/danat-hotels.php |
| | Millennium Hotel | 02 626 2700 | www.milleniumhotels.com |
| | Sheraton Abu Dhabi Resort & Towers | 02 677 3333 | www.starwoodhotels.com |
| Al Ain | Al Ain Rotana Hotel | 03 754 5111 | www.rotana.com |
| Barka | Al-Sawadi Beach Resort | +968 26 795 545 | www.alsawadibeach.com |
| Dubai | Al Qasr Hotel | 04 366 8888 | www.jumeirah.com |
| | Jumeirah Beach Hotel | 04 348 0000 | www.jumeirah.com |
| | Mina A'Salam | 04 366 8888 | www.jumeirah.com |
| | Palace of One&Only Royal Mirage ▶ p.526 | 04 399 9999 | www.oneandonlyroyalmirage.com |
| | Ritz-Carlton Dubai, The | 04 399 4000 | www.ritzcarlton.com |
| Fujairah | Al Diar Siji Hotel | 09 223 2000 | www.aldiarhotels.com |
| Musandam | Golden Tulip Resort Khasab | +968 26 730 777 | www.goldentulipkhasab.com |
| | Khasab Hotel | +968 26 730 271 | na |
| Muscat | Al Bustan Palace InterContinental | +968 24 799 666 | www.al-bustan.intercontinental.com |
| | Al Falaj Hotel Muscat | +968 24 702 311 | www.omanhotels.com |
| | The Chedi Muscat | +968 24 524 400 | www.ghmhotels.com |
| | Crowne Plaza Muscat | +968 24 660 660 | www.cpmuscat.com |
| | Grand Hyatt Muscat | +968 24 641 234 | www.muscat.hyatt.com |
| | Holiday Inn Muscat | +968 24 487 123 | www.holiday-inn.com |
| | Hotel InterContinental Muscat | +968 24 680 000 | www.interconti.com |
| | Radisson SAS Muscat | +968 24 487 777 | www.radissonsas.com |
| | Sheraton Oman Hotel | +968 24 772 772 | www.starwoodhotels.com |
| Nizwa | Falaj Daris Hotel | +968 25 410 500 | www.falajdarishotel.com |
| Ras Al Khaimah | Al Hamra Fort Hotel | 07 244 6666 | www.alhamrafort.com |
| | Ras Al Khaimah Hotel | 07 236 2999 | na |
| Salalah | Hilton Salalah Resort | +968 23 211 234 | www.salalah.hilton.com |
| | Holiday Inn Salalah | +968 23 235 333 | www.holiday-inn.com |
| Sohar | Sohar Beach Hotel | +968 26 841 111 | www.soharbeach.com |
| Sur | Sur Mercure Hotel | +968 25 543 777 | www.mercure.com |
| Umm Al Quwain | Flamingo Beach Resort | 06 765 1185 | www.flamingoresort.ae |

# XVA ART HOTEL

Located in the historical district of Bastakiya, XVA Art Hotel combines all the characteristics of an art-inspired modern boutique hotel with the architectural splendor of a 100-year old house.

Artists and Designers like British designer Sameh El Shahat, Dubai's fashion guru Zayan Ghandour, Sharjah-based fashion designer Essa, Iraqi painter Halim Al Karim, award winning design brand Gaia&Gino, Lebanese furniture designer Nada Debs and painter Laudi Abilama have decorated our 8 rooms, blending style with functionality.

Enjoy XVA's unique and tranquil spirit while in the heart of Dubai's only pedestrian area, a step away from the Dubai Creek, its traditional souks, charming courtyards and windtowers.

**XVA Art Hotel**
For reservations email xva@xvagallery.com
For more information and rates www.xvagallery.com
Address: Building 15 A, Bastakiya Historical District, Bur Dubai, P.O. Box 37304

# Bahrain

For a change of pace head to nearby neighbour Bahrain, just a 50 minute flight away and small enough to be explored in a weekend. With traditional architecture, miles of souks, excellent shopping and some truly outstanding bars and restaurants, you can choose from a cultural escape or fun-packed break. Formula 1 fans won't want to miss the Grand Prix that usually takes place in March or April, with hotels booked up months in advance – see the *Bahrain Resident's Guide* or the upcoming *Bahrain Mini* for more on what to do there.

**Sheikh Hamad**
**Causeway**
*Sh Al Quwain*

## Novotel Al Dana Resort

*+973 1729 8008* | *www.novotel-bahrain.com*
The only city beach resort in Bahrain, the Novotel offers the Curves sports and leisure facility, a large outdoor pool and a small private man-made beach. Watersports equipment available for hire on the beach includes jet skis, water skis, windsurfers and kayaks. Jet skis are not available on Sundays and Mondays. Single annual membership fees are BD 400 for gold membership, which gives access to all the facilites, including the beach. Non-members can have access to the pool and beach, but not the health club; the fee is BD 6 per day for adults and BD 3 per day for children.

**El Seef**
*Manama*

## The Ritz Carlton Bahrain Hotel and Spa

*+973 1758 0000* | *www.ritzcarlton.com*
The hotel has one of the best beaches on the island in a man-made lagoon surrounded by lush gardens. The 600 metre private beach sweeps round the lagoon with its own island and private marina. As one would expect from a luxury five-star hotel, the annual club membership fees are very high. There's a BD 150 joining fee and single membership fees range from BD 400 for silver membership, which is only valid on weekdays, to BD 750 for platinum membership, which includes access to the Spa Health Club (ladies only). Temporary single membership for a minimum period of 2 weeks ranges from BD 28 to BD 42. One-day entry fees are BD 18 for a couple, and BD 25 for a family with two children.

# Kuwait

Kuwait is not always immediately considered as a weekend break destination (no alcohol don't forget), but the colourful and somewhat tainted heritage of this small (yet rich) country means it is still worth a visit. Kuwait may be one of the world's smallest countries but its 500km coastline has endless golden beaches that remain refreshingly tranquil. From the Grand Mosque to the Kuwait Towers there are many architectural splendours to explore, while Al Qurain House, which still shows the scars of war with its immortal bullet holes, gives you a fascinating insight into the troubled times of the Iraqi invasion. There is also Green Island, an artificial island linked by a short bridge and home to restaurants, a children's play area and a great alternative view of Kuwait's shoreline. For more information and inspiration, check out the *Kuwait Resident's Guide*.

**Fahaheel 64009**
*Mangaf*

## Hilton Kuwait Resort

*+965 225 6222* | *www.hilton.com*
Located in Mangaf, this resort has one of the best beaches and health clubs in the country. There are 143 rooms, four suites, 80 chalets, 61 studios and apartments, 52 Presidential Villas and 12 Royal Villas, plus four restaurants, two cafes, one coffee shop and two poolside bars. The resort also has a water sports pavilion and a dive centre.

**King Fahad Highway**
*Sabahiya*

## Kempinski Julai'a Resort

*+965 844 444* | *www.kempinski-kuwait.com*
Built in 2003, the Art + Tech hotel takes modern hospitality to another level with cutting edge amenities perfect for business travellers. All of the 70 rooms feature

interactive Plasma screen TVs, DVD, VCD and CD facilities, and high speed Internet access. Hotel facilities include a restaurant, lobby lounge, health club and outdoor swimming pool.

**Visas**

*Visas for Oman are required whether entering by air or road, and different regulations apply depending on your nationality and how long you want to stay. Nationalities are split into two groups –– check out the Royal Oman Police website, www.rop.gov.om for full lists (click on Services, and then Passport and Residencies). People in group one can get a visit visa at the border – it's usually free for visitors but Dubai residents are likely to incur a Dhs.60 charge. Residents from group two, however, will need to get a visa from the Oman consulate or embassy in advance for a Dhs.60 charge, which may take a few days to process. Oman does have a common visa facility with Dubai, meaning people on a Dubai visit visa will not need a separate visa to visit Oman.*

# Oman

Other options **Weekend Break** p.298

Just a few hours from Dubai, you'll find the countless attractions of Oman. It's a peaceful and breathtaking place, with history, culture, and spectacular scenery. The capital Muscat has enough attractions to keep you busy for a good long weekend, including beautiful beaches, some great restaurants and cafes, and the mesmerising old souk at Mutrah. Out of the capital you will find many historic old towns and forts, and some of the most stunning mountain and wadi scenery in the region. Salalah in the south has the added bonus of being cool and wet in the summer.

A flight from Dubai to Muscat takes 45 minutes, but when you factor in check-in times and clearing customs it's not much quicker than driving. There are daily flights from Dubai with Emirates and Oman Air, while Air Arabia flies from Sharjah. Regular flights direct to Salalah from Dubai are also available. There is also a bus service from Dubai to both Muscat and Salalah, taking six and 16 hours respectively, and costing from Dhs.50 for Dubai to Muscat.

For further information on what Oman has to offer both visitors and residents, refer to the *Oman Resident's Guide, Oman Off-Road Explorer*, and *Oman Trekking Explorer* – all from Explorer Publishing.

## Musandam

The UAE's northern neighbour, Musandam, is an isolated enclave belonging to the Sultanate of Oman, and its capital Khasab is a quaint fishing port largely unchanged by the modern world. The region is dominated by the Hajar Mountains, which run through the UAE and the rest of Oman.

It is sometimes called the 'Norway of the Middle East', since the jagged mountain cliffs plunge directly into the sea and the coastline is littered with inlets and fjords. Just metres off the shore are beautiful coral beds with an amazing variety of sea life, including tropical fish, turtles, dolphins, occasionally sharks, and even whales on the eastern side. This area offers some of the best dive sites in the Middle East, and as such is becoming increasingly popular with divers. A dhow trip into the fjords is a great way to sample the beauty of Musandam – on a full-day trip you'll see isolated coastal villages, get a chance to swim and snorkel in the calm waters, and hopefully see dolphins frolicking beside your boat. Khasab Travel & Tours operates a number of dhows, with day trips costing around Dhs.200 per person including lunch, soft drinks, and an informative guide. Call their Dubai office on 04 266 9950. Alternatively, get down to the harbour in Khasab and bargain hard with the independent dhow owners to arrange your own private cruise.

To get there by road, turn right about 30km north of Ras Al Khaimah, at the Shams Roundabout, turn right and follow the road as it loops around to the UAE exit post (Unfortunately at busy periods this is a real bottleneck). You'll have to park the car and battle your way to one of the three windows, making sure you grab an exit form to fill in as you queue – on Eid weekends you may be there over an hour. Then drive just a few hundred metres to the Oman entry point where you fill in an entry form and pay for your visa, if applicable.

Finally there's a checkpoint where cars are occasionally searched for prohibited goods such as alcohol. The officers won't empty the car though, so with a little careful packing…

**309**

The road then follows the scenic coastline until it reaches Khasab, passing some great beaches on the way. The visa/nationality rules for entering this region of Oman are the same as those outlined above, but again, you're advised to check with the embassy if in any doubt.

Another option for exploring Musandam is to hire a dhow in Dibba on the UAE's east coast and then travel north. You won't need to arrange visas as technically you're not going into Oman. The UAE Off-Road and Oman Off-Road Explorers have more Musandam info, as does the Oman Explorer – all from Explorer Publishing.

**Zighy Bay**
*Musandam*

## Evason Hideaway & Six Senses Spa At Zighy Bay
*+968 092 443 060* | www.sixsenses.com

Located in a secluded cove, shared only by a fishing village, the Evason Hideaway (newly opened in late 2007) is a little slice of paradise just across the Musandam border. Accessible by three arrival options - 4WD (hotel pickup from the base of the mountain) on a rather bumpy road that cuts over the hills down to Zighy Bay, by speed boat into the bay or, believe it or not, by paraglide. The resort has been designed in true rustic style (without compromising on luxury of course) and is made up of individual pool villas. Guests have the option to dine in their villa (by flaming torch light in private surrounds), eat in the main restaurant, enjoy a group arabic cookery lesson, have an intimate dinner atop the stone wine tower or enjoy breathtaking views in the mountainside restaurant.

**Shati Al Qurm**
*Muscat*

## InterContinental Muscat
*+968 246 80000* | www.interconti.com

This is an older hotel that has recently undergone a major facelift. The InterCon continues to be popular for its outdoor facilities, international restaurants, Al Ghazal Pub and regular entertainment in the form of dinner theatres and visiting bands. New alfresco restaurant, Tomato, is a must-try. Trader Vic's, with its legendary cocktails, is perenially popular. Some of the 265 rooms have views of Qurm Beach. The health club is one of the best in Muscat.

**Shati Al Qurm**
*Barr Al Jissah*

## Shangri-La's Barr Al Jissah Resort
*+968 247 76 666* | www.shangri-la.com

This is the largest of the hotels within Shangri-La's Barr Al Jissah Resort, with 302 bedrooms, and has been built for families. Kids will love the 'Little Turtles' club, where they can play in air- conditioned comfort or outdoors. The hotel has numerous swimming pools, including a rubber-cushioned toddlers' pool and a kids' pool in the shape of a mushroom. Babysitting services are available, so that you can enjoy the hotel's excellent restaurants.

## Qatar

Qatar once had something of a sleepy reputation, but things are changing fast. The amount of development and investment in the country means it is becoming increasingly popular with visitors. With an attractive corniche, world-class museums and cultural centres, and plenty of hotels with leisure and entertainment facilities, the capital Doha makes a perfect weekend retreat. The Doha Asian Games in December 2006 attracted thousands of visitors and put Qatar firmly in the spotlight; many new hotel, retail, leisure and entertainment projects were built especially for the event. Away from the city, the inland sea (Khor Al Udaid) in the south of the country also makes a great day trip, usually as part of an organised tour. The *Qatar Resident's Guide* has details of all these activities and many more.

**Corniche Rd**
*Doha*

## Mövenpick Hotel Doha

*+974 429 1111 | www.moevenpick-hotels.com*

This modern hotel boasts the breathtaking corniche as its vista, where guests can enjoy a morning jog or afternoon stroll. Close to both the airport and the National Museum, the hotel recently won the Silver Award for Best 4 Star Business Hotel in The Spirit of Hospitality Awards, thanks to its wireless internet service and excellent business rooms. This boutique-style hotel also attracts tourists with its excellent restaurants and leisure facilities.

**West Bay Lagoon**
*Doha*

## Ritz-Carlton Doha

*+974 484 8000 | www.ritzcarlton-doha.com*

A deluxe hotel, located 20 minutes from the airport, all of the 374 rooms and suites are exquisitely decorated, with breath-taking views over the sea or marina. The beach club provides a great selection of water sports while the luxurious spa has every pampering treatment imaginable. The hotel has a variety of restaurants, serving both international and Arabic cuisine and it also houses the Admirals Club, a very popular upscale night club.

Oman

Kuwait

Bahrain

Qatar

# Holidays From Dubai

One of the best things about living in Dubai is its central location and easy access to some wonderful holiday destinations that you may not have had the opportunity to visit had you stayed in your home country. The following holiday hotspots are just some of the amazing places that you can visit with ease from Dubai.

**Flight time:** 3 hours
**Time difference:** 2 hours behind
**Best time to visit:** Oct – Apr

## Jordan

Jordan is packed with religious and historical sites, incredible architecture, and friendly, welcoming people. You can brush up on your history by visiting the Bronze Age Citadel of Amman and a city hewn out of bare rock at Petra. If it's sun and luxury you're after, Jordan boasts an excellent choice of five-star hotels and resorts. And with Emirates, Air Arabia and Royal Jordanian Airlines all offering direct flights, it's ideal for a quick getaway.

**Flight time:** 3.5 hours
**Time difference:** 2 hours behind
**Best time to visit:** Oct – Apr

## Lebanon

Lebanon's blossoming development as a vibrant tourist destination was tragically set back when Israel invaded in July 2006. Fortunately, the conflict ended after 34 days, and Qatar Airways resumed flights into Beirut by early September 2006, followed by other airlines. Never a nation to take knock-backs lying down, Lebanon is doing everything possible to rebuild itself, but it's probably still best to check the current national safety situation before picking it for your next holiday.

**Flight time:** 4 hours
**Time difference:** 2 hours ahead
**Best time to visit:** Oct – Apr

## Egypt

Egypt is undoubtedly an ideal trip for history fans. It's one of the oldest civilisations in the world and home to famous historical sites such as the pyramids and sphinx. It also has some amazing scenery: there is the White Desert in the west, the Red Sea in the east, and, of course, the Nile. Cairo is a busy city with an active nightlife, and the resort town of Sharm El Sheikh is a popular spot for diving holidays at luxurious beach resorts.

**Flight time:** 7 hours
**Time difference:** 4 hours behind
**Best time to visit:** Oct – Apr

## Morocco

Whether you visit Casablanca, Marrakesh, Tangier or Rabat, the cities of Morocco have a similar thread running through them – a perfect balance of African and Middle Eastern cultures, with some great shopping (both traditional and modern), excellent nightlife, and superb cuisine. Marrakesh is known for its traditional Berber villages, markets and festivals while Casablanca is busy and industrialised. Emirates operates a daily flight to Casablanca.

**Flight time:** 8.5hours
**Time difference:** 2 hours behind
**Best time to visit:** Year round

## South Africa

Whether you choose the vibrant, cosmopolitan city of Johannesburg, the tropical, coastal beauty of Durban or the stylish, Mediterranean-influenced Cape Town, South Africa is a fantastic holiday destination and often referred to as 'a world in one country'. The list of things to see and do here is almost endless: whale watching, surfing, spotting some big game on a wildlife safari or wine tasting through the Cape. Emirates has two direct flights to Johannesburg each day, and Etihad has recently started a Johannesburg route from Abu Dhabi.

**Flight time:** 5 hours
**Time difference:** 1 hour behind
**Best time to visit:** Aug – Mar

## Kenya

The epic beauty of Africa and the opportunity to spot the big five on a wildlife safari is just a five-hour flight away. For a once-in-a-lifetime experience, head there between August and October to witness the annual migration, when you can observe over two million wildebeest moving over the great plains of the Masai Mara – a sight best seen from above in a hot air balloon. Both Emirates and Kenyan Airlines operate a daily flight to Nairobi.

# Holiday Hotspots

Morocco

Lebanon

Jordan

Egypt

India

**Flight time:** *3 hours*
**Time difference:**
*2 hours ahead*
**Best time to visit:**
*Oct – Feb*

## India

India is a land of contrasts, from the beautiful beaches of Goa, to the vibrant city of Mumbai, to the imposing mountains of Kashmir. Goa is probably the top holiday spot, thanks to its palm-fringed white beaches and luxurious hotels. Alternatively, travel to Agra for architecture, handicrafts and jewellery, as well as to visit the legendary Taj Mahal, or the rose pink city of Jaipur. Daily flights are operated by Emirates, Air India and Air Arabia.

**Flight time:** *6 hours*
**Time difference:**
*3 hours ahead*
**Best time to visit:**
*Aug – Feb*

## Thailand

It used to be big with backpackers but now Thailand is a popular holiday destination for all. It is blessed with beautiful beaches and numerous luxury resorts in areas such as Phuket and Koh Samui, while Bangkok is a bustling city with a dynamic population and a vibrant nightlife. Emirates operates several daily flights direct to Bangkok, where you can catch a connecting flight to Phuket and Koh Samui.

**Flight time:** *4 hours*
**Time difference:**
*2 hours ahead*
**Best time to visit:**
*Oct – Mar*

## Sri Lanka

The beauty of Sri Lanka, apart from the short flight time and negligible time difference, is that you can either have a fantastic holiday on a small budget, or a luxurious holiday of a lifetime. Capital city Colombo has its attractions, although most holiday makers head for the beautiful beach resorts. Emirates offers direct flights to Sri Lanka on a daily basis, and low-cost airline Air Arabia offers return flights for under Dhs.1000.

**Flight time:** *7 hours*
**Time difference:**
*4 hours ahead*
**Best time to visit:**
*Apr – Oct*

## Malaysia

This natural paradise, spread over hundreds of little islands, is a unique and beautiful place to visit. It has plenty of almost-untouched little villages and jungles, full of interesting communities and exotic wildlife. It also has one of the world's most progressive cities: Kuala Lumpur is bustling and attracts expats and visitors from around the globe. Emirates operates a codeshare with Malaysian Airlines, and there is a daily flight from Dubai.

**Flight time:** *4.5 hours*
**Time difference:** None
**Best time to visit:**
*Year round*

## Seychelles

Enjoying balmy weather throughout the year, the islands of the Seychelles are a perennially attractive holiday destination. The 115 islands that make up the Archipelago of the Seychelles feature beautiful white sands and vivid turquoise waters. Because it is a natural haven for wildlife, there is an emphasis on eco-tourism. Accommodation ranges from acceptable three-star hotels to luxurious five-star beach resorts.

**Flight time:** *4 hours*
**Time difference:**
*1 hour ahead*
**Best time to visit:**
*Dec – Apr for good weather;*
*Nov – Apr for diving*

## Maldives

The Maldives is undoubtedly a destination best suited to those who are looking for a relaxing beach holiday rather than an action-packed adventure. That said, many of the luxurious beach resorts offer a range of exciting watersports that will keep adrenaline junkies happy, and this one of the premier dive locations in the world. Resorts tend to be tailored, remains either to families or couples only.

**Flight time:** *6 hours*
**Time difference:** None
**Best time to visit:**
*Nov – Apr*

## Mauritius

Since Emirates started offering direct flights four times a week, Mauritius has become hugely popular. It is not a massive island, but it has enough variety for you to explore something different each day. From the endless white beaches to the clear blue seas rich with marine life, and from the hustle and bustle of Port Louis (and some great shopping), to the lush, tropical greenery of the inner countryside, Mauritius is an island of contrasts.

## United Kingdom

**Flight time:** 7 hours
**Time difference:** 4 hours behind
**Best time to visit:** Jun - Aug; Dec– Jan

Samuel Johnson once said, 'if you're tired of London, you're tired of life,' and this is still true today. Get your fix of culture, glitz and glamour by taking in a West End play; embark on a shopping extravaganza on Oxford Street; get dazzled by the lights and sights of Piccadilly Circus; and explore the many historical sites of the city. Numerous direct flights are offered by Emirates, Virgin, British Airways and Royal Brunei Airlines.

## Greece

**Flight time:** 4 hours
**Time difference:** 2 hours behind
**Best time to visit:** Apr – Jun; Sep – Oct

Postcard-perfect vistas of whitewashed chalets against a backdrop of azure skies and sea are what you can expect from Greece. A wide variety of accommodation options means you can either settle in a beach hotel or be a bit more adventurous and island hop for a couple of weeks between Corfu, Crete, and Mykonos among others.

## Russia

**Flight time:** 5 hours
**Time difference:** 1 hours behind
**Best time to visit:** Jun – Aug

For so long it was firmly hidden behind the iron curtain and off limits for visitors, but now it is one of the most up-and-coming tourist destinations for the curious traveller. Culturally, Moscow is a powerful city with a history of artistic and literary achievement. Perhaps one of the most interesting aspects of Russia is the fusion of the staid, old-fashioned, way of life, with the young, vibrant lifestyle that was ushered in following the demise of the Soviet Union in 1991. Emirates offers a direct flight from Dubai six days a week.

## Turkey

**Flight time:** 4 hours
**Time difference:** 2 hours behind
**Best time to visit:** Apr – Jun; Sep – Oct

Perfectly placed between contrasting cultures of east and west, Turkey is an extremely popular holiday destination – and one of the most reasonably priced. Istanbul is an amazing city, with an impressive cultural heritage. Alternatively, visit the bazaar and the mosques in Bursa, and the Bodrum at Halicarnassus where Herodotus, the 'father of history' was born. Turkey also offers beautiful landscapes, great weather, sun, sea and mountains.

## Cyprus

**Flight time:** 3 hours
**Time difference:** 2 hours behind
**Best time to visit:** Apr - May; Sep - Oct

It's hard to believe that this idyllic Mediterranean island is such a short flight from Dubai. Three main towns, Larnaca, Limassol and Paphos, each offer unique accommodation and leisure options, and capital city Nicosia is great for shopping and nightlife. Whether you choose to rent a self-catering apartment or stay in a luxurious hotel with full-board, a holiday in Cyprus is a huge change from Dubai. You can drive up mountains for crisp, cool air and some awesome views, and explore quiet local villages off the beaten track.

## Malta

**Flight time:** 8 hours
**Time difference:** 3 hours behind
**Best time to visit:** Feb - Jun; Sep - Oct

Malta is a country rich in history, with its oldest temple dating back to 3600BC. The medieval city of Madina (which you tour by horse and carriage), and the beautifully preserved 16th century city of Valletta are the historical highlights. There are many excellent beach resorts and hotels, as well as a lively offering of bars, restaurants and nightlife. Emirates flies direct to Malta four times a week.

### Travel Agencies

| | | |
|---|---|---|
| Absolute Adventure | 04 345 9900 | www.adventure.ae |
| Africa Connection | 04 339 0232 | na |
| Airlink | 04 282 1050 | www.airlinkuae.com |
| Al Futtaim Travel | 04 228 5470 | www.access2travel.com |
| Al Naboodah Travel | 04 294 5717 | www.uaetraveler.com |
| Al Rostamani International Exchange | 04 332 7444 | na |
| Al Tayer Travel Agency | 04 223 6000 | www.altayer-travel.com |
| Belhasa Tourism Travel & Cargo Co. | 04 295 7474 | www.belhasatravel.com |
| DNATA | 04 316 6666 | www.dnata.com |
| Emirates Holidays | 04 343 9999 | www.emirates-holidays.com |
| Kanoo Travel | 04 393 3633 | www.kanoogroup.com |
| MMI Corporate Services | 04 209 5527 | www.mmitravel.com |
| Signature Travels | 04 311 6555 | www.signaturetravel.biz |
| SNTTA Travel & Tours | 04 282 9000 | www.sntta.com |
| Turner Travel & Tourism | 04 345 4504 | www.turnertraveldubai.co |

Classes and private lessons
For children and adults
Flexible schedule
Club system
Exclusive professional instructors
Pleasant atmosphere

Learn
and Burr

# Salsa

# Quickstep

# Waltz

Viennese Waltz

# Tango

# Foxtrot

# Paso Double

# Rumba

A Partner Of

Saint-Petersburg State University of Engineering and Economics, Knowledge Village, Block 18, 2nd floor
Tel.: 04 362 53 13, 04 362 53 17, 04 362 53 19. Cell: 050 157 30 61
web: www.dancedubai.com, e-mail: info@dancedubai.com

# Activities

**Oops!**

*Did we miss anything out? If you have any thoughts, ideas or comments for us to include in the Activities section, drop us a line, and if your club or organisation isn't in here, let us know and we'll give you a shout in the next edition. Visit www.explorerpublishing. com and tell us whatever's on your mind.*

## Sports & Activities

Believe it or not, life in Dubai is not all shopping malls, restaurants, and five star hotels. Warm winters provide the perfect environment for all manner of outdoor activities, while a host of diversions are available to take your mind off the extreme heat and humidity of the summer.

Traditional sports such as tennis, golf, rugby and cricket are widely available, and for the more adventurous there's always skydiving, rockclimbing, mountain biking, wadi bashing and dune driving.

Thanks to a sprawling coastline of crystal clear waters, watersports are particularly popular too, with scuba diving, snorkelling, sailing, surfing, water-skiing, and more recently kitesurfing being firm favourites.

With so many different nationalities and cultures at play in Dubai, most sports, activities and interests are covered. Sometimes word of mouth is the best way of discovering that there are others that share your passion. If you can't find an existing club, you could always start your own.

### Activity Finder

| | | | | | | | |
|---|---|---|---|---|---|---|---|
| Aerobics Classes | p.319 | Environmental Groups | p.338 | Music Lessons | p.364 | Swimming | p.378 |
| Aqua Aerobics | p.319 | Fencing | p.339 | Netball | p.365 | Table Tennis | p.378 |
| Archery | p.319 | Fishing | p.339 | Orchestras/Bands | p.365 | Tennis | p.378 |
| Art Classes | p.320 | Flower Arranging | p.341 | Paintballing | p.365 | Thai Boxing | p.379 |
| Baseball | p.322 | Flying | p.341 | Parasailing | p.365 | Triathlon | p.379 |
| Basketball | p.322 | Football | p.342 | Photography | p.366 | Wadi & Dune Bashing | p.379 |
| Beauty Training | p.322 | Gaelic Games | p.343 | Polo | p.366 | Wakeboarding | p.380 |
| Belly Dancing | p.322 | Gardening | p.343 | Quad Bikes | p.366 | Watersports | p.380 |
| Birdwatching | p.322 | Golf | p.344 | Rollerblading/Skating | p.366 | **Spectator Sports** | |
| Boot Camp Training | p.324 | Gymnastics | p.348 | Rowing | p.366 | Camel Racing | p.382 |
| Bowling | p.324 | Hashing | p.348 | Rugby | p.367 | Golf | p.382 |
| Bridge | p.325 | Hiking | p.349 | Running | p.367 | Horse Racing | p.382 |
| Bungee Jumping | p.325 | Hockey | p.350 | Sailing | p.368 | Tennis | p.383 |
| Camel Rides | p.325 | Horse Riding | p.350 | Salsa Dancing | p.369 | **Leisure Facilities** | |
| Camping | p.326 | Ice Hockey | p.351 | Sand Boarding/Skiing | p.369 | Beach Clubs | p.384 |
| Canoeing | p.327 | Ice Skating | p.352 | Scouts & Guides | p.370 | Health Clubs | p.384 |
| Caving | p.327 | Jetskiing | p.352 | Scrabble | p.370 | Sports Clubs | p.384 |
| Chess | p.327 | Karting | p.352 | Scrapbooking | p.370 | Rates Table | p.386 |
| Climbing | p.328 | Kayaking | p.353 | Shooting | p.370 | **Well-Being** | |
| Crab Hunting | p.328 | Kickboxing | p.353 | Singing | p.372 | Beauty Salons | p.388 |
| Cookery Classes | p.328 | Kitesurfing | p.353 | Skiing | p.372 | Hairdressers | p.388 |
| Cricket | p.329 | Language Schools | p.355 | Skydiving | p.374 | Health Spas | p.390 |
| Cycling | p.329 | Libraries | p.356 | Snooker | p.374 | Massage | p.398 |
| Dance Classes | p.329 | Martial Arts | p.359 | Snorkelling | p.374 | Pilates | p.398 |
| Desert Driving Courses | p.332 | Mini Golf | p.360 | Social Groups | p.375 | Reiki | p.398 |
| Dhow Charters | p.333 | Mothers & Toddlers | p.360 | Softball | p.376 | Stress Management | p.399 |
| Diving | p.334 | Motocross | p.362 | Speedboating | p.377 | Tai Chi | p.399 |
| Dragon Boat Racing | p.337 | Motorcycling | p.362 | Squash | p.377 | Yoga | p.399 |
| Drama Groups | p.338 | Motor Sports | p.362 | Summer Camps | p.377 | | |
| Dune Buggy Driving | p.338 | Mountain Biking | p.362 | Surfing | p.377 | | |

*Slimming made easy!*

*Body Solutions (04 282 4122) is the only place in Dubai offering the revolutionary HypoxiTherapy, a fast acting way to lose cellulite and fat by exercise combined with vacuum suction. This method is immediate and painless, can be directed exactly where you want to lose weight, and shows visible results after the first session, with reductions of one inch upwards. They have a number of machines around Dubai; check out www.hypoxitraining.com.*

## Aerobics & Fitness Classes

Step, pump, aqua and conventional aerobics classes are offered at many beach, health and sports clubs. For a complete list of up to date classes, times and instructors, check with the clubs – see the table to the right for more details. Prices vary from club to club but average around Dhs.25 per class for members and Dhs.30 for non-members.

## Aqua Aerobics

With so many fantastic swimming pools at hotels and health clubs, aqua aerobics is far more a pleasure than a chore. It's also a good workout for people with knee or lower back injuries, osteoporosis sufferers and pregnant women. For some truly exotic exercise, you can cycle your pool noodle around the waterfalls and palm trees at Pharaohs' Club (04 324 0000).

## Archery

### Dubai Archers
050 450 9819 | www.dubaiarchers.com

Small, friendly and informal, the Dubai Archers Club meets at Dubai Country Club on Friday and Saturday afternoons from 15:00 until dark. They have a target range with nine targets up to 90m, and a 3D 'animal range.' Coaching is available and club equipment is on hand for novices. There's a Dhs.20 entry charge for non-Country Club members, and an equipment rental fee of Dhs.20.

### Hatta Fort Hotel
04 852 3211 | www.jebelali-international.com

Hatta Fort Hotel's archery range is 25 metres long, with eight targets. Archery fans can enter the hotel's annual competition, and the Dubai Archers Club also holds its annual archery tournament at this venue. Assistance is available at the hotel for this challenging sport.

### Jebel Ali Shooting Club
04 883 6555 | www.jebelali-international.com

As well as excellent clay shooting facilities, Jebel Ali Shooting Club also boasts indoor and outdoor archery ranges with equipment for both men and women. The outdoor range is huge at 5,000 square metres and can accommodate up to 12 archers at the same time. Instruction is given to beginners who have never tried archery before.

| Aerobics & Fitness Classes | | |
| --- | --- | --- |
| Name | Phone | Type of Class |
| Aviation Club | 04 282 4122 | Body Balance |
| | | Body Combat |
| | | Body Pump |
| | | Spinning |
| | | Step |
| The Big Apple | 04 319 8661 | Body Pump |
| | | Spinning |
| Dubai Country Club | 04 333 1155 | Spinning |
| Fitness First | 04 358 0344 | Body Attack |
| | | Body Balance |
| | | Body Combat |
| | | Body Pump |
| | | Spinning |
| Fitness Planet | 04 398 9030 | Body Balance |
| | | Body Combat |
| | | Body Pump |
| | | Spinning |
| Nautilus Academy | 04 397 4117 | Body Balance |
| | | Body Combat |
| | | Body Pump |
| | | Spinning |
| Pharaohs' Club | 04 24 0000 | Body Pump |
| | | Spinning |
| | | Step |
| Quay Healthclub | 04 366 8888 | Body Balance |
| | | Body Pump |
| | | Spinning |

*Sharjah Wonder Golf Club*
*Sharjah*
*Map 16 B3 169*

*Dubai-Hatta Rd*
*Hatta*
*Map 1 F2*

*Nr Jebel Ali Golf Resort & Spa*
*Jebel Ali*
*Map 3 A2 63*

## Art Classes

Other options **Art & Craft Supplies** p.410 **Art Galleries** p.258

*Town Centre*
*Jumeira*
*Map 7 D1*

### Café Ceramique

*04 341 5008 | www.cafe-ceramique.com*

Part cafe, part artist studio, Café Céramique offers a novel art and eating experience. Pick a tasty bite from the menu and a blank piece of pottery, and get creative. Once you've finished your masterpiece it'll need glazing and firing – the cafe takes care of this for you, and you're given a time and date on which to pick up your pot. Events offered include Art4fun Workshops and the Kidz4art Summer Camp. A second branch can be found in Mall of the Emirates (04 341 0144).

*Mall of the Emirates*
*Al Barsha*
*Map 6 A3*

### Dubai Community Theatre & Arts Centre

*04 351 3400 | www.dubaitheatre.org*

The Dubai Community Theatre & Arts Centre (DUCTAC) is a modern, non-profit-making cultural and arts facility serving the varied communities within Dubai. In addition to a 540 seat two-level theatre and a 190 seat studio theatre/rehearsal space, the centre features art galleries, classrooms and studios for painting, sculpture, photography, calligraphy, pottery, dance, music, and just about every other art form and craft you can think of. With a cafe, art supplies shop, and lending library, DUCTAC is fast becoming a hub for the arts in Dubai.

Located at Mall of the Emirates, the centre officially opened for business in November 2006. Keep an eye on the website for details of upcoming performances, exhibitions, workshops and events.

*Nr Town Centre*
*Jumeira*
*Map 7 D1*

### Dubai International Art Centre

*04 344 4398 | www.artdubai.com*

As one of the first art-centred establishments to reach Dubai, the centre is a haven of artistic tranquillity. Classes are offered in over 70 subjects, including painting and drawing, dressmaking, etching, pottery and photography. Courses last six to eight weeks, and prices vary according to the materials required. The DIAC also holds regular exhibitions showcasing the members' works. Annual membership fees start at Dhs.250, but classes are open to non-members too.

*Jumeirah Centre*
*Jumeira*
*Map 7 F1*

### Elves & Fairies

*04 344 9485 | jim@mailme.ae*

This craft shop for adults and children specialises in stencils, rubber stamps and face painting. They also deal in decorative paint effects and stock paints, glazes, colourwashes, varnishes and brushes, as well as cross-stitch, mosaics and decoupage. They run regular workshops for children and adults on all things crafty, including the popular new activity of scrapbooking.

*St 17a, Beh Dubai*
*Garden Center*
*Al Quoz*
*Map 10 D1*

### Jam Jar

*04 341 7303 | www.jamjardubai.com*

At the Jam Jar you'll be equipped with unlimited paint, brushes, music and drinks, and let loose to freely express yourself on canvas. Whether you've never painted before or are something of a closet Picasso, inspiration, creativity and fun is what it's all about. Private painting parties can be arranged, and Jam Jar hosts regular exhibitions and competitions. The 'Jam-To-Go' service even brings the experience to you – a novel idea for your next garden party or corporate event.

**TOGETHER,** WE CAN GO FURTHER

Sun & Sand is proud of the UAE's sterling achievements and its iconic growth as one of the 21st century's greatest success stories.

At Sun & Sand, we are not only inspired but commited to follow in our great nation's steps diligently.

For over 29 years, we have lived up to our reputation as the leading provider for quality sports and Lifestyle Brands in the UAE.

With continued growth, we also have ambitious plans to open up many stores in GCC countries and indeed across the world.

سن اند ساند سبورتس
SUN & SAND SPORTS

UAE, SAUDI ARABIA, DOHA, MUSCAT, OMAN, QATAR & KUWAIT

## Baseball

**Nr Nad Al Sheba Club**
*Nad Al Sheba*
*Map 2 E3*

### Dubai Little League

*04 332 4429* | www.dubailittleleague.org

Dubai Little League Baseball is a non-profit organisation run by parent volunteers. Every year they field over 20 baseball teams, consisting of 350 boys and girls between the ages of 4 and 18, and this year they have a new all-girls slow pitch softball programme. Previous experience or knowledge is not necessary, it's all about learning to play as a member of a team and enjoying some outdoor exercise.

## Basketball

Basketball courts can be rented at the Aviation Club and Dubai Country Club, or you can go down to Safa Park (04 349 2111) and get regular pick up games on Wednesday, Thursday and Sunday evenings. You'll also find courts beside Diyafah Street in Satwa, near Rydges Plaza hotel. Organised club basketball is, however, limited.

## Beauty Training

Other options **Beauty Salons** p.388

**Wafi Residence**
*Umm Hurair*
*Map 10 E4*

### Cleopatra & Steiner Beauty Training Centre

*04 324 0250* | www.cleopatra-steiner.com

This is the Middle East's first internationally endorsed training facility, and offers long and short term courses in health, beauty and holistic therapy. Courses include anatomy and physiology, body massage, nail and skin treatments, reflexology, hairdressing and aromatherapy. Qualifications are recognised by CIDESCO, CIBTAC, and City & Guilds.

## Belly Dancing

Other options **Dance Classes** p.329

Belly dancing is not only an ancient Arabic art but also great fun and a good way to keep fit. The Ballet Centre (04 344 9776) holds belly dancing lessons on various mornings and evenings, and the Nautilus Fitness Centre (04 331 4055) at the Crowne Plaza teaches oriental belly dancing on Sunday and Tuesday evenings. Groups of seven or more ladies can also arrange lessons at home from Isabella (050 651 2273).

## Birdwatching

Other options **Environmental Groups** p.388

Thanks to the ever-increasing greenery, Dubai attracts many bird species not easily found in Europe or the rest of the Middle East. Over 80 species breed locally, and during the spring and autumn months, over 400 species have been recorded on their migration between Africa and Central Asia. The many parks and golf clubs are often the best birdwatching sites, where parakeets, Indian rollers, little green bee eaters and hoopoe can easily be spotted. Other species found in the Emirates include the striated scops owl, chestnut bellied sandgrouse, Saunders' little tern and Hume's wheatear. Outside Dubai, the mangrove swamps in Umm Al Quwain and Khor Kalba are good places for birdwatching. Khor Kalba is the only place in the world where you can spot the rare white-collared kingfisher. Canoe trips through the mangroves can be arranged by tour companies, see the Desert Rangers and their entry on p.327. The Ras Al Khor Wildlife Sanctuary at the end of Dubai Creek was off-limits to the public for many years. In 2005 though, three bird hides were opened, allowing the public access to the site. See next page.

# Get in gear...
## for an incredible year

If every weekend you scratch your head for something new and exciting to do then this book is a must. From a royal hammam to a Musandam hike it's time to get off your...

**365 Must-Do Experiences UAE & Oman**
The weekend just got a whole lot more exciting

Abu Dhabi • Amsterdam • Bahrain • Barcelona • Beijing • Berlin • Dubai • Dublin • Geneva
Hong Kong • Kuala Lumpur • Kuwait • London • Los Angeles • New York • New Zealand • Oman
Paris • Qatar • Shanghai • Singapore • Sydney • Tokyo • Vancouver

**EXPLORER**
www.explorerpublishing.com

**Various locations**

## Emirates Bird Records Committee
*050 642 4358 | www.uaeinteract.com/nature*

The Emirates Bird Records Committee puts together information about birds in the UAE and maintains a checklist. A weekly round up of bird sightings and a monthly report is available via email upon request. For more information contact the committee chairman, Simon Aspinall.

**Ras Al Khor**
*Map 2 F3*

## Ras Al Khor Wildlife Sanctuary
*04 206 4240*

This is the only nature reserve within the city, and a superb place to see Greater Flamingos, as well as many other shore birds and waders. On an average day in winter you can find up to 15,000 birds, including up to 1,500 flamingos. Dubai Municipality is increasingly concerned about the protection of these birds and their ecosystem, and you'll see police patrolling the area around the clock. The three new hides from where you can watch the birds come with telescopes and binoculars provided. You can also read information on the types of birds it is possible to see, and pick up a guide to the sanctuary. One of the hides is situated beside Ras Al Khor Road, the other two off Oud Metha Road. All three are manned, have their own car parks, and are free to visit for small parties. Groups of more than 10 may need to contact the Environment Department at Dubai Municipality (04 206 4240) to arrange permits.

## Boot Camp Training

The lethargy of Dubai living can be hard to break, and so when the opportunity came up for the city's pampered expats to get kicked into shape, many took advantage. Boot Camps are hardcore fitness programmes for those in a rut, or those that want to go from vaguely healthy to super fit. They normally take place at sunrise on the city's public beaches and parks, and tend to involve burly men telling flabby expats to jog, sprint, squat and heave.

**Various locations**

## Fitness O2
*050 955 6129 | www.02fitness.net*

This firm offers a similar product, at the same price (Dhs.950 for 12 sessions over four weeks) as Physical Advantage, but mixes in a few Thai boxing moves (non contact) to get you kicking and swinging (and possibly imagining your instructor on the end). It has also begun sessions in Ski Dubai (Dhs.1,250 for a month, or Dhs.120 for a one off) for those that fancy getting sweaty in the cold.

**Various locations**

## Physical Advantage
*04 311 6570 | www.physicaladvantage.ae*

A four week course, costing Dhs.950 per person and offering three sessions a week. Sessions last an hour or more, and start at either 06:00 or 20:00. Exercises will include jogging and sprinting along the beach, squats, sit ups, push ups and running with a 'gun' (usually plastic piping filled with sand). A basic fitness test in the first session decides which section you should be in.

## Bowling

**Behind American Hospital**
Oud Metha
*Map 10 E2* 11

## Al Nasr Leisureland
*04 337 1234 | www.alnasrleisureland.ae*

Al Nasr Leisureland has an eight-lane bowling alley with various fast food outlets and a bar that serves alcohol. Booking is recommended since there are regular league games that take place during the week. The entrance fee is Dhs.10, and each game costs Dhs.7 – this includes shoe rental.

## Dubai Bowling Centre

**Nr Al Shabab Club**
*Al Mamzar*
*Map 12 B3* 🇮🇹

*04 296 9222 | www.dubaibowlingcentre.com*

The biggest bowling centre in Dubai, this modern venue has 36 state-of-the-art computerised lanes, which are enjoyed by recreational and competitive bowlers alike. Several of Dubai's clubs and leagues are based here and the centre hosts regular competitions. The range of facilities is excellent and includes an equipment shop, snooker and billiards, amusements and video games, and a number of cafes and dining options.

## ThunderBowl

**Nr Jct 1,**
**Shk Zayed Rd**
*Al Wasl*
*Map 7 D3* 🇮🇹

*04 343 1000 | road.tb@eim.ae*

ThunderBowl has 20 fully computerised Brunswick lanes, a snooker and pool hall, a pro-bowling shop, Indian and Arabic restaurants and a cyber games cafe. Everyone is welcome to use the facilities, and there is a fun and lively atmosphere. Large groups (minimum 100 people) can hire out all 20 lanes and enjoy the added bonus of an ultraviolet extravaganza with 'cyber bowling' (must be booked a week in advance – call for further details). Games cost Dhs.15 per person or Dhs.80 per hour on weekdays and Dhs.100 per hour on weekends. Shoe rental is Dhs.2

## Bridge

### Dubai Bridge Club

**The Village**
*Jumeira*
*Map 7 F1*

*050 658 6985 | olavo786bridge@yahoo.com*

The Dubai Bridge Club is an organisation with members from the UAE, Poland, Iran, France, India, Syria, Turkey, Pakistan and the UK. The club organises regular tournaments; contact Olavo D'Sousa for more info.

### Dubai Ladies Bridge Club

**Dubai Intl**
**Women's Club**
*Jumeira*
*Map 7 D1*

*04 344 2389*

Ladies-only bridge mornings are held at 09:00 on Sundays and Wednesdays. Registration ends at 08:45, and games start promptly at 09:00. For further details, contact Marzie Polad on 050 659 1300 or Jan Irvine on 050 645 4395.

## Bungee Jumping

For adrenaline junkies, bungee jumping is available in Dubai at certain times of the year. During the Dubai Shopping Festival (DSF) there are various attractions and fun-fairs dotted around town, and the one on Al Seef Road by the creek usually has bungee. For more information, check the daily press for details as DSF approaches.

## Camel Rides

When in Arabia, riding a camel is like riding a London bus – it's a must-do and a bumpy ride too. You could opt for a short camel ride as part of a desert tour (see Main Tour operators p.283) or a hotel and beach resort package, but for a more memorable experience you should go on a longer guided camel ride in the sand dunes. On such tours there are stops for rests, refreshments and photos, so that you can remember your experience long after the aches subside.

### Al Ain Golden Sands Camel Safaris

**Hilton Al Ain**
*Al Ain*
*Map 1 E3*

*03 768 8006*

Al Ain Golden Sands Camel Safaris offer a selection of tours that include a camel ride over the dunes of Bida Bint Saud. The rides usually last one to two and a half hours, and all tours include transfers from Al Ain, Arabic coffee and dates, and soft drinks.

**325**

*Got a 4WD?*

Use it for what it was made for. The UAE offers SUV owners a real chance to push their vehicles to the limits and experience nature first hand. The **UAE Off-Road Explorer** is your complete guide to offroading in the UAE. From dune bashing and wadi driving to hiking and mountain biking, this all-inclusive guide will give you all you need to know about your local wilderness.

# Camping

Other options **Wadi & Dune Bashing** p.379, **Outdoor Goods** p.441

Constant sunshine and an awe-inspiring array of locations make camping a much-loved activity in Dubai and the UAE. In general, warm temperatures and next to no rain means you can camp with much less equipment and preparation than in other countries, and many first-timers or families with children find that camping becomes their favourite weekend break. For most, the best time to go is between October and April, as in the summer it can get unbearably hot sleeping outside.

Choose between the peace and tranquillity of the desert, or camp among the wadis and mountains next to trickling streams in picturesque oases. Many good campsites are easily accessible from tarmac roads so a 4WD is not always required.

Although the UAE has low rainfall, care should be taken in and near wadis as flash floods can and do occur (remember, it may be raining in the mountains miles from where you are).

You should consider taking the following equipment:

• Tent
• Lightweight sleeping bag (or light blankets and sheets)
• Thin mattress (or air bed)
• Torches and spare batteries
• Cool box for food
• Water (always take too much)
• Camping stove, or BBQ and charcoal if preferred
• Firewood and matches
• Insect repellent and antihistamine cream
• First aid kit (including any personal medication)
• Sun protection (hats, sunglasses, sunscreen)
• Jumper/warm clothing for cooler evenings
• Spade
• Toilet rolls
• Rubbish bags (ensure you leave nothing behind)
• Navigation equipment (maps, compass, Global Positioning System (GPS)
• Mobile phone (fully-charged)

For the adventurous with a 4WD, there are endless possibilities for camping in remote and beautiful locations all over the UAE. The many sites in the Hajar Mountains (in the north near Ras Al Khaimah or east and south near Hatta or Al Ain), and the huge sand dunes of Liwa in the south are highly recommended. These routes require some serious off-road driving but offer a real wilderness camping experience. For more information on off-road adventuring and places to camp, refer to the *UAE Off-Road Explorer*.

*Various Locations*

## Absolute Adventure

04 345 9900 | www.adventure.ae

For companies looking to give their employees a treat while enhancing teamwork and problem solving skills, Absolute Adventure organises corporate camping trips. Departing from their base in Dibba, a boat takes large groups to a nearby cove where they'll camp in tents and participate in team-building activities. All of the equipment and food is taken care of, including sunshades, shower tents and toilet tents.

**Blue Banana**

For a present with a difference, Blue Banana offers a range of Gift Experiences including driving, flying, and sporting activities, plus exciting adventures and pampering spa days. Visit www.bluebanana arabia.com for details.

## Canoeing

Other options **Kayaking** p.353, **Outdoor Goods** p.441

Canoeing is a great way to access hidden places of natural beauty and get close to marine and bird life in the UAE. At Khor Kalba Nature Reserve on the east coast, tours are available and canoes can be hired. If you have your own canoe, other worthwhile areas to visit include the coastal lagoons of Umm Al Quwain, selected areas around Ras Al Khaimah and mangrove-covered islands north of Abu Dhabi. Many of these areas are on their way to becoming protected reserves, so treat them with respect and do not litter. Adventurous paddlers occasionally go to the Musandam in sea-touring canoes where it is possible to visit secluded bays and view spectacular rocky coastlines with fjord-like inlets and towering 1,000 metre cliffs. Also see Khor Kalba in the Exploring section on p.297.

*Beh Dubai Garden*
*Centre*
*Al Quoz*
*Map 6 B3*

### Desert Rangers  ▶p.287

*04 340 2408 | www.desertrangers.com*

Desert Rangers offers trips through the mangroves at Khor Kalba Nature Reserve. Only a basic level of fitness is required and this is a suitable activity for people of all ages. A guide accompanies you on your trip. Trips usually cost Dhs.300 per person.

## Caving

Other options **Out of Dubai** p.290

The cave network in the Hajar Mountains is extensive and much of it has yet to be explored. Some of the best caves are located near Al Ain, the Jebel Hafeet area and just past Buraimi near the Oman border. Many of the underground passages and caves have spectacular displays of curtains, stalagmites and stalactites, as well as gypsum flowers.

At present there are no companies offering guided tours, and caving is limited to unofficial groups of dedicated cavers. Within the region, caving ranges from fairly safe to extremely dangerous, but either way you should always be well-equipped and accompanied by an experienced leader.

Check weather forecasts to find out about recent rainfalls and be warned that flash floods occur regularly at certain times of the year. The Hajar Mountain range continues into the Sultanate of Oman, where it is higher and even more impressive. In Oman, the range includes what is believed to be the second largest cave system in the world, as well as the Majlis Al Jinn Cave – the second largest chamber in the world. A word of warning though, no mountain rescue services exist, therefore anyone venturing out into mountains should be reasonably experienced, or go with someone who knows the area.

## Chess

Other options **Scrabble** p.370

*Nr Al Shabab Club*
*Hor Al Anz*
*Map 12 B3*

### Dubai Chess & Culture Club

*04 296 6664 | www.dubaichess.com*

This club is involved in all aspects of chess and cultural programmes. Members can play chess at the club seven nights a week and competitions are organised on a regular basis. International competitions are also promoted including the Dubai International Open, Emirates Open and Dubai Junior Open, attracting representatives from Asia, Arabia and Europe. Annual membership is Dhs.100 for Nationals and Dhs.200 for expats.

**327**

## Climbing

For those who feel at home on vertical cliffs or hanging from rocky precipices, excellent climbing can be found in various locations around the UAE, including Ras Al Khaimah, Dibba, Hatta and the Al Ain/Buraimi region. The earliest recorded rock climbs were made near Al Ain and Buraimi in the late 1970s; since then more than 600 routes have been climbed and named. These vary from short outcrop routes to difficult and sustained mountain routes of alpine proportions. New routes are generally climbed 'on sight', with traditional protection. Most are in the higher grades – ranging from (British) Very Severe, up to extreme grades (E5). Due to the nature of the rock, some climbs can feel more difficult than their technical grade would suggest. Many routes, even in the easier grades, have loose rock, poor belays and difficult descents, often by abseil, making them unsuitable for total novices. However, there are some easier routes for new climbers, especially in Wadi Bih and Wadi Khab Al Shamis. To meet like-minded people head to Wadi Bih where you're sure to find climbers nearly every weekend, or go to the indoor climbing wall at Pharaohs' Club, where most of the UAE climbing fraternity hangs around (ahem). For more information contact John Gregory on 050 647 7120 or email arabex@eim.ae. Another excellent resource is www.globalclimbing.com, which features a wealth of information for anyone interested in climbing in the UAE.

**Beh Dubai Garden Centre**
*Al Quoz*
*Map 6 B3*

### Desert Rangers ▶ p.287
*04 340 2408 | www.desertrangers.com*

Desert Rangers offers rock climbing trips to well-established locations throughout the Emirates, that are suitable for absolute beginners or experienced climbers. Trips include instruction, all necessary safety equipment and lunch. The cost is Dhs.400 per person, and there is a minimum of four people per trip.

**Pyramids**
*Umm Hurair*
*Map 10 E4*

### Pharaohs' Club
*04 324 0000 | www.waficity.com*

The indoor climbing wall at Pharaohs' Club lets climbing enthusiasts improve their skills, and offers a range of courses for kids and adults of all abilities, as well as public sessions for experienced climbers. Lessons cost Dhs.50 per hour, and are limited to six people per instructor. The wall consists of varied climbing routes, and crash mats are present for bouldering.

## Cookery Classes

Many hotel restaurants hold occasional cookery demonstrations or classes, so look out for events advertised in the media. The Shangri-La (04 343 8888, p.43) can organise classes for groups of 10 or more people, by special arrangement. Speak to someone in the F&B department for more info. The Blue Elephant (04 282 0000, p.562) in Al Bustan Rotana has been known to hold cooking classes during the summer, as has Sushi Sushi (04 282 9908, p.548). Gordon Ramsay's Verre at the Hilton Dubai Creek (04 227 1111, p.518) also stages occasional demonstrations and master classes.

## Crab Hunting

**Nr Lamcy Plaza**
*Al Karama*
*Map 10 D2*

### Lama Desert Tours
*04 334 4330 | www.lamadubai.ae*

This unusual tour takes you to Umm Al Quwain where you head out to sea to hunt crabs, and then enjoy a dinner consisting of your own catch of the day. The cost is Dhs.280 per person (minimum six people) and includes return transfers, soft drinks, snacks and the traditional (if you can call crabs traditional) dinner.

**328**

## Cricket

With such a mixture of nationalities and cultures in Dubai, cricket is a passion shared across many communities. Many organisations have their own cricket teams for inter-company competitions and the sport is becoming more popular in schools. If your company doesn't have an existing team, then the favourite choice for 'western' expats is the Darjeeling Cricket Club (04 333 1746). International matches are regularly hosted in the Emirates, especially at the grounds in Sharjah where it's possible to see some of the world's best teams in action.

*Mountain biking at sunset*

*Nr Int 4, Shk Zayed Rd*
*Al Quoz*
*Map 6 B3* 19

## Insportz

*04 347 5833 | www.insportzclub.com*

This indoor sports centre located behind Dubai Garden Centre near Interchange Four is a handy little club with cheap prices and good equipment and facilities. There are three main net courts with a scoreboard, and one side court, available for playing a social game, as part of a league, or just for practice. There's also a small outlet for refreshments. Contact the centre for booking inquiries and prices.

## Cycling

Other options **Sports Goods** p.477, **Mountain Biking** p.362, **Cycling** p.56

Dubai is not a very bicycle-friendly city but there are plenty of areas where you can ride, and it can be a great way to explore as well as keep fit. The pedestrian areas on both sides of the creek are pleasant places for a spin, especially in the evening, and riding through the souks can also be an experience. Clubs and groups of cyclists generally ride at the weekends, and early mornings and evenings when roads are quieter and the temperatures are cooler. If you have no choice but to ride in busy areas, exercise a lot of care and attention. Although helmets are not legally required, it is recommended that you wear one considering how crazy Dubai traffic can be. Outside the city limits the roads are flat until you near the mountains. Jebel Hafeet near Al Ain, the Hatta area of the Hajar Mountains, and the central area in the mountains near Masafi down to the coast at either Fujairah or Dibba, offer interesting paved roads with better views. The new road from Hatta through the mountains to Kalba on the east coast is probably one of the most scenic routes in the country.

*Various locations*

## Dubai Roadsters

*04 339 4453 | www.wbs.ae*

To join Dubai Roadsters you need nothing more than a safe bike, cycling helmet, pump and spare tubes. The average distance covered on a Friday ride is 65 to 100 km, while weekday rides are about 30 to 50 km. There are no membership fees. Email wolfi@wbs.ae to be added to the club's mailing list.

## Dance Classes

Other options **Salsa Dancing** p.369, **Music Lessons** p.364, **Belly Dancing** p.322

Whether it's the Polka, Salsa or Bharatnatyam, all dancing tastes are catered for in Dubai. In addition to established dancing institutions, many health clubs, restaurants

**329**

and bars hold weekly sessions in flamenco, salsa, samba, jazz dance, ballroom and more. Some health clubs also offer dance-based aerobic classes (see p.319).

## Al Naadi Club

**Al Ghurair City**
*Deira*
*Map 9 C4*

*04 205 5229* | *wilson@alghurairgroup.com*
Ballet lessons leading to Royal Academy of Dancing examinations are taught by Sally Bigland, who also teaches Latin American dance to adults. Karate classes for boys and girls aged 6 and older, and swimming lessons for children and adults are also on offer. Tennis and squash is available seven days a week.

## The Ballet Centre

**Behind Jumeira Plaza**
*Jumeira*
*Map 7 F1*

*04 344 9776* | *www.balletcentre.com*
The Ballet Centre offers Royal Academy Ballet and Imperial Society of Teachers Tap classes. The centre also has classes for modern, Spanish, Irish and jazz dancing, and not forgetting belly dancing too. For aerobics fans, there are various sessions for all levels of fitness.

## Ceroc Dubai

**Various locations**

*050 428 3061* | *www.cerocarabia.com*
Ceroc modern jive is a stylish partner dance similar to salsa but with no tricky footwork. This makes it very easy to learn, and unlike other partner dances it can be danced to many different musical styles such as club & chart hits, old classics, swing, Latin & rock 'n' roll. Regular classes, workshops, social dance nights and private tuition are available. Partners are rotated regularly so there's no need to bring one, and no special footwear or clothing is required. Call Des on the above number for more information.

## The Dance Centre ▶p.331

**Various locations**

*www.thedancecentre.ae*
The Dance Centre has over 19 studios throughout Dubai, catering to people living in Emirates Hills, Arabian Ranches, Jumeira, Bur Dubai, Mirdif and many more areas. It specialises in classes for children from the age of 3 up to 19. The centre is affiliated to the Royal Academy of Dance in London (RAD), teaching its ballet syllabus and offering their Graded Examinations, alongside the Imperial Society of Teachers of Dance (ISTD) syllabus with examinations in Modern, Jazz, Tap and Disco/Freestyle. Contact the above website or 050 877 5918 for more information.

## Dance Dubai ▶p.316

**Block 18**
*Knowledge Village*
*Map 5 D2*

*04 362 5317* | *www.dancedubai.com*
Russia's rich heritage as a country is dancing and is brought to Dubai at St Petersburg State University in Knowledge Visit. It offers classes, lectures, private lessons and workshops given by Russian professional dancers, in disciplines ranging from ballroom to Latin for both children and adults. For more details you can contact  Mr. Anton on 050 157 3061.

## DanceHorizons

**Various locations**

*04 360 7691* | *dancehorizons@gmail.com*
Dance Horizons is a specialist ballet school that offers the Royal Academy of Dance Examination syllabus for beginners through to professional level. There is a Specialized Music and Movement programme for children aged 4 years and older. Classes are held at Horizon School and Safa School in Jumeirah (near Safa Park) in fully equipped ballet studios with sprung floor, barres and mirrors, and are led by highly qualified, RAD registered, teaching staff.

# Turning Pointe
## dance studios
Formerly *The Dance Centre*

"With studios all over Dubai, we're in your neighbourhood."

All types of dance classes for 3yrs - 18yrs.
For further information, please contact us on:
Tel: 04 **338 8412/3** | **info@turningpointe.ae** | www.**turningpointe**.ae

**Various locations**

## Dubai Liners
*050 654 5960 | difromdubai@yahoo.com*
Although traditional line dancing involves a strong country and western music theme, Dubai Liners teaches a more modern version, using a wide variety of music including disco, rock 'n roll, salsa, jazz, R&B, waltz, and ballads. Classes for beginners and intermediate students are on Saturday and Tuesday evenings, from 19:00 to 22.00, and people of all ages and fitness levels are welcome. Contact Diana for more details.

**Capitol Hotel**
*Al Satwa*
*Map 8 B2*

## Savage Garden
*04 346 0111 | caphotel@eim.ae*
Savage Garden is a Latin American restaurant and nightclub that sports a Latino band and food. You can also partake in Salsa and Merengue dance classes. Daily classes (except Fridays) are offered from 20:00 to 21:00 for beginners and 21:00 to 22:00 for intermediate and advanced dancers. Classes cost Dhs.35.

**Various locations**

## Swing Dancing
*04 367 2217 | www.lindyswing.com*
Swing, or to give it its correct name Lindy Hop, was invented by New York's African American community in the 1930s. It is an energetic partner dance involving intricate footwork and jazz steps from dances like the Charleston. With music from jazz greats like Count Basie, Duke Ellington and Glen Miller to dance to, swing has enjoyed a huge resurgence over the last decade. Call Des on 050 428 3061 for details of classes and events.

## Desert Driving Courses
Other options **Wadi & Dune Bashing** p.379

For those who want to master the art of driving a 4WD in the desert without getting stuck (and learn how to get yourself out when you do), several organisations offer desert driving courses with instruction from professional drivers. Vehicles are provided on some courses, while others require participants to bring their own (this is usually cheaper). Picnic lunches and soft drinks are often included as part of the package.

**Opp Municipality**
**Garage**
*Al Rashidiya*
*Map 11 D3*

## Al Futtaim Training Centre
*04 285 0455 | www.traininguae.com*
The Desert Campus Training Course gives off-road driving enthusiasts the knowledge and experience to venture safely into the desert. It starts with a three hour classroom session covering the basics of your vehicle and is followed by five hours of supervised off-road driving where you take your own 4WD up and down the dunes. Costs are Dhs.300 per person or Dhs.450 for two people in one car.

**Beh Dubai Garden**
**Centre**
*Al Quoz*
*Map 6 B3*

## Desert Rangers ▶ p.287
*04 340 2408 | www.desertrangers.com*
Desert Rangers offer lessons for anyone wanting to learn how to handle a car in the desert. If you are just starting out you'll be taught the basics of venturing off-road. There are also advanced classes that tackle challenging dune scenarios.

**Beh Al Bustan Centre**
*Al Qusais*
*Map 12 B4*

## Emirates Driving Institute
*04 263 1100 | www.edi-uae.com*
The Emirates Driving Institute offers a one-day desert driving course for Dhs.200 (Saturday to Thursday), or Dhs.250 on Fridays. The institute also offers a one-day defensive driving course for Dhs.300, or Dhs.350 on Fridays. Participants receive certificates on completion of all courses. Call to find your nearest branch.

*Shangri-La Hotel*
*Trade Centre 1*
*Map 7 E3*

## Off-Road Adventures  ▶ p.281

*04 405 2917 | www.arabiantours.com*

Off-Road Adventures provides exciting safari tours with the focus on safety, exclusivity and personnel expertise. In addition to off-road driving courses (Karim's speciality), the company also arranges fun drives, treasure hunts, camping tours, camel safaris and sand boarding.

## Dhow Charters

Other options **Boat & Yacht Charters** p.277, **Dinner Cruises** p.510

An evening aboard a dhow, either on Dubai Creek or sailing along the coast, is a wonderfully atmospheric and memorable experience. Contact one of the companies below to find out more about dhow charters. Alternatively, large independent groups can charter a dhow from the fishermen at Dibba on the east coast, to travel up the coast to Musandam. If you're prepared to haggle you can usually knock the price down substantially, especially if you know a bit of Arabic. Expect to pay around Dhs.2,500 per day for a dhow large enough to take 20 – 25 people, or Dhs.100 per hour for a smaller one. You'll need to take your own food and water, as nothing is supplied onboard except for ice lockers that are suitable for storing supplies. Conditions are basic, but you'll have the freedom to plan your own route and to see the beautiful fjord-like scenery of the Musandam from a traditional wooden dhow. The waters in the area are beautifully clear and turtles and dolphins can often be seen from the boat, although sometimes unfavourable weather conditions can seriously reduce visibility for divers. If you leave from Dibba (or Daba), Omani visas are not required, even though you enter Omani waters. It is also possible to arrange stops along the coast and it's worth taking camping equipment for the night, although you can sleep on board. This kind of trip is ideal for diving but you should hire any equipment you may need before you get to Dibba (refer to the *Underwater Explorer* for dive shop rentals, and see Diving on p.334). If diving is not your thing, you can just spend the day swimming, snorkelling and soaking up the sun.

*Nr Al Garhoud Bridge*
*Umm Hurair*
*Map 13 C1*

## Al Boom Tourist Village

*04 324 3000 | www.alboom.ae*

Al Boom Tourist Village operates nine dhows on the creek, ranging from single-deckers with room for 20 people, right up to the huge triple-decker Mumtaz with a capacity of 350 passengers. Al Boom claims that this is the biggest dhow currently operating on the creek. They offer a variety of packages, so prices vary accordingly. As well as the usual dinner cruises, late-night trips can also be arranged.

*Dibba Port*
*Sharjah*
*Map 1 F1*

## Al Marsa Travel & Tourism & Charters

*06 544 1232 | www.musandamdiving.com*

Al Marsa has two purpose-built dhows that are suitable for divers and tourists. You can relax on the sundeck for a day trip and discover fishing villages, or go on an overnight voyage and explore the Musandam fjords. Prices start at Dhs.370 for divers and Dhs.300 for non-divers.

*Nr DCCI Bld*
*Deira*
*Map 11 B1*

## Creek Cruises

*04 393 9860 | www.creekcruises.com*

The Malika Al Khor and Zomorrodah dhows can be chartered for any occasion, and are suitable for groups of 20 to 150 people for dinner, and more for cocktail parties when seating is not required. Facilities include an air-conditioned deck, majlis, sound system and dance floor. The charter fee is Dhs.1,500 per hour (minimum two hours) and catering can be provided from Dhs.80 per person. For enquiries contact the above number, or try 050 552 8993.

## Tour Dubai ▶ p.513

*Opp Dubai Municipality HQ*
*Deira*
*Map 9 C4*

*04 336 8406* | www.tour-dubai.com

Creekside Leisure offers a variety of charter packages that range from romantic dinners for two, to corporate hospitality for up to 200 guests. The dhows are licensed and offer catering, live entertainment and business facilities. A two-hour dinner cruise costs Dhs.150 and includes a welcome drink, food, and soft drinks.

## Khasab Travel & Tours

*Warba Centre*
*Deira*

*04 266 9950* | www.khasabtours.com

Sailing north from Dibba (no Omani visa is required) the cruise follows the coastline where steep rocky cliffs rise out of the sea. You'll pass small fishing villages that are accessible only by boat, and will hopefully see dolphins and turtles. Prices start at Dhs.200 per adult for a full-day cruise including lunch and refreshments.

## Diving

Other options **Snorkelling** p.374

The UAE's coastal waters are home to a variety of marine species, coral life and even shipwrecks. You'll see some exotic fish, like clownfish and seahorses, and possibly even spotted eagle rays, moray eels, small sharks, barracuda, sea snakes and stingrays. Most of the wrecks are on the west coast, while the beautiful flora and fauna of coral reefs can be seen on the east coast.

There are many dive sites on the west coast that are easily accessible from Dubai. Cement Barge, Mariam Express and the MV Dara wrecks are some of the more popular dive sites. Off the east coast, a well-known dive site is Martini Rock, a small, underwater mountain covered with colourful soft coral, with a depth range of three to 19 metres. North of Khor Fakkan is the Car Cemetery, a reef that has thrived around a number of cars placed 16 metres below water. Visibility off both coasts ranges from five to 20 metres.

Another option for diving enthusiasts is to take a trip to the the Musandam. This area, which is part of the Sultanate of Oman, is often described as the 'Norway of the Middle East' due to the many inlets and the way the sheer cliffs plunge directly into the sea. It offers some spectacular dive sites. Sheer wall dives with strong currents and clear waters are more suitable for advanced divers, while the huge bays, with their calm waters and shallow reefs, are ideal for the less experienced. Visibility here is between 10 and 35 metres. If you plan to travel to Khasab, the capital of the Musandam, you may not be able to take your own air tanks across the border and will have to rent from one of the dive centres there. You may also require an Omani visa. Alternatively, from Dibba on the UAE east coast, you can hire a fast dive boat to take you anywhere from five to 75 kilometres up the coast. The cost ranges between Dhs.150 and Dhs.500, for what is usually a two-dive trip.

There are plenty of dive companies in the UAE where you can improve your diving skills. Courses are offered under the usual international training organisations.

## 7 Seas Divers

*Nr Khor Fakkan*
*Souk East Coast*
*Khor Fakkan*
*Map 1 F1*

*09 238 7400* | www.7seasdivers.com

This PADI dive centre offers day and night diving trips to a variety of sites around Khor Fakkan, Musandam and Lima Rock. Training is provided from beginner to instructor level, in a variety of languages including Arabic, English, German, Dutch, Italian and Russian. The centre provides diving equipment for you to buy or rent.

Underwater Dubai

**Nr Iranian Hospital**
*Al Wasl*
*Map 7 F1*

## Al Boom Diving

*04 342 2993 | www.alboomdiving.com*

Al Boom's Aqua Centre on Al Wasl Rd is a purpose-built school with a fully outfitted diving shop. There's a variety of diving courses on offer, both here, and at their PADI Gold Palm Resort at Le Meridien Al Aqah Beach Resort (09 204 4912) near Fujairah.

**Oceanic Hotel**
*Khor Fakkan*
*Map 1 F1*

## Divers Down

*09 237 0299 | www.diversdown.ae*

Divers Down is a PADI Five Star Gold Palm Resort that offers courses from beginner to instructor level, and organises pleasure dives three times a day in the tropical waters of the Gulf of Oman. The centre is open seven days a week, and transport is available. Check the website for rates and diving information.

**Heritage & Diving**
**Village**
*Al Shindagha*
*Map 9 B1*

## Emirates Diving Association

*04 393 9390 | www.emiratesdiving.com*

Based at the Heritage & Diving Village by Dubai Creek, the aim of this non-profit organisation is to conserve, protect and restore the UAE's marine resources by promoting the importance of the environment. The association looks after the well-being of UAE corals as part of its coral monitoring project, and organises annual Clean-Up Arabia campaigns. A quarterly newsletter, Divers for the Environment, details their current activities and the website has lots of useful info. Divers are encouraged to join, with membership costing just Dhs.60 per year.

**Nr the Harbour**
*Dibba*
*Map 1 F1*

## Nomad Ocean Adventures

*050 885 3238 | www.discovernomad.com*

Nomad offers a range of trips and excursions. For qualified divers a single dive with all equipment included starts from Dhs.320, while beginners can try the Discover Scuba Diving programme for Dhs.400. The company can also organise all manner of tailor-made trips that in addition to offering diving (both scuba and snorkelling) can also incorporate dhow trips and overnight stays at traditional Arabian camps. For details speak to Christophe on his UAE mobile, or try +968 26 836 229 (Oman landline).

**Jumeirah Beach**
**Hotel**
*Umm Suqeim*
*Map 6 B1*

## The Pavilion Dive Centre

*04 406 8827 | www.thepaviliondivecentre.com*

This PADI Gold Palm IDC Centre is run by PADI Course Directors offering an extensive range of courses from beginner to instructor. Daily dive charters for certified divers are available in Dubai, and dive charters to the Musandam region of Oman can be organised upon request. Two dives with full equipment in Dubai are priced at Dhs.300, and two dives with full equipment in Musandam cost Dhs.490 including transport and lunch. Courses offered include Discover Scuba Diving (Dhs.250), Open Water (Dhs.1,850), Adventures in Diving (Dhs.1,400), Instructor Development IDC (Dhs.5,000) and many more.

*An evening swim*

**Sandy Beach Hotel**
**& Resort**
*Fujairah*
*Map 1 F1*

## Sandy Beach Diving Centre

*09 244 5555 | www.sandybm.com*

This dive centre is managed by Sandy Beach Hotel and offers a qualified team of instructors and support staff. It is open all year round for diving and accommodation, and the retail store stocks diving gear. The famous Snoopy Island is alive with hard corals and marine life, and is an excellent spot for snorkelling and scuba diving.

*Al Badiyah Beach*
**East Coast**
*Dibba*
*Map 1 F1*

## Scuba 2000

*09 238 8477* | *www.scuba-2000.com*

This east coast dive centre is open all year round and provides daily trips to dive sites at Dibba and Khor Fakkan. Standard courses are available for beginners and advanced divers. Costs range from Dhs.350 for Discover Scuba to Dhs.1,600 for Open Water, and teaching materials are available in a variety of languages.

**DWTC Apts, Block C**
*Trade Centre 2*
*Map 7 F3*

## Scuba Dubai

*04 341 4940* | *www.scubadubai.com*

For those wishing to arrange their own diving and snorkelling trips, equipment can be rented from Scuba Dubai on a 24 hour basis, collecting one day and returning the next. Rates for Thursday, Friday and Saturday are the same as renting for one day because the shop is closed on Fridays. Note that original diving certification must be shown for all scuba equipment rentals. Scuba Dubai is open from 09:00 to 20:30 Saturday through Wednesday, 09:00 to 19:00 on Thursday and is closed Fridays.

**Fujairah Intl**
**Marine Club**
*Fujairah*
*Map 1 F2*

## Scuba International

*09 222 0060* | *scubaint@emirates.net.ae*

Scuba International (PADI Five Star) offers activities for both divers and non-divers that include recreational dive charters, snorkelling trips and diver training (Discover Scuba dive costs Dhs.300). They can also arrange modern dhow excursions, sundowner cruises, and day trips.

**Sana Bld**
*Al Karama*
*Map 8 D4*

## Scubatec

*04 334 8988* | *www.scubatec.net*

Scubatec is a Five Star IDC licenced by PADI and TDI. Lessons are provided in Arabic, English, German or Urdu, and the company offers a full range of courses from beginner to instructor level. A variety of dive trips is available in Dubai and on the east coast.

**Shj Wanderers**
*Sharjah*
*Map 2 F2* 169

## Sharjah Wanderers Dive Club

*06 566 2105* | *www.sharjahwanderers.com*

Sharjah Wanderers Dive Club is part of Sharjah Wanderers Sports Club, which means that members automatically get to benefit from other sporting and social activities. The club is a member of the British Sub Aqua Club and follows its training, certification and diving practices. Clubhouse facilities include a training room, social area, equipment room, compressors, dive gear and two dive boats.

## Dragon Boat Racing

**Le Meridien**
**Mina Seyahi**
*Al Sufouh*
*Map 5 C1*

## Dubai Flying Dragons

*www.dubaidragons.com*

Light sleeper? Fancy getting out of bed before the sun rises for a bit of on-water action, Chinese style? If so, Dubai Flying Dragons has your name all over it. Training sessions in the ancient eastern sport of dragon boat racing are held several mornings a week, or if you can't face the early start, on a Saturday evening. It's a good way to be sociable (through regular get togethers) as well as to get yourself extremely fit, and for the serious there is also the opportunity to participate in international dragon boat competitions.

**337**

## Drama Groups

*Performances at*
*DUCTAC*
*Al Barsha*
*Map 6 A3*

### Dubai Drama Group
*www.dubaidramagroup.org*
The DDG has recently enjoyed a renaissance and now performs at the Community Theatre in the Mall of the Emirates (DUCTAC). Members range from actors, singers and dancers, to behind the scenes personnel like directors, costumiers, writers and scene shifters. Four productions are staged each year, and there are workshops, monthly social events, and an internet forum.

*Dubai Media City*
*Al Sufouh*
*Map 5 C2*

### Scenez Group
*04 391 5290* | *www.scenezgroup.com*
Dubai's arts scene is promising, and new ways to get involved occasionally spring up. Scenez group offers budding talent the opportunity to get involved in theatre and production through its workshops and events. Young actors between 6 and 16 can experience the world behind the scenes and onstage with courses featuring scriptwriting, costume design, acting and mime. Previous performances have included The Wizard of Oz at The Dubai Community Theatre & Arts Centre (DUCTAC), and even involved workshops in juggling and clownery.

## Dune Buggy Driving
Other options **Karting** p.352, **Quad Bikes** p.366

Bouncing over the dunes in a buggy is exhilarating, addictive, and definitely one of the best ways to experience the desert. Popular in just about every area of desert close to roads at the weekend, a particularly busy location is behind Al Ain airport, where locals and expats go to take advantage of the wide open spaces. Desert Rangers in Dubai offer dune buggy tours, where you can enjoy all the thrills and spills of this extreme sport in the safest possible way – they provide training, all the safety equipment you'll need, and an experienced leader to guide you through the dunes. Alternatively, you can hire quad bikes from independent companies, most commonly found at the 'Big Red' area on the road from Dubai to Hatta. Unlike dune buggies though, quad bikes have no roll bar so be very careful – accidents do occur. The area around this landmark sand dune gets pretty crazy on Fridays, when off-roading enthusiasts head there in large numbers for a bit of dune bashing.

*Dubai Garden Centre*
*Al Quoz*
*Map 6 B3*

### Desert Rangers
*04 340 2408* | *www.desertrangers.com*
After a brief safety lecture you will be taken on a buggy drive through a series of desert dunes. Desert Rangers promise to make this an unforgettable experience while ensuring safety is a top priority. This is not to be mistaken for quad biking which has clocked up a few unsurprising accidents over the years. Safaris can be combined with a BBQ dinner at an Arabic campsite. Costs start at Dhs.385 per person.

## Environmental Groups
Other options **Voluntary & Charity Work** p.102

People don't generally chain themselves to palms or dunes here, but over the last few years environmental issues have gradually become more

| Environmental Groups | |
|---|---|
| American Women's Association | 050 725 7652 |
| British Community Assistance Fund | 04 337 1413 |
| Club for Canadians | 04 355 6171 |
| Egyptian Club | 04 336 6709 |
| German Speaking Women's Club | 050 459 1885 |
| Indian Association | 04 351 1082 |
| Italian Cultural Association | 050 684 2310 |
| Norwegian Centre | 04 337 0062 |

**Scenez Arts & Drama Academy**
*Young actors and thespians now have a chance to show off and build on their talents with this new academy. Youngsters aged 6 to 12 go through a series of practical courses in acting, mime, script writing, backstage management, and costume designing. One – hour courses take place twice weekly, and culminate in a public performance. For details call 050 356 2709.*

important in the UAE. However, as is always the case, far more needs to be done by all sections of the community. Leading the way, HH Sheikh Mohammed bin Rashid Al Maktoum, Crown Prince of Dubai, has established a prestigious international environmental award in honour of HH Sheikh Zayed bin Sultan Al Nahyan, late President of the UAE. The award, which was first presented in 1998, goes to an individual or organisation for distinguished work carried out on behalf of the environment.

On an everyday level there are increasing numbers of glass and plastic recycling points around the city. *The Khaleej Times* sponsors bins for collecting newspapers for recycling; these are easily spotted at a variety of locations, but mainly outside shopping centres.

In addition, the government of Dubai is gradually taking action with school educational programmes and general awareness campaigns. However, overall, there seems to be very little done to persuade the average person to be more active environmentally, for instance by encouraging the reduction of littering.

If you want to take action contact one of the environmental groups that operate in the Emirates. These range from the Emirates Environmental Group to the flagship Arabian Leopard Trust. They always need volunteers and funds.

*Emirates Academy* ◀
*Opp. Wild Wadi*
*Jumeira*
*Map 6 B2*

## Dubai Natural History Group
*04 349 4816 | valeriechalmers@hotmail.com*

Dubai Natural History Group was formed to promote interest in flora, fauna, geology, archaeology and the natural environment of the Emirates. Meetings are held on the first Sunday of each month and speakers give lectures on a range of natural history topics. Regular trips are organised and the group maintains a library of natural history publications. Annual membership costs Dhs.100 for families and Dhs.50 for individuals.

*Crowne Plaza* ◀
*Trade Centre 1*
*Map 7 F2*

## Emirates Environmental Group
*04 331 8100 | www.eeg-uae.org*

This is a voluntary, non-governmental organisation devoted to protecting the environment through education, action programmes and community involvement. Current members include individuals and corporate members, schools and government organisations. Activities include regular evening lectures on environmental topics, and special events such as recycling collections and clean-up campaigns. Annual membership costs Dhs.50 for adults and Dhs.20 to 30 for students.

## Fencing

*Mina A'Salam* ◀
*Umm Suqeim*
*Map 6 A1*

## Dubai Fencing Club
*04 050794 4190 | www.dubaifencingclub.com*

The Dubai Fencing Club is the first club of its kind in the UAE, providing individual and group training sessions in Epee and Foil for adults and juniors of any level. Training is conducted by experienced fencing coaches. All fencers receive the necessary basic equipment such as masks, gloves and weapons. For advanced fencers, the club offers three fencing paths with electrical scoring systems and electrical weapons. The club meets at Madinat Jumeirah, in the Quay Health Club in Mina A'Salam Hotel.

## Fishing
Other options **Crab Hunting** p.328, **Boat & Yacht Charters** p.277

Fishing has become increasingly popular in the region in recent years, and subsequently the government has introduced regulations to protect fish stocks off the UAE coast. However, you can still fish, as long as you have the right permit or you

**339**

charter a licensed tour guide. The most productive fishing season lasts from September to April, although it is still possible to catch sailfish and queenfish in the summer months. Fish commonly caught in the waters off Dubai include king mackerel, tuna, trevally, bonito, kingfish, cobia and dorado or jacks.

Beach and surf fishing is popular along the coast, and in season you can even catch barracuda from the shore. Any beach along the Dubai coastline will be a reasonable fishing spot, and you should definitely try fishing from the end of the promenade on the Jumeira Beach Corniche. The creek front in Creekside Park is also popular, although you may want to think twice before putting these fish on the barbie! Alternatively, on a Friday, you could hire an abra for the morning (either at the Bur Dubai or Deira landing steps) and ask your driver to take you out to the mouth of the creek for a bit of fishing. Always agree on a price before you leave. If you want to splash out you could consider a deep-sea fishing trip with one of the charter companies listed.

## Bounty Charters

*Various locations*

*050 552 6067* | *bountycharters@hotmail.com*

Bounty Charters has a fully equipped 36 foot Yamaha Sea Spirit game fishing boat captained by Richard Forrester, an experienced game fisherman from South Africa. The company offers full day sailfish sessions, half day bottom fishing or night fishing charters as well three to five-day trips to the Musandam Peninsula.

## Club Joumana

*Jebel Ali Htl*
*Jebel Ali*
*Map 2 D4*

*04 883 6000* | *www.jebelali-international.com*

Four and eight-hour fishing trips are available for up to seven people per boat. The captain, tackle, equipment, soft drinks, water, Danish pastries and croissants are included as part of the package as you try to catch barracuda, lemonfish, trevally, hammour and kingfish. Call for current prices.

## Dubai Creek Golf & Yacht Club

*Opp Deira City*
*Centre Mall*
*Al Garhoud*
*Map 11 B4*

*04 295 6000* | *www.dubaigolf.com*

Take a trip on the club's Sneakaway Yacht into the Arabian Gulf and experience big game sports fishing. The fully equipped 32ft Hatteras carries up to six passengers and rates include tackle, bait, ice, fuel and a friendly crew. Trips cost Dhs.2,550 for four hours, Dhs.3,150 for six hours and Dhs.3,550 for eight hours .

## Dubai Voyager

*Fishermen Port 2*
*Jumeira*
*Map 6 C2*

*04 348 1900* | *www.dubaivoyager.com*

Based at the Fishing Village in Umm Suqeim, this company operates a fleet of reliable and fully equipped fishing boats, captained by qualified and experienced South African crew. Full safety gear is installed. Soft drinks, water, ice, bait and all fishing gear is supplied. Rates are Dhs.2,000 for four hours (morning or afternoon), Dhs.2,500 for six hours (morning or afternoon) or Dhs.3,000 for eight hours (full day). Alternative contact: 050 886 6227.

## Le Meridien Mina Seyahi

*Al Sufouh Rd*
*Al Sufouh*
*Map 5 C1*

*04 399 3333* | *www.lemeridien-minaseyahi.com*

Fishing trips take place on the custom-built Ocean Explorer and Ocean Luhr. Sailfish are the main prize, and Le Meridien Mina Seyahi supports the tag and release scheme. While you are welcome to bring your own gear, the boats are fully equipped with 20, 30 and 50 lb class tackle.

### Oceanic Hotel

*Beach Rd*
*Khor Fakkan*
*Map 1 F1*

09 238 5111 | *www.oceanichotel.com*

Fishing trips from the hotel head to a favourite local spot where catches are guaranteed. For hotel guests the catch of the day can then be cooked according to your taste by the hotel chef (a nominal cleaning fee is charged). Non-guests can take their catch home with them. The cost is Dhs.125 per person (minimum of six people per boat) for three hours and trips leave from 14:00 onwards.

## Flower Arranging

Other options **Gardens** p.427, **Flowers** p.426

### Ikebana Sogetsu Group

*Hamriya, Opp*
*Syrian Consulate*
*Al Hamriya*
*Map 12 A3*

04 262 0282 | *fujikozarouni@hotmail.com*

Ikebana is the art of Japanese flower arranging. Dubai's Ikebana Sogetsu Group was formed by Sogetsu members in 2000, and attempts to deepen cultural understanding among the city's multinational society through exhibitions, demonstrations and workshops. Classes are taught by Fujiko Zarouni, a qualified teacher from Japan.

## Flying

Other options **Hot Air Ballooning** p.282, **Plane Tours** p.286

### Dubai Flying Association

*Dubai International*
*Airport*
*Al Garhoud*
*Map 11 F4*

04 351 9691

The Dubai Flying Association (DFA) is a registered, non-profit group that aims to provide flying time to members at cost price. Membership costs Dhs.500 per annum and the association welcomes UAE Private Pilot Licence holders to join. The DFA has also taken up operations at Umm Al Quwain Airfield, but please note that the DFA is not a flying school and does not offer sightseeing or pleasure flights.

### Emirates Flying School

*Terminal 2,*
*Dubai Int Airport*
*Al Twar*
*Map 14 A1*

04 299 5155 | *flying@eim.ae*

This flying school is the only approved flight training institution in Dubai. With six Piper aircraft, the school offers private and commercial pilot's licences, and will convert international licences to UAE licences. The average cost for a Private Pilot Licence course is Dhs.38,000. Gift vouchers (Dhs.500) are available for those interested in experiencing flying for the first time.

### Fujairah Aviation Centre

*Fujairah Int'l Airport*
*Fujairah*
*Map 1 F2*

09 222 4747 | *www.fujairahaviation.ae*

Fujairah Aviation Centre is accredited with Civil Aviation Authorities in the UAE and UK. Facilities include single and twin-engine training aircraft, an instrument flight simulator and a workshop for repairs. Training is offered for Private and Commercial Pilot Licences, instrument rating and multi-engine rating. The centre also offers pleasure flights and sightseeing tours, and has aircraft available for hire to licence holders.

*Flying over the desert*

Dubai – Ras Al
Khaimah Highway
Ras Al Khaimah
Map 1 E1

## Jazirah Aviation

07 244 6416 | www.uaeflyingclubs.com

Approved by the General Civil Aviation Authority, Jazirah Aviation club is dedicated solely to microlight/ultralight flying. They offer flight training courses as well as pleasure flights lasting from 10 minutes to an hour. A complete Microlight Pilot's Licence course, with around 25 hours flying time, will cost in the region of Dhs.8,000.

Umm Al Quwain
Airport
Map 1 E1

## Micro Aviation Club

04 050350 4289 | microaviation@hungary.org

Micro Aviation Club offers training courses in microlight flying, paragliding, and paramotoring. Their office is located at Dubai Men's College, within Dubai Academic City. Courses start from Dhs.3,500, with an annual registration fee of Dhs.250.

17km North of
UAQ on RAK Rd
Umm Al Quwain
Map 1 E1

## Umm Al Quwain Aeroclub

06 768 1447 | www.uaqaeroclub.com

The club offers flying, skydiving, skydive boogies, paramotors and helicopter training. The facilities include a variety of small aircraft, two runways, eight hangars with engineering services, a pilot's shop and a briefing room. Sightseeing tours are available in Cessna aircraft, with prices starting from Dhs.350 for 30 minutes.

## Football

Like most places around the world, football (or soccer) is a much-loved sport here in the emirates, and evenings and weekends will often witness impromptu games in parks, open areas, and even on the beach. If you fancy a kick-around, InSportz in Al Quoz has indoor five-a-side pitches, and some university campuses are willing to rent out their outdoor and five-a-side pitches. More details below, or see Sports Clubs on p.384. Gaelic Football fans should contact Dubai Celts GAA – their details can be found in Gaelic Games on p.343.

Various locations

## DHL Dubai Amateur Football League

050 458 1087 | www.dxb.leaguerepublic.com

The DHL Dubai Amateur Football League, also known as the 'Expat League', hosts 23 teams in two divisions. Teams compete in 11-a-side league and cup games between September and April at various locations, and seven-a-side games during the summer. If you're keen to pull on those boots once more, check out the different teams via the website.

Various locations

## Dubai Football Academy

04 282 4540 | www.esportsdubai.com

The Dubai Football Academy provides comprehensive training to youngsters in a fun and enjoyable environment, with training sessions held at various locations including the Dubai Country Club and Jumeira Primary School. Players are encouraged to join one of the teams competing in the Dubai Junior Football League. Full details of prices, schedules and venues can be found on the website, or alternatively contact Academy Director Gareth Mordey on 050 698 0048.

Various Locations

## Dubai Irish

050 465 1087 | hayes_conor@yahoo.ie

Dubai Irish consists of players of all nationalities and participates in the Dubai Amateur Football League. Despite competing in the more competitive division 1, the team welcomes all players to come out and train with them. Training sessions vary from week to week during the season depending on that week's game schedule.

**Jebel Ali Shooting Club**
*Jebel Ali*
*Map 3 A2*

## Dubai Women's Football Association
*050 396 5069 | dubaiwf@hotmail.com*

This is a seven-a-side league for women looking to play football, get fit and have fun. There are three divisions which cater for all levels of experience, but you will need to be over 16 years old to participate. Games are on different days of the week depending on which division you are in. They are always on the look out for new talent and welcome new players of all levels. If you are interested and would like some further information, call Philippa on the number above or Nehal on 050 454 3806.

*Beach football*

**Various locations**

## International Football Academy
*04 362 5231 | www.intlfootballacademy.com*

The International Football Academy offers high standards of football training by experienced FA-qualified coaches. Boys and girls of all ages are welcomed, with the academy providing tailored coaching programmes to schools and local communities as well as existing teams. The aim is to increase footballing skills, confidence and team building. The Operations Director is ex-professional footballer Sean O'Shea, while the training programmes are planned by respected coach and ex-Northern Ireland international Iain Dowie.

**Jumeirah Beach Hotel**
*Umm Suqeim*
*Map 6 B1*

## UAE English Soccer School of Excellence
*04 406 8800 | masty57@hotmail.com*

The ESSE now operates at four venues in Dubai – Safa Park, Jumeirah Primary School, Trade Centre Apartments and the Lakes Club at Emirates Hills. They have over 575 students enrolled, and the fees for each training session range from Dhs.35 to Dhs.45 depending on the age of the child and how many sessions you sign up for. Kids from 4 to 16 are welcome, and training takes place at various times throughout the week except Fridays. Speak to James on the above number for more info. The ESSE operates during school terms and camps are organised during the holidays.

## Gaelic Games

**Dubai Exiles**
*No Area Listed*
*Map 16 C3*

### Dubai Celts GAA
*www.dubaicelts.com*

Dubai Celts GAA Club holds games and organises training in men's and ladies' Gaelic football, hurling and camogie. In addition to monthly matches within the UAE, international tournaments are held in Bahrain (November) and Dubai (March) each year. Training sessions are held every Saturday and Tuesday at 19:00.

## Gardening

Other options **Gardens** p.427

**Shk Rashid, Villa 52, Street 6C**
*Jumeira*
*Map 7 B2*

### Dubai Gardening Group
*04 344 5999 | bomi@eim.ae*

The Dubai Gardening Group was established in 2000 and aims to share its love and knowledge of gardening in a friendly and informal atmosphere. During the cooler months, trips to greenhouses, nurseries and members' gardens are arranged. Speakers, who are experts in various fields, address the meetings and, where possible, give practical demonstrations.

**343**

## Golf

Dubai is fast becoming one of the world's premier golfing destinations, with excellent weather and top class facilities. The number of international standard courses grows every year, with recent additions including Al Badia within Festival City and the Arabian Ranches Golf Club.

Emirates Golf Club hosts the annual Dubai Desert Classic tournament, which is part of the European PGA Tour and attracts such big names as Tiger Woods, Ernie Els, Ian Woosnam and Colin Montgomerie. There are also several local monthly tournaments and annual  competitions open to all, such as the Emirates Mixed Amateur Open, the Emirates Ladies' Amateur Open (handicap of 21 or less), and the Emirates Men's Amateur Open (handicap of five or less).

Dubai Golf operates a central reservation system for those wishing to book a round of golf on any of the major courses in the emirate. For further information visit www.dubaigolf.com or email booking@dubaigolf.com.

The future looks good for Dubai's golfers too; Nakheel is working with Greg Norman to develop six new courses based within residential communities, and Golf World at Dubailand promises four 18-hole courses plus an academy and driving ranges.

**Festival City**
**Ras Al Khor**
*Deira*
*Map 13 D3*

### Al Badia Golf Resort

*04 232 5778 | www.albadiagolfresort.com*

Al Badia was designed by world-renowned golf course designer Robert Trent Jones II. Lying at the heart of the Festival City project beside the creek, this new golf resort enjoys great views over the Dubai skyline. The 7,250 yard Par 72 Championship Course has extensive water features including 11 lakes, as well as a very plush clubhouse, and the grass used is salt-tolerant, meaning it can be irrigated with sea water.

**Arabian Ranches**
*Map 2 E4* **32**

### Arabian Ranches Golf Club ▶ p.345

*04 366 3000 | www.arabianranchesgolfdubai.com*

Designed by Ian Baker-Finch in association with Nicklaus Design, this par 72 grass course uses the natural desert terrain and features indigenous shrubs and bushes. Facilities include a Golf Academy with floodlit driving range, an extensive short game practice area, and GPS on all golf carts. Within the clubhouse there is the Ranches Restaurant and Bar as well as 11 luxury guest rooms overlooking either the golf course or the lake. Bookings can be made via the website and reservations are open 24 hours, seven days a week

*Montgomerie Golf Club*

*Emirates Golf Club*

# A MEMORABLE GOLFING EXPERIENCE

**ARABIAN RANCHES GOLF CLUB DUBAI**

## ARABIAN RANCHES GOLF CLUB - DUBAI'S GOLFING PARADISE

Designed by Ian Baker-Finch Signature Golf Courses in association with Nicklaus Design - it doesn't get better than this. The Arabian Ranches Clubhouse is open for reservations 24 hours, 7 days a week. Enjoy an unforgettable game of golf on the 18 hole par 72 Golf Course and relax in one of our 11 luxurious Guest Rooms with beautiful views overlooking either the Golf Course or the lake. An ideal place to stay and play all year round.

For further details and reservations please call **04 366 3000** or alternatively request a booking online at **www.arabianranchesgolfdubai.com**

**EMAAR**

## Dubai Creek Golf & Yacht Club

*Opp Deira City*
*Centre Mall*
*Al Garhoud*
*Map 11 B4*

*04 295 6000* | *www.dubaigolf.com*

The Creek Golf & Yacht Club has recently undergone a major redevelopment, with a challenging new front nine redesigned by Thomas Björn. The par 71 championship course is open to all players holding a valid handicap certificate, and those who are new to the game are encouraged to join the Golf Academy manned by PGA-qualified golf instructors. There is also a new nine-hole par three course, a floodlit driving range and extensive short game practice facilities, and the iconic clubhouse has undergone extensive refurbishment too.

## Emirates Golf Club

*Int 5, Shk Zayed Rd*
*Media City*
*Emirates Hills*
*Map 5 C3*

*04 380 2222* | *www.dubaigolf.com*

Emirates Golf Club has two 18 hole championship courses to choose from. The 6,857 yard, par 71 Majlis Course was the first grass course in the Middle East and plays host to the annual Dubai Desert Classic. The Wadi Course reopened in October 2006 after undergoing a major redesign by Nick Faldo and IMG Design. The club also offers the Peter Cowen Golf Academy, along with two driving ranges and dedicated practice areas.

## Montgomerie Golf Club ▶ p.347

*The Montgomerie*
*Emirates Hills*
*Map 5 B3*

*04 390 5600* | *www.themontgomerie.com*

The Montgomerie is set on 200 acres of land and was designed by Colin Montgomerie and Desmond Muirhead. The 18 hole, par 72 course has some unique characteristics, including the mammoth 656 yard 18th hole. Golfing facilities include a driving range, putting greens, a floodlit par three course and a swing analysis studio, while the newly opened clubhouse boasts guest rooms, a spa, and various bars and restaurants.

## Nad Al Sheba Club

*Nad Al Sheba*
*Nad Al Sheba*
*Map 2 E3*

*04 336 3666* | *www.nadalshebaclub.com*

Nad Al Sheba club was the first fully floodlit 18 hole golf course in the Middle East, and golfers can stay out on the course until midnight every night. The club shares its location with the famous horse racing venue, and the back nine are actually situated within the perimeter fence of the racecourse. The golf course and popular clubhouse have both undergone refurbishment and redevelopment, and the golf academy offers a range of courses including the chance to 'learn golf in a week.'

## The Resort Course

*Jebel Ali Hotel*
*Jebel Ali*
*Map 2 D4*

*04 883 6000* | *www.jebelali-international.com*

Situated in the landscaped gardens of the Jebel Ali Golf Resort and Spa, this nine hole, par 36 course offers golfers the opportunity to play alongside peacocks and with views of the Gulf. Renowned for its good condition all year round, the Resort Course is also home to the Jebel Ali Golf Resort & Spa Challenge, the curtain raiser to the annual Dubai Desert Classic.

## Sharjah Golf & Shooting Club

*Nr University City*
*Sharjah*
*Map 2 F2*

*06 548 7777* | *www.golfandshootingshj.com*

Offering a range of membership options Sharjah Golf and Shooting Club is a great option for a spot of out-of-town golf. The club offers a range of membership options from Dhs.3,000 to Dhs.9,500 per annum. A top end membership provides access to all club facilities, unlimited midweek golf and use of the academy throughout the week, while budget-priced options allow you access to the driving range, short game area and putting range academy throughout the week and a 20% discount on green fees.

# At The Montgomerie, Dubai, you are never just a visitor.

We pride ourselves on providing you, our VIP Guest, with a seamless 5-star experience, whether it be playing our Colin Montgomerie-designed championship golf course, staying in our stylish 20-room boutique hotel, dining in our award winning restaurant, enjoying a private golf clinic, or luxuriating in the Angsana Spa. We make it our responsibility to ensure that you want for nothing from the moment you arrive.

CREATING EXTRAORDINARY EXPERIENCES

THE
## MONTGOMERIE
DUBAI

P.O. Box 36700, Dubai, UAE   Tel +9714 390 5600   Fax +9714 360 8981
Email info@themontgomerie.ae   www.themontgomerie.com

TROON GOLF ®

*Emirates Golf Club*
*Emirates Hills*
*Map 5 C3*

## UAE Golf Association

*04 399 5060 | www.ugagolf.com*

This non-profit organisation is the governing body for amateur golf in the UAE. It is overseen by the General Authority of Youth & Sports and actively supports junior players and the development of the national team. The Affiliate Membership rate is Dhs.200 for a year, and the UGA Handicap Scheme costs Dhs.595. The website has a comprehensive calendar of forthcoming events.

## Gymnastics & Trampolining

*Various locations*

## DuGym

*050 553 6283 | www.dugym.com*

DuGym offers gymnastics and trampoline coaching to children of all ages and abilities. Established by Suzanne Wallace in 2000, the club now operates at a number of locations including the Dubai Country Club, Jumeirah English Speaking School and Emirates International School. Classes are held from Sunday to Thursday – contact Suzanne on the above number for more details.

*Villa 520, Jumeira*
*Beach Rd*
*Jumeira*
*Map 6 F1*

## My Gym

*04 394 3962 | www.my-gym.com/dubai*

If you are looking for innovative ways to get the kids active, My Gym offers a range of activities to keep your tots on their toes. My Gym offers a variety of events ranging from 'Mommy and Me' programmes for babies aged six weeks and up to gymnastics, dance and general fitness alongside fun-filled private birthday parties and camps; children up to the age of 13 can participate. A two hour per week class and play session will cost Dhs.1,000 for 10 weeks. Parents can also participate in classes with their children if preferred, but independent classes are offered.

## Hashing

Other options **Running** p.367, **Pubs** p.588

Sometimes described as drinking clubs with a running problem, the Hash House Harriers are a worldwide family of social running clubs. The aim of running in this setup is not to win, but to merely be there and to take part. The original club was formed in Kuala Lumpur in 1938 and is now the largest running organisation in the world. Hashing consists of running, jogging or walking around varied courses, often cross-country, laid out by a couple of 'hares'. It's a fun way to keep fit and meet new people, since the clubs are invariably very sociable affairs.

*Various locations*

## Barbie Hash House

*04 348 4210 | hasher@deserthash.net*

Meeting on the first Wednesday of every month (except in summer), this is a girls only gathering with a Barbie theme, which means pink dress code with a tiara. Each time around 20 to 25 members get together for a social evening that involves hashing, champagne, a meal and singing their Barbie song. Cost is Dhs.10.

*Various locations*

## Creek Hash House Harriers

*04 050451 5847 | www.creekhash.net*

This is a men only hash that meets each Tuesday in a different location. Start times are usually 45 minutes before sunset and runs last 40 to 50 minutes. Further information can be obtained from Ian Browning on the above number or Richard Holmes (050 644 4285). Information on weekly runs can be obtained at www.creekhash.net.

*Various locations* ◄ Desert Hash House Harriers

*050 454 2635*

The Desert Hash House Harriers meet every Sunday evening at various locations around Dubai. Runs start an hour before sunset and last about 50 minutes. Fees are Dhs.50 for men and Dhs.30 for women and include food and beverages. Contact Stuart Wakeham (above number) for details, or try Alan Permain on 050 457 1603.

*Various locations* ◄ Moonshine Hash House Harriers

*050 850 3662*

Moonshine Hash House Harriers run once a month on the night of the full moon. The run/walk creates a thirst, which is then quenched upon return to the alehouse for traditional hash ceremonies. Fees are Dhs.10 per hash. Contact Talga on the above number for details.

## Hiking

Other options **Outdoor Goods** p.441, **Out of Dubai** p.290

Despite Dubai's flat terrain, spectacular hiking locations can be found just an hour outside the city limits. To the north, the Ru'us Al Jibal Mountains contain the highest peaks in the area and stand proud at over 2,000 metres. To the east, the impressive Hajar Mountains form the border between the UAE and Oman, stretching from the Musandam Peninsula to the Empty Quarter Desert, hundred of kilometres to the south.

Most of the terrain is heavily eroded due to the harsh climate, but there are still places where you can walk through shady palm plantations and lush oases. Routes range from short, easy walks leading to spectacular viewpoints, to all-day treks over difficult terrain, and can include major mountaineering. Some hikes follow centuries old Bedouin and Shihuh mountain paths, a few of which are still being used.

One of the nearest and easiest places to reach is the foothills of the Hajar Mountains on the Hatta Road, near the border of Oman. After passing through the desert, the flat stark, rugged outcrops transform the landscape. Explore any turning you like, or take the road to Mahdah, along which you'll find several options.

Other great areas for hiking and exploring include Al Ain and its surroundings, many places in Wadi Bih (the mountainous route from Ras Al Khaimah to Dibba), and the mountains near the east coast. The mountains in the UAE don't generally disappoint, and the further off the beaten track you get, the more likely you are to find interesting villages where residents live much the same way as they did centuries ago.

For somewhere a bit further afield see the *Oman Trekking Explorer*, a guide book with

*Hiking in the Hajars*

pull-out maps covering major signed routes in Oman. As with any trip into the UAE 'outback', take sensible precautions. Tell someone where you are going and when you should be back and don't forget to take a map, compass, GPS equipment and robust hiking boots. Don't underestimate the strength of the sun – take sunscreen, and most importantly, loads of water. For most people, the cooler and less humid winter months are the best season for serious mountain hiking. Be particularly careful in wadis (dry riverbeds) during the wet season as flash floods can immerse a wadi in seconds. Also note that there are no mountain rescue services in the UAE, so anyone venturing out into the mountains should be reasonably experienced or accompanied by someone who knows the area.

**349**

*Behind Dubai*
*Garden Centre*
*Al Quoz*
*Map 6 B3*

## Desert Rangers

*04 340 2408* | *www.desertrangers.com*

Desert Rangers offer hikes for individuals and groups of up to 100 people by dividing them into smaller teams and taking different trails to the summit. A variety of routes are offered according to age and fitness. Locations include Fujairah, Dibba, Masafi, Ras Al Khaimah and Al Ain, with prices starting at Dhs.275 per person.

## Hockey

Other options **Ice Hockey** p.351

*Kings School*
*Umm Suqeim*
*Map 6 B2*

## Dubai Hockey Club

*055 966 8762* | *www.dubaihockeyclub.com*

Dubai Hockey Club (DXBHC) is made up of men and woman of all abilities and from all around the world (members hail from Ireland, England, Australia, Holland, South Africa, Canada, and elsewhere).

Matches take place on Sunday, Tuesday and Wednesday evenings at 20:00 on a floodlit pitch. The Club also plays in local tournaments on grass as well as arranging friendly matches throughout the year. Annual international tours are also organised to locations such as Singapore, Hong Kong, and the UK.

*Shj Wanderers*
*Sharjah*
*Map 2 F2* **169**

## Sharjah Wanderers Hockey Club

*06 566 2105* | *www.sharjahwanderers.com*

The club was born as a part of the Sharjah Contracts Club in 1976. The hockey section became the first mixed team in the Gulf, and has always retained a strong mixed club atmosphere. The approach at the club is to play sport within a friendly, but competitive, environment.

## Horse Riding

Other options **Polo** p.366

*Jebel Ali Htl*
*Jebel Ali*
*Map 2 D4*

## Club Joumana

*04 883 6000* | *www.jebelali-international.com*

Located at Jebel Ali Golf Resort and Spa, this riding centre has five horses, air-conditioned stables and a paddock overlooking the Arabian Gulf. Keith Brown, the resident riding instructor, gives half-hour private lessons from Tuesday to Sunday, and one-hour desert rides can be arranged for experienced riders. The stables are closed during the summer months.

*Various locations*

## The Desert Equestrian Club

*050 309 9770*

Horse lovers will be hard pushed to beat the excitement of being out there among the dunes, galloping over sandy tracks with the camels. Riders will be back at the stables before sundown, gritty, exhilarated and with colour in their cheeks, ready to give the horses a much-needed hose down. If you've got your own horse, the Desert Equestrian Club offers livery services for Dhs.1,500 a month, while accomplished riders can pay Dhs.100 to take one of the stable's horses out for a jaunt (accompanied by a member of staff so there's no fear of not finding your way back). Those keen to learn can take a private lesson for Dhs.80 for adults (approximately 30 minutes long) and Dhs.50 for children under 16. During the hottest months, the hours are from 06:00 until 08:00 and from 18:00 until 21:00, Monday to Saturday. Contact Anna on the above number for bookings or further information.

### Dubai Polo & Equestrian Club

*Arabian Ranches*
*Emirates Rd*
*Map 2 E3*

*04 361 8111* | *www.poloclubdubai.com*

Located near the Arabian Ranches off Emirates Road, this riding centre has five horses, air-conditioned stables and a paddock overlooking the Arabian Gulf. Keith Brown, the resident riding instructor, gives half-hour private lessons from Tuesday to Sunday, and one-hour desert rides can be arranged for experienced riders. The stables are closed during the summer months.

### Emirates Riding Centre

*Nr Camel Race Track*
*Nad Al Sheba*
*Map 2 E3*

*04 336 1394* | *emrc@eim.ae*

The Emirates Riding Centre has 147 horses and the facilities include an international size floodlit arena, riding school, dressage and lunging ring. It's also possible to take along children and small toddlers and let them have a ride. The club hosts at least two competitions and three riding school shows per month, as well as gymkhanas from October to May. The centre also has regular clinics and stable management courses.

### Jebel Ali Equestrian Club

*Jebel Ali Village*
*Jebel Ali*
*Map 4 C3*

*04 884 5566* | *jaridingclub@yahoo.com*

Fully qualified instructors teach children and adults, from beginner to advanced levels, at Jebel Ali Equestrian Club. For more experienced riders, dressage, jumping and hacking are on offer, and gymkhana games, with competitions, are held on a regular basis. Newcomers can try a one-day lesson, after which a 10-lesson package will cost Dhs.500 for children and Dhs.800 for adults, plus a Dhs.120 annual registration fee.

### Sharjah Equestrian & Racing Club

*Jct 6, Al Dhaid Rd*
*Sharjah*
*Map 2 F2*

*06 531 1155* | *www.forsanuae.org.ae*

This riding centre was built in 1984 under the supervision of Sheikh Sultan bin Mohammed Al-Qassimi, member of the Supreme Council and Ruler of Sharjah. Facilities include a floodlit sand arena and paddock, a grass show jumping arena and hacking trails into the desert. The club houses 250 horses, and riding must be arranged by appointment. Annual membership is Dhs.1,000 per person, or Dhs.2,000 for a family. Membership benefits include discounted riding lessons, plus preferential rates at the club's hotel, chalets, and recreational facilities.

## Ice Hockey

Other options **Ice Skating** p.352

### Dubai Mighty Camels Ice Hockey Club

*Al Nasr Leisureland*
*Oud Metha*
*Map 10 E2*

*04 050450 0180* | *www.dubaimightycamels.com*

Ice hockey has been a fixture on the local sports scene ever since Al Nasr Leisureland opened in 1979. The club presently has over 120 members and has regular social get-togethers from September to May. The club also hosts an annual tournament in April, which regularly attracts up to 20 teams from the Gulf, Europe and the Far East.

### Dubai Sandstorms Ice Hockey Club

*Al Nasr Leisureland*
*Oud Metha*
*Map 10 E2*

*04 344 1885* | *www.dubaisandstorms.com*

This club was established to provide boys and girls (6 to 18 years) with the opportunity to learn how to play ice hockey. The club's emphasis is on teamwork and sportsmanship, and previous experience is not necessary. Practice sessions are held twice a week and matches are played against teams from Dubai, Abu Dhabi, Al Ain and Oman. For further details email Robin Proctor on rproctor@eim.ae.

**351**

## Ice Skating

Other options **Ice Hockey** p.351

*Behind American Hospital*
*Oud Metha*
*Map 10 E2*

### Al Nasr Leisureland

*04 337 1234 | www.alnasrleisureland.ae*

Open to the public (except when in use by clubs), the rink is part of the Leisureland complex that comprises a bowling alley, fast food outlets, arcade games and shops. Entrance fees are Dhs.10 for adults and Dhs.5 for children under 10, while skate rental charges are Dhs.10 for two hours. The ice rink opens for two-hour sessions at a time, starting at 10:00, 13:00, 16:00 and 19:00.

*Nr Hyatt Regency*
*Deira*
*Map 9 D1*

### Galleria Ice Rink

*04 209 6550*

Located in the centre of a shopping mall, the Galleria Ice Rink is a busy place. Fees for public sessions are Dhs.25 per person (including skate hire) or Dhs.15 if you have your own skates.

*Catching air*

Membership rates start at Dhs.300 per month, or Dhs.1,200 per year, and members are entitled to unlimited skating. Lessons are available for non-members and start at Dhs.80 per half hour.

## Jetskiing

Other options **Beach Clubs** p.384

Officially, jetskiing has been shut down in Dubai, primarily to maintain the peace and quiet, and also to protect swimmers and avoid accidents. Keen jetskiers have been waiting for the Municipality's review of the situation for some time. However, in the meantime, unofficial operators are still hiring out jetskis from Mamzar Lagoon. If you do manage to get your hands on a machine in Dubai waters, it may be worth checking that your medical insurance covers you for this potentially dangerous sport before you rev away, as accidents do happen. You may also want to consider whether you have any personal liability insurance in case you injure a third party.

## Karting

Other options **Dune Buggy Driving** p.338

*Nr Arabian Ranches*
*Dubailand*
*Map 2 E4*

### Dubai Autodrome

*04 367 8700 | www.dubaiautodrome.com*

Wannabe Alonsos of any age or gender should head to this new Kartdrome to burn some rubber and let off steam. After a safety briefing you'll take to your powerful 390cc kart (there are smaller 120cc karts for the kids) and hit the tarmac on the exciting 1.2km circuit. Each kart has a transponder allowing you to see the overall winners and losers, and lap times. With overalls, gloves and helmets supplied, it's a great option for parties or team-building exercises. Those with their very own karts can also use the track at certain times of the week, and full garaging and maintenance packages are available.

**Nr Jebel Ali**
**Golf Resort & Spa**
*Jebel Ali*
*Map 2 D4*

## Emirates Kart Centre

*04 282 7111 | www.emsf.ae*

Operated by the Emirates Motor Sports Federation, this kart centre has a floodlit, 0.8km track with straights, hairpins and chicanes. Professional and junior karts are available, and you can take part regularly without buying any equipment. The centre is open seven days a week.

## Kayaking

Other options **Canoeing** p.327

**Al Aqah, Btn Dibba**
**& Khorfakkan**
*Fujairah*
*Map 1 F1*

## Sandy Beach Hotel & Resort

*09 244 5555 | www.sandybm.com*

The Beach Hut at Sandy Beach offers a variety of watersports equipment for rent or sale. For those who want to paddle out to Snoopy Island, single kayaks are available for hire at Dhs.30 per hour, or you could go for a two-seater for Dhs.50. It's a great way to see the abundant marine life (including the occasional turtle and shark) without getting too wet.

## Kickboxing

Other options **Martial Arts** p.359, **Thai Boxing** p.379

**Emirates Towers**
*Shk Zayed Rd*
*Map 7 F3*

## Raifet N Shawe

*050 495 4446 | rifshawe@emirates.net.ae*

Raifet Shawe has been teaching kickboxing professionally for around 10 years. Currently a Black Belt 4th Dan in karate and kickboxing and a black beld in Judo, his methods of teaching include forms of karate, kickboxing and muay thai. Classes are thorough, concise and most importantly, enjoyable. Beginners will find themselves learning quickly, especially if attending his three weekly classes held at the Big Apple gym in the Emirates Towers (04 319 8660). Group classes are held on Mondays, Wednesdays and Saturdays from 17:30 to 18:30. Rates are reasonable and class length is usually an hour. Contact him directly for further information or to set up private classes.

## Kitesurfing

Other options **Beaches** p.267

Kitesurfing is an extreme sport that is swiftly gaining popularity. It's not windsurfing, it's not wakeboarding, it's not surfing and it's not kite flying. In fact, it's a fusion of all these disciplines, with a few other influences thrown in for good measure. At the moment kiting is allowed on the stretch of beach near the old Wollongong University premises, but is most popularly practised at the Jebel Ali Public Beach, on the left-hand side of the Jebel Ali Hotel. You'll need a licence too. The rules and regulations are prone to change without warning, so check with the Dubai Kite Club for the latest info.

*Kitesurfing*

353

Activities

## Dubai Kite Club

*DIMC*
*Al Sufouh*
*Map 5 B1*

*050 618 0612* | *www.dubaikiteclub.com*

The Dubai Kite Club regulates the sport of kitesurfing, mountain board kiting, power kiting and display kiting. To kitesurf in Dubai you are now required to hold a licence – the police carry out spot-checks and may punish offenders. Membership of DKC (Dhs.200 per year) automatically grants the licence, plus a number of other benefits such as third party liability insurance. To join you'll need passport copies and photos, a medical certificate from a clinic confirming that you're fit enough to participate in an extreme watersport, and a completed application form (available on the website). Take everything along to the office at DIMC and your membership card/licence will be ready within a week. For the latest information call the number above. You may also want to check out www.fatimasport.com when looking to buy equipment.

## Language Schools

Other options **Learning Arabic** p.222

## Alliance Française

*Opp Our Own English*
*High School*
*Umm Hurair*
*Map 10 E3*

*04 335 8712* | *www.afdubai.com*

The Alliance Française is a non-profit organisation supported by the French Government, with the goal of promoting French language and culture. The Alliance in Dubai offers special morning classes for ladies, afternoon classes for children and evening classes for everybody. It also offers Arabic language classes for foreigners. In addition, it offers evening French language classes for adults at the Lycée Georges Pompidou in Sharjah. Terms run from September to June, but intensive courses are also held during the summer for both adults and children. Alliance Française offers DEL/DALF and TEF degrees.

## Arabic Language Centre

*Trade Centre*
*Trade Centre 2*
*Map 10 A1*

*04 308 6036* | *alc@dwtc.com*

A division of the Dubai World Trade Centre, this language school was established in 1980 to teach Arabic as a foreign language. Courses, from beginner to advanced levels, are held five times a year, last 30 hours, and cost Dhs.1,650 (inclusive of all materials). Specialist courses can be designed to meet the requirements of the hotel, banking, hospital, motor and electronics industries.

## Berlitz

*Nr Dubai Zoo*
*Jumeira*
*Map 7 E1*

*04 344 0034* | *www.berlitz.com*

The Berlitz method has helped more than 41 million people acquire a new language. A variety of language courses are offered and can be customised to fit specific requirements, such as 'English for banking' or 'technical English'. Instruction is in private or small groups, from kids to adults. Additional training includes translation and self-teaching. See the website for more details.

## British Council

*Nr Maktoum Bridge*
*Umm Hurair*
*Map 11 A2*

*04 337 0109* | *www.britishcouncil.org/uae*

The British Council is the world's largest education and cultural relations organisation. In the UAE there are three centres, in Dubai, Abu Dhabi and Sharjah. In addition to teaching English to adults, children, professionals and teacher training programmes, the British Council administers professional, academic and vocational examinations, and advises students looking for study opportunities in the UK. Students are supported by learning zones which provide multimedia learning resources, including a lending library and audio books, videos and DVDs, and access to the internet. From a creative

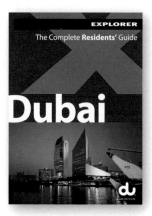
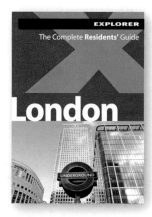
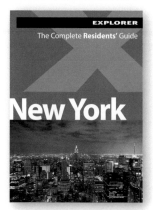

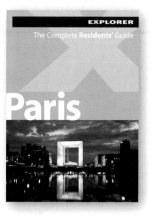

# Tired of writing your insider tips…

## …in a blog that nobody reads?

The Explorer Complete Residents' Guide series is growing rapidly, and we're always looking
for literate, resident writers to help pen our new guides. So whether you live in Tuscany or
Timbuktu, if writing's your thing, and you know your city inside out, we'd like to talk to you.

Apply online at www.explorerpublishing.com

Abu Dhabi · Amsterdam · Bahrain · Barcelona · Beijing · Berlin · Dubai · Dublin · Geneva
Hong Kong · Kuala Lumpur · Kuwait · London · Los Angeles · New York · New Zealand · Oman
Paris · Qatar · Shanghai · Singapore · Sydney · Tokyo · Vancouver

**EXPLORER**

www.explorerpublishing.com

perspective, the British Council is active in supporting arts, music, science and sports projects which help young people from the UAE and the UK to connect with each other. Call toll free 800 225522 or visit the website for more info.

## Dar El Ilm School of Languages

**Exhibition Hall 4**
*Trade Centre 1*
*Map 7 E3*

*04 331 0221 | darelilm@eim.ae*

Now in its seventeenth year, Dar El Ilm offers language courses to students of all ages and abilities, with an emphasis on making learning fun. Adult and children's tuition is offered in English, French, German, Italian, Spanish and Arabic. With fees starting at Dhs.900, adult courses last 15 hours and run eight times during the academic year. Lessons for children are also offered at Dhs.63 per hour.

## El Ewla Language Academy

**Knowledge Village,**
**Block 2B**
*Al Sufouh*
*Map 5 D2*

*04 391 1640 | elewlainfo@partners.kv.ae*

El Ewla, meaning 'the first' in Arabic, is a language and training institute. El Ewla's language programmes (Arabic, English, French) are offered to individuals, companies and government institutions. Classes focus on every language aspect including grammar, vocabulary, use of idioms and improving your accent and pronunciation. Special exam programmes and corporate packages are also available.

## ELS Language Center ▶ p.357

**Al Hai Bld**
*Deira*
*Map 11 D3*

*04 294 0740 | www.elsmea.com*

Sessions at ELS last four weeks and prices range from Dhs.2,100 for the standard 48 hour session, to Dhs.4,000 for a super intensive 100 hour session. Unlike traditional forms of English language instruction, ELS concentrates on applying language patterns through group work and problem solving. Along with their standard programmes, they offer a children's programme, TOEFL training and business English courses.

## Goethe-Institut German Language Center

**Nr Sea View Hotel**
*Bur Dubai*
*Map 8 E2*

*www.goethe.de/dubai*

The Goethe-Institut is Germany's cultural institution and operates worldwide. The Dubai centre provides German language courses, from beginner level upwards. Tailor-made courses can be designed to meet the specific need of educational and corporate institutions and companies. The centre also offers classes for teenagers and individual courses, as well as internationally recognised exams.

## Polyglot Language Institute

**Al Masaeed Bld,**
**Behind Radisson**
**SAS Hotel**
*Deira*
*Map 9 C4*

*04 222 3429 | www.polyglot.ae*

Polyglot Language Institute offers courses in modern languages, as well as secretarial and computer skills for individuals and companies. Courses offered include Arabic, general and business English, French, Spanish, Italian, German, TOEFL preparation, office skills, typing, and secretarial and computer studies. Courses last six to 10 weeks and all materials are provided. Courses range between Dhs.1,450 to 1,750.

## Libraries

Other options **Second-Hand Items** p.444, **Books** p.414

## Alliance Française

**Opp Our Own**
**English High School**
*Umm Hurair*
*Map 10 E3*

*04 335 8712 | www.afdubai.com*

The Alliance Française multimedia library has over 12,000 French books (including a children's section), plus 50 daily, weekly and monthly French newspapers and magazines, 2,000 videotapes, 150 CD-ROMs, 100 Audio CDs and 3,000 DVDs.

# ELS Language Centers
## The effective English language learning solution!

- **Improve conversation & writing skills**
  ### General English courses
- **Develop your child's confidence in English**
  ### Children's after-school & holiday classes
- **Enhance your business skills**
  ### Professional Business English
- **Prepare skills for test taking**
  ### iBT-TOEFL / IELTS preparation

Approved by the Ministry of Education.
All teachers are native English-speakers

enter sessions start every four weeks for all levels ● Tailor made business courses also available.

To register or to find out more, **call**

| | |
|---|---|
| Abu Dhabi | Tel : 02-6426640 |
| Dubai | Tel : 04-2940740 |
| Al Ain | Tel : 03-7623468 |
| Fujairah | Tel : 09-2244731 |

**Website : www.elsmea.com**

*We Teach English To The World*

## Archie's Library

*Pyramid Bld,*
*Nr Burjuman*
*Al Karama*
*Map 8 F4*

*04 396 7924 | abcl180@hotmail.com*

Archie's Library is stocked with 45,000 English fiction, non-fiction, classic, cooking, health and fitness, and management books. A selection of children's books and comics is also available, along with the latest magazines. The annual membership fee of Dhs.75 (plus a Dhs.100 refundable deposit) entitles you to borrow four books at a time for 14 days. Reading charges vary from Dhs.1 to Dhs.7. The library is open 365 days a year, and they also have a branch in Sharjah (06 572 5716).

## Dubai Municipality Public Libraries

*Various Locations*

*04 852 1022 | www.dm.gov.ae*

The Municipality is in the process of rebranding some of Dubai's public libraries as e-Libraries; look out for the big brown road signs directing you to the nearest branch. The e-Library in Umm Suqeim was the first, with many of the books having made way for banks of shiny new PCs, and it is now home to an ICDL training and test centre. The ICDL (International Computer Driving Licence) is a computer skills competency standard recognised around the world. Covering all aspects of computer use (such as file management, word processing, and spreadsheets), students take seven tests (one theoretical and six practical), and upon passing the course will receive a personalised certificate, or 'licence'. Contact the Umm Suqeim branch for details of fees and timings. Libraries also offer internet access – it's just Dhs.3 for one hour, or Dhs.5 for two hours, but members pay nothing.

It's not all computers though, as Dubai's libraries do still have selections of English language books to borrow. The Al Ras and Safa branches are perhaps your best bet. Library membership costs Dhs.200, but Dhs.150 of that is refundable. Family membership is Dhs.250 (including a refundable Dhs.200). To apply you'll need passport and visa copies, and photos.

The libraries website has a facility allowing you to search the entire catalogue, and you can even apply for membership online by uploading your photos and scanned copies of your passport.

A new public library has recently opened in Al Twar, and construction has just been completed on a further library in the Mankhool area.

Additionally, a new Central Library is planned. To be built on the banks of Al Mamzar Lagoon, this new building will resemble a huge book when complete.

Public library locations and contact numbers:

Al Ras (04 226 2788), Hatta (04 852 1022), Hor Al Anz (04 266 1788), Rashidiya (04 285 8065), Safa (04 394 7279), Umm Suqeim (04 348 9572), Union House (04 345 2929).

## Juma Al Majid Cultural & Heritage Centre

*Nr Dubai Cinema*
*Deira*
*Map 11 F1*

*04 262 4999 | info@almajidcenter.org*

This is a non-profit reference library and research institute that focuses on Islam. It has a collection of 500,000 cultural media items that range from heritage to current world issues, plus 3,000 periodicals and out of print publications. Books cannot be taken home, but you can use the reading room or make photocopies. There's no fee to use the library.

## Old Library, The

*Mall of the Emirates*
*Al Barsha*
*Map 6 A3* 19

*04 341 4777 | www.dubaitheatre.org*

The Old Library, established in 1969, is the oldest English language library serving the expatriate community in Dubai, and is now part of the Dubai Community Theatre & Arts Centre (DUCTAC), located near Magic Planet on the second level of the Mall of the Emirates. The library has a collection of over 13,000 adult fiction and reference books as well as an extremely well-stocked children's section and specialist sections for romance and the Middle East. Reading sessions for children are conducted on Saturday mornings. The Old Library is a non-profit making organisation run entirely by volunteers. New volunteers are always welcome to train as librarians or to assist with maintaining the book collection. Donations of second-hand books are always welcome, as funds raised from book sales and subscriptions are used to cover operational expenses and the purchase of new books.

Timings: 10:30 to 13:30, 15:00 to 19:00. Closed Fridays and public holidays.

## Martial Arts

Other options **Kickboxing** p.353, **Thai Boxing** p.379

Whether you're a black belt Bruce Lee wannabe or just fancy trying your hand at karate there are various fitness centres in Dubai where you can hone your martial arts skills, be it judo, which is a great form of self defence, or aikido, which combines joint locks and throws with the body movements of sword and spear. Check with the club to find out what disciplines they teach.

### Dubai Aikido Club

*Dubai Karate Centre*
*Al Wasl*
*Map 6 E2*

*04 344 7797 | www.aikido.ae*

Aikido is a self defence martial art that also trains the mind. The Dubai Aikido Club was established in 1995 and is affiliated with the International Aikido Association. Classes for both children and adults are held throughout the week at the Dubai Karate Centre. The membership fee is Dhs.200 for kids and Dhs.250 for adults. For further information contact John Rutnam, the chief instructor, on the above number.

### Dubai Karate Centre

*Nr Emirates Bank*
*Al Wasl*
*Map 6 E2*

*04 344 7797 | www.dubaikarate.com*

At the Dubai Karate Centre a team of black belt, JKA qualified instructors teach shotokan, taekwondo, aikido, muay thai and judo, and there are also courses in self defence. The club is a member of the Japanese Karate Association (JKA) and offers tuition for everyone from beginners to black belts. There is a Dhs.100 registration fee and Dhs.200 monthly membership fee.

### Golden Falcon Karate Centre

*Behind Sony Jumbo*
*Al Karama*
*Map 10 D1*

*04 336 0243 | www.goldenfalconkarate.com*

Established in 1990, this karate centre is affiliated to the International Karate Budokan and UAE Judo, Taekwondo and Karate Federation. The centre is open throughout the week and students can choose class times to suit their schedules. Official certificates are issued from international headquarters to successful grading candidates. Membership prices are between Dhs.100 and Dhs.200 per month, depending on how many days a week you plan to train.

### Golden Fist Karate Club

*Al Riffa Plaza,*
*Nr Ramada R/A*
*Downtown Bur Dubai*
*Map 8 F3*

*04 355 1029 | goldenfistkarate.net*

Golden Fist provides training in a number of martial arts, including karate and kung fu, with students receiving official certificates upon passing each grade. The club offers flexible timings with classes running throughout the day and well into the evening. A nine-month black belt crash course is also available. You can sign up for between two and six classes a week, with the monthly fee ranging from Dhs.100 to Dhs.250. Discounts are available if you pay in advance.

**359**

## Taekwondo

*The Ballet Centre*
*Jumeira*
*Map 7 F1*

*04 344 9776* | www.balletcentre.com

The Ballet Centre's taekwondo arm is run by Fabun, a 7th dan black belt. This form of martial art teaches children and adults mental calmness, courage, strength and humility, courtesy, integrity, perseverance, self-control and indomitable spirit. Lessons take place on Sundays, Tuesdays and Thursdays. The beginners' membership fee is Dhs.670 for 14 weeks, but you can also pay on an hourly basis (Dhs.35).

## XMA

*Nr Int 2, Shk Zayed Rd*
*Al Quoz*
*Map 7 A3*

*04 339 5588* | www.xmafitness.com

XMA focuses on your personal development as well as fitness, and aims to increase your confidence alongside your agility and martial arts skills. As well as kickboxing lessons, they offer stretch and tone classes, black belt clubs and ladies only classes. Open six days a week, from 07:30 to 22:00, you're guaranteed to find a class to suit you.

## Mini Golf

Other options **Golf** p.344

## Aviation Club, The

*Nr Tennis Stadium*
*Al Garhoud*
*Map 13 E1*

*04 282 4122* | www.cftennis.com

This nine-hole pitch and putt course is located between the tennis stadium and the clubhouse. With manicured fairways and greens, each hole is a reasonable challenge for beginners and accomplished golfers. The course offers putting variety, and holes differ from 40 to 82 yards. Free for members, non-members can play mini golf for Dhs.150.

## Hatta Fort Hotel ▶ p.291

*Dubai-Hatta Rd*
*Hatta*
*Map 1 F2*

*04 852 3211* | www.jebelali-international.com

Set against the backdrop of the Hajar Mountains, the Hatta Fort Hotel has a mini golf course, a chipping green, and a driving range where golfers can practise their swings. Guests at the hotel can use the course for free, but visitors need to pay. Prices are available upon request and activities can be combined with an outing to the pool or with a barbecue.

*Mini golf*

## Hyatt Golf Park

*Hyatt Regency*
*Deira*
*Map 9 D1*

*04 209 6802* | www.dubai.hyatt.com

The Hyatt offers a nine-hole pitch and putt grass course (Dhs.15 for one round) or an 18 hole crazy golf course (Dhs.10 per person). For the pitch and putt you'll need your own clubs, and golf balls are sold at Dhs.8 each. Clubs and balls are provided for the crazy golf though. The park is floodlit in the evenings and the clubhouse overlooks a small lagoon. No membership required.

## Mother & Toddler Activities

There are a number of mother and baby/toddler activity groups in Dubai that are great when you are a new mum and a million miles away from your friends and family support network.

**Various Locations** ◀ French for Toddlers
*050 698 5165*
This is a language programme for babies and toddlers from the age of 6 months. Designed for both French and non-French speakers, it takes the form of a structured educational play and music group with songs, games and action rhymes. Research shows that children who are exposed to a second language in their early years are more likely to achieve fluency in languages and improve their learning ability.

**Various Locations** ◀ Funky Monkeys
*050 698 5165*
Funky Monkeys dance classes are aimed at developing a child's attention, balance and coordination through carrying out dance moves and actions to children's songs and music. The idea is to encourage a natural love of activity and allow kids to channel their boundless energy. The classes are suitable for children between 2 and 6 years old. Other classes and activities offered by the organisers include Little Scholars, a child development and IQ stimulation class for children from three months to three years; Little Scholars Phonics, introducing the letter sounds of the English language using a variety of fun activities; and Music, Singing & Rhyme, a fun music class where children are encouraged to play instruments, sing songs, and move in time to the music. Class locations and timings vary – contact Holly for details.

**Opp Choithram** ◀ Kidz & Mumz
*Al Garhoud*
*Map 13 D1*
*050 451 0225 | shalini@eim.ae*
The aim of this group is to allow mums and their children to engage together in creative and educational activities such as arts and crafts, games, reading, writing, story telling, and cooking and baking. A 'MumZ Forum' also allows the grown-ups to discuss different aspects of their children's development. The current age group of the 'kidz' is between 2 and 5.

**Nxt to Al Manara Rd** ◀ Mother to Mother
*Umm Suqeim*
*Map 6 D2*
*050 452 7674*
This is a non-profit support group for mums of children up to 3 years. They meet every Wednesday morning at the Alphabet Street Nursery. For more information contact Ilsie at the above number.

**Le Meridien Mina** ◀ Mothers & Miracles
*Al Sufouh*
*Map 5 C1*
*050 794 1439 | rjvrensburg@hotmail.com*
Mothers and Miracles offers a structured, interactive learning programme, designed to stimulate children between 3 months and 3 years, in the areas of intellect, emotions, creativity, physical movement, social interaction and music. The programme, developed by a leading early childhood educationalist, encourages the active participation of the parent in each session, guiding and encouraging the child through each activity. For more details, contact Ronel by phone or email above.

**Wafi City** ◀ Mums & Tots Group
*Oud Metha*
*Map 10 D4*
*050 656 5837 | anncassidy100@hotmail.com*
This well-established, informal mums' group has been going for over 15 years. All mums (and dads) are welcome, and the focus is on meeting like-minded people and making friends. The meetings take place in a huge hall that is crammed with toys to keep the kids busy while mums chat over coffee. This group is highly recommended, especially if you're new to Dubai or new to motherhood. Contact Ann for more info and directions. The cost is Dhs.20 per meeting, which includes tea/coffee, biscuits, and snacks for the kids.

**361**

## Motocross

Other options **Quad Bikes** p.366

*Behind Kart Club*
*Jebel Ali*
*Map 4 C3*

### Dubai Motocross

*050 452 7844 | www.mydubaimotocross.com*

Dubai Motocross (DMX) runs classes for Cadets, Juniors, 65ccs, 85ccs, 125ccs and adults. The new Jebel Ali Motocross Park features two tracks (one for juniors and one for seniors) along with other facilities that make it fun for the whole family to enjoy a day at the track. The club organises 12 individual championship events per year, with an entry fee of Dhs.100 for members and Dhs.200 to 250 for non-members.

## Motorcycling

*Al Muragabat Street*
*Deira*
*Map 11 D1*

### UAE Motorcycle Club

*04 266 9922 | www.uaedesertchallenge.com*

The UAE Motorcycle Club is the UAE's FIM representative. Regular Motocross and off-road enduros are held between September and April, and activity centres at the DMX Club and in Umm Al Quwain host quad and drag races. Call the number or keep an eye on the website for details of upcoming events.

## Motorsports

*Nr Arabian Ranches*
*Dubailand*
*Map 2 E4*

### Dubai Autodrome

*04 367 8700 | www.dubaiautodrome.com*

The home of motorsport in Dubai, the Autodrome (part of Dubailand, on Emirates Road) has six different track configurations, including a 5.39km FIA-sanctioned GP circuit, state-of-the-art pit facilities and a 7,000 seat grandstand. The venue hosts a variety of events throughout the year, including rounds of the FIA GT Championship. But how long before Dubai gets a Formula 1 Grand Prix?

*Nr Aviation Club*
*Al Garhoud*
*Map 13 E1*

### Emirates Motor Sports Federation

*04 282 7111 | www.emsf.ae*

For rally and racing enthusiasts in the UAE, the Federation organises a variety of events throughout the year ranging from the 4WD 1000 Dunes Rally to the Champions Rally for saloon cars. Other events include road safety awareness campaigns and classic car exhibitions. Federation membership is Dhs.200 per year, although non-members can enter races for a fee. Check the website for a full calendar of events.

## Mountain Biking

Other options **Cycling** p.329

Away from the cities, the UAE has a lot to offer outdoor enthusiasts, especially mountain bikers. On a mountain bike it's possible to see the most remote and untouched places that are not even accessible in 4WDs. For hardcore, experienced mountain bikers there is a good range of terrain, from the super-technical rocky trails in areas like Fili and Siji, to mountain routes like Wadi Bih, which climb to over a thousand metres and can be descended in minutes.

The riding is mainly rocky, technical and challenging. Even if you are an experienced biker, always be sensible and go prepared – the sun is strong, you will need far more water than you think, and it's easy to get lost. For further information on mountain biking in the UAE, including details of possible routes, refer to the *UAE Off-Road Explorer*.

# THE BEST REASON YET TO
# RIDE RED

It's the many years of experience, advanced 4-stroke technology and unparalleled reliability that have made Honda off-road bikes the finest on earth! Choose from one of the widest range of off-road bikes and ATVs, including the class leading CRF450R and TRX450R. Experience a piece of the action - visit your local Trading Enterprises - Honda showroom and 'Ride Red'.

**HONDA**
**PERFORMANCE FIRST**

**trading enterprises**

**Dubai** Airport Road (04) 2954246, Dubai Festival City Showroom (04) 2066300, Sheikh Zayed Road (04) 3472212, Fleet Sales (04) 3409958 **Sharjah** (06) 5597833 **Ajman** (06) 7446543 **RAK** (07) 2351881 **Al Ain** (03) 7211838 **Fujairah** (09) 2223097 **Abu Dhabi** (02) 6763300 **UAQ** (06) 7666694
e-mail:tradingent@alfuttaim.ae     www.tradingenterprises.com     www.al-futtaim.com

An **Al-Futtaim group** company

www.**honda**uae.com

**Various Locations** ◄ Hot Cog MTB
*www.hot-cog.com*
Hot Cog MTB is an active group of enthusiasts who ride every weekend, all over the country, all year round. They also camp, hike and barbecue, and new riders are always welcome. See the website for more information.

## Music Lessons
Other options **Dance Classes** p.329, **Music, DVDs & Videos** p.449, **Singing** p.372

**Opp Karama** ◄ Crystal Music Institute
**Municipality**
*Al Karama* 04 396 3224 | *crystalmusicinstitute@hotmail.com*
*Map 10 E1* Recognised by the UAE Ministry of Education, the Crystal Music Institute courses are designed mainly for children and are available for a variety of instruments. Children take periodic examinations, which are conducted by the Trinity College of Music in Dubai.

**Stalco Bld, Zabeel Rd** ◄ Dubai Music School
*Al Karama* 04 396 4834 | *www.glennperry.net*
*Map 10 E1* Dubai Music School offers guitar, piano, organ, violin, brass, drums, singing and composing lessons for beginners and serious amateurs. Lessons last for one hour, and students take Trinity College of London examinations to get certification. Monthly fees range from Dhs.200 to Dhs.395, and there's a Dhs.50 registration fee.

**Nr Mazaya Centre** ◄ Juli Music Centre
*Shk Zayed Rd* 04 321 2588
*Map 7 D3* In addition to selling a wide variety of musical instruments including new and used pianos, brass, woodwind, strings, and percussion, Juli Music Centre also offers tutoring to students of all experience levels. Contact the shop for details of fees and which instruments are offered.

**Jumeira Plaza** ◄ Jumeirah Music Center
*Jumeira* 04 349 2662 | *www.kindermusik.com*
*Map 7 F1* Opened in 2004, the Jumeirah Music Centre now boasts more than 300 members. Lessons are offered in piano, guitar, flute, violin, drums, and voice. All children are welcome to audition for the choir, which puts on a big concert every year. Music lessons are also available to adults.

**Sana Fashion Bld** ◄ Sruthi Music & Dance Training Center
*Al Karama* 04 337 7398 | *sruthimusic@hotmail.com*
*Map 8 D4* Education is available for a variety of instruments including piano, electric organ, guitar, drums, violin, accordion and tabla, and students can register with Trinity College of Music (London) and take exams in Dubai. Lessons are also offered in Carnatic and Hindustani vocals, as well as dance from Indian styles such as Bharatnatyam or Kathak, to western dance styles like disco and jive.

**Sheikh Zayed Road** ◄ Vocal Studio, The
050 698 0773 | *www.bravodubai.com*
The Vocal Studio offers vocal instruction and a range of singing related activities for adults and youngsters. The centre offers ABRSM and Trinity College (London) syllabus exam preparations, and grades range from beginner to advanced. Students are also encouraged to take part in recitals and concerts, and are also featured in musical productions with visiting international guest artists. For more information email doremivs@eim.ae.

## Netball

*Mirdif Tennis Centre*
*Mirdif*
*Map 15 A1*

### Dubai Netball League
*050 450 6715 | www.dxbnetball.com*
There are over 18 teams in three divisions at the club, and players range from beginners to experts. Matches are played from September to May on Wednesday nights. During the season, players are selected for the Inter-Gulf Netball Championships, a tournament that features teams from throughout the Gulf. Although they currently play in Mirdif, they plan on moving to the new courts at Silicon Oasis.

## Orchestras & Bands
Other options **Music Lessons** p.362, **Singing** p.372

*Horizon School*
*Al Wasl*
*Map 7 C2*

### Dubai Chamber Orchestra
*04 349 0423 | www.dubaiorchestra.org*
The Dubai Chamber Orchestra was founded by a group of musicians residing in the UAE. The group comprises many different nationalities and meets regularly to rehearse. Its aim is to give at least two public performances a year. For more information, contact Linda Brentano on 050 625 2936.

*Horizon School*
*Al Wasl*
*Map 7 C2*

### Dubai Wind Band
*04 348 3631*
This is a gathering of over 50 woodwind and brass musicians. Abilities range from beginners to grade eight plus, and all levels and ages are welcome. The band is in popular demand during December for seasonal singing and music engagements at clubs, malls and hotels. For further information, contact Peter Hatherley-Greene. Alternative number: 050 651 8902.

## Paintballing
Other options **Shooting** p.370

*WonderLand*
*Umm Hurair*
*Map 13 C1*

### Pursuit Games
*04 324 4755 | www.paintballdubai.com*
This is a fun game for teenagers and adults where bullets are replaced by paintballs. Club experts break groups up into two teams and give safety demonstrations before equipping participants with overalls, facemasks, special guns and paintballs. Costs start at Dhs.75 for a two-hour game, and include 100 paintballs, gun and gas.

## Parasailing
Want an aerial view of the Palm Jumeirah but can't afford a helicopter? Then pop down to the beach for a spot of parasailing. The area around the Marina is the place to be – the Sheraton Jumeirah Beach (04 399 5533) has a watersports and activity centre, and Nautica 1992 (050 426 2415) operates from the Habtoor Grand. Summertime Marine Sports (04 331 1483) also offer flights from the open beach near Le Meridien Mina Seyahi. All use specially designed boats with winches and a launch pad on the back, meaning you no longer have to sprint down the beach (or get dragged through the sand) in order to get airborne – all very sensible. You can expect to pay around Dhs.250 for a 15 to 20 minute ride, or Dhs.350 for a tandem ride.

### Paintballing
If you want to maintain a great work environment, why not take your office mates on a team building exercise? Paintballing is sure to improve, boost or destroy relations in the office. Find out if you're brave enough to smoke out the 'silent but deadly' types.

Note of caution: It is advisable for the boss to wear extra padding.

**365**

## Photography

Gulf Photo Plus and UAE Photo are web-based communities where local photography enthusiasts can exchange tips and ideas, post their pictures, and buy and sell equipment. Competitions, workshops, exhibitions and events are held at regular intervals throughout the year.

| Photography | |
|---|---|
| Gulf Photo Plus | www.gulfphotoplus.com |
| UAE Photo | www.uae-photo.com |

## Polo

Other options **Horse Riding** p.350

*Arabian Ranches*
*Emirates Rd*
*Map 2 E3*

### Dubai Polo & Equestrian Club

*04 361 8111 | www.poloclubdubai.com*

With two full-size pitches, this new club at Arabian Ranches is set to become a regular venue for both local and international polo events. A wide selection of polo coaching is offered, from beginner to advanced level, and ranging from 20-minute lessons to six-day courses. The club has over 300 stables and livery is available. Keep an eye on the website or call the club for details of forthcoming events.

*Shk Maktoum Rd*
*Abu Dhabi*
*Map 1 E1*

### Ghantoot Racing & Polo Club

*02 562 9050 | www.emiratesracing.com*

With six international standard polo fields (three of which are floodlit), two stick and ball fields, three tennis courts, a swimming pool, gym, sauna and restaurant, this club has first-class facilities for the entire family. Non-members are welcome to dine at the restaurant or to watch polo matches that take place between October and April.

## Quad Bikes

Other options **Dune Buggy Driving** p.338, **Motocross** p.362

Quad bikes are available to hire from a number of firms operating around the 'Big Red' sand dune on the Dubai – Hatta road; after a bit of haggling you should pay around Dhs.100 for half an hour. You won't necessarily be allowed out into the dunes unaccompanied as most have their own fenced-off area, but for an extra fee you may be given permission to tackle the big stuff on your own. Beware though – unlike dune buggies, quad bikes have no roll cages or seatbelts, so be careful hurtling over sand dunes when you've no idea what's on the other side.

## Rollerblading & Rollerskating

Other options **Beaches** p.267, **Parks** p.268

Dubai's many parks provide some excellent locations for rollerblading. Creekside Park and Safa Park have wide pathways, few people and enough slopes and turns to make it interesting. Alternatively, check out both sides of Dubai Creek, the seafront near the Hyatt Regency Hotel or the promenades at the Jumeira Beach Corniche and in Deira along towards Al Mamzar Beach Park, where the views are an added bonus.

## Rowing

The Dubai Rowing and Sculling Club was founded in 2005 at the Dubai Water Sports Association (DWSA) complex on the creek, but moved to DIMC when DWSA was forced to close due to construction. The club has coxed fours and both double and single sculls, and also has two ergometers. Activities include regular regattas, indoor rowing competitions, coaching camps and social events.

*DIMC*
*Al Sufouh*
*Map 5 B1*

## Dubai Rowing and Sculling Club (DRSC)

*050 854 8334 | www.dubairowingandscullingclub.com*

The Dubai Rowing and Sculling Club was founded in 2005 at the Dubai Water Sports Association (DWSA) complex on the creek, but moved to DIMC when DWSA closed. The club has coxed fours and both double and single sculls, and also has two ergometers. Rowing usually takes place early morning, and other activities include regular regattas, indoor rowing competitions, coaching camps and social events.

## Rugby

*Al Ain Road*

### Dubai Exiles Rugby Club

*04 333 1198 | www.dubaiexiles.com*

The Exiles is Dubai's most serious rugby club and has become a bastion for the sport. The club has a 1st and 2nd XV team who compete in the AGRFU leagues, as well as veterans, U19s, ladies, girls U17s and a minis and youth section. The Exiles also host the annual Dubai International Rugby 7s Tournament, which attracts international teams from all the major rugby playing nations. For further information on playing rugby call the club, or email enquiries@dubaiexiles.com. As of late 2007, the club was due to move premises to new fields on the Al Ain road – contact Exiles for further details.

> **Exiled Exiles**
>
> The 2007 Dubai Rugby 7s was the last event held at the Exiles Club in Al Awir. The several teams that trained there have been promised a new, larger complex on the Al Ain Road. Although the exact location of its replacement is unknown, the new complex will have several pitches, a gym and a bar. The new pitches are scheduled to be completed by Spring 2008.

*Al Ain Road*

### Dubai Hurricanes

*050 626 6107 | www.dubaihurricanes.com*

Originally formed as a purely social outfit, Dubai Hurricanes now compete in the Dubai 7s tournament. The club sports a ladies team and invites new players of all abilities to join their ranks. Training sessions are held on Sunday and Tuesday evenings. Contact club captain, Chris Gregory (050 626 6107), for more details. The club is based at the Exiles ground in Al Awir until the end of 2007, which is then set to move to the new Dubai Rugby Grounds on the Al Ain road in early 2008.

## Running

Other options **Hashing** p.348

For over half the year Dubai's weather is perfect for running and many groups and clubs meet up for runs on a regular basis. There are several major running events, usually held annually, such as the Round the Creek Relay Race, the Dubai Marathon, and the epic Wadi Bih Race. In the latter, each runner in a five-member team runs a portion of the 70 km route between Ras Al Khaimah on the west coast to Dibba on the east. The terrain is arduous, featuring mountains that top out at over a thousand metres (depending on the erratic rules at the border posts on the day itself). For more information on the Round the Creek Relay Race, contact John Harringon (050 645 0587) and for more information on the Wadi Bih Race, email John Young at jcyoung@eim.ae. The Dubai Marathon is usually run in January every year, and aside from the official marathon-distance run around the city of Dubai, there is also a 10km road race and a 3km charity run. For more information, or to register online, visit www.dubaimarathon.org.

**367**

## Dubai Creek Striders

*Opp Exhibition*
*Hall no 4*
*Trade Centre 1*
*Map 7 F3*

04 321 1999 | www.dubaicreekstriders.com

This medium to long-distance running club organises weekly outings on Friday mornings. Distances and routes differ each week, but normally consist of 10km runs during the summer and 32km winter training runs that form part of the build up to the annual 42.2km Dubai Marathon. The club chairman, Malcolm Murphy, can be reached via the above number. Otherwise, check the website for details of the weekly training runs and forthcoming events.

## Dubai Road Runners

*Safa Park*
*Al Wasl*
*Map 7 B2*

04 340 3777 | www.dubai-road-runners.com

Come rain or shine, 100% humidity or 50°C temperatures, Dubai Road Runners meet every Saturday at 18:30 outside gate 4 of Safa Park. The object of the meeting is to run a 3.5 or 7km track around the park. A Dhs.5 entrance fee is charged, and for an added bit of fun runners predict their times, with a prize being awarded to the winner. Additional runs and events are organised too – check the website for the full schedule.

## Stride for Life

*Various locations*

050 657 7057 | www.strideforlife.com

This is an aerobic walking and running programme designed to allow people of all abilities and fitness levels to take part in regular, enjoyable, safe exercise. After an initial one-on-one meeting to assess lifestyle and current fitness, an exercise programme is recommended and you then attend the group sessions that take place three times a week (Saturday, Monday and Wednesday) at various locations. Stride for Life also teaches Nordic Walking, conducts mall walking programmes on behalf of several malls around Dubai, and puts together focused 'training journeys' for novices, in preparation for first time participation in long distance events (half and full marathons). At present these are either at the Lakes Club or Safa Park. Progress is tracked continuously, and members receive computerised feedback monthly, plus a follow up meeting every 12 weeks. The fees are very reasonable – if you join for a year it works out at about Dhs.10 per session.

## Sailing

Other options **Boat & Yacht Charters** p.277

Temperatures in winter are perfect for sailing, and taking to the sea in summer serves as an escape from the scorching heat. Membership of one of Dubai's sailing clubs allows you to participate in club activities and to rent sailing and watersports equipment. You can also use the leisure facilities and the club's beach, and moor your boat at an additional cost. There's a healthy racing scene for a variety of boat types, and long distance races such as the annual Dubai to Muscat race, held in March. The traditional dhow races are also an exciting spectacle. See Dhow Racing – Annual Events (p.71) for more details.

## Bluesail Dubai

*Nr British Embassy*
*Downtown Bur Dubai*
*Map 9 B3*

04 397 9730 | www.bluesailyachts.com

Bluesail are the most highly qualified Royal Yachting Association tidal sailing school in the Middle East, offering RYA power and tidal sail training for all levels of ability, from novice through to Yachtmaster. They have 42ft sail yachts and a new 21ft Yamaha powerboat, which are used for instruction. Bluesail's Fast42 yachts are entered in the Middle East's racing calendar annually, so budding race crew are encouraged to apply for tuition. Each of the Bluesail instructors is RYA Yachtmaster Ocean qualified.

**Umm Suqeim Beach**
Umm Suqeim
Map 6 F1

## Dubai Offshore Sailing Club
*04 394 1669 | www.dosc.ae*

DOSC is a Royal Yachting Association Training Centre, providing dinghy and keelboat courses throughout the year. Members can take advantage of marina moorings, storage, launch facilities, and sail training, alongside an active social calendar.

**Various locations**

## Fun Sports
*050 465 7311*

Fun Sports offers multi-hull sailing training with professional instructors, to both beginners and those with some experience. The company operates from the following beach clubs: Hilton Dubai Jumeirah, Habtoor Grand Resort & Spa, and the Ritz-Carlton Beach Club.

**Nr Habtoor Grand Resort & Spa**
Al Sufouh
Map 5 B1

## Jebel Ali Sailing Club
*04 399 5444 | www.jebelalisailingclub.com*

This club is recognised by the RYA to teach and certify sailing, windsurfing and powerboat licences, and instruct in kayaking. Races are held on most Fridays for toppers, lasers, catamarans and cruisers. Topper coaching takes place every Wednesday afternoon, while cadet club takes place on Thursdays. The annual club membership is Dhs.2,000 (single) and Dhs.3,000 (family).

## Salsa Dancing

Other options **Belly Dancing** p.322, **Dance Classes** p.329

**Dubai Marine Beach**
Jumeira
Map 7 F1

## El Malecon
*04 346 1111 | www.dxbmarine.com*

Saturday night is Salsa night at Malecon, with lessons available between 20:00 and 22:00 and costing Dhs.30. If you're dining in the restaurant they're free of charge, making this a cheap and enjoyable way to burn off the calories.

**Various locations**

## Salsa Dubai
*050 848 7188 | www.salsanight.com*

Salsa Dubai is fronted by Phil, who has 13 years experience in Cuban, New York and Spanish dance styles. Classes are tailored to the individual, so everyone can progress at their own speed. Members also have the opportunity to learn the famous La Rueda Cuban dance. Nights out are organised at Latin venues to enjoy live bands. Call the above number or check the website for more details on classes and locations.

## Sand Boarding/Skiing

Sandboarding is not as fast or smooth as snowboarding but it can be a lot of fun. Head out into the desert in your 4WD, climb a big dune and feel the wind rush past you as you carve down the sandy slopes. A popular sandboarding spot is 'Big Red', the huge dune halfway along the E44 towards Hatta.

Boards are usually standard snowboards, but as the sand wears them down they end up being good for nothing else. Some sports stores sell sandboards, but they are really nothing more than cheap, basic snowboards. As an alternative for children, a plastic sled or something similar proves to be just as much fun.

All major tour companies offer sandboarding experiences, along with basic instructions, and will also provide 4WD taxi services back to the top – most important! Sandboarding can be done as part of another tour or you can opt for a half day session, which will cost between Dhs.175 and Dhs.200.

## Scouts & Guides

*Various locations*

### British Guides in Foreign Countries

Various groups for girls of different age ranges include Rainbows (5 to 7), Brownies (7 to 10), Guides (10 to 14), and Young Leaders and Rangers (14 to 26). For more information call Jane Henderson (04 340 8441) for the Jumeira packs, Liz Smith (04 395 4640) for the UAE Senior Section, or Mary Dunn (04 348 9849), the Dubai District Commissioner.

*Various locations*

### Scouts Association (British Groups Abroad)

050 654 2180 | www.scoutbase.org.uk

The Scout Association aims to encourage the development of youngsters through weekly activities and outings. The scout groups are broken up by age: Beavers (6 to 8), Cubs (8 to 10½), Scouts (10½ to 14), Explorer Scouts (14 to 18) and Scout Network (18 to 25). Activities for younger groups include games, badge activities, sports, competitions and outings. For general enquiries, the group contact is Dawn Tate.

## Scrabble

Other options **Chess** p.327

*Al Maskam Bldg*
*Al Karama*
*Map 10 D1*

### Dubai Scrabble League

050 653 7992 | alicoabr@eim.ae

This club meets once a week for friendly games between players of all levels. Regular competitions are held, and players also attend competitions in Bahrain, Singapore and Bangkok. The UAE Open (held every year in March/April) is the qualifier for the Gulf Open held in Bahrain. For more information, contact Selwyn Lobo.

## Scrapbooking

*Holiday Centre Mall*
*Trade Centre 1*
*Map 7 F2*

### Emirates Scrapbook

050 565 0892 | www.emiratesscrapbook.com

Scrapbooking is the preservation of your photographs and memories in archive-quality albums, using photo-safe materials. This rewarding hobby helps you create a lasting family treasure and preserve a record of your time in the country. At Emirates Scrapbook there's always someone willing to help you get started, and supplies are available at the scrap centre. For more details speak to Mary Watt.

## Shooting

Other options **Paintballing** p.365

*Dubai-Hatta Rd*
*Hatta*
*Map 1 F2*

### Hatta Fort Hotel

04 852 3211 | www.jebelali-international.com

Clay pigeon shooting is one of many activities offered by Hatta Fort Hotel, which is located just an hour's drive from Dubai. More frequently visited as an overnight retreat from the hustle and bustle of Dubai, the Hatta Fort Hotel also features a rock pool and Friday barbecue for guests or day visitors. See Hatta Fort Hotel in Weekend Breaks for more information (p.298).

*Nr Jebel Ali Golf*
*Resort & Spa*
*Jebel Ali*
*Map 3 A2*

### Jebel Ali Shooting Club

04 883 6555 | www.jebelali-international.com

The Jebel Ali Shooting Club has five floodlit clay shooting ranges that consist of skeet, trap and sporting. Professional shooting instructors give comprehensive lessons and experienced shooters are welcome to try their hand at clay shooting or

**370**

**For your next event, use our imagination.**

**It works overtime.**

As proud winners of the prestigious

**MEBA 2007 Small Business of the Year Award**

AND

the coveted **Lloyds TSB Business Growth Award 2007,**

Flying Elephant continues to provide the finest in

corporate and family events, ensuring that we never

compromise on the areas that have made us successful.

Call us and discover the many ways

we can bring your event to life.

Corporate Events   ✦   M.I.C.E. Events   ✦   Teambuilding Events   ✦   Corporate Family Days

Themed Events   ✦   Entertainment   ✦   Product Launches   ✦   Event Rentals

Mascot Fabrication   ✦   Keeko Kids   ✦   Royal Events   ✦   Balloon Decoration

# Flying Elephant

The region's largest supplier of corporate and family entertainment

Tel: +9714 347-9170    Fax: +9714 347-9171    info@flyingelephantuae.com    www.flyingelephantuae.com

archery. Members and non-members are welcome. Refreshments are available at Shooters restaurant and corporate or group activities can be arranged. Prices available on request.

**Nr RAK Airport**
*Ras Al Khaimah*
*Map 1 E1*

## Ras Al Khaimah Shooting Club
*07 236 3622*

This club welcomes interested parties that want to learn how to shoot, whether it's shotguns or long rifles. The club boasts a 50 metre indoor and 200 metre outdoor rifle range, and has a canteen selling snacks and soft drinks. If you ring them you may want to have an Arabic speaker standing by. Otherwise, just drop by the next time you're in RAK.

## Singing
Other options **Music Lessons** p.364

**Various Locations**

## Dubai Harmony
*04 348 9395 | seewhy@eim.ae*

Barbershop-style singing varies greatly from other kinds of group singing. Finding the right part for your voice is the initial step, but any woman with average singing ability, with or without music or vocal training, will find a part that fits her vocal range. Dubai Harmony has 50 female members who get together for weekly rehearsals.

**Various Locations**

## Dubai Singers & Orchestra
*04 349 1896 | dubaisingers@yahoo.com*

This is a group of amateur musicians who meet regularly to create music in a variety of styles, including requiems, choral works, Christmas carols, musicals and variety shows. Membership is open to everyone and no auditions are required, except for solo parts. Membership fees are low and sheet music is provided.

## Skiing & Snowboarding

**Mall of the Emirates**
*Map 6 A3*

## Dubai Ski Club
*04 344 9897 | www.dubaiskiclub.com*

To coincide with the opening of its first ski slope, Dubai got its very own ski club to go with it. The club now has over 900 members. Skiers and snowboarders meet twice a week at Ski Dubai: Tuesdays 10:00 – 12:00 and Saturdays 18:00 – 20:00. Membership benefits include a reduced fee for the slope pass and use of the 'advance booking' lane when purchasing tickets, plus regular special offers on equipment, clothing, accessories and holidays.

**Mall of the Emirates**
*Al Barsha*
*Map 6 A3*

## Ski Dubai ▶ p.373
*04 409 4000 | www.skidxb.com*

When temperatures outside are melting your sunglasses, it's now possible to go sub-zero with a visit to Ski Dubai. The huge tube extending behind and above the Mall of the Emirates is home to five slopes to suit all skill levels, from gentle beginner slopes to the world's first indoor 'black' run. There's also a 90m long quarter pipe to get some serious air, and let's not forget the largest indoor snow park in the world – perfect if you fancy a snowball fight in the middle of July. The slope has both chair lifts and tow lifts, and there's a well-stocked retail shop selling skis, boards, and clothing. Strict rules ensure only suitably skilled skiers and boarders can take to the slopes, but for those that don't make the grade, lessons are offered with qualified instructors.

Tel: +971 4 409 4000 | www.skidxb.com

**ESCAPE EVERY DAY**

SKI DUBAI
سكي دبي
an unforgettable snow experience

Entrance to the Snow Park is Dhs.40 for adults and Dhs.30 for children. Prices for a two-hour Slope Pass start at Dhs.115 for adults and Dhs.100 for kids, and this includes all equipment and clothing (except gloves).

## Skydiving

**17km North of UAQ on RAK Rd**
*Umm Al Quwain*
*Map 1 E1*

### Umm Al Quwain Aeroclub
*06 768 1447 | www.uaqaeroclub.com*

In addition to pilot training, helicopter flying, hangar/aircraft rental, paramotors and microlights, the club also operates as a skydive school and boogie centre. You can enjoy an eight level accelerated free fall parachute course (Dhs.6,000) and train for your international parachute licence. Alternatively, try a tandem jump with an instructor from 12,000 feet for Dhs.800.

## Snooker

**Sana Bld**
*Al Karama*
*Map 8 D4*

### Billiard Master
*04 335 2008 | www.uaebilliard.com*

Billiard Master has 18 billiard tables in spacious surroundings and two private snooker tables. The club organises annual inter-club leagues as well as international tournaments, and they are also the official organiser of the Billiards Championships in Dubai. Other facilities include computer games and an internet cafe.

**Nr Post Office**
*Al Karama*
*Map 10 F1*

### Dubai Snooker Club
*04 337 5338 | www.dubaisnooker.com*

The Dubai Snooker Club has 15 snooker tables and eight pool tables, along with three private snooker rooms that can be rented by groups. Tables are rented out at Dhs.20 per hour, and the club organises five tournaments a year. The club is open to the public, with no membership required.

## Snorkelling
Other options **Diving** p.334

Snorkelling is a great way to see the varied marine life in the Arabian Gulf, or on the east coast at popular places such as Snoopy Island, near Sandy Beach Motel. Another good spot is the beach north of Dibba village where the coast is rocky and coral can be found closer to the shore. Closer to home, the sea off Jumeira Beach has a fair amount of marine life. Most hotels or dive centres rent equipment (snorkel, mask and fins) but costs vary greatly so shop around. Check out the revised 3rd edition of the Underwater Explorer for further information on where to go snorkelling in the UAE.

**Beach Rd**
*Khor Fakkan*
*Map 1 F1*

### Oceanic Hotel
*09 238 5111 | www.oceanichotel.com*

The Oceanic Hotel, on the UAE's east coast, offers a boat ride out to Shark Island, or guests can snorkel and swim off the hotel beach. Equipment hire is Dhs.30 per hour for guests, and the boat trip is Dhs.35. Visitors are obliged to pay an entrance fee of Dhs.45 for adults and Dhs.25 for children.

**Al Aqqa, Btn Dibba & Khorfakkan**
*Fujairah*
*Map 1 F1*

### Sandy Beach Hotel & Resort
*09 244 5555 | www.sandybm.com*

For those who want an exhilarating snorkelling experience, the Beach Hut is a good place to start. Snoopy Island, the house reef, is just off their private beach and is an excellent place to enjoy the underwater world. Equipment is available for sale, or you can rent an entire set for Dhs.20 per hour, or Dhs.40 for the day. Kayaks are also available for hire. Entry to the hotel costs Dhs.50.

## Scuba 2000

*Al Badiyah Beach*
*East Coast*
*Dibba*
*Map 1 F1*

*09 238 8477* | *www.scuba-2000.com*

This east coast centre offers snorkelling from the beach or by boat ride to Snoopy Island, Shark Island or Al Badiyah Rock. Snorkelling trips to these destinations cost Dhs.120 and are inclusive of fins, mask, snorkel and boots. The centre also has other watersports facilities, including diving, pedal boats and canoes.

## Scuba Dubai

*DWTC Appts, Block C*
*Trade Centre 2*
*Map 7 F3*

*04 341 4940* | *www.scubadubai.com*

Please see the entry for Scuba Dubai under Diving (p.335).

# Social Groups

Other options **Support Groups** p.200

With its cosmopolitan population, it's hardly surprising that Dubai has a large number of social and cultural groups for people from all walks of life. Some are linked to an embassy or business group, and can be an excellent way of meeting like-minded people or even for business networking. See the Business Councils & Groups table in Residents (p.99) for more details. If your particular interest or background is not covered, now is the perfect opportunity to fine tune your organisational skills and to start something new. The 'expat mum' population is also alive and well in Dubai with various Mother and Toddler groups; see p.360, and check out www.expatwoman.com for more information. You should also grab a copy of the *Family Explorer*, which has heaps of information on where to find the best 'mums and tots' groups.

## American Women's Association of Dubai

*Various locations*

*050 725 7652* | *www.awadubai.org*

The AWA is a volunteer group offering information programmes, social functions, common interest groups, and charitable activities while fostering fellowship among American women in Dubai. The organisation is open to women who are United States citizens, legal residents, or spouses of U.S. citizens.

## The Bridget Jones Club Dubai

*Various locations*

*Bridget@Expatwoman.com*

The Bridget Jones Club is a social group for single women in Dubai to meet and make like-minded friends. They currently have over 400 members of approximately 20 nationalities ranging in age from 21 to 65! The club was established a few years ago and organises various events such as a desert safari, cruise to the Musandam peninsula, belly dancing lessons, salsa classes and dinners at various restaurants. They also run a Book Club and next year will start organising sports teams including a Bridget's Netball Team. They welcome women of all ages and nationalities and are open to suggestions from members for events and activities. For more information on becoming a member email the club or check out the details on www.expatwoman.com.

## Dubai Adventure Mums

*Various locations*

*04 390 4053* | *www.dubaiadventuremums.com*

Once a month this group of women sets off without their children or partners to test themselves in new and challenging ways. The aim of this non-profit group is to offer

**375**

women a wide range of recreational activities that they may not have experienced before. Qualified instructors offer advice and teach the safest way to enjoy these new activities.

*Various locations*

## Dubai Caledonian Society

*050 293 0696 | www.scotsindubai.com*

The society provides a social focal point for Scottish expats in Dubai as well as raising money for Scottish and local charities. There are four main events every year – the St Andrew's Ball in November, the Burns Supper in January, The Chieftain's Ball in May, and the Welcome Back Ceilidh in September. Every first Sunday month the committee and members meet in the St Andrew's Snug in Rydges Plaza. Anyone can join, even non-Scots.

| Social Groups | |
|---|---|
| British Community Assistance Fund | 04 337 1413 |
| Club for Canadians | 04 355 6171 |
| Egyptian Club | 04 336 6709 |
| German Speaking Women's Club | 050 459 1885 |
| Indian Association | 04 351 1082 |
| Italian Cultural Association | 050 558 2716 |
| Norwegian Centre | 04 337 0062 |

*Various locations*

## Dubai Irish Society

*050 552 6474 | www.dubaiirishsociety.com*

Dubai Irish Society has been in existence for over 30 years and its purpose is to promote Irish culture, social events and sporting interests to its members and to a wider public. DIS organises events such as the St. Patrick's Day Ball, Rose Ball and other social and cultural events as per members' requests. The website has more details, and those interested in membership can email keith@dubaiirishsociety.com.

*Various locations*

## Dubai Manx Society

*04 394 3185 | www.dubaimanxsociety.com*

The Dubai Manx Society is a non-profit making social and cultural organisation, dedicated to bringing the traditions of the Isle of Man to Dubai. Originally formed in 1911, the international society now has branches all over the world. The website has details of forthcoming events and membership.

*Al Futtaim Training Centre*
*Al Rashidiya*
*Map 11 D3*

## Dubai Toastmasters Club

*050 454 4327 | www.dubaitoastmasters.org*

Toastmasters is a worldwide, non-profit organisation which offers its members opportunities to hone their public speaking, leadership, creative thinking, evaluation and effective listening skills. The club provides a supportive and positive learning environment that foster self-confidence and personal growth. Contact V.P. Menon for more details.

## Softball

*Metropolitan Palace Hotel*
*Downtown Bur Dubai*
*Map 7 B3*

## Dubai Softball League

*www.dubaisoftballleague.com*

The Dubai Softball League runs from September to December, and from January to May, and the only criteria is that you are over 16 years of age. Dubai usually hosts the biannual Middle East Softball Championships, held in November and April. It attracts 30 teams with over 500 players from around the Gulf. Entrance is free and food and beverages are available. Membership of the league costs Dhs.100 per player per season. Check the website for team and fixture details.

## Speedboating

Other options **Boat & Yacht Charters** p.277

**Nr British Embassy**
*Downtown Bur Dubai*
*Map 9 B3*

## Bluesail Dubai

*04 397 9730 | www.bluesailyachts.com*

You and up to four friends can experience a thrilling two-hour ride aboard either a 21ft/200hp or 34ft/450hp speedboat. The Bluesail skipper will even give you the wheel following a safety and tactics briefing. A short leisurely trip down the creek is followed by a high-octane blast out into the Gulf. All vessels are fully insured and equipped with the required safety equipment.

**Various locations**

## Fun Sports

*050 465 7311*

Speed boating in the Gulf is a great weekend activity. You can hire a boat, which is handled by a captain, and go exploring along the coast, taking in the sights of the Burj al Arab and around the outside of the Palm Jumeirah and The World islands. You'll be advised where you can and can't go when you make the booking.

## Squash

Other options **Leisure Facilities** p.384

**Various locations**

## D.H.L. Dubai Squash League

*04 343 5672 | www.dubaisquash.org*

The squash league has been active in Dubai and Sharjah since the 1970s and is run by the UAE Squash Rackets Association. About 300 competitors play three 10-week seasons at over 30 clubs. The league meets every Monday evening and each team fields four players. Contact Shavan Kumar (04 343 5672), Chris Wind (050 688 7421) or Andy Staines (04 339 1331) for more details.

## Summer Camps & Courses

While the summer used to see a mass exodus of expatriate women and their children to their home countries, today less and less people head for cooler climates and instead stay put despite the heat. With more kids in Dubai during the summer holidays, many hotels, clubs and organisations have added summer camps and activities to their annual schedule. Most language schools run summer courses for kids, see Language Schools on p.354, tour operators have a good range of family-orientated activities during the summer, see Tour Operators p.283, and not forgetting Dubai Summer Surprises which is packed with fun for all the family, see p.70. Also, venues such as Dubai Country Club, Dubai Tennis Academy and Futurekids offer good summer classes.

**Surfin' UAE**
*Scott Chambers offers surfing lessons off Jumeira Beach near the Burj Al Arab. Times and dates depend on the conditions. He can hire you a board if you don't have your own. Call 050 504 3020 or email scott@surfingdubai.com.*

## Surfing

Other options **Kitesurfing** p.353, **Beaches** p.267

Dubai is a reasonably good surfing location, and there is a dedicated group of surfers keeping their eye on the weather and tides from November to June. Swells are generally on the small side, but every now and again conditions are right and bigger waves hit the coast. Check out www.surfersofdubai.com for information on locations, current conditions, where to buy boards and where to meet up with fellow surfing dudes and dudettes. A popular destination is Oman (especially Masirah Island), where being on the open ocean and the general conditions make for more exciting swells and better surfing than in Dubai. See the *Oman Explorer* for more details.

**377**

## Swimming

Other options **Leisure Facilities** p.384, **Beaches** p.267

Dubai has some great swimming spots, whether it's at a public beach, beach club or one of the beach parks. The water is relatively clean with pleasant temperatures most of the year, although during the summer it can feel like stepping into a bath. Be warned that rip tides and undertows can catch out even the strongest swimmer, so be especially careful and never ignore flags or signs ordering you not to swim. Other hazards you may face include jellyfish, usually around the end of the summer. If you don't fancy roughing it on the beach, many hotels and clubs have swimming pools that are open for public use for a day entrance fee. Swimming lessons are widely available from health and beach clubs.

## Table Tennis

Other options **Leisure Facilities** p.384

If you are interested in playing table tennis, tables can be booked for Dhs.20 per hour, inclusive of equipment, at Insportz (04 347 5833) just off Sheikh Zayed Road behind Dubai Garden Centre. For information on Insportz, see their entry under Sports Clubs on p.384. There is a UAE Table Tennis Association based in Dubai (04 266 9362), which can provide some information on how to get into leagues and high level competitions, but unfortunately most of the local clubs only accept Emirati nationals.

## Tennis

Other options **Leisure Facilities** p.384

Dubai is firmly established on the international tennis circuit, with the annual $1,000,000 Dubai Tennis Championships attracting the best players in the world. There are plenty of venues around the city to enjoy a game. Outdoor courts are available at most health and beach clubs, many of which are floodlit. There are also indoor courts for hire at InSportz (04 347 5833).

*Nr Tennis Stadium*
*Al Garhoud*
*Map 13 E1*

### Aviation Club, The
*04 282 4122 | www.cftennis.com*

The Clark Francis Tennis Academy at The Aviation Club offers a variety of lessons and activities for all ages and abilities. A 14-week coaching course costs Dhs.650 as part of a group, or Dhs.1,000 for individuals. The club boasts a range of modern facilities, including eight floodlit Decoturf tennis courts. It also hosts the Aviation Cup and the annual Dubai Tennis Championships.

*American University*
*in Dubai*
*Umm Suqeim*
*Map 5 C2*

### Dubai Tennis Academy
*04 344 4674 | www.dubaitennisacademy.com*

The Academy offers world class training with experienced internationally qualified coaches all year round, for tennis players of all ages and abilities. The Academy's full time adult and junior programmes include private lessons, group clinics, competitions, ladies' tennis mornings and school holiday sports camps. A personal progress report and video analysis are also available.

*Int 5, Shk Zayed Rd*
*Emirates Hills*
*Map 5 C3*

### Emirates Golf Club
*04 380 2222 | www.dubaigolf.com*

The Emirates Tennis Academy is open to members and non-members, and offers coaching for all ages and skill levels. The centre has four courts, and coaching is

378

provided by qualified USPTR professionals. The academy also has two teams in the ladies' Spinneys League and one in the men's Prince League.

## Thai Boxing
Other options **Martial Arts** p.359, **Kickboxing** p.353

*Montana Centre Bld,*
*Za'abeel Rd*
*Al Karama*
*Map 10 F1*

### Colosseum
*04 337 2755*
This health and fitness club was the first to introduce the martial art of Muay Thai (Thai Boxing) to the UAE. Classes are held on Monday, Wednesday and Saturday evenings from 20:30 to 22:00. Personal training sessions are also available for children over the age of 8. The price per lesson is Dhs.40, but slightly less if you sign up for lessons in advance. Colosseum also organises competitions between different clubs in the area.

## Triathlon

*Various locations*

### Dubai Triathlon Club
*050 774 6581 | www.dubaitriclub.com*
During the winter season (October to April) the Dubai Triathlon Club organises the Dubai Triathlon Series that comprises three or four triathlons, aquathons or duathlons. Membership is not required, but all interested participants are invited to register via email.

## Wadi & Dune Bashing
Other options **Desert Driving Courses** p.332, **Camping** p.326

With the vast areas of virtually untouched wilderness in the UAE, wadi and dune bashing are very popular pastimes. To protect the environment from damage, you should try to stick to existing tracks rather than create new tracks across virgin countryside. While it may be hard to deviate from the track when wadi bashing, dunes are ever changing so obvious paths are less common. Although the sandy dunes may look devoid of life, there is a surprising variety of flora and fauna that exists.
Dune bashing, or desert driving, is one of the toughest challenges for both car and driver, but once you have mastered it, it's also the most fun. Driving in the wadis is usually a bit more straightforward. Wadis are (usually) dry gullies, carved through the rock by rushing floodwaters, following the course of seasonal rivers. The main safety precaution to take when wadi bashing is to keep your eyes open for developing rare, but not impossible thunder storms – the wadis can fill up quickly and you will need to make your way to higher ground pretty quickly to avoid flash floods.

*Fun in the dunes*

**379**

If you want a wilderness adventure but don't know where to start, contact any of the major tour companies (see Tour Operators, p.283). All offer a range of desert and mountain safaris. If you're really keen, have a go at a desert driving course (p.332). For further information and tips on driving off-road check out both the *UAE Off-Road Explorer* and *Oman Off-Road Explorer*. These fabulous books feature a multitude of detailed routes, stunning satellite images, striking photos and essential off-road directories.

## Wakeboarding & Waterskiing

**Nr the Yacht Club**
Umm Al Quwain
*Map 1 E1*

### Dubai Water Sports Association
*050 492 7445* | www.dwsa.net
Though no longer located at the creek, the DWSA still provides wakeboarding and waterskiing lessons out of their new home in Umm Al Quwain. A 15 minute lesson costs Dhs.75 and those interested can contact Henri at the above number.

**Cassells Ghantoot Hotel**
Jebel Ali
*Map 1 E2*

### The Wakeboard School
*050 768 9504* | www.thewakeboardschool.com
National champion wakeboarder Tom Ellis provides wakeboarding lessons for both beginner and advanced wakeboarders. A 15 minute lesson costs Dhs.100 or you can opt for an hour-long trip for Dhs.300 per person. Contact Tom for more information.

## Watersports

**Jebel Ali Htl**
Jebel Ali
*Map 2 D4*

### Club Joumana
*04 883 6000* | www.jebelali-international.com
Operating from the Aqua Hut on Jebel Ali Golf Resort and Spa's private beach, the club offers watersports including windsurfing, waterskiing, kayaking, catamaran and laser sailing, and banana boat rides. Special rates are available for guests and club members. Non-residents are charged an additional fee for access to the beach and pools.

**Rd 39A off Beach Rd**
Jumeira
*Map 6 D1*

### Dubai Surfski & Kayak Club
www.dskc.net
Those with a penchant for a paddle can take full advantage of the Dubai Surfski and Kayak Club's range of activities for all levels of ability. The club has a paddling school that offers training for surf ski or kayak beginners, and for the more advanced there are individual private coaching sessions. The focus of the sessions is to develop fitness and technique while encouraging safety, with sessions on the Kite Beach at the Dubai Surfski and Kayak club. The club itself runs a range of activities and challenges, including the DSKC Squall which takes place on the last Friday of every month at the Mina Seyahi and involves a 10km course along the Palm finishing at Bussola Beach. Paddlers can test their training along this course which costs Dhs.50 for singles and Dhs.60 per paddler for doubles and includes breakfast.

*Catamaran sailing*

## Spectator Sports

Dubai has been expanding its repertoire of sporting events on two fronts. In an effort to retain a sense of culture in an increasingly international city, the UAE government has made clear efforts to promote traditional sports. The best example of this can be found in the Friday camel races held throughout the country, and locally at Nad Al Sheba. On the other front, Dubai has steadily been promoting huge international events with massive prizes that not only satisfy the local population, but draw sporting enthusiasts from around the world.

*Robotic Jockeys*
*The law now prevents children from riding camels in races. In their place robotic jockeys have been tried and tested. The operators follow the race in 4WD while directing the jockeys by remote control.*

## Camel Racing

This is a chance to see a truly traditional local sport up close. Apart from great photo opportunities and the excitement of the races, you can also have a browse around the shops as most race tracks have camel markets alongside (they are dark and dusty but should not be missed). The best buy is the large cotton blankets (used as camel blankets),which make excellent bedspreads, throws and picnic blankets, and only cost around Dhs.40. It is also interesting to see the old traders sitting on the floor of their shop, hand weaving camel halters and lead-ropes. Other shops will sell buckets, pots, and general hardware items.

Races take place during the winter months, usually on Thursday and Friday mornings, at tracks in Dubai, Ras Al Khaimah, Umm Al Quwain, Al Ain and Abu Dhabi. Often, additional races are held on National Day and certain other public holidays. Races start very early (by about 07:30) and are usually over by 08:30. Admission is free.

Ras Al Khaimah has one of the best racetracks in the country at Digdagga, situated on a plain between the dunes and the mountains, about 10km south of the town. The course at Nad Al Sheba in Dubai is also a great place to visit and has a grand falconry building where one entire wall consists of a glass window overlooking the sand racing course.

## Golf

*Emirates Golf Club*
*Emirates Hills*
*Map 5 C3*

### Dubai Desert Classic

*04 380 2222 | www.dubaidesertclassic.com*

One of the highlights of the Dubai sporting calendar, this European PGA Tour event is a popular event among both players and spectators at the end of January and start of February. Tiger Woods won the 2006 competition, with Henrik Stenson taking the title off him in 2007. Tickets for the event at Emirates Golf Club sell out fast, so check the website regularly for details.

## Horse Racing

*Nad Al Sheba*
*Racecourse*
*Nad Al Sheba*
*Map 2 E3*

### Dubai Racing Club

*04 332 2277 | www.dubairacingclub.com*

A visit to Dubai during the winter months is not complete without experiencing race night at Nad al Sheba. This racecourse is one of the world's leading racing facilities, with top jockeys from Australia, Europe and the USA regularly competing throughout the season (October – April). Racing takes place at night under floodlights and there are usually six to seven races each evening. The start time is 19:00 (except during Ramadan when it is 21:00). The clubhouse charges day membership on race nights; prices change, so check the Nad al Sheba's website for details. Everyone can take part in various free competitions to select the winning horses, with the ultimate aim of taking home prizes or cash. Hospitality suites, with catering organised on request, can be hired by companies or private individuals. The dress code for the public enclosures is casual, while racegoers are encouraged to dress smart-casual in the clubhouse and private viewing boxes. General admission and parking are free and the public has access to most areas with a reserved area for badge holders and members. Nad al Sheba also plays host to the world's richest horse race, the Dubai World Cup, every March (see p.69).

Nad Al Sheba is approximately 5km south-east of Dubai, signposted from Sheikh Zayed Road at the Metropolitan Hotel junction and then from the roundabout close to the Dubai Polo Club and Country Club. You can also catch a slightly more raw form of horse racing at Jebel Ali racecourse, near the Greens, every other Friday afternoon during the season.

## Rugby

*Al Ain Road*

### Dubai Rugby 7s

*04 321 0008 | www.dubairugby7s.com*

One of the biggest events in the UAE, sport or non-sport related, the Dubai Rugby 7s attracted more than 70,000 people in 2006. The two-day event is the first stop in the IRB Sevens World series and plays host to the top 16 sevens teams in the world. The first day of the event sees regional teams go head to head while the second day lets the big boys take the pitch. Unlike 11-a-side rugby, sevens often proves more exciting for fans due to its fast pace and high scores. Tickets regularly sell out weeks in advance so make sure you plan early. For years the tournament was held at the Exiles Club in Al Awir, but that site is now gone and future events should be held at the new Dubai Rugby Grounds near the Silicon Oasis on the Al Ain Road (to be confirmed).

## Tennis

*Dubai Tennis*
*Stadium*
*Al Garhoud*
*Map 13 E1*

### Dubai Tennis Open

*04 282 4122 | www.dubaitennischampionships.com*

The Dubai Duty Free Tennis Open takes place every February at the Aviation Club in Garhoud, and is a great opportunity to catch some of the top players in the game at close quarters. The $1,000,000 event is firmly established on the international tennis calendar, and features both men's and ladies' tournaments. Roger Federer took the men's title in 2007. Tickets for the later stages sell out in advance so keep an eye out for sale details, although entrance to some of the earlier rounds can be bought on the day.

*Horse racing*

## Leisure Facilities

Wherever you are in Dubai, there is a wide variety of sport and leisure facilities available. As well as health clubs in hotels, there are many local neighbourhood gyms, often filled with serious workout fanatics. While facilities tend to be mixed, prices are generally a fraction of health club membership fees. Depending on the gym, its size, location and facilities you may find that the annual membership is at least half that of the beach clubs. Sports clubs, however, are more geared to the hard work involved with getting in shape whereas beach clubs have a little luxury thrown in for good measure! Refer to the Beach Clubs and Health Clubs table on p.386 for full details of various clubs in Dubai, including their membership rates and amenities offered.

## Beach Clubs

Other options **Beaches** p.267, **Health Clubs** p.386

Beach clubs offer a similar range of facilities to health clubs (see below) but with the added bonus of beach access. They are very popular with families on weekends, and you can swim, play sports or just lounge in the sun in a peaceful environment. Most include some excellent food and beverage outlets, so people tend to stay for the day. Generally beach clubs require you to be a member before you can use their facilities, although many also have day guest rates. Day rates sometimes include lunch, which often is a buffet so that you can get your money's worth by stuffing your face. For listings of rates and facilities of Dubai's beach clubs, see the Club Membership Rates & Facilities Table (p.386).

## Health Clubs

Most health clubs offer workout facilities such as machines and weights, plus classes varying from aerobics to yoga, while some also have swimming pools and tennis or squash courts. Fitness First, the well-known fitness chain, has opened seven health clubs throughout Dubai. See the Club Membership Rates & Facilities Table on page 386 or check out their website at www.fitnessfirst.ae

## Sports Clubs

Other options **Beach Clubs** p.384, **Health Clubs** p.384

Most of the following clubs offer a range of sporting activities, and feature a variety of facilities like swimming pools, tennis and squash courts, and golf courses. Many also have workout facilities. For details of individual sports refer directly to listings in this section of the guide.

*Al Ain Road*

### Dubai Exiles Rugby Club
*04 333 1198 | www.dubaiexiles.com*

Although primarily a rugby club, Dubai Exiles offers additional leisure facilities for hire, which include netball courts and football pitches. The club can also cater for special events and private parties. For more information email enquiries@dubaiexiles.com or check the website. The Exiles club is set for a new year move from its Al Awir location to a new stadium (yet to be confirmed) near Silicon Oasis.

### Goodbye Country Club

As of November 2007, the popular leisure location Dubai Country Club finally closed its doors at its Bukadra location as the city's unstoppable wave of development swept over it. The club, which housed tennis, squash and badminton courts, plus a swimming pool, football pitch and sand golf course, is hopeful of finding a new venue for its members, but at the time of going to print no location had been revealed. Keep an eye on www.dubaicountryclub.com for further developments.

384

**Nr Indian High School**
*Oud Metha*
*Map 10 E2 170*

## India Club
*04 337 1112 | www.indiaclubdubai.com*
Opened in 1964, this club currently has 6,500 members and seeks to provide facilities for sports, entertainment and recreation, and to promote business. Facilities include a gym, with a separate steam room and sauna for men and women, badminton, squash and tennis courts, table tennis, basketball, a swimming pool, and a variety of indoor games.

**Nr Int 4, Shk Zayed Rd**
*Al Quoz*
*Map 6 B3 19*

## Insportz
*04 347 5833 | www.insportzclub.com*
Insportz is Dubai's first indoor sports centre and features five multi-purpose courts, a cricket coaching net and cafeteria, all within the comfort of air-conditioned surroundings. Sports available include table tennis, cricket, football, basketball and hockey, and prices (inclusive of equipment) start from Dhs.20 for children and Dhs.25 for adults. There's also a complete coaching programme for juniors. The club can also be booked for functions such as a kids' party or a corporate get-together with a difference.

**Nr Sharjah English School**
*Sharjah*
*Map 2 F2 169*

## Sharjah Wanderers Sports Club
*06 566 2105 | www.sharjahwanderers.com*
This is a popular club supported by the expat community in Sharjah, Dubai and the northern emirates. Facilities include floodlit tennis courts, football, rugby and hockey fields, squash courts, swimming pool, gym, library, snooker, darts, aerobic classes, yoga, dancing for kids, netball and a kids' play area.

Mini super stars

The Quay Health Club

Art Dubai (19-22 March 2008)

## Club Membership Rates & Facilities

| Beach Clubs | Location | Area | Map | Tel |
| --- | --- | --- | --- | --- |
| Club Joumana | Jebel Ali Golf Resort & Spa | Jebel Ali | 3-A1 | 04 883 6000 |
| Club Mina | Le Meridien Mina Seyahi | Al Sufouh | 5-C1 | 04 399 3333 |
| Dubai Marine Beach Resort & Spa | Dubai Marine Beach Resort & Spa | Jumeira | 7-F1 | 04 346 1111 |
| Jumeira Health & Beach Club | Sheraton Jumeirah Beach Resort & Towers | Dubai Marina | 4-F1 | 04 399 5533 |
| Elixir Spa & Health Club | Habtoor Grand Resort & Spa | Dubai Marina | 5-B1 | 04 399 5000 |
| Oasis Beach Club | Oasis Beach Hotel | Dubai Marina | 5-A1 | 04 315 4029 |
| Pavilion Marina & Sports Club | The Jumeirah Beach Hotel | Umm Suqeim | 6-B2 | 04 406 8800 |
| Ritz-Carlton Health Club & Spa | The Ritz Carlton Dubai | Dubai Marina | 5-B1 | 04 399 4000 |

| Health Clubs | | | | |
| --- | --- | --- | --- | --- |
| Al Nasr Fitness Centre (m/f separate) | Al Nasr Leisureland | Oud Metha | 10-E2 | 04 337 1234 |
| Assawan Health Club | Burj Al Arab | Umm Suqeim | 6-B1 | 04 301 7777 |
| Aviation Club | Aviation Club | Garhoud | 13-D1 | 04 282 4122 |
| Taj Health Club | Taj Palace Hotel | Deira | 11-C1 | 04 223 2222 |
| Big Apple | Boulevard at Emirates Towers | Trade Centre 2 | 7-F3 | 04 330 0000 |
| Body Connection Health Club | Rydges Plaza Hotel | Satwa | 8-A3 | 04 398 2222 |
| Bodylines Jumeira | Jumeira Rotana Hotel | Satwa | 8-A2 | 04 345 5888 |
| Bodylines Leisure & Fitness | Towers Rotana Hotel | Trade Centre 1 | 7-E3 | 04 343 8000 |
| Bodylines Leisure & Fitness | Al Bustan Rotana Hotel | Garhoud | 13-E1 | 04 705 4571 |
| Club Olympus | Hyatt Regency Hotel | Deira | 9-D1 | 04 209 6802 |
| The Club | Dubai International Hotel Apartments | Trade Centre 2 | 7-F3 | 04 306 5050 |
| Colosseum | Montana Building, Zabeel Road | Karama | 10-F1 | 04 337 2755 |
| Creek Health Club | Sheraton Dubai Hotel & Towers | Deira | 9-B4 | 04 207 1711 |
| Dimensions Health & Fitness Center | Metropolitan Hotel | Int 2, Shk Zayed Rd | 7-B3 | 04 407 6704 |
| Creek's Gym | Dubai Creek Golf & Yacht Club | Garhoud | 9-B4 | 04 205 4567 |
| Fitness First | Various Locations | Dubai | – | 04 358 0344 |
| Fitness Planet (mixed & ladies) | Al Hana Centre | Satwa | 8-B3 | 04 398 9030 |
| Fitness Planet | Atrium Suites | Hor Al Anz | 12-A3 | 04 269 9773 |
| Griffins Health Club | JW Marriott | Deira | 11-E1 | 04 607 7755 |
| The Health Club | Emirates Towers Hotel | Trade Centre 2 | 7-F3 | 04 330 0000 |
| Hiltonia Health Club | Hilton Dubai Jumeirah | Dubai Marina | 5-A1 | 04 399 1111 |
| Inter-Fitness Dubai | Radisson SAS Hotel, Deira Creek | Deira | 9-B4 | 04 222 7171 |
| Lifestyle Health Club | City Centre Residence | Deira | 11-C3 | 04 603 8825 |
| Natural Elements | Le Meridien Dubai | Garhoud | 13-E1 | 04 702 2430 |
| Nautilus Health Centre | Metropolitan Palace Hotel | Deira | 11-C1 | 04 227 0000 |
| Pharaohs' Club (mixed & ladies) | Pyramids | Umm Hurair (2) | 10-E4 | 04 324 0000 |
| Quay Healthclub | Madinat Jumeirah | Umm Suqeim | 6-A2 | 04 366 8888 |
| u Concept Centre | Village Mall | Jumeira | 7-F1 | 04 344 9060 |
| Willow Stream | Fairmont Hotel | Trade Centre 1 | 8-A4 | 04 311 8800 |

## Club Membership Rates & Facilities

| | Membership Rates | | | | Gym | | | | | | Activity | | | | Relaxation | | | | |
|---|---|---|---|---|---|---|---|---|---|---|---|---|---|---|---|---|---|---|---|
| Male | Female | Couple | Family | Non-Members (peak) | Treadmills | Exercise bikes | Step machines | Rowing machines | Free weights | Resistance machines | Tennis courts | Swimming pool | Squash courts | Aerobics/Dance Exercise | Massage | Sauna | Jacuzzi | Plunge pool | Steam room |
| 4300 | 2900 | 7200 | 7200 | 200 | 1 | 1 | 1 | 1 | ✓ | ✓ | 4FL | ✓ | 2 | – | ✓ | ✓ | ✓ | – | ✓ |
| 10000 | 10000 | 15000 | 15000 | 250 | 10 | 4 | 1 | 2 | ✓ | 18 | 4FL | ✓ | – | ✓ | ✓ | ✓ | ✓ | ✓ | ✓ |
| 9500 | 9500 | 12300 | 13500 | 200 | 5 | 5 | 2 | 1 | ✓ | 13 | 2FL | ✓ | 4 | ✓ | ✓ | ✓ | ✓ | ✓ | ✓ |
| 8000 | 8000 | 10000 | 12000 | 120 | 3 | 4 | 3 | 2 | ✓ | 11 | 2FL | ✓ | 2 | ✓ | ✓ | ✓ | – | ✓ | ✓ |
| 12000 | 12000 | 16000 | 20000 | 200 | 8 | 3 | 2 | 2 | ✓ | 25 | 2FL | ✓ | 2 | ✓ | ✓ | ✓ | ✓ | ✓ | ✓ |
| 1200* | 1200* | 1600* | 1900* | 160 | 2 | 2 | 2 | 1 | ✓ | ✓ | 1FL | ✓ | – | – | ✓ | ✓ | ✓ | ✓ | ✓ |
| 10000 | 10000 | 15000 | 17500 | 350 | 9 | 8 | 2 | 3 | ✓ | 23 | 7FL | ✓ | 3 | ✓ | ✓ | ✓ | ✓ | ✓ | ✓ |
| 30000 | 30000 | 40000 | 50000 | 300 | 3 | 6 | 3 | 2 | ✓ | 10 | 4FL | ✓ | 2 | ✓ | ✓ | ✓ | ✓ | ✓ | ✓ |
| 1450 | 1000 | 2150 | 2650 | – | 4 | 5 | – | – | ✓ | ✓ | 4 | ✓ | ✓ | – | – | ✓ | – | – | – |
| 35000 | 35000 | 50000 | 58000 | – | 5 | 8 | 3 | 2 | ✓ | 15 | – | ✓ | 1 | ✓ | ✓ | ✓ | ✓ | ✓ | ✓ |
| 5500 | 4500 | 7500 | 8750 | – | 9 | 5 | 3 | 3 | ✓ | 16 | 6FL | ✓ | 2 | ✓ | ✓ | ✓ | ✓ | ✓ | ✓ |
| 3500 | 3000 | 5250 | 7250 | 100 | 5 | 3 | 1 | 1 | ✓ | 7 | – | ✓ | – | ✓ | – | ✓ | ✓ | ✓ | ✓ |
| 3120 | 3120 | 5280 | – | 30 | 8 | 3 | 4 | 2 | ✓ | 11 | – | ✓ | – | ✓ | ✓ | ✓ | ✓ | ✓ | ✓ |
| 2500 | 2500 | 3800 | – | – | 2 | 2 | 2 | 2 | ✓ | 9 | – | ✓ | – | ✓ | ✓ | ✓ | ✓ | ✓ | ✓ |
| 2000 | 2000 | 2800 | 3000 | 75 | 1 | 1 | – | – | ✓ | 2 | – | ✓ | – | ✓ | – | ✓ | – | ✓ | – |
| 2600 | 2200 | 3600 | 4000 | 75 | 3 | 1 | 2 | 1 | ✓ | 9 | – | ✓ | – | ✓ | – | ✓ | ✓ | ✓ | ✓ |
| 3575 | 3025 | 4500 | 5225 | 75 | 6 | 6 | 2 | 2 | ✓ | 9 | 3 | ✓ | 2 | ✓ | ✓ | ✓ | ✓ | ✓ | ✓ |
| 4200 | 3000 | 5000 | 5900 | 80 | 8 | 4 | 2 | 2 | ✓ | 10 | 3 | ✓ | 2 | ✓ | ✓ | ✓ | ✓ | ✓ | ✓ |
| 3850 | 3300 | 4950 | 6270 | 60 | 6 | 3 | 2 | 2 | ✓ | 12 | 4FL | ✓ | 3 | – | ✓ | ✓ | ✓ | ✓ | ✓ |
| 2400 | 2100 | 3600 | 4200 | – | 5 | 3 | – | 2 | ✓ | 10 | – | ✓ | – | – | ✓ | ✓ | ✓ | ✓ | ✓ |
| 3000 | 3000 | 4000 | 5400 | 75 | 2 | 2 | 2 | – | ✓ | 1 | 1 | ✓ | – | ✓ | ✓ | ✓ | – | ✓ | ✓ |
| 2400 | 2000 | 3500 | 4000 | 60 | 6 | 4 | 2 | 2 | ✓ | 19 | 1 | ✓ | – | ✓ | ✓ | ✓ | ✓ | ✓ | ✓ |
| 5500 | 5500 | – | 7500 | – | 6 | 5 | 3 | 3 | ✓ | ✓ | – | ✓ | – | ✓ | – | ✓ | – | – | ✓ |
| | | | | | 40 | 20 | 25 | 3 | ✓ | 30 | – | ✓ | – | ✓ | – | ✓ | – | – | ✓ |
| 2560 | 3390 | 4608 | 8704 | 40 | 7 | 7 | 5 | 2 | ✓ | 25 | – | ✓ | – | ✓ | ✓ | ✓ | ✓ | – | ✓ |
| 2560 | 3390 | 4608 | 8704 | 40 | 10 | 9 | 2 | 2 | ✓ | 36 | – | – | – | ✓ | ✓ | ✓ | ✓ | – | ✓ |
| 3575 | 2530 | 5060 | – | 82.5 | 7 | 6 | 4 | 2 | ✓ | ✓ | – | ✓ | 2 | ✓ | ✓ | ✓ | ✓ | ✓ | ✓ |
| 6625 | 6625 | 8980 | – | 120 | 8 | 3 | 2 | 2 | ✓ | 11 | – | ✓ | – | ✓ | ✓ | ✓ | ✓ | ✓ | ✓ |
| 4500** | 4500** | 6000** | 7500** | – | 4 | 2 | 2 | 2 | ✓ | 2 | – | ✓ | – | ✓ | ✓ | ✓ | ✓ | ✓ | ✓ |
| 3500 | 2500 | 5000 | – | 85 | 5 | 4 | 2 | 2 | ✓ | 10 | 1FL | ✓ | 2 | ✓ | ✓ | ✓ | ✓ | ✓ | ✓ |
| 3200 | 2600 | 4800 | – | 50 | 8 | 6 | 2 | 1 | ✓ | 14 | 1FL | ✓ | 2 | ✓ | ✓ | ✓ | – | ✓ | ✓ |
| 3920 | 3335 | 5290 | 6390 | 150 | 3 | 4 | 1 | 2 | ✓ | 15 | – | ✓ | 2 | ✓ | ✓ | ✓ | ✓ | ✓ | ✓ |
| 3750 | 2750 | 5000 | 5000 | 60 | 10 | 4 | 2 | 3 | ✓ | 22 | 3FL | ✓ | 2 | ✓ | ✓ | ✓ | ✓ | ✓ | ✓ |
| 6600 | 6600 | 9600 | 10800 | – | 7 | 8 | 4 | 2 | ✓ | 18 | 3 | ✓ | 2 | ✓ | ✓ | ✓ | ✓ | ✓ | ✓ |
| 10230 | 10230 | 13090 | – | – | 9 | 8 | 3 | 3 | ✓ | 12 | 5FL | ✓ | ✓ | – | ✓ | – | ✓ | – | ✓ |
| – | – | – | – | 250 | 2 | 2 | – | 1 | ✓ | 5 | – | – | – | – | ✓ | ✓ | – | – | – |
| 6000 | 6000 | 10000 | – | 250 | 5 | 4 | 2 | 2 | ✓ | 13 | – | ✓ | – | ✓ | ✓ | ✓ | ✓ | ✓ | ✓ |

* Monthly membership

** Half-yearly membership

## Well-Being

Whether it's a pampering session at a health spa, receiving meditation guidance from a guru, or a limbering body massage: whatever your definition of well-being there's a good chance that someone, somewhere in Dubai will have the necessary facilities and skills to have you feeling and looking better in no time.

*Comfort Beauty*

*When you can't face the tiresome drive to your favourite salon, Comfort Beauty will save you the hassle by visiting you at home. Offering manicures, pedicures, and top to toe waxing, appointments can be made by calling Dubai 04 332 6844, or online at www.comfort beauty.com.*

## Beauty Salons

Other options **Perfumes & Cosmetics** p.443, **Health Spas** p.388, **Beauty Training** p.322

Beauty is big business in Dubai. Salons are very popular and there is a huge variety to choose from offering every type of treatment imaginable. Services range from manicures, pedicures, waxing and henna, to the latest haircuts, styles and colours. Alternatively, you can arrange for a stylist to come to your house if you want to be truly decadent. The quality and range of treatments vary greatly, so trial and error or word of mouth is probably the best way to find a good salon.

In hotels you'll find both male and female stylists working alongside each other, but in establishments located outside hotels, only female stylists are permitted to work in ladies' salons. These salons are very private and men are not permitted inside – even the windows are covered.

There are also numerous salons aimed primarily at Arabic ladies and they specialise in henna designs, so look out for a decorated hand poster in salon windows. The traditional practice of painting henna on the hands and feet, especially for weddings or special occasions, is still very popular with UAE nationals. For tourists, a design on the hand, ankle or shoulder can make a great memento – it will cost about Dhs.30 and the intricate brown patterns fade after two to three weeks.

## Hairdressers

Dubai has a wide range of options for getting a cut, colour or restyle. At one end you have the small barber shops where gents can get a haircut (and relaxing head massage) for as little as Dhs.10, with the option of a shave with a cut-throat razor for a few extra dirhams. Ladies should be able to find salons where a basic haircut starts at around Dhs.40. At the other end of the scale you have upmarket boutiques and salons offering the latest styles and treatments to men and women, where you could pay Dhs.300 or more for a cut and blow dry. Many of the shopping malls have hairdressers, as do some of the bigger hotels. Roots in Jumeira and Al Barsha is popular, as is Hair

| Hairdressers | | |
| --- | --- | --- |
| Carla K. Styling Centre | Trade Centre 1 | 04 343 8544 |
| Cut Shape | Al Satwa | 04 398 6008 |
| Essentials | Al Wasl | 04 398 8723 |
| Hair Corridor | Al Wasl | 04 394 5622 |
| Hair@Pyramids | Umm Hurair | 04 324 1490 |
| Hairworks | Umm Suqeim | 04 394 0777 |
| Jen's Hair Studio | Marsa Dubai | 800 5367 |
| Lamcy Hair & Beauty Centre | Oud Metha | 04 335 1101 |
| Mainstream Hair Design & Beauty | Al Diyafah Rd | 04 345 0556 |
| Roots | Jumeira | 04 344 4040 |
| Sisters | Jumeira | 04 342 0787 |
| SOS Beauty Salon | Jumeira | 04 349 1144 |
| Toni & Guy | Trade Centre 2 | 04 330 3345 |
| Zouari | Al Sufouh | 04 399 9999 |

Corridor. A new concept that recently touched down at the Grosvenor House is JetSet, a ladies wash and blow-dry salon (so no cutting or colouring) with a cool airline-themed interior. If you are looking for a bridal hair stylist contact Maria Dowling on 04 345 4225 (for more information on weddings see p.92).

# Well-Being

Willow Stream

Oriental Hammam

The Palace - The Old Town

Radisson SAS

Angsana Spa Facial

Talise Spa

## Health Spas

Other options **Leisure Facilities** p.384, **Massage** p.398

*Grosvenor House*
*Al Sufouh*
*Map 5 B2* 71

### 1847

*04 399 8989* | *info@1847.ae*

In a city where the ladies seem to get all the best perks and pampering, it's about time the men were offered a little of the same. Step forward 1847, the first dedicated 'grooming lounge' for men in the Middle East. Why not start with a manicure or pedicure (or both) in the privacy of your own 'study', where you can sit back and flick through a selection of news, sports, and documentary channels on your personal LCD TV. The walls even slide back allowing you to socialise with your next-door neighbour if you wish. Follow this with a traditional shave experience – handmade, cream leather Italian barber chairs, built-in sinks, and dark panelled walls set the tone, while Master Barbers transform this mundane daily task into an art form.

For tired and aching muscles you can end your day with a full-body massage in one of the welcoming candle-lit therapy suites. The skilled masseuses offer a range of treatments, allowing you to choose a massage that will leave you dreamily relaxed or thoroughly revived and invigorated. If your schedule is back-to-back high-powered meetings then try a 'quick fix' head, neck and shoulder massage.

Clearly aimed at gents of a certain breeding, the stylish interior, discreet, professional staff, and soothing atmosphere all work to convey an air of exclusivity. So if you want to feel like a movie star or pro footballer, then head to 1847 for some head-to-toe attention. In addition to the Grosvenor House branch, there is another 1847 lounge in the Boulevard at Emirates Towers – telephone 04 330 1847.

*The Aviation Club*
*Al Garhoud*
*Map 13 D1* 33

### Akaru Spa ▶ p.391

*04 282 8578* | *www.akaruspa.com*

The Akaru Spa opened in the summer of 2005 with autumnal colours and natural decor, such as wooden fittings, orange walls and glass features, creating a truly tranquil retreat. There is a Turkish Room with sauna in dimly lit surroundings and fruit juices and water on tap. Exotic treatments range from various specialised facials and wraps to Microdermabrasion and Sunvision. During the cooler months they offer Sky Therapies including Sky Facial, Aromatic Sky Massage and Face and Body Experience which are administered on the rooftop terrace. Also on the indulging menu is Thalgo (La Beaute Marine), a range of specialised body marine treatments that utilise the riches of the ocean, with a whole host of benefits for your skin.

*Park Hyatt Dubai*
*Creekside, Deira*
*Map 11 B4* 76

### Amara Spa

*04 602 1660* | *www.dubai.park.hyatt.com*

The recently opened Amara spa is something of a breath of fresh air in Dubai's spa world. While the spa scene in Dubai is certainly sublime they tend to all follow the same formula – a paradise retreat with dimmed lighting, rose petals, candles and hypnotic music. Amara, however, is something different. Not to say that the aforementioned approach isn't heavenly but what sets this spa apart is the treatment rooms. After you arrive at the grand spa entrance there is no communal changing room or wet area, instead you are escorted directly to your treatment room which acts as your personal spa. Here you have all the facilities of a changing room (toilet, shower, hairdryer, wardrobe) as well as a relaxation corner. After your treatment, or during if you are having a scrub or wrap, you can treat yourself to a shower under the sun in your very own private outdoor shower (very liberating) with a relaxation area for you to dry off under the warm rays. The treatments are usually packaged, which is definitely a good thing as you really won't be in a hurry to leave.

...release, relax, rewind

Revolutionary
Hydradermie Facial and Lift
from GUINOT
INSTITUT • PARIS

Treatments from AED 195
For more information,
please call Isabelle 04 282 8578

Indulgent spa treatments
www.akaruspa.com

akaru
spa

The Aviation Club - P.O.Box 55400, Dubai, U.A.E - Tel. 04 282 4122 - Fax. 04 282 4751 - www.aviationclub.ae

## Angsana Spa Arabian Ranches

*311, Emirates Road*
*Arabian Ranches*
*Map 2 E4* 127

**04 361 8251** | www.angsanaspa.com

Angsana promises to be a 'sanctuary for the inner self', offering privacy and tranquillity in a retreat-like atmosphere. And unsurprisingly the promise is delivered. The minimalist Asian surroundings feature rich, dark wood, while incense, exotic oils, low light and soft music set the tone for relaxation. The impeccably trained staff work wonders on stressed, aching bodies, turning tight muscles into putty and sending overworked minds to cloud nine. Unique massages, ranging from Balinese to Hawaiian, and of course Thai, are certainly at the higher end of the scale in terms of price, but the quality of treatment ensures value for money. This Singaporean/Thai affiliate brand of Banyan Tree certainly has brought its highly reputed standards to Dubai.

Other locations include Dubai Marina (04 368 4356), Emirates Hills (04 368 2222) and The Montgomerie (04 360 9322). All spas have male and female areas; the Dubai Marina location also features a health club with outdoor pool and mixed and female-only gyms.

## Armonia Spa

*Sheraton Jumeirah*
*Beach*
*Marsa Dubai*
*Map 4 F1* 85

**04 315 3450**

Upon arriving at the spa you'll be greeted at reception and offered a complimentary beverage or juice while waiting for your treatment. You then begin with a refreshing welcome ritual, including a warm herbal aromatic foot massage using sea salt, rose petals, dried herbs, peppermint oils, and pebbles. The wood-themed interior, candles, and relaxing music help set the mood. Treatments on offer include facials, full-body massages and luxurious body wraps for both men and women. Recommended is the Well-Being massage, a 60 minute pampering session with a gentle body massage that incorporates treatment of the face and scalp. The massage may be a little too gentle for some, so don't be afraid to tell your therapist to increase the pressure if required. The spa is on the small side, and facilities not as comprehensive as some other spas in town, but this is certainly a good place to come for facials and massages.

## Assawan Spa & Health Club

*Burj Al Arab*
*Umm Suqeim*
*Map 6 B1* 35

**04 301 7777** | www.burj-al-arab.com

The Assawan Spa is situated on the 18th floor of the breathtaking Burj Al Arab. Unsurprisingly it's an elaborate affair with a mosaic domed ceiling and ornately tiled corridors. The personal service here is excellent; you are pampered from the minute you walk through the door. The Spa has female only and mixed environments, including a state of the art gym with studios (where you can take part in everything from yoga to aerobics), saunas, steam rooms, plunge pools and two wonderfully relaxing infinity pools decorated in mosaic and gold leaf tiles. You can literally swim up to the edge of the pool, put your nose to the window, and enjoy the amazing views of the Palm and the World islands.

For pure unadulterated indulgence try the caviar body treatment – at Dhs.680 it's a bit pricey but worth it. Also on offer is a 'men only' range including massage, facial, manicure, pedicure and more. If you really want to feel like royalty then this spacious and seriously sublime spa is a dream come true. You will feel like a princess, or indeed a prince.

## Cleopatra's Spa

*Pyramids*
*Umm Hurair*
*Map 10 E4* 17

**04 324 0000** | www.waficity.com

Tucked away behind the members only door of the Pharaohs' Club, Cleopatra's Spa may not have the grand entrance that some hotel spas share, but what it lacks in ostentation it makes up for in occasion. You will be led from the modest reception (literally led by the arm, which is both attentive and awkward), to the changing rooms which have all the necessary goodies but are more operational than opulent. The relaxation area, however, is more of an ancient Egyptian affair with drapes, silk cushions and majlis-style seats. There is also a small plunge pool with Jacuzzi and sauna. The treatment rooms are all comfortable, softly lit and basked in luxurious touches and the obligatory hypnotic tunes. The spa menu should satisfy all, with everything from massages (including pregnancy) and facials to body wraps and anti-ageing miracles. The big bonus is that if you book a package you get a pool pass which allows you to float round the lazy river at the Pharaohs' Club's idyllic tree-shaded pool area. There is also a separate spa for men, and while this may not be the most splendid of spas, a visit to Cleopatra's is pure pleasure.

**Nr Jumeira Mosque**
*Jumeira*
*Map 7 F1*

## Dubai Marine Spa

*04 346 1111 | www.dxbmarine.com*

Although the spa at Dubai Marine is not as plush as some other spas in Dubai, it does offer an excellent array of treatments. This is a rather compact spa and the changing rooms are a little on the small side but the treatment rooms are comfortable and fragrantly scented. The treatments available range from Guinot, Thalgo and La Phyto facial and body treatments in addition to the Ionithermie slimming treatment, manicures and pedicures. Particularly pleasurable is the Hot Stones massage that can also be combined with a facial, manicure and pedicure. It involves the use of essential oils chosen for their calming, relaxing and grounding effects that are designed to uplift and relax the body. Also on offer are full and half-day packages and a limited range of treatments for men.

**Beh Jumeirah Plaza**
*Jumeira*
*Map 7 F1* **128**

## Elche

*04 349 4942 | www.elche.ae*

It might look a bit like a healthy cafe from the outside but don't let looks deceive you. Elche utilises the healing potential of herbs, fruit and flowers in modern scientific methods – it is like a heavenly secret garden. Hungary's Molnar family are the expert herbalists behind Elche and are committed to creating a customised range of skincare products that are refreshingly fragrant (they smell good enough to eat), perfectly pampering, and most importantly produce dramatic regenerative results. Set in a walled garden this elegantly furnished retreat is warm and peaceful and the entire experience is wholly tailored to the individual. Not only will you be given an in-depth analysis by one of the professional therapists (while relaxing and enjoying their delicious refreshments) but you will also receive a client evaluation at the end of your treatment and can even have your makeup done by a professional makeup artist. The range of treatments is unique to Dubai and the mini facials are great if you need to pop in on your lunch break. For total indulgence try the Elche's No. 1 facial with paprika – guaranteed to leave you looking hot!

**Habtoor Grand**
**Resort & Spa**
*Marsa Dubai*
*Map 5 B1* **56**

## Elixir Spa & Health Club

*04 399 5000 | www.methotels.com*

Elixir Spa & Health Club at the Habtoor Grand is as exclusive and luxurious as its plethora of five-star neighbours. Based on authentic 'Touch of Arabia' treatments with east-west holistic rituals using natural products and various healing therapies, the spa will have six decadently designed treatment rooms, a dry float room, a rasul mud chamber, nail stations, a tropical airbrush sunless tanning booth, crystal steam room, Moroccan sauna and a unique wet plinth room with Vichy shower. There will also be a restful retreat where you can relax in soothing surroundings, with wistful musical overtones and herbal teas on tap. Treatments will include Arabian rituals, hydrotherapy and Ytsara massages as well as the revolutionary Karin 02 Herzog skincare treatments from Switzerland.

One&Only
Royal Mirage
Al Sufouh
Map 5 C1 95

## Givenchy Spa

*04 399 9999 | www.oneandonlyresort.com*

The emphasis in this serene setting is on understated decor, with plenty of neutral colours, natural light and soft music in the treatment rooms. The relaxation room is a haven of tranquillity and an ideal spot to savour the sensations after your treatment. While they offer a variety of massages and facials, their speciality is the Canyon Love Stone Therapy, an energy-balancing massage using warm and cool stones. The volcanic stones have been specially selected and are 'charged' in the moonlight and cleansed with salt. Stones are placed on specific points around the body, and then used to massage the skin. Other massages are available, such as Swedish, lymphatic drainage, slimming and sports massages. For high-level pampering, you could try one of the body treatments, including peels, wraps and oil baths. Only Givenchy products are used in this spa, and all are gentle and safe.

*Grand Hyatt Dubai*
*Umm Hurair*
*Map 13 C1* 54

## The Grand Spa

*04 317 1234 | www.dubai.grand.hyatt.com*

The spa may not be the biggest in Dubai but what it lacks in size it makes up for in atmosphere and attention to detail. The changing room and adjacent relaxation area have dark wooden floors and walls and are lit by rows of candles. The wet area is drizzled in rose petals and houses a Jacuzzi, plunge pool, sauna and steam room as well as spacious showers. The treatment rooms are medium in size but very comfortable, and the tranquil tunes help transport you to a higher plain. The treatments on offer range from facials, all designed with preservation and attainment of youth in mind, to massages with specialist 'aromasoul' treatments using essential oils. They also have fusion packages that allow you to combine a massage, body or hand/feet treatment, facial and a lifestyle enhancer such as pilates, circuit training, and joint flexibility – perfect for unadulterated top-to-toe indulgence.

*Nr Jumeira Mosque*
*332-5b St*
*Jumeira*
*Map 7 F1* 129

## Haven, The

*04 345 6770 | www.thehaven.ae*

The Haven is a holistic clinic dedicated to relaxation and rejuvenation for the mind , body and soul. Housed in a converted two-storey villa, the mesmerising scents, earthy decor and gentle background music will guide you into a relaxed state the moment you enter. Downstairs is a beauty and hair salon, while the candle-lit stairs lead you up to the simple and welcoming treatment rooms. There are none of the trappings of a hotel spa (steam room, Jacuzzi and relaxation area), but The Haven benefits from a wonderfully intimate aura. It offers a wide range of treatments including Thai yoga massage, Ayurvedic treatments, reflexology, aromatherapy and yoga. They also offer the increasingly popular hot stone massage. During this treatment the smooth stones are used as an extension of the therapist's hands, allowing a deeper penetrating massage that releases tension, increases circulation and induces a deep state of relaxation. No doubt you will slowly drift into a blissful sleep and when you surface in the comfortable surroundings it will be as if you have woken from a wonderful dream.

*Shangri-La Hotel*
*Trade Centre 1*
*Map 7 E3* 82

## The Health Club & Spa at Shangri-La

*04 405 2441 | www.shangri-la.com*

The Spa offers a holistic approach to healing, featuring traditional Asian treatments. The emphasis here is to restore the balance of Yin and Yang in the body with the five elements – fire, water, metal, wood and earth. The signature Chi Balance massage is 50 minutes of blissful stimulation and relaxation. The health club element includes a rooftop swimming pool, tennis courts, a squash court plus a gym. Relaxation facilities include separate spas for men and women, each with plunge pool, sauna, steam, and nine treatment rooms. A salon and barber, juice bar and boutique complete the package. Surroundings are minimalist and the treatment rooms are a little on the clinical side, while the communal areas lean more towards fitness club than spa, with too many open spaces and not enough privacy. That said, it's ideal for a healthy break for those working on the Sheikh Zayed Road strip.

**Oasis Beach Tower**
*Marsa Dubai*
*Map 5 A1* 74

## Oasis Retreat

*04 399 4444 | www.jebelali-international.com*

More of a treatment room than a spa the Oasis Retreat is hidden down some steps near the pool bar. The single, medium-sized room is decorated with candles and clad in wood with the treatment bed on the floor – which at first may seem a little basic but in some ways adds to the traditional feel of a Thai massage. Stocked with Elemis products and set to relaxing music, the lack of changing room means that you strip down in the treatment room and shower here too. The therapist will leave the room when you shower – but it is a little hard to relax as you don't know when she (or anyone else for that matter) may re-enter. The treatment range is good but there is only one therapist so it can be hard to get an appointment, especially if the hotel is busy. There is also no relaxation area so it is very much about the treatment itself and not an entire spa experience.

**One&Only**
**Royal Mirage**
*Al Sufouh*
*Map 5 C1* 75

## Oriental Hammam – Health & Beauty Institute

*04 399 9999 | www.oneandonlyresorts.com*

Having battled through the Dubai traffic you feel instantly relaxed arriving at the One & Only Royal Mirage, which is the ultimate in Arabian luxury. Welcomed by the attentive staff, you are put at ease as they explain the Oriental Hammam Experience. The surroundings are elegant but not overly opulent, with a warm traditional feel. A variety of wraps, robes and slippers are available in the changing rooms where there is soft pipe music and relaxing fragrances to set the mood. The Hammam and Spa is an impressive area with mosaic arches and intricate carvings on the high domes. The 50 minute treatment involves a variety of different experiences, including being bathed, steamed, washed with black soap, vigorously scrubbed with a loofah and massaged on a hot marble table which sounds invasive but manages somehow to be wonderfully invigorating and leaves your skin feeling as soft as cream. Also included in this treatment is free use of the Jacuzzi, plunge pools and the sensually sleep-inducing relaxation room.

**Ibn Battuta Mall**
*Jebel Ali*
*Map 4 D2* 38

## Paris Gallery Day Spa

*04 294 4000*

Conveniently located in one of Dubai's major shopping malls, Paris Gallery Day Spa combines ancient therapies with the latest technologies. They offer a wide range of treatments from total relaxation and pure indulgence to professional hair and makeup services carried out by highly trained staff. For devilishly decadent delights the new menu of chocolate and grape facials and body therapies lets you indulge in the naughty but nice without expanding your waistline! Only top quality, 78% cocoa powder and essential oils of oranges, tangerine and cedarwood are used to create your decadent face mask. The warm 'sauce' is painted onto your face and while the mask works its nourishing, energising, anti-ageing magic, you will enjoy hand and arm massage as you breathe in the sweet choc-orange aromas. A deliciously pampering treatment at Paris Gallery is the perfect way to end a shopping spree.

**395**

*The Ritz-Carlton*
*Marsa Dubai*
*Map 5 A1* 78

## Ritz-Carlton Spa

*04 318 6184 | www.ritz-carlton.com*

While the Ritz-Carlton is certainly a majestic hotel, its spa is somewhat understated. The larger treatment rooms push all the right buttons – spacious with bamboo features, running water, dimmed lights and hypnotic background music and highly professional service. If you're a member then you have the benefit of a private pool outside with a healthy spa menu and beds that have the required sink-in comfort for true relaxation. Non-members though are limited to the facilities inside the spa, the design of which seems a little ill conceived. This spa is on the petite size with a changing room, shower room (with an open entrance), and the treatment rooms all leading off a central corridor. While there is a wet room with Jacuzzi, sauna and steam room, the small relaxation area has just three beds, and feels a little claustrophobic. The range of treatments is impressive nonetheless, with an excellent selection of Balinese massages and facials, hot stone therapy, aroma body treatments, spa baths and signature spa packages.

*Al Mamzar Centre*
*Deira*
*Map 12 B4* 28

## Royal Waters Health Spa

*04 297 2053 | therwspa@eim.ae*

Located on the top floor of the Al Mamzar Centre, with separate entrances for men and women, you will receive a warm welcome from the friendly and knowledgeable staff waiting to advise you on the vast range of treatments available for health, relaxation and beauty. The spa has simple tiled decor with soft lighting and tranquil music. There are lockers and showers available and a sauna and steam room. Walk through the well-equipped gym and up on the roof you'll find the swimming pool with views of the bustling area below. You can sit and take in the surroundings as you wait for your treatment in the relaxation area. The spa offers treatments for cellulite and stretch marks, and they have a wonderful hydrotherapy circuit designed to leave you refreshed after a hard day.

*The Village*
*Jumeira*
*Map 7 F1* 91

## Sensasia

*04 349 8850 | www.sensasiaspas.com*

Tucked away on the first floor of The Village, this 'Urban Spa' is a surprising and welcome refuge from the hustle and bustle of daily life. After a chat with the friendly reception staff, you are met by your therapist and taken to one of the beautiful, Asian-inspired treatment rooms. Lighting and noise are subdued, so the process of relaxation begins long before you lie down on one of the large treatment beds. Sensasia specialises in massage, and apart from their wide range of full body massages they also offer some innovative treatments such as the 'high-heeler', an intensive pampering package for tired feet. After your treatment you have the option of spending some time in the sublime relaxation area, where you are served ginger tea and given a heated neck beanbag fragranced with essential oils. From the moment you enter to the moment you reluctantly leave, a trip to Sensasia is a heavenly experience.

*Le Meridien*
*Mina Seyahi*
*Al Sufouh*
*Map 5 C1* 69

## Solesenses Spa

*04 318 1904 | www.lemeridien.com*

The Spa is housed in a small white building (blink and you'll miss it) separated from the hotel, and once you are inside it has a nice intimate feel. There are only three treatment rooms and one makeup and manicure room, and no facilities such as a sauna or a steam room. The treatment range is a little limited – manicure, pedicure, waxing, self-tanning, reflexology and massages including Thai. Recommended are the Pro Active treatments, especially the facial range, which are particularly relaxing as

**396**

they include a head and shoulders massage. Lie back in very comfortable surroundings with low lighting and mellow music (if you don't mind pan pipes) and let the charming therapist work her magic. You will come out 75 minutes later positively glowing, feeling 10 years younger and completely relaxed. A complete range of Clarins products, including makeup and their men's range, can also be found here.

## The Spa

**Jebel Ali Golf Resort & Spa**
*Jebel Ali*
*Map 3 A1* **63**

04 883 6000 | www.jebelali-international.com

The Spa at the Jebel Ali Resort caters mainly to hotel guests, although the influx of new residents in the nearby areas could change that. An excellent level of service is offered for both men and women, in intimate and well-presented surroundings. There is a communal area with an invigorating shower, sauna, Jacuzzi and steam room (just be warned the shower leaves you not only refreshed but shivering). The changing areas are a little small but equipped with Elemis goodies, and the tranquil after-treatment area overlooks the beach. Recommended is the Royal Hammam Ritual, a 90 minute treatment in a steamy marble room that involves black soap, a henna mask, some exuberant exfoliating and a rasul mud mask before a darn good wash down. And this is literally from head to toe, give or take a corner or two! Just leave any shyness at the marble door – but not your partner, if you're brave enough to try the couples option.

## Taj Spa

**Taj Palace Hotel**
*Deira*
*Map 11 C1* **87**

04 223 2222 | www.tajpalacedubai.com

This is a relaxing and tranquil spa with a mystic and romantic atmosphere. They offer modern Ayurvedic treatments as well as popular European and far eastern ranges and natural therapies. The therapists concentrate on the body as well as the mind and methods are based on the ancient science of Ayurveda (fused with modern technology). Massage techniques, movements, herbal selection and products used are tailored to the individual guest, supporting the holistic principle that each individual has a unique body type and will therefore have different balancing needs. The changing rooms are welcoming and have a sauna and steam room, while the relaxation area is hard to tear yourself away from thanks to the spacious and sumptuous surroundings blessed with sink-in sofas and armchairs.

## Talise Spa

**Madinat Jumeirah**
*Umm Suqeim*
*Map 6 A2* **70**

04 366 6818 | www.jumeirah.com

Stepping into the Talise Spa you immediately feel a sense of calm. The atmospheric light, trickling water and neutral shades add to the feeling that you have walked out of the hectic pace of Dubai life into a tranquil oasis. Attentive staff greet you at the entrance and immediately whisk you away to the large and beautifully appointed changing rooms where you can prepare for your treatment. The treatment rooms are stand-alone studios, spacious and airy, with terracotta shaded walls, rattan blinds and ambient music at just the right level. Before or after your treatment you can enjoy the spa's other facilities including sauna, steam rooms and plunge pools, as well as a chill-out area where you can sit and sip herbal tea. The treatment list is one of the most extensive in Dubai, ranging from traditional massages to unusual therapies including flower therapy. Yoga classes are also offered.

## Willow Stream Spa & Health Club

**Fairmont Dubai**
*Trade Centre 1*
*Map 8 A4* **53**

04 332 5555 | www.fairmont.com

In keeping with the eclectic decor of The Fairmont Dubai, Willow Stream is decorated in a luxurious Greco-Roman style, with beautiful mosaics and sleek white pillars. There is a comprehensive selection of top-to-toe spa and beauty treatments using Phytomer

**397**

and Aromatherapy Associates product lines, including facials, hydrotherapy, aromatherapy and total body care. The added bonus is being able to select spa packages for that ultimate pampering session. The packages can also be tailor-made and given as gift vouchers. After a friendly welcome you'll be guided to the changing rooms where there are showers, a steam room, sauna and Jacuzzi. Soft, white towels and subtle candlelight create a wonderful sense of calm. Before or after your treatment you can use the fitness centre, the outdoor swimming pools or simply relax with a herbal tea or fresh juice. When you are ready for your treatment the knowledgeable staff will talk you through the process and give you advice so you can continue the good work at home. Near to the spa is a juice bar and an Italian restaurant where spa patrons will receive a discount.

## Massage

Other options **Leisure Facilities** p.384, **Reflexology & Massage Therapy** p.196, **Health Spas** p.390

Soothing for the body, mind and soul, a massage could be a weekly treat, a gift to someone special, or a relaxing way to get you through a trying time at work. Numerous massage techniques are available, but prices and standards vary, so it's worth doing your research into what's on offer. A full body massage will cost in the range of Dhs.100 to 300 for a one-hour session. Massages, in addition to a variety of other treatments, are available at most spas in Dubai, see Health Spas on p.390.

## Pilates

Other options **Yoga** p.399

*Shk Zayed Road,*
*Nr ThunderBowl*
*Al Wasl*
*Map 7 D3*

### The Pilates Studio

*04 343 8252 | pilates@eim.ae*

Pilates is an effective  way to tone and strengthen muscles. It was introduced to the UAE in 1998 by the owner of this studio, Catherine Lehmann, a physiologist with years of experience in Pilates. The studio offers classes for beginners and advanced students.

## Reiki

Reiki is a healing technique based on the belief that energy can be channelled into a patient. Translated as 'universal life force energy', Reiki can emotionally cleanse, physically invigorate and leave you more focused. You can learn Reiki to practise on yourself or others, directly or remotely.

*Nr Police College*
*Umm Suqeim*
*Map 6 B2*

### Archie Sharma Reiki

*04 348 8190 | archie_asharma@yahoo.com*

Archie Sharma is a Reiki master who has been practising for over 10 years and is involved in teaching and healing. She also conducts Zen meditation, is a qualified herbalist and reflexologist, and when time permits, advises on matters pertaining to Feng Shui.

*Various locations*

### Pookat Suresh Reiki

*04 285 9128*

The Pookat Suresh Reiki centre offers various degrees of attunement. In the first degree, a series of four attunements are taught by a traditional master with the aim of channeling a higher amount of universal life force energy. The second degree level teaches powerful absentee healing. For more details contact Reiki master Pookat Suresh Babu on the above number, or 050 453 9643.

## Stress Management

Other options **Support Groups** p.200

**Nr Al Wasl Park**
*Al Satwa*
*Map 7 F1*

### Sesam Omniverse Stress Management

*04 344 9880* | *www.sesam-omniverse.com*

Karin Meyer-Reumann is a counsellor, holistic healer and family display practitioner who helps people 'break patterns'. With 30 years-experience, she creates individual grids (a combination of forms and colours) that are transferred into auras so that people will attract new options into their lives while providing ways to lift energy levels.

## Tai Chi

**Musalla Towers**
*Downtown Bur Dubai*
*Map 8 F3*

### House of Chi & House of Healing

*04 397 4446* | *www.hofchi.com*

Tai Chi has been practised in China for over 2,000 years. Often referred to as meditation, it is in fact a soft martial art that is today practised by 20% of the world's population. Tai Chi is particularly beneficial to the elderly or those with impaired motor skills, since it emphasises correct posture and balance thus making it a safe exercise option for people with frail bones.

## Yoga

Other options **Pilates** p.398

Many health and fitness clubs offer yoga classes as part of their weekly schedule, catering to all levels of experience. Check the table on p.386 for a list of health club phone numbers or see below for some centres dedicated to yoga. Art of Living courses (www.artofliving.org) are also offered at various locations throughout Dubai. Ring 04 334 0105 for details of where and when.

**109, Karama Centre**
*Al Karama*
*Map 10 D1*

### Al Karama Ayurvedic centre

*04 337 8921* | *almadxb@eim.ae*

Operating for over 18 years, this centre is run by qualified professionals with expertise in the traditional systems of Ayurveda, herbal beauty care, yoga and meditation. This is a one-stop institution that has all the necessary facilities to take care of healing, rejuvenation and beauty care. Separate areas are available for men and women.

**White Crown Bld**
*Trade Centre 1*
*Map 7 F2*

### Gems of Yoga

*04 331 5161* | *www.gemsofyogadubai.com*

Gems of Yoga mixes yoga and art through yogasanas, mudras, pranayam, meditation and other stress release techniques. The centre also offers classes such as weight-watchers, desktop yoga, prenatal and postnatal yoga, therapeutic yoga, animal yoga for children, and Ashtanga Vinyasa Power Yoga from Mysore. Packages range from Dhs.650 to Dhs.2,500, and 'Yoga@home' packages are also available.

**Various Locations**

### Zen Yoga

*04 367 0435* | *www.yoga.ae*

Zen Yoga offers full-time yoga and Pilates classes in four centres: Emirates Hills, Dubai Media City, Dubai Marina and the Murooj Rotana. Studios are pristine and airy with mirrored walls to help you check your posture. Facilities include changing rooms, showers and lockers. Instructors are all highly trained and professional. Reduced rate packages of 11 or 25 classes (valid up to a year) and trial classes are available. Also, Zen donates 10% of its profits to charity

**399**

# 20th Anniversary

## The voice of British business in Dubai & the Northern Emirates

Founded in 1987, the British Business Group, Dubai & Northern Emirates, (BBG) has been promoting UK business for 20 years.

Now, with more than 1,000 members, it is the biggest and most active group of its kind in the Middle East.

Members enjoy a wide range of events, from social networking to lunches with high profile speakers. BBG member companies range from small start-ups to multinational corporations.

There are various types of membership. Visit our website or call the office for more information.

- **Breakfast meetings**
- **Speaker lunches**
- **Networking**
- **Special Interest Groups**
- **Social events**

**BRITISHBUSINESSGROUP**
DUBAI & NORTHERN EMIRATES

Check us out!
www.britbiz-uae.com

# Shopping

# Shopping

## Shopping

**Always on Sale**
The Dubai Shopping
Festival is now more
about promotions, with
raffles and scratch-
and-win offers rather
than great discounts.
Then again, discounts
are available
throughout the year
during the many sales
that take place so
frequently, so you may
never need to pay full
price for anything! The
annual shopping
festival will run from
January 24 to February
24, 2008, for more info
see the website
www.dubaishopping
festival.com.

Dubai provides innumerable opportunities to indulge in a spot of retail therapy. The city is either a shopaholic's dream or nightmare – depending on who's paying the bill. The rapid development that Dubai continues to experience is inextricably linked to shopping, and with each new development comes a new mall. The retail sector is taken very seriously, and its contribution to the emirate's economy is not underestimated. The Dubai Shopping Festival, a month dedicated to consumerism, has taken place annually for over ten years (postponed only once, in 2006, as a mark of respect following the death of Sheikh Maktoum Bin Rashid Al Maktoum).

Shopping in Dubai revolves around the malls, both big and small (see p.450), but it is also well worth checking out the ever-expanding number of independent stores, as there are some real gems. Practicality plays a large part in the mall culture, and during the hotter months they are oases of cool in the sweltering city – somewhere to walk, shop, eat and be entertained – where you can escape the soaring heat for a few hours. From the smaller community malls dotted around the city, to the mega malls that have changed the skyline, shopping opportunities abound and with most shops open until 22:00 every night, there's enough time to browse. The popularity of the malls is evident by the crowds that they pull, particularly at the weekends. It takes a brave and dedicated shopper to tackle them on a Friday evening.

In common with many countries, the cost of living is increasing and while some of what is available is still cheaper than elsewhere, groceries seem to be more expensive every week. While average prices for most items are comparable, there are not many places that can beat Dubai's range and the frequency of the sales. Cars are, on the whole, a good buy and petrol, though prices are going up, is still cheap enough to make large 4WDs practical for the school run. Electronics can be cheaper but it depends what you are used to; and Dubai is the world's leading re-exporter of gold. The variety of goods on sale is staggering and there is very little that is not available. For most items there is enough choice to find something to fit any budget, from the streets of Karama with its fake designer goods, to the shops in the malls that sell the real thing.

**Need Help? Just Ask**
Be picked up by a
resident shopaholic
and taken on a guided
tour of Dubai's
shopping hotspots. To
arrange a tailor-made
shopping trip, contact
Dubai VIP Services on
04 311 6675 or visit
www.dubaivip
service.com

Some of Dubai's most interesting shops are the independent ones (see p.475) that are springing up all over the city – they may take a bit of looking for but it is usually worth it, as what they sell is invariably more original than anything the malls have to offer. The various shopping areas, the closest that Dubai has to high streets, are great for their eclectic mix of shops. There are few other places where you can shop for fabric while waiting for your car windows to be tinted. One of the few retail sectors where Dubai is lacking is second-hand shops (see Second-Hand Items on p.444), although there are a few linked to various charities. With the population still being largely transitory, there is no shortage of second-hand goods, many of which are advertised on the notice boards in supermarkets, in the classified section of newspapers, and on websites (such as www.expatwoman.com).

Further afield, the modern malls of Sharjah are an alternative to what Dubai has to offer, the brands are pretty much the same but they are convenient for those living on that side of the city. Sharjah's souks, and the Al Arsah Souk (p.484) in particular, are more traditional than those in Dubai and are great for unique gifts. Sharjah is also renowned for its furniture warehouses, especially those selling Indian pieces, such as Lucky's, Pinky's and Khan's. Ajman is developing as the population grows, and has its own City Centre and an area with garment factories and their outlet shops. The traffic to both emirates can get pretty heavy and they are more traditional, with many companies still working split shifts ie closing between 13:00 and 16:00.

## Online Shopping

**Shop On The Hop**

The website www.quickdubai.com is a great online shopping resource that delivers food and items for the home to any Dubai address within 24 hours. You can even send a gift to someone in Dubai from anywhere in the world. If you need your shopping in a hurry, www.brownbag.ae offers a selection of goods ranging from pet food to iPods, and aims to deliver to any Dubai address within one hour. Their sister site www.fred.ae delivers fresh grocery products within three hours of ordering. If you're thirsty, www.bebida.ae delivers a variety of soft drinks to your door.

The popularity of online shopping is increasing around the world, and in an expat city like Dubai, where many residents long for the products they can get in their home countries, it is great to be able to order online. The variety of goods available, and possibly the bargain prices, make this an attractive option for anything you can't find locally. However, not all companies will ship to the UAE and if they do, the shipping charges can be prohibitive. The increasing popularity of PayPal is causing problems for many residents as the facility is only available to those with a US or UK credit card. There are often ways around this, and many sites will accept other forms of payment. eBay is a good example of a site where PayPal is preferred, making it potentially inaccessible here, but some vendors are usually willing to be flexible, especially if you explain the situation.

There should be no problems buying from sites like Amazon, although its branded packaging may sometimes be opened at customs. If you are buying DVDs or videos Benson's World (www.bensonsworld.co.uk) has much cheaper shipping rates and they use plain packaging, so often the DVDs come straight to your post box without going through the censor. Companies without representation in the region will sometimes agree to sell directly to individual customers, so it is worth emailing them. It is possible that if the UAE is not listed as a country that the site deals with, it is because they have not had customers here before, so you may get a positive response if you contact them.

There are a number of local businesses and organisations with an online presence. For electrical goods, Jacky's Electronics (www.jackys.com) has a fairly comprehensive site with good online deals; Magrudy's website (www.magrudy.com) allows for both buying and reserving books; www.uaemall.com is a site which sells items from a number of companies. There are also sites based here that will arrange delivery of gifts both here and internationally, for example, www.giftexpressdubai.com, or www.papagift.com, which deals with India, Sri Lanka and the UAE. Access to the second-hand market is available through sites such as www.dubizzle.com, www.expatgossip.com, www.expatwoman.com, www.souk.ae, www.souq.com and www.websouq.com.

Aramex (see also Shipping on p.404) can provide a 'Shop & Ship' service which sets up a mailbox in both the UK and US, great for dealing with sites which do not offer international shipping. They also offer the Web Surfer card, a prepaid MasterCard for use online – as this can be set up through the mailboxes it is a solution to PayPal problems.

## What & Where To Buy – Quick Reference

| | | | | | | | |
|---|---|---|---|---|---|---|---|
| Alcohol | p.408 | Clothes | p.421 | Home Furnishings | p.432 | Party Accessories | p.441 |
| Art | p.408 | Computers | p.424 | Jewellery, Watches & Gold | p.434 | Perfumes & Cosmetics | p.443 |
| Art & Craft Supplies | p.410 | Electronics/Appliances | p.424 | Kids' Items | p.436 | Pets | p.443 |
| Baby Items | p.412 | Eyewear | p.425 | Kids' Clothes | p.436 | Portrait Photograhers | p.444 |
| Beachwear | p.413 | Flowers | p.426 | Lingerie | p.437 | Second-Hand Items | p.444 |
| Bicycles | p.413 | Food | p.427 | Luggage & Leather | p.437 | Shoes | p.445 |
| Books | p.414 | Gardens | p.427 | Maternity Items | p.438 | Souvenirs | p.445 |
| Camera Equipment | p.416 | Gifts | p.429 | Medicine | p.439 | Sports Goods | p.447 |
| Car Parts & Accessories | p.418 | Handbags | p.429 | Mobile Telephones | p.439 | Stationery | p.447 |
| Cards & Gift Wrapping | p.418 | Hardware & DIY | p.430 | Music, DVDs & Videos | p.439 | Tailoring | p.448 |
| Carpets | p.420 | Hats | p.430 | Musical Instruments | p.440 | Textiles | p.448 |
| Cars | p.420 | Health Food | p.432 | Outdoor Goods | p.441 | Wedding Items | p.449 |

*Mall shopping in Dubai*

## Refunds & Exchanges

The policies on refunds and exchanges vary from shop to shop. There is more chance of success with faulty goods rather than with those where you have changed your mind, and it is more common to be offered an exchange or credit note rather than a refund. Even with tags attached, many stores will not even consider even an exchange unless you have the receipt. For some items such as those in sealed packages, shops insist that the packaging should be intact so that the item can be resold. This is ok if the item was unwanted however it has been known for claims for faulty goods to be rejected as the packaging has been damaged but how could you know if it was faulty if you hadn't opened it?

If you are having no success with customer services, ask to speak to the manager, as the person on the shop floor is often not authorised to deviate from standard policy whereas managers may be more flexible.

## Consumer Rights

The Consumer Protection Department (part of the UAE Ministry of Economy) was recently established to safeguard the interests of shoppers. The department keeps track of retail prices and has been known to reject planned price increases for staple goods. Consumers wishing to complain about a retailer can do so by completing the complaint form on the website www.economy.ae, by sending an email to consumer@economy.ae, or by calling the freephone hotline on 600 522225. The hotline, however, is manned by non-English speakers so you may be better off sticking to the other methods. In Dubai, the Consumer Rights Unit within the Dubai Economic Department (700 4000, www.dubaided.gov.ae), primarily deals with unfit food, but can be contacted to report faulty goods or to complain if a guarantee is not honoured.

## Shipping

The large number of both international and local shipping and courier agencies make transporting anything from a coffee pot to a car feasible. Both air freight and sea freight are available; air freight is faster but more expensive and not really suitable for large or heavy objects, whereas sea freight may take several weeks to arrive but it is cheaper and, as it is possible to rent containers, size and weight are not as much of an issue. With so many companies to choose from it is worth getting a few quotes and finding out what will happen when the goods arrive; some offer no services at the destination while others, usually the bigger ones, will clear customs and deliver right to the door. For smaller items, or those that have to be delivered quickly, air freight is better, and the items can be tracked; again, it is worth shopping around for deals, especially during Dubai Shopping Festival or Dubai Summer Surprises. Empost (286 5000), the Emirates Postal Service, offer both local and international courier and air freight services – their prices are competitive and packages can be tracked.

Several of the courier companies can arrange for items to be delivered to Dubai, and Aramex (286 5050) offers a great service called 'Shop & Ship', for those wishing to buy online. If the site doesn't offer international delivery or their postage rates are high, for a one-off payment of US$35, Aramex will set up a mailbox for you in both the UK and the US. They will arrange for delivery up to three times a week and packages can be tracked; rates for the first half kilo are US$8 and US$5.50 for additional half kilos.

### No Going Back?

*Buying a gift to send back home? Marks & Spencer (p.490) is one of the few international retailers that allows refunds and exchanges on goods bought overseas. So if granny in Scotland would have preferred a woolly scarf to those flip-flops you bought her, she can take them back to her local store, providing she has the receipt.*

## How To Pay

You'll have few problems parting with your money. Credit cards (American Express, Diners Club, MasterCard and Visa) and debit cards (Visa Electron) are accepted in all the shopping malls, supermarkets, and many of the independent shops. However, you can no longer pay for your petrol with credit or debit cards – it's either cash or a petrol card. Cash is easily accessible, and you're never far from an ATM. While credit cards are great in shops with fixed prices, if you're looking to get the most from your bargaining skills, use cash. Cash is preferred in the souks and smaller shops – try to have a variety of denominations, because it is better to hand over close to the exact amount. US dollars and other foreign currencies are accepted in some larger shops (and in the airport duty free shops), but you're likely to get a better deal if you use dirhams.

*Buyer Beware*

*Traps for the unwary shopper do exist in Dubai. Some of the international stores sell items at prices that are far more expensive than in their country of origin (you can even still see the original price tags). This can be as much as 30% higher–so beware.*

## Bargaining

Other options **Markets & Souks** p.483

Bargaining is still common practice in the souks and shopping areas of the UAE. Whether you find it fun or not, it is expected and you'll need to give it a go to get the best prices. Before you take the plunge, try to get an idea of prices from a few shops, as there can often be a significant difference for the same item, and decide how much you are willing to spend.

Once you've picked out exactly what you want, start by making the vendor aware that you are a resident and not a tourist, and that if the prices are good, you will come back to shop again. No matter how much you want the item, try to stay laidback and vaguely disinterested. The initial bid should usually be around half of what the vendor is offering. When this is rejected keep going until you reach an agreement or until you have reached your limit. If the price isn't right, say so and walk out – the vendor will often follow and suggest a compromise price. The more you buy, the better the discount and you should find that it improves further if you become a regular customer.

When the price is agreed, a verbal contract has been created and if you back out, don't be surprised if you get an angry earful from the vendor.

While common in souks, bargaining isn't appreciated in malls and independent shops; many do operate a set discount system and the price shown may be 'before discount'.

*Signs at Dubai Outlet Mall*

Welcome to **Géant** جيان

أهلاً وسهلاً بكم في

**Opening Hours:**
Saturday - Friday - 9.30 am to 12 midnight
**Géant Hypermarket**

Ibn Battuta Mall
Sheikh Zayed Road
Between Interchange 5 & 6, Dubai
Tel: 04 3685858, Fax: 04 3685050
Visit us on our website: www.geant-uae.com

It's Géant and it's for you

## What & Where To Buy

With so much choice there should be little problem finding what you need. From antiques to the latest technology, and from tools to toys, the aim of this section is to let you know what's out there and the best places to buy.

## Alcohol

Other options **On the Town** p.574, **Liquor Licence** p.90

In Dubai, it is legal for anyone over the age of 21 to buy alcohol at licensed bars, restaurants and some clubs, for consumption on the premises. This does not apply to all the emirates. However, if you wish to drink at home you will need a liquor licence (see p.90). Liquor licences are only issued to non-Muslims earning over Dhs.4,000 per month and are only valid for use in the emirate in which they were issued; the amount that you can spend each month on alcohol is determined by your monthly salary. There are two companies that operate liquor stores in Dubai: African & Eastern (A&E) and Maritime & Mercantile International (MMI). Both have branches in several locations around the city, the most handy being the ones near supermarkets. The selection is decent, and prices are not so bad: wine costs from around Dhs.20 and upwards; vodka from Dhs.60; whisky from Dhs.80; and beer from Dhs.4 to Dhs.8 per can or Dhs.100 to Dhs.135 per case. There is a catch however; alcohol is subject to 30% tax on top of the marked prices and, although this is not included in your allowance, it can be a bit of a shock at the till. The alcohol available at the airport is similar in price to the shops in town, but you don't pay the tax.

In the time-honoured tradition of there being a way round everything, there are a number of 'hole in the wall' stores close to Dubai that sell duty-free alcohol to members of the public, even if you don't have a licence. Prices are reasonable and there is no tax. You can pick up a cheap bottle of plonk from around Dhs.15, and most international brands of beer, wine and spirits are available. There are several dubious brands of whisky, brandy and vodka on sale for around Dhs.10, but drink these at your peril! Barracuda Beach Resort (www.barracuda.ae) and Centaurus International (www.centaurusint.com) are popular. MMI also recently opened a tax-free shop near Al Hamra Fort Hotel in Ras Al Khaimah. You don't need to worry about being busted buying booze illegally, but you should be careful when driving home, because it is the transporting of alcohol that could get you into trouble, especially if you are stopped within the borders of the Sharjah emirate. There have been reports of random police checks on vehicles driving from Ajman into Sharjah. Also, if you have an accident and you're found to have a boot full of liquor, your day could take a sudden turn for the worse.

### Progress in Pictures

Stunning images shed light on the beauty of contemporary Dubai, a city that epitomises diversity and development. As you explore historical highlights and innovative architecture you can only wonder in awe at what the future might hold. *Dubai: Tomorrow's City Today* is available in all good bookshops.

| Alcohol | | | |
|---|---|---|---|
| African & Eastern (A&E) ▶ p.409 | | See p.486 | www.aneme.ae |
| Centaurus International Ltd (RAK) ▶ p.411 | | 07 244 5866 | www.centaurusint.com |
| MMI ▶ p.305 | | See p.490 | www.mmidubai.com |

## Art

Other options **Art & Craft Supplies** p.410, **Art Classes** p.320, **Art Galleries** p.258

The art scene in Dubai, quiet for so long, is now enjoying rapid growth. There are galleries and exhibitions displaying traditional and contemporary art, by Arabic and international artists working in a range of media.

# location

# location

# location

## we are here

Karama a+e store
Tel: 04 3348056

## ... and here

Deira a+e store
Tel: 04 2222666

## ... and here

SPINNEYS MERDIF

a+e
we are here

## ... and here

## ... and here

a+e STORE

Wasl a+e store
: 04 3942676

## ... and here

a+e STORE

Bur Dubai a+e store
Tel: 04 3524521

## ... and here

DUBAI MARINE BEACH CLUB    PALM STRIP

MACRUDY'S MALL    SPINNEYS JUMEIRAH 1    LIME TREE

a+e
we are here

## ... and here

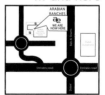
ARABIAN RANCHES

WE ARE NOW HERE

ou'll find that apartments and villas close to african+eastern stores are
rticularly sought after. This maybe because we offer some the World's finest
ers, spirits and wines. Or perhaps it's because people want easy access to our
rvice and knowledge Saturday to Thursday, between 10am and 9pm. Or
ssibly it's the fact that we can arrange new or renewed alcohol licenses and do
L the hard work. Whatever the reason, whenever you see an african+eastern
ore, you know you've found just the right part of town.

**æ**

**african+eastern**

## drink. taste. enjoy.

P.O. Box 32321 Dubai, U.A.E.
Tel: (04) 40 90 500 Fax: (04) 33 70 399

Aquarius sells locally inspired, often light-hearted, silk paintings and antique furniture. The Majlis Gallery, in a traditional windtower house, is a great venue for fine art, handmade glass, pottery and other unusual pieces. For cutting edge art, check out Five Green or XVA Gallery while the Art Source in the Al Ghazal Mall in Satwa stocks a range of original artworks. A framing service is also offered.

Souk Madinat Jumeirah has the largest concentration of boutiques selling art, glass and photographs, both originals and reproductions. The style and subjects are diverse, from traditional to modern, and Arabic to international.

Many of the galleries and showrooms have a framing service  or can recommend one. There are some excellent framing shops on Plant Street in Satwa (map 7 F2) and in Karama Market (map 10 D1) – they can frame anything from prints to sports jerseys.

## Art

| | | | |
|---|---|---|---|
| Aquarius | Jumeira | 04 349 7251 | na |
| Art & Culture | Deira | 04 221 9339 | na |
| The Art Source | Al Wasl | 04 345 3887 | www.theartsource.ae |
| Art Space Gallery | Trade Centre 1 | 04 332 5523 | na |
| Creative Art Centre | Jumeira | 04 344 4394 | na |
| Five Green | Oud Metha | 04 336 4100 | www.fivegreen.com |
| Jadis | Al Quoz | 04 347 4233 | www.jadisuae.com |
| Kenza Art Gallery | Umm Suqeim | 04 368 6603 | na |
| The Majlis Gallery | Downtown Bur Dubai | 04 353 6233 | www.majlisgallery.com |
| Mirage Glass | Various | See p.491 | www.mirage-glass.com |
| Miraj Islamic Art Gallery | Jumeira | 04 394 1084 | na |
| Mondo Art Gallery | Al Barsha | 04 341 3001 | na |
| Nakkash Gallery | Al Garhoud | 04 282 6767 | www.nakkashgallery.com |
| Profile Gallery | Jumeira | 04 349 1147 | na |
| Sharjah Art Museum | Sharjah | 06 568 8222 | www.sharjahtourism.ae |
| Soho Gallery | Downtown Bur Dubai | 04 397 5637 | na |
| Studio Al Aroosa | Jumeira | 04 344 1663 | www.studioalaroosa.com |
| The Third Line | Al Quoz | 04 341 1367 | www.thethirdline.com |
| Total Arts | Al Quoz | 04 228 2888 | www.courtyard-uae.com |
| XVA Gallery ▶ p.107 | Downtown Bur Dubai | 04 353 5383 | www.xvagallery.com |

## Art & Craft Supplies

Other options **Art Classes** p.320, **Art Galleries** p.258, **Art** p.408

There are a number of shops selling a good range of art and craft supplies. Prices can be rather expensive for some speciality items, such as mosaic tiles for example, but are reasonable for art materials. There is enough choice to keep most artists happy, from paints and crayons for children, to top quality oils. Emirates Trading, near Maktoum Bridge, stocks everything from children's crayons to industrial spray booths, and they are suppliers for Windsor & Newton and

## Art & Craft Supplies

| | | | |
|---|---|---|---|
| Al Hathboor General Trading | Al Karama | 04 286 5965 | www.alhathboor.com |
| The Art Source | Al Wasl | 04 345 3887 | www.theartsource.ae |
| Art Stop | Jumeira | 04 349 0627 | na |
| Creations Art | Trade Centre 1 | 04 331 1047 | www.artdubai.com |
| Dubai International Art Centre | Jumeira | 04 344 4398 | www.artdubai.com |
| Dubai Library | Al Rashidiya | 04 286 2400 | www.dubailibrary.com |
| Elves & Fairies | Jumeira | 04 344 9485 | na |
| Emirates Trading Est. | Various | See p.488 | www.emiratestrading.ae |
| Kazim Gulf Traders | Jumeira | 04 349 3347 | na |
| Rafi Frame Store | Al Karama | 04 337 6989 | www.dubaiframes.com |
| Wasco White Star | Jumeira | 04 342 2179 | na |

JOYEUSES FÊTES
Happy Birthday!!
Happy New Year!
Centaurus
LIQUOR WHOLESALER AND RETAILER
with Exclusive selected French wines and spirits
Merry Christmas
Enjoy!
www.centaurusint.com

Daler products. Elves & Fairies (p.320), upstairs in the Jumeirah Centre, have a huge range of decorative stamps and stencils. Wasco White Star, in the Beach Centre, have a selection of reasonably priced craft supplies, many of which are suitable for children's projects and difficult to find elsewhere. The Holiday Centre on Sheikh Zayed Road houses a few good art and craft supplies shops, such as Creations Art, and there are also some excellent shops within the Bin Sougat Mall in Rashidiya. For DIY picture-framers, Rafi Frame Store (aka Al Warda Gallery) in Karama is the place to find the necessary equipment, including mountboard.

*Second-Hand Stuff* ◀

*Second-hand baby stuff is widely available in Dubai – you just need to know where to look. There are classifieds listings on www.expatwoman.com and www.expat gossip.com, and then of course there's always the supermarket noticeboards.*

## Baby Items

The basics are all available and, while you may not find the range you would back home, you won't need to resort to putting your baby down in a drawer.

The supermarkets all stock formula, jars of food, nappies and wipes; many also sell bottles and feeding equipment. Choithram has the best selection of formulas, stocking popular UK brands SMA and Cow & Gate. If you can't find what you are looking for, ask a shop assistant because they sometimes keep certain brands behind the counter. They also have a good range of jars of baby food – they may cost double what they would back home but are great for when you can't face cooking. Large pharmacies sell baby essentials and some have breast pumps.

For nursery essentials, Baby Shop, Goodbaby and Mothercare all sell bottles, buggies, car seats, changing bags, cots, prams, rocking chairs, travel cots and pretty much everything else you'll need. Toys R Us has recently doubled the size of their baby department and now stock a wide range, from pushchairs to baby bottles, cots to travel accessories. The quality of the items is good and most conform to international safety standards. Britax and Maxi Cosi car seats are widely available and should fit most cars; all shops will offer to help fit car seats but the staff seem to be trained in the mechanics of how the seat fits in rather than whether it is the most suitable for the vehicle.

The quality of cot mattresses may vary. Mothercare can order specific sizes but plan ahead so that you get it in good time. The range of slings is pretty limited and backpacks to put your baby in are hard to find, so you may want to order these items from overseas.

Mamas and Papas products can be found in Harvey Nichols in Mall of the Emirates and the brand is expected to have its own shop in the new Dubai Mall.

IKEA has a small range of nursery furniture such as cots, changing tables and bathtubs. They also do a selection of cot sheets and blankets and some baby-safe toys.

Worth waiting for are Baby Shop's sales which they have several times a year.

Goodbaby has the largest selection of buggies and prams, including Cam, Quinny and Phil & Teds, which are not available elsewhere.

Mothercare provide an ordering service for items that you've seen online or in a UK catalogue but the delivery

| Baby Items | | |
|---|---|---|
| Baby Shop | Various | See p.486 |
| Choithram | Various | See p.488 |
| Goodbaby | Al Karama | 04 397 5653 |
| Harvey Nichols | Mall of the Emirates | 04 409 8888 |
| IKEA ▶ p.IBC | Dubai Festival City | 800 4532 |
| Just Kidding | Al Quoz | 04 341 3922 |
| Carrefour ▶ p.479 | Deira City Centre | 04 295 1600 |
| Mothercare | Various | See p.491 |
| Toys R Us | Various | See p.493 |

time is a minimum of four weeks and often longer. Just Kidding, a warehouse in Al Quoz, sells a range of baby items, furniture and clothes from Europe, including Bugaboo buggies, Little Company bags and Stokke high chairs. It's not for the budget conscious, but worth a browse.

## Beachwear

Other options **Sports Goods** p.447, **Clothes** p.421

For the amount of time spent on the beach or by the pool in Dubai, it's not surprising that there are several specialist and designer beachwear shops where a swimsuit can cost as much as a good night out. With year-round sunshine there is no real off-peak season, so end-of-season sales are a bit unpredictable. Join the Beyond the Beach mailing list though, and they'll send you advance notice of their December sales. UV protective items are a must for children, and a good idea for adults. There are limited ranges in Beyond the Beach, UV swimsuits for kids at Woolworths all year round, and a number of the larger stores and department stores carry them seasonally. Debenhams has a great range of fashion swimwear (including a full range of beach accessories, like hats, sarongs, beach towels and matching flip-flops). Heatwaves sell a good range for both adults and children, and if they don't have much stock you can leave your name and they'll let you know when a new delivery arrives. The Uniform Shop has some UV suits (they also carry Baby Banz sunglasses and hats), as does Picnico on Beach Road. Hamac's ranges include Vilebrequin swimming shorts for men and boys.

| Beachwear | | |
| --- | --- | --- |
| Al Boom Marine | Various | See p.486 |
| Bare Essentials | Jumeirah Centre | 04 344 0552 |
| Beyond the Beach | Various | See p.487 |
| Debenhams | Various | See p.488 |
| Hamac | Various | See p.489 |
| Heatwaves | Various | See p.489 |
| Oceano | Palm Strip | 04 346 1961 |
| Picnico General Trading | Jumeira Beach Road | 04 394 1653 |
| The Uniform Shop | Spinneys | 04 394 1477 |
| Woolworths | Various | See p.493 |

## Bicycles

Once you've experienced the traffic in Dubai it may not seem like the most bicycle-friendly city, but there is an active cycling scene. Both mountain biking and road cycling are popular and the equipment needed for them is available; the range is adequate but can be expensive. For serious cyclists, there are an increasing number of shops, and brands, in town – all offer a good selection of bikes and all the paraphernalia and safety equipment that you'll need, and they also repair and service bikes. Bike 'n' Rack ( on Al Khail Road), stocks Giant and a range of Thule bike racks, the Cannondale shops stock Cannondale, Mongoose, Schwinn and Fuji, and Wolfi's stocks Scott, Felt, Merida and Storck. Two recent additions are 360 Lifestyle in Oud Metha, which stocks a wide range of the excellent Specialized bikes, clothing and accessories (and also has a smaller range on show inside Studio R in Ibn Battuta, 04 366 9890), and a Trek shop in the Metropolitan Hotel.

For the casual cyclist, Toys R Us and a number of sports shops sell more basic models at reasonable prices. GO Sports has a large bike section and workshop in their store in Mall of the Emirates. If you're after a bit of nostalgia, the 'sit-up-and-beg' models – popular with gardeners and delivery cyclists – can be found in the smaller bike shops all over the city (check out Karama and Satwa). Children's bicycles are widely available in bike and sports shops, and toy shops like Baby Shop and Goodbaby have a range for tiny Lance Armstrong wannabes. Magrudy's also carries a small range of bikes

| Bicycles | | |
| --- | --- | --- |
| 360 Lifestyle | Shop 6, Al Nasr Palace | 04 337 3013 |
| Baby Shop | Various | See p.486 |
| Bike 'n' Rack | Ras Al Khor | 04 333 3556 |
| Cannondale | Various | See p.487 |
| Carrefour ▶ p.479 | Various | See p.487 |
| Go Sports | Various | See p.489 |
| Goodbaby | Al Karama | 04 397 5653 |
| Magrudy's ▶ p.415 | Various | See p.490 |
| Sun & Sand Sports ▶ p.321 | Various | See p.493 |
| Toys R Us | Various | See p.493 |
| Trek | Metropolitan Hotel | 04 407 6641 |
| Wolfi's Bike Shop | Between Jct 2-3 | 04 339 4453 |

**413**

both big and small – kids' models like their hot-pink trike complete with flower basket and handlebar tassles will take you right back to childhood. If you want to make cycling a family activity, Cannondale has a selection of children's seats, priced from Dhs.150 to Dhs.300, that they will fit for you. Both adult's and children's helmets are available at the main retailers.

## Books

Other options **Second-Hand Items** p.444, **Libraries** p.356

Book lovers of all ages are well catered for in Dubai. There are a number of English language bookshops with huge ranges of books from the latest bestsellers to obscure reference books. The logic behind the shelving system can be a little eccentric and although you'll be able to find out if a book is in stock, finding the actual item, even for the staff, can be a bit hit-and-miss. Prices of books vary but generally compete with online prices.
Magrudy's has a good range of titles and can order specific books for you. They also have a website (www.magrudy.com) on which you can order and reserve books. The popular international chain Borders opened its first Dubai store in Mall of the Emirates in late 2006, and added two more branches in 2007 in Deira City Centre abd Dubai Festival City. Jashanmal Bookstore carries an impressive range for all ages and Virgin Megastore has an interesting selection worth checking out – both have branches around Dubai. Books Plus has an excellent range of books both for adults and children, including fiction, travel, hobbies and interests. Book Worm, in the Park n Shop complex is especially good for children. They carry a huge range of children's books, and if you know about a book that children will love, they'll consider ordering it for the shop.
With Dubai's many transitory residents trying to keep their clutter (and book collections) to a minimum, the second-hand book shops have a wide choice, including a large selection of fiction, and a fast turnover. Many of their books have only been read once, and it's considerably cheaper than buying new books. Both House of Prose in Jumeira and Ibn Battuta and Book World in Karama and Satwa, buy and sell, and also have a buy-back service, where they'll give you back 50% of what you paid on books you've bought from them, regardless of how long ago it was.

## Books

| Book Park Trading | Hyatt Regency Dubai | 04 273 1361 | na |
|---|---|---|---|
| Book World | Various | See p.487 | na |
| Book Worm | Behing Park n Shop | 04 394 5770 | na |
| Books Gallery | The Village Mall | 04 344 5770 | na |
| Books Plus ▶ p.459 | Various | See p.487 | na |
| Borders ▶ p.419 | Various | See p.487 | www.bordersstores.com |
| Carrefour ▶ p.479 | Deira City Centre | 04 295 1600 | www.carrefouruae.com |
| Culture & Co | API Tower | 04 331 3114 | www.culturecodubai.com |
| Dubai Library | Bin Sougat Centre | 04 286 2400 | www.dubailibrary.com |
| Géant ▶ p.477 | Ibn Battuta Shopping Mall | 04 368 5888 | www.geant-dubai.com |
| House of Prose | Various | See p.489 | na |
| Jashanmal ▶ p.417 | Various | See p.489 | www.jashanmal.ae |
| Kazim Gulf Traders | Jumeirah Centre | 04 349 3347 | na |
| Kids Plus | Town Centre | 04 344 2008 | na |
| Magrudy's ▶ p.415 | Various | See p.490 | www.magrudy.com |
| Spinneys | Various | See p.492 | www.spinneys.com |
| Titan Book Shop | Various | See p.493 | na |
| Virgin Megastore ▶ p.451 | Various | See p.493 | www.virgin.com |
| Wasco White Star | Beach Centre | 04 342 2179 | na |
| White Star Bookshop | Beach Centre | 04 344 6628 | na |

Books make us who we are

Magrudy's
bringing you only the best

*ic sights at
Battuta mall*

There are regular charity book sales, the most notable being the ones organised by Medecins Sans Frontiers (www.msfuae.com). They are held several times throughout the year, usually in the Dune Centre in Satwa.

## Camera Equipment
Other options **Electronics & Home Appliances** p.424

From single-use cameras to darkroom equipment, photographers have got plenty of places to include on their shopping lists. In common with market forces the world over, digital models dominate the shelves. They are available in all the electronics shops, hypermarkets, and photo processing outlets; all the major brands are represented. The jury's still out on whether cameras here are cheaper than elsewhere, it really depends on where else you are looking; the prices in Singapore are often lower, and in most of Europe they will be higher. Within Dubai, prices will vary between the larger outlets, where prices are fixed, and the electronics shops of Bur Dubai. However, while you might be able to bag a bargain from the independent retailers using your superior powers of negotiation, you'll have more protection buying from the larger outlets. The most important consideration, if you are buying the camera to take to another country, is to ensure that your warranty is international: don't just take the retailer's word for it, actually ask to open the box and read the warranty to make sure.

For specialist equipment and a good range of film cameras, the main outlets are Grand Stores and Salaam Studios. Grand Stores sells Fuji, Nikon, Canon and Mamiya; Salaam Studios carry Bronica, Leica, Minolta and Pentax; they both sell a selection of filters, tripods and studio equipment. The alternative to buying locally is to use an online retailer. B&H Photo, in New York, is extremely popular, and although shipping is expensive you can group together with a few friends for a big order, and spread the delivery costs (www.bandhphoto.com).

For second-hand equipment, www.gulfphotoplus.com has an active equipment noticeboard (as well as being a great source of information and a good networking site for locally based photography enthusiasts).

Should your equipment need to be repaired, Grand Stores offers a repair service. HN Camera Repairs offer an in house repair service for all makes of camera.

| Camera Equipment | | | |
| --- | --- | --- | --- |
| Grand Stores | Garhoud | 04 282 3700 | www.grandstores.com |
| HN Camera Repairs | Jumeirah Centre | 04 349 0971 | na |
| Jacky's Electronics | Jebel Ali | 04 881 9933 | www.jackys.com |
| Jumbo Electronics | Various | See p.490 | www.jumbocorp.com |
| MK Trading Co | Deira | 04 222 5745 | na |
| National Stores | Al Falah Street | 04 353 6074 | www.nationalstore.ae |
| Plug-Ins | Various | See p.492 | www.pluginselectronix.com |
| Salaam Studios | Wafi Mall | 04 324 5252 | na |
| Sharaf DG | Various | See p.492 | www.sharafdg.com |
| United Colour Film (UCF) | Al Qusais | 04 267 5599 | www.ucfq.com |

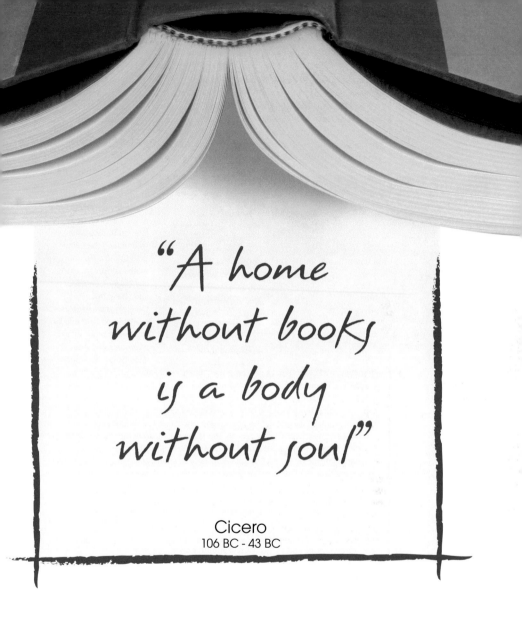

"*A home without books is a body without soul*"

Cicero
106 BC - 43 BC

# JASHANMAL BOOKSTORES

Dhabi: Abu Dhabi Mall, Level 3, Hamdan Street, Tel: 6443869, Dubai: Mall of the Emirates, Tel: 3406789, Village Mall, Jumeirah, Tel: 3445770, Caribou Coffee, Uptown Mirdiff Tel: 2888376, Dubai Marina Walk, Jashanmal Department Store, Wafi City, Level 2, Tel: 3244800, Sharjah: Sahara Centre, Tel: 5317898, Bahrain: Seef Mall, West Wing, Tel: 17581632, Al Aali Shopping Complex, Tel: 17582424

## Car Parts & Accessories

Wherever there are cars, there will be accessories for them and Dubai is no exception. ACE and Carrefour have large departments selling everything from steering wheel covers to fridges which run off the car battery. For those who enjoy tinkering with what's under the bonnet, there are a myriad of tools available in larger stores and in the smaller shops in Satwa. Off-road enthusiasts should also check out AAA for specialist sand tracks and heavy duty jacks and winches – if your car is fitted with a GPS system they can rescue you from the most remote dune or wadi. GPS systems are available from Picnico and Abdulla Mohammed Ibrahim Trading (who recommend the Garmin brand), and even from more mainstream shops like Plug-Ins, Carrefour and Sharaf DG. Car stereos are widely available, and are sold by most electronics shops, with some of the car dealerships stocking

| Car Parts & Accessories | | | |
|---|---|---|---|
| AAA | Nr Honda Trading, Rashidiya | 04 2669 989 | www.aaadubai.com |
| Abdulla Mohammed Ibrahim Trading (Amit) | Al Ras | 04 229 1195 | na |
| ACE | Various | See p.486 | www.aceuae.com |
| After Dark | Oud Metha | 04 337 8337 | na |
| Carrefour ▶ p.479 | Various | See p.487 | www.carrefouruae.com |
| Picnico General Trading | Jumeira Beach Rd | 04 394 1653 | na |
| Plug-Ins | Various | See p.492 | www.pluginselectronix.com |
| V-KOOL Emirates | Sheikh Zayed Rd, Al Quoz | 04 340 0092 | www.v-kool.com |
| West Coast Customs | Nr 3rd Interchange, Shk Zayed Rd | 04 347 2888 | www.wcc-me.com |

alternative models for their cars. To have them fitted, head either to the workshops of Rashidiya or Satwa, or AAA and the dealers – it should cost around Dhs.500 if you are providing all the parts.

Many car owners try to beat the heat by having their car windows tinted. The legal limit is 30% tint, if you get your windows tinted any darker you could be fined, and your car won't pass its annual inspection. The options range from the Dhs.75 plastic film from the workshops in Satwa, to Dhs.1,300-1,500 at After Dark (covered by a ten-year warranty), and up to Dhs.5,000 at V-Kool (also covered by warranty, and their clear film is more heat resistant than the tinted one). Al Quoz and Rashidiya are where to head if you're looking to customise your car by increasing its performance. Drivers really wishing to pimp their ride will be thrilled to hear that West Coast Customs (as featured on the MTV series) now has a showroom and workshop in Al Quoz.

## Cards & Gift Wrapping

Other options **Books** p.414, **Art & Craft Supplies** p.410

| Cards & Gift Wrapping | | |
|---|---|---|
| Al Fahidi Stationery | Various | See p.486 |
| Cadorim | The Village Mall | 04 394 3333 |
| Carlton Cards | Various | See p.487 |
| Carrefour ▶ p.479 | Various | See p.487 |
| Emirates Trading Est. | Various | See p.488 |
| Farook International Stationary | Meena Bazaar | 04 352 1997 |
| Gulf Greetings | Various | See p.489 |
| IKEA ▶ p.IBC | Dubai Festival City | 800 4532 |
| Marks & Spencer | Various | See p.490 |
| THE One | Various | See p.493 |
| Paper Moon | Various | See p.491 |
| Susan Walpole | Various | See p.493 |
| Titan Book Shop | Various | See p.493 |
| Virgin Megastore ▶ p.451 | Various | See p.493 |
| Woolworths | Various | See p.493 |

The standard greetings cards and wrapping paper are widely available, but there are also alternatives. Carlton Cards and Gulf Greetings cover most occasions and the supermarkets carry limited selections. Marks & Spencer greeting cards are good quality. For something a bit different, the Susan Walpole shops have a good selection, as do Magrudy's and THE One; there are small gift wrapping counters in several of the malls. For gift wrapping paper that won't break the bank try IKEA and Woolworths, or for elaborate wrapping that will really add a special touch to your gift, try Paper Moon. There are

# For all your favourite books...

## BORDERS®

### YOUR PLACE FOR KNOWLEDGE AND ENTERTAINMENT

Mall of the Emirates 04 3415758   Deira City Center 04 2957672
Dubai International Finance Center 04 4250371 Muscat City Center 0096895921377

handmade cards available, most readily at craft fairs. Cadorim, in The Village Mall, offer a gift wrapping service (boxes and paper) and they also have a selection of cards.

## Carpets

Other options **Souvenirs** p.445, **Bargaining** p.406

Carpets are one of the region's signature items. The ones on sale here tend to be imported from Iran, Turkey, Pakistan and Central Asia. The price of a carpet depends on a number of factors such as its origin, the material used, the number of knots, and whether or not it is handmade.

The most expensive carpets are usually those hand-made with silk in Iran. The higher the quality the neater the back, so turn the carpets over – if the pattern is clearly depicted and the knots are all neat, the carpet is of higher quality than those that are indistinct. Try to do some research so that you have a basic idea of what you are looking for before you go, just in case you happen to meet an unscrupulous carpet dealer who could take advantage of your naivety. Fortunately, crooked carpet conmen are few and far between, and most will

| Carpets | | |
|---|---|---|
| Al Orooba Oriental | BurJuman | 04 351 0919 |
| Carpetland | Opp Al Nasr Cinema | 04 337 7677 |
| Carrefour ▶ p.479 | Various | See p.487 |
| Fabindia | Al Mankhool Road, Bur Dubai | 04 398 9633 |
| Gemaco | Nr Ace Hardware, Shk Zayed Rd | 04 338 9500 |
| IKEA ▶ p.IBC | Dubai Festival City | 800 4532 |
| Kashmir Gallery | Al Ghurair City | 04 222 5271 |
| National Iranian Carpets | Various | See p.491 |
| THE One | Various | See p.493 |
| Persian Carpet House | Crowne Plaza | 04 332 1161 |
| Pride of Kashmir | Various | See p.492 |
| Quem Persian Carpets | Sheraton Dubai Creek Hotel | 04 228 1848 |
| Red Sea Exhibition | Beach Centre | 04 344 3949 |
| Total Arts | The Courtyard | 04 228 2888 |

happily explain the differences between the rugs and share their extensive knowledge with you. National Iranian Carpets have a section on their website (www.niccarpets.com) about the history and development of carpets from the various regions.

Ask to see a selection of various carpets so that you can get a feel for the differences between hand-made or machine-made, silk, wool or blend carpets. Of course, asking may not be necessary, since the moment you walk through the doors the carpet vendor will undoubtedly start unrolling carpets and laying them out at a furious pace! Carpets range in price from a few hundred dirhams to tens of thousands of dirhams. It is always worth bargaining to get a better price – make sure the seller knows you are not a tourist, and remain polite at all times to maximise the success of your haggling. Deira Tower on Al Nasr Square has a huge number of carpet outlets under one roof, and the Blue Souk in Sharjah (see p.484) also has a great range. Occasionally you might get a travelling carpet seller ringing your doorbell – he usually drives around an area in his old and battered pickup that is packed to the roof with carpets. The quality isn't great, and even if you show the slightest interest he'll be back to ring your doorbell time and time again.

Carpetland is a one-stop-shop for whatever type of carpet you are after, whether your heart is set on a Persian antique, or having shagpile laid in the bedroom, you'll be spoilt for choice. Other options, if you are looking for something practical rather than decorative, are Fabindia, IKEA, Carrefour or THE One.

## Cars

Other options **Buying a Vehicle** p.226

Cars are one of the best buys in Dubai, with prices much lower than you'd usually pay in your home country. Your time in Dubai may be the only chance you have to drive a really luxurious car, rather than a more practical model, so if you've always fantasised about driving a Rolls Royce Silver Shadow, this could be your chance. It is almost de rigeur to own a four-wheel drive, even if the only off-roading you do is to park on the pavement. Fortunately, compared to the rest of the world petrol is still pretty cheap here, so it is affordable to fill up even the thirstiest of fuel-guzzlers.

All the major car dealers are represented (see p.226) and, to make owning a car even more attractive, the interest rates for car loans are fairly low. If you are buying a new car and are after a bargain, there are usually special offers during the Shopping Festival and Ramadan. The second-hand car market is thriving (see p.227). There are garages across the city, and the Used Car Market at Al Awir is worth a look. If you would prefer to buy privately, check out the classified ads or the noticeboards at the supermarkets. The conditions are tough for cars here, especially if they have been used in the desert, so it is a good idea to have the car vetted by a garage before you hand over your money. AAA, in Al Quoz (04 347 0400) and Rashidiya (04 285 8989), look at everything from the engine to the paintwork.

## Clothes

Other options **Sports Goods** p.447, **Tailoring** p.448, **Shoes** p.445, **Lingerie** p.437, **Kids' Clothes** p.436, **Beachwear** p.413

Dubai is a haven for well-dressed shopaholics, with all the malls housing a high concentration of clothes shops. Whether you are a designer diva or a bargain babe, in Dubai it is nearly impossible to have a 'bad shopping day' where you leave tired, but empty-handed. Not only is the range of clothes amazing, but several times a year there are sweeping sales when you'll end up paying so little for a designer frock that you might as well buy two! For those events when only the very best will do, the Boulevard at Emirates Towers is the place. Having chosen the creation to be seen in, be it by Alexander McQueen, Stella McCartney, Marni or Prada, the selection of Lulu Guinness bags and Jimmy Choo shoes will enable you to complete your ensemble without having to venture beyond this enclave of exclusivity. Then again, Saks Fifth Avenue in BurJuman, and Harvey Nichols in Mall of the Emirates, are both worth a visit (or

### Clothes

| | | |
|---|---|---|
| Amichi | Mercato | 04 349 0999 |
| Armani Exchange | Various | See p.486 |
| Banana Republic | Deira City Centre | 04 294 1163 |
| Bebe | BurJuman | 04 355 4007 |
| Benetton | Various | See p.487 |
| Bershka | Various | See p.487 |
| Bhs | Various | See p.487 |
| Bossini | Various | See p.487 |
| Boutique 1 | Emirates Towers | 04 330 4555 |
| Burberry | Various | See p.487 |
| Calvin Klein | Various | See p.487 |
| Carrefour ▶ p.479 | Various | See p.487 |
| Cartoon Fashion | Al Ghurair City | 04 221 6461 |
| Century 2000 | Nr Al Nasr Cinema | 04 336 6654 |
| Cerruti | Mercato | 04 344 4041 |
| Chanel | Various | See p.487 |
| Christian Lacroix | BurJuman | 04 351 7133 |
| Club Monaco | Various | See p.488 |
| Coast | Various | See p.488 |
| Debenhams | Various | See p.488 |
| Diesel | Various | See p.488 |
| Donna Karan | BurJuman | 04 351 6794 |
| Dorothy Perkins | Various | See p.488 |
| Elle | Various | See p.488 |
| Escada | BurJuman | 04 359 1117 |
| Esprit | BurJuman | 04 355 3324 |
| Etoile | Wafi Mall | 04 324 0465 |
| Evans | Various | See p.488 |
| Eve Michelle | Magrudy's | 04 342 9574 |
| Fabindia | Al Mankhool Road, Bur Dubai | 04 398 9633 |
| Factory Fashions | Lamcy Plaza | 04 336 2699 |
| FCUK | Various | See p.489 |
| Five Green | Garden Home Building | 04 336 4100 |
| Fleurt | Mercato | 04 342 0906 |
| Forever 21 | Various | See p.489 |
| G2000 | Various | See p.489 |
| Gap | Deira City Centre | 04 295 1354 |
| Géant ▶ p.477 | Ibn Battuta Shopping Mall | 04 368 5888 |
| Gerry Webber | Various | See p.489 |
| Giordano | Various | See p.489 |
| Guess | Various | See p.489 |
| H&M | Various | See p.489 |
| Hang Ten | Various | See p.489 |
| Harvey Nichols | Mall of the Emirates | 04 409 8888 |
| Hugo Boss | Various | See p.489 |
| HyperPanda | Dubai Festival City | 04 232 5566 |
| Jaeger | Wafi Mall | 04 324 9838 |
| JC Penney | BurJuman | 04 351 5353 |
| Jennyfer | Various | See p.489 |
| Karen Millen | Various | See p.490 |
| Kookai | Various | See p.490 |

## Clothes

| | | |
|---|---|---|
| Lacoste | Deira City Centre | 04 295 4429 |
| Levis | Various | See p.490 |
| Levis Outlet | Various | See p.490 |
| Liwa | Various | See p.490 |
| Liz Clairborne | Downtown Bur Dubai | 04 351 4917 |
| Mango | Various | See p.490 |
| Marks & Spencer | Various | See p.490 |
| Marlboro Classics | Various | See p.490 |
| Massimo Dutti | Various | See p.490 |
| Max | Various | See p.490 |
| Max Mara | BurJuman | 04 351 3140 |
| Mexx | Various | See p.490 |
| Mexx for Less | Lamcy Plaza | 04 334 0096 |
| Miss Sixty | Various | See p.491 |
| Moka | Jumeirah Centre | 04 349 3800 |
| Monsoon | Various | See p.491 |
| Motivi | Various | See p.491 |
| Mr Price | Lamcy Plaza | 04 336 6656 |
| New Look | Deira City Centre | 04 295 9542 |
| Next | Various | See p.491 |
| Oasis | Various | See p.491 |
| Oltre | Various | See p.491 |
| Oui | Various | See p.491 |
| Peacocks | Various | See p.491 |
| Pierre Cardin | Twin Towers | 04 224 7774 |
| Polo Ralph Lauren | Various | See p.492 |
| Promod | Various | See p.492 |
| Pull and Bear | Deira City Centre | 04 295 3525 |
| Replay | BurJuman | 04 355 3324 |
| River Island | Various | See p.492 |
| Rodeo Drive | Various | See p.492 |
| Saks Fifth Avenue | BurJuman | 04 351 5551 |
| Sana Fashion | Al Karama Shopping Complex | 04 337 7726 |
| Splash | Various | See p.492 |
| Stradivarius | Various | See p.492 |
| Ted Lapidus | Twin Towers | 04 227 2789 |
| Topshop | Various | See p.493 |
| Topman | Deira City Centre | 04 295 1804 |
| Via Rodeo | Mall of the Emirates | 04 341 0113 |
| Wallis | Various | See p.493 |
| The White Company | Various | See p.493 |
| Woodland | Century Mall | 04 296 7890 |
| Woolworths | Various | See p.493 |
| XOXO | BurJuman | 04 355 3324 |
| Zara | Various | See p.493 |

many visits) to bag yourself some cutting-edge couture. Via Rodeo, also at Mall of the Emirates, houses outlets for Dolce & Gabbana, Emporio Armani and Versace, among others. Other designer names that you will see as you scour Dubai's many shopping malls include Karen Millen, Kenneth Cole, Calvin Klein, Donna Karan, Hugo Boss, Paul Smith, Ralph Lauren and Christian Lacroix.

Vying for the crown of Dubai's most exclusive mall, BurJuman and Wafi City both have designer labels in abundance in their many exclusive boutiques; although both also have some high-street shopping such as Marks & Spencer in Wafi and Bhs in BurJuman. The Mall of the Emirates is the 'big daddy' of shopping malls, outstripping the competition in terms of space, much of which is filled with designer names. If you have designer tastes but a limited budget, the Designers at Debenhams range is an exclusive selection of men's and women's clothing from Jasper Conran, Pearce Fionda and John Rocha. Eve Michelle (Magrudy's Mall) has a loyal following for its range of exclusive European creations for ladies. If you are into street chic, Five Green (p.475) will be a regular hangout – every corner of this unique space is dedicated to cutting-edge clothing, art and music. For everyday clothing, the choice is unlimited. Debenhams, Marks & Spencer, H&M, Zara, Woolworths (the South African one, not the UK one), Mango, Promod, River Island, Topshop, Massimo Dutti, Monsoon, Next... the list goes on and on, and these all have more than one branch around Dubai. For something a little different, you can get beautiful hand-crafted fabrics and traditional Indian clothing at Fabindia (see also p.475) on Al Mankhool Road.

Men needn't feel left out or poorly dressed: Maktoum Road (between the Clock Tower Roundabout and Al Khaleej Palace Hotel) is lined with stores selling men's designer clothing, and there are also plenty of options inside the Twin Towers Mall in Deira. There are a couple of suit shops along Diyafah Street in Satwa. Of course, most of the shops loved by ladies also have excellent men's sections, such as Debenhams, Marks & Spencer, Next, Zara and Massimo Dutti.

Bargain hunters will love Dubai... the choice is huge. Try Sana Fashions, Carrefour and Géant for really good bargains – they receive regular deliveries of factory seconds and retailer overruns, and there are plenty of well-known brands available if you get there early, such as Gap, George and Cherokee. Lamcy Plaza is a real bargain-hunter's mall... Mexx for Less, Peacocks and Factory Fashions (stocking overruns from Adams and Pumpkin Patch) are all excellent; as are Jennyfer and Mr Price. The new Dubai Outlet Mall (p.468) is a welcome addition to the shopping scene, with a number of brands offering end-of-line stock at reduced prices.

The Karama Market is perhaps the main contender for bargain shopping in Dubai: with rows and rows of shops selling designer labels, both the genuine article and some quite convincing knock-offs. There's also some pretty dreadful tat on offer and some of the clothing isn't suitable for even the most liberal of customers.

**Factory Outlets**

*There's a Benetton factory shop (04 335 2761) near Maktoum Bridge and Adidas factory shops on Airport Road (04 282 0211) and near Lamcy Plaza (04 335 4403), among others. Prices are not always lower than they are in the retail shops, so you'll probably get better bargains if you wait for the sales. The new outlet mall (p.468) is the best bet for bargain hunters.*

### Shoes & Clothing Sizes

Figuring out your size isn't rocket science, just a bit of a pain. Firstly, check the label – international sizes are often printed on them. Secondly, check the store – they will often have a conversion chart on display. Otherwise, a UK size is always two higher than a US size (so a UK 10 is a US 6). To convert European sizes into US sizes, subtract 32 (so a European 38 is actually a US 6). To convert European sizes into UK sizes, a 38 is roughly a 10. As for shoes, a woman's UK 6 is a European 39 or US 8.5 and a men's UK 10 is a European 44 or a US 10.5. If in doubt, ask for help.

*Petite & Plus Sizes*

If you are frequently frustrated by the regular sizes (UK 8 – 16) because clothes are always a little bit too big or a little bit too small, you will be relieved to know that retailers in Dubai are increasingly offering petite and plus-size lines. Petite ranges are available in Debenhams, Splash and Marks & Spencer, while Bhs, Debenhams, Liz Claiborne, Marks & Spencer, Splash and Woolworths all carry plus-size collections (look out for Evans in Debenhams and Scarlett's in Splash). For more exclusive lines for the fuller figure, try Irene Sieber, Oui Plus and Samoon (all in Wafi), or Charisma in the Beach Centre in Jumeira.

It's not only women who are frustrated at not being able to find clothes that fit. Men looking for larger sizes should head to Big & Tall (04 397 3873) on Bank Street. They cater for waist sizes from 40 plus and shirts up to 6XL.

*Window shopping*

# Computers

Other options **Electronics & Home Appliances** p.424

*Poorly PC?*
*St George Computers*
*offers all the assistance*
*you need when it*
*comes to fixing or*
*upgrading your*
*computer. Call Lee on*
*050 456 2821 to find*
*out what solutions he*
*can offer.*

In terms of technology, Dubai is no slacker – the latest computer equipment is easy to find and there's even a mall dedicated to it (Al Ain Mall in Bur Dubai). Every year Dubai hosts GITEX (the Gulf Information Technology Exhibition), the largest IT exhibition in the region. Alongside GITEX is the phenomenally popular GITEX Computer Shopper – a great place to bag the latest technology at lower prices (www.gitex.com).

If you can't wait until GITEX is held, computer equipment is on sale in a surprising number of outlets, from Carrefour to CompuMe, and all the main manufacturers are represented. CompuMe has a great website where you can order products online (www.compume.com).

The market is dominated by PCs, but Macs are available from a growing number of stores including CompuMe, PACC, Virgin Megastore and the Mac Store in Ibn Battuta and iStyle in Dubai Festival City. The UAE government has been cracking down on the sale of pirated software, and consequently the software and hardware that is available is genuine and should be of good quality.

## Computers

| | | | |
|---|---|---|---|
| Al Faris Computers | Bur Dubai | 04 393 3444 | na |
| Aptec Gulf LLC | Oud Metha | 04 336 6885 | www.aptecme.com |
| Carrefour ▶ p.479 | Various | See p.487 | www.carrefouruae.com |
| Compu-Me | Various | See p.488 | www.compume.com |
| Explorer Computers | Deira | 04 228 9625 | na |
| GBM Distribution | Jebel Ali | 04 883 5652 | www.gbmd.com |
| Interdev Information Systems | Computer Street, Bur Dubai | 04 351 4153 | www.interdev-me.com |
| iStyle | Various | See p.489 | na |
| Jumbo Electronics | Various | See p.489 | www.jumbocorp.com |
| PACC | Karama | 04 337 0070 | na |
| Plug-Ins | Various | See p.492 | www.pluginselectronix.com |
| Redington Middle East | The Atrium Centre, Bur Dubai | 04 359 0555 | www.redingtongulf.com |
| Seven Seas Computers | Bin Lahej Building, Oud Metha | 04 308 3555 | www.sscomp.co.ae |
| Sharaf DG | Various | See p.492 | www.sharafdg.com |
| Virgin Megastore ▶ p.451 | Various | See p.493 | www.virgin.com |

# Electronics & Home Appliances

Other options **Camera Equipment** p.416, **Computers** p.424

From blenders to plasma TVs, electronics are a staple of the retail sector. All the major brands are available, along with some of the lesser-known brands. If it's advice you need, you'll have to choose your store carefully – some shop assistants have excellent product knowledge while others simply read off the main selling points from the display. The good news is that there's a lot of competition, so prices are reasonable and most dealers offer warranties.

A word on warranties: some retailers offer an extended warranty system where, by paying a little bit extra you can get a year or even two added onto your warranty. Just remember to make sure your warranty is an internationally valid one if you're planning on taking your electronic items back to your home country during the life of the warranty.

Prices are often cheaper in Dubai than they are elsewhere, but it's worth your while to check whether the items will work in all areas of the world. You should also find out whether you will have to pay any import duty if you take the item back to your home country. If you're interested in second-hand items, keep checking the adverts placed on supermarket noticeboards and online classifieds (a good one worth visiting is www.expatwoman.com).

## Electronics & Home Appliances

| | | | |
|---|---|---|---|
| Agiv (Gulf) | Al Quoz | 04 223 2228 | www.agivgulf.com |
| Al Futtaim Electronics | Al Khabaisi | 04 359 9979 | www.al-futtaim.com |
| Al Ghandi Electronics | Deira | 04 337 6600 | www.alghandielectronics.com |
| Al Sayegh Brothers Trading | Deira | 04 227 4142 | www.alsayeghbrothers.com |
| Archimedia | Al Karama | 04 337 0181 | www.archimedia-me.com |
| Axiom Telecom | Various | See p.486 | www.axiomtelecom.com |
| Bang & Olufsen | Bur Dubai | 04 355 1162 | www.bang-olufsen.com |
| Better Life | Al Khabaisi | 04 268 0656 | na |
| Carrefour ▶ p.479 | Various | See p.487 | www.carrefouruae.com |
| Elekta Gulf | Jebel Ali | 04 883 7108 | www.elekta.net |
| Eros Electricals | Deira | 04 266 6216 | www.erosgroup.com |
| G & M International | Deira | 04 266 9000 | www.gnminternational.com |
| HyperPanda | Deira | 04 232 5566 | www.panda-uae.com |
| Jacky's Electronics | Al Garhoud | 04 282 1822 | www.jackys.com |
| Jashanmal ▶ p.417 | Various | See p.489 | www.jashanmal.ae |
| Jashanmal and Company | Deira | 04 266 5964 | www.jashanmal-uae.com |
| Juma Al Majid | Deira | 04 266 0640 | www.al-majid.com |
| Jumbo Electronics | Various | See p.490 | www.jumbocorp.com |
| Mohd Hareb Al Otaiba | Deira | 04 269 1575 | www.alotaibagroup.com |
| The New Store | Jumeira | 04 353 4506 | na |
| Oasis Enterprises | Deira | 04 282 1375 | na |
| Oman National Electronics | Bur Dubai | 04 351 0753 | na |
| Plug-Ins | Various | See p.492 | www.pluginselectronix.com |
| Radio Shack | Various | See p.492 | www.radioshack.com |
| Samsung Electronics | Various | See p.492 | www.samsung.com |
| Scientechnic | Deira | 04 266 6000 | www.scientechnic.com |
| Sharaf DG | Various | See p.492 | www.sharafdg.com |
| Sounds Middle East Trading L.L.C. | Bur Dubai | 04 397 6615 | www.soundsme.com |
| Universal Electricals | Deira | 04 282 3443 | www.universal-uae.ae |
| Viking Electronics | Deira | 04 223 8167 | na |
| VV & Sons | Bur Dubai | 04 353 2444 | www.vvsons.com |

## Eyewear

Other options **Sports Goods** p.447

Unless you want to spend your life in Dubai squinting against the year-round sunshine, you'll need to get yourself a good pair of sunglasses. From Dhs.10 knock-offs in Karama to Dhs.7,000 designer creations in exclusive opticians, and everything in between, you'll probably have trouble choosing just one pair. Most people have sunglasses for driving with good quality lenses and others they don't mind getting sandy at the beach.

You can buy sunglasses in fashion shops, hotel lobbies, opticians, pharmacies, petrol stations, sports shops and supermarkets, so you'll never be far from a replacement pair if you lose, break or forget yours! If you're looking for protection as well as style, the lenses need to be dark and protect against both UVA and UVB. The range of sunglasses

**425**

### Eyewear

| | | |
|---|---|---|
| Al Adasat Opticals | Lamcy Plaza | 04 335 4006 |
| Al Jaber Optical Centre | Various | See p.486 |
| City Optic | Deira City Centre | 04 295 1400 |
| Dubai Opticals | Various | See p.488 |
| Fashion Optics | Jumeirah Beach Hotel | 04 348 6559 |
| Grand Optics | Various | See p.489 |
| Grand Sunglasses | Deira City Centre | 04 295 5334 |
| Lunettes | Jumeirah Centre | 04 349 2270 |
| Lutfi Opticals Centre | Wafi Mall | 04 324 1865 |
| Opic Gallery | Deira City Centre | 04 295 3825 |
| Optic Art | BurJuman | 04 352 8171 |
| Picnico General Trading | Jumeirh Beach Road | 04 394 1653 |
| Sunglass Hut | Wafi Mall | 04 324 4277 |
| Top Visions Optics | Al Diyafah St | 04 398 4888 |
| The Uniform Shop | Spinneys | 04 394 1477 |
| Yateem Opticians | Various | See p.493 |

for children is improving, with Baby Banz and Kidz Banz available in both Picnico, on Beach Road, and The Uniform Shop, in Spinneys Centre, Umm Suqeim. For adults, a good quality pair of sunglasses, which offer a good level of protection, will cost anywhere from Dhs.100 and up. Major brands like Oakley, Ray Ban, Police and Polaroid are widely available.

For prescription glasses, the choice is just as good, with opticians in virtually every mall. Lenses cost from Dhs.80 up to Dhs.2,000 for single focus and from Dhs.150 to Dhs.5,000 for bifocal. There are a dizzying selection of frames, with most of the designer names available, and prices are from around Dhs.350 to Dhs.9,000 (and some costing as much as Dhs.18,000 which you'd want to make sure you didn't sit on).

There is a fairly comprehensive selection of contact lenses on sale, both single focus and bifocal. Prices range from Dhs.120 for a month's supply of daily single focus, to Dhs.200 for six bifocal monthly lenses.

Many opticians will do an eye test for free, particularly if you go on to buy glasses from them, but others may charge Dhs.20 to Dhs.50. As with any service, the standard of opticians can be a bit hit-and-miss, so it's worth asking around to get some recommendations.

## Flowers

Other options **Gardens** p.427

For a city in the desert, flowers are remarkably abundant. Dubai's position as an international hub means that they are transited through the airport. This has led to the opening of the Dubai Flower Centre where as well as providing cool storage, flowers are sold wholesale (www.dubaiflowercentre.com).

### Flowers

| | | | |
|---|---|---|---|
| Art & Flower | Trade Centre 2 | 04 343 3288 | na |
| Blooms | Jumeira Beach Road Nr Dubai Zoo | 04 344 0912 | na |
| Carrefour ▶ p.479 | Various | See p.487 | www.carrefouruae.com |
| Choithram | Various | See p.488 | www.choithram.com |
| Dubai Garden Centre | Btn 3rd & 4th interchange | 04 340 0006 | www.dubaigardencentre.com |
| Floramex | Al Qusais | 04 267 5850 | www.floramex-uae.com |
| Gift Express | Jumeirah Centre | 04 342 0568 | www.giftexpressdubai.com |
| Home Centre | Various | See p.489 | www.homecentre.net |
| Homes r Us | Mazaya Centre | 04 321 3444 | na |
| Intraflora | Sheikh Zayed Road | 04 332 5333 | www.intraflorame.com |
| Oleander | Jumeira Beach Road | 04 344 0539 | www.oleander.co.ae |
| THE One | Various | See p.493 | www.theoneme.com |
| Park N Shop | Al Wasl Rd | 04 394 5671 | www.parkshopdubai.com |
| Planters | Opp Hamrain Centre | 04 266 6427 | www.planters.info |
| Spinneys | Various | See p.492 | www.spinneys.com |
| Swissflora | Al Quoz | 04 340 1944 | www.swissflora.com |

The larger supermarkets have in-house florists (Carrefour, Choithram, Park n Shop and Spinneys) where the prices are usually towards the lower end of the scale; bouquets start from around Dhs.65. The quality is fairly good but the varieties available are usually limited to basics. Specialist florists often have more exotic ranges to choose from but here the sky can be the limit in terms of price. Most stores produce arrangements for formal functions, including weddings.

If you need to send flowers, many of the florists can arrange delivery; Intraflora and Gift Express can both arrange for overseas delivery. Local online options include www.emiratesflorist.com, www.flowersdubai.com and www.uaegiftshop.com, all of which deliver within the UAE.

Artificial flowers are widely available but the quality varies enormously. Home Centre and Homes r Us, in the Mazaya Centre, both have good ranges of good quality artificial flowers, and THE One has a fabulous selection of gorgeous artificial flowers; Blooms is the shop to head for if you are looking for silk flowers.

## Mini Marvels

Explorer *Mini Visitors' Guides* are the perfect holiday companion. They're small enough to fit in your pocket but beautiful enough to inspire you to explore. With detailed maps, visitors' information, restaurant and bar reviews, the lowdown on shopping and all the sights and sounds of the city, these mini marvels are a holiday must.

## Food

Other options **Health Food** p.432, **Supermarkets** p.476, **Hypermarkets** p.478, **Souks & Markets** p.483

The cosmopolitan nature of Dubai results in a huge amount of choice for consumers, and this is most apparent in the amazing array of foodstuffs available. As well as basic staples, many supermarkets specialise in foods from a particular country or region: for example, Safestway on Sheikh Zayed Road stocks a great range of American products, Spinneys keeps the Brits happy with their Waitrose range as well as other British products, and Carrefour keeps just about everybody happy by stocking products from France, the UK, USA, South Africa, the Philippines, Thailand and India, among others. Apart from the gigantic hypermarkets and well-stocked supermarkets, all areas have a few 'corner shops' that are good for bread, milk and other daily essentials. Most petrol stations have 24 hour convenience shops that sell a basic range of food items.

| Food | | | |
|---|---|---|---|
| Carrefour ▶ p.479 | Various | See p.487 | www.carrefouruae.com |
| Choithram | Various | See p.488 | www.choithram.com |
| Fred.ae | Various | na | www.fred.ae |
| Géant ▶ p.477 | Ibn Battuta Shopping Mall | 04 368 5888 | www.geant-dubai.com |
| HyperPanda | Dubai Festival City | 04 232 5566 | www.panda-uae.com |
| Lifco | Various | See p.490 | www.lifco.com |
| Lulu Hypermarket | Various | See p.490 | www.luluhypermarket.com |
| Organic Foods & Café | Various | See p.491 | www.organicfoodsandcafe.com |
| Park N Shop | Al Wasl Rd | 04 394 5671 | www.parkshopdubai.com |
| Safestway | Shk Zayed Road | 04 343 0412 | na |
| Spinneys | Various | See p.492 | www.spinneys.com |
| Union Co-Op | Various | See p.493 | na |

## Gardens

Other options **Hardware & DIY** p.430, **Flowers** p.426

For a city on the edge of the desert, Dubai is amazingly green. A surprisingly large number of plant species thrive here, although not without help. With very little annual rainfall and rapidly diminishing groundwater, if you want to create your own oasis, it's

427

going to need plenty of water. If you are living near the coast you may be able to save on the DEWA bill by having a well bored in your garden and a pump installed. Keep an eye on it though, if your plants start to wilt it means the water may have become saline. For many the answer is to have an irrigation system installed so that watering the garden is as easy as turning on the tap. Many residents have a gardener (an industrious chap who rides around a particular area on his bicycle and services several gardens every day). When you move into an area, you'll have gardeners touting for your business not long after the delivery trucks have left. Alternatively you can get a garden service, such as Berkeley.

Even if you are living in an apartment the world of horticulture is open to you and pots are widely available so you can turn your balcony into a mini garden to be proud of. To buy plants, you should definitely visit the nursery area (currently to your right just before the Garhoud Bridge, as you head towards Deira, but there are plans to move it). They sell a great range of plants, pots, soil and compost. As with any informal shopping in Dubai, the more you buy the better the discount. Plant Street, in Satwa, also has a number of nurseries that are great for basics but the range is limited. You'll see a number of independent nurseries in various areas (as you drive along the Beach Road, for example), with prices roughly the same as in the nursery area. Of course, the larger retailers like IKEA, Spinneys and Carrefour sell plants too, as well as a range of gardening equipment. For budget tools, Plant Street is hard to beat, with rakes for around Dhs.10. Serious gardeners might find ACE a good source of gardening tools and furniture, and they have a particularly good range of irrigation equipment.

The Dubai Garden Centre, between Junctions Three and Four on Sheikh Zayed Road, has everything you need for gardens. It sells everything from plants to furniture to tools to irrigation systems, and is staffed by knowledgeable people who can tell you why your wisteria is wilting. If you are starting your garden from scratch (freehold buyers pay attention!), they offer a landscaping and planting service.

If it's just garden furniture you're after, try ACE, Carrefour, IKEA, or Home Centre. You can pick up wooden garden furniture quite reasonably, but if you can't store it properly during the harshest months of summer you will probably have to revarnish it every year or two. Parasol in Al Quoz also stocks a range of quality outdoor furniture. Once you've got your garden all green and kitted out with some comfy garden furniture, you are well on your way to making the most of the idyllic alfresco lifestyle

## Picture Perfect

*Images of Abu Dhabi and the UAE* shares the aesthetic and lush wonders of Abu Dhabi in breathtaking images that capture the marvels of the capital emirate and the diversity of its landscapes as well as the changing vistas throughout the seven emirates of the UAE.

## Gardens

| | | | |
|---|---|---|---|
| ACE | Various | See p.486 | www.aceuae.com |
| Berkeley | Trade Centre 1 | 04 339 3111 | na |
| Carrefour ▶ p.479 | Various | See p.487 | www.carrefouruae.com |
| Dubai Garden Centre | Al Quoz | 04 340 0006 | www.dubaigardencentre.com |
| Floramex | Al Qusais | 04 267 5850 | www.floramex-uae.com |
| Hennessey | Al Quoz | 04 347 0379 | www.hennesseyllc.com |
| Home Centre | Various | See p.489 | www.homecentre.net |
| IKEA ▶ p.IBC | Dubai Festival City | 800 4532 | www.ikeadubai.com |
| In-Step Trading Co. | Deira | 04 285 5996 | na |
| THE One | Various | See p.493 | www.theoneme.com |
| Parasol | Umm Suqeim St | 04 347 9003 | www.parasoldubai.com |
| Royal Gardenscape | Al Quoz | 04 340 0648 | roycon@emirates.net.ae |
| Spinneys | Various | See p.492 | www.spinneys.com |
| Stone Gallery | Al Quoz | 04 347 2525 | na |
| Suncoast | Sheikh Zayed Road, Al Quoz | 04 339 4730 | www.suncoastllc.com |
| Those Pool Guys | Al Quoz | 04 339 0418 | www.thosepoolguys.com |
| Union Co-Op | Various | See p.493 | na |

that is common in Dubai. All you need now is a good barbecue, which can be found in hypermarkets, supermarkets, hardware stores and garden centres. Prices start at around Dhs.25 for a disposable model, and range up to Dhs.20,000 for a state-of-the-art, six-burner beast.

If you decide to splash out and install your own pool, you can choose between an above-ground or below-ground pool. Above-ground pools, available in Carrefour, are cheaper and portable, although not very sturdy for the long term. Although it's a big investment (starting from around Dhs.65,000 for a fibreglass pool and Dhs.85,000 for a concrete one), getting a below-ground pool is worth it in the long run. There are several companies that, for a monthly fee, will take care of routine pool maintenance for you (such as Those Pool Guys).

## Gifts

With so many expats enjoying a high standard of living in Dubai, with more disposable income to spend on gadgets and luxuries for themselves, it can be difficult to buy gifts as many people already seem to have everything. Fortunately, Dubai has all bases covered with gift items that range from small to large, cheap to expensive, run-of-the-mill to bizarre, and practical to indulgent. Lifestyle, Harvest Home, Magrudy's, Susan Walpole and The Warehouse all stock some interesting pieces with broad appeal. Debenhams and Next have some interesting toys for big boys as well as their ranges of other gift-worthy items. Many malls have little stalls selling novelty gift items and Arabian knick-knacks. You'll have no worries if you need to buy a gift for a child, as Dubai is full of toy stores (see also p.436) and bookshops (p.414). For something different, try Stuck on You, an Australian franchise selling labels and personalised items for children (www.stuckonyou.biz). For extra-special gifts, try Rivoli. And if your budget stretches to jewellery, then what could be more exciting than giving something beautiful wrapped up in the distinctive blue and white packaging from Tiffany & Co?

| Gifts | | |
|---|---|---|
| Debenhams | Various | See p.488 |
| Gift Express | Jumeirah Centre | 04 342 0568 |
| Harvest Home Trading | Jumeirah Centre | 04 342 0225 |
| Lifestyle | Various | See p.490 |
| Marks & Spencer | Various | See p.490 |
| Melangé | Jumaira Plaza | 04 344 4721 |
| Music Room | Beach Centre | 04 344 8883 |
| Next | Various | See p.491 |
| Rivoli | Various | See p.492 |
| Sunny Days Trading | Jumeirah Centre | 04 349 5275 |
| Susan Walpole | Various | See p.493 |
| Tiffany & Co | Various | See p.493 |
| Virgin Megastore ▶ p.451 | Various | See p.493 |
| Warehouse | Jumaira Plaza | 04 344 0244 |
| Woolworths | Various | See p.493 |

If online gift shopping is your thing, Gift Express (www.giftexpress.com) delivers a range of items within the UAE and overseas. And Blue Banana (www.bluebananaarabia.com) is a gift service that specialises in adventure package gift certificates; you can even give someone the gift of flying in a MiG-25 to the edge of space, if you have a spare Dhs.58,000 to spend. If you want to send Christmas presents to family members back home, you can order on Amazon (www.amazon.com or www.amazon.co.uk) and have it all delivered for you.

Most shops issue gift vouchers. Debenhams issues vouchers but does not accept those issued in overseas branches of Debenhams, Marks & Spencer will accept vouchers issued in the UK (there are two types of voucher issued, and the Dubai branch of M&S will only accept the ones for franchise branches).

## Handbags

Local ladies love their handbags and the humble handbag has become a major status symbol, especially since it is often the only item visible when dressed in the long black abaya. As a result, you can get some amazing creations (both in terms of craftmanship and in price) at various exclusive boutiques around Dubai. For the latest Louis Vuitton or Tod's handbag, head for BurJuman where both have stores.

**429**

## Handbags

| Accessorize | Various | See p.486 |
|---|---|---|
| Bally | Mall of the Emirates | 04 341 0280 |
| Benetton | Various | See p.487 |
| Burberry | Various | See p.487 |
| Carrefour ▶ p.479 | Various | See p.487 |
| Coach | Various | See p.488 |
| Debenhams | Various | See p.488 |
| Elegance | Wafi Mall | 04 324 2266 |
| Eve Michelle | Magrudy's | 04 342 9574 |
| Louis Vuitton | BurJuman | 04 359 2535 |
| Monsoon | Various | See p.491 |
| Next | Various | See p.491 |
| Tod's | Various | See p.493 |

If you're addicted to designer handbags but don't have the money to support your habit, various shops in Karama sell knock-offs. The price for a really good copy handbag is not that cheap at still around Dhs.300 to Dhs.400 but sometimes the quality is so good that it is nearly impossible to distinguish between the copy and the real thing. Shop owners selling copy handbags are the focus of a crackdown to stamp out this illegal trade, and as a result if you want to view the handbags you will be taken into a back room so that you can see them behind closed (and sometimes even locked) doors. For the less label-conscious, handbags are sold in most fashion, luggage and accessories shops, including Accessorize, Monsoon, Benetton, Next, Debenhams, Bally and even Carrefour.

## Hardware & DIY

Other options **Outdoor Goods** p.441

With a number of companies offering handyman services (see Domestic Services on p.164), it may be easier and cheaper to find a 'man who can' rather than invest in the tools and materials you need for DIY jobs. However, if you enjoy tinkering with tools and doing odd jobs around the house, there are plenty of outlets where you can buy your toolkit. Both ACE and Speedex on Sheikh Zayed Road stock comprehensive ranges of tools, along with all the nails, nuts, bolts and screws you need. Carrefour has a DIY section and in Satwa there are numerous independent shops selling everything from the rustiest nail to the shiniest drill bit. Dragon Mart, in International City, has a section for builder's merchants and here you can find baths, tiles, power tools and other hardware items.

## Hardware & DIY

| ACE | Various | See p.486 | www.aceuae.com |
|---|---|---|---|
| Carrefour ▶ p.479 | Various | See p.487 | www.carrefouruae.com |
| Dragon Mart | International City, Emirates Rd | 04 368 7205 | www.chinamexmart.com |
| Speedex | Nr Oasis Centre | 04 339 1929 | na |

## Hats

The Dubai World Cup is not just the highlight of the horse racing season, it is the fashion event of the year, when no outfit is complete without a hat. Some shops, including Debenhams, have hats year round, great for weddings, but most shops stock them between January and March. Oasis Fashions creations tend toward the full-on feathery and flowery and are aimed at race goers. Eve Michelle stocks a selection of designer hats in different styles for those looking to make a bold statement. Their main collection arrives in time for the races with a small selection available year round. Sunny Days sells hats year round, made by local milliner Lynn Holyoak, whose stunning creations are very reasonably priced. Malls, including BurJuman and Wafi, get in on the act by hosting displays in the run up to World Cup night. For high-street style, Accessorize has hats for all seasons, with accessories to match.

If you are looking for something functional rather than fashionable, options are rather limited but the beachwear shops have small collections. Beyond the Beach and Studio R have surfwear styles, while Heatwaves has UV protective models for adults and children.

## Hats

| Accessorize | Various | See p.486 |
|---|---|---|
| Beyond the Beach | Various | See p.487 |
| Debenhams | Various | See p.488 |
| Eve Michelle | Magrudy's | 04 342 9574 |
| Heatwaves | Various | See p.489 |
| Oasis | Various | See p.491 |
| Studio R | Various | See p.493 |
| Sunny Days Trading | Jumeirah Centre | 04 349 5275 |

Copper wall panel (5m high) · Art paint effects

**MacKenzie Associates**

ART & SPECIALIST DECORATION

MURALS · SCULPTURE
SPECIALIST PAINTING

'no 2 sterility, yes 2 creativity…'

F. MacKenzie – Artist · Designer

Art details · gold panel (1.5m high)

Tel 04 334 8825  Fax 04 335 3529  PO Box 34275  Dubai  UAE

info@dubaimurals.com  www.dubaimurals.com

# Health Food

Other options **Food** p.427, **Health Clubs** p.384

The range of health and speciality food is increasing, and although prices are generally high it is worth shopping around as costs vary from shop to shop. Shops selling sports supplements, energy bars and protein powders are often classified as health food shops and some are now diversifying into selling speciality foodstuffs.

Good Health, at the Nutrition Centre, sells both and they have a small selection of gluten-free and wheat-free products. Nutrition Zone specialises in vitamins, health supplements and detoxifying products from Holland & Barrett. They also carry a range of health food, grains, gluten and wheat-free products, as well as Green & Blacks chocolate and some ecological household products. Their prices are reasonable and below those of the supermarkets for many items. The main supermarkets stock increasing varieties of speciality foods and they all carry products for diabetics, Choithram has possibly the widest range. Choithram also stocks dairy-free, gluten-free and wheat-free products ranging from bread to icecream. Spinneys carries a limited selection of organic fruit and vegetables and, through their partnership with Waitrose, an organic range which includes beans, pulses, biscuits and fruit juice. They also stock some items from Waitrose's 'Perfectly Balanced' calorie and fat counted range. Park n Shop's health food range includes breads made from spelt or rye flour which are less allergenic than wheat; they even make spelt hot cross buns and mince pies. Carrefour's range is increasing and, as well as the basic range that most supermarkets carry, have some own-brand organic products.

Organic Foods and Café go to the source for every item in their stores and their product range is constantly evolving. Some products are quite expensive but they carry a good selection, including bread, seafood, frozen meals, and fresh produce. Many products are cheaper than in the supermarkets and not available elsewhere. The cafes, attached to the Satwa and Emirates Hills stores, use only products that they stock in the shops and many of the dishes are suitable for vegetarians and vegans.

Dubai hosts the annual Middle East Natural & Organic Products Expo, which sees over 300 companies from 35 countries exhibiting a range of natural products and treatments. See www.globallinksdubai.com for details.

| Health Food | | |
|---|---|---|
| Carrefour ▶ p.479 | Various | See p.487 |
| Choithram | Various | See p.488 |
| GNC | BurJuman | 04 352 6771 |
| Healthy Eating | Nr Princeton Hotel | 04 286 5777 |
| Nutrition Centre | Jumeirah Centre | 04 344 7464 |
| Nutrition World | Palm Strip | 04 345 0652 |
| Nutrition Zone | Jumeirah Town Centre | 04 344 5888 |
| Organic Foods & Café | Various | See p.491 |
| Park N Shop | Al Wasl Rd | 04 394 5671 |
| Planet Nutrition | Various | See p.491 |
| Spinneys | Various | See p.492 |

## Home Furnishings & Accessories

Other options **Furnishing Accommodation** p.160, **Hardware & DIY** p.430

This is one of Dubai's most buoyant retail sectors, perhaps because the seemingly unlimited supply of new villas and apartments all need to be furnished. For more and more people, Dubai is home rather than a limited-term posting, and this has led to an increased interest in home furnishings and accessories.

Most tastes are catered for, from ethnic pieces to the latest designer concepts and specialist children's furniture stores. IKEA, in an enormous showroom in Dubai Festival City, is perhaps the city's best known furniture store, and sells some great furniture at great value. Their selection is suitable for most budgets, and they sell everything from Dhs.1 tealight holders to Dhs.20,000 kitchens. On a slightly higher-end level, THE One covers all aspects of home furnishing and is great for Christmas decorations. Marina

**Interior Desires**

*If your interior design is lacking inspiration, then there are some excellent glossy magazines available to lend a hand.* Emirates Home, Identity *and* Inside Out *may inspire you to transform your home into a palace fit for a sheikh.*

Gulf stocks a good range of Arabian-style furniture and accessories, from lamps and bedding to chests and huge dining tables. They have a warehouse outlet in Al Quoz. And So To Bed is one of the UK's top linen shops. Their Dubai branch is opposite BurJuman and although it is not for the budget shopper, they sell some beautiful beds and bed linen. Another British company renowned for quality is The White Company, now with several branches.

Cottage Chic in the Holiday Centre next to the Crowne Plaza packs a good selection of home furnishings into its small shop space, including items from Rachel Ashwell's Shabby Chic range.

For top-class Italian leather furniture try Natuzzi, who have opened their largest international branch between Junctions Two and Three on Sheikh Zayed Road. The craftmanship is of such a high standard that their products can be classed as investment furniture rather than something to change when you redecorate.

Memoires in Wafi Mall is quite a spectacular retail experience. Selling a variety of antiques and knick-knacks for the home, it is sublimely decorated in 'medieval' style with a maze-like layout of themed rooms, and the end result is more like that of a museum than a store.

If you want to add some exotic touches to your home, there are plenty of items from India and the Far East. Safita Trading has a good range at competitive prices. Panache Interiors at Jumeira Centre offers design services, interior decoration, ready made home accessories and goodies made of natural fibres that make great gifts.

The industrial area between Junctions Three and Four of Sheikh Zayed Road is home to a number of furniture warehouses, many of which sell pieces crafted from Indonesian teak. For authentic warehouse shopping, try Lucky's and Pinky's – these hot, dusty warehouses located near the Sharjah border are piled to the rooftops with higgledy-piggledy pieces of Indian teak furniture. Don't be put off though – prices are excellent and after a good polish the furniture looks fabulous! Fabindia on Al Mankhool Road stocks an interesting range of hand-crafted bed linen, table linen, fabrics and accessories from India.

Genuine antiques are available but very rare (and therefore very expensive). Many antique pieces come from Oman and Yemen; Al Jaber Gallery is known for genuine Emirati pieces.

Children's furniture is a growth market. IKEA has a great range of reasonably priced kids' furniture, and their range of bunkbeds is consistently popular. Their children's section is good to visit even if you are not buying; while you browse around your kids can play

## Home Furnishings & Accessories

| | | |
|---|---|---|
| Aati | Al Karama | 04 337 7825 |
| Al Huzaifa Furniture | Umm Hurair | 04 336 6646 |
| Al Jaber Gallery | Various | See p.486 |
| And So To Bed | Nr BurJuman | 04 396 2022 |
| Antique Museum | Al Quoz | 04 347 9935 |
| Apollo Furniture | Al Quoz | 04 339 1358 |
| Art Of Life | Al Quoz | 04 340 6755 |
| Bafco Trading LLC | Al Karama | 04 335 0045 |
| Bayti | Deira City Centre | 04 294 9292 |
| Bedrooms 4 kids | Satwa | 04 398 9640 |
| Bhs | Various | See p.487 |
| Bombay | Various | See p.487 |
| Carpe Diem | Jumeira | 04 344 4734 |
| Carre Blanc | Deira City Centre | 04 295 3992 |
| Carrefour ▶ p.479 | Various | See p.487 |
| Casa Marakesh | Wafi Mall | 04 342 0981 |
| Chen One | Century Plaza | 04 342 2441 |
| Cottage Chic | Holiday Centre Mall | 04 331 3308 |
| Cozy House | Al Quoz | 04 340 4596 |
| Daiso | Lamcy Plaza | 04 335 1532 |
| Desert River | Satwa | 04 345 4541 |
| Design Diva | Al Quoz | 04 347 6507 |
| Ethan Allen | Jumeira | 04 342 1616 |
| Exotica | Al Quoz | 04 340 2966 |
| Fabindia | Bur Dubai | 04 398 9633 |
| Fauchar | Wafi Mall | 04 324 6769 |
| Feshwari | Various | See p.489 |
| Georg Jensen | Wafi Mall | 04 324 0704 |
| Grand Stores | Garhoud | 04 282 3700 |
| Guess Home | BurJuman | 04 355 3324 |
| Habitat | Various | See p.489 |
| Harvest Home Trading | Jumeirah Centre | 04 342 0225 |
| Home Centre | Various | See p.489 |
| Homes r Us | Mazaya Centre | 04 321 3444 |
| IKEA ▶ p.IBC | Dubai Festival City | 800 4532 |

with all the display toys. Kidz Inc. are the sole agents for Haba – this German, hand-made, wooden furniture doesn't come cheap but all pieces meet European and American safety standards and come with a five-year warranty. Especially good is their range of themed beds are especially good (think pirate ships and flowery glades), with matching furniture and accessories. Feshwari can custom-make furniture for you, from sofas and beanbags to ottomans and cushions. They specialise in designer upholstery fabrics (such as Designers' Guild, Sheila Coombes, Andrew Martin and Jim Thompson Silk), curtains and blinds. Plant Street in Satwa has a couple of fabric shops that can reupholster just about anything, should you have furniture that is beginning to look a little bit tired.

For accessories rather than large pieces of furniture, there are plenty of shops that will help you add the finishing touches to your home. Zara Home's fresh, European designs are now available in a number of malls. Next (the branch at Mall of the Emirates) has a small home accessories section at the back of the shop. Debenhams is good for homewares, bedding and kitchenware – this is where you can buy the entire range of Jamie Oliver's cookware. Kitchenalia junkies will love Tavola and Harvest Home, which have some unusual items you hadn't realised you couldn't live without.

For something unique, Mackenzie Associates can assist you with some amazing finishing touches to your home, including murals, trompe l'oeils and sculptures (see p.431).

The transient nature of some of Dubai's population results in an active second-hand furniture market. Items are advertised in the classified sections of the local newspapers but the supermarket noticeboards are the best source; they are also where to keep an eye out for garage sales.

| Home Furnishings & Accessories | | |
|---|---|---|
| ID Design | Various | See p.489 |
| IKEA ▶ p.IBC | Dubai Festival City | 800 4532 |
| Interiors | Umm Hurair | 04 337 0116 |
| Irony Home L.L.C. | The Village Mall | 04 342 2145 |
| Jotun Paints | Al Quoz | 04 339 5000 |
| KA International | Dubai | 04 345 9988 |
| Kas | Mercato | 04 344 1179 |
| Kidz Inc. | Al Quoz | 04 340 5059 |
| KKids | Jumaira Plaza | 04 344 4753 |
| Liwa | Various | See p.490 |
| Lucky's | Sharjah | 06 534 1937 |
| Marina Gulf | Various | See p.490 |
| Marlin | Various | See p.490 |
| Memoires | Wafi Mall | 04 324 3001 |
| Natuzzi | Al Quoz | 04 338 0777 |
| Pan Emirates | Al Quoz | 04 324 8061 |
| Panache Furnishing | Jumeirah Centre | 04 344 3677 |
| Persepolis | Al Karama | 04 334 2824 |
| Petals | Petals | 04 340 2201 |
| Pier Import | Mazaya Centre | 04 343 2002 |
| Pinky's | Sharjah | 06 534 1714 |
| Pride of Kashmir | Various | See p.492 |
| Safita Trading Est | Al Quoz | 04 339 3230 |
| Sara – Villeroy & Boch | Various | See p.492 |
| Showcase Antiques | Umm Seqeim | 04 348 8797 |
| Tanagra | Various | See p.493 |
| Tavola | Various | See p.493 |
| THE One | Various | See p.493 |
| Warehouse | Jumaira Plaza | 04 344 0244 |
| Western Furniture | Al Karama | 04 337 7152 |
| The White Company | Various | See p.493 |
| Wicker | Al Karama | 04 337 5544 |
| Woolworths | Various | See p.493 |
| Zara Home | Various | See p.493 |
| Zen Interiors | Al Barsha | 04 340 5050 |

## Jewellery, Watches & Gold
Other options **Markets & Souks** p.483

Dubai is the world's leading re-exporter of gold and you'll find at least one jewellery shop in even the smallest malls, and large areas dedicated to shops selling it. From trinkets for toddlers to multi-million dirham gold and diamond creations, Dubai has it all. Gold is available in 18, 21, 22 or 24 carats and is sold according to the international daily gold rate. This means that for an identical piece, whether you buy it in Emirates Towers or the Gold Souk, there will be very little difference in the price of the actual gold. Where the price varies is in the workmanship that has gone into a particular piece.

## Jewellery, Watches & Gold

| | | |
|---|---|---|
| Al Fardan Jewels | Various | See p.486 |
| Al Futtaim Jewellery | Various | See p.486 |
| Al Liali | Various | See p.486 |
| Bin Hendi Jewellery | Various | See p.487 |
| Breitling Watches | Various | See p.487 |
| Cartier Middle East | Emirates Towers, Level 36 | 04 330 0333 |
| Chopard | Wafi Mall | 04 324 1010 |
| Citizen | Nr Fish RA | 04 271 5607 |
| Claire's | Various | See p.488 |
| Damas Jewellery | Various | See p.488 |
| Debenhams | Various | See p.488 |
| Eve Michelle | Magrudy's | 04 342 9574 |
| Fossil | Various | See p.489 |
| Golden Ring | Deira City Centre | 04 295 0373 |
| Guess | Various | See p.489 |
| Mahallati Jewellery | Various | See p.489 |
| Mansoor Jewellery | BurJuman | 04 355 2110 |
| Marks & Spencer | Various | See p.490 |
| Montblanc | Various | See p.491 |
| Next | Various | See p.491 |
| Omega | Various | See p.491 |
| Paris Gallery | Various | See p.491 |
| Philippe Charriol | BurJuman | 04 351 1112 |
| Prima Gold | Various | See p.492 |
| Pure Gold | Various | See p.492 |
| Raymond Weil | Deira City Centre | 04 295 3254 |
| Rivoli | Various | See p.492 |
| Rolex | Mall of the Emirates | 04 341 1222 |
| Rossini | Various | See p.492 |
| Silver Art | Deira City Centre | 04 295 2414 |
| Swarovski | Wafi Mall | 04 324 0168 |
| Swatch | Various | See p.493 |
| TAG Heuer | Various | See p.493 |
| Tanagra | Various | See p.493 |
| Tiffany & Co | Various | See p.493 |
| Watch House | Various | See p.493 |

While gold jewellery may be the most prevalent, silver, platinum, precious stones, gems and pearls are all sold, either separately or crafted into jewellery. Most outlets can make up a piece for you, working from a diagram or photograph. Just ensure that you are not obliged to buy it if it doesn't turn out quite how you had imagined. Many of the world's finest jewellers are represented in Dubai. Cartier and Tiffany & Co. are well known as creators of some beautiful jewellery and watches. Fabergé jewellery is amongst the elite collection in Saks Fifth Avenue's jewellery department. Graff and DeBeers are among the world's top diamond retailers and produce pieces just waiting to become a girl's best friend.

The Gold Souk is great in terms of choice. A traditional gift is a pendant with your name spelled out in Arabic, or some jewellery crafted with black pearls. The recently expanded Gold & Diamond Park (at junction four on Sheikh Zayed Road) has branches of many of the same shops but in a calmer atmosphere. You can still barter, and there is an added bonus of cafes to wait in while the jeweller makes any alterations. This is also a good spot to head for if you are looking for engagement or wedding rings and, like the outlets in the Souk, you are able to commission pieces. Costume jewellery and watches can be found in most department stores as well as Eve Michelle and the beautiful Swarovski range in Tanagra. Accessorize has a great range of every-day pieces which echo the colours and fashions of the season, and Next has a small range of mostly silver pieces. For children, Claire's Accessories is like an Aladdin's Cave for girly girls, with inexpensive jewellery and hair accessories.

All the major brands of watches are available in Dubai, so whether you're in the market for a Rolex, Breitling, Tag Heuer, Swatch, Casio or Timex, you have many models to choose from.

*All you could ask for and more*

## Kids' Clothes

| Adams | Various | See p.486 |
|---|---|---|
| Dar Al Tasmim Uniforms | Umm Suqeim | 04 394 1477 |
| Debenhams | Various | See p.488 |
| Gap | Deira City Centre | 04 295 1354 |
| Factory Fashions | Oud Metha | 04 336 2699 |
| H&M | Various | See p.489 |
| Ladybird | Various | See p.490 |
| Marks & Spencer | Various | See p.491 |
| Monsoon | Various | See p.491 |
| Mothercare | Various | See p.491 |
| Next | Various | See p.491 |
| Okaidi | Deira | 04 295 9923 |
| Peacocks | Various | See p.491 |
| Prémaman | Bur Dubai | 04 351 5353 |
| Pumpkin Patch | Various | See p.492 |
| Saks Fifth Avenue | BurJuman | 04 351 5551 |
| Sana Fashion | Al Karama | 04 337 7726 |
| Shoe Mart | Various | See p.492 |
| Woolworths | Various | See p.493 |
| Zara | Various | See p.493 |

## Kids' Clothes

Other options **Clothes** p.421

Finding kids' clothing in Dubai is child's play – from high-end designer fashions (Christian Lacroix and Armani) down to factory seconds from Sana, there is something to suit all tastes and budgets. In the middle, there are great children's departments in Debenhams, Marks & Spencer, Next and Woolworths.

For babies and younger children, Mothercare, Woolworths and Next carry the essentials and have some great outfits at reasonable prices. Okaidi and Pumpkin Patch sell bright, colourful and practical clothes that children love – the beauty of these clothes is that they are designed for children rather than trying to make them look like miniature adults. Monsoon's ranges for boys and girls are great for party clothes and are especially loved by little girls. Online store Kid Eternity (www.kid-eternity.com) offers a range of clothing brands that are not widely available in Dubai. The majority of children's clothes shops also stock shoes and there are some specialist stores. Pablosky stocks a range of colourful shoes for babies and children while Magrudy's and Shoe Mart have children's sections.

For party costumes check out Early Learning Centre or Toys R Us, year round, and the supermarkets and hypermarkets in the run up to festive events like Halloween and Christmas; the craft fairs are another good source. If all else fails, buy the material and have a truly unique costume made by one of the city's numerous tailors (see p.448). Children grow out of their clothes so quickly that its worth waiting for the sales; prices are often greatly reduced and you can restock their wardrobe at a fraction of the cost.

## Kids' Items

Dubai is a child-friendly city, not least because there is a high concentration of shops selling toys. There is something for everyone, from hi-tech baby learning laptops to cheap plastic tat (which your kids will probably prefer, despite your best intentions!), but remember that not all toys conform to international safety standards and therefore should only be used under supervision.

Baby Shop, the Toy Store and Toys R Us cater to all age groups from babies to teens, and sell international brands including Little Tikes and Fisher Price. Early Learning Centre and Imaginarium stock a range of educational toys and toys that stimulate play and imagination. Magrudy's sells toys for younger children, including Little Tikes and the Whoozit range, as well as a good range of games and puzzles. Park n Shop has a great toy department with some good 'pocket money' toys. For educational and wooden toys, try the little shop on the ground floor of Children's City, IKEA and Haba – they all carry good quality toys that are built to last. For inexpensive birthday presents and stocking fillers, Carrefour and Géant both have toy departments, and little shops around Karama and Satwa are excellent for cheap toys (just don't expect them to last a long time). For a unique gift for children of all ages, you can get a customised teddy bear made at The Bear Factory: just choose your teddy, and they will stuff it, dress it and name it according to your preference.

### Toys R Us

The largest toy shop in Dubai, Toys R Us has a huge range catering to children of all ages. The opening of an in-house branch of Ladybird, offering everyday children's wear from the UK, is a welcome addition. As well as toys and a staggering variety of dolls, there are bikes for both adults and children, baby essentials including buggies and car seats and an area for DVDs, videos and computer games. Check out the huge flagship store at Dubai Festival City (p.456) and the new opening in Times Square Centre (p.472).

**436**

## Kids' Items

| | | |
|---|---|---|
| Adams | Various | See p.486 |
| Baby Shop | Various | See p.486 |
| Bear Factory | Al Barsha | 04 347 5399 |
| Book Worm | Jumeira | 04 394 5770 |
| Carrefour ▶ p.479 | Various | See p.487 |
| Children's City | Umm Hurair | 04 334 0808 |
| Dar Al Tasmim Uniforms | Umm Suqeim | 04 394 1477 |
| Dragon Mart | Al Awir | 04 368 7205 |
| Early Learning Centre | Various | See p.488 |
| Géant ▶ p.477 | Jebel Ali | 04 368 5888 |
| Geekay | Deira | 04 295 2140 |
| Goodbaby | Al Karama | 04 397 5653 |
| Hobby Centre | Deira | 04 295 5512 |
| HyperPanda | Dubai Festival City | 04 232 5566 |
| IKEA ▶ p.IBC | Dubai Festival City | 800 4532 |
| Imaginarium | Umm Hurair | 04 324 8055 |
| Kidz Inc Haba | Al Quoz | 04 340 5059 |
| Lego Store | Jebel Ali Village | 04 368 5217 |
| Little Me | Jumeira | 04 345 6424 |
| Lola et Moi | Jumeira | 04 345 4774 |
| Magrudy's ▶ p.415 | Various | See p.490 |
| Mothercare | Various | See p.491 |
| Ovo Kids | Deira | 04 295 5900 |
| Park N Shop | Al Wasl | 04 394 5671 |
| Pumpkin Patch | Various | See p.492 |
| Toy Store & B Avenue | Jumeira | 04 349 3490 |
| Toys R Us | Various | See p.493 |
| The White Company | Dubai Festival City | 04 232 5506 |

Hobby Centre will appeal to all those who prefer a little more interactive action with their toys, from build-your-own, wind-up vehicles to remote-controlled planes and cars. This is the place for serious model enthusiasts. Those who prefer to get their entertainment from a TV and a games console will not be disappointed by what the city has to offer – most electronics stores stock a wide range of games for the various platforms. Try Geekay and Carrefour, both of which have a good selection at reasonable prices.

# Lingerie

Other options **Clothes** p.421

Dubai has a huge range of lingerie outlets. Nayomi is a regional retailer selling a range of functional and sexy underwear. They offer a bridal chest full of lacy, frilly, silky goodies, including the ultimate in bedroom glamour – high-heeled fluffy slippers!

Top European brands are also available, such as Agent Provocateur at Saks Fifth Avenue and Janet Reger in the Boulevard at Emirates Towers.

Bendon, in Mall of the Emirates, caters to women of all sizes. In the same mall, K-Lynn is a well-known Lebanese boutique carrying lines to suit everyone.

Secrets Boutique in the Bin Sougat Centre specialises in larger size bras. It may be worth visiting their website, www.secretsgroup.com, before you head over to the shop. If you want a fitting you should also call in advance.

## Lingerie

| | | |
|---|---|---|
| Bare Essentials | Jumeirah Centre | 04 344 0552 |
| Bendon | Mall of the Emirates | 04 341 3373 |
| Bhs | Various | See p.487 |
| Carrefour ▶ p.479 | Various | See p.487 |
| Debenhams | Various | See p.488 |
| K-Lynn | Mall of the Emirates | 04 341 0083 |
| La Belleamie | Beach Centre | 04 349 3928 |
| La Perla | Various | See p.490 |
| La Senza | Various | See p.490 |
| Marks & Spencer | Various | See p.490 |
| My Time | BurJuman | 04 351 3881 |
| Nayomi | Various | See p.491 |
| Saks Fifth Avenue | BurJuman | 04 351 5551 |
| Secrets Boutique | Bin Sougat Centre | 04 285 6602 |
| Triumph | Various | See p.493 |
| Women'secret | Various | See p.493 |
| Woolworths | Various | See p.493 |

Debenhams, Marks & Spencer and Woolworths are famed for their lingerie, from every day basics to sets for special occasions, and they all offer fitting services. Debenhams stocks the renowned Floozie collection, as well as a small Calvin Klein range. La Senza has a super-girly and fun selection of reasonably priced lingerie and pyjamas.

# Luggage & Leather

Dubai residents generally travel a lot, so luggage is widely available. At the lower end, Carrefour is a great starting point with its huge selection and reasonable prices. Just a tip though... so many Dubai travellers buy their luggage from Carrefour that you might have a bit of trouble identifying your suitcase among the hundreds of other Carrefour suitcases on the conveyor belt. Sports shops sell good ranges of kit bags and trolley bags, usually in bright, sporty colours.

**437**

## Luggage & Leather

| | | |
|---|---|---|
| Aigner | Various | See p.486 |
| Aristocrat | BurJuman | 04 355 2395 |
| Bally | Mall of the Emirates | 04 341 0280 |
| Benetton | Various | See p.487 |
| Calonge | Al Ghurair City | 04 228 4232 |
| Carrefour ▶ p.479 | Various | See p.487 |
| Chanel | Various | See p.487 |
| Francesco Biasia | Mercato | 04 349 9622 |
| Furla | BurJuman | 04 352 2285 |
| HyperPanda | Dubai Festival City | 04 232 5566 |
| IKEA ▶ p.IBC | Dubai Festival City | 800 4532 |
| Jashanmal ▶ p.417 | Various | See p.489 |
| La Valise | Deira City Centre | 04 295 5509 |
| Leather Palace | Various | See p.490 |
| Louis Vuitton | BurJuman | 04 359 2535 |
| Mohd Shareif | BurJuman | 04 355 3377 |
| THE One | Various | See p.493 |
| Porsche Design | Various | See p.492 |
| Sacoche | Deira City Centre | 04 295 0233 |
| Sun & Sand Sports ▶ p.321 | Various | See p.493 |
| Tod's | Various | See p.492 |

At the higher end of the luggage market, designer labels are widely available. Try BurJuman for Aigner, Bally, Tod's and Louis Vuitton. Or if you like the labels but not the prices, a good rummage around the Karama Market can unearth some quite convincing knock-offs.

Leather clothing is not overly popular in such a warm climate, but people often buy leather coats and accessories for trips to colder climes. For reasonably priced leather jackets imported in bulk from the subcontinent, try Karama Market. For more luxurious options, try Timberland (outlets inside Sun & Sand sports shops), Massimo Dutti, and other designer boutiques.

Leather furniture is available in most home furnishing outlets, but Natuzzi specialise in leather. Their enormous store, between junctions two and three on Sheikh Zayed Road, has something for most tastes. IKEA and THE One also have leather collections.

## Maternity Items

Fortunately pregnant women no longer have to suffer months of dressing in large, shapeless smocks or wearing their husband's shirts over leggings. These days, with many retailers jumping on the maternity fashion bandwagon, mums-in-training can look as stylish as everyone else. Dorothy Perkins and Topshop are great for fun, fashionable items, and Debenhams, Marks & Spencer, Mothercare and Woolworths also stock good selections of maternity clothes.

## Maternity Items

| | | |
|---|---|---|
| Arabian Home Health Care | Oud Metha | 04 335 1230 |
| Baby Shop | Various | See p.486 |
| Debenhams | Various | See p.488 |
| Dorothy Perkins | Various | See p.488 |
| Formes | Wafi Mall | 04 324 4856 |
| Great Expectations | Palm Strip | 04 345 3155 |
| Jenny Rose | Various | See p.489 |
| Just Kidding | Al Quoz | 04 341 3922 |
| Marks & Spencer | Various | See p.490 |
| Mothercare | Various | See p.491 |
| New Look | Deira City Centre | 04 295 9542 |
| Pumpkin Patch | Various | See p.492 |
| Topshop | Various | See p.493 |
| Toys R Us | Various | See p.493 |
| Woolworths | Various | See p.493 |

Formes, Great Expectations and Jenny Rose carry the latest styles, and might be the best places to find speciality items such as swimwear, underwear and evening wear.

As well as buggies and nursery furniture, Just Kidding carries Noppies maternity wear from Holland. Pumpkin Patch now also stocks a limited maternity range – hold out for the sales if you can. For other maternity items like cool packs, creams and bras, you'll have to shop around in Mothercare, or Baby Shop, Debenhams, Marks & Spencer and Jenny Rose – ranges vary and may be limited. Baby Shop and Mothercare stock a range of breast pumps, or you could try one of the larger pharmacies if you want a really heavy duty one. Storage bags for breast milk are widely available (Playtex and Avent brands). Boppy breastfeeding pillows are available in Toys R Us, and Arabian Home Health Care, opposite Rashid Hospital also stock pillows for breast feeding – you need to ask for them when you go in.

Some essential accessories for pregnancy may not be available here – one example is a 'Bump Belt', which redirects your car seatbelt under your bump, and which can be ordered online (try www.halfords.co.uk or www.jojomamanbebe.co.uk).

## Medicine

Other options **General Medical Care** p.178

The UAE has a more relaxed policy on prescription drugs than many other countries and most can be bought over the counter. If you know what you need it cuts out the hassle of having to see a doctor just so that you can get a prescription. Pharmacists are willing to offer advice, although they may be reluctant to suggest antibiotics. Always tell the pharmacist if you have any pre-existing conditions or are taking other medication, as they don't always ask.

| Medicine | | |
|---|---|---|
| Al Wasl Pharmacy | Jumeira | 04 344 8333 |
| Life Pharmacy | Al Wasl | 04 344 1122 |
| Safa Society Pharmacy | Al Wasl | 04 394 6618 |
| Yara Pharmacy | Deira | 04 222 5503 |

Certain medications do require a prescription, and some medications (such as codeine and temazepam) are banned here even though they are widely available over the counter in other countries. It's a crime to have these medicines in your possession or to take them, unless you can produce an official prescription from your doctor in your home country (but even then you might end up at the police station while it is translated into Arabic). So unless it is absolutely necessary and there's no alternative, avoid medications that are banned in the UAE.

Supermarkets and petrol station convenience stores sell basic medications such as Panadol or ENO. They also stock basic first aid equipment such as plasters, gauze and antiseptic cream. You might find it frustrating that certain common medications from your home country are not available here (such as Gaviscon for Infants, for example). You can however bring these into the country for your own personal use.

There are pharmacies all over the city and a number are open 24 hours a day.

## Mobile Telephones

Other options **Telephone** p.170

| Mobile Telephones | | | |
|---|---|---|---|
| Aptec Mobiles | Various | See p.486 | www.aptecmobiles.com |
| Axiom Telecom | Various | See p.486 | www.axiomtelecom.com |
| Carrefour ▶ p.479 | Various | See p.487 | www.carrefouruae.com |
| Cellucom | Various | See p.487 | www.cellucom.com |
| Jacky's Electronics | Various | See p.489 | www.jackys.com |
| Jumbo Electronics | Various | See p.490 | www.jumbocorp.com |
| Plug-Ins | Various | See p.492 | www.al-futtaim.com |
| Sharaf DG | Various | See p.492 | www.sharafdg.com |

Every mall seems to have at least one or two outlets selling mobile phones (but usually more). Major electronics shops sell the leading brands but the mobile specialists are Axiom Telecom and Cellucom, both of which have servicing and repair facilities and issue their own warranties, as well as the standard manufacturers' ones – Cellucom's also covers accessories.

While there's no real market for second-hand mobile phones, they are sometimes advertised on supermarket noticeboards, websites and in the newspapers. As models become obsolete so quickly, and basic handsets are so cheap, buying a used phone is not the preferred option.

For convenience, the major retailers can now also issue subscriptions to Etisalat and du's pay-as-you-go schemes.

## Music, DVDs & Videos

Unless you're a music connoisseur with particularly eclectic tastes, you should be able to find a music range here that will satisfy you. The advantage to shopping for music in such a multi-cultural society is that you can open yourself up to new genres that you've never heard before – Arabic dance music for example, is popular. Everything has to go through the censor, so any music or DVDs deemed offensive will not be sold here, unless it can be edited to make it more acceptable.

**439**

Vinyl fans and those into electronic mixing should head for speciality shop Ohm Records – everything they stock comes from independent labels. They also sell processors and turntables, as well as record bags and a select line of street wear. The selection of DVDs and videos is mainstream, very Hollywood, with few independent films. Bollywood films are extremely popular and available in most shops. Of course, online shopping is an alternative and you should be able to get more variety on sites such as Benson's World (www.bensonsworld.co.uk) and Amazon (www.amazon.com and www.amazon.co.uk). Amazon's postal charges are often more expensive, and their packaging is branded so may occasionally be opened by an inspector at the post office, although this is happening less frequently. Benson's World send your DVDs in plain packaging, so they are often delivered directly to your post box without passing through the censor.

Retailers generally won't order titles not on the lists approved for the UAE. Diamond Audio Vision has a fairly good range and often has sales; they will try to order items listed in the catalogues but are not always reliable. Disco 2000 have a pretty good range, especially BBC and children's titles; they also have a rental section. Magrudy's have a selection of BBC titles and can order from the catalogue. Carrefour have good value bargain bins and although they are usually filled with mainstream Hollywood, there are occasional gems and BBC children's titles. In common with the rest of the world, video is being phased out as a format, and DVD is now prevalent.

### Music, DVDs & Videos

| Al Mansoor | Wafi Mall | 04 324 4141 |
| Al Meher Recordings | Bur Dubai | 04 353 1278 |
| Carrefour ▶ p.479 | Various | See p.487 |
| Diamond Audio Vision | BurJuman | 04 352 7671 |
| Disco 2000 | Spinneys | 04 394 0139 |
| Géant ▶ p.477 | Ibn Battuta | 04 367 0456 |
| Ohm Records | Opp. BurJuman | 04 397 3728 |
| Plug-Ins | Various | See p.492 |
| Spinneys | Various | See p.492 |
| Virgin Megastore ▶ p.451 | Various | See p.493 |

## Musical Instruments

Other options **Music Lessons** p.364, **Music, DVDs & Videos** p.439

There was a time when good musical equipment was hard to find in Dubai, but things are changing. Juli Music, on Sheikh Zayed Road, stocks a good range of instruments and can also arrange lessons for you. Particularly useful is their 'hire before you buy' policy. Sowira Pianos offer rental and sales on a range of new and used pianos. The Music Room is run by an experienced music teacher, and has the widest range of sheet music in Dubai. Here you'll find a range of instruments including clarinets, flutes, violins, trumpets and guitars, and their associated accessories. They are agents for Steinway & Sons pianos, but if you don't have the space for a grand piano they also stock Kawai grand, upright and digital pianos. Prices for pianos are considerably lower than elsewhere in the world. Thomsun Music House stocks a wide range of mainly Yamaha instruments, from pianos to drum kits and guitars, and they also sell mixing desks and equipment for digital music-making. (Their Ibn Battuta branch is called Thomsun Pure Music). Carrefour, Géant and the larger supermarkets stock basic keyboards and guitars, which are fine for beginners.

### Musical Instruments

| Carrefour ▶ p.479 | Various | See p.487 |
| Fann Al Sout Music | Deira | 04 271 9471 |
| Géant ▶ p.477 | Ibn Battuta Shopping Mall | 04 367 0456 |
| House of Guitar | Al Karama Shopping Complex | 04 334 9968 |
| JS Music | Ibn Battuta Shopping Mall | 04 366 9715 |
| Juli Music | Sheikh Zayed Road | 04 321 2588 |
| Jumeirah Music Equipment | Jumaira Plaza | 04 344 3855 |
| Melody House Musical Instruments | Deira | 04 227 5336 |
| Mozart Musical Instruments | Al Karama Shopping Complex | 04 337 7007 |
| The Music Chamber | Crowne Plaza Centre | 04 331 6416 |
| Music Room | Beach Centre | 04 344 8883 |
| Sadek Music | Souk Madinat Jumeirah | 04 368 6570 |
| Sowira Pianos | Mazaya Centre | 04 343 9188 |
| Thomsun Music House | Various | See p.493 |
| Zak Electronics | Zabeel Road | 04 336 8857 |

**440**

## Climb Every Mountain

*Global Climbing is a brand new company created to meet all UAE residents' climbing needs. As well as importing climbing and caving equipment into Dubai, their new website, www.globalclimbing.com, will soon have route information and useful climber tips.*

## Outdoor Goods
Other options **Camping** p.326, **Hardware & DIY** p.430, **Sports Goods** p.447

With miles of desert, mountains and coastline, and year-round sunshine, spending time in the great outdoors is a popular pastime in the UAE. With temperatures cooler on higher ground, the hardiest adventurers are still out there in the heat of the summer. For everyone else, the weather of the cooler months is ideal for exploring. While there are no specialist camping shops, the basic gear is readily available in Carrefour, Géant, ACE and Picnico. It is all suitable for weekend campers, but would not withstand extremes, so if you are intending anything more strenuous you should consider ordering kit online.

Picnico are outdoor specialists, stocking a good range of Coleman and Campingaz equipment like cooler bags, tents and accessories. They also stock GPS systems and rock climbing gear. They have one of the largest ranges of hydration packs, and are stockists for Dakine (kite surfing kit) and angling equipment. GPS equipment can also be found in Sharaf DG – the Times Square branch has the biggest selection. For outdoor sports enthusiasts there are a number of options (see Sports Goods on p.447). Fishing equipment is also widely available from shops such as Al Hamur Marine, GO Sport and Picnico.

Serious climbers and hikers should consider getting their boots and equipment from overseas, as a very limited range of boots are available and are often aimed more towards the fashion market. While hydration packs (backpacks that you can fill with water, complete with a long tube and mouthpiece) are becoming more widely available in sports shops, anything larger than a day pack should be bought overseas. Hiking accessories for those people with small children, such as backpack carriers, are not widely available here and should be bought online or from overseas.

| Outdoor Goods | | | |
| --- | --- | --- | --- |
| ACE | Various | See p.486 | www.aceuae.com |
| Al Hamur Marine | Jumeira | 04 344 4468 | na |
| Carrefour ▶ p.479 | Various | See p.487 | www.carrefouruae.com |
| Géant ▶ p.477 | Ibn Battuta | 04 367 0456 | www.geant-dubai.com |
| Go Sports | Various | See p.489 | na |
| Harley-Davidson | Sheikh Zayed Rd | 04 339 1909 | www.harley-uae.com |
| Picnico General Trading | Jumeira Beach Road | 04 394 1653 | na |
| Sharaf DG | Various | See p.492 | www.sharafdg.com |
| ULO Systems | Sharjah | 06 531 4036 | www.ulosystems.com |

## Party Accessories
Other options **Parties at Home** p.594, **Party Organisers** p.594

Party accessories are available, on a small scale, in most supermarkets and toy shops but there are a number of specialist stores that stock everything for children's or adults' parties. If you want a party at home but without the bother, there are a number of companies who will do it for you. You can always have children's parties at one of the various play centres around town, if your house won't stand up to an afternoon of messy toddlers buzzed up on too much sugar.

The Party Centre, in Garhoud, is enormous and stocks pretty much everything you will need, no matter what the occasion. This is a one-stop shop for decorations and party accessories, and they even sell children's fancy dress outfits. Partyzone, in the Beach Centre, and The Balloon Lady cover the basics. Carrefour, Park n Shop and Toys R Us all sell themed party essentials, such as paper cups, gift bags, balloons and plates. The range isn't huge and tends to be either Winnie the Pooh, Barbie or Mickey Mouse, so if your child has a preference you may have to order online.

For certain occasions, like Halloween and Easter, specialist shops and even supermarkets (Park n Shop, Carrefour and Spinneys) really get into the spirit of things,

**441**

*Shady style*

selling a range of costumes, sweets and accessories. Costume ranges tend to be a bit limited though – chances are that your child won't be the only arabian princess or swashbuckling pirate. In Disguise, in Satwa, has a slightly bigger selection or you can shop online for costumes, party accessories and weird and wacky gifts at www.bonkers.ae. Purchases are delivered to your door within two days.

Fabric is inexpensive and it doesn't cost much to hire the services of a tailor, so you can easily have a costume made.

For that all-important birthday cake, the choice is great. For adult's cakes, try Lenôtre, Coco's or Boulevard Gourmet at the InterContinental for some yummy options. For children, you can get a customised cake made at Park n Shop (choose from one of their designs or take your own picture in and they will scan it onto edible paper and put it on top of your cake). Baskin Robbins makes a range of icecream party cakes, or Caesars does some elaborately iced creations.

For party entertainment, Flying Elephant can provide bouncy castles, soft-play areas and more. Tumble Time are bouncy castle specialists, and Harlequin provide marquees, tables and chairs and even outdoor cooling units.

Planet Hollywood, Café Céramique and The Jam Jar all cater for children's parties, as do many of the hotel clubs. For entertainment at an adult's party, try Andy the Entertainer – his acts range from the amazing (magic tricks and fire eating) to the bizarre (encasing his whole body in a big balloon).

## Party Accessories

| | | | |
|---|---|---|---|
| Andy the Entertainer | na | 050 840 1770 | www.andystuartentertainments.com |
| Balloon Lady | Jumaira Plaza | 04 344 1062 | www.balloonladyuae.com |
| Baskin Robbins | Various | See p.486 | www.baskinrobbins.com |
| Boulevard Gourmet | Radisson SAS Hotel, Deira Creek | 04 205 7317 | na |
| Caesars | Karama Centre | 04 335 3700 | www.caesars-uae.com |
| Café Ceramique | Town Centre | 04 341 5008 | www.cafe-ceramique.com |
| Carrefour ▶ p.479 | Various | See p.487 | www.carrefouruae.com |
| Coco's | Shk Zayed Rd | 04 332 6333 | na |
| Elves & Fairies | Jumeirah Centre | 04 344 9485 | na |
| Flying Elephant ▶ p.595 | Jct 3, Shk Zayed Rd | 04 347 9170 | www.flyingelephantuae.com |
| Fun Island | Deira | 04 227 8273 | na |
| Gulf Greetings | Various | See p.489 | www.gulfgreetings.com |
| The Jam Jar | St 17a, Al Quoz | 04 341 7303 | www.jamjardubai.com |
| Lenôtre | Spinneys | 04 349 4433 | www.lenotre.fr |
| Magrudy's ▶ p.415 | Various | See p.490 | www.magrudy.com |
| Papermoon | Mina Rd, off Diyafah St | 04 345 4888 | na |
| Park N Shop | Al Wasl Rd | 04 394 5671 | www.parkshopdubai.com |
| The Party Centre | Opp Welcare Hospital | 04 283 1353 | na |
| Partyzone | Beach Centre | 04 344 4158 | na |
| Planet Hollywood | Wafi City | 04 324 4777 | www.planethollywood-dubai.com |
| Spinneys | Various | See p.492 | www.spinneys.com |
| Toys R Us | Various | See p.493 | www.toysrus.com |
| Tumble Time | na | 050 352 1212 | www.tumbletimedubai.com |

## Perfumes & Cosmetics

Other options **Markets & Souks** p.483

| Perfumes & Cosmetics | | |
|---|---|---|
| Ajmal Perfumes | Various | See p.486 |
| Amouage ▶ p.405 | Paris Gallery | See p.491 |
| Arabian Oud | Various | See p.486 |
| Areej | Various | See p.486 |
| Body Shop | Various | See p.487 |
| Boots | Various | See p.487 |
| Debenhams | Various | See p.488 |
| Jashanmal ▶ p.417 | Various | See p.488 |
| L'Occitaine | Ibn Battuta | 04 368 5505 |
| Lush | Deira City Centre | 04 295 9531 |
| MAC | Various | See p.490 |
| Make Up Forever | Wafi Mall | 04 324 2364 |
| Makeup etc. | Mazaya Centre | 04 343 3531 |
| Mikyajy | Various | See p.491 |
| The Nature Shop | Deira City Centre | 04 295 4181 |
| Paris Gallery | Various | See p.491 |
| Pixi Cosmetics | Mall of the Emirates | 04 341 4747 |
| Rasasi | Various | See p.492 |
| Red Earth | Various | See p.492 |

Perfumes and cosmetics are big business here, from the local scents like frankincense and oudh, to the latest designer offerings. The department stores and local chains (such as Areej and Paris Gallery) stock the most comprehensive ranges of international brand perfumes and cosmetics.

Body Shop, MAC and Red Earth are found in many of the city's malls, while Boots now has several branches. This sector has been joined by Pixi Cosmetics in Mall of the Emirates. L'Occitaine in Ibn Battuta Mall is also worth seeking out for their natural skincare products.

Larger supermarkets and pharmacies all stock skincare products and some make-up. Anti-allergenic ranges are available at some of the larger pharmacies. Most needs are covered but if yours aren't, specialist retailers often have online shopping facilities.

Local perfumes and scents tend to be strong and spicy – shops selling these products can often be smelled before they are seen as many burn incense in the doorways. Amouage produces some of the world's most valuable perfumes, with scents made with rare ingredients. They can be found in airports and on board Emirates flights as well as in Paris Gallery outlets. Ajmal and Arabian Oud outlets are found in most malls, but they cater to the Arab population and don't always have English-speaking shop assistants on duty.

Prices for perfumes and cosmetics are similar to those in some other countries, although certain nationalities might find perfume is cheaper here than in their home country. There are no sales taxes, so there is rarely a difference between Duty Free and shopping mall prices.

## Pets

Other options **Pets** p.164

Most supermarkets carry basic ranges of cat, dog, bird and fish food, although the choice is limited. If yours is a particularly pampered pet you might end up bringing some special treats home with you after your next trip. If your pet has specific dietary requirements, many of the veterinary clinics (p.166) carry specialist foods.

| Pets | | |
|---|---|---|
| Animal World | Jumeira | 04 344 4422 |
| Pet Land | Al Quoz | 04 338 4040 |
| Pet Zone | Trade Centre 1 | 04 321 1424 |
| Pet's Delight | Various | See p.491 |

Pet shops are a bit on the dismal side here – standards are low and animals are usually in tiny cages without water for long periods. The pet shops along Plant Street in Satwa are notoriously the worst offenders and animals purchased there are often malnourished and diseased. Dubai Municipality has laid down regulations and if they are contravened the shop will be closed down for a day; hardly a strong motivation for these shops to clean up their acts. Even the pet shops that most animal lovers can bear to go into have a long way to go before standards are acceptable. Petland and Petzone, on Sheikh Zayed Road, and Animal World, on Jumeira Beach Road, are the most acceptable. All sell a range of pet accessories, food, animals, birds and fish.

If you are looking for a family pet, consider contacting Feline Friends or K9 Friends (see p.167) who have hundreds of fluffy, friendly cats and dogs all looking for homes.

**443**

## Portrait Photographers & Artists

Many of the photography shops in Dubai also have a portrait studio where you can get attractive family or individual portraits done. Alternatively, there are several independent portrait photographers that can take beautiful pictures of you and your family – the advantage of using an independent photographer is that they can do the portraits at the location of your choice, be it in your home or garden or on the beach. Many shopping malls have 'roving' portrait painters who set up a stall from time to time. They can either do a genuine likeness (working from a sitting or a photo), or a caricature. Try Souk Madinat Jumeirah and Deira City Centre. See also Weddings (p.449).

| Portrait Photographers & Artists | | |
|---|---|---|
| Belina Muller | 050 769 7650 | na |
| Charlotte Simpson | 050 428 3660 | www.hotshotsdubai.com |
| Henk Bos | 050 626 3724 | www.henkbos.com |
| Karen Bullock | 050 458 1846 | na |
| Robeya Polley | 050 494 4297 | www.robeya.com |
| Stu Williamson Photography | 04 348 8527 | www.stuwilliamson.com |
| Sue Johnston | 050 565 5519 | www.imageoasisdubai.com |

## Second-Hand Items

Other options **Cars** p.420, **Furnishing Accommodation** p.160, **Books** p.414

There is an active second-hand market in Dubai, as people are always leaving, redecorating or downsizing and need to get rid of their stuff. Supermarket noticeboards are a great place to start, as many people post 'for sale' notices with pictures of all the items. Garage sales are also popular on Fridays and you'll notice signs going up in your neighbourhood from time to time. The White Elephant Sale, held twice a year at the Dubai Country Club, is a great place to buy (or sell) second-hand children's items. There are also a number of websites with classifieds sections. Try www.expatwoman.com, www.dubizzle.com, www.souq.com, and www.websouq.com. There are a number of second-hand shops, often linked to churches and special needs schools, but the opening hours can be somewhat eccentric. The Holy Trinity Thrift Shop gives you back 50% of what your items sell for, so you can even make money out of being charitable! It is good for high-quality items and books in particular, and proceeds go towards a number of orphanages supported by the church. The Al Noor shop raises funds for the Al Noor School for Special Needs and is good for second-hand clothing. All donations in good condition are accepted. The Dubai Charity Centre, behind Choithram in Karama, is the biggest of the charity shops. This store supports the students who attend The Dubai Centre for Special Needs, and finances a number of places for those who are unable to afford them. It stocks a good range of clothes, books and toys. The Rashid Paediatric Therapy Centre, behind the American Academic School in Al Barsha, has a decent range of items and raises money for projects at the centre.

| Second-Hand Items | | |
|---|---|---|
| Al Noor Shop | Shk Zayed Rd | 04 340 4844 |
| Dubai Charity Association | Al Rigga Rd | 04 268 2000 |
| Dubai Charity Centre | Al Karama | 04 337 8246 |
| Holy Trinity Thrift Shop | School Rd | 04 337 8192 |
| House of Prose | Various | See p.489 |
| Rashid Paediatric Therapy Centre | Al Barsha | 04 340 0005 |

House of Prose is a second-hand bookshop, with branches in Jumaira Plaza and Ibn Battuta. If you are looking to clear some space on your bookshelves, House of Prose buys books, in good condition, that they will be able to sell. Any books bought from them will be worth 50% of the purchase price if returned in good condition.

## Shoes

Other options **Beachwear** p.413, **Clothes** p.421, **Sports Goods** p.447

The choice of shoes available in Dubai is enormous, unless you are a woman with outsized feet. Designer labels like Jimmy Choo and Gucci mingle with middle-of-the-range creations from Bally, Milano, Faith and Nine West, which mingle with cheap-as-chips flipflops and sandals in the big hypermarkets. Apart from the dedicated shoe shops, department stores like Debenhams, Marks & Spencer and Woolworths all have shoe departments. For stylish shoes that won't break the budget, Shoe Mart, Brantano Shoe City and Avenue all carry fashionable and practical shoes, as do the many shoe shops in Karama Market.

You'll probably find that sports shoes are cheaper than in your home country, but you might not be able to get the latest styles. Studio R is good for active-wear shoes and sandals. Birkenstocks are widely available and Scholl shoes can be found in shoe shops and larger pharmacies. Pharmacies also stock supports, powders and specialist plasters.

For children's shoes, Magrudy's Shoe Shop stocks Clarks, Start-Rite and Elephanten, and they provide a foot measuring service. Pablosky has branches in many of the malls, and Ecco stocks a good range of children's shoes. Because of the weather, children spend a great deal of time in sandals, which are widely available. If you are planning a trip to colder climes, it can be hard to find good winter shoes for little feet – so if you see a pair, grab them.

## Souvenirs

Other options **Carpets** p.420

From fridge magnets to antique wooden wedding chests, the range of souvenirs available is incredible. Many souvenirs are regional rather than local, and many are mass produced in India, Pakistan and Oman. Souvenir and gift shops are widely available, and there is at least one outlet in every mall. The best prices are to be had in the souks and shopping areas, where bargaining is encouraged and expected – make sure the vendor knows you are not a tourist, and be firm but reasonable while you haggle. Being rude won't help. The more you buy, the better the discount, and if the vendor gets to know you over time he will give you special discounts on every visit.

As you would expect, camels feature heavily; cuddly toys, wooden carvings, camel pot stands, and even carvings made from camel bones are all widely available and are great as novelty presents. Perhaps the frontrunner for the 'tackiest souvenir' prize are plastic alarm clocks in the shape of a mosque – they are available in various colours

| Shoes | | |
| --- | --- | --- |
| ALDO | Various | See p.486 |
| Aqua Shoes | Al Ghurair City | 04 221 3340 |
| Avenue | Opp BurJuman | 04 397 9983 |
| Bally | Mall of the Emirates | 04 341 0280 |
| Brantano | Various | See p.487 |
| Carrefour ▶ p.479 | Various | See p.487 |
| Cesare Paccioti | Wafi Mall | 04 324 3227 |
| City Shoes | Karama Centre | 04 337 8010 |
| Clarks | Various | See p.488 |
| Debenhams | Various | See p.488 |
| Domino | Various | See p.488 |
| Ecco | Various | See p.488 |
| Escada | BurJuman | 04 359 1117 |
| Eve Michelle | Magrudy's | 04 342 9574 |
| Faith | Various | See p.488 |
| Florsheim | Various | See p.489 |
| HyperPanda | Dubai Festival City | 04 232 5566 |
| Jimmy Choo | Emirates Towers | 04 330 0404 |
| Kenneth Cole | Mall of the Emirates | 04 341 0320 |
| Magrudy Shoe Shop | Magrudy's | 04 344 4192 |
| Marelli | Al Ghurair City | 04 227 0933 |
| Mario Bologna | BurJuman | 04 352 9726 |
| Marks & Spencer | Various | See p.490 |
| Milano | Various | See p.491 |
| Manolo Blahnik | BurJuman | 04 351 5551 |
| Nine West | Various | See p.491 |
| Pablosky | Various | See p.491 |
| Philippe Charriol | BurJuman | 04 351 1112 |
| PrettyFIT | Various | See p.492 |
| Rockport | Deira City Centre | 04 295 0261 |
| Shoe Bazar | Al Faheidi St | 04 353 0444 |
| Shoe City | Deira City Centre | 04 295 0437 |
| Shoe Mart | Various | See p.492 |
| Spring | Various | See p.493 |
| Studio R | Various | See p.493 |
| Tod's | Various | See p.493 |
| Topshop | Various | See p.493 |
| Valencia | Various | See p.493 |
| Vincci | Various | See p.493 |
| Woodland | Century Mall | 04 296 7890 |
| Woolworths | Various | See p.493 |

**445**

*Cartoon keyrings*

(the fluorescent green one is particularly splendid) and wake you up with a very loud call to prayer. Best of all, they only cost Dhs.10.

Coffee pots are symbols of Arabic hospitality and another popular souvenir item – small enough to be tucked in to a suitcase or big enough to blow your baggage limits. Prices vary enormously from Dhs.100 for a brand new, shiny one, to several thousand dirhams for a genuine antique.

Traditional silver items, such as the traditional Arabic dagger ('khanjar'), are excellent souvenirs, and are available both framed and unframed. Of course, if you buy a khanjar you shouldn't attempt to transport it back home in your hand luggage. Silver wedding jewellery is chunky and ornate, and is often framed.

Wooden items are popular and representative of the region. Trinket boxes (often with elaborate carvings or brass inlays) are beautiful and start from around Dhs.10. Elaborate Arabic doors and wedding chests, costing thousands, are also popular. The doors can be hung as art, or converted into tables or headboards.

While carpets are a good buy, it is worth doing some research before investing. For a smaller, cheaper option, many shops sell woven coasters and camel bags, or you can buy a Persian carpet mouse pad.

You can hardly walk through a mall or shopping area without being offered a pashmina – they are available in an abundant range of colours and styles. Most are a cotton/silk mix and the ratio dictates the price. In many shops the shelves are stacked high and the staff are happy to take the place apart till the perfect shade is found. It is a good idea to check out a few shops before buying as prices vary and, as with most items, the more you buy the cheaper they are. For a decent quality pashmina, prices start from around Dhs.50.

Shisha pipes make fun souvenirs and can be bought with various flavours of tobacco, such as apple or strawberry. Both working and ornamental examples are on sale, prices start from around Dhs.75 in Carrefour. If you are into smells, the heavy local perfume and incense make good gifts and are widely available in outlets like Arabian Oud (branches in most of the big malls).

For book lovers, there are a number of great coffee table books with stunning photos depicting the diversity of this vibrant city. Grab a copy of *Dubai: Tomorrow's City Today*, *Impressions Dubai*, or *Images of Dubai and the UAE*. *Dubai Discovered* is a concise pictorial souvenir of Dubai and is available in five languages (English, Japanese, French, German and Russian).

If you've scoured the souvenir shops in Dubai and still can't find what you're looking for, head for Souk Al Arsah in Sharjah (p.484), where you can shop for traditional items in a traditional setting.

## Souvenirs

| Al Jaber Gallery | Various | See p.486 | na |
| Arabian Oud | Various | See p.486 | www.arabianoud.com |
| Carrefour ▶ p.479 | Various | See p.487 | www.carrefouruae.com |
| Creative Art Centre | Nr Choithram | 04 344 4394 | www.arabian-arts.com |
| Falcon Gallery | Mina Road, Near Port Rashid | 04 345 3369 | www.falcongallery.com |
| Showcase Antiques | Opp Dubai Municipality | 04 348 8797 | www.showcaseantiques.net |

## Sports Goods

Other options **Outdoor Goods** p.441

The development of Sports City (part of Dubailand) will rocket Dubai into the sports limelight. Sport is already big business in Dubai, and whatever sport you are into, chances are that it is played here. Basic sports equipment is well covered – the many sports shops stock clothing and footwear, as well as equipment for 'core sports' like running, basketball, cricket, football, swimming, badminton, squash and tennis.

| Sports Goods | | |
| --- | --- | --- |
| 360 Sports | BurJuman | 04 352 0106 |
| Adidas | Various | See p.486 |
| Al Boom Marine | Various | See p.486 |
| Alpha Sports | Deira City Centre | 04 295 4087 |
| Cannondale | Various | See p.487 |
| Carrefour ▶ p.479 | Various | See p.487 |
| Dubai Surfski Kayak Club | Umm Suqeim | 050 813 3207 |
| Emirates Sports Stores | Wafi Mall | 04 324 2208 |
| Go Sports | Various | See p.489 |
| Golf House | Various | See p.489 |
| Intersport | Times Square | 04 341 8214 |
| Knight Shot Inc. | Nr Mazaya Centre | 04 343 5678 |
| Magrudy's ▶ p.415 | Various | See p.490 |
| Picnico General Trading | Jumeira Beach Road | 04 394 1653 |
| Profit Free Sports | Nr Lamcy Plaza | 04 337 3799 |
| Royal Sporting House | Deira City Centre | 04 295 0261 |
| Scuba Dubai | DWTC Appts, Block C | 04 341 4940 |
| Sketchers | BurJuman | 04 352 0106 |
| Sport One Trading | BurJuman | 04 351 6033 |
| Studio R | Various | See p.493 |
| Sun & Sand Sports ▶ p.321 | Various | See p.493 |
| ULO Systems Ltd | Sharjah | 06 531 4036 |
| Wheels Trading | Sahara Tower, Shk Zayed Rd | 04 331 7119 |
| Wolfi's Bike Shop | Between Jct 2-3 | 04 339 4453 |

GO Sport, at Ibn Battuta and Mall of the Emirates, has the most comprehensive collection of sports goods. Apart from equipment for the above sports, they also stock cycling, camping, equestrian and golfing equipment. Studio R combines active-wear clothing labels with serious sports equipment – they are stockists for New Balance footwear and have large Speedo and Reebok collections. Sun & Sand Sports have outlets all over the city, and their larger branches have Nike and Timberland departments. They also stock home gym equipment, from treadmills to rowing machines, as well as a limited range of pool and snooker tables (although the specialists for pool and snooker tables and equipment are Knight Shot Inc.). Golf is extremely popular and clubs, balls and bags are available in most sports shops. Golf House and the pro shops are the best places for decent kit. The clubs that organise specialist sports, such as Dubai Surfski Kayak Club (www.dskc.net), can often be approached for equipment. Kite surfing is a sport that has become popular very quickly and the equipment is now being stocked in shops; Al Boom Marine stocks North Kites at the Jumeira Beach Road showroom, and Picnico, next door, stocks Dakine. Al Boom also stocks equipment for other watersports, including waterskiing and diving.

Profit Free Sports is a factory outlet for Sun & Sand Sports and is great for end-of-range clothes, shoes and equipment. Studio R and Adidas also have factory shops – the Studio R factory shop is on Sheikh Zayed Road and there are some excellent bargains to be had; and Adidas has factory shops on the Airport Road and near Lamcy Plaza, and although their prices are slightly lower than in their retail stores, the difference is not huge. Karama Market has several sports shops with decent ranges that are often cheaper than the bigger stores – just remember, if the item you are buying is much cheaper than normal, it could be a fake.

## Stationery

Whether you are looking for a pencil sharpener or professional standard plotting paper, there are stationery shops all over the city. For basic school and personal stationery, Carrefour and Union Co-Op carry extensive ranges, particularly at the

**447**

## Stationery

| | | |
|---|---|---|
| Books Plus ▶ p.459 | Various | See p.487 |
| Carrefour ▶ p.479 | Various | See p.487 |
| Compu-Me | Various | See p.488 |
| Dubai Library Distributors | Various | See p.488 |
| Emirates Trading Est. | Various | See p.488 |
| Kazim Gulf Traders | Jumeirah Centre | 04 349 3347 |
| Montblanc | Various | See p.491 |
| Office Mart | Orange Bld, Zabeel Road | 04 335 9929 |
| Office Outlet | Umm Suqeim Bld, Shk Zayed Rd | 04 338 8444 |
| Union Co-Op | Various | See p.493 |
| World of Pens | Town Centre | 04 349 1022 |

beginning of the school year. Dubai Library Distributors and Kazim Gulf Traders should have everything that you will need for personal or home office use. Offices are well served by Emirates Trading Est., Office Mart and Office Outlet, all selling wide ranges of stationery. If a ballpoint pen just isn't appropriate, World of Pens and Mont Blanc stock luxury models that will add style to your signature.

## Tailoring

Other options **Souvenirs** p.445, **Tailors** p.448, **Deira** p.135, **Clothes** p.421, **Bur Dubai** p.133, **Textiles** p.448

## Tailoring

| | | |
|---|---|---|
| Al Aryam Tailor | Al Satwa | 04 349 2434 |
| Ali Eid Al Muree | Jumeira Beach Road | 04 348 7176 |
| Couture | Deira | 04 269 9522 |
| Dream Boy | Downtown Bur Dubai | 04 352 1840 |
| Dream Girl | Various | See p.488 |
| Eves | Nasser Square | 04 228 1070 |
| First Lady | Al Faheidi St | 04 352 7019 |
| Future Tailors | Al Satwa | 04 349 8723 |
| Garasheeb | Al Karama Shopping Complex | 04 396 8900 |
| Kachins | Carpet Souk | 04 352 1386 |
| Khamis Abdullah Trading & Embroidery | Al Rashidiya | 04 285 2543 |
| La Donna | Al Wahida Rd | 04 266 6596 |
| Ma Belle | Opp Buy & Save Supermaket | 04 269 6500 |
| Monte Carlo | Behind York Hotel | 04 352 0225 |
| Montexa | Al Satwa | 04 349 4037 |
| Oasis | Various | See p.491 |
| Regency Tailors | Bur Dubai | 04 352 4732 |
| Royal Fashions | Al Karama | 04 396 8282 |
| Stitches | Jumeira | 04 342 1476 |
| Tailorworks | Satwa | 04 349 9906 |
| Vanucci Fashions | Al Ghusais | 04 263 2626 |
| Whistle & Flute | Al Satwa | 04 342 9229 |
| Yoginir'z Tailoring & Fashion Design | Musalla Rd, Nr Dubai Museum | 04 355 5105 |

There are so many tailors in Dubai, and word of mouth is the best way to find a good one. They can be found in most areas, but the area around the Dubai Museum in Bur Dubai, or the main street in Satwa, are good places to start. A good tailor will be able to make a garment from scratch (rather than just make alterations), either from a photo or diagram or by copying an existing garment. If he doesn't get the garment spot on, he will happily make the necessary alterations. Dream Girl tailors, in Meena Bazaar and Satwa, have huge followings and they are great for all tailoring jobs from taking up trousers to making ball gowns. Skirts cost around Dhs.50 and dresses from around Dhs.80, depending on how basic the pattern is. For those living on the Deira side, Khamis Abdullah Trading & Embroidery, in Rashidiya, is one of the least expensive in town, with skirts starting from around Dhs.30. Dream Boy, near the museum, is good for shirts and suits, as are Kachins and Whistle & Flute; shirts usually start from Dhs.30 and suits from around Dhs.500.

## Textiles

Other options **Souvenirs** p.445, **Tailoring** p.448

You have three options if you are looking for fabric: the Textile Souk (near Al Fahedi Street), Satwa, or the shopping malls (most of which have at least one fabric outlet). Prices start from a few dirhams for a metre of basic cotton. The Textile Souk can get busy and parking is difficult, but the sheer range of fabrics is worth it. Deepaks, in Satwa, is renowned for its huge selection of fabrics and helpful staff. There are several haberdashery shops in the same area should you wish to buy matching buttons, bows or cotton.

## Textiles

| | | |
|---|---|---|
| Abdulla Hussain | Al Ghurair City | 04 221 7310 |
| Al Masroor (Gents) | Deira City Centre | 04 295 0832 |
| Damas (Ladies) | Al Ghurair City | 04 221 6700 |
| Deepak's | Plant Street, Satwa | 04 344 8836 |
| Feshwari | Various | See p.489 |
| IKEA ▶ p.IBC | Dubai Festival City | 800 4532 |
| Meena Bazaar Fashions | Downtown Bur Dubai | 04 353 9304 |
| Mostafawi | Deira | 04 225 5678 |
| Ratti | Bef Meena Bazaar Bur Dubai | 04 353 8143 |
| Regal Traders | Various | See p.492 |
| Rivoli Textiles | Downtown Bur Dubai | 04 335 0075 |
| Royalex | Downtown Bur Dubai | 04 351 8800 |
| Yasmine (Ladies) | Al Diyafah St | 04 398 8476 |

Plant Street in Satwa is the place to go for upholstery fabrics; IKEA also stocks a range of fresh and vibrant fabrics that can be used for cushions, curtains or bedding.

## Wedding Items

If you are planning a Dubai wedding, you can choose to work with a wedding planner (see also p.92) or do it yourself. For books and magazines on etiquette, traditions and fashions of weddings, Magrudy's has a large selection, and Marks & Spencer has a limited range of books.

For the latest off-the-peg wedding gown fashions, Saks Fifth Avenue has a fabulous department stocking designer dresses by Vera Wang and Reem Acra. They keep some gowns in stock, but others can be ordered (allow around four months for delivery). The bride will attend a number of fittings; alterations are done in-house and are up to couture standards. The Wedding Shop also sells off-the-peg dresses in a range of styles.

There are several specialist bridal designers with workshops in Dubai. Arushi is renowned as one of the best. The bride can either provide the fabric or it can be selected during the first meeting with the designer. Gowns take around one month to make, but as Arushi is so popular, there is often a waiting list. If you want to get your dress made but are on a tighter budget, some of the city's tailors are able to work from pictures to create your ideal dress. Bridal accessories and shoes are available at Saks Fifth Avenue and The Wedding Shop.

## Wedding Items

| | | |
|---|---|---|
| Amal & Amal | Jumeirah Centre | 04 344 4671 |
| Arushi | Beach Rd, opp Dubai Zoo | 04 344 4103 |
| Cadorim | The Village Mall | 04 394 3333 |
| Cocomino | Bin Sougat Centre | 04 286 1514 |
| Debenhams | Various | See p.488 |
| Dream Girl | Various | See p.488 |
| Elegance | Diyafah St | 04 349 1613 |
| Enigma | Downtown Bur Dubai | 04 397 4114 |
| Eve Michelle | Magrudy's | 04 342 9574 |
| Formal Wear | Diyafah St | 04 345 5185 |
| Lenôtre | Spinneys | 04 349 4433 |
| Magrudy's ▶ p.415 | Various | See p.490 |
| Marks & Spencer | Various | See p.490 |
| Monsoon | Various | See p.491 |
| THE One | Various | See p.493 |
| Saks Fifth Avenue | BurJuman | 04 351 5551 |
| The Wedding Shop | Jumeirah Centre | 04 344 1618 |

For the groom, there are several shops where formal wear can be hired, including The Wedding Shop and Elegance and Formal Wear, on Al Diyafah Street. Bridesmaid's dresses are sold in the children's department of Saks Fifth Avenue. Debenhams and Monsoon both sell suitable ranges, as does Cocomino; if the style or shade you are looking for aren't available, have them made up by a tailor. Monsoon also sells hair accessories and pretty shoes suitable for young bridesmaids.

Wedding guests have many options when it comes to choosing the ideal outfit. Mothers of the bride and groom, and guests, are well catered for at Debenhams and Monsoon, among many others.

The Wedding Shop sells everything but the cake, and is a great place to get your confetti, guest books and photo albums. Amal & Amal and Chic Design both make bespoke wedding stationery, and Cadorim and Enigma do tailor-made favour and ring boxes. Magrudy's and Susan Walpole stock invitations, guest books and photo albums. As well as offering wedding planning services, several of the hotels can be commissioned to make the wedding cake; Lenôtre also creates them. Most of the city's florists can turn their hands to wedding bouquets and arrangements, discuss your requirements with them to find out what will be available.

Debenhams and THE One both offer wedding list services. For any items that you can't find here, www.confetti.co.uk accept international orders.

**449**

## Places To Shop

The following section features Dubai's main shopping malls, with information and store directories for each. The table below also lists a selection of the city's smaller malls.

## Shopping Malls

Shopping malls are not just places to shop; a definite mall culture exists here and they are places to meet, eat and mingle. Many malls provide entertainment and people of all ages can spend hours in them. Recent changes to the law have resulted in a smoking ban in all of Dubai's malls (and some of the bars attached to them) which has been welcomed across the city.

With so much choice out there, malls make sure they can offer something unique to shoppers to draw the crowds. In terms of architecture, Ibn Battuta is remarkable – six distinct architectural styles reflecting the sights of Egypt, China, India, Persia, Tunisia and Andalusia. Mall of the Emirates has got their unique selling point covered – a community theatre and a huge ski slope has made this one of the busier malls. Deira City Centre is the old kid on the block and yet is still consistently popular because of its excellent range of outlets, huge cinema multiplex and wide range of food outlets. Wafi City and BurJuman have cornered the market for exclusive boutiques and designer labels. Despite the choice of shopping centres on offer, more are planned with The Walk at Jumeirah Beach Residence and Dubai Mall due to open in 2008. The latter is currently growing into what will be the world's largest mall but of course, things move quickly in the UAE, so this record breaker will soon have its crown stolen with the opening of Mall of Arabia in 2009 as part of Dubailand, boasting over 1,000 retail outlets and 10,400 car park spaces.

Special events are held during Dubai Shopping Festival, Dubai Summer Surprises and Ramadan, with entertainment for children and some special offers in the shops. These are peak shopping times and an evening in the larger malls at this time is not for the faint-hearted. Most of the malls have plenty of parking – often stretched to the limits at the weekends; all have taxi ranks and many are handy for bus routes.

| Shopping Malls | | |
|---|---|---|
| Al Ain Centre | Downtown Bur Dubai | 04 351 6914 |
| Al Bustan Centre | Al Qusais | 04 263 0000 |
| Al Ghazal Complex & Shopping Mall | Al Wasl | 04 345 3053 |
| Al Ghurair City | Deira | 04 222 5222 |
| Al Hana Centre | Al Satwa | 04 398 2229 |
| Al Khaleej Centre | Downtown Bur Dubai | 04 355 5550 |
| Al Manal Centre | Deira | 04 227 7701 |
| Al Mulla Plaza | Al Qusais | 04 298 8999 |
| Al Rais Center | Downtown Bur Dubai | 04 352 7755 |
| Beach Centre | Jumeira | 04 344 9045 |
| Bin Sougat Centre | Al Rashidiya | 04 286 3000 |
| Boulevard at Emirates Towers | Trade Centre 2 | 04 319 8999 |
| BurJuman ▶ p.453 | Downtown Bur Dubai | 04 352 0222 |
| Century Mall | Al Mamzar | 04 296 6188 |
| Century Plaza | Jumeira | 04 349 8062 |
| Deira City Centre ▶ p.455 | Deira | 04 295 1010 |
| Dubai Outlet Mall | Al Ain Road | 04 367 9600 |
| Galleria Shopping Mall | Deira | 04 209 6000 |
| Gold & Diamond Park | Al Quoz | 04 347 7788 |
| Hamarain Centre | Deira | 04 262 1110 |
| Holiday Centre Mall | Trade Centre 1 | 04 331 7755 |
| Ibn Battuta Shopping Mall | Jebel Ali | 04 362 1900 |
| Jumeirah Centre | Jumeira | 04 349 9702 |
| Jumaira Plaza | Jumeira | 04 349 9119 |
| Karama Centre | Al Karama | 04 337 4499 |
| Lamcy Plaza | Oud Metha | 04 335 9999 |
| Magrudy's Shopping Mall | Jumeira | 04 344 4193 |
| Mall of the Emirates ▶ p.461 | Al Barsha | 04 409 9000 |
| Mazaya Centre | Al Wasl | 04 343 8333 |
| Mercato | Jumeira | 04 344 4161 |
| Palm Strip | Jumeira | 04 346 1462 |
| Reef Mall | Deira | 04 224 2240 |
| Souk Madinat Jumeirah | Umm Suqeim | 04 366 8888 |
| Spinneys | Umm Suqeim | 04 394 1657 |
| Times Square | Al Quoz | 04 341 8020 |
| Town Centre | Jumeira | 04 344 0111 |
| Twin Towers | Deira | 04 221 8833 |
| The Village Mall | Jumeira | 04 344 4444 |
| Wafi Mall ▶ p.98 | Umm Hurair | 04 324 4555 |

**MEGASTORE**

Music DVDs Books Electronics Games Multimedia Boutique

Mall of the Emirates • Deira City Center • Mercato • Burjuman • Abu Dhabi Mall

www.vmeganews.com

## Shopping Malls – Main

### BurJuman ▶ p.453

*04 352 0222 | www.burjuman.com*

BurJuman is a firm favourite in Dubai, and has always been renowned for its blend of designer and high-street brands, attracting many a well-heeled shopper. The newer area, anchored by Saks Fifth Avenue, has attracted even more big names and BurJuman offers other outlets exclusive to the mall such as Valentino and Hermes. The original area houses many famous brands, as well as some interesting smaller shops. There is a Fitness First gym with a pool on site too.

BurJuman has been active in organising activities for the Dubai Shopping Festival and Dubai Summer Surprises and is also heavily involved with the Safe & Sound breast cancer awareness programme; during October (breast cancer awareness month) it gets decked out in pink ribbon and organises a walkathon to raise money for this worthy cause.

**Insider Tip**
For gift-wrapping, head to the Customer Service Counter on level two.

The outlets within the mall are a mixture of clothing, electronics, home decor and sports goods. There are a few shops on the ground level that are often overlooked, including ACE (hardware & DIY store) and a pharmacy. There's also branches of Yo! Sushi and Dôme down there too.

Within the mall, there are enough designer shops to keep even the most dedicated fashionista happy, including Fendi, Just Cavalli and Christian Dior. For everyday fashion, Massimo Dutti and Zara lead the way. If you are into music or DVDs, the independent music shops sell a good range and they often have sales, and there is a branch of Virgin Megastore for those with mainstream tastes and for ticket sales for local events. Home decor stores include THE One and Zara Home.

There are two foodcourts and numerous cafes, well arranged for people watching, including the popular Pavillion Gardens on the third floor and Paul on the ground floor where you can dine outside during the cooler months. There is a taxi rank outside the mall and plenty of underground parking but it does get pretty full at peak times.

*Dramatic design*

KS FIFTH AVENUE • CHANEL • DIOR • LOUIS VUITTON • PRADA • HERMES • FENDI • CARTIER • VALENTINO • EMANUEL UNGARO • CHAUMET

AHMED SEDDIQI & SONS • BANG & OLUFSEN • CANALI • VERTU • BAUME & MERCIER • BCBG • MAXAZARIA • CALVIN KLEIN • DONNA KARAN • ESCADA • ETRO • FRATELLI ROSSETTI • HUGO BOSS

HOME TO THE FINEST LUXURY BRANDS IN THE WORLD. SHOP FROM HEAD TO TOE.

BURJUMAN

ST CAVALLI • DOLCE & GABBANA • TIFFANY & CO. • GIANFRANCO FERRE' • CHRISTIAN LACROIX • SHANGHAI TANG • CHOPARD • PAUL SMITH

## Deira City Centre ▶ p.455

**04 295 1010 | www.deiracitycentre.com**

A stalwart of Dubai's mall scene, this is a great place to go to get a feel for the real cosmopolitan nature of the city. Deira City Centre is popular with residents and visitors alike, particularly at the weekends. The three floors offer a huge and diverse range of shops where you can find anything from a postcard to a Persian carpet. There's an 11 screen cinema, a children's entertainment centre, a jewellery court, a textiles court and an area dedicated to local furniture, gifts and souvenirs. Deira City Centre is anchored by a huge Carrefour hypermarket, a Debenhams department store, and a large Magrudy's bookshop (beyond the cinema). Most of the high street brands are represented, including the recent additions of Gap (currently one of only two outlets in Dubai), Next, Pull and Bear, Club Monaco and River Island in the new extension, as are a number of designer boutiques which are mainly on the top floor. The City Gate section (on the same level as car parks P2 and P3) is dominated by electronics retailers, although there is also a pharmacy and information desk. The mall has two foodcourts: one on the first floor, around the children's entertainment area, serving mainly fast food, and one on the second floor, featuring several good sit-down restaurants. Bin Hendi Avenue features some excellent restaurants, including the Noodle House and Japengo. There are a number of coffee houses, including Paul and three Starbucks, so you're never far from a caffeine kick. The facilities for mothers and babies are tucked away on the top floor, near the entrance to car park P4, and in the centre of the ground floor. There are four car parks but its popularity means that, at weekends, spaces are scarce. P4 is usually the quietest of the car parks. The taxi ranks are in the City Gate section.

**Insider Tip**

* The Starbucks on the top floor of Debenhams is a haven from the crowds and noise of the mall.

* There is a left luggage area on the second floor, near the men's prayer room at the Debenhams end, which is great if you don't want to be weighed down by bags while you browse.

*Another busy day at Deira City Centre*

# Get more
## in the **heart** <sup>of</sup> the **City**

Over 370 stores • Family leisure & entertainment centre • Free shuttle bus service to select hotels • Luggage storage facility • Souvenirs • Currency exchange, full service banking & ATMs • Postal, courier & business services • Dubai Tourism counter • Wheelchairs & baby strollers • Car rental counters • Wi-Fi service throughout the mall

**Shop until midnight on weekends**

DEIRA
**CITY CENTRE**
www.deiracitycentre.com

BinHendi Avenue | Brantano Shoe City | Carrefour | Debenhams Department Store | Forever 21 | Gap
H&M | Jawad Home | Liwa Trading | Magrudy's | New Look | Next | Paris Gallery | Sharaf DG
Splash | Studio R | Sun & Sand Sports | Virgin Megastore | Woolworths | Zara

## Dubai Festival City

*04 213 6213* | *www.dubaifestivalcity.com*

Dubai Festival City describes itself as 'a city within a city' and is a 13 acre retail and entertainment destination a short drive from the airport, set along over 3km of creekside corniche.

When complete it will offer 600 retail outlets (including 25 flaghip stores) and 100 restaurants including 40 alfresco dining options. With five hotels on site there will be over 2,500 hotel rooms available as well as residential suites but if you want to stay longer there will be a range of homes and even a school.

As for retail therapy, the Power Centre is the first dedicated household shopping complex in the world. It houses some of the biggest names in homeware, such as The White Company and The Red Carpet, as well as electronic stores, including Al Falak Electronics. In addition, it is home to HyperPanda (p.478), the largest IKEA in the UAE, and boasts a large Plug-Ins as well as the largest ACE store outside of North America so is an ideal stop when you've moved into a new home, or just looking to spruce up your existing abode. You'll also find a branch of the Dubai London Clinic here, a pharmacy, banks and dry cleaners.

The Power Centre is linked to Festival Waterfront Centre by a 25,000 square foot marketplace selling gold from all over the world. The Festival Waterfront Centre has dramatic water features, performance spaces and many international brands. Most of this bright and airy mall might feel a little empty but that's just because everyone is in IKEA. At the time of going to print it wasn't fully open but, with a flagship Toys R Us store, Brit favourite Marks & Spencer and designers like Marc by Marc Jacobs on offer, it won't be long before other retailers are greeting the crowds.

It's not just shopping though; Fitness First gym, Grand Cinema and a ten-lane bowling alley are on site so this is a place where you can happily spend an entire day, before dining (choose from family favourites at Romano's Macaroni Grill, Steam Sum Dim Sum and everything in between) then relax in one of the licensed bars.

*Alfresco dining at night*

*Floors of stores*

# Dubai's first generation tell all...

Just half a century ago Dubai was merely a village where hope and pride was the emirate's wealth. These first-hand stories tell of a time before the skyscrapers.

**Telling Tales**
An oral history of Dubai

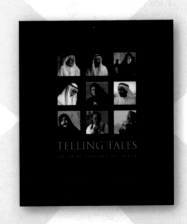

Abu Dhabi · Amsterdam · Bahrain · Barcelona · Beijing · Berlin · Dubai · Dublin · Geneva
Hong Kong · Kuala Lumpur · Kuwait · London · Los Angeles · New York · New Zealand · Oman

**EXPLORER**

# Ibn Battuta Shopping Mall

04 362 1900 | www.ibnbattutamall.com

Ibn Battuta is one of the newest and largest malls in Dubai. It is huge, but the maps that you can pick up from information kiosks will help you find your way around. Named after 14th century explorer Ibn Battuta who spent 29 years travelling throughout the Middle East and Asia, the mall is divided into six zones, each based on a country that he visited (China, India, Egypt, Tunisia, Andalusia and Persia). Each zone has distinctive architecture representative of that country. Guided tours that illuminate the mall's more unusual features, such as the full-size replica of a Chinese junk and Al Jazari's Elephant Clock, are available.

The range of outlets is staggering, with most international brands represented here. There are a several anchor stores, including Debenhams and Géant hypermarket. Shops are loosely grouped: China Court is dedicated to entertainment, with several restaurants and a 21 screen cinema – this has the UAE's first IMAX screen, which is often used to show regular films.

The fashion conscious should head for India Court for the likes of Fitz & Simons, H&M, River Island and Topshop. Persia Court is styled as the lifestyle area, anchored by Debenhams – when you get to Starbucks, look up to see the ceiling detail. Egypt Court is for sporty types; Tunisia Court is anchored by Géant, so this is where to head for the weekly shop, and finally, Andalusia Court covers life's necessities such as banking, dry cleaning, key cutting, and DVD and video rental.

The foodcourts are at either end of the mall. There are several restaurants in China Court (including the excellent Finz) and a group of fastfood outlets in Tunisia Court. There are several restaurants and coffee shops dotted around in other areas of the mall. To reward the kids for trailing round after you, there's a Fun City in Tunisia Court. There are ATMs in most of the courts so refuelling your wallet shouldn't take too much effort.

This is an enjoyable mall to wander around but because of its size it can be a long way back if there's something you've missed. The taxi points are by the entrance to each court so if you really can't face walking back to the car with all that shopping, you could always get a cab. There are 10 car parks, so parking shouldn't be a problem; the numerical order of the car parks is a little eccentric, so remember which zone you came in through.

*Chill out and look up*

**458**

AED **25-30** EACH

DAN BROW
DAN BROWN
DAN BROWN

STEPHEN KING

STEPHEN KING    THE GUNSLI

STEPHEN KING

STEPHEN KING

**ROBIN COOK**

Books Plus gives you the incredible chance to own best-selling titles of your favourite authors for as little as Dhs. 25 each. Keep checking out your nearest Books Plus store for the season's best bargains, all round the year. And grab them before the racks get empty!

5 stores across the UAE
Lamcy Plaza Tel: 04 3366362, 3349514 ▪ Town Centre, Jumeirah Tel: 04 3442008 ▪ Spinneys Mall, Jumeirah Tel: 04 940278 ▪ Greens Centre Tel: 04 3674388 ▪ Al Reef Mall, Deira Tel: 04 2227547 ▪ Dubai Marina Tel: 04 3606196 ▪ Ibn attuta Mall, China Court Tel: 04 3685375 ▪ Al Jimi Mall, Al Ain Tel: 03 7633503 ▪ Arabian Ranches Tel: 04 3606198 Greens Community Tel: 04 8853250 ▪ Springs Community Center Tel: 04 3605703 ▪ George Mason University Tel: 7 2225526 ▪ Mirdif Tel: 04 2886735 ▪ Dubai Festival City Tel: 04 2325563 ▪ Academic City Tel: 04 4291393

**B⬢⬢KSPLUS**
BOOKS ▪ STATIONERY ▪ NOVELTIES
*"Reader's No. 1 Choice"*

## Mall of the Emirates ▶ p.461

*04 409 9000* | *www.malloftheemirates.com*

This is the big one... you will need to grab a map as you go in, and if you see a shop that you want to go into, don't put it off until later - it's too far to go back! Mall of the Emirates is more than a mall, it's a lifestyle destination. It houses the indoor ski slope (Ski Dubai, see p.372), the Kempinski Mall of the Emirates Hotel (p.41) and the Dubai Community Theatre & Arts Centre (p.320).

There are over 400 outlets selling everything from forks to high fashion here. The mall is anchored by Carrefour hypermarket (at least as big as the one in Deira City Centre), Dubai's largest branch of Debenhams, Harvey Nichols (London's trendiest department store), and Centrepoint, which is home to Baby Shop, Home Centre, Lifestyle, Shoemart and Splash. There is also a Cinestar cinema where you can treat yourself to a film in Gold Class which involves enormous leather armchairs and waiter service throughout. Nearby, the huge Magic Planet includes a bowling alley, a myriad of games and rides, just in case the kids haven't used up enough energy walking round the mall.

Label devotees should head for Via Rodeo, to get their fix of designer labels such as Burberry, Dolce & Gabanna, Salvatore Ferragamo, Tod's and Versace. If you're more into street chic, there are two H&M stores as well as Phat Farm, the New York clothing line that will add a bit of bling to your wardrobe. With skiing now possible in Dubai, a whole new area of fashion has opened up; check out Rampage and Staff for the coolest slope styles. You're spoiled for choice when it comes to homeware, with Home Centre, Marina Gulf, BoConcept, B&B Italia, THE One, and Zara Home, to name but a few.

For entertainment head to Virgin which has a bookshop and many international magazines alongside CDs, DVDs, mobile phones and computers. You'll also find a range of Apple products and accessories.

Of course, you'll need to keep your energy up so it's fortunate there is a wide range of dining options from the Swiss chalet feel of Après (p.524) to the three separate foodcourts.

Whatever you're looking for, you'll want to come back again and again, not least because you're unlikely to make it round in one day. Should you fancy a marathon shopping trip, Mall of the Emirates is open from Sunday to Wednesday 10:00-22:00, Thursday to Saturday: 10:00 to midnight and Carrefour opens 09:00 to midnight every day. And don't forget there's always mall walking here to keep you fit.

*Shopping on a grand scale*

# Welcome to the desert.

Sun and sand is plentiful in Dubai, but for snow and shopping make a trip to Mall of the Emirates, Dubai's finest shopping resort and the largest mall in the Eastern Hemisphere. With over 450 stores housing the world's leading brands, Ski Dubai - an Alpine themed snow resort, a 14-screen cineplex, a two level family entertainment zone with indoor rollercoasters, and over 75 cafés and restaurants, there are plenty of reasons for you to visit us.

Opening hours: 10am – 10pm (Sun – Wed), 10am – midnight (Thu – Sat)
Carrefour, CineStar and restaurant hours may vary. Please ask for details.
Interchange 4, Sheikh Zayed Road. Tel: 04 409 9000 www.malloftheemirates.com

## Mercato

*04 344 4161 | www.mercatoshoppingmall.com*

Mercato is the largest mall in Jumeira, with over 90 shops, restaurants, a cinema and cafes. As you drive along the Jumeira Beach Road, the Renaissance-style architecture really makes Mercato stand out and once inside, the huge glass roof provides a lot of natural light and enhances the Mediterranean feel.

The mall is anchored by Spinneys which has a dry cleaners, photo lab and music shop, a large Virgin Megastore (that has a decent book department) and a new Gap outlet which replaced Home Centre. There is a good mix of designer boutiques and high-street brands in the mall and shops range from the reasonably priced Pull and Bear, to the more exclusive Hugo Boss; there's even a shop dedicated to Barbie. With Topshop and Next on site, Mercato makes many British expats feel at home while Massimo Dutti and Mango have cornered the European market.

The layout is more interesting than many of the malls and it's worth investigating the 'lanes' so you don't miss anything.

There is a foodcourt and a number of cafes and restaurants, including Paul, a French cafe renowned for its patisserie, and Bella Donna, an Italian restaurant where you can dine alfresco. The cinema and large Fun City play area near the food court should keep most of the family occupied. There is a mother and baby room, tucked away near Costa Coffee on the upper floor, in addition to ATMs, a money exchange, and a branch of HSBC (they don't handle money but can offer advice and do the paperwork) and a shoe repair shop.

The atrium at Mercato Mall

# Where first impressions…
## are made to last

Through the spice souks, waterways and valleys of skyscrapers this fascinating photography book depicts the many architectual wonders of Dubai.

**Impressions Dubai**
Go beyond the picture postcard

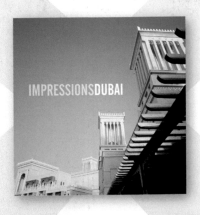

Abu Dhabi • Amsterdam • Bahrain • Barcelona • Beijing • Berlin • Dubai • Dublin • Geneva
Hong Kong • Kuala Lumpur • Kuwait • London • Los Angeles • New York • New Zealand • Oman
Paris • Qatar • Shanghai • Singapore • Sydney • Tokyo • Vancouver

**EXPLORER**
www.explorerpublishing.com

## Souk Madinat Jumeirah

*04 366 8888* | *www.madinatjumeirah.com/shopping*

Part of the Madinat Jumeirah complex, which also incorporates the Mina A'Salam and Al Qasr hotels, Souk Madinat Jumeirah really doesn't feel like a mall. It's a recreation of a traditional Middle Eastern marketplace, complete with narrow alleyways and authentic architecture. The blend of outlets is unlike anywhere else in Dubai, with boutique shops, galleries, cafes, restaurants and bars. It is one of Dubai's hotspots, so spend some time wandering through the souk before enjoying an evening out dining, drinking and dancing.

The layout, in keeping with traditional souks, can be a little confusing. There are location maps throughout and the main features are signposted (the signposts are quite subtle - look up). If you're really lost, a member of staff will be able to point you in the right direction.

The souk is best appreciated if you have time to walk around and enjoy the experience. During the cooler months the doors and glass walls are opened to add an alfresco element and there is shisha in the courtyard.

With an emphasis on unique brands, there are a large number of speciality outlets which aren't found anywhere else in Dubai. The souk is home to the greatest concentration of art boutiques in the city including Gallery One (selling photos with a local flavour) and Mirage Glass. The stalls in the outside areas sell souvenirs, some tasteful and some tacky.

There are more than 20 waterfront cafes, bars and restaurants to choose from, including some of Dubai's hottest night spots and you'll find The Meat Co, Trader Vic's, Jambase and BarZar here to name a few. There's also the impressive Madinat Theatre (www.madinattheatre.com) which has seen international and regional artists perform everything from ballet to comedy since it opened.

Getting lost at a modern souk

New buildings in an old style

## Wafi Mall  ▶ p.98

**04 324 4555** | *www.waficity.com*

Wafi is possibly Dubai's most exclusive mall. Part of the larger Wafi City, with its Egyptian theme and designer boutiques, this mall really stands out. The distinctive building has three pyramids forming part of the roof and a large stained glass window. Two of the pyramids are decorated with stained glass, depicting Egyptian scenes – best viewed during daylight.

Wafi has been extended several times since it opened, with further development ongoing. The layout makes this one of the more interesting malls to wander round, and the mall rarely feels busy. There are often exhibitions held throughout and the atrium is home to a huge tree at Christmas – it even snows!

Wafi seems to become more exclusive with each extension and the store directory now reads like a who's who in design, be it jewellery or couture. Imaginarium, a children's toy shop, has some great traditional toys and a separate kid-sized door! There's a large Marks & Spencer and a branch of Jashanmal to browse in when you're taking time out from the likes of Nicole Farhi or Versace.

There are a number of cafes and restaurants, including Biella, where you can enjoy your meal in the alfresco dining area. The children's entertainment area, Encounter Zone, is very popular and has age-specific attractions.

If you feel the need for pampering, or an evening out, head across to the Pyramids complex where there are some excellent bars, restaurants, a club and a renowned spa. The most recent construction added the five-star Raffles Dubai hotel, a new underground carpark and 90 new shops, including the largest Topshop in the UAE and popular LA retailer Kitson. Future work includes a 100,000 square foot department store and Khan Murjan, which will be an underground souk with around 200 units where, as well as shops, artisans will have workshops and will create pieces onsite.

*Stained glass inside Wafi Mall*

*Ancient design at Wafi Pyramids*

## Shopping Malls – Other

**Corner Al Diyafah St**
**& Al Wasl Rd**
*Al Wasl*
*Map 8 A2* **30**

### Al Ghazal Complex & Shopping Mall
04 345 3053
The Al Ghazal Centre is a new low-key shopping hub just finding its place on the Dubai shopping map. It's a range of shops situated in a large office building and can often feel deserted, but the ground floor is sometimes used at weekends for craft fairs featuring stalls with jewellery, photography and home accessories which get the crowds through the doors. From Alina Baby's Dream and Bambini for kid's clothes, Damas for jewellery, Giordano for cheaper high street clothes and the self-explanatory Ahmed Al Maghribi Perfumes, as well as NStyle for your mani-pedi, Shoes Avenue for, um, shoes and Mr Ben"s Closet for costumes. Al Ghazal has enough smaller stores to make it a worthwhile pit stop for those little essentials and treats.
Other outlets include: Adidas, Barocco, Brazil One, Century 2000, Century Home, Claire's, Cutest Fashion, Daphne, Dazzle, FAE, Gulf Optiks, Le Carmen, Little Luxuries, Marble Slab , Redstar, Revolution, S.O.S, Telefonika and Watch Me.

**Al Riqqa Rd**
*Deira*
*Map 9 C4*

### Al Ghurair City
04 222 5222 | www.alghuraircity.com
Al Ghurair City is Dubai's oldest mall, the one that set the ball rolling. If you are in Deira, chances are that you will head to Deira City Centre but, for a change of scene, Al Ghurair is worth a look. It was refurbished in 2003, and now houses an eight-screen cinema, a Spinneys , and a range of shops. The layout of the two-storey mall has the maze-like quality of a souk. There are a number of international brands, including Bhs, Book Corner and Mothercare, along with smaller boutiques. When you need a break, there are coffee shops and food outlets, and a Fun Corner to keep children occupied.
Other outlets include: Aldo, Benetton, Bhs, Bossini, Esprit, FCUK, French Connection, Guess, La Senza, Mexx, Nine West, Paris Gallery, Plug-ins, Red Earth, Starbucks, Sun & Sand Sports, Swatch and Triumph.

**Jumeira Beach Rd,**
**Nr Dubai Zoo**
*Jumeira*
*Map 7 E1*

### Beach Centre
04 344 9045 | beachctr@hotmail.com
Located on Jumeira Beach Road, this unassuming mall is home to a number of interesting independent shops selling everything from books to furniture and jewellery. Notably, the mall includes two branches of White Star Bookshop, one stocks craft materials and the other specialises in teachers' supplies. It also houses Charisma, an independent plus-size women's clothes shop, and Jenny Rose for fashionable maternity wear. The Music Room, at the back on the second floor has the largest supply of sheet music in Dubai and a selection of instruments. With Kuts 4 Kids, a children's hairdressers, and an opticians, pharmacy and Cyber Café, this is a good community mall.
Other outlets include: Bossini, Crystal Gallery, Dubai Desert Extreme, Hobby Land, Kids to Teens, Party Zone, Photo Magic, Sports House, Studio Al Aroosa, World of Art and Yateem Opticians.

**Airport Rd**
*Al Rashidiya*
*Map 13 F4*

### Bin Sougat Centre
04 286 3000 | sougati@aol.com
Located on Airport Road in Rashidiya, this mall is really convenient for Mirdif dwellers. The long, two-storey building, with impressive glass skylights, is packed with outlets selling everything from beanbags to paint brushes. Spinneys is the anchor store with all the essentials, including a pork section and ready meals, an in-house photo processors, a dry cleaner, DVD rental and two ATMs. For creative types, there is a branch of Emirates Trading, an art supplies store with a great range of professional

standard equipment, as well as Brush & Bisque-It, where you can paint your own designs onto ceramic items then fired for you. Dubai Library Distributors is excellent for stationery, especially school stuff. The Balloon Lady, on the first floor, is a whole shop dedicated to party supplies, from balloons to fancy dress outfits. If you are looking for furniture, head to the basement for Orient Curios Furniture where they keep larger pieces including wardrobes and cabinets. Or for something a little more unusual, RelaxSit sells beanbag chairs for adults and children. There is a small branch of Jumbo Electronics, concentrating mainly on mobile phones but they are able to order other items for you. Cocomino is the pick of the children's clothes shops – if you have to dress up your little one for a wedding this is a good place to start as their lines are fairly formal. If you are looking for pampering, try Nugoosh (follow the henna footprints), a ladies salon which offers henna, facials, body waxing and hairdressing. Secrets Boutique is the city'e first lingerie shop dedicated to larger sizes. The range is limited but it's still a welcome addition to the retail scene.

Most culinary tastes are catered to, with branches of Costa Coffee, Pizza Express, Dôme, Automatic restaurant, Gazebo Indian Restaurant, and a fish and chip shop. There is ample parking both in front and behind the mall, although it is hard to find a space at certain times on Fridays when the mosque next door is busy.

Other outlets include: Al Ansari Money Exchange, Al Jaber Optical, Baskin Robbins, Damas Jewellers, Dubai Leisure Holidays, House of Translation, KFT (fabric and carpets), Lily's flower shop, London Café, Kuts 4 Kids, Network Zone, San Marco and Union National Bank.

## Boulevard at Emirates Towers

*Shk Zayed Rd,*
*Emirates Towers*
*Trade Centre 2*
*Map 7 F3*

04 319 8999 | www.jumeirah.com

The Boulevard houses some of Dubai's most exclusive boutiques and popular restaurants and bars. The area links the Emirates Towers Hotel and Emirates Towers Offices, and is accessible from both. Boutiques include Cartier, Gucci, Yves Saint Laurent, and Boutique 1 (which stocks Stella McCartney, Alexander McQueen, Prada and Jimmy Choo shoes – so exclusive it has its own entrance from the car park!). If you're into more than shopping, there's also a health club and 1847, a men-only spa. Should you need to recharge, there are cafes (some with wireless internet access), licenced restaurants (Scarlett's and The Noodle House), and the ever-popular early evening hangout, The Agency.

This is one of the first malls in Dubai to introduce paid parking, at a costly Dhs.10 per hour, but if you have to think before paying for parking, this is not the mall for you.

Other outlets include: Ajmal, Areej, Azza Fahmy, Bottega Veneta, Cartier, Custo Barcelona, Damas, D. Porthault, Emporio Armani, Ermenegildo Zegna, Europcar, Flower@the towers, Lanvin, N-Bar, Sergio Rossi and Yves Saint Laurent.

## Dragon Mart

*International City*
*Emirates Rd*
*Al Awir*
*Map 2 F3* **21**

04 368 7205 | www.chinamexmart.com

Central to what will become Dubai's China Town, Dragon Mart is part of International City; a residential and commercial development beside the Hatta Road. It is reportedly the largest concentration of Chinese traders outside China. The centre is open from 10:00 to 23:00, but many of the shops don't open till 17:00, so the mornings are quiet. The huge number of outlets sell a mix of anything made in China. The mall is divided into zones by commodity, but these demarcations have been blurred. From building materials to toys, household items to quad bikes, everything is available, and cheaper than elsewhere in the city. The quality isn't great, but if you're looking for something cheap and for the short haul, you can't go wrong.

At over one kilometre in length, it takes about three hours to have a good look round.

**467**

There is no foodcourt as such, although there is a restaurant, a cafe, and several little foodstands at regular intervals – helpful for when those hunger pangs strike as you make the great trek around this vast retail space.

## Dubai Outlet Mall

*Dubai – Al Ain Rd*
*Map2 F3* **1**

04 367 9600 | *www.dubaioutletmall.com*

In a city where the emphasis in on excess, it is refreshing (not only for the wallet) to find a mall dedicating to saving money. Dubai's first 'outlet' concept mall may be quite a way out of town, but bargain-hunters will find it's worth the drive. Only 20 minutes down the Al Ain road, it is quickly becoming the place for hard-up fashionistas and frugal families to stop off and spend up. Big discounts on major retailers and labels are available with price tags seemingly missing a zero; think T-shirts for under Dhs.30 and Karama-esque prices for Marc Jacobs handbags. High street shops including Massimo Dutti and Dune sit alongside designer names such as Tommy Hilfiger and DKNY, with city style and sports casual equally catered for. Pick up trainers from Adidas, Nike and Puma, reduced eyewear from Al Jaber or Magrabi, jewellery from Damas, cosmetics from Paris Gallery and a range of electronics and homeware from more than 10 different outlets.

In addition to more shops you can shake a credit card at, several pharmacies and even a barbers, you'll also find a few spots to refuel including Starbucks, Stone Fire Pizza Kitchen and Automatic as well as the usual foodcourt suspects. And to keep the little ones engaged there's Chuck E Cheese's – a US institution serving up ample portions of food and entertainment.

Other outlets include: Adams, Aldo, Converse, Diesel, Espirit, Fashion For Less, G-Star, Giordano, Guess, Kenneth Cole, Levi's, Mango, Monsoon, Nine West, Phat Farm, Pierre Cardin, Planet Nutrition, Price Less, Pumpkin Patch, Replay, Samsonite, Sports World Outlet, Studio R and Timberland.

## Jumaira Plaza

*Jumeira Beach Rd,*
*Nr Jumeira Mosque*
*Jumeira*
*Map 7 F1*

04 349 9119 | *www.dubaishoppingmalls.com*

The 'pink mall' on Jumeira Beach Road has an interesting range of independent shops that are definitely worth a browse. It is dominated on the ground floor by a children's play area and the Dôme Cafe; the play area is really only suitable for younger children. Downstairs, there's an eclectic mix of outlets selling everything from furniture to beachwear. House of Prose is a popular second-hand book shop; Heatwaves has a good, if expensive, selection of UV protective beachwear; there are a number of home decor, trinket and card shops, and a small branch of the Dubai Police – great for paying fines without having to queue. Upstairs, Aquarius sells silk paintings of local scenes; and Melangé has an interesting selection of clothing, jewellery and soft furnishings from India. Those not wishing to browse the shops can sit and watch the fish.

This is a busy area and parking spaces can be hard to find; there is parking under the mall but the entrance is quite tight, especially for larger cars or four wheel drives.

Other outlets include: Aquarius, Art Stop, Balloon Lady, Blue White, Falaknaz Habitat, Girls' Talk Beauty Centre, Heatwaves, Kashmir Craft, KKids, Susan Walpole, Safeplay and The Warehouse.

## Jumeirah Centre

*Jumeira Beach Rd,*
*Nr Jumeira Mosque*
*Jumeira*
*Map 7 F1*

04 349 9702 | *www.dubaishoppingmalls.com*

This mall seems to pack a lot in to a small space. There are branches of several established chains including Benetton, Mothercare, Studio R and Sun & Sand; and a number of independent shops. The stationery shop, on the ground floor, has a good range of stationery and art supplies. Upstairs, independent shops abound and include Elves & Fairies (a crafts and hobbies shop), Panache (for accessories made only from natural materials), Sunny Days (a boutique selling a range of gift items), and the Wedding Shop that does exactly what it says on the door.

There are also some interesting clothes shops, and a gallery here. Harvest Home has shops on both levels selling an interesting range of gifts and kitchenalia. The branch of the Coffee Bean & Tea Leaf has a terrace where you can enjoy an alfresco coffee.

Other outlets include: Blue Cactus, Caviar Classic, Cut Above, Flower Box, Harvest Home, HN Camera repairs, Kazim Gulf Traders, Lunnettes, Mothercare, Nutrition Centre, Panache, Photo Magic, Rivoli, Sunny Days, The Barber Shop, The Wedding Shop and Thomas Cook.

## Lamcy Plaza

*Nr EPPCO HQ*
*Oud Metha*
*Map 10 D2*

*04 335 9999 | lamcydxb@eim.ae*

Home to five floors of open-plan shopping, with a wide range of outlets, Lamcy is consistently popular. As the only mall open at 09:00 seven days a week, it's the place to head for if you need a Friday morning shopping fix. It can be a bit tricky to find your way around at first, with the escalators from the first to second floors hidden away behind a shoe shop, but once you get the hang of it Lamcy is great for shopping in many different shops without having to walk for miles.

Entertainment dominates the ground floor, with a huge foodcourt and one of Dubai's best play areas, Loulou Al Dugong's. There is also a pharmacy, a money exchange, a florist and a post office counter, as well as a fascinating feng shui shop that is crammed with interesting knick-knacks. Towards the back of the ground floor (behind Paris Gallery), there's a photo developing outlet, a key cutting service and a driving school.

The first floor is for women's fashion and shoes and includes Dorothy Perkins (good value fashion), Guess, Jennyfer and Hush Puppy. The second floor is great for mums and kids, with Mothercare, Pumpkin Patch and The Toy Store. Mexx for Less, as the name suggests, sells discounted Mexx clothing for men, women and children, and Peacocks and Mr Price are also great for reasonable fashions. Factory Fashions is well worth a look as it carries Adams and Pumpkin Patch overstocks.

Men and sporty types should head for the third floor where there are several men's clothing and sports shops. This is the destination for bargain hunters too; Daiso is a Japanese store where everything costs Dhs.5 – there are some great bargains to be had here but you'll have to sort through quite a bit of tacky stuff first. The top floor is dedicated to the Hypermarket, which sells everything from kitchenware and bedding to clothes and groceries.

Parking is limited and Lamcy offer a unique service to combat it; if you have to park further away, look out for a red people carrier with Lamcy written on it, it offers a pick-up and drop-off service to the mall.

Other outlets include: Al Jaber Optical Centre, Adams, Aldo, Athlete's Foot, Books Plus, Bhs, Bossini, City Sports, Dorothy Perkins, Giordano, Golf House, Guess, Hang Ten, Hush Puppies, Jennyfer, La Senza, Mothercare, Mexx For Less, Monsoon, Nine West, Peacocks, Pumpkin Patch, Rivoli, Shoe Mart, Swatch and Watch House.

## Magrudy's Shopping Mall

*Nr Jumeira Mosque*
*Jumeira*
*Map 7 F1*

*04 344 4193 | www.magrudy.com*

The Magrudy's Shopping Mall, on Beach Road between Jumeirah Centre and Spinneys, comprises a collection of shops around a central courtyard. The shaded ground floor packs a lot into a small area. The Magrudy's Gift Shop sells a good selection of cards (this is a good place to look for seasonal decorations and cards), gifts, stationery, shoes

**469**

and the uniforms for a number of schools. The children's shop has bikes, books, toys and games all under one roof and for more reading material head to the recently renovated Magrudy's book shop.

There's also a small health food shop and a pharmacy. Eve Michelle is a clothes and accessories shop with a loyal customer base – a great place to find a hat for the races. It's also the only store in Dubai where you will find clothes by European designers including Fenn Wright Manson, Tuzzi and Frank Usher. The patisserie, Gerard, is a popular place to sit outside and enjoy a coffee, their croissants are legendary. Above the shops are a number of medical practices and a beauty salon.

*Green Community*
*Emirates Hills*
*Map 2 D4* **20**

## The Market

*04 885 3500*

Located in the Green Community, The Market has proved to be a welcome addition to the area among residents who previously had quite a trek to get their supplies. Among the stores on offer is Choithram supermarket, ACE (hardware and DIY store), Damas jewellery, Emirates Bank, and Athlete's Foot, as well as an impressive range of other outlets and cafes. Other outlets include: Bossini, Dôme Café, Grand Optics, Hour Choice, Jumbo Electronics, Karisma, McDonald's, Nine West, Oasis Greetings, Oriental Stores and Plug-ins.

*Jumeira Beach Rd*
*Opp Jumeira Mosque*
*Jumeira*
*Map 7 F1*

## Palm Strip

*04 346 1462* | *www.dubaishoppingmalls.com*

Styled as Jumeira's mall by the beach, Palm Strip is across the road from Jumeira mosque. More of an arcade than a mall, the majority of outlets are independent retailers. Upmarket boutiques dominate, with lingerie, beachwear, fashion and shoes, for men, women and children; and speciality shops for Arabic perfumes (Rusasi), maternity wear (Great Expectations) and chocolate (Jeff de Bruges).

If you are looking for a little pampering, there are two beauty salons and a branch of N-Bar, a walk-in nail bar (which is always busy, so even though you don't need to have an appointment, you will usually have to wait).

For home furnishings, Zara Home has an outlet here selling bright and stylish accessories, and of course THE One has a huge outlet just across the road.

Palm Strip is often quiet during the day, getting a little more lively in the evenings with the popular Japengo Café. If you want to catch up on your emails, head to F1 Net Café, especially if you're also into motor racing. If the shaded parking at the front is full, there's an underground car park, with access from the side.

Other outlets include:Beyond the Beach, Elite Fashion, Escada Sport, Gianfranco Ferre, Gulf Pharmacy, Hagen-Dazs, Little Me, Mask, My Time Ladies Salon, Northern Chic, Oceano and Starbucks.

*Salahuddin Street*
*Deira*
*Map 9 D4*

## Reef Mall

*04 224 2240* | *www.reefmall.com*

Reef Mall has rapidly become a popular place to go for those living on the Deira side of the Creek. This surprisingly large mall is anchored by Home Centre, Lifestyle, Splash and The Baby Shop. Among many other outlets are branches of Cellucom, i2 and the Athlete's Foot.

There's a huge Fun City here, which is often quiet during the day. It's a great place where everyone from toddlers to teens can burn off a bit of energy . There's a small foodcourt, several cafes and a supermarket. With ample underground parking, this is a very convenient mall, and a great alternative to Deira City Centre for Deira's residents.

Other outlets include: Bossini, Damas, Grand Optics, Giordano, Karisma, Oasis Greetings, Nayomi, Cellucom, Digi 4 U, The Athlete's Foot, Bossini, Nine West, Charles & Keith, McDonald's, The Coffee Bean & Tea Leaf, and Dome Café.

# Not big, but very clever…

Perfectly proportioned to fit in your pocket, these marvellous mini guidebooks make sure you don't just get the holiday you paid for, but rather the one that you dreamed of.

## Explorer Mini Visitors' Guides
Maximising your holiday, minimising your hand luggage

Abu Dhabi • Amsterdam • Bahrain • Barcelona • Beijing • Berlin • Dubai • Dublin • Geneva
Hong Kong • Kuala Lumpur • Kuwait • London • Los Angeles • New York • New Zealand • Oman
Paris • Qatar • Shanghai • Singapore • Sydney • Tokyo • Vancouver

**EXPLORER**
www.explorerpublishing.com

*Al Wasl*
*Umm Suqeim*
*Map 6 F2* **23**

## Spinneys

***04 394 1657*** | *www.spinneys.com*

This small mall just off Al Wasl Road centres around a large Spinneys supermarket (surprisingly). There is a small number of other shops including Early Learning Centre and Mothercare, Tavola (for kitchenalia), and Disco 2000, which is one of Dubai's better music and DVD shops. There are branches of both MMI and A&E (the alcohol shops) here, along with cafes and a large Fun Corner play area for children. A real neighbourhood centre, it gets quite busy at weekends and the small carpark is nearly always full.

Other outlets include: Arabella Pharmacy, Areej, Arts Palace, Axiom Telecom, Baskin Robbins, Beyond the Beach, Books Plus, Café Havana, Champion Cleaners, Damas, Emirates Bank, Gulf Greetings, Hair Works, The Healing Zone, The Indian Pavillion, Lunettes, Marina Gulf Trading, Photo Magic, Starbucks and Uniform Shop.

*Interchange 3½*
*Sheikh Zayed Road*
*Map 6 C3*

## Times Square Center

***04 341 8020*** | *www.timessquarecenter.ae*

This relatively small mall is bright, modern and set to attract bigger crowds as the various outlets open up to the public. Sharaf DG is the big draw with deals on electronics. You'll also find a large Intersport, several home stores, Toys R Us and even V-Moto should you feel the need to pick up a scooter on a Saturday afternoon. The Chillout ice lounge (not licensed) is a unique spot to have a sub-zero drink while wearing boots and a coat. In addition to the foodcourt, there is also the world's first Lamborgini Café, Caribou Coffee and Extreme Freshies Café where you can eat lunch while watching snowboarding on the screens. There's also a pharmacy, mini supermarket and ATM.

Other outlets include: InWear, Joe Bloggs, JYSK, Sanrio (Hello Kitty), Trek, Watch Square and Yellow Hat

*Jumeira Beach Rd*
*Jumeira*
*Map 7 D1*

## Town Centre

***04 344 0111*** | *www.towncentrejumeirah.com*

Town Centre is a community mall on Jumeira Beach Road, next to Mercato. With an interesting blend of outlets, this is the place to head to for a little time out. There are several cafes, including Café Céramique where you can customise a piece of pottery while you dine. For those after a bit of pampering, there's Feet First (reflexology and massage for men and women), Kaya Beauty Centre, Nail Station and SOS Salon. There are also clothing shops including Heat Waves (for beachwear) and DKNY, a large branch of Paris Gallery, an Empost counter and an Etisalat machine.

Other outlets include: Al Jaber Optical, Bang & Olufsen, Bateel, Books Plus, Bayti, Calonge, Damas, DKNY, Marie Claire, Nine West, Nutrition Zone, Papermoon, Paris Gallery, Simply Healthy and World of Pens.

*Jumeira Beach Road*
*Jumeira*
*Map 7 F1*

## The Village Mall

***04 349 4444*** | *www.thevillagedubai.com*

The Village Mall, with its Mediterranean theme, has more of a community feel than many of the malls in Dubai. The niche boutiques are great if you're looking for something a bit different, whether it's clothing or something for the home. With pampering opportunities for both men and women, and Sensasia Urban Spa (p.396), this is one of the more relaxing malls. Peekaboo, the children's play area, is bright and fun for younger children – they also run activities. There are a number of places to eat, including Shakespeare & Co, Thai Time, the Village Kitchen and Tony's New York Deli.

Other outlets include: Books Gallery, Boots, Cadorim, Candella Clothing, Edouard Rambaud Designs, Exotica Flowers, Irony Home, Julian Hairdressing for Men, Lollipop, Magrabi Optical, Offshore Legends, OXBOW Sportswear, Peekaboo, S*uce, Sisters Beauty Lounge and Tayyiba Beachwear.

## Department Stores

Department stores are now a standard feature of Dubai's larger malls. This is an expanding sector – rumour has it that London's famous Harrod's department store may be the next big name to enter the fray. The scope of department stores is representative of Dubai's shopping scene, from the epitome of chic, Saks Fifth Avenue, in BurJuman, to Avenue, just across the road, which caters for the more budget conscious.

**Opp BurJuman**
*Downtown Bur Dubai*
*Map 8 F4* 9

### Avenue

*04 397 9983*

This independent store, on the other side of Trade Centre Road from BurJuman, is good for those on a budget. Selling men's, women's and children's clothes and shoes, lingerie, luggage, some items for the home, sunglasses and watches, Avenue has the basics covered. This may not become one of your regular stops, but it is worth a look.

**Deira City Centre**
*Deira*
*Map 11 C3* 35

### Debenhams

*04 294 0011* | *www.debenhams.com*

A stalwart of the British high street, Debenhams has three stores in Dubai: Deira City Centre, Ibn Battuta and Mall of the Emirates. The stores all stock perfumes and cosmetics, clothing for men, women and children, and homewares. There are a number of brands with concessions within the stores, including Evans for plus-size clothing, Liz Claiborne, Oasis and Dorothy Perkins. There's a good selection of homeware, including Jamie Oliver's cookware. Debenhams is renowned for selling good quality items at reasonable prices. This ethos continues in the Designers at Debenhams ranges by John Rocha, Jasper Conran and Pearce Fionda – a great way for the budget conscious to own designer chic. Fans of Italian fashion will be happy to know that the Ibn Battuta and Mall of the Emirates branches of Debenhams stock Motivi. For other branches, see the directory on p.486.

**Ibn Battuta**
**Shopping Mall**
*Jebel Ali*
*Map 4 D2* 2

### Fitz & Simons

*04 368 5598* | *www.fitzandsimons.com*

This bright and spacious store sells quality European brands, with a guarantee that each collection will be limited, keeping it exclusive. With fashion for ladies and men, lingerie, kitchenware, and home decor accessories, the store's brands include Gerry Weber, Oui and Olsen, Camel Active and Windsor Man, Luisa Cerano, Sem Per Lei and Windsor Woman. Casa Marrakesh has interesting home accessories.

**Mall of the Emirates**
*Al Barsha*
*Map 6 A3* 19

### Harvey Nichols

*04 409 8888* | *www.harveynichols.com*

Dubai simply couldn't call itself a luxury destination without its own Harvey Nichs. Since the largest Harvey Nich's outside the UK opened here in February 2006, Dubai's label junkies have taken to their local branch like designer-coat-wearing ducks to Gulf waters. It contains a large selection of high-rolling fashion (for men, women and kids), food, beauty and homeware brands. Here's where you'll find Jimmy Choo, Diane Von Furstenburg, Juicy Couture, Hermes and Sergio Rossi, rubbing shoulders with other swish brands. On the top floor is the popular Almaz by Momo, restaurant, juice bar and shisha cafe.

*Smoke-free shopping*

BY LAW

## Jashanmal ▸ p.417

*Wafi Mall*
*Umm Hurair*
*Map 10 D4* **73**

**04 324 4800** | *www.jashanmal.ae*

One of Dubai's original department stores, with branches in Al Ghurair City, Mall of the Emirates and Wafi City. Jashanmal is the importer for several brands including Burberry, Clarks shoes and Mexx. With books, cameras, fashion, gifts, housewares, household and kitchen appliances, and luggage, the stores are worth a look. For other branches, see the directory on p.386.

*Browsing at Dubai Festival City*

## Marks & Spencer

*Dubai Festival City*
*Garhoud*
*Map 13 D2* **50**

**04 206 6466** | *www.marksandspencer.com*

One of the best known brands from the UK, M&S, as it is known, sells men's, women's and children's clothes and shoes, along with a small, but ever popular, selection of food. They are famous for their underwear, as worn by the majority of women in Britain, and have a reputation for quality. The Dubai stores carry selected ranges which include Per Una – high street chic – as well as more classic lines. The cafe is a great place to sit and relax; the food is good and the portions generous, particularly the children's menu. The Dubai Festival City branch opened in 2007 and is the largest M&S outside the UK. As well as offering extensive fashion and homewares, the DFC shop also has an espresso bar and a bakery. The other Dubai branches are in Wafi Mall (p.465) and the Al Futtaim Centre (next to Reef Mall, p.470) in Deira. For contact details see the directory on p.486.

## Next

*Deira City Centre*
*Deira*
*Map 11 C3* **35**

**04 295 2280**

Next is a popular British chain that was founded in 1982 and now has over 500 stores worldwide, including 11 stores right here in the UAE. They sell a range of high-quality clothes for men, women and children, as well as shoes, underwear, accessories and homeware. It's a great place to go clothes shopping for all occasions, whether you need casual daywear, office outfits or even semi-formal evening wear. The kids' clothing section is lovely and you'll find some beautiful items for children of all ages, from newborns to teenagers. For other branches, see the directory on p.486.

## Saks Fifth Avenue

*BurJuman*
*Downtown Bur Dubai*
*Map 8 F4* **8**

**04 351 5551** | *www.saksfifthavenue.com*

Anchoring the extension to BurJuman is the second-largest Saks Fifth Avenue outside the US. The name is synonymous with style, elegance, and the good life, encapsulated here in two floors of paradise for the label conscious. Even in Dubai's cultured retail sector, this store has an added air of sophistication. The first level is all about pampering, with cosmetics and perfumes, designer sunglasses and the Saks Nail Studio; it also houses the D&G Boutique, the children's department (Petit Bateau and designer clothes for little ones), the men's store, and the chocolate bar and cafe. The second level is dedicated to shopping – here you'll find the designer boutiques including Christian Dior, Jean Paul Gaultier and Prada. This is where to head for accessories, jewellery – including Tiffany and Fabergé – and an exclusive bridal salon which stocks Vera Wang gowns. For those looking for something a little different, head for Agent Provocateur (lingerie with a twist) – ignore the discreet exterior, the lingerie on display inside is anything but! The Fifth Avenue Club is a personalised shopping service, where members can browse the store with the guidance of a consultant. If you are into top designers, this will become a home from home.

**Deira City Cetnre** ◀
*Deira*
*Map 11 C3* **35**

## Studio R

*04 351 5551*

With branches in several of the larger malls, Studio R sells a selection of brands, catering to those with an active lifestyle. With a range of well-known clothing labels (Quiksilver, Rockport and Union Bay), and sports brands (Adidas, New Balance, Reebok and Speedo), Studio R has created its own niche. They are also stockists for Teva, who do a range of great, practical sandals. Studio R has sales throughout the year, when prices are heavily discounted. For other branches, see the directory on p.486.

## Independent Shops

This is a blossoming sector of the retail market. These independent stores and boutiques are opening, predominantly in converted villas, all over the city; Jumeira Beach Road is seen as the most popular address, although many more can be found in the more traditional shopping areas.

**Al Mankhool Road,** ◀
**Bur Dubai**
*Downtown Bur Dubai*
*Map 8 E2* **6**

## Fabindia

*04 398 9633* | *www.fabindia.com*

Beginning as a company that exported Indian handcrafted soft furnishings and clothes, Fabindia is now one of India's leading retail chains. The products are made in the villages, creating a livelihood for many and supporting rural communities. The branch in Dubai, on Mankhool Road, is one of only two outside India. A riot of bright colours and subtle hues, the clothing ranges for men and women combine Indian and western styles. From capri pants to kurtas, the cotton-based designs are guaranteed to add a splash of colour to any wardrobe. The soft furnishings, including sheets, table cloths and cushion covers, add an ethnic touch to your home. They also sell a beautiful range of rugs and hard-wearing dhurries to liven up dreary white floor tiles. The rolls of fabric, sold by the metre, are a great alternative to standard upholstery. The prices are very reasonable, especially as everything is handcrafted; shirts from around Dhs.40, large table cloths from Dhs.120 and quilts from Dhs.300.

**Garden Home** ◀
**Building**
*Oud Metha*
*Map 10 F2* **18**

## Five Green

*04 336 4100* | *www.fivegreen.com*

This is the best independent clothes shop in Dubai. Styled as an urban living boutique, it's the place to go for cutting-edge fashion and art. Street chic jeans, printed tees, shirts and trainers from labels including Paul Frank, GSUS and Boxfresh mix with creations from Dubai-based designers. The soundtrack to your retail experience is provided by top US labels like BBE, Compost and Soul Jazz. Five Green's inspiring space plays host to a number of exhibitions throughout the year from both home-grown and international talent. It may be expensive, but it is unique within the city.

**Al Karama** ◀
**Shopping Complex**
*Al Karama*
*Map 10 D1* **16**

## Sana Fashion

*04 337 7726*

Sana Fashion, on Trade Centre Road at the edge of Karama, is something of an institution. Renowned for branded clothing at bargain basement prices, it is well worth sorting through the racks to find the hidden gems. There are regular deliveries, especially in the run up to the festivals of Eid and Diwali, and word soon gets round, so if you see something you like, buy it – chances are it'll be gone before you go back. The shop is actually spread between two shops, and over two floors (the upper floor is linked). The huge ladies department has rack after rack of everything from lingerie to linen trousers. Prices start at around Dhs.20; an expensive item may cost up to Dhs.120. The children's department, girls on the ground floor and boys upstairs, caters for children from newborns to teens. It is not uncommon to find Gap bodysuits

**475**

starting from around Dhs.15. The men's section, upstairs, has a good range of casual wear and work shirts and trousers – good if you work outside or somewhere that your Armani suit wouldn't last a minute. Prices are super reasonable, with shirts starting at around Dhs.30 and trousers starting from around Dhs.50.

Much of Sana's stock is seconds and overruns from factories in both the UAE and India, so what they have depends on what's available. Sometimes you'll go there and find nothing but tat, but sometimes you'll leave with bags full of great bargains. But if you persevere, this a great value store, especially for children's clothing.

## Supermarkets

**Various**

### Choithram
*See p.488* | *www.choithram.com*
With 12 branches, Choithram is technically Dubai's largest supermarket chain. Their supermarkets are renowned for stocking items that can't be found elsewhere, but unfortunately they are also known for being expensive. You'll find a selection of British, American and Asian products, as well as a range of baby food. They have excellent freezer sections, although you'll pay top dollar for your favourite foods from home.

**Various**

### Lifco
*See p.490* | *www.lifco.com*
Although not the largest of the city's supermarkets, Lifco stocks a great range of items in terms of convenience. It is a good place to go for fresh olives. They regularly have items on special, where you can buy two or three items banded together for a discount.

**Various**

### Organic Foods & Café
*See p.491* | *www.organicfoodsandcafe.com*
A welcome addition to Dubai's food shopping options, Organic Foods & Café has a product range that's under constant review. All items are organically produced, so prices for fresh items can be expensive, although other items are competitively priced. You can dine in at the Satwa branch until 22:00 and 21:00 in The Greens, where there are also regular coffee mornings for mums and new arrivals in Dubai. They sell bread, vegetables, seafood, coffee, tea and body care products

**Al Wasl Rd**
*Al Wasl*
**Map 7 A2 40**

### Park n Shop
*04 394 5671* | *www.parkshopdubai.com*
Although it is small and just one single shop (rather than a chain), Park n Shop is worth a trip simply because it has the best bakery and butchery in the city. The bakery sells a huge range of wheat-free breads (made with alternatives such as spelt), as well as a range of delicious, delectable and incredibly fresh goodies, including reputedly the best jam doughnuts in Dubai. Famous for their birthday cakes, come Christmas time this is where you'll get your mince pies. The butchery sells a range of marinated cuts ideal for the barbecue, and they also have a Christmas ordering service for your turkey and ham. Prices of other items in the shop are higher, but they have products that you won't always find elsewhere.

**Various**

### Spinneys
*See p.492* | *www.spinneys.com*
With branches across Dubai from Mirdif to the Marina, you're never far from a Spinneys. Products are competitively priced (although many items are more expensive in Spinneys than they are at one of the larger hypermarkets). They have a great range of South African and Australian, as well as British and American items. They stock a

Opening Hours:
Saturday - Friday - 9:30 am to 12:00 midnight

**Géant Hypermarket**

Ibn Battuta Mall
Sheikh Zayed Road
Between Interchange 5 & 6, Dubai
Tel: 04-3685858 Fax 04-3685050
Visit us on our website: www.geant-uae.com

It's Géant and it's for you

# Together for a better Environment

**Plastic damages our environment.
It's a Non-Bio Degradable substance
which keeps destroying our
Eco System. Burning it will emit
toxic fumes that can poison
the environment.**

# Say NO to plastic bags

**For only 5.00AED, we will strive
to protect the environment.
Do your share by picking up our
reusable JUTEBAGS
from our counters.**

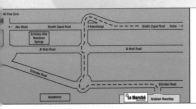

**Le March Supermarket**
Arabian Ranches, Community Center
Emirates Road, Tel: 043618358, Fax: 043618373
Visit us on our website: www.lemarche-dubai.com

Opening Hours:
Saturday - Friday 7:30 am - 10:00 pm

selection of Waitrose products (Waitrose is a UK supermarket renowned for its quality), and the freezer section and vegetarian options are both very good. Also worth a try are items from the deli counter which are great for picnics along with the ever popular roasted chickens.

*Various*

## Union Co-op
**See p.493**

This local chain sells a diverse range of goods. They have some of the best fruit and vegetables, and because they are always busy the turnover is quick and the produce fresh. There is a bulk-buy section, which can save you money as long as you can eat your way through a plate of cucumbers before they go soft! Some branches incorporate 'Hot Breads' bakeries, selling a freshly baked range of pies, cakes, samosas and croissants. The big branch on Al Wasl Road is open 24 hours a day.

# Hypermarkets

*Ibn Battuta*
*Shopping Mall*
*Jebel Ali*
*Map 4 D2* **2**

## Géant ▶ p.477
*04 367 0456* | *www.geant-dubai.com*

Géant is the hypermarket at Ibn Battuta Mall. Their range is very similar to that of Carrefour, a massive number of items are carried and there's a good selection. In addition to the foodstuffs, there are clothes, electronics, household goods, outdoor goods and stationery. A great bonus for anyone living near Jebel Ali.

*Dubai Festival City*
*Garhoud*
*Map 13 D2* **50**

## HyperPanda
*04 232 5566* | *www.panda-uae.com*

At an enormous 175,000 sq.ft, the HyperPanda is owned by the Saudi-based Savola Group and located at Dubai Festival City. It may not have quite the varied selection of produce found in other hypermarkets, but it does have the first hypermarket healthcare centre in the UAE and a strong electronics department. The parking facilities are good and allow easy access to other Dubai Festival City outlets.

*Al Karama*
*Map 10 E1* **17**

## Lulu Hypermarket
**See p.490** | *www.luluhypermarket.com*

The Lulu Hypermarkets, in Al Barsha, Karama and Qusais, are great for those on a budget. These stores, especially the smaller branch, which is in Karama, have an Aladdin's cave quality about them. There's not much that they don't sell, from luggage and electronics to food and clothing. They stock a good range of home appliances and have an area set aside with lots of colourful saris.
For other branches, see the directory on p.486.

*Deira City Centre*
*Deira*
*Map 11 C3* **35**

## Carrefour ▶ p.479
**See p.487** | *www.carrefouruae.com*

There are now four branches of this French hypermarket chain, all of which are enormous. As well as aisles piled high with all sorts of foodstuffs, they carry fairly comprehensive ranges of electronics, household goods, luggage, mobile phones, and white goods. They also sell camping gear, car accessories, clothes and shoes for men, women and children, garden furniture, hardware and tools, music, DVDs and videos, and stationery.
The range of foodstuffs is enormous – they offer a good range of French products (it's the best place to get crusty, freshly baked French sticks) and have a small health food section. Carrefour is renowned for its competitive pricing and special offers. For other branches, see the directory on p.486.

# Carrefour

## THE FIRST PLACE TO EXPLORE WHEN YOU ARE IN THE UAE.

Ras Al Khaimah

Ajman

Dubai
Al Shindagha

Sharjah

Dubai
Al Mamzar

Dubai
City Center

Abu Dhabi
Marina Mall

Dubai
Mall of the Emirates

Abu Dhabi
Airport Road

Al Ain

**EXPLORE 10 STORES**

## Visit www.carrefourme.com and win!

Deira City Centre, PO Box 60885, Tel: 04 295 1600, Fax: 04 295 1601 - Al Shindagha, PO Box 44272, Tel: 04 393 9395, Fax: 393 5604 - Al Mamzar Century Mall, PO Box 86677, Tel: 04 203 5699, Fax: 04 203 5578 Mall of the Emirates, PO Box 37044, Tel: 04 409 4899, Fax: 04 409 4888
Abu Dhabi Airport road, PO Box 31905, Tel: 02 449 4300, Fax: 02 449 4364 - Marina Mall, PO Box 4933, Tel: 02 681 7100, Fax: 02 681 4266 Ajman Ajman City Centre, PO Box 3098, Tel: 06 743 4111, Fax: 06 743 5200
Al Ain Al Jimi Mall, PO Box: 23333, Tel: 03 762 0044, Fax: 03 7624151 Sharjah Sharjah City Centre, PO Box 38100, Tel: 06 533 2333, Fax: 06 539 8891 Ras Al Khaimah Manar Mall, PO Box 2656, Tel: 07 228 5555, Fax: 07 227 0525

**MAF** HYPERMARKETS
MAJID AL FUTTAIM GROUP

Carrefour  Low prices and so much more!

# Streets & Areas to Shop

Other options **Bur Dubai** p.133, **Karama** p.250, **Satwa** p.254

## Al Faheidi Street

Central to Bur Dubai's traditional shopping area, and bordering the Textile Souk, Al Faheidi Street is the location of Dubai's electronics souk. This area is always busy but it really comes to life at night – if you're not sure if you're in the right place, just head for the neon lights. Electronics shops abound with top global brands such as Canon, JVC, LG, Panasonic, Philips and Sony available. Prices are negotiable and competitive but the vendors know the value of what they're selling. Don't make your purchases at the first shop you go into; rather take the time to look around at the range and prices available. Although goods are often cheaper here, if you are making a big purchase it may be worth it to pay that little bit extra and buy from a major retailer, so that you have more security if something goes wrong.

Al Faheidi Street is part of the commercial area that runs from the Bastakiya area all the way to Shindagha and takes in Dubai Museum and the Textile Souk. A great place to wander round in the cooler evenings, it's perfect for a bit of local colour and some great shopping. This area has a good range of inexpensive places to eat, including some fantastic vegetarian restaurants near the museum, as well as various outlets at the nearby Astoria and Ambassador hotels.

## Al Karama Shopping Complex

Karama is one of the older residential districts, and it has a big shopping area that is one of the best places to find a bargain. The main shopping area is the Karama Complex, a long street running through the middle of the district. It is lined by veranda-covered shops on both sides, and most display some goods outside to entice you in. The area is best known for bargain clothing, sports goods, gifts and souvenirs. While you wander round, you will quickly become aware of the reason for Karama's popularity and notoriety, as you will be offered 'copy' watches and handbags at every shop. If you show any interest you will be whisked into a back room to view the goods – if you have a specific model in mind, ask and they may be able to get it for you. If you're not interested, a simple 'no thank you' will suffice, or even just ignore the vendor completely – it may seem rude, but sometimes it's the only way to cope with the incessant invitations to view 'copy watches, copy bags'. Prices are negotiable in many of the shops in Karama; exceptions include the Benetton luggage shop and City Shoes (near Emirates Bank) and their prices are fixed, but very reasonable and they always have special offers.

Much of the clothing comes from the Far East, so check the sizes before you buy – they tend to be on the smaller side. There's always a huge range of T-shirts, shoes, shorts, and sunglasses at very reasonable prices. There are several shops selling gifts and souvenirs, from toy camels to mosque alarm clocks and stuffed scorpions to pashminas – Gifts Tent is one of the larger outlets and has a wide range, including every colour of pashmina imaginable – they are happy to take most of them out so you can find exactly the right shade.

With loads of small, inexpensive restaurants in the area serving a range of cuisines, you won't go hungry; Shezan, near Choithram, has good Indian and Chinese food. For fresh produce, head for the large fish, fruit and vegetable market.

## Satwa

Satwa, one of Dubai's original retail areas, has something of a village feel about it. Primarily arranged over four roads, the area is best known for its fabric shops and tailors, but in reality, it's like Aladdin's cave. The shops tend to cater to the lower end of the market and are great fun to look around. Popular reasons to visit Satwa include buying traditional majlis seating and getting your car windows tinted. The pick of the fabric shops is Deepaks, with an amazing range, reasonable prices and helpful staff. Shop around, because whatever you are looking for there's bound to be more than one outlet selling it and prices vary. If you are looking to brighten up your house or garden, there are a number of shops on 'Plant Street' with good indoor and outdoor plants. This is also the street for upholstery and paint, with both Dulux and National Paints outlets and several upholstery shops. Animal lovers are probably better off giving the pet shops a wide berth – conditions are awful, despite regulations, and the animals are often in a sorry state.

Diyafah Street is a great place for an evening stroll. There's an eclectic mix of shops and fast food outlets but, for some reason, there is a fairly high shop turnover so don't count on finding the same outlets twice. Al Mallah, the popular Lebanese restaurant recognisable by its green umbrellas and neon lighting, is highly recommended for delicious and authentic local food (the best falafel in Dubai, if not the world!). Along Diyafah Street you'll also find a huge bookshop, an off-road motorbike gear shop and a shop hiring formal evening wear, both men's and women's.

Satwa is renowned for its fast food outlets and reasonably priced restaurants. Ravi's is an institution in Dubai, serving good Pakistan food at incredible prices; Mini Chinese has been going for years and serves great Chinese food, and if you're looking for healthy food, the Organic Foods and Café, opposite Rydges Plaza, has rapidly established itself as one of the city's best speciality outlets. Rydges Plaza Hotel has a number of popular, licenced bars and restaurants.

Satwa is also home to some great cheap-and-cheerful salons, where you can get various treatments at low prices. They might not be as smooth as the upper-end salons, but are great for a quick treatment. Try Pretty Lady (04 398 5255) or Honeymoon (04 398 3799).

## Sheikh Zayed Road

*Btn Trade Centre & Jebel Ali*
*Trade Centre 1*
*Map 7 F3*

More than just the highway connecting Abu Dhabi and Dubai, Sheikh Zayed Road, between the Trade Centre and Jebel Ali, is rapidly developing into the city's largest shopping district. The area is a mixture of industrial and retail units which, due to the size and nature of the buildings, house some of the city's larger independent stores. Beginning at the Trade Centre end, this portion of the highway is flanked by some of Dubai's tallest buildings. While they are interesting to look at in themselves, it is worth checking out what is happening at ground level. On the left side are Emirates Towers (home to Boulevard at Emirates Towers – see p.467), a number of sports shops and an Axiom Telecom repair centre; while on the right are the Holiday Centre, Lifco supermarket, and a number of cafes and fast-food outlets.

The left-hand side of the stretch between Junction One (Defence Roundabout) and Junction Two (Safa Park) is home to Emaar's new Downtown district and the Burj Dubai. The massive Dubai Mall is scheduled to open in late 2008 – keep an eye on www.thedubaimall.com for the latest news. On the right-hand side are Safestway supermarket, the Mazaya Centre and a number of used-car dealers.

After Junction Two, the right-hand side of the road is residential while on the left-hand side there are a number of retail outlets and car dealerships. Behind the Pepsi factory is an outlet called Safita, which sells wooden Indian furniture – they have a decent selection and their prices are better than most. Further along is the former site of the Oasis Centre, which is currently being rebuilt after a fire. For those looking to make improvements on their homes, ACE and Speedex (both p.430) will have the equipment to do the job. For the sporty, there's Wolfi's Bike Shop (p.413). The area between Junctions Three and Four looks, at first glance, to be dominated by industrial units but there are some real gems waiting to be discovered. Innovative Kidz is where to head for if you are looking for great quality furniture, puzzles and toys for children – it's not cheap but it everything is built to last. Just Kidding has all the latest baby equipment, furniture and fashions from Europe as well as a maternity wear. The warehouse has been imaginatively laid out with various model rooms and the team can recreate the effects in your own home. The Courtyard, near the Spinneys warehouse, is home to a collection of interesting shops and galleries, in a very tasteful setting; there's even a coffee shop. This is the area to head for if you have green fingers or enjoy the alfresco lifestyle; Dubai Garden Centre has everything for the garden pretty much covered. There are a number of used car dealers and vehicle repair workshops. The Gold & Diamond Park, right by junction four, has much of the choice of the Gold Souk, but you can browse in air-conditioned comfort.

Those feeling the heat should head to Mall of the Emirates (p.460) where you can indulge in a spot of shopping and skiing. There is little else other than high rise-buildings but there are a few shops around the Greens, including a branch of Organic Foods & Café (p.476). Dubai Marina is where you'll find the weekend Marina Market (www.marinamarket.ae) during the cooler months, and The Walk, a new outdoor shopping area beneath the Jumeirah Beach Residence towers. There is another mall under construction at the Marina too. It's then not far to Ibn Battuta Mall, with a good variety of shops and interesting architecture. After that you'll be hard pressed to part with your cash until you reach Abu Dhabi; be sure to have a copy of the *Abu Dhabi Explorer* on hand when you arrive.

**Mirdif**
**Map 15 B2**

## Uptown Mirdif

Bearing in mind that three years ago the only shopping that could be done in Mirdif itself was getting milk and bread from Ali Akhbar's cornershop, it's hardly surprising that Uptown Mirdif has fast become the centre of eating, socialising, and of course shopping for many a Mirdif dweller. With a Spinneys, an A&E, a money exchange, a bank (Lloyds), a pharmacy and a florist, it is well-equipped enough to meet all your daily needs. But it is also home to the kind of shops full of things you just have to have, whether you need them or not. Bedu, La Senza, Pumpkin Patch, Adams, Mothercare, Kamiseta, and Beyond the Beach will keep you and the kids dressed to the nines, and you can kit yourself out with the best shoes, bags and accessories from Brantano, Aldo, Claire's Accessories and Nine West. There's also a huge Paris Gallery which is stocked full of beautiful things, and it seems that it has yet to pull the crowds, so it's great if you're shy and like to do your shopping in solitude. Cosmetics chain Faces also has a branch here, and it's almost impossible to walk in and walk out without having spent a fortune on must-have goodies by Benefit or Urban Decay.

If you've just moved into a new villa in the area, or you want to spruce up your old one, 2XL has some lovely furniture and their kitchen section is full of great gadgets that you just know will turn you into an award-winning chef. Howard's Storage World and Stokes are also great for kitchen stuff.

The cafe culture that was once the sole pleasure of Jumeira Janes has finally arrived in Mirdif – Uptown has a Caribou Coffee (Explorer tip: try the smoothies), where you can play boardgames, browse in the bookshop, or read magazines while you savour your tall double decaf skinny cinnamon latte, a Central Perk (yes, it's just like the one in the TV show and features an excellent healthy food menu), a Starbucks, a Mugg & Bean and a Le Pain Quotidien. In terms of other food outlets, there's Gourmet Burger Kitchen (shame on you if you haven't tried their blue cheese burger yet), Da Shi Dai for innovative Chinese cooking with not a shake of MSG in sight, and Pane Caldo for interesting Italian yummies in a cool setting. And then of course there's the foodcourt – probably one of the best in Dubai, with Mcdonalds, Burger King, KFC and Hardees all

**482**

*Uptown Mirdif*

fighting for your chicken nugget cravings, as well as Pizza Hut, Da Gamas, ARZ Lebanon, Zaatar W Zeit, Automatic, a Chinese takeaway, an Indian takeaway, and a branch of Fresh, where you can get the ultimate paradox: healthy fast food.

After all that eating, you can burn it all off in the Mirdif branch of Fitness First, or you can take a course of slimming therapy at VLCC (they can also sort out your skin and hair).

Even if you don't have a penny to spend, Uptown has a sense of community that sees plenty of families down there in the late afternoon, so expect to see all the neighbourhood kids riding their bikes, scooting round on scooters, or impressing their mates in their new pair of heelies.

## Markets & Souks

Other options **Bargaining** p.406, **Bur Dubai** p.133, **Deira** p.135

There are a number of souks and markets in Dubai. The souks are the traditional trading areas, some more formally demarcated than others. In keeping with tradition, bargaining is expected and cash is the best bargaining tool.

Parking around the Gold Souk, Spice Souk and Textile Souk is limited, so if possible it is better to go to these areas by taxi or, if you are visiting all three, park on one side of the Creek and take an abra (water taxi) to the other side – great value at Dhs.1 each way.

Markets are an increasingly popular concept in the city; they are usually based around crafts and are often seasonal. The Marina Market (see below) is the first to take place on a regular basis. Craft fairs are held throughout the year, mainly in the Mazaya Centre and The Holiday Centre (at the Crowne Plaza). The stalls are filled with hand-made items and are a great place to stock up on presents. There are also a number held at the schools in the run up to Christmas.

*Nr Shindagha Tunnel*
*Deira*
*Map 9 C1* 13

### Fish Market

The Fish Market in Deira is hard to ignore if you're in the area, especially during the hotter months – maybe not the best place to visit if you don't like the smell of fish. To get the freshest fish for your evening meal, and to experience the vibrancy of this working market, head down early in the morning or late at night as the catch is coming in. There is an incredible range of seafood on display. The emphasis is on wholesale but the traders are usually more than happy to sell to individuals and, for those of a squeamish disposition, the fish can be cleaned and gutted for you.

As well as the market there's a seafood restaurant and a museum dedicated to the history of the fishing village that Dubai used to be.

*Nr Used Car Market,*
*Dubi – Hatta Rd*
*Map 9 C1* 29

### Fruit & Vegetable Market

There are a number of small fruit and vegetable markets around the city, like the one in Karama. The main market is now located off Emirates Road in Al Awir. It is a wholesale market but, like the Fish Market, the traders are usually happy to sell by the kilo rather than the box. There is a huge variety of produce on offer and it is usually fresher than in the supermarkets. Be sure to haggle, you can often tell if you have paid more than the trader thinks the goods are worth if they give you freebies. The location is not overly convenient for most people but it is worth a look if you are out that way. It is well signposted as you drive along the Dubai-Hatta Road. Mornings are the best time to visit.

## Gold Souk

*Baniyas Rd*
*Deira*
*Map 9 B1*

This is Dubai's best-known souk and a must-do for every tourist. There is a huge number of shops and many of them have branches in other parts of town. Whether you are looking to make a special purchase or just want to window shop, a wander through the Gold Souk is a great experience. The meandering lanes are lined with shops selling gold, silver, pearls and precious stones. These can be bought as they are or in a variety of settings. This is definitely a place to try your bargaining skills but don't expect a massive discount. Gold is sold by weight according to the daily international price and so prices will be much the same as in the shops in malls – the price of the workmanship is where you will have more bargaining power. Most of the outlets operate split shifts, so try not to visit between 13:00 and 16:00 as many outlets will be closed. The Gold Souk is always busy, and it is shaded, but there is added sparkle when you visit in the evenings, as the lights reflect on the gold and gems.

If you are more interested in buying than enjoying the souk experience, the Gold and Diamond Park, by junction four on Sheikh Zayed Road, has a far calmer atmosphere. There are branches of many of the outlets which are also found in the Gold Souk but here they are quieter and the whole area is air conditioned. There's also a cafe if you'd like a break while you decide which pieces you can't live without.

## Marina Market

*Marina Walk*
*Dubai Marina*
*Map 5 B2* 42

**050 244 5795** | www.marinamarket.ae

This venture is the brainchild of Roslynne Bourguignon, a long-term expat who couldn't believe Dubai didn't have any outdoor markets similar to those common in the UK. Originally a Friday affair, the Marina Market now operates on a Friday and Saturday, from October to April at the picturesque Marina Walk. It features around 50 stalls selling a range of items, predominantly crafts, clothing and home accessories. The setting makes this an enjoyable place to head at the weekend, as you can wander around the stalls before adjourning to one of the cafes or restaurants. Things get started at 11:00 and wind up around 19:00. The organisers recently expanded the concept and added outdoor weekend markets at two further locations – Uptown Mirdif and Burj Dubai Old Town. See the website for more details.

## Sharjah Central Souk

*Nr Corniche*
*Sharjah*
*Map 2 F2* 71

www.sharjah-welcome.com

Situated beside the lagoon, the Sharjah Central Market – or Blue Souk – is an unmissable sight. Consisting of two long, low buildings running parallel to each other and connected by footbridges, the souk is intricately decorated and imaginatively built according to Islamic design.

Each building is covered and air-conditioned to protect shoppers from the hot sun, with one side selling a range of gifts, knick-knacks, furniture, carved wood and souvenirs, and the other given over almost entirely to jewellery stores. There are over 600 individual shops, and the upper floors have a traditional souk feel with narrow passages and staircases. The souk also has shops selling a fabulous range of carpets from all over the world. For visitors and residents, a half-hour trip into the Blue Souk can easily turn into half a day.

## Souk Al Arsah

*Nr Bank St*
*Sharjah*
*Map 2 F2* 78

www.sharjah-welcome.com

This is probably the oldest souk in Sharjah. It has been renovated in recent years, so although the shops are still in a style reminiscent of old market places, the souk is covered (to provide shelter from the sun) and air-conditioned. Around 100 tiny shops line a labyrinth of peaceful alleyways, selling goods such as silver jewellery, perfumes, spices, coffee pots and wedding chests. There is a small coffee shop where you can get Arabic coffee and sweets. Shop closing times do vary, with some closing by 20:30 and others remaining open until 22:00.

## Spice Souk

*Nr Gold Souk*
*Deira*
*Map 9 A2*

With its narrow streets and exotic aromas, a wander through the Spice Souk is a great way to get a feel for the way the city used to be – it makes the modern city that Dubai has become seem a long way away. The number of spice shops is diminishing, due in part to hypermarkets, like Carrefour, having areas dedicated to spices and the supermarkets selling a wider range. Most of the stalls sell the same ranges and the vendors are usually happy to advise on the types of spices and their uses. This is unlikely to be where you do your shopping on a regular basis, but the experience of buying from the Spice Souk is more memorable than picking a packet off a shelf. You may even be able to pick up some saffron at a bargain price. The shops operate split shifts but whether you visit in the morning or the evening, this is a bustling area of the city.

## Textile Souk

*Nr Abra Station*
*Downtown Bur Dubai*
*Map 9 A2*

The Textile Souk, in Bur Dubai, is stocked with every fabric and colour imaginable. The textiles are imported from all over the world, with many of the more elaborate coming from the subcontinent and the Far East. There are silks and satins in an amazing array of colours and patterns, velvets and intricately embroidered fabrics; basic cottons can sometimes be harder to find but you can always try Satwa (p.254). Prices are negotiable and there are often sales, particularly around the major holidays, Eid and Diwali, and the shopping festivals. It is worth having a look in a few shops before parting with your cash as they may have different stock and at better prices. The mornings tend to be a more relaxed time to browse.

Meena Bazaar is the shop that most taxi drivers head for if you ask for the Textile Souk; they have an amazing selection of fabrics from raw silk to metallic net and plain cotton but be prepared to haggle. Rivoli has a range of textiles for men on the ground floor and for women upstairs. The assistants are keen to offer the 'best discount' but it is always worth haggling to see if the price will drop further. Rivoli also runs a tailoring shop in Karama, where you will get a discount on pieces made up with fabric from the shop.

There are a number of tailoring shops around the Textile Souk, including a branch of Dream Girl, which is renowned for their service. Before choosing a tailor, check out their finished pieces as some are better at certain styles of clothing.

*Going for gold*

*Rich finds at the textile souk*

| | |
|---|---|
| **Accessorize** | Deira City Centre (04 295 0725), Mall of the Emirates (04 340 9052), Wafi Mall (04 327 9801) |
| **ACE** | BurJuman (04 355 0698), Dubai Festival City (04 206 6660), Green Community (04 885 3208), Sheikh Zayed Rd (04 338 1416) |
| **Adams** | Lamcy (04 337 6002), Uptown Mirdif (04 288 8424), Mercato (04 349 2272), BurJuman (04 351 0068), Al Ghurair City (04 223 7004), Deira City Centre (04 294 5576) |
| **Adidas** | BurJuman (04 359 0995), Deira City Centre (04 295 4151), Ibn Battuta Shopping Mall (04 366 9777), Al Ghurair City (04 227 8936) |
| **African & Eastern (A&E)** | Dubai Marina (04 368 3981), Spinneys (Ramada) (04 359 0730), Nr Choithrams, Al Karama (04 334 8056), Mirdif (04 288 2715), Spinneys (04 394 2676) |
| **Aigner** | Mall of the Emirates (04 341 4747), BurJuman (04 351 5133), Deira City Centre (04 295 4149) |
| **Ajmal Perfumes** | Emirates Towers Hotel (04 330 0600), Mall of the Emirates (04 341 4151), Hamarain Centre (04 269 0102), Deira City Centre (04 295 3580), Al Ghurair City (04 222 7991), |
| **Al Boom Marine** | Jumeira Beach Road (04 394 1258), Ras Al Khor, nr Coca Cola (04 289 4858) |
| **Al Fahidi Stationery** | Al Faheidi St (04 353 5861), Opp Al Khaleej Hotel, Nasr Square (04 222 8641) |
| **Al Fardan Jewels** | Deira City Centre (04 295 4238), Hamarain Centre (04 269 9882) |
| **Al Futtaim Jewellery** | Mall of the Emirates (04 341 4499), BurJuman (04 351 1275), Deira City Centre (04 295 2906) |
| **Al Jaber Gallery** | Mall of the Emirates (04 341 4103), Ibn Battuta Shopping Mall (04 366 9795), Deira City Centre (04 295 4114) |
| **Al Jaber Optical Centre** | Al Ghurair City (04 224 9444), Deira City Centre (04 295 4400), Lamcy Plaza (04 336 0773), Mall of the Emirates (04 341 1322), Mercato (04 349 3938) Town Centre (04 342 9933), Opp Hamarain Centre (04 266 7700) |
| **Al Kamda** | Al Wasl (04 343 0808), Deira (04 266 4200) |
| **Al Liali** | BurJuman (04 351 0075), Ibn Battuta Shopping Mall (04 368 5384), Jumeirah Centre (04 342 0909), Mercato (04 344 5055) |
| **ALDO** | Lamcy Plaza (04 334 8486), Mercato (04 344 7995), Uptown Mirdif (04 288 7471), Mall of the Emirates (04 341 0360), Ibn Battuta (04 368 5243), Dubai Festival City (04 232 6196), Al Ghurair City (04 223 8851), Deira City Centre (04 295 7885) |
| **Aptec Mobiles** | Arabian Ranches (04 360 8040), Deira (04 271 3331), Nr Lamcy Plaza (04 334 1166) |
| **Arabian Oud** | Deira (04 225 8334), Deira City Centre (04 295 6767), Wafi Mall (04 324 4118) |
| **Areej** | Mall of the Emirates (04 341 4747), Mercato (04 344 6894), Emirates Towers Hotel (04 330 3340) |
| **Armani Exchange** | Deira City Centre (04 295 1165), Mercato (04 344 2118), Palm Strip (04 345 9944) |
| **Axiom Telecom** | Al Ghurair City (04 227 0683), Deira City Centre (04 295 1888), Ibn Battuta Shopping Mall (04 366 9960), Jebel Ali (04 887 2293), Mall of the Emirates (04 340 6746), Mercato (04 342 0083), Nr Dusit Dubai, Shk Zayed Rd (04 321 0600), Town Centre (04 342 2996) |
| **Baby Shop** | Abu Hail Center (04 266 1519), Zabeel Rd (04 337 8075), Al Karama (04 335 0212) Mall of the Emirates (04 341 0604), Reef Mall (04 224 3343) |
| **Bang & Olufsen** | Bur Dubai (04 353 1678), Jumeira Beach Rd (04 342 2344) |
| **Baskin Robbins** | Al Ghurair City (04 222 5910), Deira City Centre (04 224 9112), Jumeirah Centre (04 349 4569) |

| | |
|---|---|
| **Benetton** | Al Ghurair City (04 227 6048), BurJuman (04 359 1600), Deira City Centre (04 295 2450), Factory Outlet (04 335 2761), Jumeirah Centre (04 349 3613), Mall of the Emirates (04 341 4646) |
| **Bershka** | Mercato (04 344 8645), Mall of the Emirates (04 347 5399), Deira City Centre (04 295 8440) |
| **Beyond the Beach** | Mercato (04 349 0105), Palm Strip (04 346 1780), Souk Madinat Jumeirah (04 366 6822), Spinneys (04 394 2977), Ibn Battuta Shopping Mall (04 368 5211) |
| **Bhs** | Al Ghurair City (04 227 6969), BurJuman (04 282 2555), Lamcy Plaza (04 335 8334) |
| **Bin Hendi Jewellery** | Deira City Centre (04 295 2544), Jumeirah Beach Hotel (04 348 7030) |
| **Body Shop** | Jumeirah Centre (04 344 4042), Mall of the Emirates (04 341 0551), |
| **Bombay** | Wafi Mall (04 324 5255), Mercato, Level 1 (04 344 5994) |
| **Book Corner** | Dune Centre (04 345 5490), Galleria Shopping Mall (04 209 6453), Jumaira Plaza (04 344 0323) |
| **Book World** | Nr Bikanervala, Beh Pizza Inn (04 396 9697), Opp Satwa Flower Shops (04 349 1914) |
| **Books Plus** | Academic City (04 429 1393), Emirates Hills (04 367 4388), Spring Community Centre (04 360 5703), Spinneys (04 394 0278), Reef Mall (04 222 7547), Lamcy Plaza (04 336 6362), Ibn Battuta Shopping Mall (04 368 5375), Town Centre (04 344 2008), Emirates Hills (04 367 4388), Ibn Battuta Shopping Mall (04 368 5375), Dubai Marina (04 368 3986), Dubai Festival City (04 232 5563), Arabian Ranches (04 361 8643), Mirdif (04 288 6735), Green Community (04 885 3250), Knowledge Village (04 367 8642) |
| **Boots** | Al Diyafa St (04 398 9913), Deira City Centre (04 294 3990), Ibn Battuta Shopping Mall (04 368 5936), Mall of the Emirates (04 340 6880), The Village Mall (04 349 9112) |
| **Borders** | Deira City Centre (04 294 3344), Dubai Festival City (04 425 0371), Mall of the Emirates (04 341 5758) |
| **Bossini** | Beach Centre (04 349 0749), Lamcy Plaza (04 334 2484), BurJuman (04 351 6917), Al Ghurair City (04 221 5917), Cosmos Lane, Meena Bazaar (04 352 4817) |
| **Brantano** | Deira City Centre (04 295 0437), Mall of the Emirates (04 341 3394) |
| **Breitling Watches** | Deira City Centre (04 295 4109), Dubai Duty Free (04 206 6444), Mall of the Emirates (04 341 1165), Wafi Mall (04 324 3530) |
| **Burberry** | BurJuman (04 351 3515), Deira City Centre (04 295 0347), Mall of the Emirates (04 340 5559) |
| **Calvin Klein** | BurJuman (04 352 5244), Mall of the Emirates (04 340 3448), Deira City Centre (04 294 8729), Dubai Festival City (04 232 6767) |
| **Cannondale** | Al Barsha (04 882 1660), Al Quoz (04 339 1333) |
| **Carlton Cards** | Deira City Centre (04 294 8707), Lamcy Plaza (04 336 6879) |
| **Carrefour** | Al Shindagha (04 393 9395), Mall of the Emirates (04 409 4899), Century Mall (04 203 5699), Deira City Centre (04 295 1600) |
| **Cartier** | BurJuman (04 355 3533), Emirates Towers, Level 36 (04 330 0333) |
| **Cellucom** | Jebel Ali (04 368 5151), Mall of the Emirates (04 341 0503), Al Sufouh (04 367 2788), Downtown Bur Dubai (04 355 3443), Al Bada'a (04 345 1445), Deira (04 273 3107) |
| **Chanel** | BurJuman (04 355 7388), Wafi Mall (04 324 2086) |

**487**

| | |
|---|---|
| **Choithram** | Al Rais (04 352 4012), Al Wasl Rd (04 394 3852), Beach Rd (04 344 2424), Bur Dubai (04 352 0435), Dubai Tower (04 223 2488), Green Community (04 885 2299), Greens (04 366 3160), Holiday Centre (04 331 1377), Hyatt Regency (04 209 6455), Jebel Ali (04 884 6242), Karama (04 337 1021), Lakes (04 380 1010), Rashidiya (04 282 5494), Springs (04 360 6626), Umm Suqueim (04 348 1864). |
| **Claire's** | Deira City Centre (04 295 7277), Mall of the Emirates (04 340 7575), Wafi City (04 324 2830)Al Ghurair City (04 221 5542), Mercato (04 344 2889) |
| **Clarks** | Al Ghurair City (04 2277 7780), Deira City Centre (04 294 8266), Mall of the Emirates (04 340 3449) |
| **Club Monaco** | Deira City Centre (04 295 5832), Wafi City (04 398 4149) |
| **Coach** | Emirates Towers Hotel (04 330 1020), Mall of the Emirates (04 409 8932) |
| **Coast** | Deira City Centre (04 294 0011), Ibn Battuta Shopping Mall (04 368 5900), Mall of the Emirates (04 340 7575) |
| **Compu-Me** | Al Garhoud (04 282 8555), Mall of the Emirates (04 341 4442) |
| **Damas Jewellery** | BurJuman (04 352 5566), Deira City Centre (04 295 3848), Gold Centre Bldg, 3rd floor (04 226 6036) |
| **Dar Al Tasmim Uniforms** | Rashidiya Factory (04 285 9624), Spinneys (04 394 1477) |
| **Debenhams** | Deira City Centre (04 294 0011), Ibn Battuta Shopping Mall (04 368 5900), Mall of the Emirates (04 340 7575) |
| **Diesel** | BurJuman (04 351 6181), Deira City Centre (04 295 0792), Mercato (04 349 9985) |
| **DKNY** | BurJuman (04 351 3788), Deira City Centre (04 295 2953), Mall of the Emirates (04 341 4343) |
| **Domino** | Al Ghurair City (04 221 0298), BurJuman (04 352 3340), Mercato (04 344 9407) |
| **Dorothy Perkins** | Ibn Battuta Shopping Mall (04 368 5900), Lamcy Plaza (04 334 0740), Mall of the Emirates (04 340 7575) |
| **Dream Girl** | Al Karama (04 337 7287), Al Satwa (04 349 5445), Downtown Bur Dubai (04 352 1841) |
| **Dubai Library Dist** | Bin Sougat Centre (04 333 9998), Opp Post Office, Satwa Rd (04 331 6635), Safia Branch, Al Muteena St (04 262 5552), Shk Zayed Rd (04 339 4966) |
| **Dubai Opticals** | BurJuman (04 351 0051), Deira City Centre (04 295 4303) |
| **Early Learning Centre** | Deira City Centre (04 295 1548), Spinneys Centre (04 394 1204), Wafi Mall (04 324 2730), Souk Madinat Jumeirah (04 368 6519), BurJuman (04 359 7709), Mercato (04 344 8463), Mall of the Emirates (04 341 4177) |
| **Ecco** | Al Ghurair City (04 221 3340), Deira City Centre (04 295 2797), Mall of the Emirates (04 341 3838), Mercato (04 344 3374), Reef Mall (04 224 2252) |
| **Elle** | Deira City Centre (04 295 1551), Ibn Battuta Shopping Mall (04 366 9950), Reef Mall (04 222 2323) |
| **Emirates Trading Est.** | Bin Sougat Centre (04 284 4594), Nr Al Nasr Cinema (04 337 5050), Jumeira (04 344 1052) |
| **Esprit** | Deira City Centre (04 295 0524), Al Ghurair City (04 221 9463), BurJuman (04 355 3324) |
| **Evans** | Al Ghurair City (04 222 8261), Deira City Centre (04 294 0011), Ibn Battuta Shopping Mall (04 368 5900), Mall of the Emirates (04 340 7575) |
| **Faith** | Deira City Centre (04 294 0011), Ibn Battuta Shopping Mall (04 368 5951), Mall of the Emirates (04 340 7575) |

| | |
|---|---|
| **FCUK** | Mall of the Emirates (04 341 1116), Al Ghurair City (04 227 3848), Deira City Centre (04 295 0413) |
| **Feshwari** | Sheikh Zayed Rd (04 339 3559), Al Satwa (04 344 5426) |
| **Florsheim** | BurJuman (04 351 5353), Deira City Centre (04 295 3988) |
| **Forever 21** | Deira City Centre (04 295 2031), Ibn Battuta Shopping Mall (04 368 5232), Mall of the Emirates (04 341 3412) |
| **Fossil** | BurJuman (04 352 8699), Deira City Centre (04 295 0108) |
| **G2000** | Al Ghurair City (04 221 5023), BurJuman (04 355 2942), Reef Mall (04 224 1119) |
| **Gerry Webber** | Deira City Centre (04 295 4914), Wafi Mall (04 324 3899) |
| **Giordano** | BurJuman (04 351 3866), Deira City Centre (04 295 0959), Karama Centre (04 336 8312), Wafi Mall (04 324 2852), Al Ghurair City (04 223 7904) |
| **GO Sports** | Ibn Battuta Shopping Mall (04 368 5344), Mall of the Emirates (04 341 3251) |
| **Golf House** | BurJuman (04 351 4801), Deira City Centre (04 295 0501), Lamcy Plaza (04 334 5945) |
| **Grand Optics** | Mall of the Emirates (04 341 0351), Carrefour (04 393 6133), Deira City Centre (04 295 4699) |
| **Guess** | Mall of the Emirates (04 341 1177), Deira City Centre (04 295 2577) |
| **Gulf Greetings** | Al Bustan Centre (04 263 2771), Spinneys (04 394 0397), Wafi Mall (04 324 5618), BurJuman (04 351 9613), Deira City Centre (04 295 9627), Mall of the Emirates (04 347 6888) |
| **H&M** | Deira City Centre (04 295 7549), Ibn Battuta Shopping Mall (04 364 9819), Mall of the Emirates (04 341 5880) |
| **Habitat** | Jumaira Plaza (04 344 7456), Near Spinneys Distribution Centre (04 340 4996), Near Spinneys Distribution Centre (04 340 4996) |
| **Hamac** | Ibn Battuta Shopping Mall (04 368 5410), Dubai Marine Beach Resort & Spa (04 345 1167) |
| **Hang Ten** | Mall of the Emirates (04 341 3322), BurJuman (04 351 9285), Deira City Centre (04 295 5449) |
| **Heatwaves** | Ibn Battuta Shopping Mall (04 366 9722), Jumaira Plaza (04 344 9489), Le Meridien Dubai (04 399 3161), Town Centre (04 342 0445) |
| **Home Centre** | Mercato (04 344 2266), Reef Mall (04 222 7755) |
| **House of Prose** | Ibn Battuta Shopping Mall (04 368 5526), Jumaira Plaza (04 344 9021) |
| **Hugo Boss** | Emirates General Market (04 295 5281), Mercato (04 342 2021), Twin Towers (04 227 7177) |
| **ID Design** | Mall of the Emirates (04 341 3434), Sharjah Road (04 266 6751) |
| **iStyle** | Dubai Festival City (04 232 9979), Ibn Battuta Shopping Mall (04 366 9797) |
| **Jacky's Electronics** | Deira City Centre (04 294 9480), Ibn Battuta Shopping Mall (04 368 5080), Al Garhoud (04 282 1822) |
| **Jashanmal Bookstores** | The Village Mall (04 344 5770), Mall of the Emirates (04 340 6789), Wafi Mall (04 324 4800) |
| **Jenny Rose** | Beach Centre (04 349 0902), Mall of the Emirates (04 341 0577) |
| **Jennyfer** | Ibn Battuta Shopping Mall (04 368 5125), Al Ghurair City (04 227 1208), Lamcy Plaza (04 337 2924) |

**489**

| | |
|---|---|
| **Jumbo Electronics** | Mall of the Emirates (04 341 0101), Media City, Bld 2, Unit-Retail 4 (04 336 7999), Opp. Ramada Hotel (04 352 3555), Qusais (04 261 6626), Shk Zayed Road (04 332 8315), Wafi Mall (04 324 2077), Karama (04 336 9208) |
| **Karen Millen** | Deira City Centre (04 295 5007), Palm Strip (04 345 6703) |
| **Kookai** | Wafi Mall (04 324 9936), Deira City Centre (04 295 2598) |
| **La Perla** | BurJuman (04 355 1251), Mall of the Emirates (04 341 3070) |
| **La Senza** | BurJuman (04 351 5353), Lamcy Plaza (04 335 3580), Mall of the Emirates (04 340 7004) |
| **Leather Palace** | BurJuman (04 351 5251), Al Ghurair City (04 222 6770), Hamarain Centre (04 266 7176), Mall of the Emirates (04 341 0814) |
| **Levis** | BurJuman (04 351 6728), Deira City Centre (04 295 9943), Mall of the Emirates (04 341 4050) |
| **Levis Outlet** | Al Khaleej Centre (04 359 6770), Mall of the Emirates (04 341 4747) |
| **Lifco** | Al Garhoud (04 286 8685), Nr Al Moosa Tower (04 332 7899) |
| **Lifestyle** | Downtown Bur Dubai (04 351 0177), Reef Mall (04 227 4009), Ibn Battuta Shopping Mall (04 368 5699), Mall of the Emirates (04 341 0523) |
| **Liwa** | BurJuman (04 351 5353), Deira City Centre (04 295 3988) |
| **Liz Claiborne** | Deira City Centre (04 294 0011), Ibn Battuta Shopping Mall (04 368 5900), Mall of the Emirates (04 340 7575) |
| **Lulu Hypermarket** | Deira (04 298 8876), Nr Dubai Municipality (04 336 7070) |
| **MAC** | Deira City Centre (04 295 7704), Ibn Battuta Shopping Mall (04 368 5966), Mercato (04 344 9536), Wafi Mall (04 324 4112), BurJuman (04 351 2880) |
| **Magrudy's** | Jumeira Beach Rd (04 344 4192), Spinneys (04 351 1777), Ibn Battuta Shopping Mall (04 366 9770), Deira City Centre (04 295 7744) |
| **Mahallati Jewellery** | Mall of the Emirates (04 341 0787), Mercato (04 344 4771), Gold Souk (04 226 7023) |
| **Mango** | BurJuman (04 355 5770), Deira City Centre (04 295 0182), Mall of the Emirates (04 341 4324) |
| **Marina Gulf** | Deira City Centre (04 295 9570), Spinneys (04 394 2541), Al Barsha Rd (04 347 8940), Souk Madinat Jumeirah (04 368 6050), Mall of the Emirates (04 341 0314) |
| **MMI** | Mall of the Emirates (04 341 0371), Spinneys (04 352 3091), Silicon Oasis (04 326 4583), Nr Al Hamra Fort Hotel (07 244 7403), Khalid Bin Waleed Street, Bur Dubai (04 393 5738), Ibn Battuta Shopping Mall (04 368 5626), Green Community (04 885 4550), Al Maskan Bldg, Al Karama (04 335 1722), Umm Suqeim (04 394 1678), Deira (04 294 0390), Shk. Zayed Road (04 321 1223) |
| **Marks & Spencer** | Dubai Festival City (04 206 6466), Salah Al Din Rd, Al Futtaim Centre (04 222 2000), Wafi Mall (04 324 5145) |
| **Marlboro Classics** | Ibn Battuta Shopping Mall (04 368 5590), BurJuman (04 351 3288), Mall of the Emirates (04 341 0545) |
| **Marlin** | Sheikh Zayed Rd (04 338 6866), Port Rashid Rd (04 334 6664) |
| **Massimo Dutti** | BurJuman (04 351 3391), Deira City Centre (04 295 4788), Mall of the Emirates (04 341 3151), Mercato (04 344 7158) |
| **Max** | Khalid Bin Al Waleed Str (04 397 5111), Abu Hail Center (04 266 8660), Ibn Battuta Shopping Mall (04 368 5435) |
| **Mexx** | Mall of the Emirates (04 341 1990), BurJuman (04 355 1881), Deira City Centre (04 295 4873) |

| | |
|---|---|
| **Mikyajy** | Deira City Centre (04 295 7844), Ibn Battuta Shopping Mall (04 366 9834), Mall of the Emirates (04 341 4277), Souk Madinat Jumeirah (04 366 8888) |
| **Milano** | Mercato (04 344 9517), Deira City Centre (04 294 0011), Al Ghurair City (04 222 8545), Ibn Battuta Shopping Mall (04 368 5981), Mall of the Emirates (04 340 7575) |
| **Mirage Glass** | Nr Gold & Diamond Park (04 347 0320), Souk Madinat Jumeirah (04 368 6207) |
| **Miss Sixty** | Mall of the Emirates (04 311 4600), Wafi Mall (04 324 1998) |
| **Monsoon** | Mall of the Emirates (04 341 0479), BurJuman (04 355 2205), Deira City Centre (04 295 0725), Wafi Mall (04 327 9801) |
| **Mont Blanc** | Mall of the Emirates (04 341 4451), Ibn Battuta Shopping Mall (04 368 5584), BurJuman (04 355 7377), Deira City Centre (04 295 4308), Wafi Mall (04 327 9970) |
| **Mothercare** | Mall of the Emirates (04 340 7575), Lamcy Plaza (04 334 0742), Spinneys (04 394 0228), Ibn Battuta Shopping Mall (04 368 5921), Deira City Centre (04 295 9061), BurJuman (04 352 8916), Al Ghurair City (04 223 8176), Jumeirah Centre (04 349 4019) |
| **Motivi** | Mall of the Emirates (04 340 7575), Ibn Battuta Shopping Mall (04 368 5900) |
| **Mr Price** | Reef Mall (04 224 0244), Lamcy Plaza (04 335 9999) |
| **National Iranian Carpets** | Al Nasr Square, Deira Tower (04 221 9800), Deira City Centre (04 295 0576), Mall of the Emirates (04 341 1904), Souk Madinat Jumeirah (04 368 6003) |
| **Nayomi** | Ibn Battuta Shopping Mall (04 366 9832), Wafi Mall (04 324 5141), Lamcy Plaza (04 335 8841), Al Ghurair City (04 227 2337), Mercato (04 344 9120) |
| **Next** | BurJuman (04 351 0026), Deira City Centre (04 295 2280), Ibn Battuta Shopping Mall (04 368 5971), Lamcy Plaza (04 335 0262), Mall of the Emirates (04 340 3898), Mercato (04 344 8016) |
| **Nine West** | Mall of the Emirates (04 341 0244), Al Ghurair City (04 221 1484), Town Centre (04 344 0038), Mercato (04 349 1336), Ibn Battuta Shopping Mall (04 368 5097), BurJuman (04 351 6214), Lamcy Plaza (04 337 4575), Deira City Centre (04 295 6887) |
| **Oasis** | Deira City Centre (04 294 0011), Ibn Battuta Shopping Mall (04 368 5956), Mall of the Emirates (04 340 7575), Wafi Mall (04 324 9074) |
| **Oltre** | Ibn Battuta Shopping Mall (04 368 5900), Mall of the Emirates (04 340 7575) |
| **Omega** | Deira City Centre (04 295 3623), Mall of the Emirates (04 341 4545) |
| **Organic Foods & Café** | Opp Al Hana Centre (04 398 9410), Greens (04 361 7974) |
| **Oui** | Wafi Mall (04 324 2167), Deira City Centre (04 295 3906) |
| **Pablosky** | Lamcy Plaza (04 336 2583), Mercato (04 344 7816), Reef Mall (04 224 2252), Ibn Battuta Shopping Mall (04 368 5085), BurJuman (04 359 6330) |
| **Paper Moon** | Al Ghurair City (04 223 4415), Al Mina Rd, Nr Capitol Hotel (04 345 4888), Town Centre (04 344 5998) |
| **Paris Gallery** | BurJuman (04 359 7774), Wafi Mall (04 324 2121), Town Centre (04 342 2555), Lamcy Plaza (04 336 2000), Ibn Battuta Shopping Mall (04 368 5500), Deira City Centre (04 295 5550), Al Bustan Centre (04 261 1288), Hamarain Centre (04 268 8122) |
| **Peacocks** | Lamcy Plaza (04 337 7321), Ibn Battuta Shopping Mall (04 368 5931) |
| **Pet's Delight** | Arabian Ranches (04 361 8184), Emirates Hills (04 361 7767) |
| **Planet Nutrition** | Deira City Centre (04 294 5889), Spinneys (04 394 4108) |

**491**

**Plug-Ins** ◄ Al Ghurair City (04 228 3657), BurJuman (04 351 3919),
Souk Madinat Jumeirah (04 368 6131)

**Polo Ralph Lauren** ◄ Deira City Centre (04 294 1200), BurJuman (04 352 5311)

**Porsche Design** ◄ Mall of the Emirates (04 341 0899), Deira (04 222 8806),
Jumeirah Beach Hotel (04 348 0648), Deira City Centre (04 295 7652)

**PrettyFIT** ◄ Deira City Centre (04 295 0790), Mercato (04 344 0015)

**Pride of Kashmir** ◄ Souk Madinat Jumeirah (04 368 6109), Mercato (04 342 0270),
Mall of the Emirates (04 341 4477), Deira City Centre (04 295 0655)

**Prima Gold** ◄ BurJuman (04 355 1988), Deira City Centre (04 295 0497)

**Promod** ◄ BurJuman (04 351 4477), Deira City Centre (04 295 7344),
Mall of the Emirates (04 341 4944), Mercato (04 344 6941)

**Pull and Bear** ◄ Deira City Centre (04 295 3525), Mercato (04 344 0518),
Mall of the Emirates (04 341 4234)

**Pumpkin Patch** ◄ Uptown Mirdif (04 288 7629), Mall of the Emirates (04 341 3633),
Lamcy Plaza (04 337 1006), Dubai Outlet Mall (04 425 9843), Dubai Festival City
(04 232 6620), Al Ghurair City (04 234 0931), BurJuman (04 351 0445)

**Pure Gold** ◄ Ibn Battuta Shopping Mall (04 368 5584), Mercato (04 349 2400)

**Radio Shack** ◄ Deira City Centre (04 295 2127), Mall of the Emirates (04 341 3337)

**Rasasi** ◄ BurJuman (04 351 2757), Deira City Centre (04 295 0670),
Al Ghurair City (04 222 9109)

**Red Earth** ◄ Al Ghurair City (04 227 9696), Bin Sougat Centre (04 285 8653),
Deira City Centre (04 295 1887), Mercato (04 344 9439)

**Regal Traders** ◄ Al Satwa (04 353 2320), Downtown Bur Dubai (04 355 1742)

**River Island** ◄ Deira City Centre (04 295 4413), Ibn Battuta Shopping Mall (04 368 5961),
Mall of the Emirates (04 340 9115)

**Rivoli Group** ◄ BurJuman (04 355 5191), Ibn Battuta Shopping Mall (04 368 5583),
Mall of the Emirates (04 341 3121), Mercato (04 344 6918), Wafi City (04 324 6675)

**Rodeo Drive** ◄ Al Bustan Rotana Hotel (04 282 4006), Mall of the Emirates (04 340 0347),
BurJuman (04 355 5204), Boulevard at Emirates Towers (04 330 3500)

**Rossini** ◄ Deira City Centre (04 295 4977), Wafi Mall (04 324 0402)

**Samsung Electronics** ◄ Downtown Bur Dubai (04 334 4973), Muraqqabat Rd (04 271 5599),
Salahuddin Rd (04 266 0640)

**Sara – Villeroy & Boch** ◄ Deira City Centre (04 295 0408), Wafi Mall (04 324 0100), BurJuman (04 351 7775)

**Sharaf DG** ◄ Times Square Center (04 341 8060), Deira City Centre (04 294 8483),
Ibn Battuta Shopping Mall (04 368 5115)

**Shoe Mart** ◄ Lamcy Plaza (04 337 9811), Near Jumbo Showroom (04 351 9560)

**Spinneys** ◄ Trade Centre Rd, Nr Bur Juman Centre (04 351 1777), Mercato (04 349 6900),
Mazaya Centre (04 321 2225), Bin Sougat Centre (04 286 2442), Al Wasl Rd (04 394
1657), Al Ghurair City (04 222 2886), Mirdif (04 288 0335), Oud Metha (04 335 7321),
Jumeira (04 367 4801), Dubai Marina (04 367 4810), Nr Ramada Htl (04 355 5250)

**Splash** ◄ Nr Maktoum Bridge (04 335 0525), Reef Mall (04 222 2512), Nr BurJuman (04 351
1130), Mall of the Emirates (04 341 0644), Deira City Centre (04 295 0553)

**Spring** ◄ Lamcy Plaza (04 334 7952), Mall of the Emirates (04 341 0311),
Reef Mall (04 228 4462), Ibn Battuta Shopping Mall (04 368 5244)

**Stradivarius** ◄ Deira City Centre (04 294 1221), Mall of the Emirates (04 341 3999)

| | |
|---|---|
| **Studio R** | Jumeirah Centre (04 344 1756), Lamcy Plaza (04 336 5651), Ibn Battuta Shopping Mall (04 366 9890), Deira City Centre (04 295 0261), BurJuman (04 351 3435), Jumeirah Beach Hotel (04 348 0830) |
| **Sun & Sand Sports** | Souk Madinat (04 368 6120), Al Ghurair City (04 222 7107), BurJuman (04 351 5376), Deira City Centre (04 295 5551), Ibn Battuta (04 366 9777), Jumeirah Centre (04 349 5820), Mall of the Emirates (04 341 0933), Bur Dubai (04 351 6222) |
| **Susan Walpole** | Mercato (04 344 8551), Mall of the Emirates (04 341 3227), Deira City Centre (04 294 3007), Dubai Festival City (04 375 0182) |
| **Swatch** | Al Ghurair City (04 224 8556), BurJuman (04 359 6109), Deira City Centre (04 295 3932), Ibn Battuta Shopping Mall (04 368 5580), Mall of the Emirates (04 341 4453), Wafi Mall (04 324 0518) |
| **Tag Heuer** | Wafi Mall (04 324 3030), BurJuman (04 355 9494) |
| **Tanagra** | Deira City Centre (04 295 0293), Wafi Mall (04 324 2340) |
| **THE One** | Mall of the Emirates (04 341 3777), BurJuman (04 351 4424), Wafi Mall (04 324 1224), Jumeira (04 342 2499) |
| **Tavola** | Umm Suqeim (04 394 8150), Mall of the Emirates (04 340 2933), Town Centre (04 361 8787) |
| **Thomsun Music** | Btw Oman Insurance & Mashreq Bank (04 266 8181), Wafi Mall (04 324 2322) |
| **Tiffany & Co** | Deira City Centre (04 295 3884), Mall of the Emirates (04 341 0655), BurJuman (04 359 0101) |
| **Titan Book Shop** | Radisson SAS Hotel, Deira Creek (04 227 1372), Holiday Centre Mall (04 331 8671) |
| **Tod's** | BurJuman (04 355 4417), Mall of the Emirates (04 341 3033) |
| **Topshop** | Deira City Centre (04 295 1804), Ibn Battuta Shopping Mall (04 368 5946), Mall of the Emirates (04 340 7212), Mercato (04 344 2677), Wafi Mall (04 327 9929) |
| **Toys R Us** | Deira (04 224 0000), Dubai Festival City (04 206 6552), Times Square Center (04 341 8383) |
| **Triumph** | Deira City Centre (04 295 2756), Mercato (04 344 4707) |
| **Union Co-Op** | Al Rashidiya (04 285 7514), Dubai (04 331 2314), Al Wasl (04 394 5999), Downtown Bur Dubai (04 398 0944), Ghesais (04 261 3100) |
| **Valencia** | Mall of the Emirates (04 341 3020), Twin Towers (04 221 6104), Deira City Centre (04 295 0990), Baniyas Centre, Al Maktoum St (04 223 2772) |
| **Vincci** | Deira City Centre (04 295 7684), BurJuman (04 351 7246) |
| **Virgin Megastore** | BurJuman (04 351 3358), Deira City Centre (04 295 8599), Mall of the Emirates (04 341 4353), Mercato (04 344 6971) |
| **Wallis** | Mall of the Emirates (04 340 7575), Deira City Centre (04 294 0011), Ibn Battuta Shopping Mall (04 368 5976) |
| **Watch House** | Mall of the Emirates (04 341 0354), BurJuman (04 352 8699), Deira City Centre (04 295 0108) |
| **The White Company** | Deira City Centre (04 295 6180), Dubai Festival City (04 232 5506), Mall of the Emirates (04 341 0493), Wafi City (04 327 9110) |
| **Women'secret** | BurJuman (04 359 9447, Deira City Centre (04 295 9665) |
| **Woolworths** | Deira City Centre (04 295 5900), Ibn Battuta Shopping Mall (04 368 5104) |
| **Yateem Opticians** | Al Diyafah Rd (04 345 3405), BurJuman (04 352 2067), Al Ghurair Centre (04 228 1787), Bur Dubai (04 353 5333), Boulevard at Emirates Towers (04 330 3301) |
| **Zara** | BurJuman (04 351 3332), Deira City Centre (04 294 0839), Mall of the Emirates (04 341 3171) |
| **Zara Home** | BurJuman (04 359 5598), Mall of the Emirates (04 341 4184), Palm Strip (04 346 0020) |

SOME EXPERIENCES FILL YOU UP.
OTHERS LEAVE YOU HUNGRY FOR MORE.

Welcome to a delectable hotel experience. At The Palace, splendour is on the menu wherever you go. Thiptara serves the most exotic Royal Thai cuisine. Ewaan is a fresh breeze of Mediterranean delights. And Asado brings you live music and premium Argentinean meat cuts.
**The Palace - The Old Town. It's not all you need. It's all you want.**

www.sofitel.com

THE PALACE
THE OLD TOWN
For reservations call: +971 4 428 7800

# Going Out

# Going Out

### Single In The City

*Dubai, like many cities, is not the easiest place to meet people if you're single. But help is at hand: Table 4 Six (www.table4six.net) is a social service that will match you with like-minded people for a group dinner, and there is also he Bridget Jones Club (p.375) – a raucous club for single girls.*

## Going Out

As you'd expect from a bustling multicultural metropolis, Dubai has a wide range of options when it comes to eating, drinking, and socialising. With almost 300 independent reviews, this Going Out section covers restaurants, cafes, bars, pubs, and clubs, and provides details of cinemas, theatres, and live entertainment venues throughout the city.

From Arabic to Vietnamese, and from Indian to Italian, the city really does dish up the world on a plate. And whether you're after five-star finery or cheap and cheerful you'll find somewhere to suit. Bar flies won't be disappointed either, with plenty of high-class hangouts and no-nonsense pubs to choose from, while big-name DJs and regular dance events keep clubbers more than happy. The live entertainment scene does lag behind other cities somewhat, but with the opening of new theatres and venues, and more international names such as Kanye West being lured over to perform, it is improving all the time.

## Eating Out

### Emirati Etiquette

*Although it's definitely not expected in Dubai's Arabic restaurants, it is traditional to eat Emirati cuisine with your right hand, as this allows you to appreciate flavours more readily. In very authentic places, there are also no chairs, little in the way of cutlery and sometimes even no tables. Al Hadheera at Bab El Shams (p.503) is one place offering such a genuine experience. Every aspect of the restaurant, from the main course to the traditional desserts, and even the cooking and dining methods, is rooted firmly in tradition.*

### Eating & Drinking

Many of Dubai's most popular restaurants are located within hotels and leisure clubs, and no doubt their popularity is partly down to the fact that these are virtually the only outlets where you can drink alcohol with your meal. Look out for the Alcohol Available icon next to the reviews. There's quite a hefty mark-up on drinks, with a decent bottle of wine often costing as much as your meal.

The city has some superb independent restaurants and cafes that shouldn't be ignored just because they don't serve booze. Bottled water also seems to rocket in price in the five-star venues, and if you ask for water you'll often be given an imported brand, costing up to Dhs.40 a bottle. You should specify 'local' water when ordering, but even then you can expect to pay Dhs.10 or Dhs.20 for a bottle of water that costs less than Dhs.2 in the supermarket.

### Restaurant or Bar?

With so many competing bars and restaurants in Dubai, many venues try to be all things to all people. Bars have restaurants and restaurants have bars, clubs and cafes have a la carte food and you'll find pubs in five-star surroundings. This means

## Cuisine List – Quick Reference

| | | | | | |
|---|---|---|---|---|---|
| American | p.500 | International | p.523 | Portuguese | p.554 |
| Arabic/Lebanese | p.503 | Italian | p.538 | Russian | p.554 |
| British | p.508 | Japanese | p.546 | Seafood | p.554 |
| Chinese | p.508 | Korean | p.549 | Singaporean | p.557 |
| Dinner Cruises | p.510 | Latin American | p.549 | Spanish | p.558 |
| European | p.512 | Mediterranean | p.550 | Sri Lankan | p.558 |
| Far Eastern | p.512 | Mexican | p.551 | Steakhouses | p.559 |
| Filipino | p.516 | Moroccan | p.551 | Tex Mex | p.560 |
| Fish & Chips | p.517 | Pakistani | p.552 | Thai | p.560 |
| French | p.517 | Persian | p.552 | Turkish | p.566 |
| German | p.518 | Pizzerias | p.553 | Vegetarian | p.566 |
| Indian | p.520 | Polynesian | p.553 | Vietnamese | p.566 |

*Top Tips*
*There are more restaurants and bars in Dubai than you can shake a chopstick at, and this section is bursting with reviews of almost 300 venues. But what if the taxi is waiting and you simply don't have time to read every write-up? Well fear not – just look out for some of our recommendations in the following categories: Alfresco (p.498), Sports Bars (p.573), Cocktails (p.538), Karaoke (p.581) and Live Music (p.592).*

*Night of Romance*
*Dubai is overflowing with excellent eateries and beautiful bars. If you are looking for a truly romantic experience check out the following intimate spots perfect for candlelit liaisons: Tagine (p.551), Pierchic (p.556), Vu's (p.550), Medzo (p.550), Teatro (p.536) and La Baie (p.556).*

*Dressing Up*
*Generally speaking shorts and T-shirts are a no-no for Dubai's bars and restaurants, and even some pubs will frown at your beach-bum attire. While trainers aren't strictly out ruled it will depend on the whole ensemble. Dubai's dress code is on the smarter side - more beautiful than bohemian - so shine your shoes when you're stepping out.*

that while a certain outlet may be famed for its late-night activities, it may also have an excellent restaurant. For a list of bars with good food see p.585, for restaurants with good bars see p.542, and for bars and restaurants that transform into nightclubs, see p.591.

## Hygiene

Food and drink outlets in Dubai are subject to regular checks by the Municipality, and unclean outlets are warned to either scrub up or shut down. You can be fairly confident that wherever you eat will meet basic health and hygiene requirements.

## Special Deals & Theme Nights

Many Dubai restaurants and bars dedicate one evening a week to a promotion. Details of some of the best deals can be found in All You Can Eat & Drink on the next page. Another Dubai institution is Friday Brunch – for a set price you get to take multiple visits to a huge buffet serving both breakfast food (British fry-ups alongside continental and local choices) and lunch with roasts, curries and international dishes. For more on Friday Brunch and a list of recommended outlets, see p.573.
Ladies' Nights (p.587) are big in Dubai – usually on Tuesdays or Wednesdays, ladies get a few free drinks in various locations around town – a bit of careful planning and you can go the whole night without paying for a single drink. And of course, wherever there are crowds of tipsy ladies, the fellas are never far behind.

## Tax, Service Charges & Tipping

Look out for the small print at the bottom of your menu – you may spot the dreaded 'prices are subject to 10% service charge and 10% municipality tax'. In most hotel restaurants and bars these extras are already included, but in an independent outlet they may appear as an additional charge. The 10% service charge is perhaps incorrectly named as often it isn't passed on to the staff, and you have no option of withholding it if you receive poor service. If you want to reward the waiting staff directly then the standard rule of a 10%-12.5% tip will be appreciated, but give them cash personally, or your tip may go straight in the till.

## Restaurant Listing Structure

Dubai is growing, and with it the choice of venues for dining, drinking and dancing. Reviewing every outlet would fill a whole book in itself (check out the beautiful restaurant and bar guide Posh Nosh, Cheap Eats & Star Bars also by Explorer Publishing), so the Going Out section features a select 300 venues. Each review attempts to give an idea of the food, service, decor and ambience, while those venues that really excel get a yellow star (see right).
Primarily the restaurants have been categorised by cuisine (in alphabetic order) but if you want to go out for a specific occassion, see 'Alfresco' (p.498), 'Cocktails' (p.538), 'Karaoke' (p.581), 'Live Music' (p.592), 'Night of Romance' (p.497) and 'Sports Bars' (p.573).
If you want to plan your evening around a particular location - maybe you have guests in town and you want to dine in their hotel or a hotel nearby - then simply turn

### The Yellow Star

The natty yellow star seen to the right is our way of highlighting places that we think merit extra praise. It might be the atmosphere, the food, the cocktails, the music or the crowd, but any review that you see with the star attached is somewhere that we think is a bit special.

### Quick Reference Icons

| | |
|---|---|
| 🚫 | No Credit Cards Accepted |
| 👶 | Kids Welcome |
| 🌳 | Alfresco option |
| 🙂 | Have a Happy Hour |
| 🎵 | Live Music |
| 🍷 | Serves Alcohol |
| 🚚 | Will Deliver |

**497**

to the index at the back of this book. Each of the hotels will have a list of all its outlets and their cuisine, or you can turn to the Restaurant or Bar section on p.500. As a rule, non-English names retain their prefix (Al, Le, La and El) in their alphabetical placement, while English names are listed by titles, ignoring prefixes such as 'The'.

## Alfresco

As soon as it's cool enough (typically October until May), diners head outside. Popular spots include Al Mallah (p.503), Barasti (p.576), Boardwalk (p.526), Bussola (p.538), Century Village (various), Madinat Jumeirah (various), Medzo (p.550) and The Terrace (p.536).

### Privileged

With so much choice it's no surprise that many places offer privilege cards to keep you coming back. The benefits vary so call to find out what you get and whether you have to pay for the card. The Wafi Advantage Card is a favourite as it gives discounts on shopping and restaurants, and it's free. Dine in By Hyatt is another popular loyalty scheme - for every Dhs.10 you spend, you get Dhs.1 Collected points are converted into rewards that can be used in Hyatt outlets across Dubai.

## Hidden Charges

It doesn't happen often, but every now and then you'll find that the 'complimentary' water or bread basket that was placed on your table makes an appearance on your bill, even though you didn't actually order these items. Don't pay for stuff you didn't order, and when you get your bill read the small print - it is normal to pay 10% municipality tax and a service charge of 10-15%, but these are usually included in the menu prices.

## Vegetarian Food

Vegetarians should be pleasantly surprised by the variety of cuisine available in restaurants in Dubai. Due to the large number of the subcontinent population who are vegetarian by religion, numerous Indian restaurants offer a range of cooking styles and tasty vegetarian dishes. Try Saravana Bhavan (p.523) and Aryaas (p.520) in Karama. In other restaurants (even in steakhouses), you'll find at least one or two vegetarian options. Also Arabic food, although dominated by meat in the main courses, offers a staggering range of mezze that are mostly vegetarian.

Dubai's cafes are also great for vegetarian food. Of particular note are the Lime Tree Café, (p.570) THE One (p.571) and Celebrities (p.526), which offers fine dining and a completely separate vegetarian menu. One notable newcomer to the scene is Magnolia (p.566) in Madinat Jumeirah, which offers high-class organic, vegetarian food.

A word of warning: if you are a strict veggie, confirm that your meal is completely meat free. Some restaurants cook their 'vegetarian' selection with animal fat or on the same grill as the meat dishes. Also, in some places you may need to check the ingredients of seemingly vegetarian items.

### Room Service

Most fastfood outlets deliver, but you can also order through Room Service, which publishes a list of menus from participating restaurants, (www.roomservice-uae.com). Delivery time is between 30 minutes and an hour, with a minimum order of between Dhs.60 and Dhs.80, depending on your location. There's also a Dhs.25 delivery charge per outlet. Call toll free on 800 4788.

## All You Can Eat & Drink

While the concept of 'all you can eat and drink' may sound a little on the cheap and nasty side, in Dubai buffet deals are the best of both worlds. For an all-inclusive price you can stuff your face, get very tipsy and the food is of an a la carte standard. In the table on the left is a selection of some of the best deals in town.

### All You Can Eat & Drink

| Bamboo Lagoon, Deira | 04 262 4444 | Far Eastern |
| Benihana, Garhoud | 04 282 0000 | Sushi, Teppanyaki |
| Brauhaus, Satwa | 04 345 5888 | German |
| Come Prima, Garhoud | 04 282 0000 | Italian |
| Creekside, Deira | 04 207 1750 | Japanese Seafood, Sushi, Teppanyaki (food only) |
| Flavours on Two, Trade Centre 1 | 04 343 8000 | Asian, British, Seafood & Spit Roast, Pasta |
| Spice Island, Hor Al Anz | 04 262 5555 | Asian, BBQ, Japanese, Mongolian, Seafood, Steak |
| Sushi Sushi, Garhoud | 04 282 9908 | Sushi, Sashimi, Tempura, Teppanyaki (food only) |

### Discount Delights

The Entertainer, a book full of 'buy one, get one free' vouchers could also save you thousands of dirhams on a year of wining and dining. Call 04 390 2866 or visit www.theentertainer.ae for more information. Always check the expiry date on the book before you buy it though.

# EXPERIENCE
# AN AWARD WINNING
# FORMULA

# 10 VENUES. 1 DESTINATION.

Unrivalled by any other destination in the city, The Fairmont Dubai
offers ten diverse and unique award winning dining and entertainment venues;
all conveniently located within one fabulous location.

For more information and for restaurant reservations,
visit **www.fairmont.com/dubai** or call **+971 4 332 5555**.

## American

Other options **Tex-Mex** p.560

*Sheikh Issa Tower*
Trade Centre 1
Map 7 F2

### Applebees ▶ p.501

*04 343 7755* | www.anemco.com

Applebee's is very much an all-American family restaurant where huge portions are offered up by enthusiastic, smiley staff in a bright, welcoming setting. Big screen TVs are scattered around the restaurant showing the latest US sports and the walls are filled with photos and souvenirs of the US of A. The menu consists of all you'd expect, with the focus on Tex-Mex grills, burgers and sandwiches, but there are also sufficient options to keep vegetarians happy. The desserts are particularly impressive and the kids' menu has plenty to choose from. To finish off, the Oreo milkshake is a fine way to end your calorie overload. Wrap up warm though – the air conditioning here works a bit too well.

*Saleh Bin Lahej Bld*
Al Garhoud
Map 11 C4 129

### Chili's

*04 282 8484* | www.chilis.com

If you're looking for a fast-paced meal in a buzzing and frenetic atmosphere, then get down to Chili's. Decorated with Americana knick-knacks, the restaurant is bright and lively with TVs, music, and plenty of seating in booths or at the 'bar'. The varied menu offers soups, salads, steaks, fajitas, and sandwiches. There's a low-carb menu and inexpensive kids' dishes, along with table activities to keep them busy. A popular destination with families and groups of friends, they also offer home delivery and takeaway.
Other Locations: Al Ghurair City (04 229 6760); BurJuman (04 352 2900); Deira City Centre (04 295 9559); Dubai Internet City (04 390 1495); Jumeirah Beach Centre (04 344 1300); Mall of the Emirates (04 341 3344); Sahara Centre, Sharjah (06 531 8890); Dubai Home Delivery (04 282 8303).

*The Jumeirah
Beach Hotel*
Umm Suqeim
Map 6 B1 17

### Go West

*04 406 8999* | www.jumeirah.com

If you like steaks and Tex-Mex, big portions and calorific courses (starters are as big as the mains; mains are more like shared platters and desserts make your top button pop) all wrapped up in a cowboy hat then you'll love Go West. Television screens show old classic westerns and there are a few prized wagon booths (which are pretty life-like) that seal the deal. Kids will love the attention to detail and the live music focusing on light rock 'n roll adds a bit of fun for the oldies! The staff come wearing big grins and accommodating attitudes, adding neatly to the fun of the affair.

*Uptown Mirdif*
Map15 B2 82

### Gourmet Burger Kitchen

*04 288 9057*

Dubai loves its fast food, but how much does it like its 'healthy' fast food? Quite a lot if the success of Gourmet Burger Kitchen in Mirdif is anything to go by. An extension of the GBK chain that has proved so popular in London, this branch follows the same simple formula – good juicy meat, fresh produce, an eclectic choice of toppings and sauces, and wholesome fries, all served in a pleasant loungey setting. The menu is scribbled on the blackboard, you simply pick your favourite, from among many others: avocado and bacon, chilli, cajun, blue cheese, Jamaican and lamb. Unusually, vegetarians are well catered for; there are three excellent choices: falafel, aubergine and goat's cheese, and portabella (mushrooms, sweet red peppers, rocket). There's miniature burgers for kids, fresh juices with GBK milkshakes available in chocolate, vanilla, strawberry, banana and lime flavours. Slouch inside on leather sofas or head outside to enjoy one of the best locations in Uptown Mirdif's piazza. There's another branch in Dubai International Financial Centre  (800 287437).

**Open on**

**Sheikh Zayed Road**
Tel : 04 – 343 77 55

*Eatin' Good in the Neighborhood®*

*Jct 5, Shk Zayed Rd*
*Al Sufouh*
*Map 5 C2* 89

### Hard Rock Café

*04 399 2888* | *www.hardrock.com*

The Hard Rock Cafe's distinctive gigantic guitar that sits atop its entrance sets the tone for this well-known chain. Rock and roll memorabilia adorns all the walls, while the TVs in every corner cycle through various music videos. The menu is typical American/Tex-Mex fare with Texan-sized starters, and even larger main courses. In keeping with the American theme, the ethusiastic service comes with a smile, and the staff will ensure that your glasses remain filled and the kids' menu satisfies (and is equipped with crayons). The large space also suits big groups who want an order of fries and fun with their big night out!

*Opp Jumeirah Centre*
*Jumeira*
*Map 7 E1* 88

### Johnny Rockets

*04 344 7859* | *www.johnnyrockets.com*

If you want a taste of good old American food, with a 'Back to the Future' movie feel, then Johnny Rockets is just the place. This 1950s style diner offers a lively yet casual dining experience. Freshly cooked burgers and fries are washed down with probably the best milkshakes in town. It's popular with a broad cross section of society, and the real challenge is trying to get a table or a place at the counter on Friday afternoons. To ensure you control the soundtrack, get there early and bag a booth with a jukebox.
Other Locations: Mall of the Emirates (04 341 2380); Dubai Marina (04 368 2339).

*Wafi City*
*Umm Hurair*
*Map 10 E4* 73

### Planet Hollywood

*04 324 4777* | *www.planethollywood-dubai.com*

With bright colours, lots of space and super-friendly staff, this Dubai branch of the popular chain is a good place for lunch or dinner with the kids. The menu is pretty much as you would expect it – huge, American-style portions of carb-carnivore combos with some healthy and vegetarian options, but generally calorie-laden. The kids' menu will definitely put smiles on faces and have your little 'uns jumping with joy and the Friday brunch is particularly popular thanks to the movies, toys and face painting. The movie memorabilia and bright decor is so tacky that it becomes part of the fun!

*Jebel Ali Shooting Club*
*Jebel Ali*
*Map 3 A2* 216

### Shooters

*04 883 6555* | *www.jebelali-international.com*

Shooters is a peaceful retreat popular with club members and guests from nearby Jebel Ali Golf Resort & Spa. This modern western saloon with denim-clad waiters is surprisingly quiet despite the gunfire (a glass wall gives unobstructed views of the five floodlit shooting ranges below). The menu is simple yet sophisticated, mainly offering fish and steak. King-size prawns and lobster tails are a firm favourite but save room for one of the tempting traditional American desserts. Although a little off the beaten track, friendly staff ensure Shooters is a pleasant venue for quiet dining.

Planet Hollywood

Chilis (p.500)

## Arabic/Lebanese

Other options **Moroccan** p.551, **Persian** p.552, **Turkish** p.566

*Al Boom*
*Tourist Village*
*Umm Hurair*
*Map 13 C1* **38**

### Al Dahleez

*04 324 3000* | *www.alboom.ae*

Who hasn't wondered about the Al Boom Tourist Village when crossing the Garhoud Bridge? Inside you'll find Al Dahleez, an Arabic dining experience where diners can have it both ways – one restaurant, two buffets, one price. On one side you have authentic Arabic cuisine; on the other, international. Mix and match or stick with one. For an extra charge, you can add barbecue to your buffet experience. It's a good place to take out-of-town visitors for a taste of the region's culinary delicacies, and there are plenty of locals on hand to attest to the authenticity of the food and experience.

*Bab Al Shams*
*Map 2 B4* **91**

### Al Hadheerah

*04 832 6699* | *www.babalshams.com*

Set around an open Arabian courtyard, Al Hadheerah has barasti walls, canvas canopies, throw rugs, rustic furniture and oil lamps all adding to the truly traditional feel. There is a choice of low cushion seating, regular dining tables or booths and alcoves for a more private occasion. The food here is typical Arabic in a buffet theme, with live-cooking stations, wood-fired stone ovens, spit roasts, hot and cold mezze and a fresh juice bar. Entertainment includes a live Arabic band and belly dancer, a falcon display and traditional henna painting, as well as camel rides. After dinner you can retire to one of the open fireplaces and enjoy a shisha to finish off the evening.

*Nr Al Nasr*
*Leisureland*
*Oud Metha*
*Map 10 E2* **124**

### Al Koufa

*04 335 1511* | *www.alkoufa.com*

Al Koufa is a popular restaurant and nightspot, especially with the Arab population, expat and local. The interior is massive, so it is quite nice to tuck yourself away at one of tables around the side until the place fills up. It normally starts livening up around 23:00, often with live performances (which is recorded for broadcast on local TV and attracts crowds of all ages). The menu offers great Arabic food and fruit juices, including the usual range of mezze, breads and manakish, as well as some dishes not normally found in a typical Arabic/Lebanese place including the odd Emirati dish. There is a cover charge of Dhs.30 if you plan on being there when the show starts.

*Al Diyafah St*
*Al Satwa*
*Map 8 A2* **111**

### Al Mallah

*04 398 4723*

Among the multitude of small Arabic joints across Dubai, this one stands out. Situated on one of the busiest streets in town, which comes alive in the evenings, Al Mallah offers great pavement dining with an excellent view of the world and his brothers cruising by in their Ferraris, Patrols and Corollas. The shawarmas and fruit juices are excellent here (and massive), the cheese and zatar manoushi exceedingly tasty, and they have possibly the biggest and best falafel in Dubai. Grab a fruit cocktail and an evening snack, or stay a while and order a bigger meal. Another branch of Al Mallah is located on Al Mateena Road, Deira (04 272 3431).

**Emirati Cuisine**

The Department of Tourism & Commerce Marketing (DTCM) is working closely with the Emirates Culinary Guild (ECG) and a few chefs to revive Emirati cuisine throughout Dubai. Truly local food has several distinct flavours, thanks to the country's trading past. Look out for tangs of cinnamon, saffron and turmeric along with nuts (almonds or pistachios), limes and dried fruit in the different mouthfuls.

**503**

**Century Village** ◄
*Al Garhoud*
*Map 13 E1* **47**

## Al Mazaj
*04 282 9952*

A great place to go if you crave the fruity aroma of shisha smoke in the night air and the tunes of a live Lebanese band, Mazaj is one of Dubai's most renowned hookah hangouts. The restaurant has an authentically styled interior with live Arabic music, while outside, the attractive dining area is situated among the fairy lit courtyard and leafy trees of Century Village. If you are here for food, you might be best advised to stick to the starters (which are wonderful), with enough on the menu to keep a leisurely evening going. Main courses, however, are pretty standard kebab house fare although generous nonetheless.

**Boulevard at** ◄
**Emirates Towers**
*Trade Centre 2*
*Map 7 F3* **46**

## Al Nafoorah
*04 319 8088* | *www.jumeirah.com*

A refreshing and unpretentious addition to the Emirates Towers, Al Nafoorah is a crisp, colonial, and busy Lebanese restaurant. Perfect for either a power lunch or an elegant dinner, the classic and understated atmosphere is ideal. The food is excellent and the menu is extensive with pages and pages of mezze and mains to tantalise, so come in a group and share the wide selection. After dinner, you can take a stroll round the Boulevard, or you can sit out on the terrace in awe of the towers looming above, smoke shisha and let the world unwind around you.

**Al Kawakeb Bld** ◄
*Trade Centre 2*
*Map 7 E3* **112**

## Al Safadi
*04 343 5333*

This spacious restaurant may not have all the trappings of five-star dining, but in Dubai that's not necessarily a bad thing. If you have had your fill of well-polished eateries and want to experience a more 'come as you are' style of local cuisine, then Al Safadi hits the spot. It's pretty basic, but what it lacks in imagination it makes up for in quality. The lights are bright and the customer turnover high, but relaxed dining is available outside where you can watch the world go by as you eat or smoke shisha. Another branch is on Al Rigga Road in Deira (04 227 9922).

**Beach Centre** ◄
*Jumeira*
*Map 7 E1* **80**

## Automatic
*04 349 4888*

For more than 26 years the Automatic chain of restaurants has been delivering great quality Arabic food in Dubai and throughout the Middle East. The usual vast range of mezze is accompanied by mountainous plates of salad, while main courses offer grilled meat, fish and kebabs that are tasty, come in good sized portions and are served fresh and hot to your table by the efficient and friendly waiting staff. The atmosphere is more minimalist in style but still clean and bright, with family friendly amenities that attract a mixed clientele.
Other locations: Jumeirah Tower (04 321 4465), Al Abbas Building (04 359 4300), Al Khalij Centre (04 355 0333), Al Riqqa St (04 227 7824), Bin Sougat (04 286 3022), Abu Hail Centre (04 265 0101), Jebel Ali Free Zone (04 881 0800).

**JW Marriott Hotel** ◄
*Deira*
*Map 11 E1* **18**

## Awafi
*04 607 7977* | *www.marriott.com*

If you can get over the slight whiff of chlorine, this is a lovely setting for a laid-back bite to eat. Situated

**Ramadan Timings**
During Ramadan, opening and closing times of restaurants change considerably. Because eating and drinking in public is forbidden during daylight hours, many places only open after sunset, then keep going well into the early hours. Restaurants in some hotels remain open, but will be screened off from public view. Live entertainment is not allowed, while some nightclubs remain open, dancefloors are closed.

# Restaurants

Asado (p.559)

Le Traiteur (p.512)

St Tropez Bistro (p.518)

Cubo (p.540)

The Terrace (p.536)

Focaccia (p.542)

around the Marriott's rooftop pool you can enjoy top-quality Arabic food underneath the stars with atmospheric, but not intrusive, traditional music soundtracking your evening. The menu includes the usual fare, with an ample selection of hot and cold mezze, grilled items, sandwiches and a selection from the tandoori oven. For those with a sweet tooth, the dessert selection is unfortunately limited, although you can enjoy a natural sugar rush by picking a delicious fresh juice. The atmosphere is extremely casual with low Arabic-style seating available and of course, a wide shisha menu.

*Grand Hyatt Dubai*
*Umm Hurair*
*Map 13 C1*

## Awtar

*04 317 1234* | *www.dubai.grand.hyatt.com*

The decor at this sophisticated Lebanese restaurant is the epitome of opulent Arabic elegance, with booths tastefully swathed in gold muslin, impeccably dressed tables and low lighting from ornate lanterns all conspiring to create an ambience of refined luxury. Smiling and helpful waiters hover attentively while you choose from an appealing selection of well-presented mezze. The main courses do not quite live up to the same standard, and can quite confidently be ignored in favour of double helpings of the tasty starters and traditional desserts. A band accompanies the refined clink of classy cutlery and after 22:00 a brightly attired belly dancer takes to the stage.

**Stretch In Style**

If you're feeling a bit flash (or are on a stag or hen party), you can rent a stretch Hummer or Lincoln from Dubai Exotic Limo so that you can arrive at your destination in style. See p.56.

*Bastakiya*
*Downtown Bur Dubai*
*Map 9 A2* 

## Bastakiah Nights

*04 353 7772* | *bastakr@eim.ae*

There are some meals where mood is almost as important as the food itself. Bastakiah Nights, a haven in the concrete jungle of Bur Dubai, combines the two effortlessly. As you enter the heavy wooden doors you are reminded that, despite the glitzy malls and luxurious hotels, this is still very much Arabia. The food is delectable, and you can choose from fixed menus or the various a la carte offerings. This is a magical place where local cuisine mingles with authentic local culture. There's no alcohol on the menu, but you'd be a fool to let that put you off.

*Fakhreldine*

*Park Hyatt Dubai*
*Creekside, Deira*
*Map 11 B4* 

## Cafe Arabesque

*04 602 1234* | *www.dubai.park.hyatt.com*

Cafe Arabesque is a lush, impeccably situated, elegant restaurant with opulent but tasteful decor, wonderful Middle Eastern cuisine and an unforgettable abundance of delectable mezze. Four tables, representing Jordan, Lebanon, Syria, and Turkey, are loaded with a dozen diverse mezze which are hardly cheap at Dhs.90 but unmissable nonetheless and made more affordable by the main courses which are generally half the price. Attractive Arabian

**506**

architecture, comfortable seating and pleasing views over the creek make dining here feel like a special occasion. End the evening by taking a moonlit stroll around the beautiful hotel and gardens, resplendent with water features and Arabesque charm.

**Marina Walk**
*Marsa Dubai*
*Map 5 B2* **57**

## Chandelier

*04 366 3606* | *www.chandelier-uae.com*

Set in the vibey Marina Walk, Chandelier has a stylish, modern interior and a very pleasant outdoor section. The alfresco lounge area overlooking the fountain has comfy seating with views out over the marina, making it a great spot for shisha after your meal. The food is good, with the menu offering an interesting mix of standard and unique fare, and a full range of (non-alcoholic) cocktails and juices. Service here is renowned as being leisurely, but as this is a great place to linger over a meal or a shisha, this is no great burden. Particularly atmospheric on the weekends when it's often packed.

> ### Cultural Meals
> Bastakiya is a great place to eat and simultaneously soak up local culture. This traditional part of the city is best experienced by strolling through the streets, visiting the museums and dining at one of the many cafes. A cultural and culinary experience rolled into one.

**Mövenpick Hotel**
*Bur Dubai*
*Oud Metha*
*Map 10 D3* **24**

## Fakhreldine

*04 335 0505* | *www.movenpick-hotels.com*

It can be disappointing when you go to a five-star Lebanese restaurant and the (very expensive) mixed grill you order tastes exactly the same as the Dhs.15 one you normally get from your local street cafe. No such worries with Fakhreldine – from your first dip into their creamy hummus to the last crumb of Arabic sweets at the end, the quality is apparent and the bill is less painful. The menu is extensive and gives you the opportunity to try many new dishes that you won't easily find anywhere else, and yet it still features the old favourites for those with less adventurous tastes. The decor is impressive, as is the gyrating belly dancer, making this a restaurant worth the glad-rags.

**Heritage &**
**Diving Village**
*Al Shindagha*
*Map 9 B1* **54**

## Kan Zaman

*04 393 9913* | *www.alkoufa.com*

With some of the best night views of Dubai creek, Kan Zaman offers an excellent Arabic menu and a rare chance to try some local food. As well as a full range of the usual Arabic mezze and mains on offer, there are also some traditional dishes from the Emirates. Local breads are served either with honey and dates or cheese, and the starters are good to share. Portions are large, but prices are low so it's great if you are in a group and can share a whole host of different dishes. There is seating available inside, but dining outside with the waterfront views is what draws the crowds night after night.

**Nr HSBC**
*Beach Rd*
*Jumeira*
*Map 7 C1* **94**

## Reem Al Bawadi

*04 394 7444* | *aymanshj@eim.ae*

The interior of this popular venue is traditionally decorated, with three majlis areas near the entrance where you can enjoy shisha and coffee before or after your meal. The food is Arabic, and the menu features all the usual fare plus some speciality dishes not found in many other restaurants around Dubai. They don't serve alcohol, but the place is always busy because of its reputation for good food and great shisha. A definite cultural experience, it's a perfect spot for newcomers or visitors to grab a slice of real Arabia.

**507**

# British

**Grosvenor House**
*Marsa Dubai*
*Map 5 B2* **10**

## Rhodes Mezzanine

**04 399 8888** | www.grosvenorhouse.lemeridien.com

Gary Rhodes is a British celebrity chef with vertical hair and a zealous mission to stop Johnny Foreigner carping on about the stodginess of UK cuisine. Four of his restaurants have picked up Michelin stars, while two brassieres have collected Bib Gourmand, the firm's award for moderately priced food. Mezzanine is not moderately priced, but the food is Michelin quality. The simple menu focuses on modern British classics, such as jam roly-poly, an excellent ox tail cottage pie and pork belly. Parts of the wine list run into four figures, but you can find decent bottles for around Dhs.200. The 'private' dining room is a large, white goldfish bowl in the centre of the room, which seats up to 10. A three course meal, with cheaper wines, should cost around Dhs.500 per head.

# Chinese

Other options **Far Eastern** p.512

**Radisson SAS Hotel**
*Deira Creek*
*Deira*
*Map 9 B4* **27**

## The China Club

**04 205 7333** | www.interconti.com

The China Club serves far eastern delights in a formal setting, where crisp table linen and subtle Asian decor set the tone, and top-notch waiters cater to your every whim. If you're in a small group request one of the booths lining the walls, or if in a large party then take your seat at one of the large tables in the centre. The extensive menu (which includes an impressive selection of carefully planned set menus) allows you to try exotic dishes, and there is also the usual Chinese favourites if you're feeling less adventurous. A dignified wine trolley provides a good choice of liquid refreshment.

**Nr Clock Tower R/A**
*Al Maktoum Rd*
*Deira*
*Map 11 C2* **128**

## China Sea

**04 295 9816**

China Sea is a hidden gem, offering truly authentic Chinese food at very reasonable prices. One side of the restaurant is a display area of fish and crabs in tanks as well as multitudes of different vegetables in chiller cabinets. At the back the workings of the kitchen are visible behind large glass windows. Even the noodles are prepared in full view. Start with a block of dough, add skilled stretching and folding and its amazing how fast a pile of fresh fine noodles can be created. This may not be the place for a cozy romantic meal but it's great for tasty and inexpensive Chinese food.

**Opp American Hospital**
*Oud Metha*
*Map 10 E2* **125**

## Chinese Treasure

**04 336 2525** | www.chinesetreasuredubai.com

In China, red is a lucky colour which considering everything from the ceiling to the lanterns and the tablecloths to the napkins at Chinese Treasure is red, should make it a pretty lucky find. Which could be the case depending upon how you look at it. It's above one of Dubai's seediest bars and there are so many mirrors you won't know if you're coming or going. The buffet is well rounded with appetisers, soups, and many choices of flavourful and clean Chinese food without MSG. The atmosphere may be a bit tacky for some, but many will find this place festive and perfect for quirky nights.

**Uptown Mirdif**
*Mirdif*
*Map 15 B2* **75**

## Da Shi Dai

**04 288 8314** | www.da-shi-dai.ae

A walk along the cobbled pathways of Uptown Mirdif will bring you to this refreshing Chinese eatery - it is beautifully decorated with serene tones and beautiful glass features rather than the red-lantern kitsch you might expect from a Chinese restaurant in a shopping centre. The food is refreshing too: gone are the large plates of glutinous noodles, oily fried rice and bright orange sweet and sour dishes, and in their place is a menu full of delectable Chinese specialities, all in small portions. Any one by itself would not satisfy, but the idea is to order a selection and enjoy various tastes in one sitting. And the idea works: load your table with delights such as crispy fried garlic prawn dumplings, bang bang chicken, spring onion cakes, a range of cheung feung, and a selection of noodle and rice dishes, and you won't be left hungry by the end. Da Shi Dai exceeds all expectations and definitely warrants many a return visit.

### Ramada Hotel
*Downtown Bur Dubai*
*Map 8 F3* **28**

## Dynasty

*04 351 9999* | *www.ramadadubai.com*

Dynasty serves standard but not dazzling Chinese cuisine. Szechuan, Cantonese and Peking dishes, with their characteristic degrees of spice, allow diners with diverse tastes to enjoy variations on a cuisine. A choice of four set menus enables the novice to experiment without committing to the comprehensive (but not overwhelming) a la carte menu. A neat, sophisticated space without any of the red lantern and lacquer decor usually associated with this cuisine, Dynasty is quietly tucked away at the far end of the hotel atrium, beneath the magnificent stained-glass window. Ultimately, like many hotel Chinese restaurants, the superior environment does not necessarily guarantee food or service of a very high standard.

### Nr Lamcy Plaza
*Oud Metha*
*Map 10 D2* **120**

## Lan Kwai Fong

*04 335 3680*

If you judge a good Chinese restaurant by the number of Chinese inside, then Lan Kwai Fong is worth exploring. Located between Lamcy Plaza and the Mövenpick Hotel, the restaurant's exhaustive menu includes a vast array of dim sum, clay pot, seafood, meat, duck and noodle dishes. The quality ingredients are fresh while the service might be a little on the casual side. The interior is a little dated, yet typical of any local suburban Chinese restaurant. Patrons can watch the kitchen staff at work through the big glass window at the rear of the seating area. Lan Kwai Fong is an unpretentious, inexpensive Chinese restaurant suitable for informal and casual dining occasions.

### Shangri-La Hotel
*Trade Centre 1*
*Map 7 E3* **32**

## Shang Palace

*04 405 2703* | *www.shangri-la.com*

Choose to people-watch from the balcony overlooking the Shangri-La's bustling entrance, or take a quieter position inside the circular dining room. The menu is extensive and has several entries not found in Dubai's typical Chinese restaurants. The food is delicious and the attentive and knowledgeable staff are available to guide newcomers through the numerous options. Familiar dishes are well prepared, and set menus are available. With shark fin soup, live seafood, dim sum and then some, this is certainly a place for something different. A well stocked bar also makes this a suitable venue in which to start an evening, or round one off.

### Mina A'Salam
*Umm Suqeim*
*Map 6 A1* **162**

## Zheng He's

*04 366 1599* | *www.jumeirah.com*

Zheng He's superb take on Chinese delicacies, together with its exquisite waterside spot, ensure a constant stream of Dubai's more affluent dwellers enjoying a taste of the orient. Exciting combinations used in dim sum and mini-roll starters are divine and complemented well with tangy dips and sauces. Traditional dishes with a twist are too good to pass up, while marinated fish and stir-fried meat are taken to new heights and the duck is arguably the best in town. The wine list is as thick as it is pricey, but in terms of culinary experience you certainly get what you pay for at Zheng He's.

**509**

# Dinner Cruises

Other options **Dhow Charters** p.333, **Creek Tours** p.248,
**Boat & Yacht Charters** p.277

*Radisson SAS Hotel*
*Deira Creek*
*Deira*
*Map 9 B3* **27**

## Al Mansour

*04 205 7333 | www.radissonsas.com*

This two-hour trip features an international buffet (alcohol available) and the traditional treats of live Arabic music and shisha. The buffet dinner, served on the rather dark lower deck, is a tribute to the variety of tourists who ride this dhow, with a mixture of Arabic, Indian, and European dishes. Shisha pipes are available on the outdoor upper deck, and can add to the atmosphere of watching both sides of the creek from a new vantage point. Be sure to consider the weather when booking the cruise, as even the air-conditioned dining area can be quite warm in summer.

*Nr British Embassy*
*Downtown Bur Dubai*
*Map 9 B3* **34**

## Bateaux Dubai ▶ p.511

*04 399 4994 | www.bateauxdubai.com*

From the moment you're welcomed aboard the sleek, glass-topped Bateaux Dubai, you become aware this is no ordinary creek cruise. The intimately lit interior reveals cosy tables sporting crisp white table linen and silver cutlery, and a baby grand piano. No matter where you sit, the full-length windows afford splendid views of the city beyond, and between courses you are encouraged to go out on deck and enjoy the open air. Diners choose three courses from the small but varied international menu, and the quality of the food (and drink) lives up to the five-star surroundings. A top pick for a romantic dinner or tourist treat. Departure is prompt so don't get left behind.

*Nr DCCI Building*
*Deira*
*Map 11 B1* **127**

## Creek Cruises

*04 393 9860 | www.creekcruises.com*

Whether you're the trendiest of talent spotters, the laziest of couch potatoes or the biggest of bar crawlers, you can't live in Dubai and not go on a dinner cruise. You might think it cheesy, you might think it should be reserved for tourists in white socks but the fact is the Dubai Creek is this city's most natural landmark. Sip your bar basic drink, fill up at the standard 'authentic' Arabian buffet, enjoy the live music and belly dancer, be mesmerised by the creekside sights and just go with the flow.

*Opp Dubai*
*Municipality HQ*
*Deira*
*Map 9 C4* **101**

## Creekside Leisure

*04 336 8406 | www.tour-dubai.com*

This floating majlis is an authentic dhow with a delightful upper deck, where guests can recline on traditional Arabic-cushioned seating and relax with a drink, watching the world drift by. Downstairs in an air-conditioned, glass-sided cabin, an adequate international buffet (with an Arabic slant) is served half way through the two-hour cruise. The route takes passengers up to the head of the creek at Shindagha, before turning around and cruising to the Maktoum Bridge then back to its original mooring by the Twin Towers in Deira.

*Nr British Embassy*
*Downtown Bur Dubai*
*Map 9 B3* **37**

## Danat Dubai Cruises

*04 351 1117 | www.danatdubaicruises.com*

After boarding the luxury Danat vessel you head up the creek towards Shindagha with drink in hand (try to bag one of the two sofas on the front deck for the best view). Whenever you feel hungry you can go back inside for the buffet – admittedly not the most spectacular range of dishes, but the food is secondary to the experience here. Cheerful staff (easily identified by their loud, Hawaiian shirts) do a great job of seeing to

**510**

**bateaux dubai**
*A Unique Cruise Experience*

A MEMBER OF

JEBEL ALI INTERNATIONAL
HOTELS

# A Unique Dinner Cruise Experience

Get a one-of-a-kind feel of the fascinating sights and sounds of Dubai Creek onboard the luxurious Bateaux Dubai. Air-conditioned comfort, elegant décor, live entertainment and personlised service enhance the occasion, as our Executive Chef serves up only the finest gourmet cuisine freshly prepared onboard.

Catch a spectacular sunset, enjoy a romantic moonlight rendezvous or treat your guests to a few magical hours – only with Bateaux Dubai.

For reservations and more information please contact:
Tel: +971 4 399 4994  Fax: +971 4 399 4995
E-mail: mail@bateauxdubai.com
Website: www.jebelali-international.com

everyone's needs, which is a tall order when the boat is full. Apart from their dinner cruise, which lasts for two and a half hours, Danat also offers a daily sundowner cruise.

**Various Locations**

## Tour Dubai ▶ p.539

*04 336 8409* | *www.tour-dubai.com*

Explore the creek during the day alongside the busy abras or after the sun goes down on a traditional dhow. For larger groups of up to 40 people a lounge bar allows relaxed conviviality. Majilis seating, regular dining and cocktail receptions are also available. Bigger boats and buffet meals are available in addition to these services. Or alternatively, for a romantic evening, charter a personal dhow, complete with your own butler, roses for your partner, champagne, five-star dining and a limousine to pick you up and drop you off home.

## European

Other options **French** p.517, **Italian** p.538, **Russian** p.554, **Mediterranean** p.550 **Pizzerias** p.553, **Portuguese** p.554, **Spanish** p.558, **German** p.518

**Hilton Creek**
*Deira*
*Map 11 C1*

## Glasshouse

*04 212 7550* | *www.hilton.com*

Get a taste of the Mediterranean at this chic brasserie which, under the creative supervision of a new manager, is vying to be the 'place to be' on the Creek. The decor is crisp and relaxing thanks to glass walls, dark woods, tasteful colours, and Mondrian-style paintings which create a sophisticated atmosphere. The menu provides Med dishes with a touch of the modern thrown in. They also offer a business lunch that will impress and a Friday Brunch is available with five free-flow drink options that range from Bubbly to Sangria. With a superb menu, excellent staff, and a modish interior, this venue has earned the right to throw stones.

**Park Hyatt Dubai**
*Creekside, Deira*
*Map 11 B4*

## Le Traiteur

*04 602 1234* | *www.dubai.park.hyatt.com*

No tricks. No gimmicks. Just nine confident chefs at work with the very finest ingredients. From toque to white shirt and dark grey tie to sturdy black shoes, the international team inspires a confidence that it lavishly repays. Its ballet of culinary art constitutes the evening's entertainment as the chefs perform in a breathtakingly beautiful kitchen. Spectators descend from an intimate bar via a dramatic staircase into a theatrically gorgeous room with soaring ceilings and a kaleidoscope of colour flickering on the walls. Though entranced by the performance in the kitchen, guests manage to respond to the calmly competent service. They order. They eat. They swoon. And they vow to return.

## Far Eastern

Other options **Polynesian** p.553, **Chinese** p.508, **Singaporean** p.557 **Thai** p.560, **Korean** p.549, **Vietnamese** p.566, **Filipino** p.516, **Japanese** p.546

**JW Marriott Hotel**
*Deira*
*Map 11 E1*

## Bamboo Lagoon

*04 262 4444* | *www.marriott.com*

The Bamboo Lagoon's staggering range of exquisite fusion cuisine demands a repeat visit. There's sushi, tempura, teriyaki, curries, steaks, stir-fries, grills, seafood, rice and noodle dishes galore. All are equally tempting and so wonderfully presented that you'll wish you hadn't eaten for a week. The bottomless buffet with numerous stalls offering diverse dishes is similar to the excellent Market Place restaurant next door, but as the name suggests, an abundance of bamboo, straw, water features, dainty bridges and

**512**

REFINED AND ELEGANTLY UNDERSTATED

THE FINEST THINGS IN LIFE COME TOGETHER AT THE TERRACE,
LIKE PREMIUM BEVERAGES OR FRENCH OYSTERS, CAVIAR AND SALMON FROM THE
SENSUAL RAW BAR, AND THE SMOOTH CHILLOUT TUNES OF DJ LADY RED.

PARK HYATT DUBAI™

Dubai Creek Golf and Yacht Club, PO Box 2822, Dubai, UAE
TELEPHONE +971 4 602 1234  FACSIMILE +971 4 602 1235  dubai.park.hyatt.com

other oriental trappings pervades. At 21:00 a band takes to the stage and grass-skirted singers serenade diners with low key renditions of tropical Polynesian tunes and entertaining cover versions.

## Beachcombers

*The Jumeirah*
*Beach Hotel*
*Umm Suqeim*
*Map 6 B1*

04 406 8750 | www.jumeirah.com

Located right on the beach with fantastic views of the Burj Al Arab, this breezy seaside shack hosts atmospheric far eastern buffets every night. There are live-cooking stations for stir fries and noodles, and overall there is a huge range of delicious Oriental cuisine – the peking duck, curry hotpots and satay are highly recommended. Although the food is excellent, and the staff are friendly and skilled, what you will remember most about Beachcombers is the idyllic location.

## Eauzone

*One&Only*
*Royal Mirage*
*Al Sufouh*
*Map 5 C1*

04 399 9999 | www.oneandonlyroyalmirage.com

If the weather prevents using the tranquil poolside tables, the floor-to-ceiling windows still offer a great view of the coast, unless it's past sunset and then you'll just be looking into a mirror! The international cuisine has a clearly Asian twist, giving traditional dishes a new breath of life, and keeping a healthy feel to the food. Staff are refreshingly upfront about the dishes, happily answering any questions and providing insight into the tastiest offerings. Teppanyaki is available as is a set five-course menu, but the crowning glory has to be the passion fruit souffle, which among other devilishly decadent deserts, is no less than sublime.

## Mun Chi

*Habtoor Grand*
*Resort & Spa*
*Marsa Dubai*
*Map 5 B1*

04 399 5000 | www.habtoorhotels.com

You certainly can 'munch' a lot at Mun Chi: the contemporary Asian menu covers Thai, Chinese, Indonesian and Vietnamese dishes. The restaurant overlooks the sea, tropical gardens and the beach, so you can watch the waves of the Arabian Gulf draw in and out during the day, and at night the view transforms into a sparkly sea of fairy-lit trees and the lounge music is replaced by dance. It has a seriously stylish interior and a cool ambience that should ensure it is busy for the foreseeable future. A night at Mun Chi is definitely money well spent.

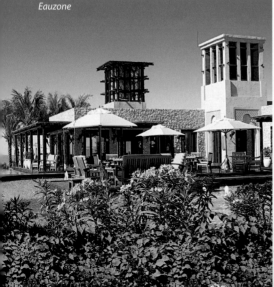
Eauzone

Mun Chi

# Work Visas p.54
# Weekend Breaks p.155

Written by residents, the London Explorer is packed with insider info, from arriving in the city to making it your home and everything in between.

**London Explorer Residents' Guide**
We Know Where You Live

Abu Dhabi · Amsterdam · Bahrain · Barcelona · Beijing · Berlin · Dubai · Dublin · Geneva
Hong Kong · Kuala Lumpur · Kuwait · London · Los Angeles · New York · New Zealand · Oman
Paris · Qatar · Shanghai · Singapore · Sydney · Tokyo · Vancouver

**EXPLORER**
www.explorerpublishing.com

### The Noodle House

*Boulevard at Emirates Towers*
*Trade Centre 2*
*Map 7 F3* **96**

**04 330 0000** | www.jumeirah.com

The Noodle House is a refreshingly relaxed affair. Just turn up and wait for the first available spot at one of the long communal tables. You order by ticking your desired dishes on the pads provided (after some advice from the friendly, clued-up staff, if required). The food is speedy and superb, with big portions of mouthwatering far eastern delights, and all reasonably priced too. The modern funky decor and exciting open show kitchen just add to the vibrant atmosphere. It might not be intimate and it may be fast food but it's all so fabulously done. Other branches are located in the Souk Madinat Jumeirah (04 366 6730), which has the added bonus of a terrace for alfresco eating, and Deira City Centre (04 294 0085).

### White Orchid

*Jebel Ali Htl*
*Jebel Ali*
*Map 3 A1* **15**

**04 804 8604** | www.jebelali-international.com

Although the White Orchid appeals primarily to the patrons of the Jebel Ali Golf Resort & Spa, its not such a long way from the new developments of Dubai and well worth the drive. Both indoor with its wood decor and high ceilings, and outside on the terrace overlooking the landscaped gardens, provide a relaxed atmosphere, complemented by the live music from the adjacent piano bar. The superb Asian fusion of Thai and Chinese cuisine is accompanied by smiley and attentive service. The deliciously prepared Big Tiger Prawns with Mushroom, Leek, Spring Onions, Garlic & Red Chili Sauce are not to be missed.

### Wox

*Grand Hyatt Dubai*
*Umm Hurair*
*Map 13 C1* **9**

**04 317 2222** | www.dubai.grand.hyatt.com

Noodle houses have become very fashionable in recent years, and Wox takes the concept to the next level. Here you can choose to sit around the noodle bar or at one of the individual tables – either way you will get to enjoy the sights, sounds and smells of live cooking. Just place your order from the simple (but comprehensive) menu and sit back while your meal is prepared in a flurry of sizzling woks and steaming pots. All your favourite Asian noodle and rice dishes are there, bracketed nicely by some interesting appetisers and desserts. The food prices are surprisingly reasonable, but the alcoholic beverages will definitely take their toll on your final bill.

### Yum!

*Radisson SAS Hotel*
*Deira Creek*
*Deira*
*Map 9 B3* **27**

**04 205 7333** | www.radissonsas.com

Yum! is exquisite and efficient all rolled up in a stack of noodles and served in a modern, funky setting. The kitchen is inspired by different far eastern cuisines, such as Chinese, Japanese, Thai or Vietnamese so there's something for every taste. The atmosphere is relaxed and casual with an open kitchen where you can see how your food is prepared. The dishes may not be highly innovative but due to the variety it is no surprise that some dishes are more authentic than others. The portions are generous and perfectly presented, making this a good spot for a casual lunch or speedy dinner.

## Filipino

Other options **Far Eastern** p.512

### Tagpuan

*Karama Centre*
*Al Karama*
*Map 10 E1* **29**

**04 337 3959**

Tagpuan ('meeting place' in Tagalog) brings traditional Filipino fare to Dubai. The tiny tables inside the small restaurant can fill up pretty quickly but the outside area on the terrace offers more space, weather permitting. For those seeking out new and interesting food, the menu offers a range of simple but tasty versions of Filipino home favourites including Adobong Pusit (squid), Tapa (fried marinated beef) Fried Tilapia (fish) or Pinakbet (mixed vegetables including bitter gourd). Prices are good value, especially the daily combo of two dishes with rice for Dhs.15. In Dubai you can virtually eat around the world – so don't forget the Philippines.

## Fish & Chips

You may not find a 'chippy' on every street corner in Dubai, but if you're really hankering for some good old fish and chips there are a few choices at your disposal. The Chippy is a real 'home from home' chip shop, where the interior may be a little drab but the food is just what

| Fish & Chips | |
| --- | --- |
| The Chippy | 04 343 3114 |
| Fish Supper | 04 286 1789 |
| Fryer Tuck | 04 344 4228 |
| Mirdiff Fish & Fries | 04 288 1812 |
| The Plaice | 04 286 8233 |

you'd expect – crispy battered fish and great chips. The Plaice (next door to the Irish Village) has a nice outside area, a varied menu (fish and chips are the main event, but you'll also find pies, prawns, chicken and even haggis), and since they serve alcohol you can even wash your meal down with a nice cold beer. For real 'a-fish-ionados', however, the newest place in Dubai could well be the best, so try a trip to Fish Supper in Rashidiya to test it out for yourselves. The Irish Village (p.590), Barasti Bar (p.576), The Boardwalk (p.526) and the Dhow and Anchor (p.588) also deserve a special mention for the quality of their fish and chips.

## French

**Le Meridien Dubai**
*Al Garhoud*
*Map 13 E1* **20**

### Café Chic
*04 282 4040* | *www.lemeridien-dubai.com*
Subtle art deco decor blends quietly with the sound of mellow jazz that fills Café Chic. Comfortable upholstered dining chairs surround each table and signal the restaurant's desire to pamper its guests. The chef provides distinctive treats before your ordered courses: a small cup of soup before the starter, a taste of pate before the main course, a sweet trio before dessert. As delectable as the generous primary courses are, you will find yourself eager as well for these tiny samples of great cooking. If the point is eating in an elegantly civilised way, every heft of the fork should bring satisfaction, and at Café Chic it most certainly does.

**Off Street 77B**
*beh Al Rabee*
*Kindergarten*
*Jumeira*
*Map 7 B2* **58**

### La Maison d'Hôtes
*04 344 1838*
La Maison d'Hôtes is Middle East meets Morocco in decor with its covered terrace with chunky wood furniture and cushioned benches, but in taste it's refreshingly français. Starters include everything from fresh salads and homemade soups to delectable foie gras, beef carpaccio and goats' cheese numbers, while mains include succulent duck, beef, fish, and pasta. Vegetarians be warned - this is French territory, and the menu is more meaty than leafy, but with the fresh bread and gazpacho delivered before you even receive your order, you'll quickly realise there is little to disappoint, especially the desserts. Open for lunch from 12:30-15:00 and dinner from 20:30, it's reasonably priced gourmet food which is all very French, and all very good.

**Emirates Golf Club**
*Emirates Hills*
*Map 5 C3* **52**

### Le Classique
*04 380 2222* | *egc@dubaigolf.com*
Le Classique, the dining equivalent of championship golf at Emirates Golf Club, asks gentlemen to dress in coat and tie. No serious diner, gentleman or not, should pass up the opportunity. Beginning with beverages in the handsome lounge, well-dressed

**517**

patrons move into the lavish dining room set comfortably under a silk tented ceiling featuring a large chandelier resembling twisted vines. Velvet panels and Roman shades adorning vast windows add to an environment quite reminiscent of Hollywood's finest country-club sets. A talented pianist sings marvellous old standards and honours requests. In that romantic setting the professional staff serves from a creative and delicious menu assembled by Le Classique's veteran chef.

**Jebel Ali Hotel** ◀
*Jebel Ali*
*Map 2 A1* **87**

## Signatures

*04 883 6000* | *www.jebelali-international.com*

This particular restaurant has something for everyone in terms of choice. Although a bit on the expensive side, the experience is well worth that extra dirham or two. The atmosphere is sophisticated and stylish both inside and out and whether the weather permits alfreso dining or not, you'll feel like you are dining under the stars. The staff are very knowledgeble about all aspects of the comprehensive menu and can help the less-experienced guests with the most delicious of choices. An elegant restaurant with a well selected wine list makes this worthy of special occasion status.

**Century Village** ◀
*Al Garhoud*
*Map 13 E1* **47**

## St Tropez Bistro ▶ p.519

*04 286 9029* | sttropez@eim.ae

The St Tropez Bistro at the Century Village offers a truly authentic French meal. The sight of frog's legs and snails on the menu gives you a good idea of what to expect. The food is delicious, simple and fresh, with a home-cooked feel to it. The main courses are dominated by hearty meat dishes with an impressive selection of steaks but save room for a dessert as the créme brulée in particular is a treat. The staff are polite and knowledgeable and the background music adds nicely to the ambience. The interior of the restaurant, with walls oddly filled with photos of celebrities, is a bit cramped, so it's best to opt for the terrace if weather permits.

**Hilton Creek** ◀
*Deira*
*Map 11 C1* **12**

## Verre

*04 227 1111* | *www.hilton.com*

Gordon Ramsay's reputation precedes him, and this is definitely the case at Verre, his first foray outside the UK. You enter through sleek, sliding glass doors, but your first impressions of the decor – understated dark wood furniture and simple white table linen – may leave you wondering what all the fuss is about. However, Ramsay is a chef, not an interior designer, and at Verre it's all about the food. The exciting and enticing menu is not huge, but contains some stunning culinary creations (although vegetarians are advised to steer clear). Faultless service and the delightful canapes and between-course palate cleansers make this a truly memorable dining experience, albeit an expensive one.

## German

**Jumeira Rotana** ◀
*Al Satwa*
*Map 8 A2* **23**

## Brauhaus

*04 345 5888* | *www.rotana.com*

Brauhaus offers a great variety of German food, such as spaetzle, sausages, schnitzel and apfelstrudel. The menu and the buffet choice are excellent with lots of heavy, but solid German dishes. There's a great choice of starters and main courses and, on certain nights, a tasty cheese fondue. It is relatively popular thanks to its location next to the Boston Bar and the different themed buffet nights mean you get more sausage (as well as a selection of alcoholic drinks) for your cash. Visit during Ocktoberfest for that authentic oom-pah vibe. Basically it's a fun, authentic German experience.

**THE AVIATION CLUB**

CENTURY VILLAGE

| INDIAN | LOUNGE | FISH & CHIPS | FRENCH STEAK HOUSE | CHINESE | PERSIAN |

THIS CHARMING RESTAURANT COMPLEX WITHIN THE GROUNDS OF
THE AVIATION CLUB IS THE PERFECT VENUE FOR DINING AND ENTERTAINMENT.
BE IT A BUSINESS LUNCH, AN INTIMATE DINNER OR TO MEET WITH FRIENDS,
CENTURY VILLAGE HAS IT ALL.
THE TWELVE LICENSED OUTLETS OFFER SUPERB CUISINE
FROM AROUND THE WORLD IN AUTHENTIC SETTINGS.

| LEBANESE | PORTUGUESE | JAPANESE | CAFE´ | ITALIAN | OVEN BAKED SPECIALTIES |

THE WORLD ON YOUR PLATE

WWW.CENTURYVILLAGE.AE

The Aviation Club - P.O. Box: 55400, Dubai, U.A.E. Tel. 04 282 4122 - Fax. 04 282 4751 - www.aviationclub.ae

*Jumeirah*
*Beach Hotel*
*Umm Suqeim*
*Map 6 B1* **17**

## Der Keller

*04 406 8181* | *www.jumeirah.com*

Der Keller is one of the most popular German restaurants in Dubai, and after eating here it won't be hard to see why. The almost-retro 1970s redbrick decor seems rather strange on entry but it does give the place a cosy, almost homely feel. If you go before sundown, you can take advantage of the wonderful sea view. Food-wise, the portions are huge and very tasty, particularly the veal and steak. Fans of German beer will also be at home with a wide range of ales on offer. The main drawback is the price, but fans of German food won't want to miss it.

*JW Marriott Hotel*
*Deira*
*Map 11 E1* **18**

## Hofbrauhaus

*04 262 4444* | *www.marriott.com*

Sometimes the copy is better than the original and that could quite literally be the case with the food and experience at JW Marriott's Hofbrauhaus - it may even be better than you'd get in Munich! From the sauerkraut to the white sausage with sweet mustard and the strudel, everything here is top notch. Add in the beer hall decor, Bavarian garb for the staff and traditional accordion music and you have a recipe for a fun night out. Several German beers are on tap, along with a full selection of wines and spirits.

# Indian

Other options **Pakistani** p.552, **Sri Lankan** p.558

*Dhow Palace Hotel*
*Downtown Bur Dubai*
*Map 8 E3* **48**

## Aangan

*04 359 9992* | *www.dhowpalacehoteldubai.com*

Housed in the Dhow Palace, one of Bur Dubai's newest and fanciest hotels, Aangen is a welcome addition to Dubai's growing Indian restaurant roster. Traditionally decorated in rich wood with many elaborate ornaments nailed to the walls, the atmosphere and live in-house music combine to boast the authentic quality of the food. Savour their range of biryanis, special curries and kebabs from their charcoal-smoked clay oven, as well as some of the most divine Indian desserts outside Delhi.

*Four Points Sheraton*
*Downtown Bur Dubai*
*Map 8 F3* **53**

## Antique Bazaar

*04 397 7444* | *www.starwood.com*

The Antique Bazaar at the Four Points Sheraton lives up to its name. Beautiful chairs, some silver, some wood, are all accurately crafted copies of antique originals and surround tables enhanced by Indian antiques creating an atmosphere akin to authentic colonial India. The hypnotic sound of an Indian musical group confirms the impression and the food engages other senses with similar success. Delicious kebabs, tasty biryanis, and a large selection of vegetarian delights seem to satisfy the many customers at this deservedly popular restaurant while attentive, leisurely service gives everyone ample time to appreciate the details.

*Kuwait Street*
*Al Karama*
*Map 10 E1* **104**

## Aryaas

*04 335 5776*

Unassuming Aryaas is at the quieter end of Kuwait Street. With only an M&M machine and a few pictures to disrupt the prison-like austerity of the clean canteen tables, it's clear they aim to impress with dirt-cheap 100% vegetarian food, rather than the decor. Fortunately, the plan works, and this chain of restaurants has been serving up no-frills Indian fare since 1959. The house speciality is Thali: small pots of different flavours into which you dip as much naan bread or rice as you can physically handle. For around Dhs.10 it will provide enough food to leave you comatose for the afternoon with a satiated grin that says it all.

**Pyramids**
*Umm Hurair*
*Map 10 E4*

## Asha's

*04 324 4100 | www.asharestaurants.com*

Owned by none other than Indian superstar Asha Bhosle, this Dubai favourite offers a memorable dining experience. Decked out in Indian summer colours of reds, yellows, and oranges, this classy joint also features beaded curtains, low-level lighting, and intimate booths as well as an inviting and majestic terrace. For starters you could sit at the bar, with a view into the kitchen, and get your tastebuds tingling with a delicious cocktail from the adventurous list. Then dive into the food - the menu features a few Indian favourites, a selection of Asha's very own signature dishes picked up on her travels, and some fusion choices concocted by Wafi's resident chef. The staff will gladly help with your choices but whatever you decide you can guarantee it'll be delicious.

> ### Bargain Barjis
> With a large population from the Indian subcontinent, Dubai is home to a host of good independent Indian eateries. The areas around Karama Market and along Trade Centre Road are good starting places for some seriously cheap chow. Don't be put off by the streetside locations - give them a try and you just might stumble upon some of the city's best fare.

**Sheraton Hotel & Towers**
*Deira*
*Map 9 B4* **33**

## Ashiana

*04 207 1733 | www.sheraton.com/dubai*

With empire-inspired decor and a traditional band playing authentic tunes every night, Ashiana celebrates India's colonial era. Cosy booths around the walls are the seats of choice, unless you happen to be in a large group. Pre-starters you are treated to a basket of delicious poppadoms and exotic dips, but leave room for the generous main courses. The food is expertly prepared and the complex medley of spices unfolds in your mouth without being too fiery - the true mark of exquisite Indian cooking. The staff deserve a special mention for their genteel, anticipatory assistance. Undoubtedly one of the finest restaurants in its category, at a price that is reasonable given the high standards.

**Opp Ramada Continental Hotel**
*Hor Al Anz*
*Deira*
*Map 12 A3* **132**

## Foodlands

*04 268 3311*

It might be one of the numerous cheap and cheerful independent restaurants in town but Foodlands deserves a special mention thanks to the excellent quality of its awesome array of Indian, Persian and Arabic dishes. Great for families, singletons fed up of microwave dinners and big groups looking for a pit stop the atmosphere is relaxed with just the right level of attentive service. You can see the mastery in action through the large window between the kitchen and the restaurant which serves to get your mouth suitably watering before your fresh, sizzling meal (kebabs, naans and tasty vegetarian dishes) is presented before you. Buffet and breakfast dishes are of equal value and taste.

**Nr Mina Plaza Hotel**
*Al Karama*
*Map 8 E3* **117**

## Gazebo

*04 359 8555*

Indian food at its very best, Gazebo impresses with authentic dishes packed with flavour. The elegantly clad staff are genuinely friendly and the service is absolutely top notch. Choosing from the menu is a challenge as it's so vast, but it has a fantastic

*Asha's*

selection of charcoal grilled specialities such as the chunky chicken kebabs and marinated leg of lamb, masses of mouth-watering curries to choose from and stacks of biryanis. The salads and side dishes are all bursting with zingy freshness, the breads fantastically tasty and the lassis and fresh fruit kulfis deliciously sweet accompaniments to your meal. All in all it's a great value Indian experience.

**Taj Palace Hotel**
Deira
Map 11 C1

## Handi

*04 223 2222* | www.tajpalacehotel.co.ae

You can get a mean curry at Handi - and no ordinary curry at that. The elaborate silver peacock-shaped Thali dish offers four curries and kebabs for Dhs.90, including biryani, salad, dessert and lassi. The lamb curry with cashew and cardamom, or the chicken with tomato and fenugreek are so savoury you're bound to order more. For biryani lovers there is a special treat - individual copper pots are sealed to keep the flavour in the pot, and when the seal is broken the aroma will transport you to Rajasthan. The decor is rich and elegant with private dining rooms available and live Indian music.

**Grosvenor House**
Marsa Dubai
Map 5 B2 **10**

## Indego

*04 399 8888* | www.grosvenorhouse.lemeridien.com

A suitably stylish match for the Grosvenor House, Indego has a cool, low-lit interior with various areas screened off by elegant wooden partitions. The menu offers Indian dishes with a contemporary international twist, such as the wild mushroom biryani that comes with a flaky pastry crust and a side order of dhal. The desserts continue the theme - don't miss the saffron and strawberry Indian tiramisu with cardamom ice cream. Eating here is evidence of why consultant chef Vineet Bhatia was the first Indian chef in the world to be awarded a Michelin star.

**Opp Fuddruckers**
Al Garhoud
Map 11 C4 **105**

## India Palace

*04 286 9600* | sfcdxb@eim.ae

Stepping through perhaps the most elaborately carved wooden doors in Dubai, you'll be transported back to the time of the Moghul Dynasty at this deservedly popular Garhoud eatery. Low lighting, traditional sitar music and beautiful ornate wooden panelling create a tranquil respite while upstairs there are private booths for a more intimate dining experience. A mouth-watering selection of starters complements a wide range of sturdy curries, fragrant rice dishes and vegetable accompaniments while a delectable grill selection will appeal to hungry carnivores. After dinner spend your many left over dirhams on handmade bangles and necklaces at the craft stall.

**Cyclone Bld**
Oud Metha
Map 10 E2 **126**

## Khazana

*04 336 0061* | www.sanjeevkapoorskhazanadxb.com

Indian celebrity chef Sanjeev Kapoor's spacious, popular eatery specialises in cuisine from the north of his home country. All dishes are well prepared and served in big portions, but the prawn curry and chicken tikka are famous. Other delicacies include grilled tandoori seafood, a variety of rice dishes and some hearty gravy-based dishes with meat and fish, as well as Anglo-Indian novelties like 'British Raj Railroad Curry'. With such excellent food and its relaxing ambience (friendly waitresses wearing traditional dress and attractive decor), it's no surprise that Khazana is so popular.

### Celebrity Chefs

Does food prepared by famous hands really taste better? Head to Verre (p.518), Gordon Ramsey's restaurant, Mezzanine (p.508), in the hands of Gary Rhodes since summer 2007 or Indego (p.522) by Vineet Bhatia (the only Indian chef to claim a Michelin star), and find out. For a more reasonably priced option try Sanjeev Kapoor's Khazana (p.522).

# Restaurants

**One&Only
Royal Mirage**
*Al Sufouh*
*Map 5 C1* 25

## Nina

*04 399 9999* | *www.oneandonlyroyalmirage.com*

Guests already smitten with the One&Only Royal Mirage will fall head over heels in love with Nina. Enter the large, luxurious dining room through beaded curtains to see tables circled toward the inviting bar and surrounding a lower level featuring velvet banquets. Massive chandeliers and graceful candelabra cast their muted light on faux marble walls and tiled circular arches, reminiscent of palatial Indian splendour. Persistently percussive music accompanies conventional Indian main courses flanked by inventive starters and desserts. The staff know the ingredients of each dish and provide diners more than ample time to reflect on the food and the lively scene.

**Marina Walk**
*Marsa Dubai*
*Map 5 B2* 57

## The Rupee Room

*04 390 5755* | *www.therupeeroom.com*

Occupying a prime spot along the popular Marina Walk, the Rupee Room offers a wide selection of north Indian dishes in comfortable and relaxed surroundings. The indoor dining area spills out on to the covered walkway, and a wooden staircase leads to the mezzanine level. The glass-fronted kitchen allows you to keep an eye on the action between courses. Weather permitting, the best tables are those outside, providing marina views and the chance to watch the world go by. With so much in its favour, it's unfortunate that the food can sometimes be less than inspiring, and the service a little confused.

**Karama Park Square**
*Al Karama*
*Map 10 E1* 81

## Saravana Bhavan

*04 334 5252*

Taking its name from the famous and much-loved hotel Saravana Bhavan in Chennai, India, this unassuming restaurant in Karama Park Square is arguably the best of the area's south Indian restaurants. Squeezing in as many customers as possible over its two floors, Saravan prefers elbow-to-elbow dining on tables decorated only with a bottle of mineral water. The menu is long enough to keep demaning Indian expatriates interested but it's the thalis that draw big crowds – for around Dhs.10 you can get a plate packed with colour and flavours, dal and chapatti. Fine Indian food doesn't come much cheaper.

**Al Murooj Rotana
Hotel & Suites**
*Trade Centre 2*
*Map 7 E3* 2

## Zaika Restaurant

*04 321 1111* | *www.rotana.com*

Spread across two floors, Zaika has private rooms on the mezzanine floor and a classic, yet relaxed, dining space on the ground level. Zaika has a traditional ambience, gracefully enhanced by an idyllic view over the lagoon and a warm decor that evokes India's timeless elegance. The cuisine stays true to the ancient methods of Indian cooking, using the flavours and styles that have made this one of the world's most popular cuisines. From start to finish the dining experience is rich with perfection; the classic dishes deliciously tender and free of any fusion or modern interpretation.

## International

**Creek Golf Club**
*Al Garhoud*
*Map 11 B4* 49

## Academy

*04 295 6000* | *www.dubaigolf.com*

Millions of people look at golf courses on TV screens. Surely it's much better to sit in the Academy Snack Bar and look through the surrounding glass at the beautiful, renovated Dubai Creek golf course? You will then be closer to the real thing and even closer to professional staff serving a wide assortment of international appetisers, sandwiches, salads, main courses, and beverages of all sorts. The cheerful colour scheme fits in well with the view of luscious green and happy golfers. If one contemplates joining the 18 hole set, browsing through the golf shop located at the end of the room could lead to the Academy becoming a regular joint - which isn't necessarily a bad thing.

**Hyatt Regency**
*Deira*
*Map 9 D1*

## Al Dawaar

*04 317 2222* | www.dubai.regency.hyatt.com

While you may think a revolving restaurant is far more tack than taste, don't be too hasty in dismissing Al Dawaar. There is nothing corny about this surprisingly sophisticated Arabic buffet restaurant, so you shouldn't knock a culinary revolution until you've tried this one. The minimalist decor with dark wood tables and immaculate white tablecloths complement the modern makeover of the Hyatt Regency. The buffet is ample rather than over-the-top, with dainty starters, a la carte-style mains and an unrivalled dessert table. As you enjoy the un-buffet-like buffet cuisine the slow revolution (it takes one hour and 45 minutes to do a complete turn) gives you an interesting window on this side of town, the beginnings of the gargantuan Palm Deira and the glistening ocean beyond.

**Bab Al Shams**
*Map 2 B4*

## Al Forsan

*04 832 6699* | www.jumeirah.com

Al Forsan boasts impressive decor, with polished concrete floors, deep red walls, rich persian tapestries and chunky, dark-wood furniture. You can fill your plate from the delectable buffet, small in comparison to some Dubai buffets but adequate nonetheless, featuring a good range of Arabic dishes as well as some more suitable for conservative tastes. The a la carte menu is similarly small but comprehensive, and features a great children's menu. It may take a while before Dubai's convenience-driven public cottons on to the idea of a 45 minute drive to Bab Al Shams for dinner, but the Al Forsan experience is well worth it.

**Burj Al Arab**
*Umm Suqeim*
*Map 6 B1*

## Al Muntaha

*04 301 7600* | www.jumeirah.com

It would be difficult to find a more impressive setting and a better view than at the top of Burj Al Arab. The mostly Mediterranean cuisine comes a la carte, and is presented with flair to match Burj Al Arab's lauded luxury. The restaurant's Friday brunch, served buffet-style, is one of Dubai's most opulent. There is also live music and an excited buzz that takes away any pretense that you might expect from such a posh spot.

**Mall of the Emirates**
*Al Barsha*
*Map 6 A3*

## Après ▶ p.525

*04 341 2575* | www.mmidubai.com

To accompany its first indoor ski resort, Dubai now has its very own alpine ski lodge in the shape of Après. Divided into three distinct areas, there's the large restaurant, a comfortable bar area, and the lodge lounge complete with a cosy fireplace and a view of the slope that is mesmerising. Although it is hard to keep your eyes on your plate, the varied menu offers good wholesome fare including steaks and pasta - perfect for respite and replenishment after a hard day on the slopes, and

*Après*

**FIRST FLOOR - MALL OF THE EMIRATES**

*Contact us 04 341 2575*

the fondue sharing events just add to the Swiss ski-chalet atmosphere. During the day this venue is popular with shoppers and families, whereas at night the vibe is more suitable to both chilling and partying. The wide-ranging cocktail list certainly helps you to do both.

*Al Qasr Hotel*
*Umm Suqeim*
*Map 6 A1*

## Arboretum

*04 366 8888* | www.jumeirah.com

Tempting variety, excellent presentation, an impressive setting and delicious flavours come together to put Arboretum at the top of the all-you-can-eat list. After tackling the Asian, Middle Eastern and western salads and appetisers you'd be forgiven for thinking the meal was over, but a wide variety of seafood, meat and pasta dishes (with a live-cooking station) still awaits. By this time you really will be full, which is a shame because the desserts are absolutely fantastic. The whole experience feels pleasantly different to Dubai's other buffets – more like eating a la carte food in a buffet setting. The a la carte menu is available 24 hours a day, with the buffet available at traditional meal times.

*Creek Golf Club*
*Al Garhoud*
*Map 11 B4*

## Boardwalk

*04 295 6000* | www.dubaigolf.com

Positioned on wooden stilts over the creek, Boardwalk offers patrons a spectacular view virtually unmatched in Dubai. Ideal in the cooler months, although seating inside is also available, this is as close as you can get to dining on the creek without being on a boat. The menu consists of a comprehensive array of starters, salads, meats, seafood, and vegetarian dishes, as well as desserts. Servings are generous and well presented while the drinks list contains a standard array of wines and beers and a huge selection of cocktails and mocktails. Equally suitable for both intimate dinners or large groups, unfortunately the restaurant doesn't take reservations but you can always grab a drink at QD's (p.584) while you wait.

*Fairmont Dubai*
*Trade Centre 1*
*Map 8 A4*

## Cascades

*04 311 8000* | www.fairmont.com

Cascades may be in a hotel lobby but this isn't just any hotel lobby. The restaurant is ensconced amidst the illuminated glass constructions of the Fairmont's breathtaking lobby; transparent elevator pods and water-features cascade serenely all around walls lavishly bedecked with angular windows, rhomboid mirrors, coloured spotlights, and artsy projections. The food is generally excellent, ample and well-presented with a variety of international dishes (Arabic, Iranian, Indian, Mediterranean and seafood) to suit every palate. Beware of the devilishly tempting, delicious desserts and cocktails. A versatile choice, Cascades is ideal for a trendy dinner, a business lunch, an extended brunch or a spot of indulgent tippling, nibbling and elevator watching.

*One&Only*
*Royal Mirage*
*Al Sufouh*
*Map 5 C1*

## Celebrities ▶ p.527

*04 399 9999* | www.oneandonlyroyalmirage.com

In keeping with its regal location, Celebrities offers some of the finest food in Dubai with views to match. Overlooking palatial gardens and candlelit waterways, the dining room is in the style of a stately drawing room while the terrace is inviting in the cooler months. The modern style of nouveau European food is minimally sized but in beautifully presented portions with superb attention to detail. The menu changes regularly and there is also a five-course set menu (including wine) which changes daily. The live band have an unusual medley of French jazz and karaoke hits, but this shouldn't detract from the romance.

# One&Only
## Royal Mirage, Dubai

# Dubai's most stylish beach resort

Celebrities is the resort's most elegant evening venue, perfect for those special moments. A grand entrance staircase leads to a classically chic restaurant overlooking the impressive esplanade, featuring stylish international cuisine and a musical quartet. Located in The Palace at One&Only Royal Mirage.

The Palace    *Residence & Spa    Arabian Court

For reservations or more information please contact
One&Only Royal Mirage, Dubai, UAE.  Telephone + 971 4 399 99 99   oneandonlyroyalmirage.com

**Aviation Club, The**
*Al Garhoud*
*Map 13 E1* **44**

## The Cellar ▶ p.535

*04 282 4122 | www.aviationclubonline.com*

The Cellar at the Aviation Club should be on every Dubai dining list. Lively but elegant, straightforward but sophisticated, grand but economical – it offers a lovely dining experience. The international menu has some favourites and some innovations and the wine list, with special bargains on Saturday and Sunday evenings, shows a surprisingly unusual range. Diners enjoy their own space, sometimes created by soft gauze curtains, in an extraordinarily well-lit room of soaring arches and unexpected stained glass. The outside space is also pleasantly relaxed with just a glimmer, and whisper, of the more raucous Irish Village across the pond. People clearly enjoy the Cellar, which is no surprise seeing as it's classy but not for too much cash.

**Nr Jumeirah**
**Beach Hotel**
*Jumeira*
*Map 6 B1* **84**

## Chalet

*04 348 6089*

It seemed that the recent widening of the Beach Road had spelled the end for Chalet, but regulars rejoiced when it reopened after a rejuvenating refurb. The interior is clean and modern, with no more than a dozen tables packed into the compact space (beware the unisex toilet which embarrasses first-timers who think they've walked into the wrong bathroom). The menu takes diners on a world tour, with stops in China for noodles and India for curries, but most people are here for the sturdy Arabic offerings including shawarma and the usual mezze suspects. On any given evening you'll see a real mixed bunch of punters including neighbourhood locals and expats, clued-up tourists discovering another side of Dubai, and sandy sunbathers fresh from the beach. It may have lost its lawn, and perhaps some of its shabby charm, but Chalet is still a dependable choice for affordable Umm Suqeim fare.

**Radisson SAS Hotel**
*Dubai Media City*
*Al Sufouh*
*Map 5 C2* **28**

## Chef's House

*04 366 9111 | www.radissonsas.com*

Typical of an international eatery, the Chef's House has a neat variety of Middle Eastern, Indian and Asian cuisine with a better buffet selection (cold and hot, and everything from a kebab to a crudite) than its rather meagre a la carte menu. The eatery serves what it calls 'business style' breakfasts, but is better suited to family lunches and leisurely dinners. Located in the Radisson SAS Hotel by Dubai Media City, the Chef's House is a comfortable choice for that can't-think-what-to-have meal.

**Novotel World**
*Trade Centre 2*
*Map 7 F3* **37**

## Entre Nous

*04 332 0000 | www.novotel.com*

You should enter Entre Nous with an eager appetite as their international buffet and theme nights are loaded with stirring and scrumptious foods. This upscale cafe is an ideal place for entertaining clients, impressing the in-laws, or just lunching with friends. The relaxing atmosphere will help you linger the day or night away. You can also watch the chef prepare your fare while you try to decide how to fill up your plate. The buffet boasts a variety of appetisers, soups, fresh breads and assorted starters. You can also opt for the a la carte menu and explore the excellent choices of steaks and gourmet burgers.

**Towers Rotana**
*Trade Centre 1*
*Map 7 E3* **70**

## Flavours on Two

*04 343 8000 | www.rotana.com*

Located on the second floor of Sheikh Zayed Road's Towers Rotana, Flavours on Two (get it?) – previously known as Gardinia – offers one of Dubai's best, most reasonable and most diverse all-you-can-eat-and-drink buffets, in one of the most stylish and contemporary settings. With decor that screams urban chic, full of shiny chrome,

**528**

# Destination
## New
## Dubai

246 rooms designed in a contemporary style with chic interiors. An extensive choice of trendy bars and speciality restaurants, unique recreation options and some of the best conference and meeting facilities. Its close proximity to the beach and the city's vibrant shopping areas make it the perfect destination to mix business with pleasure.

**Best 4 star Business Corporate Hotel 2006 MENA**
**Best New 4 star Hotel in 2006 MENA**
**Arabian Hotel Investment Conference Award 2007**
**ACN Arab Technology Award 2007**

Radisson SAS Hotel, Dubai Media City
PO Box 211723, Dubai, United Arab Emirates
Tel: +971-4-366-9111, Fax: +971-4-361-1011
info.mediacity.dubai@radissonsas.com
mediacity.dubai.radissonsas.com

wooden floors, simple leather seating and twisty metal wine racks, the venue is large enough to comfortably accommodate raucous groups, business lunches and nervous daters. The all-inclusive menu varies in theme every day of the week, but the quality remains consistently high.

### IKEA  ▶ p.IBC

*Dubai Festival City*
*Deira*
*Map 13 D2* **50**

04 800 4532 | www.ikeadubai.com

In its new Festival City location, the IKEA restaurant has more tables and more facilities, but the same great concept: unpretentious food at low prices. With canteen-style self service, each day of the week brings a different Meal of the Day, Soup of the Day and Vegetarian Meal. The standard dishes (including Swedish meatballs) are still available most days, and there's a range of pre-packed salads, sandwiches and cold plates. You could also just take the edge off your hunger with a coffee and muffin combo for just Dhs.4. The daily kids' meal usually stays the same for the whole year and offers simple choices like chicken nuggets and chips.

### The Junction

*Traders Hotel Dubai*
*Deira*
*Map 11 E2* **72**

04 265 9888 | www.shangri-la.com

Traders Hotel in Deira is owned and operated by the Shangri-La group, and this ground floor restaurant certainly reflects the quality and attention to detail of its better known corporate kin. The clean, simple, elegant decor suggests Asian and Arabic influences, and the atmosphere is pleasant and calming. The Junction's speciality is the buffet, with breakfast and lunchtime deals at reasonable prices, while weekend evenings are reserved for a themed buffet. Friday is seafood night, and the prawns are particularly recommended, with numerous methods of cooking on offer including battered, barbecue and tandoori. With great tasting desserts to finish, Deira residents and visitors may want to add this to their favourites list.

### Keva

*Al Nasr Leisureland*
*next to Chi At The Lodge*
*Oud Metha*
*Map 10 E2* **85**

04 334 4159

The revitalisation of Chi@The Lodge has breathed new life into the area around Al Nasr Leisureland in Oud Metha. There's nothing new about Keva's trendy Asian-inspired decor and slick furnishings, but the truly international menu, which includes everything from butter chicken to lamb chops and sushi, and good cocktails make it a worthwhile spot for a drink or a bite if you're heading to the latest edition of The Lodge. There's a quiet dining area or a more buzzy bar lounge for those readying themselves for the club next door. Keva offers a different theme each night of the week; there's even free mojitos for ladies on Tuesday nights when the sax player joins the resident DJ. Keva's business lunch guarantees to be served and cleared within an hour, is available 12:30 to 15:00 and the location offers a handy escape, even for DIFC dwellers.

### The Kitchen

*Hyatt Regency*
*Deira*
*Map 9 D1* **14**

04 209 1234 | www.dubai.regency.hyatt.com

Hidden away in the Hyatt Regency in Deira, The Kitchen opened its doors in 2005 and is nowhere near as popular as it should be. Great food and a

### High Class Pig Outs

Buffet restaurants often get a bad press for offering cheap chow in even cheaper surroundings. In Dubai, however, buffets are more like ready-made a la carte meals, and should by no means be discounted. Even better, they are often a more affordable way of stuffing your face with first-class fodder. The following are a few of Dubai's best buffet restaurants: Al Dawaar (p.524), Al Muna (p.524), Cascades (p.526), The Market Café (p.531), The Market Place (p.531), and Meridien Village Terrace (p.531).

bird's-eye view of the chefs at work, make it a must-see while the menu spans Asian, Mediterranean, American and even Scottish, and the lackadaisical pretension of the food and the relalaxed atmosphere is a refreshing change. Prices are surprisingly low, something accentuated by the free dessert buffet which has to be seen to be believed. Two metre marshmallows, reams of gateaux, cakes, ice creams, chocolate, pastries and even a flowing chocolate fountain will turn savoury lovers into sweet adulterers!

**Grand Hyatt Dubai**
*Umm Hurair*
*Map 13 C1* **9**

## The Market Café

*04 317 1234 | www.dubai.grand.hyatt.com*
Not exactly a buffet, not exactly a typical a la carte eatery, this bustling and popular restaurant does what it says on the tin – it's a market-style restaurant. Diners wander from station to station selecting their style of food as well as their specific starters, entrees, desserts and drinks. Mix and match or stay within the Italian, Asian, Arabic or International cuisines on offer. It's a different twist on a buffet – more creative, more fun, but the bottom line is great food and great service. Plus, you'll enjoy the decor of the Grand Hyatt's greenhouse layout which is part rainforest and part underwater fantasy.

**JW Marriott Hotel**
*Deira*
*Map 11 E1* **18**

## The Market Place

*04 262 4444 | www.marriott.com*
'Eat and Drink' nights are big in Dubai, and The Market Place is a definite contender for the leader of the pack. The restaurant itself is friendly and welcoming with relaxed, bistro-style decor in a large, open-plan setting. No sooner have you sat down than the waiter brings what will undoubtedly be the first beverage of many – drinks are free-flowing and you won't sit with an empty glass for long. Drinks aside, it is the food that distinguishes this buffet restaurant; with several live-cooking stations and a most impressive buffet of starters and desserts. The various theme nights all have one thing in common – five-star cuisine in seemingly endless supply.

**Le Meridien Dubai**
*Al Garhoud*
*Map 13 E1* **20**

## Meridien Village Terrace

*04 282 4040 | www.lemeridien-dubai.com*
Beautifully lit at night, the large Meridien Village Terrace manages to feel intimate for couples but is also perfect for larger groups. Each night there is a different culinary theme, be it Caribbean, Mexican, BBQ or Arabic, and there's always plenty of delicious staples such as roast beef on offer for those with a specific hankering. Numerous live-cooking stations, including made-to-order crepes, keep the food wonderfully fresh, and a great choice of drinks are replenished with alarming regularity. It may be yet another buffet in Dubai but the variety, value, quality and setting of the Meridien Village Terrace is an absolute treat capable of wooing even the most pretentious of foodies. From October through to May, few places in the city will give you so much pleasure for just Dhs.140 (Dhs.160 on Thursdays).

**Al Qasr Hotel**
*Umm Suqeim*
*Map 6 A1*

## Napa

*04 366 8888 | www.jumeirah.com*
Napa is a sleek and stylish Californian restaurant where the French, Italian and Spanish influenced food tastes as good as it looks and unsurprisingly, seeing as it's named after a wine region, the wine list will impress connoisseurs. Dishes are adventurous and the desserts are a must, especially Napa's avante-garde marshmallow 'smores and possibly the finest chocolate brownie in Dubai. The service is knowledgeable but far from snooty, despite the posh-nosh prices and dress code. The interior is uncluttered and tastefully decorated in soothing tones. If you've had enough of checked table cloths and cliched menu choices, Napa is a refreshing opportunity to splurge on something a little different.

**531**

*Montgomerie*
*Golf Club*
Emirates Hills
*Map 5 B3* **63**

## Nineteen

*04 390 5600* | www.themontgomerie.com

Still need convincing that golf is cool? Head to Montgomerie's flagship restaurant, Nineteen, where slick, pared-back modernism sends members-only fustiness the way of wooden clubs. Situated in a miniature White House, the restaurant would be pitch black save for a pink back-lit bar, 70s kitsch lampshades, and subtle lights that single out your table. In contrast, the show kitchen is loud, proud and slightly out of context. Choose from a perfectly balanced Thai-influenced menu and, like a pro perfecting his swing, see the food get better with each course.

*Hilton Jumeirah*
Marsa Dubai
*Map 5 A1* **13**

## Oceana

*04 399 1111* | www.hilton.com

Your first decision should be what night to visit Oceana, a difficult choice thanks to the interchanging themes of equal temptation, while your second will be what delicious dish to devour. If, for example, you choose Fish Night, forgoing Arabic, French and Mexican Nights, you might select as many as thirty superb options, cold and hot, to satisfy your piscean yearning. The decor is akin to glamorous dining rooms of 1930s cruise ships – lots of chrome and wood with Art Moderne furniture and lighting fixtures that ensure visibility while still providing you a shadowed privacy. Despite being a buffet, the attentive staff makes you forgive the self-service.

*Four Points Sheraton*
Downtown Bur Dubai
*Map 8 F3* **53**

## Promenade

*04 397 7444* | www.starwood.com

The Promenade Restaurant resides in the hotel lobby of the Four Points Sheraton and promotes itself (rather strangely) as a 'chic French-styled cafe'. On selected days and during lunch and dinner times, the Promenade offers guests a chance to watch their food being cooked at the live-cooking stations but the selection of dishes from the a la carte menu is limited and the international buffet is basic. The food, however, is well presented and the staff are attentive and responsive. The mains are rather expensive but the various cuts of meat and the selection of shellfish and fish are cooked on the grill to specific requirements which will appeal to fussy diners.

*Mall of the Emirates*
Al Barsha
*Map 6 A3* **19**

## Seasons

*04 341 2483* | www.mmidubai.com

Swiftly swarming every area in Dubai, from Internet City to Ibn Battuta, Seasons is a chain of cafes serving healthy dishes to hungry shoppers and lunch-breakers. The international menu offers the usual array of soups, salads and sandwiches, as well as items from the grill that are all elegantly presented. Gadget geeks will love the service system: you're given a buzzer/pager which flashes when you need to trot up and collect your food. With a bright and fresh interior, Seasons is a great healthy and reasonably priced alternative to typical flyby lunch and dinner options.
Other Branches: Dubai Internet City (04 391 8711), Ibn Battuta (04 368 5630).

*Mall of the Emirates*
Al Barsha
*Map 6 A3* **19**

## Sezzam

*04 341 3600* | www.sezzam.com

Sezzam's open-plan concept may seem a little confusing, but once you've got the hang of it you could eat here every night of the week and have a different experience every time. There are three kitchens: 'Bake' serves up pizzas, lasagne and roasts; 'Flame' offers grilled meats and seafoods; and 'Steam' serves up Asian cuisine. Your waiter will talk you through each kitchen's offerings and even suggest the best place to sit, depending on what kind of food you're in the mood for (this is the point where you should mention if you want to have a drink, because they have a specially allocated area for

## DUBAI
## GREEN COMMUNITY

**SINCE WE WENT TO THE COURTYARD, WE GOT RID OF THAT BIG PIECE OF WHITE FURNITURE IN THE KITCHEN.**
Come and relax in the welcoming atmosphere of the Green Community. A variety of dining options to suit all occasions offering you plenty of occasions to share good moments between friends and family and, also, to make new friends! You will enjoy it so much that you might just decide to get rid of your oven as well!

**IT'S THE MARRIOTT WAY.**℠

For restaurant reservations call **04 885 2222** or visit www.marriottdiningatcy.ae

Courtyard by Marriott Dubai
Green Community
Dubai Investment Park, PO Box 63845
Dubai, United Arab Emirates
Fax: +971 4 8852525

that!). Confusion aside, the food, once you get it, is excellent and even the fussiest of diners should be able to find something tasty.

*Metropolitan Palace*
*Deira*
*Map 11 C1*

## Sketch

*04 227 0000 | www.methotels.com*

Located in a rather unremarkable Deira hotel, this intimate and very funky restaurant and bar is a wonderfully surprising venue. Relax with a fabulous cocktail while perusing the inventive menu, then enjoy the delicious food from the very talented chefs. Portions are large and beautifully presented, and the service is professional yet friendly. Less adventurous diners may choose from the section offering steaks, poultry and seafood with accompanying vegetables and carb of choice, but do leave room for the outstanding desserts. The restaurant offers promotions which change on a regular basis.

*Fairmont Dubai*
*Trade Centre 1*
*Map 8 A4*

## Spectrum on One

*04 311 8000 | www.fairmont.com*

With probably the most diverse menu in Dubai, Spectrum on One caters for a variety of tastes throughout each course. It features both adventurous and familiar dishes from southern Asia, coastal Thailand, Japan, India and Europe, which lives up to its slogan promising the opportunity to 'taste a nation' – although it's more like eat your way round the globe. Although the restaurant is on the large size, the clever architecture, which utilises mirrors, separations and mixed seating, means you don't feel like you're in a dinner hall. The seating and decor changes with the cuisine theme of various open kitchens. There is also a divine bar hidden within the restaurant with an impressive wine cellar and cigar selection that's perfect for an aperitif or post-dinner lingering.

China Club (p.508)

The Cellar (p.528)

Spice Island (p.536)

...delightfully delectable gastronomy

Saturday Brunch. Wine Evenings. Friday Brunch.
Contact Chris at 04 282 9333

The Aviation Club - P.O.Box 55400, Dubai, U.A.E - Tel. 04 282 4122 - Fax. 04 282 4751 - www.aviationclub.ae

**Renaissance Hotel**
*Hor Al Anz*
*Map 11 E1*

## Spice Island ▶ p.537

*04 262 5555 | www.renaissancehotels.com*

When it comes to choice, it doesn't come much better than Spice Island. From Italian to Mongolian, diners of every taste will be satisfied by the mouthwateringly varied buffet. Particularly popular with after-work gatherings, the atmosphere is guaranteed to be lively, aided by an eclectic decor that shouts fun, and a buffet deal that (for Dhs.149) allows you to drink as many house beverages as you can stomach. It's bound to satisfy even the pickiest of punters and bookings are advisable, especially on weekends. The Friday and Saturday brunch is also hugely popular with families (it is smoke-free and includes a kid's area with balloons and face painting) and those looking for some hangover grease.

**Le Meridien Mina**
*Al Sufouh*
*Map 5 C1*

## Tang

*04 399 3333 | www.lemeridien-minaseyahi.com*

This is a spot for inquisitive foodies rather than hungry feeders. Tang's menu is designed to tickle the tastebuds through concept dining, doing away with the traditional starter, main and dessert, in favour of little stabs of flavour. Dishes are a mix of modern Oriental and French, with trendy influences from New York and London. Diners have an option of taster or sharing portions. The head waiter recommends three or four dishes per person of the former (around Dhs.90 each) or six or seven of the latter (around Dhs.50 each). Dishes are grouped in three sections: cold, fish and meat, and an even spread across these gives an impressive range of tastes.

**Towers Rotana**
*Trade Centre 1*
*Map 7 E3*

## Teatro

*04 343 8000 | www.rotana.com*

The open sushi kitchen that greets you as you enter Teatro is just the start of the global culinary journey that awaits. A true fusion of cultures and tastes, the menu is a mix of Japanese, Chinese, Indian and European. Whether you plump for pizza, sushi, noodles or a curry, the food is guaranteed to please, and the chef's dessert selection is a must for indecisive sweet lovers. The decor is dark, moody, modern and hip, and the window seats offer surprisingly interesting views over Sheikh Zayed Road. One word of warning, the air conditioning can be on the cold side, so don't forget your pashmina.

**Park Hyatt Dubai**
*Creekside, Deira*
*Map 11 B4*

## The Terrace

*04 602 1234 | www.dubai.park.hyatt.com*

Sweep through the Park Hyatt's vast green grounds, away from Deira's hustle and horns, through the high-ceilinged palace of a hotel, and you'll reach The Terrace – a place positively humming with wealth. But not in a showy, vulgar way – the Terrace oozes classy money, like a millionaire wearing his weekend wardrobe (Ralph Lauren, of course). Awash in icy, contemporary white, chrome and wood, the voguish space-age interior extends out through shiny conservatory doors to a awning-adorned terrace. Get yourself down there for sunset, sink into one of the huge couches and, with a cocktail in one hand and oysters in the other, salute the good life.

**Hilton Jumeirah**
*Marsa Dubai*
*Map 5 A1*

## Wavebreaker

*04 399 1111 | www.hilton.com*

Between the pool and the beach at the Hilton Jumeirah is the Wavebreaker bar. Serving snacks, light meals, kids meals and a variety of mocktails and cocktails, Wavebreaker is a great place to get away from it all. The staff are friendly and laid back, just like the setting itself, and the sandwiches and snacks are big enough to satisfy any appetite. There's a playground and bouncy castle nearby to keep the kids amused, while you can sit and watch the beach action from a distance. Try going at sunset, when it's quiet, cool and the view is stunning.

**536**

UNIQUELY RENAISSANCE®

# SPICE ISLAND

An international buffet restaurant with six live cooking stations featuring Mexican, Chinese, Korean, Japanese, Thai, Italian, Indian, Arabic and Mongolian dishes, with a variety of cheese and an extensive dessert buffet for a terrific finish.
UNIQUELY RENAISSANCE℠

**TEE TOTAL**
Inclusive of soft drinks
**Dhs. 149/-**

**THE ORIGINAL GRAND BUFFET**
Inclusive of regular house beverages
**Dhs. 189/-**

**PREMIUM EXPERIENCE**
Inclusive of a large selection of premium beverages
**Dhs. 245/-**

Add Dhs. 99/- to Grand or Premium Package and get unlimited sparkling wine

## Friday & Saturday Non-Smoking Family Brunch

Packages starting at **Dhs. 139** (all inclusive)
Kids from 6 to 12 years **Dhs. 69**

"Prices are subject to change without further notice"

WHAT'S ON AWARDS 2007
WINNER IN THE CATEGORY
FAVOURITE INTERNATIONAL
SPECIALITY RESTAURANT

"Awaken your Senses"

## Italian

Other options **Mediterranean** p.550, **Pizzerias** p.553

**Grand Hyatt Dubai**
*Umm Hurair*
*Map 13 C1* **9**

### Andiamo!

*04 317 1234 | www.dubai.grand.hyatt.com*

The most eye-catching feature of Andiamo is the colourful fiery mosaic surrounding the pizza oven, which hints at the fresh-baked delights contained within. This chic modern Italian features Miro-style lamps, an abundance of mirrors, wood and stark colours offset by black-clad serving staff dashing around like smiley ninjas. The starters are pretty, delicious and generous; the pizzas are thin and crispy, fresh and tasty. The desserts are adventurous and memorable, particularly the unexpected delight of the cheese and balsamic concoction. Andiamo's clientele are mainly hip young things and the ambience so relaxed, you could easily forget to check the prices.

**Hilton Jumeirah**
*Marsa Dubai*
*Map 5 A1* **13**

### BiCe

*04 399 1111 | www.hilton.com*

Put the book down and make a reservation now. With excellent food and a delightful atmosphere, BiCE is hugely popular and rightly so. Live piano music complements the 1930s art deco furnishings, while the huge windows offer stellar views over the pool and of the Jumeirah Beach Residence (which will be even better once completed!). The menu offers a great mix of traditional Italian comfort food and nouvelle cuisine, with good-sized portions to satisfy almost every appetite, and flavours for the most discerning palates. Discreet and observant staff can offer advice on all aspects of the menu, including the extensive wine list which changes every few months. It's tricky, but try to save room for dessert.

**Wafi Mall**
*Umm Hurair*
*Map 10 D4* **73**

### Biella Caffé Pizzeria

*04 324 4666 | www.waficitirestaurant.com*

Perfect for a business or ladies' lunch, or even for a teetotal dinner, this quaint Italian bistro has a clean modern interior and leafy exterior (with outdoor air-conditioning units making alfresco dining a year-round option). The food might not win too many prizes for originality but the trusty traditional pasta and pizza dishes are all exquisitely crafted and sumptuously satisfying. Especially worth a mention are the seafood options which are most definitely prize winners in both taste and magnitude. Although the tablecloths start out pearly white, the rich sauces soon take care of that, and if you spill some down your front the staff will appear with a can of stain remover in a jiffy! Another branch is in the Mall of the Emirates (04 347 3414).

**Le Meridien Mina**
*Al Sufouh*
*Map 5 C1* **21**

### Bussola

*04 399 3333 | www.lemeridien-minaseyahi.com*

After a short buggy ride from the hotel to the beach you'll be welcomed at Bussola by friendly, helpful staff. The interior is light and airy, with smart wooden furnishings and floor-to-ceiling windows, so you can't help but appreciate the shoreline vistas. Alternatively, the outdoor terrace gets you even closer to the sea. A Sicilian

**Cocktails**

If you're partial to multihued drinks with exotic names, here's a selection of Dubai's coolest and classiest bars that will leave you stirred but not shaken: Bahri Bar (p.575),

# TOUR Dubai

*Dubai's First*
*Arabian Dhow Cruises*

## Floating Functions - A unique experience for every event.

- Sail on the creek with Dubai's premier Dhow cruise operator
- Exclusive Dhow charters - Fully licenced to serve beverages
- Dhow capacities ranging from 30 to over 180 guests
- Choice of catering options - Arabic entertainment options
- Fitted with Govt. approved safety equipment

### DAILY DINNER CRUISES
- 2 Hours Cruising - 5 Star Buffet Dinner
enna Painting - Incl. Mineral water / Soft Drinks
Transfers can be arranged on request

### GUIDED CREEK TOURS
Four times daily : 11.30, 13.30, 15.30, 17.30
Pre-recorded commentary in English
Incl. Mineral water or soft drink

## Also available: Safaris & Sightseeing Tours

**Tel: 04 3368407 / 9 Fax 04 3368411**
Email: admin@tour-dubai.com Web: www.tour-dubai.com

*Jumeirah*
*Beach Hotel*
*Umm Suqeim*
*Map 6 B1*

## Carnevale

*04 406 8999* | *www.jumeirah.com*

Carnevale, one of two Italian restaurants at JBH, is formal but friendly, with amiable staff and a balcony with great views for alfresco dining. The rich and impressive menu offers a range of pasta, poultry and meat, with fish and seafood dishes perhaps the speciality of the house. It helps having an Italian manager and head chef, as does the use of authentic ingredients like the finest olive oil and the freshest mozzarella. The food is tasty and very attractively presented, and the quality of the whole experience is very high. Slightly expensive but definitely worth a visit on special occasions.

*Radisson SAS Hotel*
*Dubai Media City*
*Al Sufouh*
*Map 5 C2* 28

## Certo

*04 366 9111* | *dubai.radissonsas.com*

Certo is less Mama's home-cooked masterpiece and more suave Italian businessman in a bespoke suit. Which is perfectly appropriate, given its location in the heart of Dubai Media City. Trendy account execs will feel right at home in this handsome setting with its wood and faux-croc skin panels, chrome and glass. Meanwhile, burnt-out creatives will love the double volume glass-walled wine cellar where ruby merlots and grassy chardonnays rest on high metal shelves. Call for takeaway if you're in a hurry.

*Al Bustan Rotana*
*Al Garhoud*
*Map 13 E1* 1

## Come Prima

*04 282 0000* | *www.rotana.com*

With friendly staff, a broad menu of distinctive Italian food, lunch specials, and wine-inclusive offers four nights a week, you shouldn't wait for a special occasion before sampling Come Prima. While the room doesn't shout Italy, the serene atmosphere is a good place for a quiet dinner conversation. The food is an adventurous Italian selection with a lot more than your basic bolognese and alfredo. The menu is built upon a foundation of nice pasta dishes, complemented by a varied selection of meat and fish. The staff can explain the less-familiar items and advise on the surprisingly extensive wine list.

*Ibis World*
*Trade Centre 2*
*Map 7 F3* 55

## Cubo

*04 332 4444* | *www.ibishotel.com*

Cubo's decor is contemporary, romantic, and tasteful with mirrors, candles, and modern art. The room is divided with flowing material and the lighting is subdued, while paper placemat menus, paper napkins, and family-like service create a Trattoria feel. The music is low-key jazz lounge and creates a relaxed atmosphere that is ideal whether you want to entertain a client, book a large table for a party, or get cosy with your significant other. A seemingly unlimited menu makes it hard to choose, the prices are right and the portions are large, so there

*Come Prima*

# Is getting lost your usual excuse?

Whether you're a map person or not, this pocket-sized marvel will help you get to know the city like the back of your hand – so you won't feel the back of someone else's.

**Dubai Mini Map**
Fit the city in your pocket

Abu Dhabi · Amsterdam · Bahrain · Barcelona · Beijing · Berlin · Dubai · Dublin · Geneva
Hong Kong · Kuala Lumpur · Kuwait · London · Los Angeles · New York · New Zealand · Oman
Paris · Qatar · Shanghai · Singapore · Sydney · Tokyo · Vancouver

**EXPLORER**
www.explorerpublishing.com

will be plenty to share. Wednesday and Thursday are buffet nights with unlimited house beverages.

**JW Marriott Hotel**
*Deira*
*Map 11 E1* **18**

## Cucina
*04 262 4444 | www.marriott.com*

With its faux-Tuscan farm decor, Cucina adds a touch of the rustic to Dubai's usual glitz. A solidly traditional Italian menu gives you all the Italian culinary standards and a reasonably priced wine list, with decent house wine, helping you keep the budget in check. The pizzas are very good and pasta dishes, while not exemplary, are still honest to Italian kitchens. If you like an old fashioned sing-a-long, then be sure to get there in time for the staff's renditions of Italian classic tunes.

**Millennium**
**Airport Hotel**
*Al Garhoud*
*Map 13 E1* **61**

## Da Vinci's
*04 282 3464 | www.millenniumhotels.com*

This rustic Italian trattoria favours wholesome decor with checked tablecloths, an abundance of quirky Leonardo related flair, and even a dummy pianist. DaVinci's interior is three-tiered and spacious enough to accommodate smokers, non-smokers and large parties. Discounts are offered for early evening dining and there is a great value three-course business lunch special. There is a reasonable choice of no-fuss pasta, pizza, meats, fish, soups and Mediterranean starters which may not be especially inspiring but are suitably hearty. The drinks are affordable and the wine list well populated. Da Vinci's has a fun after work party atmosphere which really kicks in on weekend evenings – so you might need to book ahead.

> **Wine Lists**
>
> You will find that the majority of fine dining restaurants in Dubai have excellent wine lists but there are a few places that deserve a special mention for their wine cellars. These include The Agency (p.575), The Cellar (p.528), Pierchic (p.556), Spectrum on One (p.534), Teatro (p.536), Verre (p.518) and Vintage (p.587). All you have to do is keep track of the dirhams (wine can be pricey) and make the right choice.

**Metropolitan**
*Downtown Bur Dubai*
*Map 7 B3* **59**

## Don Corleone
*04 343 0000 | www.methotels.com*

A 'traditional' Italian right down to its red and white chequered table cloths and plastic vines, Don Corleone may not have reached kitschdom yet, but it's not far away. The restaurant, like the hotel, has been around a few years and the decor may not be as modern as some Dubai diners have come to expect. It does have a cosy feel though, and there is a terrace for alfresco eating on winter evenings. The antipasti are fine, as are the meat and fish dishes, but the real star of the slightly limited menu has to be the excellent home-made pasta dishes.

**Hyatt Regency**
*Deira*
*Map 9 D1* **14**

## Focaccia
*04 317 2222 | www.dubai.regency.hyatt.com*

Focaccia transports you to a quaint Italian village where you can check in, relax and eat to your stomach's content. Designed as an Italian farmhouse, you can pick a room – library, kitchen, lounge or patio (if you're in the mood for alfresco) and revel in the attentions of friendly staff who will help you order from a delicious menu which, while not overly extensive, will still have you struggling to decide what to order. Meals always commence with a healthy dose of fresh foccacia bread accompanied with the usual roasted garlic, balsamic vinegar and oil, but don't over-indulge as the food is unpretentious, hearty in portion and never disappointing.

*Secret Ingredients*

**Rydges Plaza Hotel**
*Al Satwa*
*Map 8 A3*

## Il Rustico

*04 398 2222 | www.rydges.com*

This little gem is a genuine Italian restaurant both in look and feel, with a Mediterranean tiled floor, dark brown wooden doors and intimate seating. The space is cosy and whether you're catching up with friends, romancing over candlelight or getting together for a family gathering, Il Rustico will make you feel Italian. The food is disconcertingly good and the chef's larder contains everything you could want from pasta, pizzas and salads, all of which are freshly made on the premises, and the deserts taste as good as they look. It may not be the poshest of restaurants or the finest of dining but Il Rustico is a little corner of Italy in a little corner of Rydges Plaza hotel.

**Radisson SAS Hotel**
*Deira Creek*
*Deira*
*Map 9 B4*

## La Moda

*04 205 7333 | www.interconti.com*

La Moda is still a deservedly popular choice for great Italian food in a trendy, if somewhat austere setting, where mood lighting softens the hard, clean lines of the glass and wood decor. As larger parties frequent La Moda, the ambience is lively, perfect for a convivial evening with friends shared over bowls of pasta and pizza, or the more sophisticated seafood options, accompanied by a glass or two from a wide and varied wine list. Don't be surprised to find yourself still chatting over coffee in the wee small hours. La Moda is just that sort of chilled out place where time doesn't matter.

**Mövenpick Hotel**
*Bur Dubai*
*Oud Metha*
*Map 10 D3*

## La Veranda

*04 336 6000 | www.movenpick-hotels.com*

With undoubtedly one of the best value all-you-can-eat deals in town, La Veranda firstly becomes well-known to many through their buffet night, but it is worth a visit at other times of the week. Located on the mezzanine level of the Mövenpick Hotel, the 'terrace' area offers views over the brightly lit lobby. On Tuesday nights, the place gets packed with hungry diners in search of a bargain Italian feast, when Dhs.75 gets you access to the stacked, delicious antipasti buffet, unlimited pasta and pizzas, as well as bottomless red and white house wine. The a la carte menu offers a good range of starters and mains, with seafood dishes and pizzas cooked in their wood-fired oven.

**Emirates Towers**
*Trade Centre 2*
*Map 7 F3*

## Mosaico

*04 319 8088 | www.jumeirah.com*

Situated on the ground level of the Emirates Towers Hotel, this is a step up from your average lobby restaurant. The decor is smart, modern and well-lit, and the name refers to the huge mosaic covering the whole floor area. The professional and friendly staff are happy to recommend dishes and accommodate requests. The menu offers the usual Italian fare with pizza, pasta and seafood dishes, all well presented and most importantly, very tasty. It may lack the atmosphere to make it the first choice for a romantic night out, but Mosaico is a sure-fire bet for high quality Italian food.

**Uptown Mirdif Mall**
*Mirdif*
*Map 15 B2*

## Pane Caldo

*04 288 8319 | www.pane-caldo.ae*

Uptown Mirdif is home to a variety of excellent restaurants and Pane Caldo may just be the leader of this very delicious pack. With modern design (all white and orange to match their corporate colours) and on-the-ball staff the restaurant has an inviting atmosphere, whether you choose to dine inside or alfresco. The menu is lip-licking tempting with antipasti options that tick the taste bud list and pizza and pasta dishes that are right on the mark when it comes to flavour. The deserts are quite literally to die for. The kids menu comes with colouring, a puzzle and an origami car, this is a great sustenance stop for families out on an Uptown shopping spree.

*Excite*

Kempinski Hotel Mall of the Emirates invites you to discover the world's first and truly complete shopping resort. Situated right next to the hotel, Mall of the Emirates brings you the ultimate in leisure and entertainment with Magic Planet and Ski Dubai, and over 450 international retail brands for an unforgettable shopping adventure, along with 393 luxurious rooms and suites in the hotel. Experience the extraordinary at Kempinski Hotel Mall of the Emirates.

P.O. Box 120679 · Dubai · United Arab Emirates
Tel +971 4 341 0000 · Fax +971 4 341 4500
reservations.malloftheemirates@kempinski.com · www.kempinski-dubai.com

Kempinski Hotel
Mall of the Emirates

DUBAI

*Kempinski*

HOTELIERS SINCE 1897

KEMPINSKI - LEADERS IN LUXURY FOR 110 YEARS

**Dusit Dubai**
*Trade Centre 2*
*Map 7 E3*

## Pax

*04 343 3333* | *www.dusit.com*

Take the lift to the 24th floor to reach this palazzo-style restaurant which boasts imposing Roman columns. Sit down on tables set in window alcoves overlooking the traffic on the Sheikh Zayed Road. The menu offers a comprehensive range of Italian, Roman and Mediterranean dishes. There is no background music, which is unfortunate as you feel the need to speak in hushed tones for fear of disturbing the silence. The food is tasty but not sensational, although you can expect extra attentive service when the restaurant is not busy.

**Souk Madinat**
**Jumeirah**
*Umm Suqeim*
*Map 6 A2* 68

## Segreto

*04 366 8888* | *www.jumeirah.com*

Finding your way around the Madinat is confusing enough at the best of times but hunting down the entrance to Segreto (under ground level near the Malakiya Villas) is the ultimate challenge. Once found, the decor is very clean, with smooth lines, pristine presentation, and warm sandy tones to keep it on the soft side of modern. Your dining journey begins with sweet champagne cocktails (Dhs.95 a pop) and delicious breads. The food is aesthetically appealing, if a little on the bland side, and the portions are more suited to a catwalk model than a rugby lad. But at least you feel a little like a celebrity in a top-secret eatery.

**Sheraton Hotel &**
**Towers**
*Deira*
*Map 9 B4* 33

## Vivaldi

*04 207 1717* | *www.sheraton.com/dubai*

If you desire more than just penne and pizza, then this restaurant is a good choice. Romantic and intimate, the stained glass windows, terracotta walls and wooden rafters surround the busy, open kitchen. The terrace opens during the cooler months for fantastic views of abras and dhows waltzing up and down the Dubai Creek. The menu includes all the usual suspects and is delivered by efficient and pleasant staff. Perfect for family, friends, and date nights, there is also live music with everything from classical to modern Roma. Reservations are essential, but if you need to wait for a table, the lounge is perfect for an atmospheric aperitif.

## Japanese

Other options **Far Eastern** p.512

**Al Bustan Rotana**
*Al Garhoud*
*Map 13 E1* 1

## Benihana

*04 282 0000* | *www.rotana.com*

An evening around the teppanyaki tables at Benihana makes for a fast and fun social dining experience. The chefs never fail to impress with their lightning-fast slicing and dicing skills (plus the odd bit of juggling), keeping you entertained while constantly filling your plate with the next tasty treat they've prepared. The main attractions are the good value all-you-can-eat nights – Sunday and Wednesday for teppanyaki (Sunday is steak, chicken, fish and veg, while Wednesday is exclusively seafood), and Tuesday and Saturday for sushi. Costing Dhs.139 including wine, beer and soft drinks, these nights are always popular so be sure to book your place at the table.

**Sheikh Zayed Road**
*Beh Sketchers*
*shoe shop*
*Nr Trade Centre 2*
*Map 7 E3* 136

## Bento-Ya

*04 343 0222* | *www.bentoya.info*

Bento-Ya is a compact, double storey, casual restaurant, that's great for a quick dinner or lunch. The Japanese chef lures in an impressive number of fellow expatriates, which is always a good indicator of just how genuine your meal is going to be (irrespective of the decor). Happily, everything is as expected, with very fresh, good quality options.

**546**

Come for authentic platters of maki, great sushi and bento boxes filled with various meat (try the teriyaki pan-fried beef), fish and egg dishes. The average price of a meal for two with soft drinks is Dhs100-200. Open Sunday to Thursday from 12:00-15:00 and 14:30-23:30, Fridays from 17:30-23:00, and Saturdays from 12:00-15:00 and 18:30-23:30.

### Creekside

*Sheraton Hotel &*
*Towers*
*Deira*
*Map 9 B4* **33**

*04 207 1750* | *www.sheraton.com/dubai*

A warm welcome awaits you at this above-average Japanese venue inside the Sheraton Creek. Depending on what day of the week it is (sushi and teppanyaki theme nights, as well as all-you-can-eat are a regular occurrence), and your mood, you can choose to sit either around one of the teppanyaki stations, at the sushi bar, or at an individual table. If weather permits you can also sit out on the terrace and enjoy spectacular views of the creek; Creekside's excellent waiters will keep you supplied with delicious food and your choice of beverage from the wine list. All food is expertly prepared by Japanese chefs, and the teppanyaki lets you watch a charismatic chef creating succulent dishes.

### Kiku

*Le Meridien Dubai*
*Al Garhoud*
*Map 13 E1* **20**

*04 282 4040* | *www.lemeridien-dubai.com*

This is one of Dubai's most popular Japanese joints, and it is regularly packed with Japanese guests (always a good sign), sushi lovers or novices looking to expand their cuisine catalogue. The restaurant has a choice of dining areas from the traditional private tatami rooms to the teppanyaki bar, sushi counter and tables. The diverse menu offers standard staples such as sushi, sashimi, tempura and teppanyaki which sit alongside some more unusual delicacies. Particularly worth trying are the set meals which are surprisingly good value considering the number of dishes that arrive at your table. Good food, comfortable surroundings and a generally enjoyable experience.

### Miyako

*Hyatt Regency*
*Deira*
*Map 9 D1* **14**

*04 317 2222* | *www.dubai.regency.hyatt.com*

Miyako is filled with Japanese patrons, night after night, all enjoying astoundingly good food. Those in the know and business people wanting to close important deals also frequent this excellent eatery. It's certainly not Dubai's cheapest Japanese option, but the standard of food, decor and impeccable service ensure patrons leave feeling they got what they paid for and more; and they always come back for more. Whether it's melt-in-the-mouth sushi, delectable teppanyaki or tempura cooked to perfection, the flavours are subtle and the high standards the same as you'd expect from a superior Tokyo restaurant.

### Noodle Sushi

*Above Safestway*
*Al Wasl*
*Map 7 C3*

*04 321 1500* | *seawfood@yahoo.com*

Conveniently located over Safestway on Sheikh Zayed Road, Noodle Sushi is one of the four theme restaurants surrounding Sea World. The decor is refined and striking, in black and bamboo tones, and you can sit at the live sushi station and watch the artistry, or order from a varied menu. If one of your diners is not a big fan of Japanese the staff will arrange a meal to be brought from the Sea World section. Both open seating and individual booths are available. The menu includes reasonably priced Bento (complete Japanese meals in lacquered boxes), as well as a wide assortment of sushi, sashimi, tempura and tasty Japanese dishes.

### Sushi

*Grand Hyatt Dubai*
*Umm Hurair*
*Map 13 C1* **9**

*04 317 1234* | *www.dubai.grand.hyatt.com*

A stroll through the oasis-like lobby leads you to the almost secret hideaway that is Sushi, a venue for lovers of sushi and sashimi. Artfully prepared in the open kitchen,

**547**

portions are determined by the number of pieces you feel like indulging in. This is evidently a popular venue for far eastern expatriates looking for some home style food which gives you some reassurance that the careful preparation and the melt in your mouth morsels are indeed high quality. Although there are not many seats, the restaurant is not tight and tables are well spaced to allow privacy, if not intimacy. Staff are welcoming and informative but not obtrusive. The pacing of the meal allows you to linger if you wish. The relaxing copper tones, dark woods, tactile pottery and the pleasing sounds of the hanging water feature help to create a pleasing experience.

*Century Village*
*Al Garhoud*
*Map 13 E1* **47**

## Sushi Sushi
*04 282 9908*
An intimate venue located in Century Village, this Japanese restaurant is decorated in a funky, modern style with low lighting and comfy couches. There is also a fabulous outdoor terrace for cooler evenings. Offering a very comprehensive menu of sushi and sashimi, non-sushi eaters are equally well catered for with some alternative Japanese dishes. Tuesday night allows you to choose all the sushi you can eat from the conveyor belt, washed down with unlimited Tiger beer, for Dhs.125. With good food, reasonable prices, and an enjoyable atmosphere, this is a popular choice. Reservations are recommended, especially on Tuesdays.

*Boulevard at*
*Emirates Towers*
*Trade Centre 2*
*Map 7 F3* **46**

## tokyo@the towers
*04 319 8088* | *www.jumeirah.com*
In keeping with its ultra-modern surroundings, the often-used mock-traditional Japanese look has been eschewed in favour of a Tokyo-style contemporary design. The restaurant has some stylish Japanese garden features along the corridor next to elegantly partitioned tatami rooms, with seating on traditional floor cushions. You can also dine at the windows overlooking the mall, at the sushi bar or at the teppanyaki table. The menu is good, featuring a wide range of all the Japanese usuals, and for something different the 'ankimo' and 'spider' are must tries. The teppanyaki table serves up hot, freshly grilled food, and other staples such as tempura, grilled dishes and the bento lunch sets are also worth trying.

*Crowne Plaza*
*Trade Centre 1*
*Map 7 F2* **4**

## Wagamama
*04 305 6060* | *www.wagamama.ae*
Modelled on a traditional Japanese ramen bar, Wagamama's contemporary, streamlined design works well for a quick bite or more leisurely dining experience. Orders are taken and electronically sent directly to the kitchen where they are immediately and freshly prepared; thus, if you want to linger over your meal, it is wise to order one course at a time. The menu is extensive and covers a wide variety of generously served noodle and rice dishes. The friendly hustle and bustle atmosphere is created by the shared seating at long tables with benches. Smokers: you'll have to leave the cigs at the door.

*Ascot Hotel*
*Downtown Bur Dubai*
*Map 8 F2* **43**

## Yakitori
*04 352 0900* | *www.ascothoteldubai.com*
For those in search of truly authentic Japanese food, there is no better place in Dubai than Yakitori. The restaurant is in the style of a Japanese diner, in stylish red and black. The extensive menu offers an unrivalled choice of food, which clearly delights the almost entirely Japanese clientele. Aficionados will enjoy the usual sushi and tempura, as well as a variety of noodle choices, set meals, and the signature yakitori dish. You may find venues with more subtle ambience, but very rarely with such a choice of quality food.

## Korean

Other options **Far Eastern** p.512

*Zomorrodah Bld*
*Al Karama*
*Map 10 E1* 122

### Seoul Garden Restaurant

*04 337 7876 | seoulgarden@empal.com*

Here you sit tucked away in your own private room, and each table is equipped with the traditional Korean barbecue – which you should definitely put to good use by ordering at least one beef dish. As is the Korean way, most main courses are served with various complimentary side dishes to enhance the meal. Your waiters are literally at your fingertips as a table-mounted button brings a friendly and helpful smile upon command. Cool ginger tea and sweet melon dessert accompany every meal and provide a unique and satisfying finish.

## Latin American

Other options **Mexican** p.551

*Dubai Marine Beach*
*Jumeira*
*Map 7 F1* 5

### El Malecon

*04 346 1111 | www.dxbmarine.com*

Designed with the in-crowd in mind, Malecon's high turquoise walls (interestingly covered in graffiti) and low lighting creates a sultry Cuban atmosphere that builds up slowly during the course of the evening, helped along by the live music and some of Dubai's best Salsa dancers. Big windows overlook the glowing Dubai Marine lagoon and while the menu isn't massive (the signature paella is the best choice), the clientele is pretty delicious. With neighbouring venues bringing in the sophisticated sheep as the clock ticks on, Malecon is a great place to start the night, dip into en route or end a liquid shoreline sojourn.

*Al Murooj Rotana*
*Hotel & Suites*
*Trade Centre 2*
*Map 7 E3* 2

### Latino House

*04 321 1111 | www.rotana.com*

Keep this venue in mind for those guests you need to impress, be it the in-laws, the boss, or even just your partner in gourmet indulgence. The seafood and steak mains are undoubtedly the swaggering stars of the menu but don't rule out the pleasures of a dalliance with the appetisers and desserts. Follow your waiter's lead and he'll ensure you sample the highlights of this establishment's take on Nuevo Latino cuisine. The plush, low-lit setting may be better suited to intrigue than to indulgence, but once more people discover Latino House, it's sure to become as lively as its food.

*Hilton Jumeirah*
*Marsa Dubai*
*Map 5 A1* 13

### Pachanga

*04 399 1111 | www.hilton.com*

Pachanga unites nations by bringing Mexican, Argentinean, Cuban and Brazilian cuisines together under one roof. The rotating spits in the open kitchen grab your attention as you walk in, offering a clue to the meat-focused fare on the menu. The food is pricey but very good, and the bar serves great cocktails to get the evening going. A big draw is the authentic house band that injects a bit of Latin spirit and tempts diners to get up and dance off their desserts. Check for themed salsa and tango nights in advance, and be sure to book early as tables are soon snapped up.

*El Malecon*

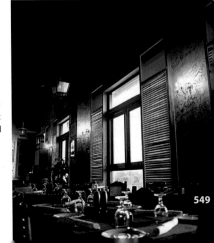

## Mediterranean
Other options **Italian** p.538, **Spanish** p.558

**Sofitel City Centre**
*Al Garhoud*
*Map 11 C3* 35

### La Villa
*04 294 1222* | *www.accorhotels.com*

La Villa at the Sofitel Hotel strikes images of sunny southern France. Warm yellow walls bear murals, prints, and paintings of fruits and vegetables, and enclose beautifully appointed tables with fresh flowers under subtle lighting. The food is prepared with the freshest ingredients, and comes by way of a gracious staff. The Dhs.69 Business Lunch, served Saturday to Wednesday, is a hit with diners who can then round off their meal with a winning dessert and choice of satisfying beverages. For a definite change of scenery, take the short walk from busy Deira City Centre to tranquil France at La Villa.

**Pyramids**
*Umm Hurair*
*Map 10 E4* 65

### Medzo
*04 324 4100* | *www.waficitirestaurants.com*

If the temperature is in the 40s but you fancy a fix of alfresco dining, Medzo is the place. A couple of rather clever outdoor air-conditioning units make it possible to enjoy the pleasant terrace without perspiring into your pasta. That's not to say you should avoid eating inside, as the decor is modern, classy, and lit just low enough to ensure an intimate setting. As for the food, a good selection of delicious Mediterranean dishes will not disappoint, neither will the one or two adventurous dishes. Add in a good wine list, friendly professional staff and desserts to die for, and you'll soon realise why Medzo is such a Dubai favourite.

**No. One Tower**
*Trade Centre 1*
*Map 7 E3*

### Olive House
*04 343 3110*

Olive House is a marvellous corner of the Mediterranean situated on Sheikh Zayed Road. Its 18 tables tend to stay occupied although diners come and go, having eaten sandwiches, pizzas, mezze or salads and, almost surely, icecream. All of the delicious dishes also pass over the counters in a busy takeaway trade. The friendly and prompt service makes this an ideal place for a quick meal, especially given the reasonable prices and the convenient location. While this strip of Sheikh Zayed Road may be home to a wide variety of eateries, Olive House is one of the finest in terms of simple, fresh and delicious cuisine.

**Oasis Beach Tower**
*Marsa Dubai*
*Map 5 A1* 137

### Oregano
*04 399 4444* | *www.jebelali-international.com*

The Mediterranean farmhouse theme at Oregano takes its origin rather seriously. Prospective diners may be put off by the rural kitsch of checked upholstery, ruffled curtains, dried flowers, and autumn colours. But beyond the decor Oregano should be famed for its admirable ingredients, professionally prepared and generously served by competent staff eager to please. The hosting Oasis Beach Hotel reinforces the idea of basic practicality, but the varied and lip-licking menu with favourites from Italy, France and Spain is what makes the real impression.

**Emirates Towers**
*Trade Centre 2*
*Map 7 F3* 7

### Vu's
*04 319 8088* | *www.jumeirah.com*

A stylish and elegant eatery, this is fine dining at its best and with one of the most sensational views in town. The food is modern European cuisine, which means you'll find a variety of original dishes with recognisable influences. The menu is finely compiled with some dishes certain to impress. You can start with caviar linguine for example and the signature dishes are lobster and roast pigeon. Each dish is exquisitely presented in more manageable portions than you might find elsewhere. You'll leave feeling more than satisfied but not about to burst. Be warned, dining in the highest restaurant in the Middle East (both in terms of quality and of skyscraping) comes at a price.

## Mexican

Other options **Tex Mex** p.560

**Nr Spinneys Centre**
*Umm Suqeim*
*Map 6 F2*

### Maria Bonita's

*04 395 4454*

In a city with so many hotel restaurants, Maria Bonita stands out as a friendly, comfortable, well-worn neighbourhood eatery. Serving traditional Mexican (of which there aren't so many choices in town) and Tex-Mex dishes, it draws its customers back time and time again. Though you will have to sacrifice having a cerveza with your meal, the flavourful and well-prepared nachos, quesadillas and fajitas plus the relaxed, laid back atmosphere make it more than worthwhile. Perfect for families, couples, or small groups, you can enjoy the patio or inside, watching the tortilla machine churn out the flat bread. There is also another branch called Casa Maria (04 885 3188) in the Green Community.

## Moroccan

Other options **Arabic/Lebanese** p.503

**Shangri-La Hotel**
*Trade Centre 1*
*Map 7 E3* 32

### Marrakech

*04 405 2703* | *www.shangri-la.com*

This classy eatery offers a tempting menu of Moroccan fare for discerning diners. Smooth arches and lamps incorporated into the design of the main eating area add to the sense of tranquility, while a rather strident duo belts out folksy traditional tunes on a small stage area at the front of the restaurant. Starters, served on beautiful blue ceramic tableware, are generously portioned and bursting with flavour, while waiters reveal piping hot mains with a flourish from beneath silver tagines. There is a good selection of meat, seafood and vegetarian options to choose from which can be accompanied by perfectly light and fluffy couscous.

**Souk Madinat**
**Jumeirah**
*Umm Suqeim*
*Map 6 A2* 68

### Shoo Fee Ma Fee

*04 366 6335* | *www.jumeirah.com*

You know by now that the views at some of the Madinat outlets are breathtaking, but even as you walk out onto the terrace at Shoo Fee Ma Fee you'll still find the postcard-perfect view mesmerising. The menu places an emphasis on authentic Moroccan cuisine, and it must be the only place in Dubai where you can choose between roasted goat leg (for two), camel kofta or a mixed platter of grilled lamb, chicken and camel. Vegetarians: you might not like it! After your meal, you can relax in the comfortable upstairs area and enjoy pastries, shisha and live entertainment.

**One&Only**
**Royal Mirage**
*Al Sufouh*
*Map 5 C1* 25

### Tagine

*04 399 9999* | *www.oneandonlyroyalmirage.com*

Tagine is the kind of place you can imagine local royalty lingering in one of the intimate booths. The entrance alone screams exclusivity – beneath ground level, through an enormous wooden door, past a majlis area soaked in rich embroidery and incense smoke and a small but inviting bar, perfect for pre- or post-dinner drinks. The large half-moon booths bejewelled in satin cushions are a must if you want to really immerse yourself in a Moroccan fantasy. The food is whole-heartedly true to its name with authentic mezze, aromatic tagines, spicy kebabs and exotic couscous which all come in fish, chicken, lamb or vegetable packages.

**551**

## Pakistani
Other options **Sri Lankan** p.558, **Indian** p.520

*Various locations*

### Karachi Darbar
Quite possibly the cheapest place in Dubai for tasty, good quality food, this Indo-Pakistani chain is a perennial favourite. The simple decor, plain menus, and utilitarian settings may not pull visitors in off the street, but that's their loss. The no-nonsense but friendly service, the range of food and the generous portions make this exceptional value for money. With the Pakistani dishes on the menu, it adds a little something different in comparison to the range usually offered by restaurants from the subcontinent. Dining options and facilities around town do differ, but some, like the Karama branch, offer dining outside. Definitely worth seeking out.
Branches at: Karama Shopping Centre, near the large car park (04 334 7272); Bur Dubai, near HSBC (04 353 7080); Qusais Road (04 261 2526); Naif Road, near Hyatt Regency Hotel (04 272 3755); Satwa (04 349 0202); Hor Al Anz, behind Dubai Cinema (04 262 5251); Al Qusais, Sheikh Colony (04 263 2266); Rashidiya (04 285 9464).

*Nr Satwa R/A*
*Al Satwa*
*Map 8 A3* **113**

### Ravi's
*04 331 5353*
Ravi's has gained something of a legendary status among western expats and seems to be on a lot of tour guides' itineraries, despite being one of the cheapest eateries in the book. This 24 hour diner offers a range of Pakistani curried favourites and rice dishes, such as biryani, alongside more quirky dishes like fried brains. The venue is basic and, while most people opt for the choice of eating outside with all of Satwa life on show to keep you entertained, dining is also available in the main restaurant or in the quieter family section.

## Persian
Other options **Arabic/Lebanese** p.503

*Al Durrah Tower*
*Trade Centre 1*
*Map 7 F2* **108**

### Al Borz
*04 331 8777*
One of Tehran's best kebab houses has finally crossed the Gulf and set up shop on Sheikh Zayed Road, providing Dubai residents the chance to sample their famous kebabs and rich rice specialities. The lunch buffet including soups and desserts, is an ideal introduction to Iranian cuisine and is moderately priced. A family setting and large portions make Al Borz popular with Iranians and those who love Persian fare. The takeaway and delivery service is good.

*Nr Rydges Plaza*
*Al Satwa*
*Map 8 A3* **114**

### Pars Iranian Kitchen
*04 398 4000* | *pars@eim.ae*
The first thing you'll notice is the huge, garish neon sign pulsating above the restaurant. Don't be put off though, as Pars offers a traditional laid-back atmosphere a million miles from the modernity suggested by the neon. The menu is limited, but all the old favourites are there including hummus, moutabel, tabbouleh, and a selection of grilled meats and kebabs. But forget the food, because here it's all about location. A delightful front garden, enclosed by a fairy light-entwined hedgerow, is home to low tables and soft, Arabic-cushioned bench seats, perfect for enjoying a leisurely shisha with a group of friends. Another branch in the Wilson building (04 398 8787), near the Dubai World Trade Centre, offers slightly more luxurious indoor dining, and Pars can also be found in the food court at the Mall of the Emirates.

**Hyatt Regency**
Deira
Map 9 D1 14

## Shahrzad

*04 317 2222 | www.dubai.regency.hyatt.com*

Shahrzad offers a sophisticated menu in an alluring setting. Step inside and enjoy traditional Iranian decor with marble fountains, palatial ceilings, Oriental carpets, hanging rustic lights, and mystical music. Dishes include unique blends of meats, seafood, fruit, vegetables, and herbs, but be careful not to fill up on the hot, seeded bread, fresh mint, basil, and feta that greet you upon arrival. The service is excellent and very accommodating to vegetarians, who may find the menu a bit spartan. The entertainment is hypnotic and enveloping. Live music is on offer every night from 21:00. Ensure a quieter evening by reserving a 'balcony' seat. There are also quaint tea and shisha rooms for more intimate conversation.

## Pizzerias

Other options **Italian** p.538

Sometimes nothing else on the menu can compete with a good pizza, and you'll find a good variety in Dubai. The following table lists places where you'll find good, reliable fare – obviously you'll get pizzas at most Italian restaurants (see p.538), but those listed really stand out (marked with an 'R' on the table). Competition is fierce and opinion is divided on who does the best, but the only way to really know is to sample them for yourself.

Of course, takeaway pizzas are pretty good too – a few favourites are marked with a 'T' in the table.

| Pizzerias | |
| --- | --- |
| 800Pizza | 8007 4992 |
| Biella Caffé Pizzeria | 04 324 4666 |
| Casa Mia | 04 282 4040 |
| Cucina | 04 262 4444 |
| Il Rustico | 04 398 2222 |
| Italian Connection | 04 335 3001 |
| La Moda | 04 391 2550 |
| Papa Johns | 04 335 2523 |
| Pastamania | 04 390 8672 |
| Pizza Express | 04 355 2424 |
| | 04 394 5616 |
| | 04 285 2393 |
| Pizza Hut | 800 6500 |
| Pizzeria Uno Chicago Grill | 04 294 8799 |
| Round Table Pizza | 04 396 6999 |
| | 04 398 6684 |
| | 04 282 0666 |
| | 04 881 0808 |

## Polynesian

Other options **Far Eastern** p.512

**Metropolitan Palace**
Deira
Map 11 C1 23

## Tahiti

*04 205 1364 | www.methotels.com*

This restaurant is small and a bit worn around the edges. If you like toy monkeys swinging from the rafters and beach shack decor, then this is the place for you, although it is a bit of a bamboo overkill. The main draw here is the theme nights with the all-you-can-eat-and-drink buffet for Dhs.125. Alternatively Teppanyaki fans can opt to sit around the wooden boat which houses the traditional Japanese live-cooking station. Here you can choose from three different tasty set menus and watch the chef throw your food in the air before presenting it in perfection on your plate. Other entertainment includes Polynesian dancers.

**Souk Madinat**
**Jumeirah**
Umm Suqeim
Map 6 A2 68

## Trader Vic's

*04 366 5646*

Trader Vic's is more of a Dubai rite of passage than just another eating and drinking venue. Until you've been through the doors and experienced the vibey atmosphere, you just can't consider yourself a seasoned night-lifer. The good news is that you have various options to earn your Trader Vic's badge: you can linger over a delicious, Asian-inspired meal, or munch your way through some very moreish snacks (crispy wontons, prawns and other oriental finger foods), or even just savour a few of their famously exotic cocktails (served in shrunken heads or adorned with feathers). And you can earn it in two locations – one in the Crowne Plaza on Sheikh Zayed Road (04 331 1111), and one with a waterside terrace in the Madinat.

## Portuguese

*Nr Crowne Plaza Hotel*
Sheik Zayed Rd
Trade Centre 1
Map 7 F2 **105**

### Nando's

*04 321 2000* | *headoffice@nandosuae.ae*

Worldwide chain Nando's is famous for its peri-peri chicken (and they're proud of it, judging by the number of peri-peri puns on the menu), which ranges from the mild to the extra hot with a 'sideline' of curly fries. The menu is limited and the service a little rusty but the takeaway downstairs is a good option for residents of the many neighbouring towers. Just don't order the bowl of nuts as your starter (only one of three choices) – why pay Dhs.7 when you can get them free in a bar down the road! Other Locations: Nr Al Ghurair City (04 221 1992), The Greens Centre (04 360 8080).

## Russian

*Nr Lamcy Plaza*
Oud Metha
Map 10 D2 **119**

### Russian Home Restaurant

*04 334 6050*

The Russian Home Restaurant lacks a bit of atmosphere, but is a great place to go for... Russian home cooking. Relax in diner-style booths while you peruse the gargantuan menu. Famous dishes like Russian salad and Borsht are available, but thanks to the large menu there is also a good selection of other dishes including side dishes of mashed potato, cabbage, dumplings and filled breads. Drinks (all non-alcoholic) range from the mundane to the downright unusual (like 'kvas', a drink made by fermenting yeast and rye flour). The service is very friendly, despite the language barrier. Open 24 hours a day.

*Ascot Hotel*
Downtown Bur Dubai
Map 8 F2 **43**

### Troyka

*04 352 0900* | *www.ascothoteldubai.com*

There are few surprises left in Dubai, but if there are any at all then this place is definitely one of them. Troyka offers old-world Russian charm in a unique, mesmerising setting. Upon entering, the first thing you will notice is the murals of rural winter wonderlands – perfect on a hot night. The low ceilings, dim lighting, red roses and candles add to the intimate mood. The service is attentive and the staff are adorned in traditional clothing. There is plenty of room with long tables for families and parties or small tables for more romantic evenings. The Tuesday night buffet is all-inclusive and comprises time-honoured delicacies from Russian cuisine. A band plays every night from 22:30 and a extravagant Live Vegas-style cabaret begins at 23:30.

## Seafood

*Heritage & Diving*
*Village*
Al Shindagha
Map 9 B1 **54**

### Al Bandar

*04 393 9001* | *www.alkoufa.com*

Its idyllic location on the edge of the creek is score one for Al Bandar, a terrific venue offering good international seafood for a more 'dress-down' clientele. This is the perfect venue to ease guests and visitors into the Arabian experience and certainly a breath of fresh air from the overwhelmingly plush restaurants in five-star hotels that can be stifling at times. The choice of seafood is pleasantly varied and the prices all cheap and cheerful. Tradition is the theme with the added photographic thrill of the resident camels nearby.

*Burj Al Arab*
*Umm Suqeim*
*Map 6 B1* **3**

## Al Mahara

*04 301 7600* | *www.jumeirah.com*
Your visit to Al Mahara starts with a simulated submarine ride that takes you 'under the sea' to dine among the fish – it's a bit flash, but fortunately once you 'disembark' the restaurant is an elegant area curled around a huge aquarium full of amazing sea life. The menu's offerings are almost exclusively seafood creations, all prepared with great talent and innovation by some of Dubai's top chefs. The presentation and flavours are sublime, just what you'd expect from the mighty Burj Al Arab. It's fine dining at its finest, with prices to match – for most people this will only ever be a 'special occasion' restaurant (and it is pretty special). Gentlemen are required to wear a jacket for dinner.

*Shangri-La Hotel*
*Trade Centre 1*
*Map 7 E3* **32**

## Amwaj

*04 343 8888* | *www.shangri-la.com*
Amwaj is a fine restaurant in every sense. The minimal decor cleverly depicts a marine theme yet remains sophisticated and refined. An immaculate sushi bar greets you on arrival, and the open kitchen allows you to watch tantalising dishes being prepared. The menu is exciting and unusual, offering endless fish and seafood creations, and the vegetarian and meat alternatives are equally impressive. Adventurous diners should definitely leave room to sample the chocolate ravioli dessert and should consider the tasting and set menus. Although a little pricey, dining at Amwaj is a wonderful culinary experience. Advance booking is advised.

*Le Meridien Mina*
*Al Sufouh*
*Map 5 C1* **21**

## The Dhow

*04 399 3333* | *www.lemeridien-minaseyahi.com*
From the moment you walk down the candlelit path and step aboard this permanently moored traditional dhow you know you're in for a special treat, whether you dine in the air-conditioned lower deck or go alfresco and enjoy the view of the marina and the ocean from the top deck. The menu focuses heavily on seafood, starting with fresh oysters and a tantalising choice of sushi and sashimi. Don't overindulge though – you'll need plenty of room for the main course, which you can select from a huge range and have cooked in a number of different ways. The dhow's location in the marina means no disconcerting ocean motion.

*The Dhow*

**555**

**AS Hotel**
*Deira Creek*
*Deira*
*Map 9 B4* **27**

## Fish Market

*04 205 7333 | www.interconti.com*

Accompanied by a member of staff clad in plastic gloves and clutching a wicker shopping basket, diners select fresh fish and other natural ingredients and request the style of cooking. While you wait for your tailor-made dinner to arrive you can snack on a bowl of french fries and soak up the creekside view (make sure to request a table next to the window when reserving). The menu is somewhat limited and a little on the simplistic side and while it's certainly novel, seafood aficionados may prefer a little less emphasis on the supermarket and more on the fish restaurant.

**Ritz-Carlton**
*Marsa Dubai*
*Map 5 A1* **31**

## La Baie

*04 399 4000 | www.ritzcarlton.com*

In Dubai's 24 hour a day milieu, it's easy to forget how to luxuriate over a meal. La Baie reminds you. If the music doesn't massage away stress, the wine list showcases some stunning tension relievers. With two very different chefs behind the scenes (Japanese-Korean Randy Joung and French Cederic Darthial) the resulting food is an exciting mix of traditional and imaginative seafood, with dishes including red snapper vanilla carpaccio and seared turbot with roast squash. Staff are unhurried, and knowledgeable of both the menu and personal space. Intimate yet spacious, La Baie is still relatively unknown, and is an ideal choice for either special occasions or a classic dining experience.

**The Jumeirah**
**Beach Hotel**
*Umm Suqeim*
*Map 6 B1* **17**

## Marina

*04 406 8181 | www.jumeirahbeachhotel.com/dining/marina*

Negotiating the long walkway extending from Jumeirah Beach Hotel justifies a ride in one of the ever-available carts. Already feeling quite at sea, cruising patrons climb to the top deck, 360º, to brave the breezes with a bracing beverage. Stunning views of the coast and its remarkable hotels encourage lingering, but the prospect of dining in the Marina below keeps traffic on the stairway brisk. In the restaurant guests inspect the shiny fish recumbent in icy displays and the even more gorgeous, though less edible, fish swimming in their sparkling tanks. Since the glass of the restaurant effectively blocks the view enjoyed outside, patrons concentrate on the fish, cooked largely under Asian influence.

**Al Qasr Hotel**
*Umm Suqeim*
*Map 6 A1* **41**

## Pierchic

*04 366 8888 | www.jumeirah.com*

Pierchic could quite possibly be Dubai's most amazing restaurant, which is a rather bold statement considering its array of awe-inspiring adversaries. There are good reasons, however, for staking this claim. Firstly the breathtaking location – Pierchic is situated at the end of a long wooden pier that juts into the Arabian Gulf and affords front-row seats of an unobstructed Burj Al Arab. Secondly the superior seafood, which is meticulously presented and delicately cooked. And thirdly, the first-class wine menu reads like a sommelier's wishlist. Waxing lyrical about Pierchic is easy, but nowhere is perfect – if you're not a fan of rich, fancy food that comes in small packages then you might think you're not getting value for money (as it doesn't come cheap). Just remember what you're really paying for is the incredible surroundings, especially if you request a table on the terrace where you can soak up the atmosphere as the waves dance beneath you.

**Souk Madin**
**at Jumeirah**
*Umm Suqeim*
*Map 6 A2* **68**

## Pisces

*04 366 8888 | www.jumeirah.com*

Pisces is a plush modern seafood restaurant with subtle decor, pleasingly professional service, and creatively delicious food, always artistically presented. The attentive staff glide between beautifully set tables arranged spaciously to maintain intimacy. Diners feel the majesty of the dramatically illuminated windtowers of the Al Qasr Hotel as seen from the windows of the Souk Madinat Jumeirah. Pisces' perfectly presented fish is exactly what one would expect at a virtually perfect restaurant. Once you have finished, be sure to visit the outdoor bar upstairs that will give you a breathtaking view of the Madinat waterways in all their man-made glory.

**Mall of the Emirates**
*Al Barsha*
*Map 6 A3*

## Salmontini
*04 347 5844*
If you like salmon and snow: this unique eatery might just be your idea of heaven. Located in a cosy cranny of the Mall of the Emirates, the lilac, pink and slate chic interior of Salmontini is fashioned around large windows overlooking Dubai's indoor ski slope. Choose from every imaginable working of Scottish salmon, from smoked and grilled to cured and poached. Prices are not cheap, but they do offer all-inclusive deals on different nights of the week. You can even pop in if you totally despise salmon, as their menu lists other fish too.

**Above Safestway**
*Al Wasl*
*Map 7 C3*

## Sea World
*04 321 1500* | *www.seaworld-dubai.com*
This is a top-notch venue offering the freshest seafood in pleasantly decorated surroundings, so don't be put off by the giant red neon lobster that flashes outside, or its location above a supermarket. It's a simple concept: choose your 'catch' from the market stall, and have it cooked to perfection by the talented chefs. Service is excellent, easily rivalling the best five-star hotels, but the real surprise is the price, which is considerably lower than you'd pay for the same thing elsewhere. No alcohol.

**Mina A'Salam**
*Umm Suqeim*
*Map 6 A1*

## The Wharf
*04 366 8888* | *www.jumeirah.com*
The Wharf is fronted by magical (though man-made) waterways, where abras transfer guests from one elegant eatery or beautiful bar to the next. Both the outdoor deck, decorated with sailing paraphenalia, and the spacious interior, with an equally nautical atmosphere, are appealing. Sadly, The Wharf's cuisine is not as mesmerising. There's steak and a smattering of Arabic dishes, alongside plentiful pizza, but you've come expecting an ocean's worth of seafood not Sinbad's leftovers. Even the live lobster and crabs sizzling on the grill behind seem a little put out. To compound the contradictions, the bill crashes down on your table and stares up with a smirk.

# Singaporean
Other options **Far Eastern** p.512

**Grand Hyatt Dubai**
*Umm Hurair*
*Map 13 C1*

## Peppercrab
*04 317 2222* | *www.dubai.grand.hyatt.com*
While it has to be said that the food at Peppercrab is excellent (if a little pricey), the restaurant itself doesn't quite live up to the hype. When you are paying pretty big bucks for your black pepper crab (which comes with aprons and a whole host of utensils for meat extraction) you want the dining experience to be extra special. The restaurant is open at the front and the lighting is a little bright, while the modern oriental style trimmings are a touch bland. Your best bet is to request a seat in the back rooms – at least then you can rip open your dinner in private!

---

**Dinner & Drinks**

Dubai has a number of restaurants that deserve a special mention for their bars. For example Trader Vic's (p.553) is primarily a restaurant but is also renowned for its cocktail bar. Other eateries that are worth visiting for a drink include Bussola's upstairs terrace (p.538), Malecon (p.549), Seville's (p.558) and Spectrum on One (p.534). For a great wine selection, try The Cellar (p.528).

---

**557**

*Nr Bur Juman Centre*
*Downtown Bur Dubai*
*Map 8 F4* **116**

## Singapore Deli Café

*04 396 6885* | *singapuredeli@yahoo.co.uk*

From bowls of steaming noodles to traditionally cooked Nasi Goreng, the authentic Asian dishes available at Singapore Deli Café are consistently excellent. The casual atmosphere and the high standard of home-style cooking draws a large crowd of regular customers, including many local Indonesians and Malaysians who come for a taste of home. Prices are very reasonable, and this is one independent eatery that should definitely be on your must-do list if you're a fan of good Asian food.

*Oasis Beach Tower*
*Marsa Dubai*
*Map 5 A1* **13**

## Singapura

*04 399 4444* | *www.jebelali-international.com*

Kitsch decor sets the scene at this friendly and incredibly casual restaurant. So casual in fact, that the menu doesn't strictly adhere to anything in particular and you could probably turn up in your slippers. Asian treats have been given a European twist and will suit easy-going tastebuds – especially those partial to seafood. It's fitting that one of Dubai's most laid-back beach hotels has incredibly friendly staff, who are only too happy to natter or help you make your choice of Chinese, Singaporean and Thai dishes.

# Spanish

Other options **Mediterranean** p.550

*Al Qasr Hotel*
*Umm Suqeim*
*Map 6 A1* **41**

## Al Hambra

*04 366 8888* | *www.jumeirah.com*

Al Hambra's exposed brickwork and vaulted ceilings make for a more than passable Spanish restaurant, and the food, which fuses Andalusia with Morrocco, is strong. Vegetarians are left with a skimpy choice, but for everyone else the seafood paella is a must. A duo of talented mariachis provides the perfect mood to accompany your meal, and may have you stopping off to rent the Desperado DVD on the way home. It's not cheap, and you may want to save it for special occasions, but Al Hambra could just become your new favourite Spanish restaurant in Dubai.

*Wafi City*
*Umm Hurair*
*Map 10 D4* **65**

## Seville's

*04 324 7300* | *www.waficityrestaurants.com*

Upon arriving in Seville's you will quickly find that this is the perfect place for kicking back and enjoying the lively atmosphere. The restaurant attracts a mixed crowd who are either there to enjoy the delicious tapas menu, or the well-stocked bar, or (more frequently) both. In the early evening the place is perfect for romance with a candlelit dinner, live acoustic guitar and the alfresco rooftop garden and bar. Later in the evening the atmosphere picks up and you will find the location an ideal spot for a fun night out with friends as the music continues, the drinks flow and that indefinable Mediterranean magic works its charms.

# Sri Lankan

*Opp Lulu Supermarket*
*Al Karama*
*Map 10 E1* **123**

## Chef Lanka

*04 335 3050*

Chef Lanka is the best chance to try Sri Lankan food in Dubai. It is a smart, clean little restaurant offering good value and great tasting food. There is a 'thatched' hut housing the daily buffet, but authentic dishes are cooked to order in the kitchen, allowing you to specify the spiciness. Alternatively, eat from the buffet for just Dhs.8 at lunch or Dhs.20 at dinner. It also does a mean nasi goreng.

## Steakhouses

Other options **American** p.500

### Asado

**The Palace**
Downtown Burj Dubai
Map 7 D4 **139**

*04 428 7888* | *www.sofitel.com*

So, the boss is in town or it's your anniversary. How do you strike the balance between impressive and showy? A restaurant called Asado in the shadow of the (current) tallest building in the world is the answer. Men will love the hefty steaks and women won't fail to appreciate the ladies' menu (on which no prices are marked) and luxurious ski lodge decor. From the signature bife de chorizo steak to the feather-light chocolate soufflé, the menu is well planned and beautifully executed. Add in charming service, live music and an extensive wine list and you'll be talking about it for days.

### The Exchange Grill

**Fairmont Dubai**
Trade Centre 1
Map 8 A4 **8**

*04 311 8000* | *www.fairmont.com*

Peer around the glass partition at Exchange Grill and you're confronted by excess – outsized leather armchairs, fussy modern art installations and a floor-to-ceiling chandelier. Offering Dubai residents and visitors an even more exciting dining and leisure destination since its refurbishment, the menu strikes a balance between the classic and the innovative. Both lunch and dinner menus offer the best quality beef, but also pays tribute to some of North America's finest eateries.

### JW's Steakhouse

**JW Marriott Hotel**
Deira
Map 11 E1 **18**

*04 262 4444* | *www.marriott.com*

Set in an intimate, out-of-the-way part of the hotel, JW's Steakhouse meets your expectations from the moment you walk through the door. Chefs can be seen cleaving huge chunks of meat in the open kitchen and once you are shown to your stately leather armchair, a huge menu offering an impressive range of steaks and seafood awaits. Salads are prepared fresh at your table and desserts, simple and generous, are worth it, if you can face them!

### Legends Steakhouse

**Creek Golf Club**
Al Garhoud
Map 11 B4 **49**

*04 295 6000* | *www.dubaigolf.com*

Membership of the Creek Golf club is not a requirement in order to savour Legends' relaxing atmosphere, deep comfortable seats and good quality food. The finely prepared, imaginative international cuisine includes a range of steaks and seafood, and accompanied by an extensive wine list. The decor is modern, with a ceiling that stretches right to the top of the building's distinctive white sails. In the cooler months seating is also available on the large veranda, with great views overlooking the creek.

### M's Beef Bistro

**Le Meridien Dubai**
Al Garhoud
Map 13 E1 **20**

*04 282 4040* | *www.lemeridien-dubai.commer*

The sophisticated simplicity of M's decor betrays the real reason diners hungrily visit this quiet corner of the Meridien Village – namely, to gorge on hunks of red meat. The menu is extensive enough for the discerning carnivore, but straightforward enough for those seeking decent, uncomplicated food. Carpaccio, tartar, tenderloins and ribeyes star in a mouthwatering portfolio of meats and the only downside is choosing which to go for. The intimate ambience makes for an altogether pleasurable dining experience.

**55**

*Grand Hyatt Dubai*
*Umm Hurair*
*Map 13 C1*

# Manhattan Grill

*04 317 1234 | www.dubai.grand.hyatt.com*

Smiles and smooth music melt your troubles away as you leave the Hyatt's rainforest and enter the sumptuous surroundings of the Manhattan Grill. The chic decor is the only reference to the bustling cosmopolitan city outside, as the staff, the lighting and the plush seating are all dedicated to relaxation. A variety of high-quality steaks can be customised with sauces and side dishes from the menu. Non meat-eaters can enjoy a special vegetarian selection, and lamb, duck and seafood are also available. The set menu, with optional recommended wines, is a delightful option for the ultimate in restaurant pampering.

*Emirates Towers*
*Trade Centre 2*
*Map 7 F3*

# The Rib Room

*04 319 8088 | www.jumeirah.com*

The deep red upholstery and dark woods create an elegant contemporary Asian decor for the Rib Room. The menu, which is simple yet interesting and well-rounded, includes an array of excellent starters, both hot and cold, tempting entrees with delectable fish and meat dishes and a host of steaks in large and small portions. Only a few of the dishes have a slight lean towards Asian and surprisingly – there are no ribs! Excellent service, a warm intimate atmosphere and delicious food make the Rib Room a most satisfying dining experience.

## Tex-Mex

Other options **American** p.500, **Mexican** p.551

*Arabian*
*Courtyard Hotel*
*Downtown Bur Dubai*
*Map 9 A2* 42

# Barry's Bench

*04 351 6646*

Tucked away in a corner of the building and run independently of the hotel, Barry's Bench's situation in the Arabian Courtyard affords two things: views over the fort of Dubai Museum, its dhows, and wind towers – and the all-important drinks licence. You simply can't chow down on top quality Tex-Mex without simultaneously supping a cold cervesa or one of their fantastic margaritas. Decorated in true Tex-Mex style, the expansive menu offers everything from Mexican-style breakfasts to a selection of fajitas, burritos, grills, burgers and devilishly decadent desserts. As you'd expect, portions are podgy, though always piping hot and packed with flavour.

*Rydges Plaza Hotel*
*Al Satwa*
*Map 8 A3* 67

# Cactus Cantina

*04 398 2274 | www.cactuscantinadubai.com*

This ever-popular venue is a safe bet for sure-fire Tex-Mex fare. The food is tasty, with the emphasis leaning more toward the Tex than the Mex (refried beans and melted cheese with everything). Don't forget your appetite, as the portions are muy grande. With booths around the edges and plenty of tables squeezed into the floor space, this wouldn't be a good choice for an intimate meal. The lively atmosphere is aided and abetted by a pumping soundtrack and energetic staff. Weekends see the joint jumping, with crowds attracted by value-for-money meal deals and generous jugs of moreish margaritas.

## Thai

Other options **Far Eastern** p.512

*Dusit Dubai*
*Trade Centre 2*
*Map 7 E3* 6

# Benjarong

*04 343 3333 | www.dusit.com*

Supposedly the Dusit's signature restaurant, this Thai eatery is a little on the cold side. Which is not a reference to the over exuberant air-conditioning that you find in

Restaurants

Drinking Dubai Style

many a five-star restaurant, but rather the atmosphere – or lack there of. Benjarong's decor is very regal Thailand, the food is deliciously concocted and perfectly presented. The staff here however are cordial, but verging on lackadaisical, the result being that this restaurant lacks a bit of pizzazz. There is no denying that the menu is certainly tempting, with classics and a few inventive twists, and if you love Thai food you'll certainly enjoy, but you can't help thinking that there are better places in town.

### Blue Elephant

**Al Bustan Rotana**
*Al Garhoud*
*Map 13 E1* **1**

*04 282 0000* | *www.rotana.com*

Walking into The Blue Elephant is like travelling to Thailand without the hassle of jetlag. Sitting at bamboo tables, gazing into a lagoon and surrounded by verdant tropical greenery, the smell of orchids is evocative of exotic far eastern climates. The menu showcases an array of superb Thai food, spiced to your liking, with distinctive Oriental ingredients and traditional flavours. The artistic presentation, often in individual bamboo baskets, adds to the authentic experience. The enthusiastic sawadee (Thai welcome) on arrival is indicative of the attentive and knowledgeable interest shown by the staff throughout. This popular restaurant richly deserves its excellent reputation and consequently booking is recommended.

### Lemongrass

**Nr Lamcy Plaza**
*Oud Metha*
*Map 10 D2* **121**

*04 334 2325*

Located just across from Lamcy Plaza, Lemongrass ranks among the better (and certainly cheaper) Thai restaurants in Dubai. The innovative and user-friendly menu offers a typical range of starters, soups, salads, noodles, curries, stir-fries and desserts, and for those who can't take the heat, spice levels can be tailored to individual preferences. While the food delivers fresh and authentic flavours, servings could perhaps be more generous. There's no alcohol, but the refreshing fruit mocktails more than compensate. The setting is bright, inviting and comfortable, and the service polite and unobtrusive. For intimate dinners or small groups, Lemongrass provides decent Thai food at very reasonable prices.

### Pai Thai

**Souk Madinat Jumeirah**
*Umm Suqeim*
*Map 6 A2* **68**

*04 366 8888* | *www.jumeirah.com*

From the abra ride through the Madinat's beautiful canals, to the brightly lit venue itself, Pai Thai is an experience to remember. Outdoor seating (available in the cooler months) is a delightful way to enjoy the views, while the spacious interior keeps you cool on the hottest of evenings. The nouvelle cuisine on offer is a delicious change of pace from Dubai's standard Thai restaurants. Most classic Thai dishes are available for purists, but the real beauty here is the opportunity to try a twist on a familiar favourite, with the menu holding new choices for almost every palate.

### Royal Orchid

**Marina Walk**
*Marsa Dubai*
*Map 5 B2* **57**

*04 349 6417* | *orchid04@eim.ae*

The Royal Orchid offers good quality Thai and Chinese food at a reasonable price. There's a two-tier interior dining area and an outdoor terrace overlooking the marina for the cooler months. The staff (and there are lots of them) are friendly and willing to help you choose from the extensive menu. A good option is the 'Magic Wok', where the chef will prepare your favourite meat, fish or vegetables in the sauce of your choosing. Portions are on the large side so go hungry beforehand and try one of the starters, in particular the stir fried black pepper chicken wings. Also handy for a takeaway or delivery if you live in the area.

*Le Meridien Dubai*
*Al Garhoud*
*Map 13 E1*

### Sukhothai

*04 282 4040* | *www.lemeridien-dubai.com*

Bedecked with dark wood-panelled walls and authentic Thai artefacts, this charming restaurant is a perfect venue for a romantic occasion or a special treat. The menu is extensive, offering all the usual favourites including curries and a good seafood selection, and the food is top notch although not cheap. Service from the traditionally dressed waiting staff is attentive but not intrusive. The restaurant does have an outdoor seating area, which is quite pleasant in the cooler months, but the atmosphere and ambience inside is so good it would be a shame to miss it any time of the year.

*Pyramids*
*Umm Hurair*
*Map 10 E4*

### Thai Chi

*04 324 4100* | *www.waficityrestaurants.com*

If you're always wanting the best of both worlds, then you may find your Nirvana at Thai Chi. It would be more correct to say that this is actually two separate restaurants under one roof: the Chinese restaurant, with relaxed, bamboo decor and a menu of authentic delicacies; and the Thai restaurant, with completely different, more formal decor and a selection of Thailand's best-loved dishes. But here's the genius of Thai Chi: no matter where you sit in the restaurant, you can order from both kitchens – so it's perfect for groups of people with different food preferences. On the whole it's a delightful venue, particularly the outdoor terrace, which is only open during winter.

*Park Hyatt Dubai*
*Creekside, Deira*
*Map 11 B4*

### The Thai Kitchen

*04 317 2222* | *www.dubai.park.hyatt.com*

Thai Kitchen is intertwined around four live-cooking areas where all the ingredients are displayed and prepared by the Thai chefs. The decor is stylish and modern with dark walls and teak wood floors contrasting well with the large soft lights. Although relatively short, the menu consists of a good range of Thai delicacies each prepared to maximise the rich authentic flavours. Portions are purposely small so that you can order a variety and share a plethora of taste sensations. Combined with the palacious grandness of the Park Hyatt, Thai Kitchen is a welcome addition to the restaurant scene.

*Sukhothai*

# Sunday through to Saturday...
## paint the town whatever colour you like

A comprehensive collection of Dubai's many eclectic venues with impartial reviews and arresting photography. It's at home on the coffee table while you're out on the town.

**Posh Nosh, Cheap Eats & Star Bars**
The perfect appetizer to eating out in Dubai

Abu Dhabi · Amsterdam · Bahrain · Barcelona · Beijing · Berlin · Dubai · Dublin · Geneva
Hong Kong · Kuala Lumpur · Kuwait · London · Los Angeles · New York · New Zealand · Oman
Paris · Qatar · Shanghai · Singapore · Sydney · Tokyo · Vancouver

**EXPLORER**
www.explorerpublishing.com

# Turkish

Other options **Arabic/Lebanese** p.503

*Taj Palace Hotel*
*Deira*
*Map 11 C1* **69**

## Topkapi

*04 223 2222* | www.tajhotels.com

Topkapi is one of only two Turkish restaurants in Dubai but aside from the Istanbul-style interior and waiters in traditional garb, this has many Arabic adversaries in town. The usual fare of mezze dominates the menu although there is a bit of a Turkish twist. What does score bonus points is the appeasing decor with an open kitchen and cushion-laden benches adding to the proceedings. The food is average but the prices are certainly affordable and the everyday buffet is a particular bargain. The staff are extra-friendly, knowledgeable and all wearing a permanent smile.

# Vegetarian

*Madinat Jumeirah*
*Umm Suqeim*
*Map 6 A2* **22**

## Magnolia

*04 366 8888* | www.madinatjumeirah.com

Tucked away in the furthest corner of the Madinat, next to the Talise Spa and the restaurant's own organic gardens, Magnolia is pretty far off the beaten track, but definitely worth seeking out. Arriving at the venue by abra, its remoteness will clearly never see it thronged with clamouring diners. Instead, for vegetarians and those interested in trying some healthy dining and cutting edge gastronomy, Magnolia is Dubai's first fine dining vegetarian restaurant. You don't have to be vegetarian to dine here - open-minded non-vegetarians will also enjoy the experience. From the complimentary appetisers, between-course amuse bouches right down to the main courses, dishes are made from an interesting blend of familiar and unusual home-grown vegetables and herbs, and surprise with their creativity and fantastic flavour.

# Vietnamese

Other options **Far Eastern** p.512

*Shangri-La Hotel*
*Trade Centre 1*
*Map 7 E3* **32**

## Hoi An

*04 343 8888* | www.shangri-la.com

Named after an ancient Vietnamese port renowned for its silk, jewellery and spice trade, Hoi An proudly reflects this exotic influence and offers traditional Vietnamese ingredients combined and presented with a unique, western twist. Novices can opt for a set meal, which with the excellent guidance of well-informed staff, allows for a gourmet experience. The decor is stately-home-meets-far-eastern-tea-house, where the traditional orange walls and bright turquoise shutters blend unobtrusively with the elegant wooden tables well-placed on rugs. As Hoi An is a compact restaurant, it is always busy and the overriding ambience is of eating in a private dining room, particularly appropriate for quieter business occasions or an intimate dinner.

*Grand Hyatt Dubai*
*Umm Hurair*
*Map 13 C1* **9**

## Indochine

*04 317 1234* | www.dubai.grand.hyatt.com

A fusion of exotic flavours awaits the adventurous diner at Indochine. This popular restaurant serves a blend of Vietnamese, Thai, Cambodian and Laosian dishes, which offer some exciting and unusual a la carte choices, especially the imaginative salads and expertly seasoned soups. The predominantly dark wood and bamboo decor is cleverly counter-balanced by the high ceilings, tall windows and well-placed tables, giving an ambience of air and space. Dining is limited to the evening only, and as it is clearly a favourite haunt of both couples and groups, booking is recommended.

## Cafes & Coffee Shops
Other options **Afternoon Tea** p.572

Whether you're taking a break from shopping or work, catching up with friends, or fancy a quiet spot to sit and read the paper, you'll be spoilt for choice by the variety of venues around Dubai to grab a quick cuppa and a light bite to eat. The following section encompasses cafes and coffee shops, internet cafes and shisha cafes.

**JW Marriott Hotel**
*Deira*
*Map 11 E1* **18**

### Atrium Cafe
*04 262 4444* | *www.marriott-middleeast.com*
The Atrium Cafe is another in a long line of good eateries in the bustling JW Marriott. Offering the best in business cafe sophistication, with its leather seats, international newspapers and beautifully presented cake and sandwich counter, the cafe also excels in offering a relaxed space for everyone. A good choice of tasty and well-packed veggie and non-veggie gourmet sandwiches, salads, attractive cakes, croissants and brioches, and the choice of the hot and cold a la carte menu, make this elegant and quiet coffee house the right choice for breakfast and for lunch, alone or with others.

**Bastakiya**
*Downtown Bur Dubai*
*Map 9 A2* **3**

### Basta Art Café
*04 353 5071* | *bastaartcafe@yahoo.com*
The courtyard of the Basta Art Café is a quiet sanctuary amid the frenzy of the Bastakiya area. Sit on majlis-style low cushions, or under one of the white cotton canopies while you look through the rustic menu. The food here really stands out from other Dubai cafes, since it is prepared with healthy eating in mind. Each menu item bears a description of what vitamins and minerals it contains, as well as the calorie count. A sister outlet is located in the Arabian Ranches (04 362 6100), with wicker tables and chairs creating a similarly rustic atmosphere. Works of art hang in pride of place, with various artists being showcased (and sold) each month.

**Marina Walk**
*Nr Yacht Club*
*Map 5 A2* **140**

### Berts Cafe
*04 422 4126*
Serving healthy juices and simple cafe fare, Berts is a good option for a quick bite in New Dubai. Its location on the waterfront in Dubai Marina is doubly appealing; outside spacious loungers let you soak up the sun and see the snaking water; inside the low-slung leather couches and slightly subterranean feel bring to mind a London DJ bar designed for long, lazy lunches. The vibe is relaxed, with live music at weekends, open mic nights during the weekm sport on unobtrusive screens and an attempt to recreate someone's library around the back. The smoothies, made with fresh fruit and frozen yoghurt, are recommended. Better still, the waitress won't tire of you replying 'Good Morning' (blackberries and blueberries) when she takes your order. There's another branch in the Greens Centre, The Greens.

**Town Centre**
*Jumeira*
*Map 7 D1* **90**

### Café Ceramique
*04 341 5008* | *www.cafe-ceramique.com*
This popular cafe is a great place to spend an hour unleashing your creative side. Choose an item from the vast selection of pottery, select your colours, and get to work with an array of brushes, sponges and stencils. The finished article is then glazed in house to be collected at a later date. The menu, although giving plenty of choice, is of the snack variety with plenty of salads, bagels, sandwiches and desserts. Children's birthday parties are catered for and Thursday mornings are particularly hectic but come mid-week, grab a mag or paper, have a light lunch and unleash your inner artist! Another branch can be found in Mall of the Emirates (04 341 0144).

**567**

*Various Locations* ◀

## Costa ▶ p.569

*04 344 5705* | *www.mmidubai.com*

Despite being a chain, Costa is still able to offer patrons the perfect brew as well as an ideal location for a get together and a chat. Fashionable bucket seats allow you to take the weight off your feet and relax as your goodies arrive at your table. Fresh pastries, salads, sandwiches and other snacks complement the long list of trendy tea and coffee blends. Other locations: Bin Sougat Centre (04 286 1992); Century Village (04 286 9216); City Tower II, Shk Zayed Rd (04 331 2499); Deira City Centre (04 294 0833); DNATA Airline Centre, Shk Zayed Rd (04 321 0978); Dubai International Airport (Viewers Gallery – 04 220 0179 & Terminal 2 04 299 6358); Dubai International Airport (Concourse I 04 220 0224 & II – 04 220 0225); Dubai Internet City (04 391 8896); Madinat Jumeirah (04 368 6199); Ibn Battuta Shopping Mall (04 368 5631); The Greens Centre (04 368 3385)

*Wafi City* ◀
*Umm Hurair*
*Map 10 D4* **73**

## Elements

*04 324 4252* | *www.thomaskleingroup.com*

Located in the upmarket Wafi Mall, this cafe is a perfect pitstop for a snack while shopping. Housing a multitude of artefacts and artwork on the walls, all of which are for sale, this funky, modern eatery serves a varied menu with an Arabic influence, together with pizzas, salads and sandwiches. Find yourself a comfy couch, or venture out on to the lovely air-conditioned terrace, and indulge in one of the fabulous juices or a fruit-flavoured shisha. Promotional events feature throughout the week and include afternoon tea, dim sum nights, buffet lunches and cheese nights.

*Wafa Tower* ◀
*Trade Centre 1*
*Map 7 E3* **100**

## French Connection

*04 343 8311* | *farida@fcdubai.com*

Two floors, wide windows, cheerful decor and lots of sunshine make French Connection an excellent location for a quick bite or a leisurely coffee, while surfing wireless on your laptop at no additional cost. The breakfasts range from pastries and breads to the full British affair. There are a wide selection of salads and tasty sandwiches made from a variety of wholegrain home-made breads. And of course, the usual range of well prepared coffees will keep you going from early to late. If you have a sweet tooth you will be in awe of the range of cakes and pastries, which are freshly prepared in the bakery. Other branches are behind Spinneys next to BurJuman.

*Magrudy's* ◀
*Jumeira*
*Map 7 F1* **36**

## Gerard's

*04 344 3327* | *gerard07@eim.ae*

An institution in the Jumeira café scene, the courtyard setting gives this popular coffee spot its unique atmosphere. Frequented by a cross section of Dubai society, it is where the 'yummy mummies' head between the school run and the first exercise class of the day. As the day progresses the core clientele slowly changes, and by evening it is popular with Emirati men as a place to meet with friends and discuss the day's activities over coffee. There's a good selection of croissants, pastries and chocolate covered dates, and take away trade is brisk.
Other locations: Al Ghurair City (04 222 8637).

*Bank Street* ◀
*Nr York International*
*Downtown Bur Dubai*
*Map 8 E3* **141**

## Hakaya Cafe

*04 352 8213*

Stories passed from elders to youngsters, from generation to generation.' This, the menu informs you, is the meaning of 'Hakaya.' And, from the state of the lovingly lived-in floral couches, they're not lying about how many years have been spent in this cosy Arabic hideout, spinning yarns and playing computerised solitaire. Tucked away from burly Bank Street, this first-floor cafe quietly overlooks the neon-lit action below, and feels like

**568**

# TRUE ITALIAN HOSPITALITY
# ACROSS THE UAE

**Dubai:** Deira City Centre • Mall of the Emirates • Mercato Mall • Ibn Battuta Mall, China Court • Bin Sougat Mall, oppositeAirport Expo • Madinat Jumeirah • Dubai Festival City, Atrium & Festival Square • The Meadows • Nuran Greens, The Greens • Arabian Ranches • Green Community • Nuran Al Majara, Dubai Marina • Dubai Internet City, Bldgs 3 & 13 • DNATA AirlineCentre, Sheikh Zayed Rd • Grosvenor Tower, Sheikh Zayed Rd • City Tower II, Sheikh Zayed Rd • Al Murooj Complex, SheikhZayed Rd • Dubai International Financial City • Dubai Silicon Oasis, Villa Complex • Academic City, University Rd • The Aviation Club, Dubai Tennis Stadium • Emirates Aviation College Crew Training • Dubai Intl. Airport, Terminal 1-Arrivals & Departures • Dubai International Airport, Terminal 2 **Sharjah:** Sharjah Intl. Airport • Sharjah City Centre **Ajman:** Ajman City Centre **Abu Dhabi:** Carrefour, Airport Rd • Blue Towers, Muroor Rd • Platinum Hotel Apartments, Khalid Bin Al Waleed Rd • Al Wahda Mall, Ground Level

a treehouse for shisha-smoking grown-ups – mainly because there's a huge plastic tree shooting up the middle of it. The menu is seriously eclectic, offering everything from pasta, pepper steak and pizza to every fruit juice and flavoured coffee imaginable, as well as, rather interestingly, valet service. But Hakaya Café is really all about the shisha – it has one of the largest selections of flavours in the city, from grape to cappuccino to rose. Go after 22:30 and you'll find live Arabic music and the venue at its smokiest.

**Mall of the Emirates**
*Al Barsha*
*Map 7 E3* **19**

## Japengo Café
*04 341 1671* | *www.binhendi.com*
Japengo Café offers a Japanese-western hybrid menu that impresses with top-notch food and drink in a bright, minimalist setting. The meals are excellent and include sushi, salads, sandwiches, hot dishes and fresh juices. Crab cakes and chicken dumplings are a treat and the assorted yakitori is superb – even better washed down with a fresh Kiwi juice. The portions are generous and the prices reasonable, although drinks and water are a bit more expensive. Lunch or dinner, this is no fuss fare with a little flai.
Other Locations: Ibn Battuta (04 362 1900), Wafi Mall (04 324 5411), Dubai Ladies Club, Jumeira (04 349 6878), Palm Strip (04 345 4979)

**Nr Jumeira Mosque**
*Jumeira*
*Map 7 F1* **103**

## Lime Tree Cafe
*04 349 8498* | *limetree@eim.ae*
Set in a converted villa on the Beach Road, this amazing cafe has become somewhat of a Dubai institution. The understated decor features trendy plastic chairs, dark wood tables and lime-green washed walls, upon which hang numerous chalk boards touting the day's delicious, home-cooked meals. Enjoy an alfresco coffee break on the patio or the upstairs balcony, if the weather is not too sticky. With a definite nod towards Mediterranean cuisine, there's plenty of paninis filled with wholesome ingredients like roast vegetables, halloumi cheese and roast chicken, as well as delicious couscous salads, satay kebabs and the best quiches in the city. There's another branch in China Court of Ibn Battuta mall (04 366 9320).

**Boulevard at**
**Emirates Towers**
*Trade Centre 2*
*Map 7 F3* **46**

## Lipton T-Junction
*04 330 0788* | *www.thomaskleingroup.com*
The modern decor, bursting with orange and yellow tones, gives a cheerful welcome to the T-Junction. This tea bar leans heavily on the tea theme, and tea, in its many forms, finds its way into nearly every drink and dish on the menu. If you're peckish, try the salads or sandwiches, some of which feature chicken cooked in green tea (interesting and quite pleasant!). The signature drinks should not be missed – Spice Cha' (Assam tea infused with sweet spices), Cha'latte (Assam tea infused with ginger and orange) or Berry T-Licious (a blend of teas and berry juices).

**Nr Welcare Hospital**
*Al Garhoud*
*Map 11 C4* **130**

## MORE
*04 283 0224* | *www.morecafe.biz*
If you're bored of Dubai but don't have time for a holiday, this charming bistro-style eatery will transport you right into the trendy parts of London or Paris. With polished concrete floors, a high, warehouse-style ceiling, sturdy wooden tables and comfortable chairs upholstered in either lime green, deep purple or soft brown leather, the decor invites lingering. The menu is simple yet comprehensive – salads, soups and sandwiches dominate, although there is a small selection of main courses. Whether you sit at an individual table or at the long communal tables, the eclectic mix of clientele makes MORE great for people watching. A some-time art exhibition space, More attracts an eclectic crowd of chattering media types and young families. The branch at Al Murooj Rotana (04 343 3779) is more spacious, but similarly stylish.

**Beach Rd**
*Jumeira*
*Map 7 F1* 142

## THE One

*See p.493* | www.theoneme.com

Tucked away on the first floor of THE One, this small cafe is decorated in the same funky style seen throughout the store. The menu is extensive and imaginative (but does offer reliable classics if you're not feeling particularly adventurous) and the food is always of high quality. The freshly squeezed juices are fabulous and the cakes outstanding, and there's a kids menu with home-cooked alternatives such as pizza and sandwiches. With friendly and attentive service, this is a perfect spot for refuelling mid-shop, or for catching up with friends over a relaxed, reasonably priced lunch.

**Grand Hyatt Dubai**
*Umm Hurair*
*Map 13 C1* 9

## Panini

*04 317 1234* | www.dubai.grand.hyatt.com

As a place to meet up with friends or business associates for a lunch on the run, you can't go wrong with Panini. Set among the tropical indoor 'rainforest' in the impressive lobby of the Grand Hyatt, complete with lush greenery and jungle mist, the surroundings are spectacular. The food may not be out of this world, but it's good for a quick bite. The signature paninis are a little plain so consider this when choosing your fillings, and order a zesty, freshly squeezed fruit juice to liven up your lunchtime. Afterwards, have a browse around the gorgeous deli inside, which sells a range of heavenly treats to take home, both sweet and savoury.

**Fairmont Dubai**
*Trade Centre 1*
*Map 8 A4* 8

## Pronto

*04 332 5555* | www.fairmont.com

Hotel lobby cafes often get bad press, leaving them frequented merely by hotel guests waiting for their tour guide or business meetings who sit for hours over one coffee. Fairmont's Pronto, however, should not be pigeonholed into Dubai's lacklustre hotel cafe culture. Mainly because its deli-style cuisine is worthy of a lingering lunch, while the sushi and Arabic selections cater for a variety of palates and, most important for some, it serves alcohol and incredible cakes. Not only are the sofas comfy and the staff forever smiling, but they also offer complimentary wireless internet connection during lunch. Whoever said you should never mix business with pleasure had obviously never been to Pronto.

**Al Attar Business Tower**
*Sheikh Zayed Rd*
*Trade Centre 2*
*Map 7 E3* 99

## Shakespeare & Co.

*04 331 1757* | shakesco@eim.ae

Shakespeare & Co would probably be more at home on a Parisian side street than behind a giant skyscraper on Sheikh Zayed Road. However, the fact that it's here is a bonus not a burden. Its truly unique eccentricity, a shabby chic decor that mixes floral designs with lace and wicker that would make aristocracy feel at home, makes a refreshing change from the sometimes superficial qualities of so many Dubai eateries. The food is an equally eclectic mix, combining Arabic, Morrocan and continental dishes with a splendid selection of sandwiches and some of the finest smoothies in town.
Other Locations: The Village Mall (04 344 62528), Al Wasl Road (04 394 1121), Gulf Tower (04 335 3335)

**JW Marriott Hotel**
*Deira*
*Map 11 E1* 18

## Vienna Cafe

*04 262 4444* | www.marriott.com

This small cafe has a slightly fusty Austrian charm. There's lots of wood panelling and delicate tablecoths not readily associated with Deira. Still, it blends well with the grandeur of the JW Marriott. With a passing array of people either entering or leaving the hotel, coming and going on business, or just ambling around the shopping complex, this makes a wonderful place to sit and enjoy a slow cuppa and watch the world go by. There is also a good selection of food on offer, from light salads to steaks.

**571**

## Shisha Cafes

Other options **Arabic/Lebanese** p.503

Despite regular media mummerings about a ban on shisha smoking outside, it's common to see people, both male and female, young and old, relaxing in the evening with a coffee or juice and a shisha pipe. For visitors and residents, even non-smokers, it's a popular experience. Many of the Arabic cafes and restaurants around town have shisha available; it often

| Shisha Cafes | | |
| --- | --- | --- |
| Al Koufa | Oud Metha | 04 335 1511 |
| Al Mazaj | Al Garhoud | 04 282 9952 |
| Awafi | Deira | 04 262 4444 |
| Elements | Umm Hurair | 04 607 7760 |
| Fakhreldine | Oud Metha | 04 336 6000 |
| Kan Zaman | Al Shindagha | 04 393 9913 |
| QD's | Al Garhoud | 04 295 6000 |
| Reem | Al Bawadi Jumeira | 04 394 7444 |
| Samari Restaurant & Café | Al Satwa | 04 345 4511 |
| Shakespeare & Co. | Trade Centre 2 | 04 331 1751 |
| Shoo Fee Ma Fee | Umm Suqeim | 04 366 8888 |

makes a perfect end to a meal, especially when seated outdoors in the cooler months. If you fancy buying your own then Karama market (p.480) and the souks in Deira (p.483) are a good place to start, but most souvenir shops and larger supermarkets also sell them.

## Afternoon Tea

Other options **Cafes & Coffee Shops** p.567

**Ritz-Carlton**
*Marsa Dubai*
*Map 5 A1* **31**

### The Lobby Lounge

*04 399 4000* | www.ritzcarlton.com

Dubai's very own Tea at the Ritz is an exquisite experience from the moment you step into the austere lobby until you lick the very last morsel of cream from your lips. Delicate finger sandwiches and dainty pastries, succulent scones with clotted cream and a selection of jams, a fabulously colonial selection of teas and the fine china are all deliciously regal. It may feel exclusive, but all are welcome, and if you can even swap your brew for a hot chocolate. In addition there is an all-day menu, as well as an inviting cocktail list.

**Burj Al Arab**
*Umm Suqeim*
*Map 6 B1* **3**

### Sahn Eddar

*04 301 7777* | www.jumeirah.com

A great way to enjoy a peek inside the interior of the world's tallest and most lavish hotel with what has to be the best view in town. Service is truly superb, making you feel like Dubai royalty, with the personable staff serving up an endless feast of delicious sandwiches, scones, cakes, sweets, chocolates and a pot of your choice of the finest fragrant teas. It may be an expensive cuppa but this is an experience that no visitor or Dubai resident should miss. Although the Sahn Eddar cafe in the lobby may be the primary location for afternoon tea, you can choose the Skyview Bar if you want to maximise on the jaw-dropping factor with stunning vistas 200m above the sea.

## Internet Cafes

Whether you want to get online while enjoying a drink or bite to eat, or you just don't have a connection at home, there's a number of cafes and eateries around town with PCs available for customers to use, or with Wi-Fi connections allowing you to use your own. Most charge for the privilege, with prices around Dhs.15-Dhs.20 per hour, but you may find places where the connection is free if you're eating and drinking.
Current hotspot locations include: French Connection, Sheikh Zayed Road; Coffee Bean & Tea Leaf, Jumeira (Beach) Road; Spot Café, Bur Dubai and Al Jalssa Internet Cafe, Al Ain Centre, Berts and MORE Cafe.

# Bakeries

Bakeries in Dubai offer a wonderful range of pastries, biscuits and Lebanese sweets. Arabic breads include 'borek', flat pastries, baked or fried with spinach or cheese, and 'manakish', which is hot bread, sometimes doubled over, and served plain or filled with meat, cheese or 'zatar' (thyme seeds). Biscuits are often filled with ground dates or pistachios.

## Friday Brunch

| Friday Brunch | | |
|---|---|---|
| Al Muntaha | Umm Suqeim | 04 301 7600 |
| Al Qasr | Madinat Jumeirah | 04 366 6730 |
| Carters | Oud Metha | 04 324 4777 |
| Double Decker | Trader Centre 2 | 04 321 1111 |
| Glasshouse | Deira | 04 227 1111 |
| Irish Village | Al Garhoud | 04 282 4750 |
| JW Marriott | Deira | 04 607 7977 |
| Legends | Al Garhoud | 04 295 6000 |
| Long's Bar | Trade Centre 1 | 04 343 8000 |
| More | Nr Welcare Hospital | 04 283 0224 |
| Pax | Trade Centre 2 | 04 343 3333 |
| Planet Hollywood | Umm Hurair | 04 324 4777 |
| Rock Bottom Café | Downtown Bur Dubai | 04 396 3888 |
| Spectrum on One | Trade Centre 1 | 04 311 8000 |
| Spice Island | Hor Al Anz | 04 262 5555 |
| The Boston Bar | Al Satwa | 04 345 5888 |
| The Cellar | Al Garhoud | 04 282 4122 |
| The Market Place | Deira | 04 262 4444 |
| Waxy O'Conner's | Downtown Bur Dubai | 04 352 0900 |
| Yalumba | Garhoud | 04 282 4040 |

# Friday Brunch

An integral part of life in Dubai, Friday brunch is a perfect event for a lazy start to the weekend, especially once the really hot weather arrives. Popular with all sections of the community, it provides Thursday night's revellers with a gentle awakening, and often much-needed nourishment. For families, brunch is a very pleasant way to spend the day, especially since many venues organise a variety of fun activities for kids, allowing parents to fill themselves with fine food and drinks, and to simply relax. Different brunches appeal to different crowds; some have fantastic buffets, others are in spectacular surroundings, while some offer all you can eat at amazing prices. Hint: Saturday brunches tend to be less boozy and a bit cheaper.

*Sports Bars*

*The glitz and glamour of Dubai's bars is all very well, but sometimes all you want is a joint where you can catch the big match and enjoy a pint with your mates. These venues are recommended for supping and spectating: Aussie Legends (p.575), Boston Bar (p.578), Champions (p.579), Double Decker (p.588), Dubliners (p.588), El Paso (p.580), Fibber Magee's (p.590), Irish Village (p.590), and Scarlett's (p.585).*

# Fruit Juices

Other options **Cafes & Coffee Shops** p.567

Fresh juices are widely available, either from shawarma stands or juice shops. They are delicious, healthy and cheap, and made on the spot from fresh fruits such as mango, banana, kiwi, strawberry and pineapple. Yoghurt is also a popular drink, often served with nuts, and the local milk is called 'laban' (a heavy, salty buttermilk that doesn't go well in tea or coffee). Arabic mint tea is available, Arabic coffee however, (thick, silty and strong) is extremely popular and will have you buzzing for the rest of the day.

# Shawarma

Other options **Arabic/Lebanese** p.503

Shawarma is a popular local snack consisting of rolled pita bread filled with lamb or chicken carved from a rotating spit, vegetables and tahina sauce. You'll see countless roadside stands offering shawarma for as little as Dhs.3 each, and they make a great alternative to the usual fast-food staples. In residential areas, the small cluster of shops beside a mosque is often a good place to look for your local shawarma outlet. These cafes and stands usually sell other dishes, such as 'foul' (a paste made from fava beans) and 'falafel' (or ta'amiya), which are small savoury balls of deep-fried chickpeas. Many also offer freshly squeezed fruit juices for around Dhs.8. For a really unique version, check out Al Shera'a Fisheries Centre, next to Marks & Spencer in Deira (04 227 1803), the only place in town that offers fish shawarmas.

## On The Town

Dubai has plenty to offer once the sun sets. This section covers it all, including details of cultural entertainment such as theatre and movies, as well as bars, pubs and nightclubs.

Social nights out in Dubai tend to start late, with people usually not leaving home until after 21:00. Even on weeknights, kick off is surprisingly late. Arabic nightclubs or restaurants, where there is usually live music and belly dancing, are largely deserted before 23:00.

Both nights of the weekend, Friday and Saturday, are particularly busy, but you will also find many promotions and theme nights held during the week to pull in the crowds. Ladies' nights are particularly popular (see p.587).

In general, cafes and restaurants close between 23:00 and 01:00, with bars and nightclubs split between those that close 'early' at 01:00 and those that go on until 03:00.

## Door Policy

Even with the mix of nationalities in Dubai, there are certain bars and nightclubs that have a 'selective' entry policy. Sometimes the 'members only' sign on the entrance needs a bit of explaining. Membership is usually introduced to control the clientele frequenting the establishment, but is often only enforced during busy periods. At quieter times, non-members may have no problems getting in, even if not accompanied by a member. Some places seem to use the rule to disallow entry if they don't like the look of you or your group. Large groups (especially all males), single men and certain nationalities are normally the target. You can avoid the inconvenience, and the embarrassment, by breaking the group up or by going in a mixed-gender group. If you do find yourself being discriminated against it's not worth arguing with the doorman – it won't work. Most companies do everything to avoid bad publicity, so try taking the issue up with the local media instead.

## Dress Code

While many bars have a reasonably relaxed attitude towards dress code, some places will not allow you in if you are wearing shorts and sandals, while others require a collared shirt and have a 'no jeans or trainers' policy. In general, nightclubs are more strict, so dress to impress.

Blue Bar (p.578)

Rooftop Lounge & Terrace (p.585)

# Bars

Other options **Pubs** p.588, **Nightclubs** p.591

**The Jumeirah**
**Beach Hotel**
*Umm Suqeim*
*Map 6 B1*

## 360°
*04 348 0000 | www.jumeirah.com*
Like a static carousel for grown-ups, 360° is a two-tiered circular rooftop, rebelliously partying above the more demure Marina Seafood Market (and therefore formerly known as Marina Roof Deck). With a bar at its heart, the place boasts striking panoramic views of the Arabian Ocean and light-throwing Burj that will scorch into memory and put even the grumpiest expat in a decent mood. Late afternoon arrivals (it opens at 16:00) can laze on a catalogue of white seating, including mouldable podgy beanbags, low cubic couches and wooden reclining benches, as they suck whichever colourful shisha flavour they fancy. Happenin' house DJs spin come the weekends, while scruffy chic stylistas sup cocktails – until they start spinning too.

> ### Booze With A View
> As soon as temperatures cool off, (typically from October to May) the city's chic set head straight outside to soak up Dubai's alfresco bar scene, complete with beautiful views.
> Kick off the evening with a glass of wine at the romantic Rooftop Terrace (p.585), followed by martinis at stylish Sho Cho's (p.585), mojitos at Uptown (p.586), and an open-air bop at 360°(p.575) or Trilogy (p.593) Just remember to glug enough water between cocktails.

**Boulevard at**
**Emirates Towers**
*Trade Centre 2*
*Map 7 F3*

## The Agency
*04 330 0000 | www.jumeirah.com*
Proving that wine bars are no longer just a fad, The Agency always attracts a crowd of Dubai's young and beautiful. With a 33 page wine menu, you might do well to take one of the 'flights' available (four different glasses of wine) and revisit some of your favourites. The cafe facade 'outside' and the dark wood and brick interior could be from any great wine-producing region, as could the tasty tapas-style snacks served at lunch and dinner. This is a great place to meet after work and warm up to a night on the town, although it can get smoky and you shouldn't plan on any intimate heart-to-heart conversation. There's another branch at Madinat Jumeirah (04 366 6730).

**Rydges Plaza Hotel**
*Al Satwa*
*Map 8 A3* 67

## Aussie Legends
*04 398 2222 | www.rydges.com*
In the style of a friendly, chilled-out local, Aussie Legends offers some of the best bar music in Dubai as well as regular appearances from live bands and musicians. The small dance floor is sometimes known to kick off quite early on a weekend evening, and the pool table is so popular you may wait all night for a game. As well as a wide variety of drinks, the menu offers a good range of satisfyingly tasty pub grub. With numerous sporting events shown on the large screen TVs, this can be a great place to watch the big match in a lively atmosphere.

**Mina A'Salam**
*Umm Suqeim*
*Map 6 A1* 62

## Bahri Bar
*04 366 8888 | www.jumeirah.com*
Imagine you had the chance to design the perfect bar. For starters you'd include a stunning view, say, windtower rooftops, rustling palm trees, meandering canals and the towering Burj Al Arab and sparkling ocean beyond. The bar itself could perhaps have rich furnishings in brown and gold, with comfortable seating, and ornately engraved lanterns providing the intimate lighting both inside and out. On the menu you'd make sure a comprehensive cocktail selection was accompanied by wines, beers,

**575**

and delicious nibbles including Arabic hot and cold mezze and tapas. You'll probably never get the chance to build your dream bar but that doesn't matter, because someone else did, it's at Mina A'Salam and it's called Bahri Bar.

**Shangri-La Hotel**
*Trade Centre 1*
*Map 7 E3* 32

## Balcony Bar
*04 343 8888* | *www.shangri-la.com*
Overlooking the imposing main entrance and chic lobby of the Shangri La Hotel, Balcony Bar is a sophisticated little place to grab a fancy cocktail or pre-dinner fortifier. Dark, masculine wooden panelling is the order of the day, with black leather armchairs and glass-topped coffee tables surrounding the bar. The drinks list is extensive, and the cocktails are competently mixed and artfully presented. For the more extravagant pocket, there are some eye-wateringly expensive champagnes and vintage whiskies, while teetotallers can choose from a basic selection of booze-free beverages.

**Hyatt Regency**
*Deira*
*Map 9 D1* 14

## The Bar
*04 317 2222* | *www.dubai.regency.hyatt.com*
You may not be inclined to brave the patience-defying traffic of Deira simply to frequent The Bar, but if you have planned your evening at the often overlooked Hyatt Regency, this is a suitable spot to whet your whistle, and your appetite. Encased in glass and furnished with a mix of high tables, bar stools and low, soft leather armchairs, the interior is much like the rest of the hotel – unobtrusive and relaxed. The well-stocked (and staffed) bar dispenses some interesting aperitifs and after-dinner liqueurs, as well as decent cocktails, wines and bottled beers. The Bar's view over the Arabian Gulf and the Deira Palm more than make up for the trek, especially when the Hyatt's fine restaurants are in range.

**Souk Madinat**
**Jumeirah**
*Umm Suqeim*
*Map 6 A2* 68

## Bar Zar
*04 366 6348* | *www.jumeirah.com*
This two-floor bar is slick and fashionable, with the upper floor open in the middle so you can peer over at the talent below (the band that is). The faux brick walls, art-house prints, friendly staff who respond to a bit of banter, the small but ample terrace and laid-back sofas all add up to a funky bar with a relaxed urban feel. The drinks are equally eclectic – with beer cocktails (champagne or Smirnoff Ice with Guinness!), traditional (yet potent) long drinks and lagers aplenty. The food also pleases with bar snacks such as crab cakes, chicken satay, spring rolls, bangers and mash, and fish and chips.

**Le Meridien Mina**
*Al Sufouh*
*Map 5 C1* 21

## Barasti ▶ p.577
*04 399 3333* | *www.lemeridien-minaseyahi.com*
Following an extensive refurb in early 2007, Barasti has reopened with beachside beds, a downstairs bar and even more screens for the all important big games, while still retaining its casual charm. This laidback bar is a big favourite with residents and tourists alike, favoured for its meaty menu, jugs of Pimms and panoramic vistas, not to mention the fact you can turn up in flipflops or Friday finery depending on your mood.

*Barasti*

# barasti beach
## the renowned sessions for a great season
join our resident dj, martin metcalf daily from 5pm for a
tranquil blend of sounds to soothe your soul at sundown

## tuesday: **moonlight acid jazz**
a sophisticated blend of retro, modern and acid jazz
resident dj martin metcalf drops the funky beats and is joined by the
footprints jazz duo who'll be jamming along live.

## wednesday: **love latino**
a pick of classic and modern latin music, latin food & beverage specials.

## thursday: **jellyfish funk**
join dubai 92 dj ben whyte from 10pm for an enchanted selection
of funky dance, party classics and big anthems.

## friday: **lollipop city**
a truly scrumptious choice of house music and dance anthems
from 10pm dion mavath takes to the decks to pump it up for dubai's
only weekly beach party.

## saturday: **saturday sanctuary**
a majestic compound of twilight audio broadcast live on dubai 92
hosted by our resident dj, martin metcalf, a tranquil blend of sounds
to soothe your soul at sundown. from 8pm, chris fisher takes over for
a top pick of big party classics and pop anthems.

**barasti**

*Le* **MERIDIEN**

MINA SEYAHI BEACH RESORT
& MARINA

DUBAI

we love barasti beach x

www.minaeffect.com

Le Méridien Mina Seyahi Beach Resort & Marina Tel : 971 4 399 3333, www.lemeridien.com/minaseyahi

Film fans can also enjoy weekly outdoor screenings for free, kicking back on a mountain of bean bags. Perfect for sundowners, dancing and dining, Barasti is the ideal choice for groups who want it all.

**Novotel World Trade Centre**
Trade Centre 2
Map 7 F3 **37**

## Blue Bar
*04 332 0000* | *www.novotel.com*
Hidden at the back of the sometimes forgotten Novotel, the Blue Bar has a relaxed, low-key vibe with enough 'it' factor to give it cred but without any delusions of grandeur. You can opt to either pull up a stool at the large square bar, or get cosy in one of the leather sofas and armchairs. It's all very icy glass and modern fixtures, which complements the smooth tunes of the resident jazz band. If you're looking for a chilled-out venue, whether to catch up with a friend, get to know a first date or enjoy a pre or post-dinner drink, then the Blue Bar does just enough to impress the punters.

**Jumeira Rotana**
Al Satwa
Map 8 A2 **23**

## The Boston Bar
*04 345 5888* | *www.rotana.com*
This American-style pub in the Jumeira Rotana Hotel is a bit of a pick 'n' mix. They have everything from sports to quizzes and music to dancing on the bar. This bar/restaurant is great for after-work parties, watching sports, getting wild, or just ending a long day. Theme nights include Saturday and Sunday Sports, a Monday Quiz, Tuesday Ladies' Night, Wednesday two-for-one, Thursday Ladies' night, and a Friday breakfast binge. The variety of the Boston Bar makes it difficult to choose a day, so it's best to try all seven. Maybe just not all in one week!

**Dubai Marine Beach**
Jumeira
Map 7 F1 **5**

## Boudoir
*04 345 5995* | *www.myboudoir.com*
This exclusive, beautiful booty favourite can be as difficult to get into as a lady's chamber but once you get past the (judge)mental doormen – as long as you are appropriately dressed – you will be treated to a Parisian-style club/restaurant/wine bar perfect for liasisons dangeroux. Expect lots of opulent fabrics in hedonistic hues, hypnotic tunes and moody lighting. If you're dining you can expect an equally eclectic experience with trendy tastes and rich concoctions in the form of international dishes with a local twist. Theme nights promote different types of music including house, latino and R&B, in addition to great free drinks deals for ladies.

**Grosvenor House**
Marsa Dubai
Map 5 B2 **10**

## Buddha Bar
*04 399 8888* | *www.grosvenorhouse.lemeridien.com*
The long-awaited Buddha Bar launch rocked Dubai to its (still wet) foundations. With a brother bar in Beirut, an HQ in Paris, and latest addition in New York, its arrival officially stamped Dubai on the global bar map, with all the weighty authority a giant bronze Buddha centrepiece can bring. From the entrance, a seductively lit corridor leads you past private lounges and tucked-away alcoves, all perfectly decadent places to dine, lounge, and socialise. The grand hall beyond is a feast for the eyes, with its colossal Buddha centrepiece, spectacular chandeliers, and unfeasibly tall windows framed by equally impressive rich, red drapes, offering views onto the marina. With the Buddha Bar's famous mix of music, some of the best cocktails in town, and a selection of tasty Asian treats, this is set to become a firm favourite among the south-west Dubai social set.

**Pyramids**
Umm Hurair
Map 10 E4 **65**

## Carter's
*04 324 4100* | *www.waficitirestaurants.com*
Carter's serves a varied selection of bistro-esque food in any of the two indoor dining areas or, for the more ambient winter temperatures, on the alfresco terrace. Better

578

suited to large, casual groups than intimate, romantic couples, Carter's is still adept at attracting the singles crowd, who enjoy the fantastic drink deals and genuinely friendly atmosphere. The mellow background music gives way to live soft rock around 22:00, when Carter's evolves from a restaurant into a nightclub. A DJ continues into the small hours. Food is still available until late, but by then space is at a premium and the focus has shifted to the band or the still buzzing crowd surrounding the bar.

*Traders Hotel Dubai*
*Deira*
*Map 9 O4* 🟦

## Chameleon

*04 265 9888* | *www.shangri-la.com*

Chameleon is a vibrant cocktail bar with a broad spectrum of liquid refreshment and entertainment. The reasonably priced beverages range from sophisticated Martinis to lewdly named cocktails, and include an assortment of signature Chameleon drinks – many-hued concoctions which may have you licking your lips, rolling your eyes, or climbing the walls. The split-level venue is stylishly lit, and seating is available at dining tables, on bar stools or in comfy circular couches. Depending on which night you visit, the music may be provided by a live pianist or a hip DJ, occasionally accompanied by live bongo and saxophone players.

*JW Marriott Hotel*
*Deira*
*Map 11 E1* 🟦

## Champions

*04 262 4444* | *www.marriott.com*

This is just what you'd expect from a sports bar: lots of big screens for viewing your favorite sports (including Grand Prix and American football), pool tables, quiz nights, karaoke and even a live DJ spinning the hits on Thursdays. At Champions, you get all this and great US-style pub grub as well. It's a great place to meet friends and enjoy the diversion of your choice, and it helps that the staff are friendly and knowledgeable too. If you like hustle and bustle, go later as things heat up. The daytime food deals make this a good choice for lunch as well.

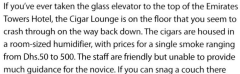

**DUI**

Drinking and driving is illegal in Dubai. There is zero tolerance; if you are caught with even a hint of alcohol in your system you will be sent to prison. Be responsible and always take a taxi - they're cheap, reliable and plentiful.

*Emirates Towers*
*Trade Centre 2*
*Map 7 F3* 🟦

## Cigar Lounge

*04 330 0000* | *www.jumeirah.com*

If you've ever taken the glass elevator to the top of the Emirates Towers Hotel, the Cigar Lounge is on the floor that you seem to crash through on the way back down. The cigars are housed in a room-sized humidor, with prices for a single smoke ranging from Dhs.50 to 500. The staff are friendly but unable to provide much guidance for the novice. If you can snag a couch there are shimmering views of Sheikh Zayed Road to be had, but the skyline is obscured somewhat by gigantic wood-panelled air-conditioners. The clientele are mainly moneyed hotel guests and the overall ambience is that of an airport with no planes.

*Fairmont Dubai*
*Trade Centre 1*
*Map 8 A4* 🟦

## Cin Cin

*04 332 5555* | *www.fairmont.com*

Cin Cin is one Dubai bar that wouldn't be so out of place in a bohemian behemoth of a city as opposed to our humble desert dwelling. Perhaps it's the arrogant impracticality: designed around a central pillar, the bar feels like a very circular, very narrow, very voguish… corridor. Lights are a running theme: pretty dot-sized ones, big bulbous ones, multi-coloured ones filched from kitsch, 1970s dance-floors, entire walls of cool blue square ones. Yet despite the stark white of the rest of the colour scheme, the bar does not over-dazzle. Instead, the modish furnishings, warehouse-high wine shelves, and walls fashioned like falling water all combine to create a backdrop as bling as Beyonce in a diamond-encrusted catsuit.

**579**

**Dubai Marine Beach**
*Jumeira*
*Map 7 F1*

## El Paso
*04 304 8120* | www.dxbmarine.com

Quiz nights, party nights, ladies' nights, karaoke nights, football nights, and live music too – what more could you want from a good all-round bar? How about great service and excellent drinks? You've got it! El Paso was previously known as The Alamo, but apart from the name change this is still the same old place, drawing a regular crowd of expats who meet and mingle to enjoy the relaxing but vibrant atmosphere. For dinner, stay for the Tex Mex or move on to one of the other outlets at the Dubai Marine Beach Resort. Open from noon until three in the morning, the bar is a good place to start or finish an evening.

**Pyramids**
*Umm Hurair*
*Map 10 D4* 65

## Ginseng
*04 324 8200* | www.ginsengdubai.com

If you've seen Sex and the City and fancy yourself as a bit of a girl about town then Ginseng is the best place to sip a sophisticated cocktail and pretend to be pretentious. Great for a girl's night out, it is dressier than neighbouring Seville's and Carter's but less affected than next-door's Chameleon. The menu is full of deliciously tempting Asian treats that lend themselves to sharing – especially the platters which you may be in danger of fighting over rather than just picking at. The cocktail menu, however, is the real draw with a variety of sweet and strong concoctions that slip down a little too easily. Two for one drink deals on Tuesdays and menu discounts on Mondays.

**Boulevard at**
**Emirates Towers**
*Trade Centre 2*
*Map 7 F3* 46

## Harry Ghatto's
*04 330 0000* | www.jumeirah.com

The singing in this small karaoke bar starts at 22:00, so you've got plenty of time before that to muster up some Dutch courage. You'll find a great list of cocktails and other beverages, although there is only a limited range of bar snacks and light meals to soak up the alcohol. There are over 1,000 songs to choose from, so whether you croon like Sinatra or rap like Eminem they can play your song here. The hostesses regularly hop up on stage and belt out a number to encourage the crowd, although with so many eager (and amazingly talented) karaoke singers in Dubai, this hardly seems necessary.

**Hyatt Regency**
*Deira*
*Map 9 D1* 14

## Hibiki Music Lounge
*04 317 2222* | www.dubai.regency.hyatt.com

Beyond the tassel-strung doors lies a karaoke lounge that will appeal to the diva in everyone. The cosy interior features a small stage, comfy seating areas, and a central bar. There are also three private rooms, with Japanese, Singaporean, and Thai themes, for those special occasions or for crooners not ready for a public performance. Singers have around 8,000 songs to choose from, and the audience can follow the action on monitors (which can also be retuned to pick up TV stations should the show fail to impress). With a nightly happy hour from 19:30 to 22:00, this friendly bar offers a great night out to its mixed clientele.

*Cin Cin (p.579)*

# Bars

**Radisson SAS Hotel**
*Dubai Media City*
*Al Sufouh*
*Map 5 C2* **28**

## Icon Bar

*04 366 9111 | www.radissonsas.com*

Icon is just that – a symbol for stylish post-work boozers everywhere. It's in Media City, so there's lots of chaps in awkward glasses, confident, hearty laughter and small groups sniggering about their absent boss. The carefully styled ambience – red leather chairs, sequined drapes, expensive looking ceramics and coffee-table house – is book-ended by big screens showing football. The bar nibbles are good if a little small; you can pick from sandwiches, imaginative salads and jacket potatoes. There's also a choice of pizzas, fired downstairs at Certo (p.540), should you be planning a long night of office gossip.

*Icon Bar*

**Hilton Creek**
*Deira*
*Map 11 C1* **12**

## Issimo

*04 227 1111 | www.hilton.com*

Issimo brings a touch of James Bond to the Dubai Creek Hilton. The long, narrow bar has a retro-futuristic feel with stark chrome, black leather, and large slanted Japanese-style panels. Electronic ambient jazz oozes from a crisp sound system and monochrome photos of Hollywood starlets bedeck the walls. The menu features a superb selection of Martinis and cocktails (all worryingly without prices). The wonderful Mangolini, a Mango and Champagne creation, is as notable as the Dhs.85 bill that follows it. Issimo's clientele is an interesting blend of moneyed hotel guests, Mafioso lookalikes, and hip young clubbers, while Saturday nights attract a different crowd with Swing dance lessons at Dhs.35 per swinger.

**Souk Madinat Jumeirah**
*Umm Suqeim*
*Map 6 A2* **68**

## Jambase

*04 366 8888 | www.jumeirah.com*

Meet, dine, drink and dance – the perfect combination for a good night out. Situated just off the main entrance to the Madinat, Jambase's tempting selection of cocktails and other alcoholic beverages is enough to kick off a good night. Although food plays second fiddle, generous portions and a varied menu selection give you the opportunity to get ready for a night of dancing with the live band. There is an authentic 50s-style jazz bar ambience accomplished by the dark wooden interior and rustic lighting and the mixture of different cultures can be felt in both the food and the music, from the jazz bars of New Orleans to the Cape of South Africa.

**Al Qasr Hotel**
*Umm Suqeim*
*Map 6 A1* **41**

## Koubba

*04 366 8888 | www.jumeirah.com*

One of the most stunning views in Dubai awaits you from the terrace of this sumptuous cocktail bar, and on a balmy winter's evening you'd be hard pressed to find a better spot for showing off to out-of-town visitors. The ever-changing light show of the Burj Al Arab, the abras drifting

### Karaoke

If you fancy yourself as a bit of a crooner and want to share your talent with the unsuspecting public, Dubai has two karaoke bars of note. Harry Ghatto's (p.580) and Hibiki Music Lounge (p.580) are both popular for a fun night out. Ear plugs are optional.

**581**

The Complete **Residents'** Guide

by on the canal, and the balconies and windtowers of Al Qasr hotel all create a magical setting. Just off the terrace is the Armoury Lounge, where you can indulge in Cuban cigars surrounded by wooden screens, lavish carpets, and antique Indian weaponry.

**Souk Madinat**
**Jumeirah**
*Umm Suqeim*
**Map 6 A2** 68

## Left Bank ▶ p.583

*04 368 6171* | www.mmidubai.com

While Left Bank's terrace by the Madinat's waterway allows romancing couples a peaceful retreat, the contemporary interior decor welcomes large groups of young and trendy professionals for a post-work or pre-club drink.

Lunch and early evening are the best times to visit for food, especially if you prefer quiet dining as opposed to being serenaded by the resident DJ. The menu is made up of simple meat and fish dishes – the coriander burger is recommended – along with a selection of nibbles and plates to share. Left Bank has a good selection of draft and bottled beers, as well as some decent wines by the glass.

*Left Bank*

**Ritz-Carlton**
*Marsa Dubai*
**Map 5 A1** 31

## Library Bar & Cigar Lounge

*04 399 4000* | www.ritzcarlton.com

The first thing that may strike you about the library bar is the lack of books. That aside, the dark wood, comfy sofas and dimmed lighting make you feel like you could be in the study of some country house. Situated just off the lobby, the bar serves a good range of cocktails including the house special 'Ritz Martini' – a delicious blend of vodka and fresh strawberries. It's a relaxing location perfect for pre-dinner drinks or a late nightcap; of course, you could even choose a cigar. The bar menu offers light bites as well as main meals, and the service is attentive yet unobtrusive.

**Towers Rotana**
*Trade Centre 1*
**Map 7 E3** 70

## Long's Bar

*04 343 8000* | www.rotana.com

Reminiscent of a workmanlike American bar, Long's fits the bawdy bar template perfectly: loads of loud, pointless paraphenailia, big screens for sport and a radio tuned permanently to the 80s and 90s chart. Earlier in the evening you can eat perfectly good pub food in the dining area, sandwiched under the stairs, but later on you'd probably rather not. Packed with punters who like their nights noisy, boozy and preferably flirty, Long's isn't subtle, sophisticated or even faintly stylish. But with staff who cover the ground brilliantly, you can be sure of swift service and several head-pounding happy hours.

**Dubai International**
**Convention Centre**
*Trade Centre 2*
**Map 7 F3** 51

## Lotus One

*04 329 3200* | www.lotus1.com

Uber-cool, hip and happening, super-trendy – whatever you want to call those 'it' places that manage to draw the social set and their sheep, Lotus One is at the top of the it-list. Basically it is very, very cool. You enter into a large, fabulously funky bar that combines Philip Stark with Café Del Mar. The glass and wood mixed floors, shiny chrome bar and intimate tables for two with chairs that swing on chains from the ceiling complement the progressive tunes courtesy of a groovy house DJ. Beyond the bar and obscured from view by wooden dividers is the spacious restaurant with a menu that jumps from Asian dishes to Aussie steaks but finds a commonality in exquisite quality.

# LEFT BANK.

WATERFRONT - SOUK MADINAT JUMEIRAH

Contact us 04 368 6171

*Radisson SAS Hotel*
*Al Sufouh*
*Map 5 C3* **28**

## Media Lounge

*04 366 9111* | *dubai.radissonsas.com*

With curvy 70s style chairs, criss-crossed windows and dangling metal decoration, the Media Lounge lives up to its name as a quiet but suitably trendy hangout for creative types. Advertising execs stop in to brainstorm over frothy coffees or juices by day, or snap open their laptops and make use of the internet access. By sundown, you'll find the frazzled post-work crowd unwinding over an aperitif or cocktail. Head up the stairs at the back and you'll find the more lively sister bar, Icon (p.581). Decent snacks are available, or you can order pizzas from Certo (p.540).

*Al Manzil Hotel*
*Downtown Bur Dubai*
*Map 7 D3* **51**

## Nezesaussi

*04 428 5888* | *www.southernsun.com*

Home to the best ribs in town, this upmarket sports bar has enough glam to keep WAGS happy while the match is on. Tastefully decked out in memorabilia, without looking like a sporty Hard Rock Cafe, Nezesaussi might be a tongue-twister but once you've been, the name is hard to forget. Boasting South African sausages, lamb from New Zealand and Australian steaks, you might think vegetarians would struggle to find something hearty on the imaginative menu, but it's not all beer and beef. Nezesaussi's menu features big salads and a decent selection of wines. Open until 02:00 at weekends.

*Creek Golf Club*
*Al Garhoud*
*Map 11 B4* **49**

## QD's

*04 295 6000* | *www.dubaigolf.com*

The food at QD's is more along the lines of elegant bar snacks than full-on dining – think nachos, thai fishcakes, satay chicken skewers and pizzas. But food is not the issue here, instead it's all about location, location, location – pull up a comfortable chair on the banks of the creek, so close to the water's edge that you can almost dip your toes in, and watch the passing abras and dhow cruises. There's no better spot for sundowners, certainly not on this side of the creek. QD's also has an excellent cocktails list, and as the sun goes down and the night wears on, it plays host to a live band who keep the fun-loving, shisha-smoking crowd entertained until the early hours.

*Aviation Club, The*
*Al Garhoud*
*Map 13 D1* **41**

## Rainbow Room

*04 282 4122* | *www.aviationclubonline.com*

It may be slightly obscured between its more famous neighbours, the Aviation Club and The Cellar, but the Rainbow Room is back and fighting its corner following a worthwhile recent refurbishment. With a pretty wooden deck around the outdoor swimming pool as well as a spacious lounge area, it's a great spot for a cool drink and quick bite from the limited but sturdy menu of salads, sandwiches, chicken, beef and fish entrees. Typically more 'chilled retreat' than 'buzzing hotspot', the Rainbow Room loosens and livens up when it hosts Laughter Factory comedy evenings, or whenever it's booked for a corporate booze-up.

*Regent Palace Hotel*
*Downtown Bur Dubai*
*Map 8 F4* **66**

## Rock Bottom

*04 396 3888* | *www.ramee-group.com*

A perennial fixture on Dubai's nightlife scene, Rock Bottom manages to meet the requirements of just about anyone fancying a good night out. Early in the evening it acts as a quiet restaurant with subdued lighting, candlelit tables, and good food at reasonable prices. Mid-evening it morphs into a hedonistic bar, popular with late night revelers who just don't want the party to end, and after 22:00 Rock Bottom really does rock. At the weekend Rock Bottom's in-house band, one of the best in Dubai, gets the dance floor jumping with and eclectic mix of live music.

**One&Only
Royal Mirage**
*Al Sufouh*
*Map 5 C1* 25

### Rooftop Lounge & Terrace
*04 399 9999 | www.oneandonlyroyalmirage.com*
One of the most spectacular hotels in Dubai hosts one of the most chilled-out bars in the city. Rooftop is a hangout for the beautiful people, which means you can expect to pay high prices for your tall drinks (although if you go during happy hour, your sundowners will be cheaper). That aside, this has a superb view of the Palm and once the island is finished, this spot will surely be the best viewing point around. Arabic cushion seats are cleverly placed around the Rooftop, promoting interaction between the clientele. If you want to kick back your kitten heels and relax under the stars with superstar style cocktails then this is the place.

**Boulevard at
Emirates Towers**
*Trade Centre 2*
*Map 7 F3* 46

### Scarlett's
*04 319 8768 | www.jumeirah.com*
Tucked away in Emirates Towers, Scarlett's has long been a favourite of both tourists and expats. The numerous big screens are great for sports fans, while the terrace in the shopping mall provides some respite from the big game bustle.
The menu is extensive, varied and very reasonably priced while the service is good enough to satisfy the crowd. Scarlett's is great for big groups who want to eat, drink and be merry. However, for a family meal out or a romantic dinner, the place is to be avoided, unless commercial dance music, drunk businessmen and plumes of cigarette smoke is your thing.

**Dubai Marine Beach**
*Jumeira*
*Map 7 F1* 5

### Sho Cho
*04 346 1111 | www.dxbmarine.com*
The Dubai Marine Beach Resort is home to a number of party places that share an impressive alfresco setting around an azure lagoon that literally sparkles under the starry night sky. It may be a Japanese restaurant but the delicate and imaginative dishes (that tend to be a little on the pricey side) are not the real reason the beautiful set flock to Sho Cho's shoreline. As the clock ticks towards midnight the ample terrace begins to fill and the happy house mixes with hints of hardcore and traces of trance. It's not quite in the ranks of Ibiza but the atmosphere has definitely got that sunshine holiday appeal.

**Hilton Jumeirah**
*Marsa Dubai*
*Map 5 A1* 13

### Studio One
*04 399 1111 | www.hilton.com*
Welcome to the sport watcher's paradise. US and European beers and spirits, tongue-wrenchingly over-salted burgers, 'bar snacks' and greasy fries are the perfect accompaniment to a night in front of the big game. TVs are scattered around the bar at unusual angles to provide punters with a multi-screen sport marathon. If the unashamedly promoted brand of beer plastered all over the walls doesn't get you in the mood, then the endless supply of salty, stale popcorn will. The price of booze isn't off-putting, and the selection is good.

**Radisson SAS Hotel**
*Dubai Media City*
*Al Sufouh*
*Map 5 C2* 28

### Tamanya Terrace
*04 366 9111 | www.radissonsas.com*
More comfortable than one would expect from a mid-city outdoor venue, the Radisson's Tamanya Terrace welcomes business visitors, tourists and media locals in a trendy mix of concrete and

---

**Bar Food**
There are quite a few bars around town that are renowned for the quality of their food. Some bars worth considering for both drinks and dinner include Boudoir (p.578), Left Bank (p.582), Buddha Bar (p.578), Carter's (p.578), Ginseng (p.580), Lotus One (p.582) and Sho Cho's (p.585).

**585**

chrome. There's music in the form of a spinning DJ, but that's for laters. Tamanya tends to tempt punters as a stopping-off point after work, though without the aid of a happy hour per se. As the clock ticks on the cocktail bar starts filling up with fun and merriment flowing. Good views, not bad nibbles, fine drinks – works just fine after a long day's slog.

*Renaissance Hotel*
*Hor Al Anz*
*Map 11 E1* **30**

## Tiki Bar

**04 262 5555** | *www.renaissancehotels.com*

If you're looking for somewhere to launch an evening of serious Dubai partying, or somewhere to round off a hard day's slog, Tiki Bar is ready, waiting and already pouring your perfect drink. One of the bar's main attractions, along with the energetic Cuban band and wakiki-style decor, is the talented barmen, who craftily concoct your own personal cocktail based on your favourite tipples and taste. If you're in a group, don't miss the cocktail packages, offering unlimited drinks for one hour starting from just Dhs.79, a fee which decreases (along with your lucidity) for every additional hour. Also try the nibbles, which arrive in a huge martini glass.

### Under Age

The law in Dubai states that drinkers must be 21 or over. If you're fortunate enough to look as though you barely remember the 80s, make sure you carry some form of ID that shows your age - a passport or driving licence is best. Even if you think you're flattering your slightly wrinkled self, it's better to be safe than sorry. Otherwise you'll be on lemonade all night, or worse still, left outside alone.

*Radisson SAS Hotel*
*Deira Creek*
*Deira*
*Map 9 B4* **27**

## Up On The Tenth

**04 205 7333** | *www.ichotelsgroup.com*

With its elevated position (the clue is in the name) this elegant cocktail bar offers terrific views over the creek and the twinkling lights beyond. With its lounge seating and dusky blue lighting, the look is New York jazz bar, and the stateside theme is confirmed by the Manhattan skyline mural adorning the walls. Jazz is regularly on the menu courtesy of the in-house band, which adds to the sophisticated atmosphere. Drinkers for whom money is no object should find the selection of champagne cocktails to their liking.

*Jumeirah*
*Beach Hotel*
*Umm Suqeim*
*Map 6 B1* **17**

## Uptown

**04 406 8999** | *www.jumeirah.com*

Take the elevator to the 24th floor to find this small but perfectly formed bar. The cool interior is classy enough, but Uptown's USP is the outdoor terrace – it's a perfect spot for 'sunset behind the Burj' photo ops and offers a cracking view along the coast with the Sheikh Zayed Road skyscrapers twinkling in the distance. The drinks come in slanted glasses and include familiar and enticing cocktails, wines for the connoisseur and bottled beers. Get there at 18:00 sharp to

*Vu's Bar*

take advantage of the half-price happy hour and cute little canapes. The menu also features some mouthwatering mocktails and a selection of tasty bar snacks should the nuts and nibbles not suffice.

**Pyramids**
*Umm Hurair*
*Map 10 E4* 65

## Vintage

*04 324 4100 | www.waficitirestaurants.com*

Vintage is a cheese and wine aficionado's dream, with the menu a veritable telephone directory of all things cheese and grape. Wines range from the most respectable plonk to a dazzling array of costly vintages, burgundies and champagnes, but despite the exclusive list this feels more like a friendly local than a stuffy wine bar. Fondue nights, on Fridays and Saturdays, offer a bottle of white or red and generous fondue for two for Dhs.145. Vintage is a small space, so reservations and smoke-free dining are not an option, and you may need to arrive early or very late to bag a stool.

**Emirates Towers**
*Trade Centre 2*
*Map 7 F3* 7

## Vu's Bar

*04 319 8088 | www.jumeirah.com*

The elevator ride to the 51st floor is an experience in itself and when the lift opens you are invited into an intimate bar that feels like a private members' club. The window space is somewhat restricted but still gives you a fabulous view across Dubai's sprawling metropolis. The sleek, chic interior features small tables with comfy low chairs by the windows, high stools around the central bar, and an inviting booth with a semi-circular red leather sofa. A comprehensive choice of imaginative cocktails and a bulging beer and wine list should ensure no one goes thirsty. Vu's is far from cheap, but for sophisticated sundowners and showing off to out-of-towners, it takes some beating.

## Ladies' Nights

| Day | Bar | Offer | Page |
|---|---|---|---|
| Sunday | Jimmy Dix | Unlimited free drinks | p.587 |
| | Carters | Two free drinks from 22:00 | p.578 |
| Monday | Icon Bar | Two free drinks | p.581 |
| Tuesday | Boston Bar | Four free drinks from 22:30 | p.578 |
| | Boudoir | Free champagne all night | p.578 |
| | Carters | Two free drinks | p.578 |
| | Double Decker | Two free drinks (that you mix yourself) | p.588 |
| | Jimmy Dix | Two free drinks | p.587 |
| | Keva | Free Mojitos | p.530 |
| | Long's Bar | Two free cocktails | p.582 |
| | Malecon | Two free drinks and free shots after midnight | p.549 |
| | Scarlett's | Two free drinks | p.585 |
| Wednesday | Boudoir | Free cocktails all night | p.578 |
| | Jimmy Dix | Free drinks all night | p.587 |
| | Long's Bar | Two free drinks from 21:00 | p.582 |
| Thursday | Aussie Legends | Free daquiris and wine | p.575 |
| | Boston Bar | Four free drinks | p.578 |
| | Boudoir | Free cocktails until midnight | p.578 |
| | Waxy O'Connors | Free bubbly and frozen cocktails and bubbly | p.590 |
| Friday | Boudoir | Free champagne all night | p.578 |
| | Scarlett's | Two free drinks for ladies. Those wearing red get three free drinks. | p.585 |
| | Lotus One | Free selected cocktails | p.582 |
| | Rock Bottom | Selected drinks Dhs.2 | p.584 |

587

## Pubs

Other options **Bars** p.575

You can't expect authenticity from Dubai's pubs, but then when they're mostly in hotels, in the desert, in the Middle East, that won't come as a surprise. What you can look forward to is some inviting, friendly spots with a decent selection of draught and bottled beers, and reliably good bar grub. Many of these mostly ersatz English and Irish places are popular when there's a big game on. And they're all comfortable, raucous and smoky enough to feel enough like the real thing.

*Sofitel City Centre*
*Al Garhoud*
*Map 11 C3* **35**

### Churchill's ▶ p.589

*04 294 1222* | *www.accorhotels.com*

While it might not be the kind of place that you go out of your way to visit, Churchill's has one distinct advantage – it is attached (via the Sofitel Hotel) to Deira City Centre so when you (or your man) gets tired of shopping you can nip in for a quick half. As close as you can get to a traditional English pub, there are TVs, a pool table and dartboard, dodgy carpets, wooden booths and obligatory tabletop nuts. The food is what you would expect from pub fare – burgers, fish and chips, pies, chicken and some worthy desserts.

*Jumeirah*
*Beach Hotel*
*Umm Suqeim*
*Map 6 B1* **17**

### Dhow & Anchor

*04 406 8999* | *www.jumeirah.com*

Slightly reminiscent of a traditional, if miniature, British pub, the Dhow and Anchor is a popular watering hole. The compact bar area can get very crowded and smoky, particularly during happy hour, or when a major sporting event is showing on the huge plasma screen TV. Just up from the bar there's a small, rather plain seating area, so if dining you're advised to try the attractive outdoor terrace, which has glimpses of the Burj Al Arab through the palm trees. A varied drinks menu includes some interesting cocktails and the usual beers, wines and spirits, while the pub grub staples include terrific curries, pies, and some of the tastiest fish and chips around.

*Al Murooj Rotana*
*Hotel & Suites*
*Trade Centre 2*
*Map 7 E3* **2**

### Double Decker Pub

*04 321 1111* | *www.rotana.com*

Double Decker is a pub themed on London transport, but thankfully the memorabilia does not overwhelm and the ambience is convivial. The largely wood-panelled interior, with an attractive glass dome at its centre, is arranged in two tiers, with seating at both levels. The upper tier houses a balcony area for the band. An adventurous cocktail and drinks menu is complemented by a superb wine list, both comprehensive and informative, and the upmarket pub food covers a broad range of tasty snacks and meals. A pleasant, horseshoe-shaped central bar, coupled with some amazing drinks deals, make this a good choice for stopping off after work, although many patrons will linger long enough to order supper.

*Le Meridien Dubai*
*Al Garhoud*
*Map 13 E1* **20**

### Dubliners

*04 282 4040* | *www.lemeridien.com*

This Irish pub is cosy, friendly, and lively, and a perfect venue for business or pleasure. Sit inside to partake in the weekly quiz, to listen to music, or to watch football. Sit outside on the romantic patio to enjoy the night air and conversation, or to stare at the front of a truck embedded in the facade of the building. The menu has many delectable choices and the dishes are fresh, tasty and reasonably priced. Save room for the Bailey's cheesecake. The pub includes some of the best beer choices in Dubai and an extensive selection of cocktails.

# Social butterflies can now...
## play their cards right

A pack of cards with impartial, snappy bar info to help you choose your location extra sharpish, with directions to get you right to the door. Small enough to fit in your pocket or purse and with discount vouchers to keep your wallet heavy.

**Dubai Star Bars**
Reshuffle your social life

Abu Dhabi • Amsterdam • Bahrain • Barcelona • Beijing • Berlin • Dubai • Dublin • Geneva
Hong Kong • Kuala Lumpur • Kuwait • London • Los Angeles • New York • New Zealand • Oman
Paris • Qatar • Shanghai • Singapore • Sydney • Tokyo • Vancouver

**EXPLORER**

www.explorerpublishing.com

**Beh White Swan Bldg**
*Trade Centre 1*
*Map 7 F2* 106

## Fibber Magee's

**04 332 2400** | www.fibbersdubai.com

Pubs on foreign shores often strive for that all-important 'rustic' feel, and many fail miserably. Fibber Magee's, though, pulls it off with aplomb. Awkwardly positioned TV screens, dark wood banisters and tables and chairs, the unique smell of years of smoke and drink-soaked carpets, and a well-stocked international drinks cabinet, appease those pub withdrawal symptoms immediately. The management takes pride in the quality and quantity of the food and the result is a tasty and fresh eating experience. Live televised sport, DJ and themed entertainment evenings, and great value food and drink promotions, makes Fibbers a popular choice for a no nonsense pint.

*Irish Village*

**Aviation Club, The**
*Al Garhoud*
*Map 13 D1* 44

## Irish Village

**04 282 4750** | www.aviationclubonline.com

Should you so desire fish and chips (in Guiness batter no less) or a bit of steak with a pint of your favourite ale to wash it down, you can get it in a warm, friendly and relaxed environment at the 'Village'. The inside covers sizeable ground but cubby holes and wooden beams give it a cosy feel, and as for the outside space, wooden benches aplenty sit on cobbled stone and are bordered by trees lit by multicoloured bulbs. Be it for a quick pint, a hearty meal, a knees-up, a hair-of-the-dog fry up or a spot of local talent (musical that is), the Irish Village is like a dear old friend.

**Habtoor Grand**
*Marsa Dubai*
*Map 5 B1* 11

## The Underground

**04 399 5000** | www.habtoorhotels.com

This English-style boozer is modelled on The Underground – the London public transport system. They've even gone to the trouble of making the bar look like a cross-section of a carriage. Luckily, the bar isn't platform-themed (no muffled cries of 'mind the gap'). Instead it has the feel of a sports social club; with live sport and pub snacks galore, and a dog-eared dartsboard. In fact, there's nothing stressful about a few pints in this laid-back basement bar. It's also the meeting place of the Dubai branch of the Liverpool supporters' club.

**Ascot Hotel**
*Downtown Bur Dubai*
*Map 8 F2* 43

## Waxy O'Conner's

**04 352 0900** | www.ascothoteldubai.com

A long bar, dark wood, Guinness on tap – what more would you expect from an Irish wannabe bar and restaurant? This one is a lively and popular Dubai watering hole and sports the usual add ons such as big screen TVs, a pool table, as well as a full menu of the kinds of food you'd expect: bangers and mash, fish and chips, burgers and sandwiches. The place livens up late and offers lots of specials including some for the ladies and hugely popular brunch on Fridays, with unbelievable prices on food and booze. Just don't be surprised if your feet stick to the beer sodden floor as the crowds thicken at the weekend.

# Nightclubs

Other options **Belly Dancing** p.322, **Dinner Cruises** p.510

Packed with all nationalities, Dubai's nightclubs are very popular from about 23:00 until well into the small hours. There are several dedicated nightclubs, as well as numerous other venues that are bars or restaurants earlier in the evening, and then later turn into the perfect place to hit the dancefloor. For authentic club nights, look out for the increasingly common visits by the cream of international DJs and the special nights held all over Dubai by various event organisers.

Additionally, since you're in the Middle East, don't forget the option of Arabic nightclubs. Here you can sample a variety of Arabic food and enjoy a night of traditional Arabic entertainment, usually with a belly dancer, a live band and singer. These venues only start getting busy very late in the evening, and can still be empty when most other nightspots are packed, reflecting the Arabic way of starting late and finishing, well… later.

> **Late & Lively**
> In addition to the dedicated clubs reviewed here, Dubai's nightlife scene also includes several bars and restaurants which transform late evening into lively joints with hopping dance floors. These include Aussie Legends (p.575), Boston Bar (p.578), Boudoir (p.578), El Paso (p.580), Malecon (p.549), Rock Bottom (p.584) and Scarlett's (p.585).

**Al Nasr Leisureland**
*Oud Metha*
*Map 10 E2* 150

## Chi@The Lodge

*04 337 9470* | *www.lodgedubai.com*

Back in the day when you could drive around Dubai and rent a flat for less than Dhs.100,000 a year, plain old The Lodge was the expat hotspot. It was like a cavernous British working men's club, with plastic chairs, sticky carpets and a beer-soaked dancefloor. Following its early 2007 revamp it Is now hugely popular with the new expat set. It has been given the Dubai sheen and now has indoor and outdoor dancefloors with lots of seating and large screens; there are VIP 'cabanas' outside and tables can be reserved indoors. The regular theme nights with fancy dress are popular and Chi is also home of the 'legendary' cheese nights with DJ Tim Cheddar. Since it reopened Dubai's live music fans have witnessed occasional concerts from has-beens like Boyz II Men and Brand New Heavies while clubbers have been treated to some big name DJs. If you needed more reasons to go, it's easy to get taxis outside, there's often a shawarma stand in the carpark and entrance is free before 23:00 on most nights.

**Mövenpick Hotel**
*Bur Dubai*
*Oud Metha*
*Map 10 D3* 24

## Jimmy Dix

*04 336 8800* | *jimmydixdxb@hotmail.com*

A friendly, unpretentious bar and nightclub with a relaxed dress code, you can always count on Jimmy Dix for a good crowd and a lively atmosphere. The DJ and talented live band always satisfy the crowds, especially on their 'Thursday Thump' weekend party. For those wishing to make a night of it, arrive early to grab a table (useful to keep hold of when the place fills up later on). The food is unexpectedly good – a mix of Tex-Mex, grills, burgers, sausage and mash, and crumbles, making this a great one-stop shop for eating, drinking, and partying. Jimmy Dix is also one of the homes of the Laughter Factory, Dubai's thriving circuit of funnymen (p.596).

**One&Only**
**Royal Mirage**
*Al Sufouh*
*Map 5 C1* 25

## Kasbar

*04 399 9999* | *www.oneandonlyroyalmirage.com*

Kasbar manages to combine the best of both worlds – the mystique and luxury of regal Arabia and the feel of an exclusive dance party. In keeping with the arabesque decor of the Royal Mirage, this is a sultry, candlelit nightclub perfect for liaisons. There is an air of old-school romance emanting from the three levels linked by a spiral

**591**

staircase. The main floor attracts toe-tappers, while the mezzanine space overlooks the dance floor, and the basement is a chill-out lounge. Excellent tunes, a glamorously funky vibe and a wonderfully unique venue make this a worthy addition to One & Only's impressive line-up.

**Emirates Towers Offices**
Trade Centre 2
Map 7 F3 109

## The Loft
*050 846 3424*

Back with a vengeance after a period of closure, this three-floored swish club reopened its doors in November 2006. Designed by the people behind the super flash Lotus One, the interior is like a showroom of designer furniture, including morphed leather seats, glass walls and huge chandeliers fashioned from shells. Hot resident and international DJs spin mainly house music, with live music on occasional Thursday nights from up and coming local performers. The venue's current lack of a dance licence does mean the mood is slightly more subdued than elsewhere, although you'll probably get away with a subtle hip-thrust or two.

**Grand Hyatt Dubai**
Umm Hurair
Map 13 C1 9

## MIX
*04 317 1234* | *www.dubai.grand.hyatt.com*

Touted as Dubai's only superclub (don't tell Trilogy), MIX has three floors of hedonistic late-night entertainment. There is a sprawling dancefloor, a lounge area (with some comfortable seating, much needed after too many hours of dancing in stilettos!), two VIP rooms, a cigar bar and a sound-proofed live music room. Various local and international DJs earn the respect of Dubai's hip crowd by belting out loud and large tunes (mostly house – but if that's not your bag you'll find some R&B upstairs). MIX can accommodate 800 clubbers – great on Thursday nights when everybody's out but during the week even a decent-sized club crowd of 300 can seem lost in such a huge space.

**Al Bustan Rotana**
Al Garhoud
Map 13 E1 1

## Oxygen
*04 282 0000* | *www.rotana.com*

Hidden beneth the Al Bustan Rotana, Oxygen is sleek, sophisticated and spacious enough to accomodate a partying crowd but equally intimate for romancing couples. It is home to a range of music styles, depending on the night, although there seems to be a slight leaning towards R&B, hip-hop and house, but you can come late and dance your kitten heels off anyway. It might be dimly lit and underground but Oxygen is more designer decadent than spit and sawdust. There are regular, generous promotions, especially for the ladies who get free-flowing champagne or complimentary drinks on certain nights.

**Wafi City**
Umm Hurair
Map 10 D4

## Plan B
*04 324 4777*

Taking over the space once occupied by the much-loved Planetarium, which after closing down in 2006 was replaced by Chameleon Arabic restaurant and bar, notable for its innovative design. The guys at Wafi took the opportunity to reinvent the space once again and in October of 2007 the aptly named Plan B opened its doors. The VIP room upstairs serves champagne and sushi, but the focus is now on

> **Live Music**
> Dubai's live music scene is currently the busiest it's ever been. From impromptu jam sessions to tight (or comedy) cover bands, these days you're spoilt for choice. Check out the sounds thumping from Aussie Legends (p.575), Bar Zar (p.576), Barasti Bar (p.576), Blue Bar (p.578), Go West (p.500), Hard Rock Café (p.502), Irish Village (p.592), Jambase (p.581), Jimmy Dix (p.591), Malecon (p.549), Rock Bottom (p.584), and Trader Vics (p.553).

dancing and not dining. Aimed at people looking for a relaxed late night hang-out (no cover charge or ridiculous drinks prices), Plan B hopes to be a refreshing change to Dubai's increasingly exclusive nightlife. The music is wide ranging, with happy hour enlivening the fervour of Saturday nights.

> **Dancing Outside The Box**
> Should you fancy wigging out to something slightly more alternative while out on the town in Dubai, scour magazine and website listings for the monthly Twisted Melons and Step On club nights. Offering some British flavour with indie, rock and whatever the DJ fancies, these are rare nights when you can jump around and feel like you're back at the student union.

**Souk Madinat Jumeirah**
*Umm Suqeim*
*Map 6 A2*

## Trilogy

**04 366 6917** | www.trilogy.ae

Dubai's original superclub, which opened its doors in 2004, remains its most popular. With three floors, a cavernous space and plenty of booty room, this glitzy high heeler has six bars, private lounges (for hire), a majlis-style chill-out terrace and a playlist of funky house. The regular thousand-strong capacity crowds enjoy the city's best line-up of international DJs. If you want to feel like a celebrity then book a VIP glass cage and sip Moet as you look at the minions making their moves below. In late 2007, Trilogy introduced a members' only policy. There are two types of membership; red is free; the other, gold, isn't. See more details on the website.

**Crowne Plaza**
*Trade Centre 1*
*Map 7 F2*

## Zinc

**04 331 1111** | www.crowneplaza.com

Zinc' up-for-it marketing remains as hyperactive, while the soundtrack is R&B, house and hip hop, with Tuesday's Housexy (Ministry of Sound) and Kinki Milinky ferrying over some of the UK's hot-shot DJs. Design-wise, there are shiny new flatscreens, louche lounge areas and glitzy mirrored walls, as well as an enlarged dance floor that's sectioned off by a mammoth bar, with sister bars ensuring the 'dancefloor to fresh drink (from the new champagne, wine and cocktail list) path' is as smooth as possible. Go between 20:00 and 23:00 for unlimited drinks deals.

Zinc

Trilogy

## Parties at Home

There are several companies in Dubai that can do all the cooking, decorating and cleaning up for you, leaving you with more time to tell witty after-dinner anecdotes. Harlequin (www.harlequinmarquees.com) offers marquees, tables and chairs, and even outdoor coolers for those summer garden parties. Flying Elephant (www.flyingelephantuae.com) helps with party decorations and venue equipment, as well as excellent children's party plans. For a novel outdoor party idea, you can get your very own shawarma stand set up in the garden, complete with shawarma maker. Several Arabic restaurants provide this service, which works out as a very reasonable and easy way to sustain hordes of party guests.

> ### Rent A Tent
> Whether you need a marquee for a thousand people or a cosy canopy for a romantic alfresco dinner, Harlequin can help. They also do event management for gatherings both big and small. See www.harlequinmarquees.com or call 04 347 0110.

## Party Organisers

Other options **Party Accessories** p.441

**Jct 3, Shk Zayed Rd**
**Al Quoz**

### Flying Elephant  ▶ p.595
*04 347 9170* | *www.flyingelephantuae.com*
Whatever your party planning needs, the folks at Flying Elephant will be happy to comply. It offers everything from adding special effects to a product launch to providing entertainment for your child's first birthday party. It has a wide variety of products to complete every occasion, be it balloons and decorations or the Gulf's largest outdoor confetti blaster. Flying Elephant also offers theme decoration, theme parties, balloon printing and balloon decoration/sculpting.

**Al Khaleej Bldg**
**Zabeel Rd**

### Mad Science
*04 337 7403* | *www.madscience.org/uae*
In addition to offering after-school activity programmes and workshops, Mad Science organises entertainment for special events and kids' birthday parties. Ideally suited to children between 5 and 12 years, the interactive, science-based shows last around an hour, and the kids get to take home a goody bag containing educational experiments.

## Caterers

For parties, special occasions, and business lunches or dinners, there are numerous options for arranging outside catering, allowing you to relax and enjoy yourself and concentrate on anything but the cooking. In addition to specialist companies, many hotels and restaurants have catering departments, so pick your favourite and ask if they can help out. Depending on what you require, caterers can provide just the food or everything from crockery, napkins, tables, chairs and even waiters, doormen and a clearing up service afterwards. You don't even have to stay at home to order catering for a function – how about arranging a party in the desert? Costs vary according to the number of people, dishes and level of service required. For a list of hotel numbers, check out the table on p.44. For restaurants and cafes, browse this section of the book.

### Light Shows

If you need to bring a splash of colour to your party or event, then consider Desert River. From huge beanbags to funky lighting and inflatable buffets, it has got a quirky collection from which to choose. See www.desertriver.com or call 04 345 4541.

| Caterers | |
|---|---|
| Emirates Abela | 04 282 3171 |
| Intercat | 04 334 5212 |
| Lime Tree Cafe | 04 349 8498 |
| Maria Bonita's | 04 395 4454 |
| Metropolitan Catering Services | 04 881 7100 |
| Open House | 04 396 5481 |
| Sandwich Express | 04 343 9922 |
| Something Different | 04 267 1639 |
| West One | 04 249 4500 |

# Planning an
# event?

# Look no further.

M.I.C.E. Events ◆ Corporate Events ◆ Teambuilding Activities
Corporate Family Days ◆ Themed Events ◆ Entertainment
Balloon Decoration ◆ Event Rentals ◆ Mascot Fabrication
Keeko Kids Parties ◆ Royal Events ◆ Product Launches
Gala Dinners ◆ Opening Cermonies ◆ Exhibitions

**Talk to us and discover the many ways we can bring your event to life.**

# Flying Elephant

The region's largest supplier of corporate and family entertainment.

For more information contact
Tel: +9714 347-9170   Fax: +9714 347-9171
info@flyingelephantuae.com • www.flyingelephantuae.com

## We're on the lookout for talent!

If you are a multi-skilled entertainer or performance artist, interested in working on corporate and family events, please email your details to careers@flyingelephantuae.com

**Shooting Stars** ◀

*Shooting Stars is an adventure video production company that produces keepsake videos . Using the latest digital technology, they can turn your child into the star of their very own video blockbuster: a popular choice is 'My Arabian Adventure' (the background tape is filmed in the dunes at Hatta). It's a unique and unusual gift to send back to the grandparents. For more information contact Shooting Stars on 04 394 1377 or 050 798 8209, or check out their website www.shootingstar.biz.*

## Cinemas

Movie-going is popular in Dubai, although screenings are limited to the mainstream – you won't find too many art house offerings. Dubai has seen an explosion in the number of screens available over the past couple of years; the biggest cinemas include a 12 screen complex in Mall of the Emirates (p.460) and a 21 screen outlet in Ibn Battuta Shopping Mall (p.458) – the latter even has the region's first IMAX screen. Mall of the Emirates also boasts the luxurious Gold Class option for selected films with a smaller theatre, enormous leather armchairs and waiter service throughout the movie. Cinema timings can be found in the daily newspapers, as well as in the 'Entertainment Plus' supplement in *Gulf News* every Wednesday. At weekends, there are extra shows at midnight or 01:00 – check press for details.

There are some common cinema annoyances widely moaned about in expatriate circles – freezing air conditioning, people talking on their mobiles or to the people sitting next to them, people switching seats mid-movie, Arabic subtitles (usually this is no problem, but if you're watching an English language film that contains some foreign language, there is no space for English subtitles so you miss out on some of the dialogue), and of course the heavy hand of the censor.

A definite cinematic highlight is Dubai International Film Festival. Improving year on year, the event runs for a week in December across various locations and showcases an impressive mix of mainstream, world and local cinema, from shorts to full features. There's usually a good range of talks and seminars from actors and directors, including Oliver Stone who showed up in 2006. See www.dubaifilmfest.com for more details.

### Alternative Screenings

While most of the cinema multiplexes only show big Hollywood movies, several bars and clubs put on screenings of older, foreign and independent films, usually early in the week and free of charge. Check out Tiger Movies at Barasti bar (04 399 3333), Movies Under the Stars at Wafi City (04 324 4100), Beach Bar at Jumeirah Beach Club Resort & Spa (04 344 5333), or the Cine-Club Alliance Française auditorium (04 335 8712). It is also worth looking in local listings magazines for details of one-off screenings at some of the city's more progressive art spaces, such as Jam Jar (www.thejamjardubai.com).

## Comedy

**Beats, Beanbags And A Barbie** ◀

*During the cooler winter months, Peanut Butter Jam at Wafi City's Rooftop Gardens (04 324 4100) is a must-do for all music fans. Resident and guest bands and performers play live acoustic music from 20:00 until midnight, with beanbags to relax on and a barbecue.*

Comedy nights in Dubai are popular with the expat crowd. The Laughter Factory organises monthly events, with comedians from the UK's Comedy Store coming over to play various venues throughout the Gulf. In Dubai these venues include Zinc at the Crowne Plaza, Jimmy Dix at the Movenpick, Rainbow Room at the Aviation Club, and the Courtyard Marriott at the Green Community. Keep an eye on www.thelaughterfactory.com for details of future shows. There are also several one-off events featuring comedians from around the world. Remember that a lot of comedy is regional, so unless you're familiar with the comedian's country, you might not get the joke.

## Concerts

Dubai hosts a number of concerts each year, and as it grows bigger it attracts bigger names. Past acts to play here include Missy Elliott, Elton John, Black Eyed Peas, Mariah Carey, Sting, and none other than Robbie Williams. These big name acts usually play at outdoor venues such as the Tennis Stadium, Dubai Autodrome and the amphitheatre at Media City. The amphitheatre recently hosted Desert Rhythm, Dubai's very own music festival celebrating cultural diversity in music. The key event for all music lovers anticipating the rise of live music in Dubai, featured a variety of smaller acts alongside big names such as Kanye West, Mika, Ziggy Marley, Joss

Stone and Madness over two days. In addition to artists at the height of their fame, Dubai also plays host to a string of groups that may be past their prime, but are nevertheless able to provide some good entertainment (think Human League, Tony Hadley, Go West and Deacon Blue). There's also been a recent rise in the number of alternative and slightly lesser-known (basically 'more cool') acts coming over for some sun. Groove Armada, 2ManyDjs and Soulwax (all part-band, part-dance acts) have all played in Dubai Autodrome, Fun lovin' Criminals and Arrested Development are also due to play at the Emirates Golf Club. Another event that goes from strength to strength is the annual Dubai Desert Rock Festival (www.desertrockfestival.com), and for the first time in 2008 will give the region's rock fans a two-day, multi-band ear bashing. Keep an eye on 9714, a promotion, events and marketing company, and general 'arts collective' for information on more upcoming gigs (www.9714.com).

## Cinemas

| Name | Tel No. | Map | Location | Languages | Screens | Normal | Special |
|------|---------|-----|----------|-----------|---------|--------|---------|
| Century Cinemas | 04 349 9773 | 5-E1 | Mercato Mall | A, E, H | 7 | 30 | – |
| CineStar | 04 294 9000 | 11-C3 | Deira City Centre | A, E, H | 11 | 30 | 40 |
| | 04 3414222 | 6-A3 | Mall of the Emirates | A,E | 12 | 30 | – |
| Galleria | 04 209 6470 | 8-D2 | Hyatt Regency | H, M, T | 2 | 20 | – |
| Grand Cinecity | 04 228 9898 | 11-D1 | Al Ghurair City | E, A, H | 8 | 25 | 30 |
| Grand Cinemas / IMAX | 04 366 9898 | 4-D2 | Ibn Battuta Shopping Mall | E, A, H | 21 | 30 | 50 |
| Grand Cineplex | 04 324 2000 | 13-D3 | Umm Hurair 2 | A, E | 12 | 30 | 50 |
| Lamcy | 04 336 8808 | 10-D4 | Lamcy Plaza | H | 2 | 20 | – |
| Metroplex | 04 343 8383 | 5-C4 | Sheikh Zayed Rd | A, E | 8 | 30 | 55 |
| Plaza | 04 393 9966 | 8-A2 | Bur Dubai | H, M | 1 | 15 | 20 |

Key:  A = Arabic; E = English; H = Hindi; M = Malayalam; T= Tamil

## Theatre

Other options **Drama Groups** p.338

The theatre scene in Dubai has always been rather limited, with fans relying chiefly on touring companies and the occasional amateur dramatics performance, but as the city grows so does its thirst for culture, and with an increase in modern facilities over the past couple of years, theatre lovers are finally finding something to cheer about. The Madinat Theatre at Madinat Jumeirah hosts a variety of performances, from serious stage plays to comedies and musical performances. Bigger events can be accommodated in the Madinat Jumeirah's arena – recent events include the production of Stomp and The Nutcracker Ballet performed by Ballet Russe, The Classical Ballet Company of Wales. Dubai's theatre space has been bolstered further with the opening of the Dubai Community Theatre and Arts Centre – see below. Young budding thespians can receive training in acting, mime, scriptwriting and costume design through the Scenez Arts & Drama Academy. Call 050 356 2709 for details.

### The Secret Is Out

Al Sahra Desert Resort is set to be the first development to open within Dubailand. One attraction already up and running is Jumana - Secret of the Desert (left), a visual extravaganza performed on a huge stage set on a lake. The show draws on Arabian folklore and fable, and offers a unique spectacle of song, theatre and dance using state-of-the-art technology. See www.alsahra.com for details.

**597**

**Mall of the Emirates**
*Al Barsha*
*Map 6 A3*

## Dubai Community Theatre & Arts Centre

*04 351 3400 | www.dubaitheatre.org*

The Dubai Community Theatre & Arts Centre (DUCTAC) is the latest, and certainly the biggest, arts facility in the region. In addition to rehearsal spaces, workshops, exhibition halls, a cafe, and a library, the complex features two fully equipped theatres. The Centrepoint Theatre can seat 543 people, while the smaller Kilachand Studio Theatre has a capacity of 196 people. Between them, the theatres aim to present a variety of entertainment; from drama, opera and classical music, to comedy and children's shows. Check the website for details of upcoming events and performances.

**Al Sahra Desert**
**Resort**

## Jumana – Secret of the Desert ▶ p.599

*04 367 9500 | www.alsahra.com*

In addition to the range of events on offer at the Madinat Theatre, a jaw-dropping contribution to Dubai's cultural scene comes from the Al Sahara Desert Resort in Dubailand. Jumana – Secret of the Desert is a remarkable show that uses around 60 acrobats and dancers in an amphitheatre capable of seating 1200. The vibrant production uses water as a backdrop to the performance and boasts the use of fireworks, large scale water effects and video projection (not to mention Omar Sharif's voice as the storyteller) in a rich, awe-inspiring show depicting Arabian folklore. Visit the website for further details.

**Souk Madinat**
**Jumeirah**
*Umm Suqeim*
*Map 6 A2*

## Madinat Theatre

*04 366 8888 | www.madinattheatre.com*

Housing a theatre within a huge complex that includes luxury hotels and a shopping centre may seem like something of an afterthought, but the Madinat Theatre is far from such mediocrity – not only is it worthy of stand-alone status thanks to its well-planned design and space (424 seats no less) but its programme has been suitably impressive. From 'treading the boards' classics to musicals and innovative comedy shows. Make sure you keep your eyes open for what comes into town next and chances are you won't be disappointed.

DUCTAC

Al Sahra- location of Jumana

# A SPECTACULAR EXTRAVAGANZA
## UNDER THE DESERT SKY

This **MUST SEE** extravaganza is one of the most spectacular open air stage shows in the world, celebrating Arabia's rich history and culture. Set in a stunning amphitheatre, the show incorporates state of the art lasers, pyrotechnics, water projected imagery, dazzling fireworks and a cast of 60 dancers, acrobats, camels & horses. Discover the secret of the desert today.

www.alsahra.com
tel: +971 4 3679500  email: reservations@alsahra.com
Storyteller's Voice **OMAR SHARIF**

HOTEL TRANSFERS • SHISHA PIT & MAJLIS
DINING • SOUK SHOPPING • CAMEL & HORSE RIDES

# DIGITALGLOBE™

C L E A R L Y   T H E   B E S T

61 cm QuickBird Imagery is the highest resolution satellite imagery available. We offer products and resorces to both existing GIS users and the entire next generation of mapping and multimedia applications.

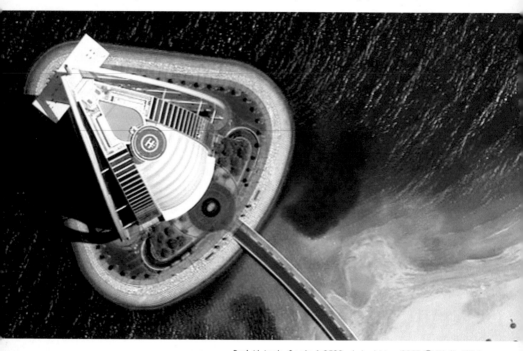

Burj Al Arab, Scale 1:2500, dated May 2003 © DigitalGlobe

## **MAPS**geosystems

### DigitalGlobe's Master Reseller serving the Middle East and East, Central and West Africa

MAPS (UAE), Corniche Plaza 1, P.O. Box 5232, Sharjah, UAE.
Tel : +971 6 5725411, Fax : +971 6 5724057
www.maps-geosystems.com

For further details, please contact quickbird@maps-geosystems.com

# Maps

# Maps

## User's Guide

The following pages contain satellite image maps of Dubai's main areas enabling you to pinpoint an exact location (and maybe even see your villa) as well as orientate yourself around Dubai.

The overview on the opposite page shows which areas are covered by the image maps, while Map 1 overleaf illustrates the whole of the UAE and Map 2 features Dubai and its neighbouring emirates. Following on from the satellite image maps, on p.602 you'll find another overview, followed by the individual Main Area maps lettered A to S.

To further assist you in locating your destination, we have superimposed information such as main roads, roundabouts, hospitals, schools, and landmarks on the maps. Many places listed throughout the book have a map reference – turn to that map to see precisely where you need to go. You will notice that some map references also have an annotation (a number in a box) which are marked on the map to aid you with your door-to-door journey. To give better visualisation, most of the maps have been orientated parallel to Dubai's coastline rather than the customary north orientation. The overview map on this page is at a scale of approximately 1:330,000 (1cm = 3.3km), all other maps range from 1:15,000 (1cm = 150m) to 1:30,000 (1cm = 300m).

**Mapophobia!**
*Many people have an irrational fear of all things cartographical, but there's really nothing to be afraid of. The fascinating satellite images in this section are good for getting your bearings - main roads and landmarks are all superimposed to help you work out where you are.*

## Technical Info

The image maps in this section are based on rectified QuickBird satellite imagery taken in 2004 and 2005. The QuickBird satellite was launched in October 2001 and is operated by DigitalGlobe™, a private company based in Colorado (USA). Today, DigitalGlobe's QuickBird satellite provides the highest resolution (61 cm), largest swath width and largest onboard storage of any currently available or planned commercial satellite. MAPS geosystems are the DigitalGlobe master resellers for the Middle East, West, Central and East Africa. They also provide a wide range of mapping services and systems. For more information, visit www.digitalglobe.com (QuickBird) and www.maps-geosystems.com (mapping services) or contact MAPS geosystems on +971 6 572 5411.

## Map Legend

| | |
|---|---|
| Ⓜ | Museum/Heritage Site |
| Ⓔ | Embassy/Consulate |
| Ⓗ | Hotel/Resort |
| Ⓢ | Shopping/Souk |
| ✈ | Airport |
| ☾ | Hospital/Clinic |
| **SALIK** | Salik Gate |
| **KARAMA** | Area Name |
| ▬▬ | Inter-Emirates Road |
| ▬▬ | Main Road |
| ▪ ▪ ▪ ▪ | U/C Road |
| )▬▬( | Tunnel |
| ▪▪ ▪▪ | Metro |
| (u/c) | Under Construction |

### Online Maps
*If you want to surf for maps online, www.ae.map24.com and www.maporama.com are worth a look. Hardcore map fans though are recommended to try Google Earth (http://earth.google.com). This amazing program (you download it from the site) combines satellite imagery, detailed maps, and a powerful search capability, allowing you to fly between various points on the globe and zoom in for incredibly detailed close-up views.*

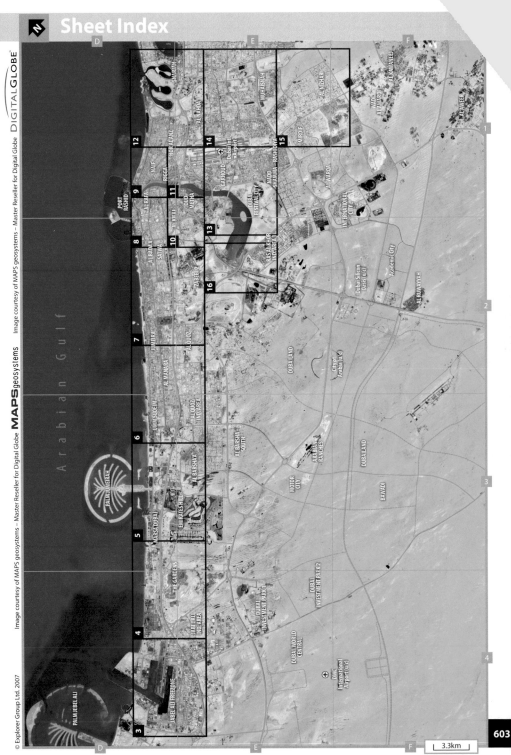

DIGITALGLOBE

Image courtesy of MAPS geosystems – Master Reseller for Digital Globe

MAPS geosystems

Image courtesy of MAPS geosystems – Master Reseller for Digital Globe

© Explorer Group Ltd. 2007

Arabian Gulf

PALM JEBEL ALI

PALM JUMEIRAH

PORT RASHID

JABEL ALI FREEZONE

JABEL ALI IND. AREA

THE GARDENS

MARSA DUBAI

EMIRATES HILLS

AL BARSHA

UMM SUQEIM

AL QUOZ IND. AREA

AL MANARA

JUMEIRA

AL QUOZ

AL BARSHA SOUTH

DUBAI INVESTMENT PARK 1

DUBAI INVESTMENT PARK 2

DUBAI WORLD CENTRAL

DWC International Airport (u/c)

MOTOR CITY

ARABIAN RANCHES

DUBAILAND

BAWADI

DUBAILAND

DUBAILAND

City of Arabia (u/c)

AL BADAA

SATWA

AL RAS

AL BADAA

AL HUDAIBA

OUD METHA

BUR DUBAI

NAIF

RIGGA

HOR AL ANZ

AL MADAD

SHARJAH

GARHOUD

Dubai Int'l Airport

DUBAI FESTIVAL CITY

RAS AL KHOR IND. AREA 1

JADDAF

NADD SHAMMA – RASHIDIYA

MUHAISNAH

AL NIZHAR

MIRDIF

AL WARQA'A

INTERNATIONAL CITY

Dubai Silicon Oasis (u/c)

Academic City

AL RUWAYYAH

WADI AL AMARDI

AL AWANEED

AL TWAR

3.3km

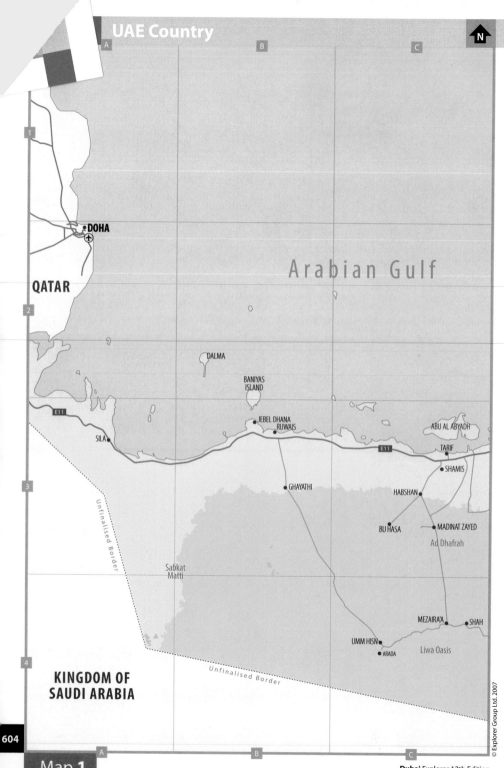

A          B          C

1

•**DOHA**
⊕

**QATAR**

A r a b i a n   G u l f

2

DALMA

BANIYAS
ISLAND

E11

ABU AL ABYADH

JEBEL DHANA
RUWAIS

E11

TARIF

SILA

SHAMIS

3

GHAYATHI

HABSHAN

Unfinalised Border

BU HASA

MADINAT ZAYED

Ad Dhafrah

Sabkat
Matti

MEZAIRA'A

SHAH

UMM HISN

Liwa Oasis

4

ARADA

Unfinalised Border

**KINGDOM OF
SAUDI ARABIA**

© Explorer Group Ltd. 2007

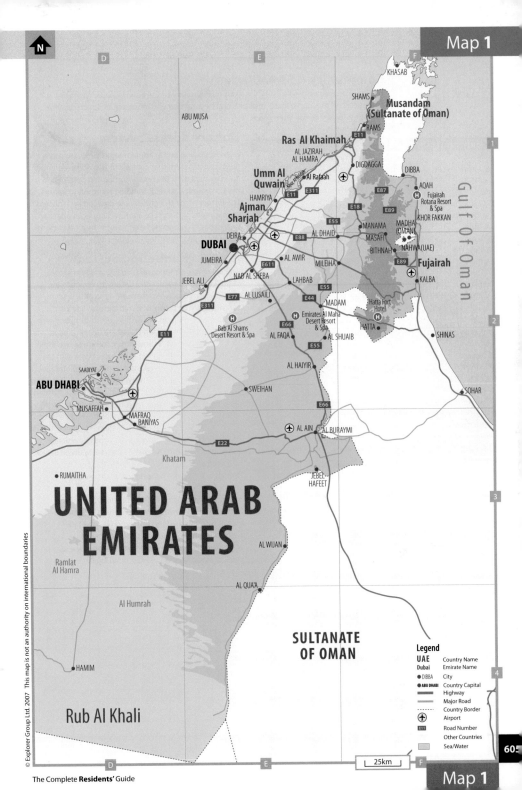

Map **1**

N

D    E    F

KHASAB

SHAMS

**Musandam
(Sultanate of Oman)**

RAMS

ABU MUSA

**Ras Al Khaimah**

AL JAZIRAH
AL HAMRA

DIGDAGGA    DIBBA

AQAH

**Umm Al
Quwain**    Al Rafaah

AQAH
Fujairah
Rotana Resort
& Spa

HAMRIYA    KHOR FAKKAN

**Ajman**

**Sharjah**    MANAMA    MADHA
(OMAN)

DEIRA    AL DHAID    MASAFI

**DUBAI**    BITHNAH    NAHWA (UAE)

JUMEIRA    AL AWIR    MILEIHA    **Fujairah**

NAD AL SHEBA    LAHBAB    KALBA

JEBEL ALI

AL LUSAILI    MADAM    Hatta Fort
Hotel

Bab Al Shams
Desert Resort & Spa    Emirates Al Maha
Desert Resort
& Spa    HATTA    SHINAS

AL FAQA    AL SHUAIB

AL HAIYIR

SAADIYAT

**ABU DHABI**    SWEIHAN    SOHAR

MUSAFFAH

MAFRAQ
BANIYAS    AL AIN    AL BURAYMI

Khatam

RUMAITHA

# UNITED ARAB
# EMIRATES

JEBEL
HAFEET

AL WIJAN

Ramlat
Al Hamra

AL QUA'A

Al Humrah

# SULTANATE
# OF OMAN

HAMIM

Rub Al Khali

G u l f   o f   O m a n

**Legend**

| | |
|---|---|
| **UAE** | Country Name |
| **Dubai** | Emirate Name |
| ● DIBBA | City |
| ● **ABU DHABI** | Country Capital |
| ▬▬ | Highway |
| ▬▬ | Major Road |
| - - - | Country Border |
| ✈ | Airport |
| E11 | Road Number |
| | Other Countries |
| | Sea/Water |

25km

605

© Explorer Group Ltd. 2007   This map is not an authority on international boundaries

## Community & Street Index

The table below contains a list of the main communities and streets in Dubai, which are referenced on the map pages. Many extend beyond one grid reference, in which case the main grid reference has been given.

| Community | Map Ref | Community | Map Ref |
|---|---|---|---|
| Abu Hail | 12-A2 | 2nd Za'abeel Rd | 10-A3 |
| Al Baraha | 9-E3 | Abu Hail Rd | 12-A2 |
| Al Barsha | 5-E4 | Airport Rd | 11-D4 |
| Al Hamriya | 12-B2 | Al Ain Rd | 2-C3 |
| Al Jafilia | 8-C3 | Al Diyafah St | 8-A2 |
| Al Mamzar | 12-C2 | Al Ittihad Rd | 12-C3 |
| Al Mizhar | 15-E2 | Al Jumeira Rd | 7-C1 |
| Al Nahda | 12-C4 | Al Khaleej Rd | 9-A1 |
| Al Quoz Ind. | 6-D4 | Al Khail Rd | 7-C4 |
| Al Quoz | 7-A3 | Al Khawaneej Rd | 15-D3 |
| Al Qusais Ind. | 14-D1 | Al Maktoum Rd | 11-C1 |
| Al Qusais | 14-C2 | Al Manara Rd | 6-D2 |
| Al Warqa | 2-F3 | Al Mankhool Rd | 8-D2 |
| Arabian Ranches | 2-E3 | Al Mina Rd | 8-B2 |
| Al Safa | 7-A2 | Al Muraqqabat Rd | 11-D1 |
| Al Sufouh | 5-E2 | Al Musallah Rd | 9-A3 |
| Al Twar | 14-B2 | Al Quds St | 12-A4 |
| Al Wasl | 7-C2 | Al Rebat St | 13-D3 |
| Bastakiya | 9-A2 | Al Rasheed Rd | 12-B3 |
| Bur Dubai | 9-A2 | Al Rigga Rd | 11-D1 |
| Deira | 9-C2 | Al Satwa Rd | 7-E2 |
| Dubai Festival City | 13-D3 | Al Sufouh Rd | 5-E2 |
| Dubai Intl Airport | 11-F4 | Al Wasl Rd | 6-E2 |
| Dubai Marina | 5-A2 | Algeria St | 15-C2 |
| Emirates Hills | 5-B3 | Amman St | 12-C4 |
| The Gardens | 4-D3 | Baghdad St | 14-C3 |
| Garhoud | 13-E2 | Beirut St | 14-C3 |
| Hor Al Anz | 12-A3 | Beniyas Rd | 9-B2 |
| Hudeiba | 8-B2 | Cairo St | 12-B2 |
| Jaddaf | 13-B2 | Casablanca St | 13-E1 |
| Jebel Ali FZ | 3-C3 | Damascus St | 14-B2 |
| Jumeira | 7-C1 | Doha St | 7-E4 |
| Karama | 10-E1 | Jumeira Rd | 6-E1 |
| Mankhool | 8-D3 | Khalid Bin Al Waleed Rd | 8-F2 |
| Mirdif | 15-B2 | Muscat St | 7-B3 |
| Muhaisnah | 14-D3 | Naif Rd | 9-D2 |
| Muraqabat | 11-D1 | Oud Metha Rd | 10-C4 |
| Muteena | 9-D4 | Riyadh St | 11-A3 |
| Naif | 9-D3 | Salahuddin Rd | 9-D4 |
| Oud Metha | 10-E2 | Sheikh Rashid Rd | 10-D1 |
| Port Rashid | 8-C1 | Sheikh Khalifa Bin Zayed Rd | 8-D4 |
| Port Saeed | 11-C2 | Sheikh Zayed Rd | 7-E3 |
| Rashidiya | 13-F4 | Tariq Bin Ziyad Rd | 11-D2 |
| Ras Al Khor | 13-B4 | Tripoli St | 15-A2 |
| Satwa | 7-E2 | Tunis Rd | 14-E4 |
| Trade Centre | 7-F2 | Umm Hurair Rd | 10-EE |
| Umm Hurair | 10-F3 | Umm Suqeim Rd | 6-A2 |
| Umm Suqeim | 6-E2 | Za'abeel Rd | 10-E1 |
| Umm Ramool | 13-E3 | | |
| Za'abeel | 10-C3 | | |

## Dubai Address System

Dubai is attempting to implement a Comprehensive Addressing System that consists of two complementary number systems – the Route Numbering System and the Community, Street & Building Numbering System. The former helps an individual to develop and follow a simple series of directions for travelling from one area to another in Dubai; the latter helps a visitor to locate a particular building or house in the city.

## Routes Numbering System

Various routes connecting Dubai to other emirates of the UAE, or to main cities within an emirate, are classified as 'Emirate-Routes' or 'E-Routes'. They comprise two or three digit numbers on a falcon emblem as shown on the UAE Map. Routes connecting main communities within Dubai are designated as 'Dubai-Routes' or 'D-Routes'. They comprise two digit numbers on a fort emblem. D-Routes parallel to the coast are even numbered, starting from D94 and decreasing as you move away from the coast. D-Routes perpendicular to the coast are odd numbered, starting from D53 and decreasing as you move away from the Abu Dhabi border.

Community, Street Numbering System

This system helps an individual to locate a particular building or house in Dubai. The emirate is divided into nine sectors:

Sectors 1, 2, 3, 4 and 6 represent urban areas.
Sector 5 represents Jebel Ali.
Sectors 7, 8 and 9 represent rural areas.
Sectors are sub-divided into communities, which are bound by main roads. A three digit number identifies each community. The first is the number of the sector, while the following two digits denote the location of the community in relation to neighbouring communities in sequential order.

Buildings on the left hand side of the street have odd numbers, while those on the right hand side take even numbers. Again, building numbers increase as you move away from the city centre. The complete address of a building in Dubai is given as Community Number, Street Number and Building Number.

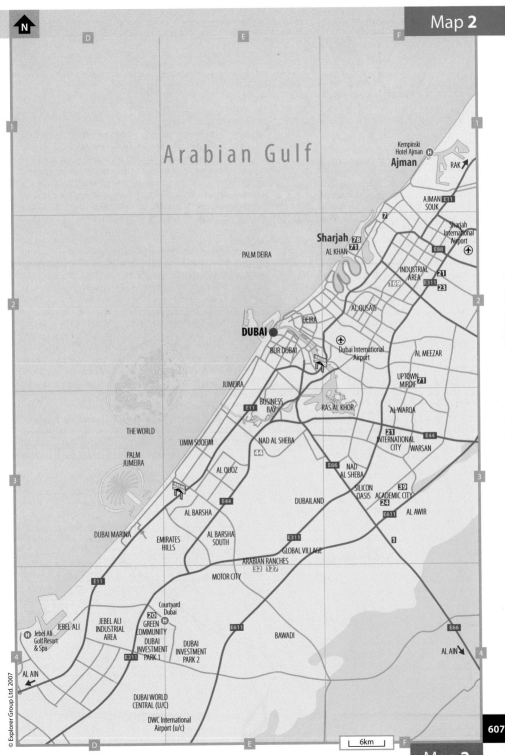

Map **2**

N

Arabian Gulf

Kempinski
Hotel Ajman H
**Ajman** RAK

AJMAN E11
SOUK

7

**Sharjah** 78
71
PALM DEIRA AL KHAN

Sharjah
International
Airport
E88
✈

INDUSTRIAL
AREA 21
169 E311 23

AL QUSAIS

DUBAI ●
DEIRA

Dubai International
Airport ✈
BUR DUBAI
AL MEEZAR

JUMEIRA
UPTOWN
MIRDIF 71

E11 BUSINESS
BAY
RAS AL KHOR
AL WARQA

THE WORLD UMM SUQEIM
NAD AL SHEBA
INTERNATIONAL
CITY 21 E44
WARSAN

PALM
JUMEIRA 44

AL QUOZ
NAD
AL SHEBA E66

SILICON
OASIS ACADEMIC CITY 39

E44
DUBAILAND 24

AL BARSHA
E611 AL AWIR

DUBAI MARINA
EMIRATES
HILLS
AL BARSHA
SOUTH
E311
GLOBAL VILLAGE
1

ARABIAN RANCHES
32 127

E11 MOTOR CITY

Courtyard
Dubai
H Jebel Ali
Golf Resort
& Spa
JEBEL ALI
JEBEL ALI
INDUSTRIAL
AREA
20
GREEN
COMMUNITY
DUBAI
INVESTMENT
PARK 1
DUBAI
INVESTMENT
PARK 2
BAWADI
E66
AL AIN ↘

E611

AL AIN ←
E311

DUBAI WORLD
CENTRAL (U/C)

DWC International
Airport (u/c)

© Explorer Group Ltd. 2007

D E F

6km

Map **3**

H 63
Jebel Ali
Golf Resort & Spa

A

B

C

1

Jebel Ali
Shooting
Club

2

JEBEL ALI FREE ZONE

3

Interchange No.9

4

Exit
13

Interchange No.8

Exit
18

SHEIKH ZAYED ROAD    E11

A

B

C

© Explorer Group Ltd. 2007

Map **3**

**Dubai** Explorer 12th Edition

Map **3**

DIGITALGLOBE

Image courtesy of MAPS geosystems – Master Reseller for Digital Globe

**MAPS**geosystems

Image courtesy of MAPS geosystems – Master Reseller for Digital Globe

© Explorer Group Ltd. 2007

DUGAS

Gas Bottling Plant

**JEBEL ALI PORT**

Cedars Jebel Ali International Hospital

Post Office

SHEIKH ZAYED ROAD

E11

Jebel Ali Industrial

**JEBEL ALI INDUSTRIAL AREA**

Jazfa/Limitless

300m

**609**

# Map **4**

Arabian Gulf

Cedars Jebel Ali
International
Hospital

**DUBAL**

SHEIKH ZAYED ROAD
E11
Exit
25
Interchange No.6

Dubal

Exit
22
Interchange No.7

**JEBEL ALI
VILLAGE**

Jebel Ali
School

Clinic

Church
Complex

Etisalat
Earth Station

**JEBEL ALI
INDUSTRIAL AREA**

© Explorer Group Ltd. 2007

General Information p.1 | Residents p.75 | Exploring p.235 | Activities p.317 | Shopping p.401 | Going Out p.495

# Map **4**

**Dubai** Explorer 12th Edition

Arabian Gulf

DEWA
Power Station

Sheraton
Jumeirah
Beach

E11 SHEIKH ZAYED ROAD

Ibn Battuta

Ibn
Battuta Mall
38 2 S

Grand
Megaplex /IMAX

Geant

Jumeirah
Islands

Dubai Multi
Commodities
Centre (u/c)

The
Winchester
School

The Gardens

Water
Reservoir

Discovery
Gardens (u/c)

Jumeirah
Park (u/c)

Al Furjan (u/c)

300m

Image courtesy of MAPS geosystems – Master Reseller for Digital Globe

Image courtesy of MAPS geosystems – Master Reseller for Digital Globe

DIGITALGLOBE

MAPSgeosystems

© Explorer Group Ltd. 2007

611

Map 4

Arabian Gulf

Oasis
Beach Resort

Le Royal Meridien
Beach Resort & Spa

Hilton Dubai
Jumeirah (H)

Ritz
Carlton (H) 78

Habtoor Grand
Resort & Spa
56 (H)

(H) 74

(H)

Jebel Ali
Sailing Club

39

Dubai
International
Marine Club

Le Meridien
Mina Seyahi
(H) 69 21

One&Only
Royal Mirage
(H) 75

Jumeirah Beach
Residence

71 (H)

Grosvenor
House

Dubai 28
Media City

Radisson SAS
Dubai Media City
(H)

**DUBAI MARINA**

(S) Marina Mall
(u/c)

Marina
Market
42 112

Dubai
Marina

American
University

(H) Palm
HardRock Cafe

Dubai
Internet City

Jumeirah
Lake Towers

Marina

Interchange No.5

Exit
33

Nakheel

**JUMEIRAH LAKE**

DMCC

Jumeirah Heights (u/c)

Emirates Golf Club

**EMIRATES HILLS 1**

**EMIRATES HILLS 2**

The Meadows

**JUMEIRAH ISLANDS**

The Montgomerie
Golf Club (H)

The Lakes

Spinneys

The Springs

**EMIRATES HILLS 3**

Dubai
American
Academy

Montgomerie
Golf Course

27

© Explorer Group Ltd. 2007

General Information p.1   Residents p.75   Exploring p.235   Activities p.317   Shopping p.401   Going Out p.495

Map **5**

Image courtesy of MAPS geosystems – Master Reseller for Digital Globe    DIGITALGLOBE

**MAPS**geosystems    Image courtesy of MAPS geosystems – Master Reseller for Digital Globe

© Explorer Group Ltd. 2007

Arabian Gulf

Trump International
Hotel & Resort (u/c)

**PALM
JUMEIRAH**

AL SUFOUH RD

Dubai
College

Dubai
Pearl (u/c)    Golden Tulip    Knowledge
Village

34  33
74
17
32

**AL SUFOUH**

Palma
Spring Village

**AL SUFOUH**

Exit
35

SHEIKH ZAYED ROAD

Exit
36

Wellington
International School

Greens
Centre

Tecom

Desert
Springs Village

**TECOM**

Golden Tulip
Al Barsha

**AL BARSHA 1**

The Greens

Dubai National
School

Regent
International
School

Al Mawakeb
School

Jebel Ali
Racecourse

**AL BARSHA 3**

**613**

Map **6**

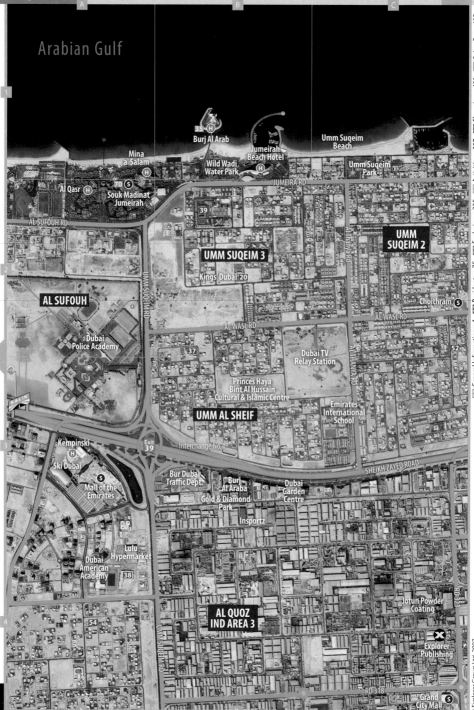

Arabian Gulf

35 H
Burj Al Arab

Mina a' Salam

Wild Wadi Water Park

Jumeirah Beach Hotel

Umm Suqeim Beach

Umm Suqeim Park

Al Qasr H

70 S
Souk Madinat Jumeirah

JUMEIRA RD

39

AL SUFOUH RD

UMM SUQEIM 3

**UMM SUQEIM 2**

Kings Dubai 20

Choithram S

**AL SUFOUH**

Dubai Police Academy

AL WASL RD

AL WASL RD

37

52

Dubai TV Relay Station

Princes Haya Bint Al Hussain Cultural & Islamic Centre

**UMM AL SHEIF**

Emirates International School

Kempinski H

Ski Dubai

Exit 39

Interchange No.4

SHEIKH ZAYED ROAD

Mall of the Emirates S

Bur Dubai Traffic Dept.

Burj Al Araba

Gold & Diamond Park

Dubai Garden Centre

Insportz

Lulu Hypermarket

Dubai American Academy

38

**AL QUOZ IND AREA 3**

Jotun Powder Coating

54

Explorer Publishing

RD 318

Grand City Mall S

⊞ General Information p.1  ⊞ Residents p.75  ⊞ Exploring p.235  ⊞ Activities p.317  ⊞ Shopping p.401  ⊞ Going Out p.495

© Explorer Group Ltd. 2007

Map **6**

DIGITALGLOBE

Image courtesy of MAPS geosystems – Master Reseller for Digital Globe

**MAPS**geosystems

Image courtesy of MAPS geosystems – Master Reseller for Digital Globe

© Explorer Group Ltd. 2007

Arabian Gulf

Dubai Offshore
Sailing Club

Miraj Islamic
Art Centre

JUMEIRA RD

42

56

44

Hint Bint
Maktoum School

Musalla
Al Eid

UMM SUQEIM 1

Denmark

AL WASL RD

Spinneys

AL SAFA 2

43

19

NMC Family
Clinic

AL MANARA

Interchange No 3

Exit
42

SHEIKH ZAYED ROAD

Exit
43

Al Quoz

Times
Square

National
Cement Factory

AL QUOZ
IND AREA 1

RD 319

RD 318

Grand Mall

Dubai American
Scientific School

National
Taxi

Oasis
Village

300m

**615**

Map **7**

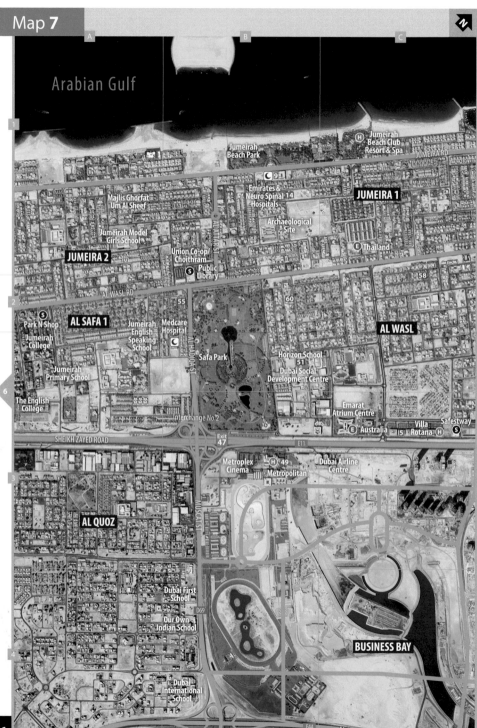

Arabian Gulf

© Explorer Group Ltd. 2007

Going Out p.495   Shopping p.401   Activities p.317   Exploring p.235   Residents p.75   General Information p.1

Jumeira Beach Park

Jumeirah Beach Club Resort & Spa

JUMEIRA RD

JUMEIRA 1

Majlis Ghorfat Um Al Sheef

Emirates & Neuro Spinal Hospitals

Archaeological Site

Jumeirah Model Girls School

JUMEIRA 2

Union Co-op/ Choithram

Public Library

Thailand

AL WASL RD

Park N Shop

AL SAFA 1

Jumeira College

Jumeirah Primary School

Jumeirah English Speaking School

Medcare Hospital

Safa Park

AL WASL

Horizon School Dubai Social Development Centre

The English College

Emarat Atrium Centre

Australia

Villa Rotana

Safestway

Interchange No.2

SHEIKH ZAYED ROAD

Exit 47

E11

Metroplex Cinema

Metropolitan

Dubai Airline Centre

AL QUOZ

MUSCAT ST

D69

Dubai First School

Our Own Indian School

BUSINESS BAY

Dubai International School

AL KHAIL RD

E44

Map **7**

N

Arabian Gulf

D  E  F

Dubai Marine
Beach Resort
& Spa

Jumeira Public
Beach

Palm Strip

Dubai
Intl
Art Centre

91  The Village

Jumeira
Mosque

129
61

1

Dubai Zoo

128

Magrudy's
Centre

Town
Centre

Mercato

11

Beach
Centre

Jumeira
Plaza

Jumeirah
Centre

Iran

Century
Plaza

Iranian
Hospital

La Maison d'Hôtes

59

AL WASL RD

8

AL WASL RD

Post
Office

Belhasa
Driving Institute

Bus
Station

AL BADA'A

57

AL SATWA RD

SATWA

2

Al Amal
Hospital

Central
Prison

Dubai
Petroleum
Company

Al Khazzan
Park

Al Moosa 2

Al Durrah

TRADE
CENTRE 1

France

Al Rostamani

Al Wasl

New Zealand

Al Salam

Satwa Park

Crowne
Plaza

No. One

Safa

Holiday Centre

Ibis

Wafa

Chelsea

Shk Ahmed

91

Shangri-La

Towers Rotana

Capricorn

Emirates
Towers

Dubai
Intl ConVention
Centre

Mazaya Centre

Thunder Bowl

Exit
52

21st Century

Al Attar

Al Ghadier

14

Novotel

Interchange No.1

DNATA

Dusit
Dubai

Al Kawakeb

Ghaya
Residence

Jumeira

The Gate

TRADE CENTRE 2

DIFC

Etisalat

3

Boulevard
Crescents (u/c)

Al Murooj
Rotana

Burj Dubai (u/c)

10

Old Town
Island

The Palace
The Old Town

Dubai
Mall (u/c)

Qamardeen

Burj Lake
Hotel (u/c)

South
Ridge (u/c)

Al Manzil

DOWNTOWN
BURJ DUBAI

ZA'ABEEL 2

4

617

300m

DIGITALGLOBE

Image courtesy of MAPS geosystems – Master Reseller for Digital Globe

MAPS geosystems

Image courtesy of MAPS geosystems – Master Reseller for Digital Globe

© Explorer Group Ltd 2007

Map **8**

N

Dubai Drydocks

**PORT RASHID**

Port Police HQ

Shell

Union House

Capitol

AL MINA RD

D75

D92

30 S
Al Ghazal

Jumeira Rotana H

Belhoul European C

Dune Centre S

AL DIYAFA RD

**HUDHEIBA**

E Sri Lanka

D73

D90

7

Satwa R/A

S Al Hana Centre

Satwa Mosque

Rydges

**AL JAFILIYA**

3

SHEIKH RASHID RD

China E

Qatar E

Monarch H

H 53
Fairmont

Exit 53

Police Station

Immigration Department

**Department of Health & Medical Services**

D88

Al Jafiliya

Za'abeel Park

General Information p.1  Residents p.75  Exploring p.235  Activities p.317  Shopping p.401  Going Out p.495

© Explorer Group Ltd. 2007

**Dubai** Explorer 12th Edition

Map 8

Map **9**

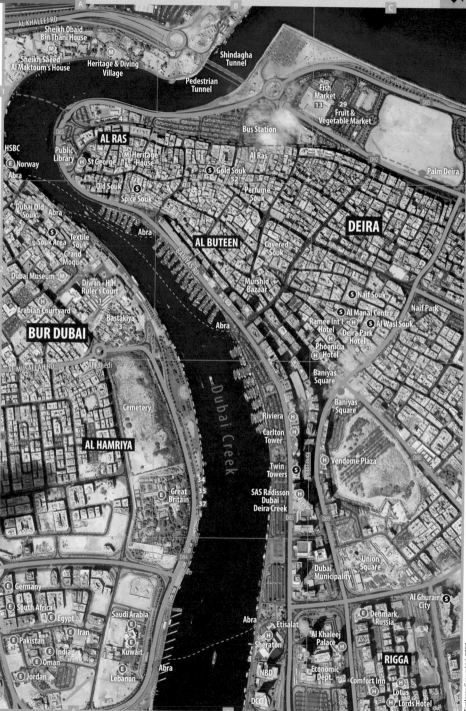

AL KHALEEJ RD

Sheikh Obaid
Bin Thani House

Sheikh Saeed
Al Maktoum's House

Heritage & Diving
Village

Shindagha
Tunnel

Pedestrian
Tunnel

Fish
Market
13

Fruit &
Vegetable Market

29

Bus Station

**AL RAS**

HSBC

Public
Library

St George

Heritage
House

Al Ras

Norway

Abra

Old Souk

Gold Souk
52

Perfume
Souk

Palm Deira

Spice Souk

**DEIRA**

Dubai Old
Souk

Abra

Textile
Souk

Souk Area

Grand
Mosque

**AL BUTEEN**

Covered
Souk

Abra

Dubai Museum

Diwan - H.H.
Ruler's Court

Murshid
Bazaar

Naif Souk

Naif Park

Arabian Courtyard

Bastakiya

Abra

Al Manal Centre

Al Wasl Souk

Ramee Int'l
Hotel

Deira Park
Hotel

**BUR DUBAI**

Phoenicia
Hotel

AL MUSALLAH RD

Al Fahedi
R/A

Baniyas
Square

Cemetery

Baniyas
Square

**AL HAMRIYA**

Riviera

Carlton
Tower

Vendome Plaza

Great
Britain

34

35

37

Twin
Towers

SAS Radisson
Dubai
Deira Creek

Dubai
Municipality

Union
Square

Germany

Al Ghurair
City

South Africa

Egypt

Saudi Arabia

Denmark,
Russia

Iran

Pakistan

India

Abra

Etisalat

Al Khaleej
Palace

Oman

Kuwait

Sheraton

**RIGGA**

Jordan

Lebanon

Abra

NBD

Economic
Dept.

Comfort Inn

Lotus

DCCI

Lords Hotel

Dubai Creek

BANIYAS RD

© Explorer Group Ltd. 2007

General Information p.1   Residents p.75   Exploring p.235   Activities p.317   Shopping p.401   Going Out p.495

Map **9**

DIGITALGLOBE

Image courtesy of MAPS geosystems – Master Reseller for Digital Globe

MAPS geosystems

Image courtesy of MAPS geosystems – Master Reseller for Digital Globe

© Explorer Group Ltd. 2007

Arabian Gulf

Palm Deira (u/c)

Hyatt Regency

Galleria Shopping Mall

Hyatt Golf Park

**CORNICHE DEIRA**

Belhoul Speciality

San Marco

**AL MURAR**

NAIF RD

D82

D88

Al Baraha Hospital

New Dubai Hospital

Musallla Al Eid

**AL BARAHA**

**NAIF**

Burj Nahar

Maktoum Hospital

D88

Nihal Hotel

46

Royal Crystal

Sea Rock

Claridge

Fish RA

Marco Polo

**MUTEENA**

Salahiddin

15

Reef Mall

SALAHUDDIN RD

Sheraton Deira

150m

Map **10**

© Explorer Group Ltd. 2007

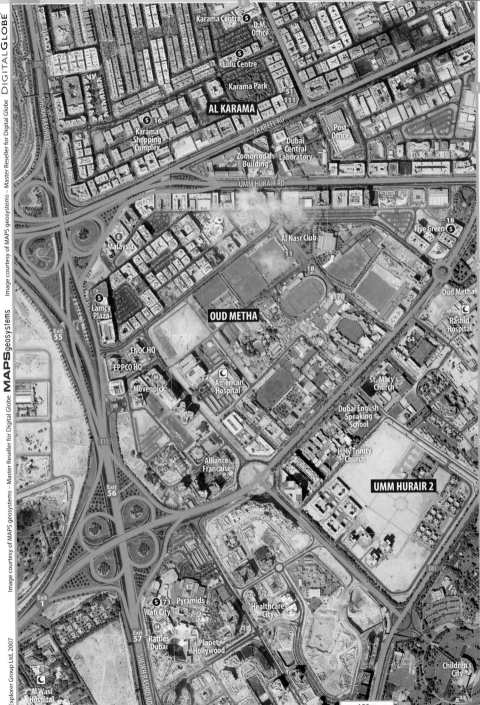

Map **10**

DIGITAL**GLOBE**

Image courtesy of MAPS geosystems – Master Reseller for Digital Globe

**MAPS**geosystems

Image courtesy of MAPS geosystems – Master Reseller for Digital Globe

© Explorer Group Ltd. 2007

SHEIKH RASHID RD

D75

Karama Centre

D.M. Office

Lulu Centre

Karama Park

51

111

**AL KARAMA**

ZAABEEL RD

S 16

Karama Shopping Complex

Zomorrodah Building

Dubai Central Laboratory

Post Office

UMM HURAIR RD

Five Green S 18

Malaysia

Al Nasr Club

11

18

170

**OUD METHA**

Oud Metha

C

Rashid Hospital

64

Exit 55

Lamcy Plaza S

ENOC HQ

EPPCO HQ

H Mövenpick

American Hospital C

St. Mary's Church

Dubai English Speaking School

E11

Holy Trinity Church

Exit 56

Alliance Francaise

**UMM HURAIR 2**

D81

Exit 1

17

S 73 Pyramids

Wafi City

Healthcare City

Exit 57

H Raffles Dubai

Planet Hollywood

SHEIKH RASHID RD

C Al Wasl Hospital

Children's City

150m

Map **11**

**Dubai** Explorer 12th Edition

© Explorer Group Ltd. 2007

General Information p.1 ☐☐ Residents p.75 ☐☐ Exploring p.235 ☐☐ Activities p.317 ☐☐ Shopping p.401 ☐☐ Going Out p.495

Map **11**

MURAQABAT

Al Rigga

Coral Deira (H)

Holiday Inn Downtown (H)

(H) Renaissance

Mövenpick Deira (u/c) (H)

Abu Baker Al Siddique

JW Marriott (H)

Traders (H)

HOR AL ANZ

AL MURAQABAT RD

(S) Hamarain Centre

TARIQ BIN ZIYAD RD

AL KHABAISI

DNATA

AL ITTIHAD RD

E11

Dubai Flower Centre

Exit 61

E11

D89

AIRPORT RD

Cargo Village

Dubai Civil Aviation Dept

DUBAI INTERNATIONAL AIRPORT

150m

Image courtesy of MAPS geosystems – Master Reseller for Digital Globe

Image courtesy of MAPS geosystems – Master Reseller for Digital Globe

DIGITALGLOBE

MAPSgeosystems

© Explorer Group Ltd. 2007

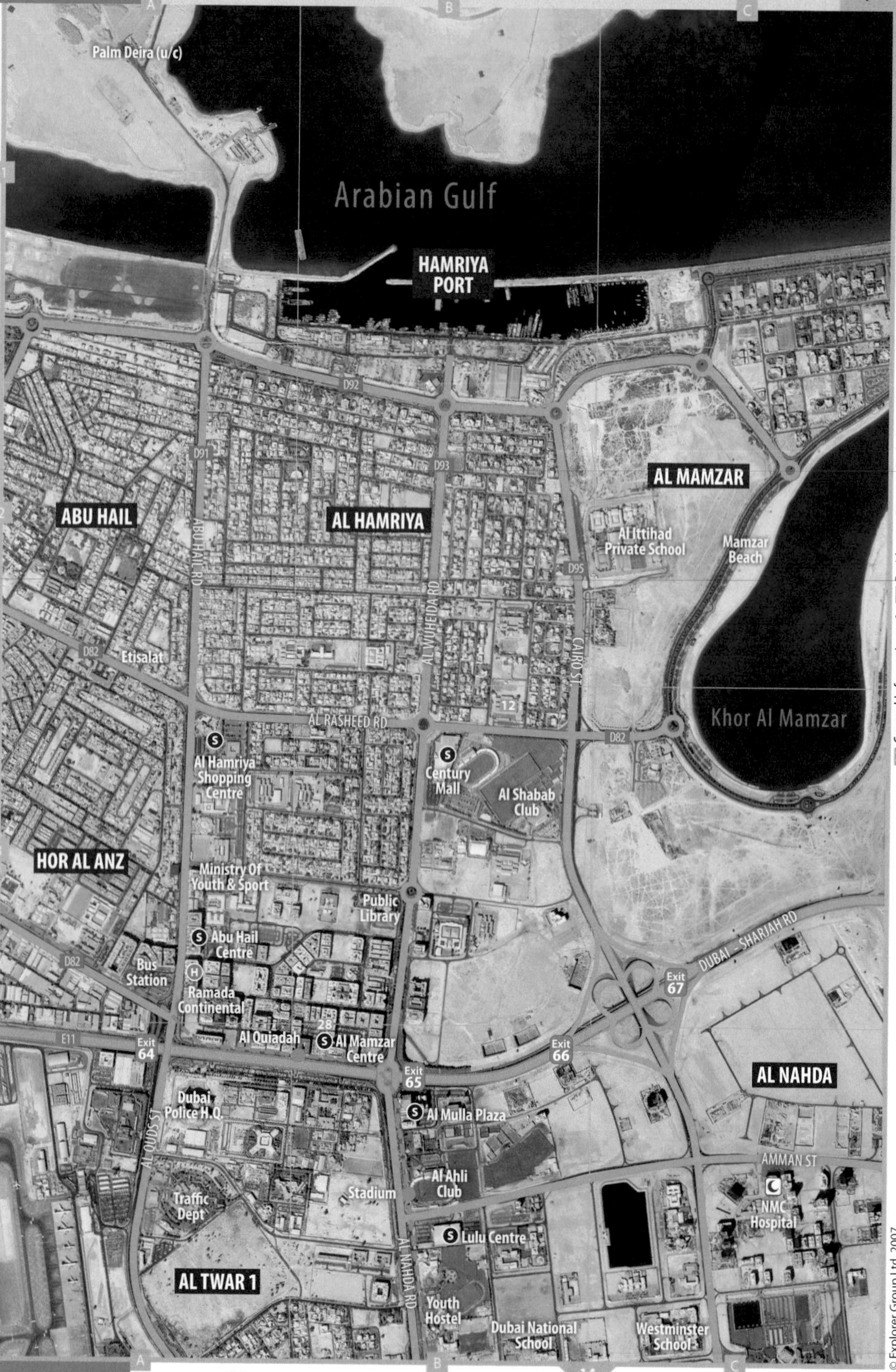
A
B
C
1
2
3
4
9
11
14
Palm Deira (u/c)
Arabian Gulf
HAMRIYA PORT
D92
D91
D93
D95
D82
E11
AL MAMZAR
ABU HAIL
AL HAMRIYA
ABU HAIL RD
AL WUHEIDA RD
Al Ittihad Private School
Mamzar Beach
CAIRO ST
Etisalat
AL RASHEED RD
12
Khor Al Mamzar
Al Hamriya Shopping Centre
Century Mall
Al Shabab Club
HOR AL ANZ
Ministry Of Youth & Sport
Public Library
Abu Hail Centre
Bus Station
Ramada Continental
DUBAI - SHARJAH RD
Exit 67
28
Al Quiadah
Al Mamzar Centre
Exit 64
Exit 66
Exit 65
AL NAHDA
Dubai Police H.Q.
Al Mulla Plaza
AL QUDS ST
AMMAN ST
Al Ahli Club
Stadium
Traffic Dept
NMC Hospital
Lulu Centre
AL NAHDA RD
AL TWAR 1
Youth Hostel
Dubai National School
Westminster School

00 General Information p.1 00 Residents p.75 00 Exploring p.235 00 Activities p.317 00 Shopping p.401 00 Going Out p.495

© Explorer Group Ltd. 2007

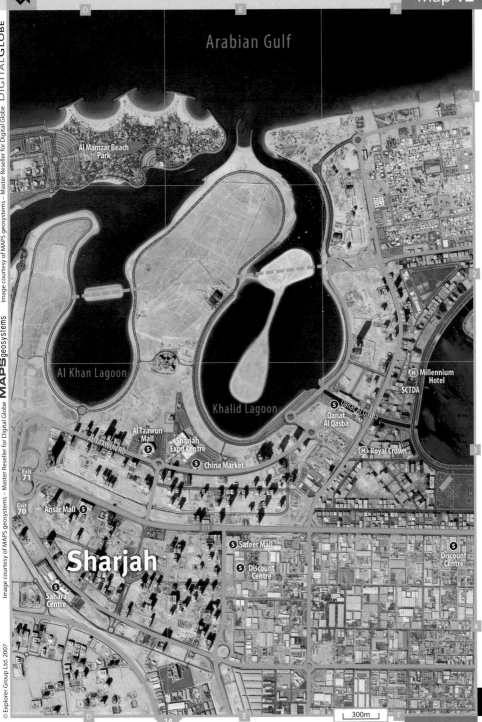

Arabian Gulf

Al Mamzar Beach Park

Al Khan Lagoon

Khalid Lagoon

(H) Millennium Hotel

SCTDA

(S) Qanat Al Qasba

Qanat Al Qasba

Al Taawun Mall

(S)

AL TAAWUN RD

Sharjah Expo Centre

(S) China Market

(H) Royal Crown

Exit **71**

Exit **70**

Ansar Mall (S)

E11

**Sharjah**

(S) Safeer Mall

(S) Discount Centre

(S) Discount Centre

(S) Sahara Centre

Image courtesy of MAPS geosystems – Master Reseller for Digital Globe    **MAPS**geosystems    Image courtesy of MAPS geosystems – Master Reseller for Digital Globe    **DIGITAL**GLOBE

© Explorer Group Ltd. 2007

300m

Map **13**

Map **13**

© Explorer Group Ltd. 2007

□□ General Information p.1 □□ Residents p.75 □□ Exploring p.235 □□ Activities p.317 □□ Shopping p.401 □□ Going Out p.495

Map **13**

Image courtesy of MAPS geosystems – Master Reseller for Digital Globe

DIGITALGLOBE

**MAPS**geosystems

Image courtesy of MAPS geosystems – Master Reseller for Digital Globe

© Explorer Group Ltd. 2007

Garhoud
Bridge

Exit
59

Marsa
Business
Park (u/c)

Marsa
Plaza

Marsa
Auto Park

Business Bay
Bridge

Crowne
Plaza

InterContinental 37

Convention
Centre

50 Dubai
Festival City

Festival Centre
Waterfront

Ikea

Festival Centre
Gateway

Hyper
Panda

ACE

Al Badia
Hillside
Village

**FESTIVAL CITY**

Universal
American
School

Four Seasons
Golf &
Country Club

Al Badia
Residences

Coca Cola

Deira
International
School
31

Bel Remeitha
Club

Aviation
College

Millennium
Airport

The Aviation
Club 33

Dubai
Tennis
Stadium

Emirates
Training
Centre

Al Bustan
Rotana

Al Garhoud
Complex 68

Le Meridien

CASABLANCA ST

American
College
of Dubai

The Cambridge
High School

**GARHOUD**

Park

DM Store

Institute of
Human Resource
& Development

Mawakeb
School

DM Transport
Garage

AL MARRAKECH ST

Emirates

Emirates
HQ

RTA

**UMM RAMOOL**

AL REBAT ST

AIRPORT RD

NAD AL HAMAR RD

D62

Nad Shamma
Park

**NAD SHAMMA**

Emirates
Post

Police
Station

Bin Sougat
Centre 31

Rashidiya
Shopping Centre

**RASHIDIYA**

Rashidiya
Station

Rashidiya
Park

Dubai International
Airport

Terminal 1

Airport
Terminal 1

Terminal 3 (u/c)

AIRPORT RD

AIRPORT TUNNEL

Airport
Expo

Dubai Airport
Royal Air Wing

D

E

F

1

2

14

3

4

**629**

Map **13**

300m

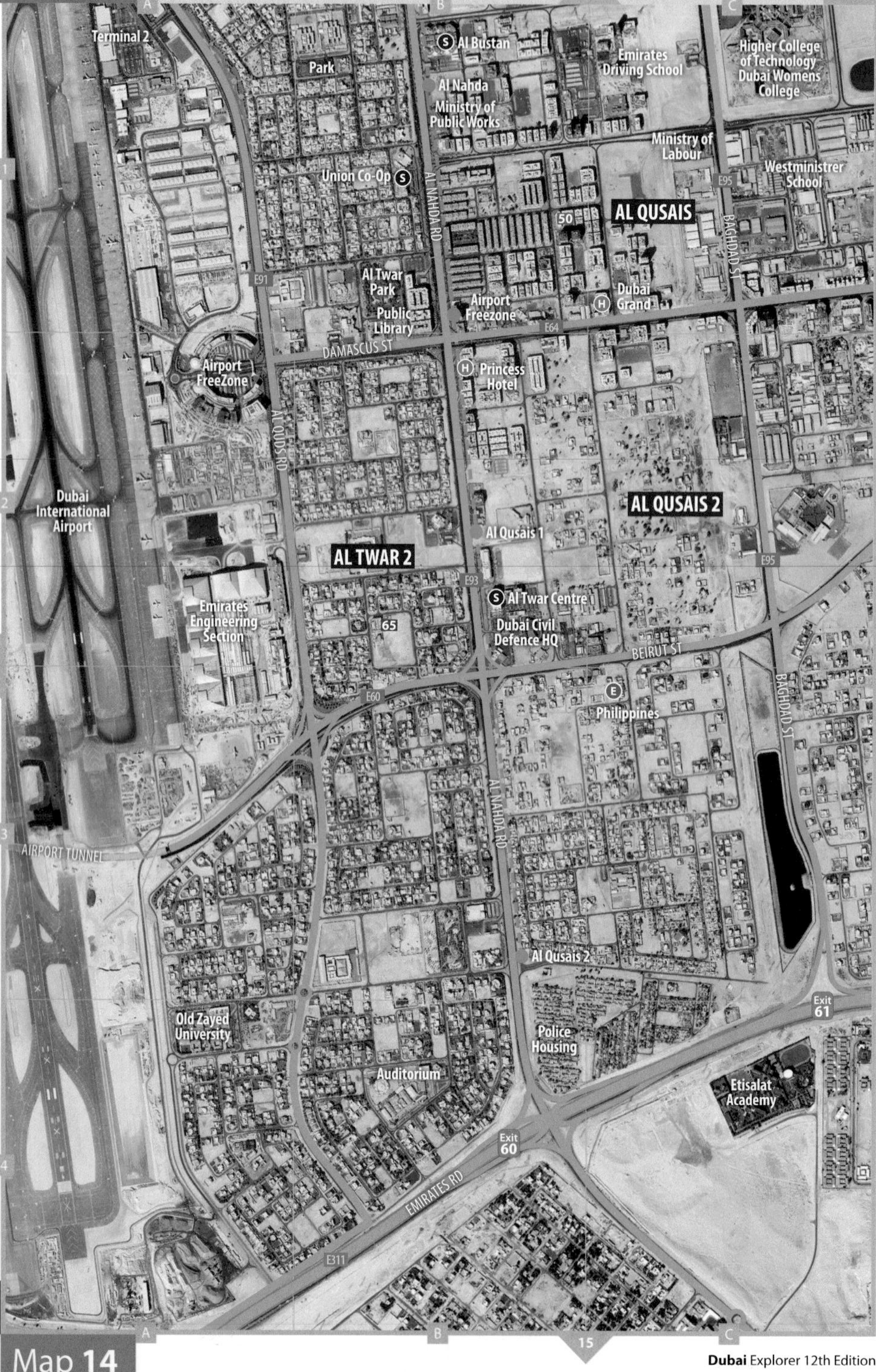
A
B
C
12
Terminal 2
Park
Al Bustan
Al Nahda
Ministry of Public Works
Emirates Driving School
Higher College of Technology Dubai Womens College
Ministry of Labour
Westministrer School
Union Co-Op
AL NAHDA RD
AL QUSAIS
50
E95
BAGHDAD ST
E91
Al Twar Park
Public Library
Airport Freezone
Dubai Grand
E64
DAMASCUS ST
Airport FreeZone
Princess Hotel
AL QUDS RD
1
2
Dubai International Airport
AL QUSAIS 2
Al Qusais 1
AL TWAR 2
E93
E95
Al Twar Centre
Emirates Engineering Section
65
Dubai Civil Defence HQ
BEIRUT ST
13
E60
Philippines
BAGHDAD ST
AL NAHDA RD
3
AIRPORT TUNNEL
Al Qusais 2
Exit 61
Old Zayed University
Police Housing
Auditorium
Etisalat Academy
Exit 60
4
EMIRATES RD
E311
15

00 General Information p.1 00 Residents p.75 00 Exploring p.235 00 Activities p.317 00 Shopping p.401 00 Going Out p.495

© Explorer Group Ltd. 2007

Al Qusais Ind Area

Zulekha Hospital

The Sheffield Private School

66

Damascus St

E64

Dubai Residential Oasis

Abattoir & Cattle Market

Beirut St

E60

Amman St

Sharjah

Muhaisnah 4

Lulu Village

Modern Renaissance School

Solid Waste Dumping Area

Dubai Transport Main Office

E311

D.M. Labour Housing

Cemetery

Tunis St

300m

© Explorer Group Ltd. 2007

Image courtesy of MAPS geosystems – Master Reseller for Digital Globe

**MAPS** geosystems

Image courtesy of MAPS geosystems – Master Reseller for Digital Globe

DIGITAL GLOBE

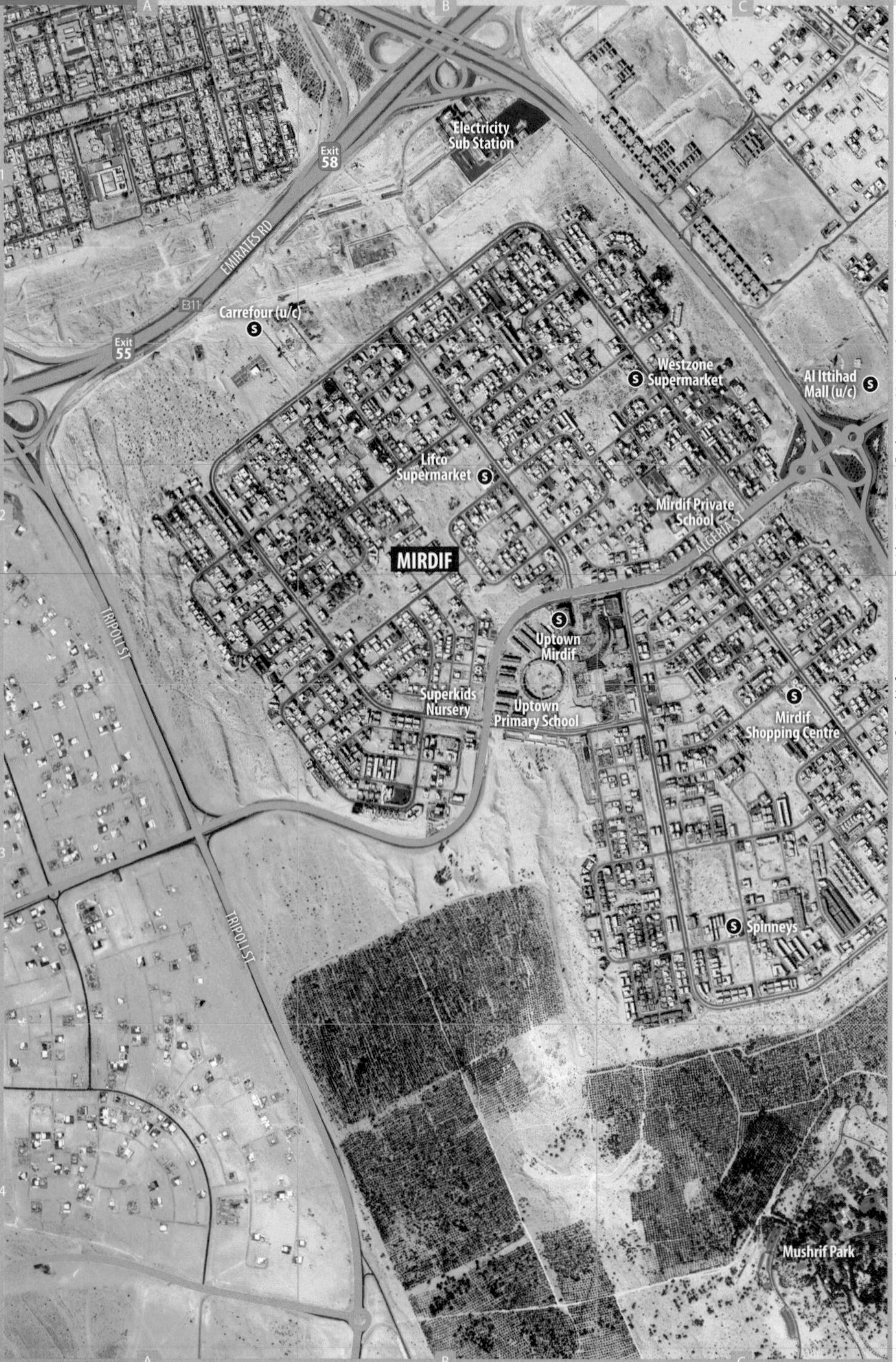

Map **15**
14

General Information p.1 · Residents p.75 · Exploring p.235 · Activities p.317 · Shopping p.401 · Going Out p.495

Exit **58**

EMIRATES RD

Electricity
Sub Station

B11

Exit **55**

**S** Carrefour (u/c)

**S** Westzone
Supermarket

**S** Al Ittihad
Mall (u/c)

**S** Lifco
Supermarket

Mirdif Private
School

ALGERIA ST

**MIRDIF**

TRIPOLI ST

**S** Uptown
Mirdif

Superkids
Nursery

Uptown
Primary School

**S** Mirdif
Shopping Centre

TRIPOLI ST

**S** Spinneys

Mushrif Park

© Explorer Group Ltd. 2007

DIGITALGLOBE

Image courtesy of MAPS geosystems – Master Reseller for Digital Globe

MAPS geosystems

Image courtesy of MAPS geosystems – Master Reseller for Digital Globe

© Explorer Group Ltd. 2007

**MADINAT BADAR**

Emirates
Co-Op Society

Al-Mizhar
American
Academy
for Girls

52

New Lamcy
Mall (u/c)

**AL MIZHAR 1**

Mirdif Private
School (u/c)

Royal
Dubai School

TUNIS RD

AL KHAWANEEJ RD

Al Mizhar
Mall

**AL MIZHAR 2**

Dubai
Municipality
Veterinary Section

300m

**633**

Map **16**

BUSINESS BAY

AL KHAIL RD

OUD METHA RD

E66

Exit
6

Exit
19

Exit
19

Exit
6

Bukadra
Interchange

Ras Al Khor
Wildlife
Sanctuary

E44

Dubai
Exiles Rugby
Club

MAIDAN (U/C)

E66

NAD AL SHEBA

NAD AL SHEBA RD

DUBAI - AL AIN RD

MANAMA RD

RAS AL KHOR
IND AREA 1

General Information p.1   Residents p.75   Exploring p.235   Activities p.317   Shopping p.401   Going Out p.495

© Explorer Group Ltd. 2007

300m

# Index

# Index

# Index

# Index

Focaccia 542

# Index

# Index

# Residents' Guides

All you need to know about living, working and enjoying life in these exciting destinations

 Abu Dhabi
 Amsterdam
 Bahrain
 Barcelona

 Beijing *
 Berlin
 Dubai
 Dublin
 Geneva

 Hong Kong
 Kuala Lumpur *
 Kuwait
 London
 Los Angeles

 New York
 New Zealand
 Oman
 Paris
 Qatar

 Shanghai
 Singapore
 Sydney
 Tokyo *
 Vancouver

## Mini Guides
The perfect pocket-sized
Visitors' Guides

## Mini Maps
Wherever you are,
never get lost again

## Photography Books
Beautiful cities caught through the lens

## Calendars
The time, the place, and the date

# Maps
Wherever you are, never get lost again

   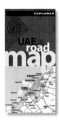 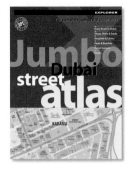

# Activity and Lifestyle Guides
Drive, trek, dive and swim... life will never be boring again

## Retail sales
Our books are available in most good bookshops around the world, and are also available online at Amazon.co.uk and Amazon.com. If you would like to enquire about any of our international distributors, please contact retail@explorerpublishing.com

## Bulk sales and customisation
All our products are available for bulk sales with customisation options. For discount rates and further information, please contact corporatesales@explorerpublishing.com

## Licensing and digital sales
All our content, maps and photography are available for print or digital use. For licensing enquiries please contact licensing@explorerpublishing.com

* Covers not final; titles released second quarter 2008

### Ahmed Mainodin
AKA: Mystery Man
We can never recognise Ahmed because of his constantly changing facial hair. He waltzes in with big lambchop sideburns one day, a handlebar moustache the next, and a neatly trimmed goatee after that. So far we've had no objections to his hirsute chameleonisms, but we'll definitely draw the line at a monobrow.

### Annabel Clough
AKA: Bollywood Babe
Taking a short break from her successful career in Bollywood, Annabel livens up the Explorer office with her spontaneous dance routines and random passionate outpouring of song. If there is a whiff of drama or a hint of romance, Annabel's famed vocal chords and nifty footwork will bring a touch of glamour to Al Quoz.

### Ajay Krishnan R
AKA: Web Wonder
Ajay's mum and dad knew he was going to be an IT genius when they found him reconfiguring his Commodore 64 at the tender age of 2. He went on to become the technology consultant on all three Matrix films, and counts Keanu as a close personal friend.

### Andrea Fust
AKA: Mother Superior
By day Andrea is the most efficient manager in the world and by night she replaces the boardroom for her board and wows the pants off the dudes in Ski Dubai. Literally. Back in the office she definitely wears the trousers!

### Bahrudeen Abdul
AKA: The Stallion
Having tired of creating abstract sculptures out of papier maché and candy canes, Bahrudeen turned to the art of computer programming. After honing his skills in the southern Andes for three years he grew bored of Patagonian winters, and landed a job here, 'The Home of 01010101 Creative Freedom'.

### Alex Jeffries
AKA: Easy Rider
Alex is happiest when dressed in leather from head to toe with a humming machine between his thighs – just like any other motorbike enthusiast. Whenever he's not speeding along the Hatta Road at full throttle, he can be found at his beloved Mac, still dressed in leather.

### Ben Merrett
AKA: Big Ben
After a short (or tall as the case may have been) career as a human statue, Ben tired of the pigeons choosing him, rather than his namesake, as a public convenience and decided to fly the nest to seek his fortune in foreign lands. Not only is he big on personality but he brings in the big bucks with his bulk!

### Alistair MacKenzie
AKA: Media Mogul
If only Alistair could take the paperless office one step further and achieve the officeless office he would be the happiest publisher alive. Wireless access from a remote spot somewhere in the Hajar Mountains would suit this intrepid explorer – less traffic, lots of fresh air, and wearing sandals all day - the perfect work environment!

### Cherry Enriquez
AKA: Bean Counter
With the team's penchant for sweets and pastries, it's good to know we have Cherry on top of our accounting cake. The local confectioner is always paid on time, so we're guaranteed great gateaux for every special occasion.

### Andrew Burgess
AKA: The Charmer
Andrew gave up his career test-driving Lamborghinis around rural Gloucestershire to move to Dubai where he now schmoozes Explorer's corporate clients and moonlights as a DJ. A lifelong Toffeeman, rumour has it he was recently involved in an attempted coup aimed at reinstating Howard Kendall.

### Claire England
AKA: Whip Cracker
No longer able to freeload off the fact that she once appeared in a Robbie Williams video, Claire now puts her creative skills to better use – looking up rude words in the dictionary! A child of English nobility, Claire is quite the lady – unless she's down at Rock Bottom.

### David Quinn
**AKA:** Sharp Shooter

After a short stint as a children's TV presenter was robbed from David because he developed an allergy to sticky back plastic, he made his way to sandier pastures. Now that he's thinking outside the box, nothing gets past the man with the sharpest pencil in town.

### Hashim MM
**AKA:** Speedy Gonzales

They don't come much faster than Hashim – he's so speedy with his mouse that scientists are struggling to create a computer that can keep up with him. His nimble fingers leave his keyboard smouldering (he gets through three a week), and his go-faster stripes make him almost invisible to the naked eye when he moves.

### Derrick Pereira
**AKA:** The Returnimator

After leaving Explorer in 2003, Derrick's life took a dramatic downturn – his dog ran away, his prized bonsai tree died and he got kicked out of his thrash metal band. Since rejoining us, things are looking up and he just found out he's won $10 million in a Nigerian sweepstakes competition. And he's got the desk by the window!

### Helen Spearman
**AKA:** Little Miss Sunshine

With her bubbly laugh and permanent smile, Helen is a much-needed ray of sunshine in the office when we're all grumpy and facing harrowing deadlines. It's almost impossible to think that she ever loses her temper or shows a dark side... although put her behind the wheel of a car, and you've got instant road rage.

### Enrico Maullon
**AKA:** The Crooner

Frequently mistaken for his near-namesake Enrique Iglesias, Enrico decided to capitalise and is now a regular stand-in for the Latin heartthrob. If he's ever missing from the office, it usually means he's off performing for millions of adoring fans on another stadium tour of America.

### Henry Hilos
**AKA:** The Quiet Man

Henry can rarely be seen from behind his large obstructive screen but when you do catch a glimpse you'll be sure to get a smile. Lighthearted Henry keeps all those glossy pages filled with pretty pictures for something to look at when you can't be bothered to read.

### Firos Khan
**AKA:** Big Smiler

Previously a body double in kung fu movies, including several appearances in close up scenes for Steven Seagal's moustache. He also once tore down a restaurant with his bare hands after they served him a mild curry by mistake.

### Iain Young
**AKA:** 'The Cat'

Iain follows in the fine tradition of Scots with safe hands – Alan Rough, Andy Goram, Jim Leighton on a good day – but breaking into the Explorer XI has proved frustrating. There's no match on a Mac, but that Al Huzaifa ringer doesn't half make himself big.

### Grace Carnay
**AKA:** Manila Ice

It's just as well the office is so close to a movie theatre, because Grace is always keen to catch the latest Hollywood offering from Brad Pitt, who she admires purely for his acting ability, of course. Her ice cool exterior conceals a tempestuous passion for jazz, which fuels her frenzied typing speed.

### Ieyad Charaf
**AKA:** Fashion Designer

When we hired Ieyad as a top designer, we didn't realise we'd be getting his designer tops too! By far the snappiest dresser in the office, you'd be hard-pressed to beat his impeccably ironed shirts.

**Ingrid Cupido**
AKA: The Karaoke Queen
Ingrid has a voice to match her starlet name. She'll put any Pop Idols to shame once behind the mike, and she's pretty nifty on a keyboard too. She certainly gets our vote if she decides to go pro; just remember you saw her here first.

**Johny Mathew**
AKA: The Hawker
Caring Johny used to nurse wounded eagles back to health and teach them how to fly again before trying his luck in merchandising. Fortunately his skills in the field have come in handy at Explorer, where his efforts to improve our book sales have been a soaring success.

**Joy Tubog**
AKA: Joyburgh
Don't let her saintly office behaviour deceive you. Joy has the habit of jumping up and down while screaming 'Jumanji' the instant anyone mentions Robin Williams and his hair sweater. Thankfully, her volleyball team has learned to utilize her 'uniqueness' when it's her turn to spike the ball.

**Ivan Rodrigues**
AKA: The Aviator
After making a mint in the airline market, Ivan came to Explorer where he works for pleasure, not money. That's his story, anyway. We know that he is actually a corporate spy from a rival company and that his multi-level spreadsheets are really elaborate codes designed to confuse us.

**Kate Fox**
AKA: Contacts Collector
Kate swooped into the office like the UK equivalent of Wonderwoman, minus the tights of course (it's much too hot for that), but armed with a superhuman marketing brain. Even though she's just arrived, she is already a regular on the Dubai social scene – she is helping to blast Explorer into the stratosphere, one champagne-soaked networking party at a time.

**Jake Marsico**
AKA: Don Calzone
Jake spent the last 10 years on the tiny triangular Mediterranean island of Samoza, honing his traditional cooking techniques and perfecting his Italian. Now, whenever he returns to his native America, he impresses his buddies by effortlessly zapping a hot dog to perfection in any microwave, anywhere, anytime.

**Katie Drynan**
AKA: The Irish Deputy
Katie is a Jumeira Jane in training, and has 35 sisters who take it in turns to work in the Explorer office while she enjoys testing all the beauty treatments available on the Beach Road. This Irish charmer met an oil tycoon in Paris, and they now spend the weekends digging very deep holes in their new garden.

**Jane Roberts**
AKA: The Oracle
After working in an undisclosed role in the government, Jane brought her super sleuth skills to Explorer. Whatever the question, she knows what, where, who, how and when, but her encyclopaedic knowledge is only impressive until you realise she just makes things up randomly.

**Kelly Tesoro**
AKA: Leading Lady
Kelly's former career as a Korean soapstar babe set her in good stead for the daily dramas at the bold and beautiful Explorer office. As our lovely receptionist she's on stage all day and her winning smile never slips.

**Jayde Fernandes**
AKA: Pop Idol
Jayde's idol is Britney Spears, and he recently shaved his head to show solidarity with the troubled star. When he's not checking his dome for stubble, or practising the dance moves to 'Baby One More Time' in front of the bathroom mirror, he actually manages to get some designing done.

**Kiran Melwani**
AKA: Bow Selector
Like a modern-day Robin Hood (right down to the green tights and band of merry men), Kiran's mission in life is to distribute Explorer's wealth of knowledge to the fact-hungry readers of the world. Just make sure you never do anything to upset her – rumour has it she's a pretty mean shot with that bow and arrow.

**Laura Zuffa**
AKA: Travelling Salesgirl
Laura's passport is covered in more stamps than Kofi Annan's, and there isn't a city, country or continent that she won't travel to. With a smile that makes grown men weep, our girl on the frontlines always brings home the beef bacon.

**Mathew Samuel**
AKA: Mr Modest
Matt's penchant for the entrepreneurial life began with a pair of red braces and a filofax when still a child. That yearning for the cut and thrust of commerce has brought him to Dubai, where he made a fortune in the sand-selling business before semi-retiring at Explorer.

**Lennie Mangalino**
AKA: Shaker Maker
With a giant spring in her step and music in her heart it's hard to not to swing to the beat when Lennie passes by in the office. She loves her Lambada… and Samba… and Salsa and anything else she can get the sales team shaking their hips to.

**Michael Dominic**
AKA: The Godfather
Master of his domain, dapper Michael rules over the bookstores of the GCC with a firm hand and a warm smile. He's got spies everywhere so woe betide a hapless shop assistant who displays an Explorer title upside down…

**Mannie Lugtu**
AKA: Distribution Demon
When the travelling circus rode into town, their master juggler Mannie decided to leave the Big Top and explore Dubai instead. He may have swapped his balls for our books but his juggling skills still come in handy.

**Michael Samuel**
AKA: Gordon Gekko
We have a feeling this mild mannered master of mathematics has a wild side. He hasn't witnessed an Explorer party yet but the office agrees that once the karaoke machine is out, Michael will be the maestro. Watch out Dubai!

**Mimi Stankova**
AKA: Mind Controller
A master of mind control, Mimi's siren-like voice lulls people into doing whatever she asks. Her steely reserve and endless patience mean recalcitrant reporters and persistent PR people are putty in her hands, delivering whatever she wants, whenever she wants it.

**Maricar Ong**
AKA: Pocket Docket
A pint-sized dynamo of ruthless efficiency, Maricar gets the job done before anyone else notices it needed doing. If this most able assistant is absent for a moment, it sends a surge of blind panic through the Explorer ranks.

**Mohammed Sameer**
AKA: Man in the Van
Known as MS, short for Microsoft, Sameer can pick apart a PC like a thief with a lock, which is why we keep him out of finance and pounding Dubai's roads in the unmissable Explorer van – so we can always spot him coming.

**Matt Farquharson**
AKA: Hack Hunter
A career of tuppence-a-word hackery ended when Matt arrived in Dubai to cover a maggot wranglers' convention. He misguidedly thinks he's clever because he once wrote for some grown-up English papers.

**Mohammed T**
AKA: King of the Castle
T is Explorer's very own Bedouin warehouse dweller; under his caring charge all Explorer stock is kept in masterful order. Arrive uninvited and you'll find T, meditating on a pile of maps, amid an almost eerie sense of calm.

### Najumudeen
AKA: The Groove
If it weren't for Najumudeen, our stock of books would be lying in a massive pile of rubble in our warehouse. Thankfully, through hours of crunk dancing and forklift racing with Mohammed T, Najumudeen has perfected the art of organisation and currently holds the title for fastest forklift slalom in the UAE.

### Rafi Jamal
AKA: Soap Star
After a walk on part in The Bold and the Beautiful, Rafi swapped the Hollywood Hills for the Hajar Mountains. Although he left the glitz behind, he still mingles with high society, moonlighting as a male gigolo and impressing Dubai's ladies with his fancy footwork.

### Rafi VP
AKA: Party Trickster
After developing a rare allergy to sunlight in his teens, Rafi started to lose a few centimeters of height every year. He now stands just 30cm tall, and does his best work in our dingy basement wearing a pair of infrared goggles. His favourite party trick is to fold himself into a briefcase.

### Noushad Madathil
AKA: Map Daddy
Where would Explorer be without the mercurial Madathil brothers? Lost in the Empty Quarter, that's where. Quieter than a mute dormouse, Noushad prefers to let his Photoshop layers, and brother Zain, do all the talking. A true Map Daddy.

### Richard Greig
AKA: Sir Lancelot
Chivalrous to the last, Richard's dream of being a mediaeval knight suffered a setback after being born several centuries too late. His stellar parliamentary career remains intact, and he is in the process of creating a new party with the aim of abolishing all onions and onion-related produce.

### Pamela Afram
AKA: Lady of Arabia
After an ill-fated accident playing Lawrence of Arabia's love interest in a play in Jumeira, Pamela found solace in the Explorer office. Her first paycheque went on a set of shiny new gleamers and she is now back to her bright and smiley self and is solely responsible for lighting up one half of the office!

### Roshni Ahuja
AKA: Bright Spark
Never failing to brighten up the office with her colourful get-up, Roshni definitely puts the 'it' in the IT department. She's a perennially pleasant, profound programmer with peerless panache, and she does her job with plenty of pep and piles of pizzazz.

### Pamela Grist
AKA: Happy Snapper
If a picture can speak a thousand words then Pam's photos say a lot about her - through her lens she manages to find the beauty in everything – even this motley crew. And when the camera never lies, thankfully Photoshop can.

### Sean Kearns
AKA: The Tall Guy
Big Sean, as he's affectionately known, is so laid back he actually spends most of his time lying down (unless he's on a camping trip, when his ridiculously small tent forces him to sleep on his hands and knees). Despite the rest of us constantly tripping over his lanky frame, when the job requires someone who will work flat out, he always rises to the editorial occasion.

### Pete Maloney
AKA: Graphic Guru
Image conscious he may be, but when Pete has his designs on something you can bet he's gonna get it! He's the king of chat up lines, ladies – if he ever opens a conversation with 'D'you come here often?' then brace yourself for the Maloney magic.

### Shabsir M
AKA: Sticky Wicket
Shabsir is a valuable player on the Indian national cricket team, so instead of working you'll usually find him autographing cricket balls for crazed fans around the world. We don't mind though – if ever a retailer is stumped because they run out of stock, he knocks them for six with his speedy delivery.

### Shan Kumar
**AKA:** Caped Crusader
Not dissimilar to the Batman's beacon, Explorer shines a giant X into the skies over Al Quoz in times of need. Luckily for us, Shan battled for days through the sand and warehouse units to save the day at our shiny new office. What a hero!

### Steve Jones
**AKA:** Golden Boy
Our resident Kiwi lives in a nine-bedroom mansion and is already planning an extension. His winning smile has caused many a knee to weaken in Bur Dubai but sadly for the ladies, he's hopelessly devoted to his clients.

### Shawn Jackson Zuzarte
**AKA:** Paper Plumber
If you thought rocket science was hard, try rearranging the chaotic babble that flows from the editorial team! If it weren't for Shawn, most of our books would require a kaleidoscope to read correctly so we're keeping him and his jazz hands under wraps.

### Tim Binks
**AKA:** Class Clown
El Binksmeisterooney is such a sharp wit, he often has fellow Explorers gushing tea from their noses in convulsions of mirth. Years spent hiking across the Middle East have given him an encyclopaedic knowledge of rock formations and elaborate hair.

### Shefeeq M
**AKA:** Rapper in Disguise
So new he's still got the wrapper on, Shefeeq was dragged into the Explorer office, and put to work in the design department. The poor chap only stopped by to ask for directions to Wadi Bih, but since we realised how efficient he is, we keep him chained to his desk.

### Tom Jordan
**AKA:** The True Professional
Explorer's resident thesp, Tom delivers lines almost as well as he cuts them. His early promise on the pantomime circuit was rewarded with an all-action role in hit UK drama Heartbeat. He's still living off the royalties – and the fact he shared a sandwich with Kenneth Branagh.

### Shyrell Tamayo
**AKA:** Fashion Princess
We've never seen Shyrell wearing the same thing twice – her clothes collection is so large that her husband has to keep all his things in a shoebox. She runs Designlab like clockwork, because being late for deadlines is SO last season.

### Tracy Fitzgerald
**AKA:** 'La Dona'
Tracy is a queenpin Catalan mafiosa and ringleader for the 'pescadora' clan, a nefarious group that runs a sushi smuggling operation between the Costa Brava and Ras Al Khaimah. She is not to be crossed. Rival clans will find themselves fed fish, and then fed to the fishes.

### Sunita Lakhiani
**AKA:** Designlass
Initially suspicious of having a female in their midst, the boys in Designlab now treat Sunita like one of their own. A big shame for her, because they treat each other pretty damn bad!

### Zainudheen Madathil
**AKA:** Map Master
Often confused with retired footballer Zinedine Zidane because of his dexterous displays and a bad head-butting habit, Zain tackles design with the mouse skills of a star striker. Maps are his goal and despite getting red-penned a few times, when he shoots, he scores.

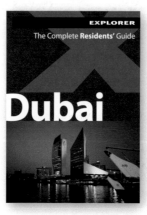
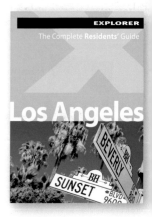

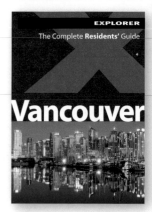

# Flick back a few pages and ask yourself…
## …would you like to see your face?

Explorer has grown from a one-man operation a decade ago to a 60+ team today and our expansion isn't slowing down. We are always looking for creative bods, from PR pro's and master marketers to daring designers and excellent editors, as well as super sales and support staff.

So what are you waiting for? Apply online at www.explorerpublishing.com

Abu Dhabi · Amsterdam · Bahrain · Barcelona · Beijing · Berlin · Dubai · Dublin · Geneva
Hong Kong · Kuala Lumpur · Kuwait · London · Los Angeles · New York · New Zealand · Oman
Paris · Qatar · Shanghai · Singapore · Sydney · Tokyo · Vancouver

# EXPLORER
www.explorerpublishing.com

The *Dubai Photography* Team
Victor Romero, Derrick Pereira, Pamela Grist, Sean Kearns, Matt Farquharson, Pete Maloney, Tom Jordan, Jane Roberts, Tim Binks, David Quinn, Hashim Moideen, Henry Hilos, Mark Grist, and special thanks to Tilo Richter for his underwater images.

## Publisher
Alistair MacKenzie
**Associate Publisher** Claire England

## Editorial
**Group Editor** Jane Roberts
**Lead Editors** David Quinn, Matt Farquharson, Sean Kearns, Tim Binks, Tom Jordan
**Deputy Editors** Helen Spearman, Jakob Marsico, Katie Drynan, Pamela Afram, Richard Greig, Tracy Fitzgerald
**Senior Editorial Assistant** Mimi Stankova
**Editorial Assistants** Grace Carnay, Ingrid Cupido, Kathryn Calderon

## Design
**Creative Director** Pete Maloney
**Art Director** Ieyad Charaf
**Design Manager** Alex Jeffries
**Senior Designer** Iain Young
**Layout Manager** Jayde Fernandes
**Designers** Hashim Moideen, Rafi Pullat, Shawn Jackson Zuzarte, Shefeeq Marakkatepurath
**Cartography Manager** Zainudheen Madathil
**Cartographers** Noushad Madathil, Sunita Lakhiani
**Design Admin Manager** Shyrell Tamayo
**Production Coordinator** Maricar Ong

## Photography
**Photography Manager** Pamela Grist
**Photographer** Victor Romero
**Image Editor** Henry Hilos

## Sales & Marketing
**Media Sales Area Managers** Laura Zuffa, Stephen Jones
**GCC Retail Sales Manager** Michael Dominic
**Global Partners Sales Manager** Andrew Burgess
**Corporate Sales Executive** Ben Merrett
**Marketing Manager** Kate Fox
**Marketing Executive** Annabel Clough
**Digital Content Manager** Derrick Pereira
**International Retail Sales Manager** Ivan Rodrigues
**Retail Sales Coordinator** Kiran Melwani
**Retail Sales Supervisor** Mathew Samuel
**Retail Sales Merchandiser** Johny Mathew, Shan Kumar
**Sales & Marketing Coordinator** Lennie Mangalino
**Distribution Executives** Ahmed Mainodin, Firos Khan, Mannie Lugtu
**Warehouse Assistants** Mohammed Kunjaymo, Najumudeen K.I.
**Drivers** Mohammed Sameer, Shabsir Madathil

## Finance & Administration
**Finance Manager** Michael Samuel
**HR & Administration Manager** Andrea Fust
**Junior Accountant** Cherry Enriquez
**Administrators** Enrico Maullon, Joy Tubog, Kelly Tesoro
**Accountants Assistant** Darwin Lovitos
**Driver** Rafi Jamal

## IT
**IT Administrator** Ajay Krishnan
**Senior Software Engineer** Bahrudeen Abdul
**Software Engineer** Roshni Ahuja

## Contact Us

### Reader Response
If you have any comments and suggestions, fill out our online reader response form and you could win prizes. Log on to **www.explorerpublishing.com**

### General Enquiries
We'd love to hear your thoughts and answer any questions you have about this book or any other Explorer product. Contact us at **info@explorerpublishing.com**

### Careers
If you fancy yourself as an Explorer, send your CV (stating the position you're interested in) to **jobs@explorerpublishing.com**

### Designlab & Contract Publishing
For enquiries about Explorer's Contract Publishing arm and design services contact **designlab@explorerpublishing.com**

### PR & Marketing
For PR and marketing enquires contact **marketing@explorerpublishing.com** **pr@explorerpublishing.com**

### Corporate Sales
For bulk sales and customisation options, for this book or any Explorer product, contact **sales@explorerpublishing.com**

### Advertising & Sponsorship
For advertising and sponsorship, contact **media@explorerpublishing.com**

**Explorer Publishing & Distribution**
PO Box 34275, Dubai
United Arab Emirates
www.explorerpublishing.com
**Phone:** +971 (0)4 340 8805
**Fax:** +971 (0)4 340 8806

## Emergencies

| | |
|---|---|
| Police | 999 |
| Ambulance | 998/999 |
| Fire | 997 |
| DEWA Emergency | 991 |
| Dubai Police HQ | 04 229 2222 |
| Municipality Emergency Number | 04 223 2323 |

## Taxi Companies

| | |
|---|---|
| Al Marmoom Tourist Taxi | 04 347 6650 |
| Arabia Taxi | 04 285 5566 |
| Cars Taxis | 04 269 3344 |
| Dubai Transport Corporation | 04 208 0808 |
| Emirates Taxi | 04 339 4455 |
| Gulf Radio Taxi | 04 223 6666 |
| Metro Taxi | 04 267 3222 |
| National Taxis | 04 339 0002 |
| Sharjah Delta Taxis | 06 559 8598 |

## Embassies & Consulates

| | |
|---|---|
| Australian Consulate | 04 321 2444 |
| Bahrain Embassy | 02 665 7500 |
| British Embassy | 04 309 4444 |
| Canadian Consulate | 04 314 5555 |
| Chinese Consulate | 04 394 4733 |
| Czech Embassy | 02 678 2800 |
| Danish Consulate & Trade Commission | 04 348 0877 |
| Egyptian Consulate | 04 397 1122 |
| French Consulate | 04 332 9040 |
| German Consulate | 04 397 2333 |
| Indian Consulate | 04 397 1222 |
| Iranian Consulate | 04 344 4717 |
| Irish Embassy (Saudi Arabia) | +966 1488 2300 |
| Italian Consulate | 04 331 4167 |
| Japanese Consulate | 04 331 9191 |
| Jordanian Consulate | 04 397 0500 |
| Kuwaiti Consulate | 04 397 8000 |
| Lebanese Consulate | 04 397 7450 |
| Malaysian Consulate | 04 335 5528 |
| Netherlands Consulate | 04 352 8700 |
| New Zealand Consulate | 04 331 7500 |
| Norwegian Consulate | 04 353 3833 |
| Omani Consulate | 04 397 1000 |
| Pakistani Consulate | 04 397 0412 |
| Philippine Consulate | 04 266 7745 |
| Qatar Consulate | 04 398 2888 |
| Russian Consulate | 04 223 1272 |
| Saudi Arabian Consulate | 04 397 9777 |
| Spanish Embassy | 02 626 9544 |
| South African Consulate | 04 397 5222 |
| Sri Lankan Consulate | 04 398 6535 |
| Swedish Consulate | 02 621 0162 |
| Swiss Consulate | 04 329 0999 |
| Thai Consulate | 04 349 2863 |
| US Consulate General | 04 311 6000 |

## Hospitals

| | |
|---|---|
| Al Baraha Hospital (Govt) | 04 271 0000 |
| Al Maktoum Hospital (Govt) | 04 222 1211 |
| Al Wasl Hospital (Govt) | 04 324 1111 |
| Al Zahra Hospital | 06 561 9999 |
| American Hospital | 04 336 7777 |
| Belhoul European Hospital | 04 345 4000 |
| Cedars Jebel Ali International Hospital | 04 881 4000 |
| Dubai Hospital (Govt) | 04 271 4444 |
| Emirates Hospital | 04 344 6678 |
| Iranian Hospital | 04 344 0250 |
| Neuro Spinal Hospital | 04 342 0000 |
| Rashid Hospital | 04 337 4000 |
| Welcare Hospital | 04 282 7788 |
| Zulekha Hospital | 04 267 8866 |

## Area & Mobile Codes

| | |
|---|---|
| Abu Dhabi | 02 |
| Ajman | 06 |
| Al Ain | 03 |
| Dubai | 04 |
| Fujairah | 09 |
| Hatta | 04 |
| Jebel Ali | 04 |
| Mobile Telephones (du) | 055 |
| Mobile Telephones (Etisalat) | 050 |
| Ras al Khaimah | 07 |
| Sharjah | 06 |
| UAE Country Code | 00 971 |
| Umm Al Quwain | 06 |

## Useful Numbers

| | |
|---|---|
| DEWA | 04 324 4444 |
| Directory Enquiries (du) | 199 |
| Directory Enquiries (Etisalat) | 181 |
| Etisalat Information | 144 |
| Fault Reports (Etisalat) | 171 |
| Operator | 100 |
| Salik | 800 72545 |
| Speaking Clock | 140 |
| To dial Explorer Publishing's Dubai office from overseas | 00 971 4 340 8805 |

## Du Contact Centre

| | |
|---|---|
| du Contact Centre (from a du phone) | 155 |
| du Contact Centre (other phones) | 055 5678 155 |
| | 04 369 9155 |

## Dubai Airport

| | |
|---|---|
| Dubai Airport | 04 224 5555 |
| Flight Information | 04 216 6666 |
| Baggage Services(Lost Property) | 04 224 5383 |